By Force of Thought

By Force of Thought

Irregular Memoirs of an Intellectual Journey

János Kornai

The MIT Press
Cambridge, Massachusetts
London, England

MIT Press books may be purchased at special quantity discounts for business or sales promotional use. For information, please email special_sales@mitpress.mit.edu or write to Special Sales Department, The MIT Press, 55 Hayward Street, Cambridge, MA 02142.

This book was set in Sabon on 3B2 by Asco Typesetters, Hong Kong and was printed and bound in the United States of America.

Library of Congress Cataloging-in-Publication Data

Kornai, János.
By force of thought : irregular memoirs of an intellectual journey / János Kornai.
    p.   cm.
Includes bibliographical references and index.
ISBN-13: 978-0-262-11302-1 (alk. paper)
ISBN-10: 0-262-11302-3 (alk. paper)
1. Kornai, János. 2. Economists—Hungary—Biography. I. Title.

HB102.K673A3   2007
330.092—dc22
[B]   2006049406

To my mother, Munyó

Contents

Preface

Even after I had written most of these memoirs, I was still unsure why I was engaged in this undertaking. What was prompting me to think back? Whom was I addressing?

I am somewhat reserved, and discuss my life rarely and sparingly. During the most exciting days of Hungary's transition from single-party state to democracy, a journalist pressed me to give, at last, a long biographical interview. "It will not interest anybody later," he argued. That was fifteen years ago, and I hope now I am not too late.

For many years my wife urged me to write my life story, but I kept putting it off. I finally sat down to the task in mid-2003, and these memoirs occupied my time and energy for the next two years to the detriment of some other projects.

My wife's insistence is motive enough. If I were asked to name the single reader for whom this book has been written, whose satisfaction and approval it is designed to win, that person has to be Zsuzsa.

I hope my autobiography will also interest many other people: my children and grandchildren and other family members, my friends, my colleagues past and present, my students, and readers of my books and articles. This is no small circle. Those who know me personally or through my previous written works already will have some impression of me. I would like them to meld that picture with the self-image I present in this account of my life. Several hundred reviews of my books can now be compared with my self-assessment. In these memoirs, I discuss how I saw my work at the time it was written and how I see it now. I have never reacted publicly to reviews. Only on rare occasions have I engaged in a dispute when I have encountered someone who disagreed with me. Here in my recollections I want to provide a comprehensive and chronological "review" of my work.

Though my memoirs are roughly chronological, this is not a diary. Each chapter is arranged around a subject, whether a single event, one of my works, or a place where I once lived. Therefore each chapter title includes the time period covered.

From chapter to chapter, these periods merge into each other and may overlap, if the topic requires it.

Readers may include some people who have not read any of my earlier writings but are simply interested in the era in which I lived. This book does not take on any of the tasks of a historian: it does not seek to give an objective, comprehensive description and an interpretation of major events. There is an extensive literature available for those wanting to study the socialist and post-socialist period in Hungary or in other formerly communist countries. I was just one participant in those eras, and not a major one. All I say about each is what impinged on my own life—the social and historical context in which the events of my life unfolded.

For those, however, who are interested in Eastern Europe, my memoirs may provide details to *complement* other sources on Eastern Europe, on the rise and fall of the communist system, and on the dilemmas facing the Eastern European intelligentsia. The various reports, diaries, and autobiographies of people who lived through the period are indispensable source materials for future scholars. Through my memoirs I try to contribute to that material, acting as a witness to what occurred. In fact, I also intended my earlier, academic writings as testimony to their historical periods, and I tried to make them as objective as possible. These memoirs are a subjective augmentation of my scholarly work. I have now tried to include what stayed out of *Economics of Shortage* or *The Socialist System* because the material was too personal in nature or because something else prevented me from stating my opinion. This book's genre allows me to present my personal credo on several ethical, political, and scientific questions. For me, it was not possible to squeeze subjective position statements and personal declarations into scholarly works on well-circumscribed topics.

I thought a great deal about what this book's title should be. I was initially inclined to call it *Understanding*.... It was myself, first of all, that I wanted to understand. I have sought to explain what I thought when and why, what influenced my thinking and actions, and then how my thinking changed. I also would like to better understand those with whom I agreed and those with whom I disagreed, those who stood by me and those who turned away.

"Understanding" can imply moral approval or at least acquiescence. That is not the kind of comprehension I have in mind. By no means am I looking to exonerate myself or to judge others here, any more than I was in my earlier academic works. I want to understand what I have experienced. Sometimes it is quite hard to discover the motives behind events, the flaws in an argument, the deep forces that motivate people, and the declared or concealed reasons for conflicts. It was no easy feat to examine my own past, and obviously it is harder still to analyze the pasts of others.

In the end, I chose a different title: *By Force of Thought*. I felt that these words most effectively summarized one of the main themes of these memoirs. I have striven neither for power nor riches but rather for a life of ideas. When from time to time I exercised some influence on the course of events, it was not because I dictated to others from a higher position or bought their cooperation at a high price. If I have had any influence on anyone or anything, I have had it through my thoughts, spoken or written.

One reader of the manuscript expressed his reservations: "It is naive to believe in the influence of argument, conviction, or thought. The real driving force behind historical events is interest." As a professional observer and analyst of social changes, I have no illusions, and I try to take into account the various causes of observed effects and handle them according to their weight. However, the dominant possessors of power and wealth are people of action, individuals who are able to choose between alternatives. There are all sorts of factors influencing them, and values, principles, and ideas are surely not among the least significant. Moreover, the course of events is certainly influenced as well by the thoughts and beliefs of the millions or hundreds of millions of those who are less powerful and rich. My whole life's work would lose its meaning if I were not convinced that thought has force.

Of course, this force of thought has its limits. Indeed this is one of the main themes of these memoirs: when and why my own thinking faltered and then was reconsidered, how others' ideas affected me, and how my line of thinking, analyses, and recommendations clashed with those of others. Thought is subject to a continuous test of strength. Every chapter recounts such tests, whether these led to success or to failure.

In the subtitle I call these memoirs "irregular," because they differ from most memoirs in two respects. While recounting the events of my life, I pause from time to time and express my thoughts on specific episodes. The emphasis is not on telling the story but on analyzing the problem and its circumstances. Such commentaries, which relate to some aspect of sociology, political philosophy, ethics, the process of research and creation, the sociology of science, or various other subjects, may be considered miniature independent essays. This book is thus a combination of memoirs interspersed with a series of essays that are more detached in nature. Hence these are "irregular memoirs."

Second, most memoirs treat the author's private life. Although I have written an account that is personal and subjective, essentially it is an *intellectual* autobiography. This term can be broadly interpreted to encompass the political and public aspects of my life, and also my friendships and other personal relations associated with my professional activities and public service.

I mention family members and family events many times throughout the book, but that private domain, with its countless pleasures and problems, is given much less space and emphasis in these memoirs than it had in my real life. The photographs may perhaps show something of this personal sphere that is not expressed in words. The book is thus an irregular autobiography also in the sense that I hardly mention what are considered strictly personal matters.

Let me say a few words about the genre and style of the book. I have spent the past fifty years writing analyses, trying to present what I have understood in clear, comprehensible arguments. I am not going to suddenly become a man of letters. Do not expect me to produce fine descriptions of scenes, recall conversations, pen portraits of friends, or offer graphic, impressionistic accounts of tense moments. Literary writers, whether by design or accident, leave problems open and thoughts unresolved. A scientific researcher cannot do that. I remain a scholar even when writing my memoirs. I try to avoid ambiguity in style, structure, and means of expression.

When I was writing my earlier books, I generally had before me a well-defined picture of those whom I was addressing, and that audience largely determined what I had to explain and what I could assume readers already knew. This time the situation is different. I trust that readers of this book will be economists and other professionals, members of older and younger generations, Hungarians and foreigners, people living in the East and in the West. I have done my best to make it easy for all to follow what I mean to say. I faced a serious dilemma at several places in the book. Should my aim be maximum precision, which would call for detailed definitions and qualifications, and a full delineation of the initial assumptions behind the theory? There was a danger that this approach would make life too hard for readers who are not economists. So should I then choose a simpler form of expression, with a concomitant danger of oversimplification? Since I am not writing an academic treatise, I preferred to risk the latter. For those who have not read any of my academic work, this book gives a sense of what I have to say in my books and articles. For those who have, perhaps it may serve to remind them of those writings. Let me apologize in advance to those who feel I have given superfluous detail in certain places.

It goes without saying that my own recollections were the most important source for this memoir. But I did not see the writing process as a test of memory: I not only relied on my own thoughts and feelings but checked the factual references as carefully as possible in other published works.

I had many sources at my disposal. As I already mentioned, I went back to the works of mine I consider the most important.* Once these appeared in print, I normally did not look at them again. Now, however, I have reread them in succession, together with many contemporary reviews and later commentaries on these primary works.

---

* The selection can be readily grasped from the table of contents. When a chapter discusses one or more of my publications in some detail, the title or titles appear as a subtitle of the chapter.

I have never kept a diary, but since I have been primarily a researcher, I have saved many notes and built up an archive of all sorts of documents. These are maintained in a form that is easy to access, catalogued in hundreds of files. I have kept most of the letters sent to me, as well as copies of my own letters. In writing this book I immersed myself in this wealth of documentation.

The material in my own collection was supplemented by research in various public archives, where my colleagues and I found much interesting information. Studying the documents of Hungary's former secret service proved to be very exciting. Recent Hungarian laws make it possible for citizens to access the material relating to them. It was a depressing and at times appalling experience to read informers' reports, records of police investigations made in preparation for political trials, and the notes of state security and intelligence officers. I describe in this volume many of the political police and secret service documents pertaining to me.

While I feel it is important to assure the reader in advance that the book is based not only on its writer's memory but on the study of other documents too, I do not want to discourage a wider audience. Its emphasis is not on giving a dry account of archival research but on the personal treatment of memories. What follows is an account of a long and adventurous intellectual journey, with light and dark episodes, and animating and embittering experiences. I hope that by the end of the book, readers will have gained a better understanding of my life, my works, and the age in which I have lived.

The Osiris Publishing House/Osiris Kiadó published the Hungarian version of my memoirs in April 2005. The present book is the translation of the Hungarian text with some modifications.

I have corrected some minor errors and inaccuracies that had been recognized only after the initial publishing of the book. I made an effort to clarify the phrasing at some places where the reactions of readers suggested that the passage was ambiguous. I also attached a glossary and a chronology to the English edition in hope of easing the way for non-Hungarian readers.

Between the completion of the Hungarian manuscript and the finalization of the English version, more than a year passed. Of course, life did not stop; but with few exceptions, the events of that period are not included in the text of the present edition.

To make reading easier, it is worth giving a bit of practical advice to the reader. At the end of the volume is a reference list limited to works mentioned in this book. It cannot, then, be considered a comprehensive bibliography covering the subject areas dealt with. For books that have been through several editions, I have listed, to the best of my knowledge, the most recent edition, adding the year of the first edition in parentheses.

The text of the book is supplemented by two types of notes: footnotes and end-notes. I chose this somewhat unusual approach to make things easier for the reader. A work neither of fiction nor of scholarship, my book belongs to an intermediate genre that justifies this solution.

The footnotes contain information that I could, in fact, have inserted in the main text, given the book's genre and style. It appears in footnotes because each represents a minor digression from the line of thought of the main text. These digressions offer illustrative examples, data, episodes, and sometimes anecdotes or jokes. I hope those who decide to read the main text will also read the footnotes.

The endnotes contain what researchers call the critical apparatus. As I explained above, this memoir is based on a broad range of material. If the source of certain information was an archival document, the endnote gives the citation in customary form. There are frequent references to published works as well. If they are simply mentioned in the text, readers may find full bibliographical data in the reference list. But if the reference in the text is less direct, or if a work is directly quoted, an endnote is supplied.*

I expect that many readers do not wish to closely track the sources of the various pieces of information. I have tried to assist them by placing those sources in end-notes. The book's points can be followed without ever consulting the endnotes. However, those who wish to follow up on one problem or another (including those doing research in the subject areas dealt with in the book) will find all the necessary information in the endnotes.

Acknowledgments

I am grateful to all who have helped me in writing my autobiography. Katalin Szabó, my full-time assistant, took on the organization and documentation related to the work cheerfully and with devoted attention, and tended the successive versions of the manuscript with great care. I was fortunate to get the efficient and patient help of four young research assistants, the historian János Molnár and the economists Gábor Iván, Noémi Péter, and László Tóth, who assisted me in collecting data and documents, clarifying sources, checking information, compiling the glossary and the index, and editing the manuscript conscientiously and resourcefully.

I would like to express thanks for the support of all who participated in preparing the book by commenting on earlier versions of the entire manuscript or parts of it,

---

* Because notes cannot themselves be annotated, the footnotes also contain the references belonging to them.

by collecting archival material, by hunting up books and articles, by clarifying certain professional problems, and in many other ways. Let me mention those from whom I received special help: Francis Bator, Tamás Bauer, Kata Csankovszki, Karen Eggleston, Hédi Erdős, Peter Eső, Ica Fazekas, Luca Gábor, Jerry Green, János Gyurgyák, Márton Karinthy, Péter Kende, János Kenedi, Anikó Környei, Éva Sz. Kovács, Mária Kovács, Zdenek Kudrna, Mihály Laki, Helga Lénárt-Cheng, Pál Lőcsei, Ilona Lukács, László Majtényi, Péter Mihályi, András Nagy, Judit Négyesi, Gábor Pajkossy, Julianna Parti, Richard Quandt, M. János Rainer, Sándor Révész, Pál Réz, Gérard Roland, Henry Rosovsky, Éva Sarnyai, Ágnes Schönner, András Simonovits, Robert M. Solow, Susan Suleiman, János Szegő, Mehrdad Vahabi, László Varga, and Sofia Weibull. My thanks also go to those not mentioned here by name, but who have assisted me by answering questions or clarifying some information.

Hungary's National Scientific Research Fund (OTKA T 046976) subsidized the costs of research, while the Institute of Economics of the Hungarian Academy of Sciences assisted in administering the OTKA support. As is true of all my work over the past fifteen years, Collegium Budapest, Institute for Advanced Study has been my workplace. It provided an inspiring environment and practical assistance to writing this book.

The translation was made by Brian McLean. I am grateful to him for his devoted work as well as for the patience and the attention with which—just as during our previous collaborations—he was willing to participate in the repeated revisions.

I would like to express my deep gratitude to Jeffrey E. Epstein for his generous donation, supporting the costs of translation and additional research needed for the completion of the publication of my memoirs in English.

I am thankful to MIT Press for undertaking the publication of my book; to its acquiring editor, Elizabeth Murry, for her encouragement and for her supportive way of accommodating my requests; and to its production editor, Matthew Abbate, for his flexible and efficient support. I was especially fortunate that Alice Falk was the copyeditor of the book, as she incorporates the best editorial virtues of high standards, precision, and empathy.

János Kornai

Budapest, May 2006

By Force of Thought

1

My Family and Youth—1928–1944

I am not Marcel Proust or Péter Esterházy. So I will not even try to convey a sense of my childhood or the ambience of my home. Like anyone else, I remember the smell of cake and the voices of parents, but I lack the literary gift that would enable me to put them before the readers of these memoirs.

So I will stay with the genre that I am used to and describe and analyze that world instead. I am going to augment that task with another: to try now, at the age of 77, to understand and analyze myself. How and why did I become what I became and am? I will mainly speak of my childhood and youth and my family, therefore, insofar as they contribute to the dual task of understanding myself and that period.

My father

My father's name was Dr. Pál Kornhauser. He was born in 1880. I bore the same surname myself until I decided of my own accord in 1945 to take the name Kornai.

My paternal grandfather, Károly Kornhauser, was a locksmith. The family lived in the town of Trencsén (Trenčín), in a region that was then part of Hungary and belongs to Slovakia now. My father was proud that part of Trencsén Bridge had been made in my grandfather's workshop. When this came up in conversation later, after I grew up, many people were surprised that a Jew in a nineteenth-century provincial town should have taken up the locksmith's trade, instead of keeping a tavern or a shop.

My father's parents died while he was still a boy. His elder brother helped him through his education, but basically it was by his own efforts that he completed his secondary education at the Piarist Gymnasium, a famous school run by the Catholic Church, before studying law at a university and becoming an attorney. I was certainly inspired by my father's example when I too became a self-made man. Like many people in the Uplands, my father was a native speaker of three languages: Hungarian, German, and Slovak. He must have been talented and industrious indeed, because he had a splendid career as a young man. His knowledge of German and his own interests oriented him toward the legal business of German companies operating in Hungary. He was briefed by them with increasing frequency and later officially became the legal adviser to the German Legation in Budapest. This was really an honorary title, as he was not employed by the German state: it meant that the legation recommended him to German companies involved in contracts or civil litigation in Hungary. My father never took cases of any other kind—not divorce, not criminal law, and not corporate law with Hungarian clients. He specialized in the Hungarian business affairs of German companies.

The family apartment and my father's office were on Akadémia utca in Budapest. It was a prestigious address, a street with the headquarters of the Hungarian Academy of Science at one end and the Parliament at the other. The building now houses the office of the Prime Minister's staff. I was there not long ago. It was a curious feeling to step into what had been my father's study and find an economist friend of mine working there. My father's office was full of Hungarian and German legal books. Neither he nor my mother collected books of any other kind. Literary works were first brought to our apartment by my older sister and then by me. I cannot report that I first learned to love and respect literature in my parents' home, as many children of the intelligentsia can.

I know from what my mother and sister told me that my father read a great deal in his youth and often went to the opera, where he was particularly fond of Wagner. By the time I was in my teens there were no traces left of this interest. All my father's attention was concentrated on his own profession.

Let us return to the German Legation. Many years after my father died, my mother mentioned that when he was appointed legal adviser to the legation, he had followed Dr. Miklós Káldor. The name sounded familiar, and I discovered that Lord Nicholas Kaldor, the great economist and adviser to the British chancellor of the exchequer, was that Hungarian attorney's son. Once I was talking to Kaldor in his Cambridge home when the conversation came around to our fathers. The subject reopened an old family resentment and jealousy in Kaldor, who was an elderly man by then. Fifty years earlier, members of the Káldor household must have cursed the young Kornhauser more than once for having stepped into the senior Káldor's shoes.

My older brother Bandi and my sister Lilly had received a lot of attention from my father when they were children. Lilly was moved by those memories, often recalling the walks she had taken with my father, the games they had played, and conversations they had had. By the time the second pair of children was born, my older brother Tomi and myself, my father no longer had the energy or patience to spend time with his children. I have no recollection of even one intimate hour with him or a single meaningful conversation. I will be returning in these memoirs several times to the fact that I did not really have masters, an observation that I first make here. I, like all boys and young men, saw my father as a model in many respects, and I still do. But in an intellectual sense, he was not my teacher or master. Though my father was a bright and knowledgeable man, he never conveyed to me in words any of his views, knowledge, or experience.

When on January 21, 1928, I was born, my father was 47 years old. The passing of the years was certainly one reason for the scant attention he paid to my brother and me. But the prime consideration behind his altered behavior was the change in his professional situation and in the political environment. I was not yet five when Hitler came to power. That ascension did not bring any sudden switch in the local network of German legations, any more than it did in many other fields. Years passed before Nazi power became totalitarian, penetrating into every cell of the system. I do not know quite when my father lost the right to use his title of "Legal Adviser to the German Legation." Initially, the only effect was that the legation stopped recommending him to any more German firms; the existing ones did not have to break with him for a while. But gradually the clients dropped away, although there were German businessmen in Hungary who remained faithful right up to my father's death.

As the number of clients dwindled, so did the family income. My father never spoke of money matters to us, but I was able to ascertain later that we lived on his accumulated wealth rather than his current earnings. We younger children did not have much sense of these financial problems. We lived prosperously in a spacious and expensive apartment in the center of town and moved every summer to a fine villa in the Rózsadomb district of Buda, the hilly side of Budapest. When we were small, we had a German governess, and the family was looked after by several servants and a gardener. To make up for some of the income lost from his legal practice, my father partly cashed in his big life insurance policy and sold family jewelry and artworks.*

---

* Not long ago my father's notes that included a detailed list of his life insurance policies came into my hands. He felt it was especially important to provide for my mother. But all his plans fell through in the end, cautious though he had tried to be. The policies he had taken out before World War I came to nothing because of the great inflation following the war. Having learned his lesson, he took out valuable new policies with a German insurance company, one of the largest in the world, at the beginning of the 1930s; they were valorized to keep up with inflation and fixed to "the value of the gold dollar." This time he felt his insurance was 100 percent secure. How could he have foreseen that the Hungarian franchise of this Berlin company would be nationalized in the 1940s by the Communist regime, which, ridiculing the principle of valorization, would set the value of one gold dollar at one forint to pay my mother a ludicrously small annuity? It was shocking to see how my father's circumspect and loving care was thwarted by history.

The feeling that he was being squeezed out of his profession was a grave trial to my father. He was still in full possession of his intellectual energies and professional expertise, and his vocation as a lawyer was extremely important to him. Far more serious were the problems and anxieties caused by the baneful historical trend that had, among other things, brought on the change in his professional and financial position. The power of Hitler was increasingly displaying its merciless side. News came of persecution of the Jews. Germany occupied Bohemia and Moravia, Austria was annexed (my father had a brother living in Vienna), the first anti-Jewish laws were passed in Hungary as well, and the war broke out.

One strict principle of my father's was not to join any political party or movement. He had bad memories from the time of the 1919 Commune, the short-lived communist rule that was accompanied and followed by terror. Nonetheless, he was far from what was known at that time as a conservative. I never heard him direct any comment against left-wingers. He subscribed to a liberal morning paper, and any other paper he bought would be liberal as well. So far as I can judge from his scattered remarks, he was liberal (as this term is understood in Europe) in his thinking. But although he would have liked to have stayed away from politics, history began to intervene is his family life—first as distant rumbles of thunder, and later as direct lightning strikes.

My father never denied being Jewish, but he did not flaunt it either. There were quite a number of Jews in his social circle, yet he had non-Jewish friends too. Although he believed in God, he was not religious and did not attend the synagogue or observe the rituals of the Jewish religion. Nevertheless, whenever he made a charitable donation, it was to the boys' orphanage run by the Jewish congregation. Perhaps he remembered being orphaned himself. He had not the remotest intention of putting a seal on his assimilation by converting to Christianity.

One thing my father was proud of was his record in World War I. He had been commissioned as a captain and won high decorations. He did not hesitate to call himself a Hungarian. After my brother Bandi had done his military service and was discharged with the rank of corporal, my father had new uniforms made for them both. They had their photograph taken looking confidently ahead as father and son in their captain's and corporal's uniforms. A year or two later, the Hungarian

---

My father gave minute instructions to his heirs about the measures to take with the insurance policies. I recognized myself in this meticulousness: I normally drum instructions into my colleagues or members of my family in the same way. Some receive my directives with gratitude, some just smile, while others feel annoyed and reject them. Where does this likeness to my father come from? Did I see manifestations of these habits as a child (I do not remember any) and follow the pattern? Or is it possible that this behavior forms part of my genetic inheritance?

gendarmerie would be loading the father into a railway truck bound for Auschwitz, while the son would be in civilian clothes enduring forced labor under Hungarian military command on the Don Bend, where he was to die of exposure or illness.

My family

My father was very generous toward us even in the years when his income was falling. I became passionate about photography as a teenager, and straightaway he bought me one of the best cameras available at the time. When I needed equipment for developing and enlarging the pictures, that was immediately provided as well. When I developed a love of books, he helped me repeatedly with sums of money. Yet the center and source of warmth in the family was not my father but my mother—Munyó, as we all called her. (Her maiden name was Aranka Schatz.)

As small children, we had kind governesses to look after us. I think back on them all fondly, and I was positively enamored of the last one, the slim, beautiful Liesl. But even if the daily tasks of looking after us were given over to a *Fräulein*, my mother found innumerable occasions to express her tenderness. She was not highly educated or cultivated, but her native wits were sharp. Her refined and interesting beauty was coupled with a natural, innate elegance. Perhaps it was Freud who wrote that self-confidence and ambition in adulthood depend largely on how much love children receive from their mothers early in life. I received vast quantities. One of the stories that Munyó gladly repeated was how I had been the one of her four children she had suffered with most during her pregnancy. When she was constantly in pain and sick, her doctor reassured her: "You will see, my good lady; this will be the child that brings you most joy." This she told me many times, even when I was small. She did not deny that I was the favorite among her four children. She rejoiced in my little successes, giving me praise and encouragement. I cannot remember her scolding me once. She never checked on my schoolwork. When I was at elementary school, if I ever complained of a setback or of difficulties in my studies, she just encouraged me and never gave advice: "You will work it out," she would say. "I am not anxious about you, you will manage." I cannot imagine a stronger inducement than that kind of maternal encouragement and unconditional trust.

Corporal punishment was quite unknown in my family. Once, as a teenager, my brother Tomi, who was three years older than me, began to wrestle with the young housemaid who worked in our house. His behavior fell short of what today would be called sexual harassment, but it went beyond what my parents considered acceptable. That night, my father came into our room and kicked—not Tomi, but the side of the bed. That kick and a few words of rebuke were enough to express his indignation. It was the most severe "punishment" of my whole childhood. Not until

1944, when I came face to face with human cruelty, did I experience or see with my own eyes the intentional infliction of bodily pain or hear angry shouts or someone being verbally abused. Utter aversion to raised voices or shouting, let alone physical indignities, beatings, or torture, was deeply instilled in me.

Life for my oldest brother Bandi, born in 1914, began cheerfully and reassuringly. As he was nearing the end of his university studies, a friend of his was preparing to emigrate to England. Bandi wanted to go as well, but my father would not allow it. I do not know exactly what my father's arguments were, but I heard later from my sister that he said we were Hungarians and our place was here. He apparently also argued that the eldest son should stay with the family. My brother was not a rebellious sort and concurred with my father's wishes. He ended his short life, as I have said, on the Russian front. I had little contact with him because of the large age difference between us, but I remember him fondly for his kindness and good humor and with an aching heart when I think of how young he died.

I had the closest sentimental and intellectual ties with my sister Lilly, born in 1919, who was nine years older than me. We would read poetry together. She introduced me to the stories of Frigyes Karinthy, one of the most popular of twentieth-century Hungarian authors, known mainly for his satirical writings. She was the first to play me Debussy and Schumann on the piano. It must have lent confidence to me—a bashful, inhibited young teenager, thin as a rake—to have a beautiful, bright older sister who took me seriously, discussed the great subjects in life with me, and took me around with her. Until the day of her death, we remained in an intimate friendship that rested not only on feelings but also on shared intellectual values. Even with the Lilly of later years, tied to a sickbed and suffering, I could easily hold a lively political discussion or talk over a shared literary experience.*

Very different was my relationship with my other brother, Tomi, who was born in 1925. For a long time, we went to the same school, and we had the same governess. We played together a lot, and as brothers will, we had little fights, friendly and less friendly. As soon as Tomi began to take an interest in girls, he broke with me altogether. We never went anywhere together, never shared friends, and never had one serious conversation. That relationship changed little when we grew up; our meetings stayed on the level of superficial banter and chat. I see in this evidence of how a common inheritance built into our brain cells and an almost identical home and

* Lilly (Mrs. Andor Gárdonyi) worked as an accountant and retired as the company's chief auditor. A firm and resolute person, she lived according to strict principles. She did not talk much about herself, but she was always sympathetic to the problems of others. It was touching to see the close relationship that the bedridden old lady formed with our daughter, Judit, and our Swedish grandchildren, Zsófi and Anna, who absolutely adored her. Lilly died in 2002.

school background do not suffice to bind two brothers closely together. The things that were individual in myself and in my brother Tomi and the ways we *differed* had a stronger effect not only on our relations but also on the development of our very different characters and life stories.*

The two parents and four children in the Kornhauser family truly loved one another, though we did not share activities or even meet every day. My father and mother were exceptionally close, but the children led their own lives, distinct from their parents and each other.

After my father's office was moved into the apartment, my mother would sometimes dress up elegantly for the evening and join the clients in the waiting room. This was her way of signaling that it was time to end a working day that was stretching far into the night. My father would then have no choice but to stop work and go out with my mother. They dined out without us nearly every evening. Family meals were almost unknown. Each person would eat lunch or dinner separately, when he or she was hungry or had time. It was rare for the family all to sit down together; the occasions when we did were largely confined to summer, in the garden of our holiday home.

To return to the subject of myself—my parents and my brothers and sister never interfered in how I divided my time, what I studied and for how long, whom I spent my spare time with, what I was reading, or what play I was going to. Occasionally we would get together, especially in the summer, and go to an open-air performance, or watch the August 20 fireworks celebrating the feast day of King Stephen, the founder of Hungary. But these shared outings were exceptional.

At the age of 13 or 14, I decided for myself that I was going to attend concerts regularly. Later I brought up the idea of learning the piano, and my father helped me to find a teacher—not just any teacher, either, for Frigyes Sándor, then an unemployed conductor, later became a great music teacher and established an orchestra. He taught me until the German occupation of Hungary in 1944 brought our lessons to an end. I decided for myself, about halfway through my secondary education, that I wanted to learn English outside school. My parents paid for each of these activities, but I did not do them on their recommendation or following their advice. These were my own ideas; I decided on them for myself.

* My older brother Tomi (Tamás Kornai) graduated from the College of Applied Arts and had planned to become a graphic artist. However, soon after he returned from doing forced labor, he changed his career and worked in the advertising business for the rest of his life. He was one of the managers of the single state-owned advertising enterprise, and then moved on to the National Savings Bank (Országos Takarékpénztár, or OTP). He was proud that his ideas had been the basis for the first advertisements for the Hungarian lottery, slogans that quickly became household words. Tomi died in 1996.

It is not easy to assess or value the effect of such an upbringing. On the one hand, I became imbued with feelings of loneliness and abandonment at being left to my own devices. On the other, I gained, once and for all, an awareness or rather a feeling that I had to shape my life *independently*, as my ideas dictated. That sense applied to matters great and small. I was not brought up to be selfish, because every member of my family tried to be tactful toward the others, saving them from disturbance or annoyance. We helped each other when we could and should, but we did not form any kind of family "community." Today I think of myself as a self-aware individualist, believing that respect for the sovereignty of the individual is among the most important of moral imperatives. At the same time, I believe that I have the primary, principal responsibility for my own life and its successes and failures. I feel a duty to help others, but I am not a "community" man. On the contrary, I resist any attempt to drive me into a collective fold. Certainly what I state consciously today, after turns and detours, an understanding to which I was helped by reading philosophical works and gaining a lifetime of observation, was embedded in me deeply by the experiences of my childhood and youth and by my family's way of life at home.

The Imperial German School

I began my studies at the Imperial German School (*Reichsdeutsche Schule*) in Budapest. Thanks to the perfect German spoken by both my parents and to the successive German *Fräulein* who had looked after me, I grew up bilingual. It was no problem for me that everything at school—apart from Hungarian language, literature, and history—was taught in German. I was admitted before the usual age, in 1933, so my entering the German school coincided with the beginning of Nazi power.

People sometimes ask how my Jewish parents could ever have sent me there. It has already been made clear that my father felt a strong attachment to the Germans. To a marked extent, he was brought up on German culture, and he studied German law alongside Hungarian. His clients were Germans and German was the language in which he did much of his work.

My father must certainly have known that Hitler and his followers were virulent anti-Semites, but like many in Germany and all over the world, he must have thought the regime would not last. How could the spirit of the Germans, the most civilized of people, put up with it? He never guessed that this road of hatred on which Germany set out would end at the gas chambers.

My parents sent me to the Imperial German School to expand my knowledge of the language and to benefit from its academic excellence. It was favored not only by German diplomats and businessmen but also by other foreigners in Hungary. My classmates were Austrian, German, American, and Turkish, as well as Hungarian. The school turned out celebrated people: Miklós Gimes, the journalist, politician, and 1956 martyr; Iván Darvas, a celebrated actor; Éva Székely, an Olympic champion swimmer; Ferenc Karinthy, a writer of novels and short stories; and Előd Halász, a highly respected Hungarian scholar of German studies.

We had patient, experienced, knowledgeable teachers. Never in the eight years I spent there did I hear a single anti-Semitic remark. Nor can I remember any word of praise for Hitler and his rule. When the order came from Berlin that the Jewish students had to leave, the parents were informed tactfully through the teacher of Jewish religious instruction that they would have to enroll their children elsewhere in the fall of 1941. Even then, those who had only one year left of the twelve were allowed to finish their studies as private pupils the following year, and so take their final examinations. It seems probable that liberal teachers in Germany trying to escape from the unbearable life at home would seek jobs abroad, for instance at the Hungarian school. Our school was an amicable island, not just in the sea of Nazism but in the Hungarian school system generally, where Hitlerite ideas were perceptibly gaining ground.

I think back to my teachers at the German school with gratitude and respect. They accustomed me to studying thoroughly and thinking straight and imparted to me a huge amount of knowledge. I still make use of all their gifts today. But I did not meet any truly great figures among my teachers. I was not taught by any master with charisma, whose personality and teaching provided a real intellectual and moral model.

One large reward I received from the Imperial German School was the friendship of a lifetime. One of my classmates from the first grade onward was Péter Kende, later a journalist, scholar, and political scientist, as well as one of the leading intellectual figures in the 1956 émigré community. We went through eight years of school and later worked together in the youth movement and in journalism. We took part together in various struggles. Though Péter's emigration to Paris put a geographical distance between us for more than thirty years, our friendship remained and continues to strengthen to this day. Few people can take pride in having, as I have, a best friend of seventy years' standing.

Seeking an intellectual path

After the German school—cosmopolitan to some extent, with its pupils of several nationalities, and coeducational, which was still exceptional in those days—I entered a new, conservative environment at the Werbőczy boys' gymnasium in Buda. Most of my classmates and the other pupils came from well-to-do middle-class homes.

The war was raging by that time. The teachers in the German school had restrained us from talking about politics and the war. Here I had a principal teacher who loudly praised Germany's conduct of the war and repeatedly predicted a German victory as the battle for Stalingrad took place in 1942–1943. He taught us three main subjects: Latin, Hungarian literature, and history. He declared in front of several of my classmates that no Jew was going to get a top mark in all three from him, and he kept his word. There were two of us Jews in the class who really deserved the top grade in all subjects, but Mr. Hegedűs was prepared to award that mark in only two of his courses, and downgraded us in the third. That was my first experience of open discrimination.

My second such experience involved not the individual prejudices of a teacher but a general state ordinance applying to all. One outward sign of Hungary's participation in the war was that all secondary school pupils received preliminary military training as members of a movement known as *Levente*. While I was still at the German school, all the boys had Levente training together. My arrival at the Hungarian school coincided with an order dividing the military training for non-Jewish and Jewish pupils. I cannot say we were treated particularly cruelly. What I found demeaning was the simple existence of a "Jewish Levente" and the exclusion and segregation it represented.

Most of the class had been together for four years when I joined them. The boys gave me a friendly reception. With some I would go to concerts and plays; with others I had discussions about books. But I did not develop close ties with anyone and tended rather to stick with the friends I had made at the German school. What I said about the atmosphere at the previous school was truer still of this one. I did not encounter one great personality among the teachers. I remember some cracks made by various teachers and some of their mannerisms, but none of them gave me lasting intellectual inspiration.

Apart from the factual information imparted, what I heard about history, philosophy, and the human spirit in school left me quite unaffected. I educated myself and developed my own tastes and ideas. Eager for intellectual influences, I consumed books at high speed. I bought books constantly and built up a fine collection.*

I joined the nearby lending library and brought home reading material from there. I found it quite difficult to decide what to read. One help was Antal Szerb's books

---

* These were carefully kept for me by family friends during the months of persecution. As soon as we came out of the cellars, I hastened to bring my books home and have them near me again. They had survived the siege of Budapest, which lasted from Christmas 1944 to mid-February 1945; the air raids; and the looting. Then all but one volume were lost only a few weeks later, when, early in 1945, Soviet soldiers suddenly ordered us to leave our apartment. The survivor is a great favorite of mine, Thomas Mann's *Tonio Kröger*.

on the history of Hungarian and of world literature. While our principal teacher spoke of them as "trash" and more or less forbade us to read them (Szerb was a Jew), I found their guidance invaluable. I complemented Szerb's works with Mihály Babits's literary history of Europe. I tried to read all the books that these guides described as great. It now seems almost incredible how much time I managed to spend on them. I was usually up at dawn and could finish all my studying for school in one or two hours. After school, I spent the whole afternoon and evening either meeting and talking to friends or reading. One week I would be in *War and Peace* and the next on to *The Brothers Karamazov*. I read Balzac and Flaubert, the classical Hungarian writers Kálmán Mikszáth and Zsigmond Móricz, the wonderful poetry of János Arany and Attila József, the brilliant Hungarian verse translations from various foreign languages of Árpád Tóth and Dezső Kosztolányi—and I could carry on for a long time listing all the books I enjoyed.

I also looked through the articles on intellectual subjects and the arts in the weekend supplements to the daily papers, again as a way of deciding what to read. Certainly it must ultimately have been an awareness of the intellectual fashions of the day that led me to the writings of Ortega y Gasset and Huizinga and Oswald Spengler. I was delighted as well to find works that gave an overview of particular spheres of intellectual life and thinking, such as Will Durant's history of philosophy. I cannot have understood more than half the real content of what I read between the ages of 14 and 16. There was no one to offer me a clear worldview—not my parents, my brothers and sister, or my teachers in the class on religion. I was open to all new ideas. I was pitched and tossed among alternative answers to the challenges of the world. One day, I would be influenced by Dostoyevsky and I felt I had to become a Christian. The next day, perhaps, I would be leafing through Anatole France, under the spell of his ironical view of the world, a view reinforced as I enjoyed Voltaire's *Candide*.

During those years, I still had no idea of what I wanted to do when I grew up. My nephew, Pál Győrfi, decided while he was still in kindergarten that he wanted to be an ambulance paramedic, and that is what he became. I had no such sense of vocation. Perhaps there were already developing in me some traits that would later be fulfilled in my research work. I liked my things to be in order. I had a strong urge to finish completely what I put my hand to. If I was taking photographs, I would concentrate all my energies on that activity. If I was collecting books, I wanted my library to contain every book considered a masterpiece. If I took to stamp collecting, my album had to be as comprehensive as possible. Even as a boy, I found chaos, untidiness, and half-completed tasks annoying.

But these characteristics and endeavors of mine had nothing to do with the direction of my intellectual interest. To extrapolate the intellectual development of my

14- to 16-year-old self (now, with hindsight) into my later years, I see a bookish egghead's profile appearing, someone who might write literary criticism or explore questions of aesthetics. There is still no sign of the man who would turn to the urgent problems of society and become a research economist twelve or fifteen years later.

I still thought then that the more knowledge I gained, the better the understanding of the world building up inside me would be. One view was being written over each day by the next, to use an image from computers. In fact, I was waiting with open heart and open mind for one true, strong intellectual impulse. And that arrived in 1945—but let us not jump so far forward. We have only reached my final years of secondary school, when the trauma of 1944 was still ahead.

1944: The fate of my father

March 19, 1944, began like any other Sunday. I was preparing to go to a morning concert with a friend. The concert was canceled; the German army had begun its occupation of Hungary.

A week or two later, my father received conscription papers, similar to the ones for Jews assigned to forced labor service. He had to present himself forty-eight hours later at a specified place with camp equipment from blanket to mess tin and with cold rations for two days. Because my father had passed his sixty-third birthday by then, he could not be conscripted into the regular labor service, which had an age limit of 60.

My parents were tormented by premonitions. They learned from telephone calls that some other well-known Jewish intellectuals and businessmen had been called up like my father. We children were not drawn into my parents' anxious discussions, but I could subsequently reconstruct, from what my mother said, the courses of action they had been weighing.

My mother came up with the idea that the two of them should commit suicide together. That was rejected; they could not abandon the other members of the family in such dangerous times. My mother asked my father if he would not try to go into hiding. Friends were prepared to make a sacrifice, including some Germans; people would give him shelter. My father dismissed this suggestion out of hand for two reasons. One was that he thought the risk was too great: he feared that if he were found there would be bloody reprisals against him and likewise against the family hiding him. The other was that his call-up was a state order that had to be obeyed. That response brings me to one of the underlying principles of my father's view of the world. He was a lawyer: not just any attorney, but a man with a consistent and passionate respect for the law. He would certainly have come across and read about cases in which morality and legal statutes came into conflict. I am sure he must have thought time and again what kind of law it was that a tyrant dictated, what kind of law it was that a sham parliament would pass while trampling on fundamental human rights. And yet, when he found himself faced with this dilemma in relation to his own life, this moral man so meticulous about honesty and incorruptibility applied the simplest formula. A state order was a state order, a command a command that had to be obeyed.

It turned out that one or two hundred prominent members of the Jewish elite in Budapest were being rounded up as hostages during the early weeks of the German occupation. At first, they were lodged at the Rabbinical Seminary on Rökk Szilárd utca, in relatively tolerable conditions and under Hungarian police control.[1] A few weeks later, their families were given permission to visit them. My mother, my sister, and I went to see him, as by that time both my brothers were in the forced labor service: Bandi, the elder, on the Russian front, and Tomi at Bor in Yugoslavia. So they could not be with us. We met in the courtyard of the seminary. My father's expression and remarks were calm and, if my memory does not deceive me, almost cheerful. Nothing emotional was said. He gave some practical advice to my mother, who up to then had been concerned only with entertaining friends and relations and with matters to do with her children, while financial affairs and the administrative side of the household were looked after by my father. These matters all fell suddenly on my mother, and my father tried to give her various kinds of information on them. Later he sent a letter proposing what to do with our apartment and instructing her where to store the files from his law practice.* Neither at the meeting nor in the letter was there a farewell from him, beyond the tender words of greeting customary in the family.

We never received another line from my father, and we never saw him again.

While he was still in the seminary building, efforts were being made on his behalf. Some of his faithful German clients formed a little delegation and went to see Ambassador Edmund Veesenmayer, the *Gauleiter* with a dreadful reputation sent to Hungary at the time of the occupation. The delegation asked the Germans to request that the Hungarian authorities send my father home. They cited the credit due to the attorney Dr. Pál Kornhauser for the way he had represented German business interests in Hungary for several decades. One member of the group later told my mother what followed: Veesenmayer flew into a rage and threatened to intern the applicants alongside Kornhauser if they did not clear out of his office right away.

* Could I have inherited the drive to always keep my files of documents and notes in meticulous order, or have I just copied my father's example?

There are only uncertain accounts of what happened to my father after that. Apparently the whole group was transferred to a camp at Horthy-liget (today's Sziget-szentmiklós), where conditions were harder but where a life of internment continued for a while.[2] This came to a sudden end when they were all put on a train taking provincial deportees to the death camp at Auschwitz.

The deaths of all the six million victims of the Holocaust were tragic and the death of every victim was preceded by a unique, individual life. Nonetheless, my father's fate was peculiar. For one thing, he was killed by the *German* reign of terror with the eager cooperation of the Hungarian authorities. His death occurred despite the fact that he had been captivated by German culture since early youth, had himself set out to promote the prosperity of German industry and commerce through his legal practice, and had himself thereby worked for honesty and legality in German-Hungarian relations. Of course he had never supported Hitler or collaborated with the Nazi authorities, but he died not because he stood aside passively but because he was a Jew.

Another peculiar aspect of my father's tragedy has been mentioned already: he was a faithful servant of *legality*, and therefore did not wish to oppose the authority of the state. He went as a defenseless lamb to the slaughter, falling victim to the most blatant and inhuman abuse of justice, the law, and the power of the state.

1944: My escape

If my father had still been at home, he would certainly have commented on what I ought to do. I do not know whose will would have been the stronger—my father's, who, as I mentioned earlier, had prevented my brother Bandi from emigrating at a critical juncture, or mine—for I was used to acting quite independently on lesser matters in life.

Since my father had gone and my mother could not and did not wish to influence my decisions, I was left to my own 16-year-old judgment. In this case, it was a matter of much greater import than what books I should read or what language I should set about learning. The year 1944 was one of life-and-death decisions.

News of deportations had begun to fly about. We had no idea then that the deportees would be killed in gas chambers; we thought they were being sent to the kind of forced labor camp that my brothers Bandi and Tomi were serving in. We had recently had news of Bandi and Tomi. We knew they were having a hard time, suffering from hunger and cold and sometimes inhuman treatment, but we were not without hope that they would survive the war.

We also heard that Jews working in arms factories would not be deported (although this rumor later proved wrong). Therefore, two friends of mine and I turned up of our own accord to work as laborers at the Nagybátony-Újlak Brickworks on the periphery of Bécsi út.* From being a secondary school student who had never done manual work and who was awkward and weak at sports, I suddenly turned into a laborer, indeed one doing very demanding and tiring physical tasks. The raw bricks, still heavy with water, were lifted by skilled, practiced workers out of a continuously operating press and placed on a trolley that ran on rails. We recruits had to push the trolleys to the sheds and stack the bricks neatly.

For a while, we went into the factory and home again in the evening, wearing the compulsory yellow star. Later, a curfew was imposed, restricting our movements. By the time the shift was over, it was too late to go home. We had no choice but to move out to the factory and sleep there in the sheds as best we could.†

This unwonted lifestyle has not left any bitter memories in me. On the contrary, it was a bit like those summer camps involving agricultural work or construction that young people would be attending by the end of the 1940s. We were motivated by fear, but we went to work there "voluntarily." We cheerfully put all our energies into the job and adapted to the conditions. It was a great relief to find that the experienced workers at the brickworks who were now our colleagues never said a disparaging word. There was not a single comment about the star glaring out from our clothes, no word of abuse against Jews. If we were clumsy, they showed us what to do or told us off, just as they would any other beginner who produced "tripe" (spoilage). One older worker invited us to his home and offered us food and drink. I saw how they lived. They had clean, orderly little apartments, but to me they seemed unbelievably poor compared with the prosperity in which my friends and I had been living. At home as well, I had always been on good terms with the domestic staff, often talking to them, visiting their homes, and meeting their families. But that had been a paternalistic relationship between an employee and a member of the employer's family. It differed altogether from this, my first real encounter with the "working class." I had suddenly stepped into a different world, leaving a life of almost hermetically sealed prosperity and comfort for one of

* Although it was not yet a conscious principle, I instinctively, or under the pressure of circumstances, started to learn that one has to choose when presented with alternatives in life. An attitude developed in me of not liking to passively submit to fate. Instead I would try to take the direction of my life into my own hands. Later I deliberately embraced this behavior as one of my basic principles of life. Of course, the resolution to make a choice does not guarantee that the decision will always be a good one. The work I did for the brick factory, for example, proved to be superfluous, as will shortly be seen.

† While I was living in the brick factory, my mother and sister had to leave our apartment on Akadémia utca. The Jews were being moved into the "star" houses, marked with a Star of David. My mother and sister were taken in by some old friends of my parents, a family who lived in one of the "Jewish houses" on Pozsonyi út.

punishing physical labor in a factory operated with obsolete technology and of meager homes. I found myself among people whom I could sincerely respect for their hard lives and natural humanity.

The Nagybátony-Újlak Brickworks later became one of the transit points for the mass deportations. It features in the stories of many people who returned after being deported, several of whom have said that they were helped by people working there. Sharp clashes took place between the clerks, gendarmes, and police carrying out the deportations on the one hand and brickyard workers on the other. Apparently, some workers even paid with their lives for their willingness to help the deportees. Unfortunately, I have not found trustworthy corroboration of that claim.

The pressure on Budapest's Jews became somewhat lighter in the summer of 1944. Deportation of the provincial Jews had been completed and word was going around that those in Budapest were not going to be deported after all. Meanwhile I found a kind doctor, István Szabó, willing to risk giving me a false certificate declaring me unfit for hard manual labor, and I was allowed to leave the brickworks.

Autumn was approaching and the beginning of the school term. I was supposed to begin the last year before the school-leaving exams. I decided I was not going to arrive in the class with a yellow star on me. To my classmates' credit, I must say that I had never heard a single anti-Semitic remark from them; but I had bad feelings about never having received any sign of sympathy from them either, any more than I had from non-Jewish friends and acquaintances at other schools. They did not visit or phone. When I ran into a couple of them after the war, I reproached them with their silence, but they looked at me uncomprehendingly, as if they could not grasp what they had neglected to do. They had often thought about me with goodwill and would like to have known what had become of me . . . The schools we had attended and the families who had raised us had not taught us how to express empathy, compassion, or solidarity.

I spent the summer and early autumn doing nothing. We moved from the "star" house to my sister's apartment under a curious deal with a gendarmerie captain, who became the official tenant. My sister agreed with him that if we perished and he and his family survived, the tenancy and the whole contents of the flat would be theirs. If we survived the storm, however, we would move back and they would go elsewhere. The latter turned out to be case, but in the summer of 1944 we had no way of telling what the future would bring. While my mother was busy in the kitchen, three of us—my sister Lilly; the captain's kind, good-humored, six-months pregnant wife; and I—would tell each other the kind of jokes enjoyed by 16-year-olds, laughing loudly like people with nothing more to lose.

On October 15, Governor Horthy, the head of the Hungarian state, issued his notorious proclamation about a cease-fire to be agreed on with the Soviet army. Soon after, bands of the Hungarian Nazis, the Arrow-Cross men, appeared in the streets. The terror lasted ten weeks on the Pest side, starting with sporadic killings and escalating into mass murder. It was another month before Germans and the Hungarian Arrow-Cross could be cleared from the Buda side.

A few days after the Arrow-Cross seized power came a mobilization order, calling up all Jews into forced labor, even those younger and older than the 18–60 age bracket liable for military service. I was among those called up and put into a labor company consisting of boys my own age and elderly men. The troops marched off from the raceway, where the new labor service men were gathering and were assigned to companies. Our quarters for the first night was a new, half-completed wing at Ferihegy Airport. There each of us used his pack as a pillow. When dawn came, an old man was lying motionless a few feet away. The turmoil and the march had been too much for him. I was seeing a dead man for the first time.

When we got to Vecsés, a small town about 20 kilometers from Budapest, we were quartered in some stables, about a hundred men lying side by side on the straw. Here there was none of the jovial camp atmosphere of the nights we had spent in the brickworks. The elderly members of the company were suffering. Anyone who had to get up in the night would stumble as he stepped over the others in the dark. Every morning, men accustomed to warm bathrooms tried to wash as best they could in ice-cold water. We were given precious little to eat. Out in the fields where we had to dig trenches, we dug up carrots for ourselves to stave off starvation. The members of the company remained strangers to each other. The time was too short for any ties of comradeship or friendship to develop. I had no one to share my cares and problems with.

Yet there too I encountered warm gestures of humanity. One day we had to churn up a family garden, because we had been ordered by the camp guards in charge of us to dig a trench there. The owners did not vent their wrath on us for the damage. On the contrary, a nice little fair-haired girl suddenly appeared with a pail of bean soup for the starving team. Márta was the girl's name and by chance I ran into her again many years later, when she was a typist in the office where I was a journalist. While sharing memories of the war, we discovered that her parents had been our guardian angels and I was one of those they had selflessly helped. It was a tiny good deed, a pail of soup. Still, this is one of several examples I give when anyone makes false generalizations about all Hungarians watching unsympathetically as the Jews were persecuted.

Already we could hear the Soviet artillery quite close when on November 2, 1944, we received an order to leave Vecsés straightaway and march toward Budapest. The company moved off on All Souls' Day, known in Hungary as the Day of the Dead— a few dozen young boys and perhaps 100 to 150 elderly men. The camp guards escorted us to the borders of Budapest. As they had during our stay in Vecsés, they kept tight discipline on the road, but they did not amuse themselves by torturing us or devising sadistic orders that would lead to a swift collapse or death. They set a fast but still bearable pace.

Since then, I have often passed the military buildings in Üllői út where the Arrow-Cross Party militiamen with their armbands and green shirts took over the company from the camp guards. A few moments later, the first new order was yelled out: "On the double!" We young ones could stand running even after a march of several miles from Vecsés to Budapest, but several of the older men began to lag behind. The Arrow-Cross youths took their rifle butts to anyone who stopped. The drive and the beatings for those who lagged behind continued along Üllői út and down to Miklós Horthy (now Petőfi) Bridge. I saw merciless treatment being meted out to those in front of me and those behind. Perhaps five or even more elderly men were beaten over the head before my eyes. When we reached the bridge, two people broke ranks and jumped into the Danube. The Arrow-Cross fired at them. I do not know whether they were hit or they got away.

We were utterly exhausted and psychologically broken when we arrived in Albertfalva, where we spent the night. It had indeed been a Day of the Dead. The 20 kilometers from Vecsés to Albertfalva was quite a distance even for people in good health. Early the next morning I decided that I would have to escape.

Luckily a good opportunity arose. Raoul Wallenberg, the heroic Swedish diplomat, at this time was carrying out his rescue campaign all over Budapest, using a number of techniques. Some people were given Swedish passports that were not exactly the same as those held by real Swedish citizens. That document had written on it the German word *Schutzpass*, meaning "protective passport," which certified that the holder was a Swedish citizen. Others had a document of less legal weight called a *Schutzbrief* (letter of safe conduct), which stated that the bearer was under the protection of the Swedish Embassy in Budapest. The former had to be respected even by the Arrow-Cross government, but the latter really had no meaning or force under international law.

I had the second type of document in my pocket: impressive looking but of little import. It had been obtained for me by a friend of the family, Ernő Wahrmann, one of my sister Lilly's admirers. Early one morning, one of the Arrow-Cross commanders gave the order for those with Swedish passports to line up. I had only a moment to decide. If I stood up with the Swedes and they noticed I did not have a genuine Swedish passport, I might be shot dead out of hand. I decided to take the risk and class myself as a Swede.

Luckily, the youngster checking the documents did not perceive the fine distinction between a *Schutzpass* and a *Schutzbrief* and left me in the Swedish squad. We were put in a truck and taken to Pest. The rest of the men remained in the original detachment, and it was whispered that they would be driven further west. I chanced to meet a survivor many years later and learned what had happened to them. By the time they reached the Austrian border, only a couple of them were still alive. Beatings, starvation, and the forced pace of the march had killed the rest.

The Swedish squad from Albertfalva was taken with several other Swedish groups to the spacious headquarters of a trade union in Pest. Although we had to sleep on the ground, what a liberating feeling it was to have nobody mistreating us. We were guarded by friendly young enlisted soldiers. Order was kept by "Swedish" officers chosen from Hungarian Jews who had once held reserve officer rank. But however tolerable the life was, I did not trust the Arrow-Cross to leave us in comfort for long. It emerged later that I was right, as this group too was driven westward after a short delay.

It was easy to escape from the Swedish house. One of the officers was a family friend and arranged for the guard to look away while I stepped out of the door.

Free again, I could walk in the Pest streets unguarded. But how free was I? Although I was not wearing a yellow star, I did not have false papers either. If any Arrow-Cross man or policeman, soldier, or civilian collaborating with them became suspicious, I could be carried off to prison and to brutal interrogation. I had to hide.

Initially, I took refuge with dear Lujza, who had been the family housecleaner. Her husband was the concierge in a large apartment house, and I slept in a room there. They did not want to leave me alone in the apartment when they went to work in the day, and so they would ask one or another of the residents to hide me. I spent one day in a tram driver's room and the next I was taken in by a prostitute. Each of them knew the incalculable risk they ran: harboring Jews or army deserters was punishable by "annihilation," as the ubiquitous posters put it. Yet they did it, and they thereby provide further examples of how wrong it is to generalize, how unjust it would be to see only sadistic Arrow-Cross villains in the Hungarians. For some Hungarians voluntarily and selflessly helped us, out of a sense of humanity, at great danger to themselves.

I could not continue for long hiding like that, finding a new place to stay every day. Again I had luck on my side. The family friend who had obtained the Wallenberg *Schutzbrief* for me now used his connections in the Jesuit order. The Jesuit fathers agreed to hide a group of Jews, including my sister's husband and me. The same friend of ours used his effective connections with the church to find refuge for my mother and sister with the Sacré Coeur Sisters. Before going to my new hiding place, I visited them, because who knew whether I would ever see them again. Without a star or identity papers, I hurried to the nunnery carrying a bunch of flowers in my hand. My mother and sister greeted me with delight and we said farewell.

The Jesuit monastery (now the premises of Rajk College, a dormitory and a place of learning for economics students) gave us a friendly welcome. Many fugitives were given asylum there by the superior,[3] Father Jakab Raile.* I was the only youngster, so I did not have a real partner for conversation. My brother-in-law and I kept up the ties proper to relations, but we were never close to each other emotionally or intellectually. Again I found myself in a community where I remained more or less alone.

One of the fathers, whose name I unfortunately forget, invited me several times to converse with him about religious beliefs, God, and the Christian and Jewish religions and philosophies. To others, we must have presented a curious sight—a Jesuit father and a lanky, disheveled teenager walking up and down the garden in lively conversation, while the artillery rumbled outside.

By that time, the Soviet army had closed around Budapest and street-by-street fighting had begun in the outer districts. We lived in the belief that the prestige of the Jesuit order would keep out the Arrow-Cross, but one morning a message came from the fathers that the Arrow-Cross had begun to search the premises. I rushed out onto the staircase and saw two armed men shouting there; I could not tell if they were soldiers or Arrow-Cross militiamen. My brother-in-law and I escaped onto the roof and lay down on the battens that the chimney sweeps used to reach the chimneys. I did not know which to be more frightened of, the raid in the building or the bombardment of the city. There was a fearful noise from the bombs falling and from the artillery firing nearby. What is more, I was anxious not to fall off the narrow plank. While the situation was frantic, there was also a hellish beauty in the skyline of the city, with flashing gunfire seen from the rooftop. And the episode had a grotesque side too, as a young Jewish bank clerk and a schoolboy bookworm clung flattened out on boards laid across the roof of a Jesuit monastery.

We survived the raid, but our hosts now wanted us to move into the cellars. We lived down there for two weeks, if I remember right, in cramped but relatively civilized conditions. The monastery supplied us with food; we were certainly better fed than most people in Budapest were at the time. Before the siege started, the houses had been linked through the air-raid shelters in their cellars by opening doorways between them where possible. One morning, the door from the cellar of the neighboring house opened and a platoon of German soldiers entered. What did they want? Was it a raid? Did they want to drive us out? No, already by then that was

* Jakab Raile was the provincial of the Jesuits in Hungary in 1944. There are no reliable data on how many people were hidden in the house. One source estimates the number at 100, another at 150. In 1992, Father Raile received the title "Righteous among the Nations" from the Israeli organization Yad Vashem. This honor is given to those who did the most to save the persecuted Jews during the Holocaust.

the least of their cares—they tried to flee. They were exhausted, broken men, dragging themselves from one cellar to the next.

Perhaps one or two days after that visit from the defeated German platoon, the Russians arrived. I will never forget the sight we saw before us. There was an inside staircase down to the cellar where we were concealed. We were living in anxiety down below, when suddenly, three men appeared at the top of the steps. There was Father Raile, the superior, in the habit of Jesuit priest. Beside him was a ramrod-straight Soviet officer in Cossack uniform. Before, I had seen a uniform like that only in operetta films, his belt of great cartridges worn on the outside across his chest. The third man with them was one of us, the cantor of a synagogue in Subcarpathia,* who was known to speak Russian and Ukrainian and was now interpreting between the Jesuit and the Soviet officer. We heard a few friendly words of greeting, and then the persecution, the hiding, and the siege of the city were over for us.

The scene continued in a bizarre way. Down the steps to us, who had been persecuted, who had hidden in the Jesuit house for weeks, and who been freed just moments before, came a couple of Russian soldiers, who with shouts of "Davay chasi!" relieved us all of our wristwatches. I did not quite understand why they were doing this or what it really meant, but I handed mine over without further ado.

We waited another day or two before all of us who had found refuge in the Jesuit house said a grateful farewell and we all went our separate ways.

I set off for the little boulevard and soon found myself in front of the main synagogue on Dohány utca. There I was astounded and moved to see frozen, naked corpses stacked by the side of the road. There were piles as high as houses of dead Jews who had perished in the ghetto around the synagogue.

I hurried on toward my sister's apartment on Pozsonyi út. I entered, and there were my mother and sister. All three of us who had been in Budapest during the siege had survived!

A chapter in my life had ended. I was only a few days short of my seventeenth birthday. I had not reached adulthood in a legal sense, but the year 1944 meant that once and for all, I ceased to feel like a child or a minor who did not bear full responsibility for myself.

* That is a region that was part of Hungary in 1944 and belongs to Ukraine now.

2

How I Became a Communist—1945–1947

I was working in Sweden in 1975. I had to travel to a meeting in New York, which meant applying for my visa at the United States Embassy in Stockholm. As required by the American law in force at that time, one question on the application asked whether I had ever in my life been a member of the Communist Party. The embassy official who took my form saw I had answered yes and suggested, kindly and helpfully: "They must have forced you to join…" "Far from it," I replied. "I joined of my own free will. I joined because those were my convictions at the time."

Half a century has passed since my Communist beliefs began to flicker and die. But still, as I record and assess my life, the question of how and why I became a Communist has lost none of its immediacy.

Grades of identification

The answer I gave to the U.S. embassy official was a slight simplification. Joining the party entails a formal declaration in writing. Though a very important and consequential act, this marks just one stage in a process of conversion, which begins outside the Communist Party and ends in complete identification with it. It usually takes quite some time, and its course is affected by each person's personality and circumstances. Moreover, conversion in countries where the Communist Party is in power differs from that in countries where the party is still struggling for power, whether as a legal or an illegal organization. I will deal here only with the case of a Communist Party in power.* The destruction of the Arrow-Cross regime in Hungary was followed immediately by a coalition government that included the Hungarian Communist Party and gave it powerful offices. (Later, after the period

---

* The Communist Party in Hungary changed its name several times. The Hungarian Communist Party (1944–1948) became the Hungarian Workers' Party (1948–1956), and then Hungarian Socialist Workers' Party (1956–1989). All these variations are covered in this book by "Communist Party."

covered by this chapter, the Communist Party managed to seize exclusive political power.)

It is worth distinguishing five grades of identification with the Communist Party, which also trace the typical route.

The first step is being *a sympathizer outside the party*. Such people are drawn to the party's ideas and ready to support specific campaigns, and they vote for the Communists in elections. They are fellow travelers, but do not accept (or have not yet accepted) the commitment signaled by party membership.

The second is being *a party member*. There is emphatically no descriptor before the phrase "party member." Such members may be ardent or reticent, hardly visible in party organizations. They may have moved from sincere sympathy with the party to accepting the duties and discipline that accompany membership. Or communist ideas may remain alien to these members, who have joined just for the advantages they expect to gain by doing so.

The third step is being *an active, committed party member*. Such members attend branch meetings regularly and take on party work. They stand by their communist convictions.

The fourth step is being *a true Communist*. This entails being a trained Marxist-Leninist, but that is not enough in itself. Think of the oft-quoted words that Stalin spoke at Lenin's funeral: "Comrades, we Communists are people of a special mould. We are made of special stuff."[1] Indeed, true Communists, true Bolsheviks, differ from non-Communists not just intellectually but in their behavior and character as well. They must behave in a "party-like" way. All interests to do with the individual, family, friends, or colleagues must be subordinated to the party's interests. True Communists must obey every order from the party in a disciplined way, even if they personally disagree with it. They must be ready to make any sacrifice the party may require of them.

There is no sharp dividing line between the third and fourth grades. Members with strong convictions would like to become true Communists. That is the human ideal before them, and an extremely "dialectical" ideal it is. True Communists are tortured by inner doubts as to whether their Marxist training is sufficient and whether they are disciplined and self-sacrificing enough. The stronger their self-critical awareness, the more their comrades see their communism as authentic, certain, and true.

The fifth step is being *a party warrior, a professional party worker*. This category covers those who serve the party full-time rather than simply devoting some of their time to party work. Such a member could be a party secretary or an employee in the party apparatus, or a factory manager or an officer in the State Security Police (Államvédelmi Hatóság, or ÁVH). The key point is that he or she has been selected for the post by the party and may be recalled by the party at any time. Whatever the job may be, the orders come from the party and the party's interests are served.

Of course, the five grades make up only an abstract model of how an individual develops into a Communist. They do not always follow a strict sequence. Several steps may occur simultaneously, wholly or in part.

Some people stop at the first or some subsequent step of identification. I went the whole course. This is my personal story, but I am sure many aspects of it are similar or identical to that of others. My story is a fairly typical one.

I was still at school in the spring of 1945, preparing for the school-leaving exams at the Reformed Church Gymnasium in the provincial town of Kiskunhalas. I had been invited by a friend to move there, where it would be easier to find food, for a couple of months. Returning to Budapest after the exams, in the summer of 1945 I started to visit the Fifth District branch of the Hungarian Democratic Youth Federation (Magyar Demokratikus Ifjúsági Szövetség, or MADISZ), a Communist-controlled organization. The first six or eight months of 1945 turned me from being remote from the Communist Party into a Communist sympathizer (first grade).

I joined MADISZ that summer and became increasingly active. My Communist sympathies grew stronger, and I formed the intention of joining the party.

By the end of the autumn, I had joined the Hungarian Communist Party and was a full-time functionary at the MADISZ Budapest headquarters. So the second and third grades overlapped: I was already an activist in a Communist-led movement by the time I joined the party. And that overlap in a sense foreshadowed my later embrace of the fifth grade, the role of a professional party warrior.

So it was the Budapest headquarters of MADISZ where my intention of becoming a true Communist began to take shape. I was later promoted and transferred to the national headquarters of MADISZ. That promotion marked the high point in my youth movement career. By the time I reached it, I saw myself as a true Communist and was seen as such by those around me. I had clearly reached the fourth or fifth grade.

I was moved in this direction by several factors: I will describe them in terms of the conversion process rather than chronologically, distinguishing the five grades where that helps the analysis along.

Reaction to the trauma of 1944

I consider the association of the Jews with leadership of the Communist Party to be gravely mistaken. It is blind stupidity and ignorance to say that Jews "have communism in their blood." Although Marx was a Jew, Engels, Lenin, and Stalin were not. Béla Kun and Mátyás Rákosi, the Hungarian Communist leaders in 1919 and after

1945, were Jews, but not the German Walter Ulbricht, the Polish Bolesław Bierut, or the Chinese Mao Zedong. And the racist charge can be refuted in reverse by listing Jewish politicians who served not the communist cause but as leaders of social democratic, liberal, or conservative parties and movements.

At the same time, many of the Hungarian Jewish intelligentsia, young and old, were propelled toward the Communist Party by the trauma of 1944.

The persecution of Hungarian Jews did not start in 1944. It grew directly out of the acts of the Horthy regime (1920–1944): its anti-Jewish laws that made anti-Semitism official policy; its alliance with Hitler, concluded as an aid to revising Hungary's borders; and its entry into World War II on Hitler's side. Many Jews therefore felt they had to support the Communist Party, which had raised the sharpest opposition to the regime and had been persecuted as an illegal organization throughout the Horthy period.

There was much talk about the Hungarian resistance movement in the weeks and months after the Liberation. The Communists proclaimed that their people had been the most active and self-sacrificing in the struggle. The truth was that the Hungarian armed resistance had been weak, ineffective, and limited in scale. I have not studied the question of the precise ratio of Communists to non-Communists among that limited body of armed resisters. In the period when I was moving toward the Communist Party, I certainly met Communists who had taken up arms against fascism. I respected and admired them, and felt remorse that I had saved just my own skin and not even tried to fight. Nor could I plead youth as an excuse. The Fifth District MADISZ included people younger than I whom everyone honored as heroes of the resistance: Homok (Ferenc Várnai) and Gabi Papp.

It was not just its past merits of resisting the Horthy regime and putting up armed resistance that made the Communist Party worthy of respect and sympathy in the eyes of a young Jewish boy. Another compelling force was anxiety about the future. Couldn't the tragedy be repeated? I am not thinking here of what the *right* answer to that question might have been; I have no desire to discuss the fate of Hungarian democracy or Hungary's relations with the democratic West. What I am trying to convey is the rough train of thought then running through my 17-year-old head (as well as the heads of many other young people who had experienced a similar trauma). Irrespective of what future socioeconomic system the Communist Party promised or what character the system in the Soviet Union possessed, the Communist Party, through its political presence, role in government, and power, offered the surest guarantee against a resurgence of fascism—and that seemed sufficient reason to support it.

That line of argument, not any affinity on the genetic level, served to enhance the Communist Party's attraction in Jewish eyes.

There was no way to separate at that time (or later) one's judgment of the Communist Party from one's verdict on the Soviet Union. Those enthusiastic about the Soviet Union also sympathized with the Hungarian Communist Party. Those who harbored distaste or hatred for the Soviet Union felt antipathy for Hungarian Communists as well.

When the Soviet forces in January–February 1945 chased out the German army and its Hungarian Arrow-Cross henchmen, I felt wholeheartedly that we had been liberated. I saw the Soviet soldiers as the people who had saved my life, and I felt gratitude for the dreadful losses they had suffered on my behalf. That sense of gratitude quite suppressed in me the recognition that many soldiers of the Red Army were behaving like ruffians and that their commanders were tolerating this behavior. The odd theft I recalled in the previous chapter, when we were robbed of our watches at the moment of liberation, was an event I found almost amusing. However, I could not smile when I discovered our apartment being pillaged on several occasions. A group of Russian soldiers wielding machine guns burst through the door, herded us into the air-raid cellar, gathered up a load of our possessions, and left. We even had a regular, who robbed us several times. (We called him *Bunker Idi*—"Go to the bunker," in Russian—because that is what he would yell as he brandished his gun and drove us down to the cellar.)

One close friend of mine told me in desperation that they had raped his mother.

I was taken several times for *malinki robot* (a little work)—digging a gun emplacement in Budapest or driving horses when I was in the provinces. Luckily, I always found my way back. By then we had heard of many civilians being taken off for little tasks and subsequently put with the prisoners of war and carried off to the Soviet Union.

What happened to me is known in psychology as the reduction of cognitive dissonance. I confined these ghastly experiences to my unconscious for many years; for if they had surfaced, they would have weakened my confidence in the Soviet Union. Or I tried to find in myself some explanation and excuse for inexcusable and unacceptable behavior. In the meantime my confidence in the Soviet Union was strengthening to the point that it eventually became a blind, unconditional faith.

Before turning to other factors behind the changes in me, let me say something more about my Jewishness. From the time I became close to the Communist Party, my Jewish identity vanished almost completely, at least from the conscious levels of my mind. An old classmate of mine at one point told me he was preparing to emigrate to Israel. The prospect left me quite cold.* I was far from holding any idea of

---

* Naturally I could have emigrated to a number of other places, not just Israel. To stay in Hungary or to emigrate was a choice that came up then and many more times during my life, and it is an issue I will discuss in greater detail in a later chapter.

vengeance for the persecution the Jews had suffered. It was immaterial to me how many Jews were in the party leadership, for their being labeled as Jewish did not make me feel closer to them. On the other hand, it never crossed my mind that this same label might make them repugnant to many in a Hungarian society long poisoned by anti-Semitism.

It seemed natural to me that the name Kornhauser—which sounded German and thus indicated a Jewish background—would have to be changed to something that sounded more Hungarian, like Kornai. Nobody actually suggested I do this. I decided to change my name of my own accord, also as part of my effort to counteract the painful experience of discrimination by "assimilating" into Hungarian society.

The erosion of my Jewish identity was facilitated, of course, by changes in Hungarian law and public life. You no longer had to declare your religion on official forms. There was no more talk about a "Christian course," with its overtones of exclusion. Crude, open manifestations of racial and religious discrimination against the Jews and segregation and confinement in ghettos disappeared from the legal system. Private, informal discrimination also faded or was dispelled.* Those two years brought an extremely rapid shift in Hungarian society toward liberalism in this respect.

I began to concern myself with my Jewish identity again when *public* anti-Semitism once more began to be visible and audible and reappeared in print. I will say more about that later in the book, when discussing the period concerned.

I said earlier that the trauma I had undergone as a Jew also pushed me toward the Communist Party. Then I said that as I came closer to the Communist Party, my Jewish identity died in me (or went into hibernation).† I see no contradiction there, and the two processes meshed psychologically as well. The more the Communist environment surrounded me, the less I felt there was any significance in having been born a Jew.

Memories of humiliation, stigmatization, and discrimination forced many Jews, including myself, to join a community that made no distinctions on the grounds of

---

* People who had moved into the apartments of Jews or received their possessions could not have been happy to see the survivors return. Those anti-Semitic to the core before 1945 retained a hatred for Jews after 1945. In the early years, there were even some pogroms, but such occurrences were generally hushed up. At least, I never was aware of anything of the kind.

† My case was not unusual. Decades later, I met "cadre children" whose parents were Jews and who had joined the Communist Party at roughly the same time as I. They told me that their parents regarded themselves as Hungarian Communists and that they had no Jewish identity whatsoever, although they were fully aware that by the Nazi laws they would be considered Jews. They almost felt embarrassed when their Jewish background came up, not because they were ashamed but because they thought it was irrelevant.

race or religion, and treated us as equals. From the very outset, Communist Party philosophy instilled in us a variety of prejudices, but these did not include racism. I was never asked in Communist circles about my creed or my parents' or grandparents' creed. I was accepted as one of them. After the dreadful trauma of discrimination, the experience of acceptance was appealing and comforting.

Intellectual conversion and acceptance of Communist political ideas

What I have tried to reconstruct above was more an *emotional* chain of cause and effect than a tight, logical sequence of ideas. It was paralleled by an *intellectual* sequence. Analyzing my own conversion reveals that this mental process was not associated with being Jewish or with the trauma of 1944. It was a case of new ideas competing with old and soon supplanting them entirely. In describing how my thinking was transformed, I emphatically want to avoid giving any impression that the acceptance of Communist ideas was the main stimulus behind my conversion. I certainly did not fit the simple pattern of a hesitant intellectual convinced by Communist political tracts and lectures that the party was the place for him.

In my account of the period up to 1944, I described my view of the world as open and flexible. I gorged myself on reading matter, and I was easily influenced by any forceful idea I encountered, until it was ousted by the next idea.

I had less time for reading books early in 1945, as I had a year's school curriculum to study in a few weeks. But I still read the papers and kept abreast of the news. The events of the war and the presence of the Soviet army drew my attention to the Soviet Union. I knew hardly anything about the subject I would later spend decades researching: how the communist system works. But I was aware of the Soviet Union's military might and I could see for myself how it was expelling the dread German army from my country. The Soviet Union was clearly creating a new world, quite different from the one I had been inhabiting. I began to believe that this new world would triumph over the old. At the same time, I could see (as I have said before) that the Soviet soldiers—the same men who had brought me liberation—were treating the civilian population roughly and often committing inexcusable crimes.

I tried to reconcile in my own mind these two elements: my belief in the future and my experiences in the present. Around that time I felt, for the first time in my life, a need to write, and I composed quite a long study—or essay, as I would call it today—titled "Seed under the Snow." The manuscript was lost, unfortunately, but I can reconstruct quite accurately what it said. I applied to the world around me the historical theory of "cultural cycles" devised by Oswald Spengler. Humanity, in Spengler's eyes, was not advancing but was undergoing cyclical change. Cultures were born and would flourish, decline, and die. This pattern, the German historian said, was demonstrated by Western culture, as the title of his seminal book *The Decline of the West* suggested. From time to time, a culture would arise, full of fresh energy and raw, barbaric forces. Then it would turn into a civilization accompanied by decadence, as its intrinsic strength weakened. The Western cultural cycle was in this latter stage, he opined.

My essay explored the idea that the Soviet Union was beginning a new cultural cycle, still at a rough, energetic, uncivilized stage. Unfortunate though it was, barbarity caused sufferings, but those very sufferings were marks of the culture's youth and freshness.

The second part of my essay echoed a poem by Endre Ady (1877–1919): I reproduced the beautiful piece in full and took over its title for my essay. Some of the lines touched me very deeply after the cataclysm of 1944: "Tortured and shredded me...I gather together from blood, moan and flame...." Another line of the poem echoed the Spenglerian view: "Let me raise my face to a new man's new world."[2]

The line of argument was strained in several places and my identification with Ady's poem was a bit grandiose. Ady in 1915 could rightly have felt that he and others like him would rescue the old values for the new world. That in part is what the title "Seed under the Snow" refers to. But what of the past's values could I, an immature young man, have saved from an inescapable new order that inevitably began with barbarity?

It was the first essay of my life, and it remained for a long time my only piece of writing to include an original thought. Mind you, it contained some of the posing of a teenage intellectual as well. Its logic was unclear and its claim unfounded, but it had some originality. I am still appalled when I begin to examine how Communist beliefs could have stifled independent thinking in me for so long.

Early in 1946, when I was already working at the Budapest headquarters of MADISZ, I showed my essay, written a couple of months earlier, to Károly Csendes, the Budapest deputy general secretary of the organization. Many years later, Csendes earned a dreadful reputation as the country's deputy chief prosecutor, but in those days he was not formidable at all. On the contrary, he seemed a quiet, understanding man. He read the study and showed it to a couple of friends at Győrffy College, a center of young left-wing intellectuals who were, as he put it, more learned than he. I understood from his comments that he was impressed with my piece. He went so far as to say he had never come across a similar piece of writing with so ambitious an aim. He was also glad I had come out in favor of the new order, although my line of argument was curious. Nonetheless, he concluded that my thoughts were confused. "You should study Marx, Lenin, and Stalin much more closely," he advised.

I had begun such study with an iron will even before he gave me that advice. Perhaps the first work I ever read by a Soviet author was Stalin's *Dialectical and Historical Materialism*—I learned much later that it originally had been published as a chapter in the standard textbook on the history of the Soviet (Bolshevik) Communist Party. I am aware that even those who call themselves Marxists nowadays think Stalin simplified and condensed his Marxism in an exaggerated, uncouth, and sometimes distorted way. But I do not intend here to offer a general assessment of Marxist philosophy or an analysis of Stalin's piece. All I want to record is how it affected *me then*, when I first read that little white pamphlet with a portrait of Stalin in a marshal's uniform on the cover.

The very fact that Stalin was simultaneously supreme head of a large country, a victorious commander in a world war, and a philosopher aroused admiration in me. My head was a confusion of fragmentary philosophies, worldviews, and schools of thought, but this little book had military precision. Each and every statement seemed correct; indeed, everything seemed to fall into place. That characterization applied to grave problems, which famous philosophers had tried to unravel or had tangled further with their tortuous arguments (as I thought then). Stalin had resolved them with finality in one terse sentence. I was attracted by the very simplicity that a sophisticated critic would have faulted: this to me was an easy-to-understand, lucid, coherent account.

Sadly, this work did not come up in critical philosophical seminars given by well-trained teachers, who could easily have shown their gullible students where the work's superficiality lay, where the author had badly contradicted himself, and where his line of argument or method of classification was lame. I did not discuss the book with anyone. I had no chance to consider the doubts of others.

I had tried in my early teens (with expert help from Antal Szerb and Mihály Babits) to pick what literature I had to read and to identify what was best and most consequential. Now I selected political writings in the same way. I assumed that the best and most significant would be the Marxist classics: writings by Marx, Engels, Lenin, and Stalin. Those I had to get to know thoroughly first. As the four had written a library full of books, I had to choose the ones that were most important. The various "selected works" were an obvious starting point, and I rapidly absorbed their contents. A year or two later, I could consider myself a well-versed Marxist, who had read all the important writings of the classic authors and knew accurately which work pronounced on which questions.

The greatest and hardest assignment was to absorb Marx's *Capital*. By then, I was working with my friend Péter Kende. He was the editor of the MADISZ paper *Magyar Ifjúság* (*Hungarian Youth*), with a desk in the organization's Budapest headquarters. I was in the same room, put in charge of matters to do with education and schooling. We often met outside work as well. First we decided, half seriously and half in jest, that we would create a "democratic legionary novel" together. We wanted to write it in the idiom of P. Howard (the pen name of a popular Hungarian novelist, Jenő Rejtő, who wrote extremely funny stories about a Hungarian serving in the French Foreign Legion) and make it democratic by taking the side of the natives against the wicked colonists. We wrote a few pages, amid much laughter, before it occurred to us that we could use our time together more fruitfully. So instead of writing a legionary novel, we decided to read *Capital* together.

We read it in German, taking careful notes. We each wrote a précis, but we went through the work almost line by line comparing our interpretations of what Marx was saying. The language presented no problems, but the text was very difficult. Neither of us had studied economics before. If we had been familiar with Ricardo or Adam Smith, we would have understood more easily what Marx borrowed from them and where he differed. This complete lack of previous preparation made the reading more laborious.

I still have my handwritten notes. I read only the first volume with Péter, over several weeks. (The second and third I studied by myself.) We went from page to page with unfaltering perseverance, thoroughly considering our notes on every sentence. Péter and I approached the work with respect and humility, as religious people would the Bible, reading it with devotion and taking every word seriously.

I did not offer a critical analysis of Stalin's work earlier and I will not go into criticism of Marx either. That task has been undertaken by others. I will make some comments on Marxism in later chapters, but here let me confine myself to saying how *Capital* struck me *then*.

It fascinated me. I was impressed above all by the clarity and logic of Marx's argument, though the line of thought was abstract and the style was often involved, in a Germanic way. If you accepted his premises, conceptual framework, and method of argument, everything fell into place. The first conclusions followed from the underlying ideas with logic sharp as a razor; they in turn could become starting points for further conclusions, and so on. In the words of Károly Csendes, Marx seemed not confused but utterly clear. (It took much time and reading and understanding before I realized what was wrong with Marx's premises and where the seemingly rigorous line of argument is slippery.) The young man who at 14 to 16 had feverishly sought enlightenment in a hundred types of reading now found it radiating like sunshine from those thousand pages.

The logic and clarity impressed me most, but I also respected and loved *Capital* for being written with passion, not gray indifference. It speaks with outrage about the treatment of child labor and the exploitation of the proletariat.

Yet Marx did not subordinate his logical analysis to his feelings. He did not ascribe the troubles of capitalism to the evil of capitalists. When I was dealing decades later with the critique of socialism, I tried to show how various disorders such as shortages and forced growth derived from the *system*, not from people's mistakes. I certainly imbibed that approach while reading *Capital*, and it affects my way of thinking to this day.

I decided while reading *Capital* that I was going to be an economist, a possibility that had never occurred to me before. I had been more concerned with literature, history, and philosophy. By the time Péter and I reached the end of our joint studies, I had no more doubts about what profession to choose. My only uncertainty concerned how I was going to put my plan into practice.

Marx's work is full of intellectual arrogance. He respects Ricardo and Adam Smith, and if he differs from them, he says so politely. But he writes with scorn of contemporaries and intellectual opponents, treating them as stupid and malevolent. "He does not even know…" "He fails even to notice…" Marx does the same in other works, and a similar arrogance, pride, and intolerance toward intellectual opponents appear in the writings of Engels, Lenin, and Stalin. I am ashamed to say I was impressed, not put off, by this trait of theirs. That was the way to handle opponents!

Another significant influence on my thinking was György (Georg) Lukács, though not such a forceful one as Marx. I came across his studies of culture in the period I am now describing.[3] Lukács's ideas about the "great realists" provided a useful, conciliatory bridge between my pre-1944 literary experiences and my freshly acquired Marxist views. What if Tolstoy and Dostoyevsky were believing Christians, and Dostoyevsky was even a zealous backer of tsarism? What if Balzac was a reactionary, or Thomas Mann an out-and-out bourgeois? No problem, György Lukács stated reassuringly. You do not need to pay any attention to whatever philosophical or political positions these authors put forward. The main thing was that they were great realists, writers portraying reality. Lukács managed to inoculate me against the harmful effects of their philosophical or political ideas, while leaving me to admire their works, as I had done when a boy.

Lukács was an absolute authority in my eyes, given added cachet by the respect that Thomas Mann had expressed for him.[4] That was another bridge between my old and new frames of mind. Reading Thomas Mann had been one of my most eye-opening and enchanting literary experiences. If Mann thought someone was great, he had to be.* So I cannot forgive Lukács for never expressing reservations

---

* I heard how Thomas Mann spoke of György Lukács with respect when I first read Lukács's works. It was not until much later, however, that I read Mann's actual comments.

about the Soviet Union. He had been there. He had seen for himself what the Soviet system was really like. He knew about the show trials, the persecution of innocent victims, and the terror. Then he returned to Hungary. How could he bear not to intimate by so much as a hint that perhaps not all was right with that system? Of course, I understand that he was afraid. But perhaps he could have kept quiet, rather than trying to cloak the crimes with his reputation. One reason why naive, gullible, inexperienced young intellectuals like me blindly believed the myths about the beauty of Soviet life was that not even György Lukács voiced any doubts.

As I progressed in my knowledge of Marxism-Leninism, I became increasingly convinced that I held the key to understanding the world. Whatever problem arose, I possessed knowledge that allowed me to solve it. Life presented no phenomenon that I could not peg into the system of coordinates provided by Marxism or refute with some argument from Marxism. This conviction also bred intellectual pride, of a more dangerous kind than that fed by an arrogant style of debate. But for me, for a young mind seeking order and clarity, it was the most attractive aspect of Marxism-Leninism.

Even when I was a teenager, descriptions of rural poverty by the group of writers researching rural Hungary and by other authors in literary works had aroused my sympathy for the life of the poor and oppressed. Developed indirectly by books, this compassion was intensified by my direct experience of 1944. I saw with my own eyes, albeit only for a couple of weeks, the kind of life the brickyard workers lived. When I started to study Marxism, that spontaneous empathy was put in its place. Political economy explained how workers and the village poor were exploited. However, this newly acquired knowledge did not encourage me to maintain an active relationship with those poor people I had come to know and love. It tended rather to encourage me to put all my energy into transforming society according to Marxist theory, which was supposed eventually to eliminate poverty once and for all.

Charismatic personalities

Another factor drawing me to the party, apart from writings, was the eloquent speech and the charisma of some Communist leaders.

I later came to know József Révai personally, but in that period, I heard him talk at meetings or give lectures on several occasions. His writings in books and in the lead articles in the party's daily paper were fully in accord with his speeches. For me, he personified the Communist intellectual at the highest level.

Révai could be an inflammatory speaker. What affected me the most was the lucid logic of his speeches and articles. He not only made clear points, I felt, but argued them convincingly and framed what he had to say in a clear structure. He was an excellent debater who confronted opponents with their own statements and tore them to bits. He expressed himself faultlessly, in well-chosen, erudite language. When I listen today to politicians expressing views with which I am in sympathy but in a disorganized, monotonous, ungrammatical, dry-as-dust way, I wish secretly that the rhetorical gifts of Révai would descend upon them.

I now know that József Révai was deceiving us on precisely the most essential matters and infecting our minds with harmful, reprehensible ideas. But he succeeded in affecting so many of us because his speeches and writings emanated his passionate conviction and faith, expressed with tight logic by a highly talented speaker and writer.

The other charismatic figure who had a formative influence on me was Ervin Hollós. His talents and his public importance did not compare with Révai's, of course; I mention him here because I was working closely with him at the time. He was general secretary of MADISZ when I was a senior staff member at the Budapest headquarters. He directed my work in the movement and I took part in the party seminar he ran. After 1956, Hollós, with the rank of lieutenant colonel, headed the police department that prepared the reprisal trials. He may have had—indeed, he probably did have—earlier contacts with the ÁVH. Then, after 1956, he became one of the main organizers of the merciless repression. But let us not run ahead. Now I am talking of the young Ervin Hollós, whom I saw and heard many times at the MADISZ headquarters on Rózsa utca.

He was not nearly as educated as Révai and did not attempt to seem so. What he conveyed to people, including me, was his inner fire of conviction. He did not have a way with words and his emphases and expressions were often unidiomatic, but there was an electric charge in what he said. He was so sure of the truth that he could not conceive how anyone could see things differently. That aura of faith was quite absent from the party bureaucrats of the Kádár period (1956–1988). And, I have to add, it is missing from many of our best present-day politicians under parliamentary democracy.

Ervin Hollós pounded into us the many ideas that we needed to become "people of a special mould" (Stalin's characterization of the *true Communist*). I first heard from him that there was one and only one criterion distinguishing a Communist from a pseudo-Communist or anyone else, and that was unconditional devotion to the Soviet Union. I repeat, to the Soviet Union, not to Marxism or to the intention of establishing a proletarian dictatorship or a classless society. A Communist was someone who showed unconditional devotion to the Soviet Union. That idea led Ervin Hollós directly to the trials that avenged the rebellion against Soviet rule.

It was Ervin Hollós who deeply imprinted in my mind the phrase "professional revolutionary." We full-timers at MADISZ (like the officials in the party and the "mass organizations") were not functionaries of a movement or employees of an organization but professional revolutionaries. There were other professional politicians as well, but nothing bound us to them, because we and only we were the revolutionaries. We shared that identity with the leaders of the Great October Socialist Revolution, the heroes of the anti-Nazi Communist movement, the commissars of the Soviet army, and the leaders of the struggles for colonial independence. The expression "professional revolutionary" gave dignity to the otherwise quite ordinary work of organizing a mass movement. What it aroused in us was not just pride but a feeling of superiority and self-satisfaction. Our work was more valuable and exalted than what nonprofessional revolutionaries or rank-and-file party members were doing. If the party is viewed as the vanguard, then we were the vanguard of the vanguard.

Belonging to a community

Let me now go back to an earlier period of my life, to the spring of 1945; I was studying in the country town of Kiskunhalas, but traveled home to Budapest several times. On one such trip, on May 1, 1945, I was walking down Andrássy út without any particular purpose when I was surprised to find myself suddenly swept along by a May Day parade. It was the first street parade I had ever seen in my life (apart from Nazi spectacles shown on newsreels). The procession was full of enthusiastic people bearing red flags, Hungarian tricolors, and banners. I felt an inclination to be among them and to join in their march.

In briefly listing biographical facts, I mentioned above that I joined the youth movement in 1945. Now, in order to demonstrate my need to belong to a community, I am returning to this event. It was the summer of 1945, and a young friend of mine suggested I go to Szent István körút 12. The house, which once belonged to the Arrow-Cross, now contained a MADISZ office and hosted interesting events. I went. Someone gave a lecture I found engaging. People were kind and friendly. I went several times to enjoy myself in the cheerful environment of enthusiastic inquiry. A couple of weeks later, I joined the work of the organization; that is how my life in the movement began.

I was attending joint excursions, afternoon dances, and youth meetings with increasing frequency. In the autumn, we went out putting up posters for the first parliamentary elections. I never had a stronger feeling, before or indeed since, of belonging to a small community than I did in the Fifth District MADISZ.

Later, what attracted me more than the small community was the idea of being part of the large community of the Party (with a very big capital "P"). By that time, it was a question of belonging to the fourth grade, which involved more than active, committed party membership. It meant becoming a *true Communist*.

An important part in this development was played by the experienced Communists whom I consciously or unwittingly imitated. There were many long-standing Communists around me. To take a single example, my immediate superior at the national headquarters of MADISZ was András Hegedűs. His career was to reach dizzy heights, as he became secretary to Ernő Gerő (the second man in the party's hierarchy), then minister of agriculture, and finally prime minister of the Hungarian People's Republic. In that capacity, it was Hegedűs who signed the Warsaw Pact in 1955 and then signed the letter calling in the Soviet troops after the 1956 Revolution broke out. Later he broke with Stalinism and gained status and respect as a sociologist and a scientific leader of considerable intellectual influence. Little of this was apparent when I first knew him. He was not a charismatic figure like Ervin Hollós, but I still saw in him an archetypal Communist in many respects, not least because his disposition was closer to my own (at that time, in any event). Hegedűs never had as much internal fire as Hollós. He was more objective and businesslike, but he too showed a Bolshevik's relentlessness and sense of infallibility. He was an extremely diligent, indefatigable worker. Hollós influenced me through his words and teachings, while Hegedűs did so by his example. Here was a pattern that I felt I might manage to emulate.

Chance influences and my own capabilities

Much later, there came periods in my life when I had a long-term goal and a conscious plan or strategy for achieving it. There was no trace of any such plan in the period I am writing about now. I outlined five grades of identification with the Communist Party at the beginning of the chapter. It never occurred to me that I wanted to go through all those stages. When I changed from being someone remote from the party to being a Communist sympathizer, I did not even know what the next step would be. I read a lot for my age and had no lack of reasoning skills, but my intellectual acumen was coupled with naiveté, superficiality, and irresponsibility. It was as if I were climbing a steep ladder with my eyes shut. These days, when reading the short, often rather self-revealing interview found on the last page of the popular Hungarian business weekly *HVG* (*Heti Világgazdaság*, or *Weekly World Economics*), I am always scandalized when people admit cynically that they joined the party only to further their careers. Some of my past thoughts and decisions bother my conscience, but I can say firmly that my actions were not motivated by any careerist cynicism of that kind.

Sometimes chance intervened. If that friend of mine had not told me about the Fifth District MADISZ—if he had instead recommended the local social democratic youth club and I had happened to find a pleasant group of people there and had a good time—who knows whether I would have stayed there.

The first task I was given in the Fifth District office was to put the membership records to rights. The papers were lying about in complete disarray. I have shown many times since that I have an aptitude for keeping records and organizing, classifying, and managing information. This was the first occasion I had a chance to use that ability, and my success soon attracted the notice of the cadre officer (in the language of the contemporary business world: the manager responsible for human resources). I was immediately entrusted with the bigger task of being the "propagandist," which meant I had to organize various educational events and meetings. That went well too.

Then chance intervened again. József Lukács, later a philosopher and member of the Hungarian Academy of Sciences but then doing work similar to mine at the MADISZ Budapest headquarters, wanted to give it up and put all his energies into his university studies. He was seeking a replacement, and when someone mentioned me we met. I remember we spent hours walking about the streets with words pouring out of Lukács as he outlined the job. My head buzzed with the names of all the people I should get in touch with and all the knowledge I would have to spread; all those names and tasks were unfamiliar to me. I was alarmed at the prospect, but I took the job. It had not even occurred to me before our conversation that I might be a full-time paid functionary in a mass movement. When the chance came, the job seemed interesting and I accepted. Seen from above, my selection arose from coordinated "cadre work." Lukács had obviously looked about the district offices, heard what district secretaries or cadre officers had to say, and chosen me. Seen from below, from my point of view, it was a chance event. Some theories of economic sociology analyze behavior as the result not of following a strategy but of seizing opportunities and advancing as the occasion allows. The model fits that stage in my career.

As I have mentioned, I received a full-time appointment at the Budapest headquarters of MADISZ in the fall of 1945. "Full-time" meant that my work record book was lodged with them, and I spent my days from early morning to late at night in the youth movement. I even received a salary, albeit in inflationary currency whose value was dwindling. My salary did not go a long way, but at least I did not have to accept money from my mother, although I continued to live with her and my sister. They probably had their own views about the cause to which I was devoting all my time and energy, but they never shared them with me. They fully accepted that I should decide what to do with my life. They betrayed a little irony only in calling me "the MADISZ," rather than using my name.*

I advanced rapidly in my career in the Communist movement. One reason was that I belonged to a category of cadres for which the Communist Party had a great demand and a very meager supply.

On the one hand, I brought with me good qualities in the form of my bourgeois past: I was well read and well mannered and had a knowledge of languages. Other aptitudes such as organizational ability and skill in human relations soon became apparent as well. On the other hand, the Communist Party could count on my absolute loyalty. It was apparent that I had nothing false in me. And being a newcomer from a middle-class background made me more eager to fit in, identify with, and follow the Communist pattern of behavior than the older, storm-weathered Communists were. All the old members of the illegal party had been in trouble with the party at some time. Not so the keen recruits like me and my peers, who were thus more dependable and pliable.

Even if reports at the time did not mention these attributes in so many words, they were recognized instinctively by the cadre officers, who pushed me further and further up the ladder.

---

* In those years, Munyó used to make ends meet by selling off pieces of the family jewelry. She started several businesses, all of which went awry. On her son-in-law's advice, she bought—at a rock-bottom price—one of Budapest's fanciest coffeehouses (named New York, it had been a legendary gathering place of writers and artists); after an abortive attempt to revive it, she was soon forced to sell it at a tremendous loss. While she owned the coffeehouse, she took great pleasure in inviting me in for a hot chocolate with whipped cream and pound cake. Munyó would sit down beside me in the huge hall decorated with the frescos of the great Hungarian painter Károly Lotz and the famous corkscrew columns, watching the hungry MADISZ downing his drink.

3

On a Communist Newspaper—1947–1955

Early in the summer of 1947, I received a message from the editors of *Szabad Nép* (*Free People*), the central daily newspaper of the Communist Party, saying they would like to take me onto their staff. I had been brought to the attention of Miklós Vásárhelyi, one of the paper's senior staff members, by Péter Kende, who by that time had been working there for a while. I was honored and excited by the invitation and had no hesitation in accepting it.

I started work at *Szabad Nép* in June 1947 and left eight years later in the summer of 1955, when I was dismissed after disciplinary proceedings. I passed the initial six years in unswerving faith and unconditional dedication to my work. The first cracks in the foundations of my worldview began to appear in 1953–1954. I will deal later with my disillusionment; here I am mainly covering those preceding six years.

Onward and upward

The paper set me to work in the domestic policy section, which was headed by Miklós Gimes. Who would have thought then that this quiet-spoken man, full of faith in communism, would become a hero of the 1956 Revolution and die a martyr on the gallows? A few days after I joined, a section meeting was called. There was a staff member who had to be upbraided for some reason, but Gimes did not feel up to delivering the rebuke and preferred to ask Miklós Vásárhelyi to do it in his jovial, but if need be caustic, style.

A couple of days later, I was given my first assignment. The newspaper had a new car that needed breaking in. There was no point in sending it out empty. My instructions came from Oszkár Betlen, one of the editors. The Feast of St. Peter and St. Paul was coming up, and the harvest in full swing. I should write a report about the swish-hush of the swinging scythes, I was told. I had never written a newspaper piece before and I had never seen up close how grain was harvested. Anyway, off we went, stopping the car here and there, and I wrote my maiden report, which appeared in *Szabad Nép* the next day.

My work appeared frequently after that—reports, interviews, and items of information. Hardly six months went by before I wrote my first editorial; it appeared in December 1947, published over my initials. It was an analysis of the investments made in the previous months.

Although I had had no economic training, it was acknowledged that I was interested in economic subjects and wanted to specialize in that field. There were others engaged on economic subjects as well, all of them working in the domestic policy section.

After about two years, I was promoted to be head of the paper's economic section. Péter Kende was put in charge of the foreign policy section at the same time. We were both 21 years old, with three or four years of party membership behind us. When the editors—Márton Horváth, Oszkár Betlen, Miklós Vásárhelyi, and Géza Losonczy—put the idea to the editor in chief, József Révai, apparently his irritable response was "What on earth are you thinking of? You want to turn the paper into a nursery?" But in the end, he agreed.

Révai shook his head over my appointment. But when Marx's *Capital* appeared in Hungarian translation and he found I was one of the few people around who had read it in the German original, he gave me the task of reviewing it.

In 1949, I was sent to the party college, where the upper ranks of the party received extension training in Marxism-Leninism. I attended meetings of the State Economic Committee, the highest economic body in the Communist Party, as the paper's permanent representative. The chairman was Ernő Gerő and the secretary István Friss. The committee deliberated all important economic decisions before they were put to the Political Committee in the form of a proposal on which a vote was taken. The chance to participate in the meetings of the State Economic Committee was a great honor. My work was also recognized in two government awards I received.

In 1952, I was called on by *Szabad Nép* to cover an official visit of a party and government delegation to the German Democratic Republic. One reason I was chosen was that I had little difficulty in translating the speeches I had to report to the newspapers. But a more important consideration would have been the complete trust in which I was held. Anyone riding with Mátyás Rákosi and Ernő Gerő on a government train had to be utterly reliable.

That brings me to an important question. What lay behind my rapid advancement in that period? I never spoke to any of my superiors about it at the time, but I will try to find an explanation. Here I am not seeking the reasons in myself, a subject I will deal with later. What I would like to reconstruct are the criteria of my superiors, drawing on my general *present-day* understanding of socialism as applied to my case.

Two main criteria govern appointments, promotions, and dismissals under the Communist system. One is loyalty to the Communist Party, the other ability. Many other factors are obviously weighed, but these two have the strongest influence. Depending on the type of post, a minimum degree of loyalty is required before an appointment can be considered, but a greater degree of loyalty than necessary may compensate for the candidate's lack in some required ability. The converse is also true: exceptional talents may help to redress an absence of political enthusiasm. Of course, the stronger a candidate is in both areas, the greater becomes the chance of rapid advancement.

An economist reading this book may find it revealing to view the dual criteria as setting up indifference curves faced by the decision maker, the two variables being loyalty and ability. The higher of the parallel indifference curves apply to higher-ranking jobs. Thus the indifference curve for a minister will be above the curve for a department head in the ministry, that of an editor in chief will lie above the curve of a trainee journalist, and so on. The indifference curves differ from country to country and period to period. The emphasis in the early, revolutionary period is on loyalty. Ability gains relatively greater importance in the later, more technocratic period. The indifference curves depend also on the field. They will show great disparity, for instance, when academics in the university world are compared to the political police. The common feature in all spheres is the duality of the selection criteria.

My rating was certainly high on both counts during and also after the "nursery" remark by Révai. In terms of ability, I had a fortunate combination of bourgeois erudition, including knowledge of languages gained at home, and a lively Marxist education. I was able to express myself rapidly and in faultless Hungarian. It soon emerged that I got on well with people. I was able to draw people out and obtain interviews with those in high places. Later, when I was in charge of a section of the paper, some leadership abilities became apparent as well.

These qualities were coupled with devoted loyalty. Those of my superiors who knew me well realized that I had identified totally with Communist ideas, despite my background and education in the *haute bourgeoisie*. When my appointment as a section editor was being considered, one of those on the staff was György Nemes, later editor of the *Irodalmi Újság* (*Literary News*). He was fifteen years older than I, with an impressive record as a journalist, a cultivated man who wrote excellently and had a degree in economics. Why was I chosen, not he? Judging solely from the situation and not from information told or whispered to me unofficially, I believe it was because they trusted me more. Youth and inexperience were an enormous advantage, not a drawback, in their eyes. My youth and lack of experience in life were likely to make me more gullible. Having no doubts, I would simply serve the cause of the Communist Party unhesitatingly and unswervingly.

Motivations

Having described how my superiors saw me, I would now like to give an "inside" report of how I experienced the period. As far as possible, I will avoid conveying my present ideas. I am concerned here with what I thought and felt *at the time*.

The main impetus behind my words, deeds, and ideas came from *faith and belief*. I had complete trust in Marxist-Leninist ideology. I was convinced that every word of it was true. I had complete confidence in the party and accepted the notion that the party embodied true ideas, pure morals, and service to humanity. It never crossed my mind that the admiration and respect I felt for Stalin or Rákosi could be classed as a "cult of personality." And because I found the logic and argumentation in their writings and speeches convincing, they reinforced my confidence in them.

One of the forces binding the bureaucratic apparatus that rules over the Communist system is *fear*. I can say that I never for a moment felt such fear during those years. I was sure that those being arrested and sentenced really were guilty. Later, when I had realized the truth and my friends and I were discussing the terrors of the Rákosi era, many refused to believe that I had had no sense of it. Unbelievable as it may sound, it is true. It is not for indifference or for keeping my head down that I need to reproach myself, but for my blindness and self-imposed isolation from news of the harsh realities.

Only on one occasion did I visit the headquarters of the ÁVH, the State Security Police, at 60 Andrássy út. It was not my task to liaise with the ÁVH, but in that one case, I had to obtain information about an upcoming trial involving a crime related to production from an officer working there. I entered the building, spoke with the officer, and left, as calm as I would have been if I had entered the Transport Ministry or a district party headquarters. I had no idea that confessions were being extracted under torture or that innocent people were being forced to make false statements. It never crossed my mind for a moment that I might ever be held there.

I was a student at the party college when I heard that László Rajk, then foreign minister, and his accomplices had been arrested, and we were briefed on the charges against them—conspiring to overthrow the Hungarian government. I accepted the announcement without demur or any idea that the charges might be false. Lightning struck around me. I knew several of the people arrested and falsely accused at that time and in years to come. Confident in my innocence, I was sure that no danger lay in store for me, although it emerged later that I was protected only by good fortune. I could have been arrested for no apparent reason at all, as many people were in those days. Having had access to certain confidential police files recently,* I have learned that one of the informants at *Szabad Nép* did denounce me on trumped-up charges.[1]

As I think back on that period later, in the appalling knowledge of what really took place, I have often felt that a comparison with a sleepwalker was just. I had stepped confidently onto a ledge several stories above the street, yet felt no fear of falling.†

Many Communist cadres were motivated by a *lust for power*. Readers will sense that I am writing these memoirs in a strongly self-critical spirit. Having examined my conscience strictly, I can say there was no trace in me of any effort to obtain power. That desire was alien to me and remained so later. I never flattered my superiors or sought to gain promotion by currying favor with them.

However, there was undoubtedly a kind of *Szabad Nép* haughtiness in me and my colleagues at the paper. We felt we were the "voice of the party"—our words were more valuable and important than those of other journalists. My manner and tone of voice when speaking to colleagues, acquaintances, or strangers remained modest and free of arrogance. But a deeper, mental layer underlies outward behavior. Our arrogance lay in a belief that we were infallible, thanks to our Marxist-Leninist learning and our position on *Szabad Nép*.‡

I did not feel any real incentive in the *privileges* we enjoyed. Nonetheless, we certainly had some material advantages over the average citizen.

---

* Unfortunately, most of the pre-1956 ÁVH archives were allegedly destroyed—or at least I could not access more of the files. For all I know, there may have been other incriminating reports against me.

† I thought the metaphor of a sleepwalker to describe this strange blindness and deafness was uniquely my invention until my attention was drawn to the autobiography of Ernő Gáll (2003, pp. 96–97), a Transylvanian intellectual, who uses the same image: "Forgoing every independent approach of a personal type, taking a completely uncritical stand. . . . My frame of mind and behavior at the time might be compared to 'ideological somnambulism' of some kind."

‡ Since then, I have often encountered this "*Wunderkind* phenomenon," a brand of self-assured intellectual arrogance—for example, among the young titans of the Hungarian political scene in the 1990s and among the young Western consultants arriving in Eastern Europe after the change of system. Perhaps I am prompted not by old age but by a retrospective assessment of my youth to say that in such cases, lack of experience in life can easily contribute to making young people overconfident and leaving them open to the influence of extreme intellectual impulses.

When I moved out of the family home—at the age of 21, which was early in those days—I was assigned a "service residence" by the newspaper office. I lived alone at the time, which meant I could move into a small studio apartment, furnished with a tasteless selection from the warehouses of the Government Commission for Abandoned Possessions. When in 1952 I got married and my wife, Teréz Laky, who was also a journalist at *Szabad Nép*, was expecting our first child, we were assigned a larger service residence—a three-room apartment in the elegant Rózsadomb district, which we furnished very modestly out of our own savings. We acquired much of our furniture very cheaply—it consisted of ungainly mass-produced pieces of low quality.

Szabad Nép staff had higher salaries than other journalists, but not much higher. When I was promoted at the newspaper, I became entitled to take holidays at resort facilities limited to employees at party headquarters. I was abroad altogether four times in my nine years there, on each occasion for a few days that were spent almost entirely on work. Three times I traveled to another socialist country and once, near the beginning of my stay at the paper, to Vienna. That was an especially memorable visit. I saw hardly any of the sights. I saved some of my expense allowance, and, with a bad conscience, purchased some pairs of fine silk stockings for my mother. I remember buying them at a Palmers store, where I was eagerly served by kind young ladies in green uniforms. I was overcome by a feeling that it was unworthy of a Communist journalist to be spending money in a place like that. Even then, some of my allowance was left over and I returned it to the office. No doubt, those who played cynical tricks with their expenses abroad in the late Kádár period will smile at such childish Puritanism.

There was a canteen for the staff of the paper, the publishing firm, and the printing press. The supplies were regular and adequate even at times when others faced serious shortages of food, although there was nothing especially lavish about what was offered. Another perquisite was the right to be treated at Kútvölgyi Hospital. The privileges were known jocularly as the three Ks: Kékestető for holidays, Kútvölgyi for medical care, and Kerepesi út for the cemetery reserved for funerals paid for by the party.

In line with the principle of "distribution according to work" generally accepted at that time by policy makers and the teachers of Marxian political philosophy, I felt entitled to the provisions we enjoyed. I did not feel we received exceptional privileges. I had spent my childhood in affluence and compared with that (or a journalist's life in the West), my way of life at *Szabad Nép* was modest. It could count as privileged only because it rose above the average in a society gripped by extreme egalitarianism.

My way of life was marked by asceticism rather than privilege. Now and again, we would go to the opera, a concert, or the theater, or would visit friends, but most of our time was spent on hard, devoted work.

I had practically no real life outside the offices of the newspaper. When our first child, Gábor, was born in 1952, I was on night duty. I thought it was self-evident that the birth of a child was not a good enough reason to cancel my night shift. I kept phoning the hospital, but I did not go and see Gabi until early the next morning. Even when I was a MADISZ (Hungarian Democratic Youth Federation) functionary and later, during my *Szabad Nép* period, the question kept coming up among peers and colleagues: should we not give up this life of "professional party worker" and start acting like proper university students instead? I never considered the matter in full, because I had my answer unhesitatingly ready. It was incomparably more important to stand my ground where the party had placed me. Many other party functionaries had no university degree, either, yet could do their jobs perfectly well.

When decades later I became a university professor in America, I would sometimes look enviously at my students as I thought of the past. We had lost in the killing pace of work the years that they were spending in carefree study, preparing for the future and enjoying the pleasures of life.

This account of my frame of mind and motivations involved the same factors that I described in the book *The Socialist System*, in the section on cohesive forces of power and motivations of the cadres. Faith and conviction, lust for power, fear, and privilege affect different individuals with different intensity. In my case, the dominant motivation was the first—faith and conviction. I do not say that I was in some sense average, but it would be equally wrong to think I was unique or exceptional in this regard; several others on the paper were similarly motivated.

Life in the newspaper office

During the years covered in this chapter, Hungary saw some epoch-making changes. When I joined the paper, the country had a coalition government and other parties had their own newspapers. But the Communist Party obliterated the competing political forces; and at the instigation and with the active help of the occupying Soviet Union, it gained a complete monopoly of power. The institutions of a totalitarian system were set up. *Szabad Nép* came to have no real rival. It was, politically speaking, the only "official" newspaper, the main mouthpiece and chief means of party propaganda. It reached every party organization and office in the country, where it was compulsory reading for every party member and every party and state functionary.

As I have emphasized before, my book is not intended to sketch the history of Hungarian politics and society. It is no more than a personal life story. So I will not even try to analyze the role of *Szabad Nép*. The aims of the next couple of pages are far more modest and narrow than that—an attempt to condense into a still picture and describe some characteristics and events in the life of the newspaper office, particularly in relation to my own life.

It was no empty platitude to say that *Szabad Nép* conveyed the voice of the party. The phone on the editor in chief's desk would often ring in the morning with Mátyás Rákosi on the line, criticizing something in yesterday's paper or giving instructions. Likewise, the voice might be that of Gerő or Révai. On other occasions, Betlen would return from some party meeting and, referring to his notes, would explain to the section editors what tasks the party leaders had assigned to the paper. I received regular instructions from István Friss, head of the economic policy department at party headquarters. In a sense, I had two masters: my superiors were at the same time the editor in chief of the paper and the head of the party economic policy department. There was similar dual control over the heads of the paper's other specialist sections.

Although the control over us was strict, it seldom extended to detail. The editor in chief and even the section heads had wide discretion. In hindsight, I am surprised to see how much freedom I had as a young man in my 20s to decide what to write and what to publish of what my subordinates wrote.

The staff of *Szabad Nép* did not work fixed hours. The day's starting and finishing time depended on the tasks to be done. If need be, we worked through the weekend as well. The discipline and sacrifice were self-evident—no one needed coercing. I do not remember a single case of someone being rebuked for laziness. And maybe I was blind to it, but I cannot remember experiencing any rancor or backbiting among the staff either. We made up the kind of team you might find in wartime, a community of comrades fighting on the front line.

I made friendships there that have lasted a lifetime. My friendship with Péter Kende became deeper still while we were working on *Szabad Nép*. For a time I shared an office with Pál Lőcsei, who was to be a leading figure of '56. We were very soon close friends and he played a large part in my political and intellectual development, as I will explain in the next chapter. We struck up a loving and lifelong friendship with Duci—Mrs. Géza Fónyi née Auguszta Majláth, who was just called Duci ("Fatty") by everyone, though in fact she was a thin, delicate woman, creator and head of the brilliant archives at *Szabad Nép*. Her small apartment, jam-packed with books, was a real place of pilgrimage. People would often drop by for a friendly chat in the *Szabad Nép* years and later, even after 1956.*

* After the revolution, there were two photographs on Duci's shelf: one of Miklós Gimes and the other of György Sárközy. There is a deeply rooted split or even chasm between two groups, those who are "urbane" and those who regard themselves as representatives of "the people," usually with roots in the Hungarian village. Duci was a one-person, living bridge between them. She had friends among the *Szabad Nép* people and later with those in Imre Nagy's circle, people associated with the urban part of the intelligentsia. She also had friends

I date from that period my abiding desire to have closer than "boss–underling" relations with those working under my direction and to develop human ties of friendship with them.

What relations people had with the others in that office depended obviously on personality. We sensed in Oszkár Betlen the merciless severity of a party warrior, and his cleverness was combined with supercilious sarcasm and coldness. On the other hand, Vásárhelyi exuded intelligence, ease, humor, and kind irony. Talking to Miklós Gimes was an intellectual pleasure, for he abounded in discerning, broad cultivation and a strong analytical ability.

My perceptions of the economy

I did not go to a school of economics or learn from the lectures of teachers there how a socialist economy ostensibly worked. My first course in the operation of the system came at first hand while I was working at *Szabad Nép*.

I gained wide-ranging experience of the operation of the type of economy I describe in my later writings as a "classical socialist system." When I attended meetings of the State Economic Committee, I saw close-up what extreme centralization of economic management meant. To take an example, the next year's production plan in a market economy depends on anonymous processes—the intentions of millions of independent market actors. Here it could be decided by Ernő Gerő, who had received from the party absolute control over the running of the economy. His decisions were prepared for him by the apparatus at the party center and in the government, which sometimes provided alternative courses. But his was the ultimate deciding voice at the meetings. I found him a cold, calculating, sharp-witted man incapable of showing human feelings. Nothing indicated that he was a trained economist, but he had an exceptional memory. In disputes over economic policy, he could quote accurately all the relevant data and information and the opinions various people had advanced. That ability greatly impressed the country's leading figures and must have boosted the respect in which he was held as a first-rate authority on economics. With my knowledge at the time, I could not ascertain how much expertise lay behind Ernő Gerő's decisiveness. I also was strongly affected by his personality, by the confidence and seriousness radiating from his words.

I would often meet and converse with ministers, deputy ministers, and senior ministry officials. These usually frank, professional discussions revealed much about

---

among the editors and staff of the journal *Válasz*, the gathering point of the "people's writers." For a long time, she was a close friend of György Sárközy, the founder and first editor of the journal, and of his wife, Márta, who later became editor, patron, and cohesive force of *Válasz*. Duci died in 1988.

how the economy was being run. I also paid frequent visits to factories, where I met managers, factory party secretaries, foremen, and workers. My direct observations were complemented by detailed accounts from my colleagues, often reporting what they had just experienced. Though there is doubt about how sincere some of my partners in conversation were, I came by a great many observations worth attending to.

Rereading my articles as I prepared to write these memoirs gave me an idea of the difficulties troubling me most at the time. I quote in parentheses—as a telling contrast—the title of or an excerpt from the relevant leading articles I wrote on the subject in question. These quotations illustrate that I was aware of the problem, but that my diagnosis was mistaken and the suggested therapy completely off the mark.

I had realized, for instance, that a centralized system could work only if executed with discipline. It was clear how often plan discipline, work discipline, and wage discipline were being flouted. I wrote various articles on the matter, but I was still seeking a solution in the wrong place. I had not understood the link between performance and incentives. I thought it was enough to explain the importance of discipline, spur people to follow instructions, or demand the imposition of punishments to make an example of the undisciplined.

When I saw how the workers, time and again, were lowering the production targets associated with their piece-wage and making fraudulent wage claims, I was bewildered to find the factory managers almost conniving with them on this. I thundered in my articles against those violating wage discipline and attacked enterprise managers and party workers who tolerated breaches of discipline. ("We need to pay great attention to the consolidation of socialist wage and working discipline," I wrote, and added, "Work contests can only really assist in accomplishing the plan ... if unjustified increase of wages and needless overtime are resisted.")[2] I failed to realize we were facing one of the inescapable problems of state ownership. Instead of wage levels being determined through conflict and agreement between the owner—the employer—and the employees, bureaucrats try to curb the wage-raising efforts of workers by imposing wage quotas.

There was evidence of all kinds of wastage and inefficient production in factories. ("Economic Efficiency—The Key Task in a Work Contest" was the title of one of my editorials.)[3] Seeking a solution, in many articles I explained the importance of economic efficiency, trying to convince enterprise managers not just to raise production quantity but to pursue higher product quality and lower costs as well. Yet the financial and moral incentives were all spurring them to increase the volume of production.

I thought that the source of the trouble was that enterprise managers were not doing their jobs well enough—that they organized production badly, were not conscientious enough, and did not listen to workers who warned them of the problems.

This criticism sometimes extended to the middle ranks of economic directors in the ministries and district party organizations. I faulted cadres who, to use the phraseology of the time, "floated in the barge of the masses," striving for popularity and not daring to be tough enough. ("Tolerating lack of discipline can only be in the interest of the enemy. Is it an unpopular task to fight staunchly and consistently for the consolidation of working discipline and make full use of working hours? Such a militant leader can be unpopular only in the eyes of a backward worker.")[4] Or, for want of another explanation, I sniffed sabotage in some shortcoming or other. That explanation was not only false but sinful, for it supported with the aid of economic rhetoric the merciless repression of ostensible "saboteurs."

Never for a moment did I think that the troubles were *systemic*, originating in the system itself. On the contrary, while perceiving many problems and faults in it, I was still convinced that socialism was superior to the capitalist system. Any difficulties would be transitory. I subscribed to Ernő Gerő's notion, taken from Stalin, that these were just growing pains. We would grow out of them! State ownership *had* to ensure higher productivity than private ownership. Central planning *must* be more efficient than market anarchy. There was utter confusion in my mind between the normative and the positive approach, the demands facing the socialist system and the realities of it.

I attached special importance to the expectation that workers in a socialist enterprise would work conscientiously, for "the factory was theirs," whereas workers in a capitalist factory were exploited and alienated from their work. This new kind of relationship to work led to work contests, voluntary offers to raise performance, and Stakhanovite achievements far above average. It was the chief explanation of the superiority of the socialist system, I believed at that time, and I therefore devoted fanatical attention to all forms of work contest. ("The triumph of socialism requires us to surpass the labor productivity under capitalism," I wrote in an editorial. "So we need to introduce widely new technology and machines, and strive for higher productivity through more vigorous work competition and the Stakhanovite movement.")[5]

My forced work pace shut me within the newspaper offices almost from dawn until far into the night. I ceased to share the daily life of other people. I was not oppressed by their day-to-day cares and hardly met anyone unconnected with my work. I, like a good Marxist, was concentrating on production, not consumption. Although I was barely aware of them from my own experience, I received some signals of problems with supplies and consequent discontent. But the signs were restrained and I was not listening for faint, distant murmurings. There were certainly people around me who knew of the grave shortcomings but refrained from speaking to me sincerely about them.

Munyó and my sister, Lilly, whom I frequently visited, at most dropped the odd hint that there were shortages. I turned a deaf ear to these. Later I kept asking Lilly why they had never spoken up more openly and sincerely. They had been afraid to discuss it, Lilly told me. It was not that they had thought for a moment I would turn against them. Rather that they had not wished to pester me, as I looked so preoccupied anyway. I would not have believed what they said, so why bother me? Much as we loved one another, an invisible wall had gradually been erected between us.

Overall, I accumulated many observations and a great deal of experience, but the way I arranged this material in my mind and organized it in terms of causal relations was based on *axioms*, as is the case with everyone. These axioms are not shaped purely by intellect. To an important extent, they are created by *meta-rational factors*: beliefs, prejudices, aspirations, desires, and moral judgments. The meta-rational factors act as doorkeepers, deciding which door will be open to an idea or impression and which closed. The doors in me were not operating properly at that time. I excluded all experiences and ideas that would have shaken my belief. The defense mechanisms described in the theory of *cognitive dissonance* had gone into operation. Information that contradicted my deep convictions was being stifled, so that I could persuade myself of the accuracy of my original view of the world and maintain my own mental peace.

If, partly under the influence of meta-rational factors, the axioms should change, the *same* body of accumulated experience will suddenly be organized differently and new chains of cause and effect appear to govern what has been experienced. I also experienced such a reorganization, as I will explain more fully in the following chapters. The process is like scattering iron filings onto a sheet of paper under a magnet. They set themselves into patterns—but move the magnet, and the patterns change.

To make another comparison, one of the well-known drawings of the Dutch artist M. C. Escher shows black wild geese in the sky flying from the left to the right side of the page. But when an observer looks at the work differently, it suddenly appears that there are white geese flying, not black, and they are moving from right to left, not left to right.

Quite a few years had to pass before I was capable of seeing the experiences I had accumulated at *Szabad Nép* with new eyes.

Intellectual emptiness

The reading I had accomplished as a teenager went almost entirely unused during those years. A quotation from one or two Hungarian historical figures or the most widely read classical poets might crop up in some of my writings. No reference to any other kind of reading can be found. Perhaps the one advantage gained from my having started out as a cultivated man was that a few writers were assigned to my section of the paper. István Örkény and Ferenc Karinthy were among the regular outside contributors. I got on with them well; they saw me not as a boss or party functionary, but as a friend with whom they could have cultured and enjoyable conversation. Each of them occasionally mentioned being dissatisfied with conditions as they were, Örkény perhaps more vociferously than Karinthy. But I cannot say they, with writers' eyes, saw the problems sooner or more clearly than I did as an economic journalist. Their vision then was as blurred by political blindness as mine.

I seldom had a book in my hand other than a work of contemporary Hungarian or Soviet literature. There would have been little time for reading anyway alongside the hectic work on the newspaper. On the other hand, I imbibed more thoroughly and methodically than before the literature of Marxism-Leninism. I had a good memory. I could back up the message of my articles with quotations that would not have occurred to others.

Looking back now, I am astonished at my lack of economic education. I took issue with the "bourgeois" theories of the time in that review I wrote of *Capital*, but my arguments rested almost entirely on secondary sources: I had not read the works I was criticizing. Others did the same. No one taught me a basic requirement of intellectual honesty—you have to examine an idea firsthand before you criticize it. Although I might have arrived at that conclusion by myself, I did not. The low level of scholarship was typified by a single event. My review of *Capital* and my excellent performance at party school were enough to have Tamás Nagy, the economist commissioned to establish the newly forming Marxist university of economics, ask me to teach at the political economy department. I declined the invitation, not because I felt unprepared but because I wanted to devote my full energies to my work on *Szabad Nép*.

Reading those writings of mine half a century later, I was not only struck by the mistakes in them. I was staggered also by their intellectual mediocrity, if that can be separated from their content.

The style was quite smooth, with hardly any of the infelicities of expression found in many newspaper articles. But they contain irritatingly simplistic praise for good results and achievements. Whenever I ran up against any problem in those days, my solution was to urge people—using the imperative mood—to overcome the mistake.

All my writings had some variety of transparent structure, with a beginning and an end. That seems to have remained a feature of my thinking. Yet the argumentation was quite dull. It is possible to argue in a clever, sophisticated way even if the conclusion is ultimately faulty, but I found hardly any examples of that in those articles.

Whether they were editorials or reports on a situation, the articles would often quote figures. Some seem replete with numbers. I am quite sure I never changed any of the figures I found in my sources to suit a purpose or goal. But I remember I did not always check the source or compare figures I wanted to use with ones elsewhere. The figures in an article are often extracted arbitrarily, or Hungarian statistics are set against those of developed capitalist countries in ways that fail to meet the basic requirements of comparability. An overall figure is compared with a partial one or an increment with state variable. I could make excuses for myself by saying no one had taught me, no one had warned me of the pitfalls of not handling data correctly. But I could have found out these rules for myself if I had not been obsessed by a desire to back up propaganda statements at all costs.

I wrote a lot and fast, which shows in the superficiality of the results. That failing did not take me fifty years to realize. When I broke with journalism a few years later and turned to scholarly research, where I could spend weeks or months addressing a single problem, I shuddered to look back on my earlier style. I began to despise journalism, with its hasty, hurried, improvised way of gathering and conveying information. I now know that this judgment too would lead to a false conclusion if generalized absolutely. There are journalists doing a conscientious job, who have checked the facts they present and who work on a highly intellectual plane. But I grew sick of it, and I hardly liked to admit to myself how long I had spent being a journalist.

Reading my writings in chronological order, I could discern no development in them. They seemed rather to become duller and more monotonous over time. I was 25 years old in 1953. What a splendid age, when many intellectuals have completed most of their university studies and written some pioneering works. I had simply turned the editorial treadmill, disgorging writings devoid of content and translating into proper Hungarian articles by colleagues or ministry or enterprise functionaries unable to express themselves. My mental state was bleaker than it had been when I had written my essay "Seed under the Snow" at the age of 17.

A moral reckoning

I do not intend this book to be an exercise in public self-criticism. My purpose is to say what has happened to me in my life and *why* things turned out as they did. Readers may pass judgment if they wish, according to their own sets of values. I make judgments as well, but inside myself, according to my own conscience. I apologize to all whom I damaged with my writings, but deeds are still more important than sincere words of apology.

Many see moral reckoning as an additive operation: some events bear a plus sign and some a minus. Adding the items produces a balance—comforting if it is positive.

This additive approach actually lies behind the idea of recompense and atonement. Some people think, "I have committed sins, but I can work them off with good deeds." I have the impression that was how my friend Miklós Gimes thought of it. He carried on fighting for the defeated revolution under cover until he was arrested. If need be, he would choose death, but he wanted to atone for the grave sins he committed in his earlier political activity.*

I respect those who adopt the principle of atonement and penance in deed, not just word, but I do not subscribe to that approach myself. I do not believe the damage someone does at one stage in life can be offset by meritorious acts in another. Sins are irreparable. Their victims may no longer be living when the ostensible recompense is made or may not be the beneficiaries of the good deeds. Even if they are alive, even if they or their descendants profit from the good deeds, the wrong that was suffered before cannot in this way be righted.

Not only had I understood that I had taken a false path in the first stage of my adult life but I stepped onto a new one with full determination. I am sure I have achieved many things in the past few decades that have benefited my fellows. But I did not do those deeds as "atonement." I keep a separate reckoning of them, while my actions during my time at *Szabad Nép* remain on the books in another account.

* It is debatable, of course, whether Gimes had any such intention of making amends and atonement.

4

Waking Up—1953–1955

Stalin's death on March 5, 1953, closed one period in the history of the Communist countries and opened another. The radical alterations that began in my political and social environment wrought, after significant intervals, changes in my worldview, ideas, and behavior as well.

The "New Course"

The turn of political events and leadership changes in the Soviet Union began to make themselves felt in Hungary a few months later. A delegation of party and state leaders was summoned to Moscow in June 1953 and sharply rebuked for the catastrophic political and economic situation that had developed in Hungary. Mátyás Rákosi, who had gladly heard himself called "Comrade Stalin's best Hungarian disciple" and who wished to be the most eminent among the Eastern European Communist leaders in carrying out Stalin's instructions, now was berated for his zealousness by the new party leaders in Moscow. Though deprived of sole authority, he was allowed to keep his position and powers as general secretary of the party, while Imre Nagy was to be prime minister. Nagy had been the first agriculture minister in the provisional government of 1945. Thus he had directed the land reform, gaining an aura among the peasantry as one who had redistributed great estates. On the other hand, he was an old Communist, exiled with Rákosi and Gerő in Moscow, where he had opposed the Rákosi-led mainstream of the party on some issues. He avoided the fate of the executed László Rajk or the imprisoned János Kádár, but he was not among Rákosi's favored few or a member of the governing clique. He stood out from the other Communist leaders for his appearance, his well-chosen words, and, above all, his closeness with and sympathy for the people.

The Hungarian party confirmed the instructions from Moscow in a momentous resolution passed at a Central Leadership meeting in June. Then came the formation of Imre Nagy's government and his program speech to Parliament as prime minister. The "June resolution," the "Imre Nagy speech," the "Government Program," the "New Course"—those expressions of the time became synonymous, all referring to the post-Stalin program of the Hungarian Communist Party. Let me summarize the program briefly, using as far as possible the contemporary phraseology:

• There had been grave errors of policy up to 1953. The problem was not with the party's ideas but with how those ideas were implemented. The errors had to be rectified, but the system's foundations would be kept unchanged.

• There had been grave errors in the party's economic policy as well. Too little attention had been paid to raising the standard of living.

• The increased targets for the five-year plan had been unrealistic. There had been excesses in forcing socialist industrialization. At the same time, the party's position on property relations was unchanged: state ownership would remain dominant.

• Distortions had appeared in agricultural policy. The goal of introducing collective farming remained correct, but those joining collective farms had to do so of their own free will (thereby observing the "voluntary principle").

• "Socialist legality" had been gravely violated. (This was party jargon for the widespread show trials, torture, mass arrests, labor camps, and other forms of brutal oppression.) Such violation could not be tolerated in the future.

• The Communist Party had become divorced from the masses. A popular front had to be formed to range the whole Hungarian people behind the party leadership.

The "New Course" program already contained many of the elements in the way of thinking known later as *reform communism*. The program broadened further in the next few months, but two factors that would be especially important in reform communism did not appear. One was *market socialism*, the partial or total removal of bureaucratic central planning and its replacement with market coordination. (Much more will be said about this later in the book.) The other was "*democratism*," a word I put in scare quotes intentionally. This tortuous term of the period expressed inconsistent desires. On the one hand, citizens were to have more say in public affairs; there was to be "workplace democracy" and "party democracy." On the other hand, the Communist Party's monopoly of power was to remain. Democratism received much greater emphasis later in the history of the development of communist ideas—for instance, in the idea of "socialism with a human face" current during the Prague Spring of 1968.

Now let me try to reconstruct my thinking in 1953–1954.

Like many other Communists, I felt a sense of great loss in the death of Stalin. I did not expect a historic turning point to follow. I thought his successors would follow Stalin's line, as they had ceremoniously promised in their funeral speeches.

When I came to read the June resolution of the Hungarian party Central Leadership and the speech of Imre Nagy, I did not realize immediately what radical changes were being introduced. I found the June program congenial, but it would be touching up my story to say I was filled with relief or enthusiasm. I was not among those who had suffered in the period before June, and I did not feel the time had come to breathe a sigh of relief. The party had decided and I would take note of its decision in a calm and disciplined way. The essential change in the party line did not surprise me as such; there had been several "new," sharply different periods in the history of the Soviet party, for instance. That was all I expected in this case. I did not attach special significance to the way Rákosi's one-man rule was giving way to two men at the top. This all offers further evidence of my political naiveté and immaturity at the time.

The first articles I wrote at the time of the New Course were not significantly different from their predecessors. They varied perhaps only in being less impassioned, more restrained, and more objective.

A meeting with an ex-prisoner

I was awakened from my reveries by some disturbing experiences.

Late in the summer of 1954, I was staying in a resort facility at Lake Balaton when I met Sándor Haraszti, who had just been released after several years in prison. He had been a Communist back in Horthy's time; and after 1945, he had become editor in chief of the other Communist newspaper, *Szabadság* (*Freedom*). We would sometimes meet and I had respectful feelings of friendship for him. He was the father-in-law of Géza Losonczy, who was tragically to die as a martyr of the 1956 Revolution. Losonczy had been one of the heads of *Szabad Nép* when I started on the paper. Our acquaintance was superficial, but he was generally known as an old and respected party member. Haraszti had been arrested in 1950 and Losonczy in 1951. It emerged later that Rákosi and his associates had wanted to include them in a public trial in which János Kádár would have been the main figure accused. That second public trial after Rajk's never took place, but the men were kept in prison until released by the advent of the New Course.

I knew nothing of what had happened to them. I accepted news of arrests with equanimity in those days. If the party decided to do that to old members, it would have checked carefully whether they were guilty or not. It did not cross my mind that the arrested might be innocent. I believed unswervingly in the party's verdicts.

Now, a few years on, sitting on the grass of a Balaton resort, I came face to face with Sándor, who related to me calmly what shameful atrocities he had suffered. They tried to force him to confess to false charges. When it turned out that simple persuasion would not work, they tortured him brutally.

When trials of this kind were being prepared, each suspect was put in charge of an officer of the ÁVH, the State Security Police, who would direct the interrogation. Sándor's officer was M. M., whom I happened to know well from 1945, when we were both members of the Communist youth movement MADISZ in the Fifth District of Budapest.* M. M. had not beaten up the elderly Sándor Haraszti himself, but he had given the orders for when and how hard he was to be hit. When I knew M. M. in 1945, he was as enthusiastic and devoted a member of MADISZ as I was. I never met him again, but I am convinced that he was not a sadist in the psychiatric sense. He was having Sándor Haraszti beaten not because he enjoyed brutality, but because it was part of the normal course of things at his place of work. Anyone branded as an enemy of the party had to have the truth extracted from them, even if doing so meant torture. And the truth is obviously the story of spying or sabotage that the investigating officer's superiors have told him, which provided the basis for suspicion and criminal charges—except that it has in fact been fabricated, it is an artificial mixture of true and false. The suspect has to be interrogated until he or she confesses that the fabricated charges are true and can be line perfect in playing the evil part assigned in the prosecution.

It was dreadful to hear all this from the one who had suffered in the drama. The tragedy was enhanced for me because I knew the other player, the one who had tortured the hero—and not as a man inherently evil, but as someone who had started life with noble intentions. I found this revelation especially shocking because it demonstrated that the tragedy was not caused by the personal characteristics of the participants. There was something fatally wrong with the system itself.

My meeting with Sándor Haraszti had undermined the moral foundations on which I had hitherto based my Communist convictions. The party had lied in saying that Haraszti was guilty, and I had believed the lie. If that trial had been based on a lie, then the others must have been as well. We were surrounded by lies and I, stupidly, had believed them without question. And, willy-nilly, I had been spreading some lies myself.

Sándor Haraszti was a man of the written word, and so am I; and although my field has changed, I have remained a man of the written word to this day. For me as for him, there is great significance in whether the things we write are true. After my meeting with Sándor Haraszti, honesty and deception, truth and falsehood were the concepts buzzing in my head.

I felt it was almost unbearable to think that people should be deliberately tortured in the twentieth century, for whatever purpose. I thought it unacceptable to torture

---

* The initials "M. M.," "N. N.," etc., here and elsewhere, are not the real initials of the individuals concerned. I will return later to the problems with revealing real names.

even criminals, let alone the innocent. Could such acts be done by a party that felt itself called to lead the progress of humanity?

I had been dealing with economic questions, planning, and production since 1947, and, as I said in the preceding chapter, I had noticed some negative economic occurrences. Yet what followed was not, as you might expect, an analysis of the problems leading to the recognition that there was something awry in Marxian political economy or planning theory or in Hungary's economic policy. My earlier view of the world was shaken when its *ethical* foundations collapsed. I felt that *all* I had hitherto believed and thought needed revision. If the ethical foundations were unsound, I could not accept without reexamination the intellectual structure resting on those unacceptable, baseless ethical foundations.

I am not saying the multiplicity of ideas then in my head disintegrated all of a sudden. I had to go from level to level in the intellectual structure and think over each element, time and time again. That took a good while. But from that day on, question marks replaced the exclamation marks at the end of all the assertions and commands in the teachings of the Communist Party, which I had accepted unquestioningly up until then.

Clarifying discussions and readings

I was lucky to find people to help me reexamine my ideas. Pál Lőcsei was the first to broach the subject of the June resolution and Imre Nagy's policies. Pál took a risk in starting such discussions, for his message was "anti-party," according to the Communist Party rule book. But he felt rightly that he could rely on our friendship. And he trusted that his arguments would have an effect on my thinking.

We had a succession of confidential conversations on a number of fundamental political issues. He had previously been in charge of the agricultural section of *Szabad Nép,* so he knew much about the field that was Imre Nagy's specialty: forced collectivization, the use of force against the peasants, and the story of the persecution of the kulaks.

I was truly appalled by the figures for imprisonment and internment that were passed on to me by Lőcsei as soon as they had come to his notice. One figure I remember was the more than 40,000 political prisoners in Hungary at the time of Stalin's death, out of a population of less than 10 million. That number included those convicted, those held before trial, and those simply detained as internees.*

---

* Mátyás Rákosi, when addressing the Political Committee of the Soviet Communist Party in June 1953, quoted the following number: the number of Hungarians in prison and internment at the time was 45,000 (Baráth 1999, p. 42). What was said at the meeting in Moscow was strictly confidential at the time, but I suppose this number must somehow have leaked out

The figure, like Sándor Haraszti's personal history, influenced me more and radical-ized my ideas to a greater extent than the recognition, say, that the raised targets of the five-year plan were unrealistic and were therefore depressing the Hungarian standard of living. At the time I still attributed the economic difficulties to errors in planning and not to a fault of the system, but the enormous extent of the political repression was already pointing to other, *underlying* troubles.

The first great thought-provoking discussions with Lőcsei left me prepared for in-tellectual guidance, which I received from Miklós Gimes. He reminded me of the day when the first news of the Berlin uprising had arrived in June 1953. We had spoken a few words on the subject at the time. I had not attached any special signif-icance to the news in the first few hours, but he had. Now, a few months later, he explained its historic significance to me. Not since the defeat of the Kronstadt upris-ing in the Soviet Union in 1921 had there been a rebellion against a socialist power by its own people. That is what the people of Berlin had attempted. Although the revolt had been swiftly put down by Soviet tanks, Gimes told me, it had to be noted that workers had attacked workers' power. (I do not want to read a prophecy into Gimes's words, but perhaps he had some suspicions that what had *begun* in Berlin would continue one day.)

I could not forget a sentence that Miklós cited to me from a conversation between him and Révai. They were discussing how the "people" had not always taken the Communist side in the history of the Soviet Union or later Eastern Europe. None-theless, it had been imperative to establish and maintain into the future the power of the Communist Party, if need be (and here Révai used the German phrase) "mit barbarischen Mitteln"—by barbaric means. I will never forget that terse expression of the Communist messianic spirit and unbridled Machiavellianism. I felt I had to break with both elements in that confession: with any idea of forcing a system on people to redeem them and with the notion that all means were permissible in the messianic cause, including intimidation, mass imprisonment, and torture.

Gimes had spent a long period in Geneva as a correspondent for *Szabad Nép*. He had been deeply influenced by its wealth, abundance, and calm and by the economic

---

from the Hungarian party headquarters and found its way to Lőcsei. I did not find the *exact* number of prisoners of the state. Another, more revealing, piece of data was reported to the party's leadership by Deputy Interior Minister László Piros and Chief Prosecutor Kálmán Czakó in November 1953 (Rainer 1999, pp. 24–25; this did not leak out at the time): almost 748,000 people were affected by the so-called amnesty actions. Everybody belonged to this category who had been released from prisons and internment camps, or was allowed to return home from places of designated residence assigned during the relocations, or had penal pro-ceedings or police investigations against them terminated. Those three-quarters of a million people amounted to a startling 8 percent of the population.

superiority of capitalism over socialism that he had experienced there. These impressions he described to me graphically.

I mentioned in the previous chapter the doors that for meta-rational reasons keep thoughts out or, conversely, let them in. After years of intellectual isolation, I began to read again. That is an understatement: I began to devour works critical of Stalinist policy.

I was still half or three-quarters a Communist at the time. The works that affect a person most strongly in the state of mind I was then in are not ones diametrically opposed to the views held hitherto by the doubter—that is, not those attacking the Communist Party from without. What swayed me most was strong criticism from within. I read in German the great book on Stalin by Isaac Deutscher and suddenly saw Stalin's personality with different eyes. I cannot recall the author or title of another book in German I read at the time that placed the history of the Soviet party in a new, socialist, but anti-Stalinist light.

I was greatly stimulated by various Yugoslav writers, including pamphlets by Edvard Kardelj.[1] These had been published after Stalin came into conflict with Tito and, in his rage, expelled the Yugoslav party from the community of Communist parties in power, thereby forcing the Yugoslav leaders to follow a separate path from Stalin's. That effort, naturally, was combined with strong criticism of Stalinism. Those Yugoslav authors were the first to introduce me to the idea that the Stalinist form of socialist economy entails *bureaucratic* centralism and that decentralized socialist economic management would be healthier and more efficient. They made no reference to Oskar Lange's study on market socialism[2] and the debate it roused in the West in the 1930s, preferring to present the idea of combining collective ownership with market coordination as their own and to phrase it in their own Marxist terminology. In the Yugoslav approach, decentralization covered two processes: a shift from a centralized form of economic management based on plan directives and the introduction of "self-management." The latter promised greater autonomy to elected district bodies and worker-elected boards in factories. The Yugoslav authors' criticism of the management methods previously employed in Yugoslavia, patterned slavishly on the Soviet ones, rang true to the negative experiences I had had with centralization. It seemed at the time that the Yugoslav ideological innovation of "self-management" would give tangible form to the New Course demand in Hungary for workplace democracy.

Many former believers in the ideology of the Communist Party broke with it in stages. The *first stage* was to turn against the brutal terror of the Stalinist regimes while retaining all the basic tenets of Marxism-Leninism, including the "dictatorship of the proletariat" (i.e., the monopoly of the Communist Party over power). Thus Stalin had committed "grave errors" and strayed from the true Leninist path, to which Communism now had to return. Other stages then followed, in which former believers understood that the *real* system that had developed in the Soviet Union and the other Communist countries embodied not only Stalin's but Lenin's and even some of Marx's basic ideas. I passed through the whole course of disillusionment with Communist ideology, but during the months described in this chapter, I was still in the first, anti-Stalinist stage, although I had begun to move further on some issues (such as centralization and the question of the market).

My first show of "insubordination"

The change that steadily took place in my thinking and view of the world began to affect my behavior as well. Up until then, I had obeyed the party's commands out of conviction, not fear. As the conviction wavered, I became less disciplined as well.

The party's instructions on what to communicate in *Szabad Nép* about the party's economic policy measures had hitherto come to me through István Friss. Friss had now been removed from his post at the party center, and Ernő Gerő himself would occasionally convey his wishes to me directly. He did so in the winter of 1953–1954, during some severe disruptions to the power supply. There were frequent unannounced power cuts during those weeks, in both factories and residential areas. *Szabad Nép* kept quiet for a good while, but eventually it became clear that something had to be said. I spoke several times on the phone to Gerő, who wanted the paper to name "objective circumstances" as the main or exclusive cause of the problems. I saw in this issue a manifestation of a dilemma that was troubling me in any case: the need to avoid lying, to tell the truth and be honest. For the first time, I contradicted Ernő Gerő, whom I had respected so much not long before. I announced that I was not prepared to write an article denying that the problems with the electricity supply were occurring because the proportions of power production to growing needs had been incorrectly assessed. Furthermore, officials were cutting off the electricity to large areas without prior thought or warning, rather than devising a rational system of electricity management. Eventually, those simple and obvious truths featured in the lead article I wrote.[3]

I later heard about Ernő Gerő's record in the Spanish Civil War, as a commissar in the Communist brigades. People had learned to be afraid of him for his mercilessness, and dozens of faithful warriors for the anti-Franco left had been executed on his orders. If I had known that at the time, I would have been scared, because by then I had knowledge of the horrors of the terror. But I had no idea I had anything to fear as I argued with Ernő Gerő over the power shortage. Nor did it ever dawn on me what the economic explanation for the shortage could be. I began to think about such matters only much later, though in hindsight it may be worth noting that my first display of "insubordination" had to do with a severe shortage. To be frank, my sole concern at the time was the choice between truth and falsehood.

Reviewing writings by Imre Nagy

It became clear to me first from my friend Pál Lőcsei's explanations and later from much other information that the "party unity" cited ceremoniously in party statements was just a rhetorical flourish. In fact there was a struggle inside the party between two groups—supporters of Mátyás Rákosi and of Imre Nagy, respectively. Of course all such struggles have personal elements as well. Despite the lip service paid to collective leadership, the classical socialist system was a personal dictatorship of a paramount leader, surrounded by a narrow clique that shared his decision making. Members of the clique, who would attend to each other's pronouncements, would experience a division of labor. Yet there was one supreme leader in whose hands power was ultimately centered. The question then was who would be top person in the Hungarian party, Rákosi or Nagy?

But the particular duel being waged in Hungary was not just a struggle for leadership between two people. It was also a battle between two lines, two political programs. Mátyás Rákosi wanted to continue the Stalinist line, with slight adjustments at most. Imre Nagy wanted to implement his June program, the specific reform communism of the New Course. It seemed for a long time as if the two sides were equally strong. Both, very importantly, had their prompters and supporters in Moscow.

A group of leading staff members on *Szabad Nép* was intent on giving decisive, active support to one side, the Imre Nagy line. In alphabetical order, the most active members were Lajos Fehér, Sándor Fekete, Miklós Gimes, Péter Kende, myself, Pál Lőcsei, Tibor Méray, and Sándor Novobáczky. Who would have thought that the events of 1956 would propel these individuals, so full of friendly feelings for each other and meeting so frequently, along such different paths? Gimes was to die a martyr's death; Fekete, Lőcsei, and Novobáczky would spend years in Kádár's prison; and Kende and Méray ended up leaders of the Hungarian political émigrés in Paris. I will not sum up my own fate in a few words here, as that is the subject of the whole book. The least expected development was that Lajos Fehér, who had stood closest to Imre Nagy, immediately joined János Kádár on November 4, 1956, and remained for the rest of his life a member of the Political Committee that Kádár headed.

To return to the end of the summer of 1954 and my own activity, my resolve to actively assist the policy of the New Course was firm. Hitherto, my articles had been almost exclusively on economic subjects, but I stepped beyond that realm on several occasions during this period.

It was in the October 6, 1954, issue of *Szabad Nép* that the long review I wrote of two recent volumes by Imre Nagy, containing selections of speeches and articles from the past ten years, appeared.[4] My piece drew attention to aspects of Nagy's thinking that *departed* from typical Stalinist political propaganda. Let me pick a few of the quotations from his writings that featured prominently: "Communists must stop ordering people about in the villages.... Arrogance and imperviousness go hand in hand with neglect of serious, purposeful, and persistent work in the party, replacing it with mere empty rhetoric.... A certain kind of 'drill' (I cannot call it anything else) is becoming more and more widespread: overemphasis on appearances, hustle and bustle, exaggerated, endless rhythmic clapping, standing ovations, words put into people's mouth in advance kill initiative."[5]

Nagy's views on agriculture were close to those once espoused in the Soviet party by Nikolay Bukharin. He thought it wrong that there was "exaggeration of the capitalist danger" and "antipathy, alienation, and even fear, in broad spheres of the party and even in its leading organizations, of developing the productive forces of small and medium-sized peasant farms."[6]

This selection presented a good picture of Imre Nagy. He was a Communist politician who would not step out of the intellectual realm of Marxism-Leninism, but would like to develop a version of it that was gentler, more approachable, and more acceptable to the peasantry than Rákosi's version. My review set out to present this picture to my newspaper's readers.

Shortly afterward, early in October 1954, the party held a Central Leadership meeting that endorsed the position of the Imre Nagy wing. By that time, we leading staff members at *Szabad Nép* had gained a great deal of inside information. We knew that this victory reflected at most the balance of power at that moment. It was by no means certain that Imre Nagy and his sincere supporters would remain in government in the longer term. We thought it had become more important still for the paper to decisively show its support of the New Course.

I wrote lead articles on the subject on two occasions. Let me quote the title of the first: "Further along the June Road with the Central Leadership Pointing the Way."[7] It expresses well the point I had reached in my political development. Like Imre Nagy, whose ideas I sought to popularize, I wanted to promote change *within* the Communist Party, reforming it so that it would continue to improve the socialist system. As for the internal struggle, I was clearly on the side of Imre Nagy and said so in my articles.

Rebellion at *Szabad Nép*

About this time, Pál Lőcsei suggested we should not limit our support for the New Course to our writings. Every article printed in the newspaper went before the editor in chief, Oszkár Betlen, or his deputy, Imre Komor, both of whom stood on Rákosi's side. Their oversight inevitably dulled the edge of our writings. Lőcsei proposed calling an extraordinary meeting of party members, at which we could state our opinions more openly and boldly. It was foreseeable that because of the central position of *Szabad Nép* in the propaganda work of the party, the comments of its leading journalists would spread widely by word of mouth.

Lőcsei was the motor behind the preparations, but I was one of the organizers too. We decided in advance who would say what. The meeting lasted two days.[8] For Lajos Fehér, *Szabad Nép*'s most important task was to speak honestly about the country's problems. He openly criticized Ernő Gerő's recent speech. Lőcsei's inflammatory talk was principally on "legality" (i.e., against brutal repression) and designed to encourage the renewal of political morals. Of the illegalities committed in previous years, Sándor Novobáczky asked, "How long will it be before those really responsible are called to account for these?" Tibor Méray focused on the problem of truth and falsehood, calling for a "cleansing storm,"[9] which duly came two years later. Kende criticized Gerő and Friss, and I Mihály Farkas, the party official then in charge of *Szabad Nép*. I stated, "It is the leadership of the party that is primarily responsible for the mistakes of *Szabad Nép*." Members of staff spoke one after the other,* sharply criticizing the party leadership and the Stalinist members of the editorial board, and demanding that the government's June program be consistently implemented and a Stalinist restoration prevented.[10]

Read with today's eyes, the criticism seems to have stopped halfway. The politicians responsible and their bad policies and decisions were rightly condemned, but not the *system* that had put these people at the top, given them limitless power, and generated their bad decisions. But the moral courage of the participants commands our respect. Everyone made sharp, radical criticisms of party leaders still in the Political Committee and in high government positions (and soon to return to absolute power). We knew our initiative would enrage them and prompt what revenge they could take.

The moral standards set by the journalists who spoke at the meeting are worthy of esteem even today, as they condemned lies and empty phrases and demanded that journalists be honest and faithful to the truth.

---

* All who spoke critically and rebelliously at that meeting and have not been mentioned yet deserve listing here: István Almási, Emil Balázs, Tibor Gallé, Ernő Gondos, Mrs. János Gyenes, Ilona Jászai, Zsuzsa Koroknai, Erzsébet Kovács, Endre Kövesi, Gábor Mocsár, Sándor Nagy, Mária Pásztor, Lajos Szilvási, Kálmán Takács, Tibor Tardos, and József Vető.

The end of my period at *Szabad Nép*

News of the *Szabad Nép* rebellion soon spread. Several copies of the meeting's minutes were reproduced and distributed. (This was a more difficult task before the era of photocopiers, let alone the Internet.) Our example certainly contributed to the holding of similar meetings in several other important organizations.

Not long after, power relations in the Communist Party began to change. Rákosi and his supporters were once again on top.

The heads of *Szabad Nép* were first called before the Political Committee on November 24, 1954, and scolded soundly for what had happened.[11] The events at the paper were frequently mentioned at subsequent Political Committee meetings as well. On December 1, those who had spoken out were repeatedly condemned.[12] The meeting, Mihály Farkas said, had "criticized the leadership of the party in an intolerable manner.... A whole series of anti-Marxist views were put forward. The meeting at *Szabad Nép* has set a precedent: similar meetings have taken place among the radio staff, in the offices of *Szabad Ifjúság*, at the Szikra Publishing House, at the universities in Budapest and Debrecen, and...among writers as well."[13] At the discussion's conclusion, Mátyás Rákosi expressed his impatience: "What do our comrades at *Szabad Nép* expect?...First of all, the press and the radio need to be ruled with a firm hand, and if need be, organizational measures will have to be taken.... We must give orders to all the papers to put an end to general imprecation of the party's past and unbridled use of open criticism."[14]

Two political commissars were assigned to the newspaper offices to restore order, and a succession of party leaders arrived to work on the journalists. What they wanted was a declaration from the party members on the paper withdrawing their previous position. This they could not obtain. It infuriated Rákosi's people that the rebels stuck to their guns.

Under such circumstances, I wanted to escape the responsibility of directing the economic section of the paper. Luckily, the post of "secretary of the editorial board" fell vacant about that time and I took it over. The secretary was responsible for the technical and administrative tasks of producing the paper. Formally, it was a high position, but the secretary did not have to write articles or commission them from colleagues.

In the meantime, preparations for "organizational measures" began at the party's central offices. Lists of those to be weeded out began to be drawn up as early as December 1954,[15] although no effective decision was reached before the political turn within the party. The Central Leadership met again at the beginning of March 1955 and passed a resolution contradicting the one affirmed a few months before.[16] Imre Nagy was branded as having "right-wing leanings" and expelled from the party. Although the party resolution of June 1953 was declared in a few empty phrases to be still valid, it was in fact withdrawn point by point and the party returned to its old political course. By that time, Rákosi's reputation was so compromised that he could not regain his absolute majority, but the victory in the struggle between the Rákosi and Nagy factions was clearly his.

It was Kende who was first dismissed, as early as December 1954; he had been deputy party secretary at the time of the meeting and bore responsibility for party affairs at the paper. Two other talented young writers, Endre Kövesi and Lajos Szilvási, were removed at the same time, although there is no knowing whether the wrath fell on them for their investigative reports or for their sharp words at the meeting.

The Political Committee came to a decision proposed by Mátyás Rákosi on April 28:[17] several leaders of the rebellious group, including myself, were fired from the staff of *Szabad Nép*.* I should add that turning us out took place in a "post-Stalinist" way. Not long before, such offenses or even lesser infractions would have earned those dismissed internment or prison, or perhaps manual labor on building sites. In our case, we were all assigned new jobs. Lajos Fehér was appointed manager of a state farm. The others found work in the press, in lowlier positions on papers with much less prestige. I was the only one who moved into an academic field.

Before they decided on our transfers, we were put through a demeaning process. It was made clear that our assignment to a new workplace would depend on our "exercising self-criticism." This was routine matter for old Communists who had returned from exile in Moscow. They had had to do whatever they were told, without hesitation or qualms of conscience. It was a new, humiliating, and shameful procedure for me. The lying words were forced out of me. I was a victim, but I had suffered a moral defeat as well. Looking back on a successful research career of half a century, I can console myself with the thought that it was worth saying those few words, if they were the price for being allowed to embark on a research career. But is there a place in such dilemmas for a cost-benefit calculation of any kind?

The defeat of the "June government program," the personal fall of Imre Nagy, and the reprisals against us were to be expected. We had clearly taken into account in advance the risk of defeat before we came out publicly in favor of the New Course. Indeed, as I intimated just now, we might have expected a worse outcome

---

* The Political Committee resolved to dismiss Lajos Fehér, János Kornai, Teréz Laky, Gábor Lénárt, Tibor Méray, Sándor Novobáczky, and Imre Patkó. Teri did not speak at the meetings: they obviously turned her out from the paper because she was my wife. Pál Lőcsei was then a student at the Lenin Institute, one of the party schools, so formally he could not be dismissed from his post at *Szabad Nép*.

and more brutal reprisals. Only two years had passed since Stalin's death. No one could foresee how much of the brutality of the Stalin period would remain and how much would abate or cease. Although I was not surprised by what happened, I found it thoroughly repellent.

To put it in a single word, the party disciplinary resolution filled me with disgust. My mental state in those months was one of disillusionment, bitterness, and horror. My earlier blind faith was dispelled once and for all. My eyes had been opened wide to what was happening. Stomach-turning lies, infamous slanders, hypocritical arguments, sly use of real and false reports compiled by informers, threats and blackmail, and mental torture and humiliation of opponents were among the "normal" weapons used in Communist factional fighting. What kind of party was this if its supreme body, the Central Leadership, bent this way and that with the wind, now adopting a specific policy and now rejecting and condemning it? I wanted to get as far as I could from this pollution. I saw the need for people within the party to take up the struggle for good against the representatives of evil, but I no longer wanted to do it.

This process of coming to my senses in 1953–1955 was accompanied by an acute loss of self-confidence. I had no right to build on my own political judgment if I could be so cruelly deceived. What had I done with my good sense and my critical faculties if I could be led by the nose for so many years? At first my feelings were only instinctive, but I steadily came to a conscious decision never again to believe in anyone without any reserve or doubt. My first reaction to any intellectual or political statement would be: Is it true? Is the argument supporting any proposal or program a sound one? Is there not some insidious intention behind it?

Having submitted myself voluntarily to iron discipline for several years, I decided I would never be a party warrior again.

I left *Szabad Nép* after eight years. I went back there for a single night in October 1956 (as I will relate later), but apart from that one occasion, I never again entered the *Szabad Nép* offices. A few years ago, papers associated with the right wing were being edited there. At the end of the summer of 2005 the building was demolished.

5

The Beginning of a Research Career—
1955–October 23, 1956

Overcentralization

I started work in the Institute of Economics of the Hungarian Academy of Sciences in June 1955. It began a new period in my life. Thereafter my vocation was research.

My first steps in that new career were taken amid remarkable events, against an unusual historical background. The mounting tension and upheaval, which was occurring openly in the political field and was even more intense beneath the surface, culminated in the 1956 Hungarian Revolution.

The background

A system of scientific and scholarly stages and degrees on the Soviet pattern began to be introduced in Hungary at the beginning of the 1950s. The first grade or level in a discipline corresponding to a research field (such as medicine or economics) was that of a "candidate." It is customary to rate a candidacy degree as equivalent to an American or Western European Ph.D. It was attained at about the same age, in each case with a book-length dissertation.*

I applied to prepare for a candidacy degree in August 1953 and I heard in December that I had been admitted. The usual requirement was a university degree, just as

---

* Content of the studies aside (as can certainly be disregarded in the case of mathematics or physics), the essential difference between the two systems appeared in the study requirements before the dissertation was submitted. American students in a Ph.D. program receive at least two years' very intense, high-standard preparation in several courses, punctuated by examinations and interactions with numerous professors. Students "aspiring" to a candidacy degree would not receive special instruction on top of their studies for their first degree. They would simply have to take a few examinations, for which they would prepare privately, and submit a dissertation that they would defend in a public debate.

Another important difference needs to be pointed out. In the Western world, the Ph.D. degree is given by universities, while under the Soviet system, the candidate's and other higher degrees are granted by the Academy of Sciences or another affiliated institution (for example, the Scientific Qualifications Committee in Hungary).

someone applying for a Ph.D. program at a Western university would be expected to have a B.A. I did not have a university degree. I had entered the school of humanities and social sciences of the Budapest University of Sciences in 1945 and attended courses mainly in philosophy and history. For a while, absentee students were still allowed; they did not attend classes but turned up at the end of the year to have their record books signed by the professors, and they postponed taking their examinations. I was one of them for two years; then, because my work at *Szabad Nép* was absorbing all my energies, I gave up the idea of completing college in the normal way. When I applied for the candidate program, the degree requirement was waived. I did not have anyone "fix" that for me, but I suppose that those deciding on my application took into consideration the high position I had held on the paper. I ultimately received my candidacy degree in 1956 without having earned a first degree at all.

The officially assigned adviser in my work for the candidate degree was Professor Tamás Nagy, second in rank to the rector of the Karl Marx University of Economics, but first in academic reputation and actual authority. He had been the translator of Marx's *Capital* into Hungarian and he held the chair of political economy at the university. He was an erudite economist (and not just in Marxism). His lectures and summaries of debates in the field were a pleasure to listen to, because he thought and expressed himself clearly and precisely. He was not a creative scholar and he left no works of lasting importance, but I, like many other economists, think back with gratitude on the support and encouragement I received from him.

Tamás Nagy left me quite free to choose my area of concentration. I was interested in questions of planning and economic management, but at that stage, I still could not express exactly what I wanted to research or how.

I passed the compulsory exams for candidacy quickly and with no difficulty. I was what was known as a "corresponding aspirant," studying in my spare time while holding a full-time job. There were also "scholarship aspirants" who could devote themselves fully to studying and writing their dissertations. Others were employed in research institutes or universities, and thus they could link their job-related activity with their work for a candidacy degree. Around 1952–1953, I twice asked my superiors to release me from *Szabad Nép*, as I would rather do research. Firmly and unhesitatingly, they had rejected those requests, saying, "The party needs you here, at *Szabad Nép*." I had obediently accepted the order.

What had prompted my desire to change careers? Back then, I still had no political motive whatsoever for wanting to keep away from the witches' kitchen of policy making. I was compelled more by an incipient distaste for the treadmill of a daily paper. I was disgusted by the superficiality and haste of journalism. I had little enough idea of what a research career would entail, but I hankered after it. One sign was that I several times volunteered to report on the formation of the Scientific Council and other academic events, although they were not in my province. I had no idea what political battles were then going on behind the scenes in science and scholarship. The only reason for these excursions was that I was drawn toward the world of scholarship.

A year or two had passed since my requests had been rejected. The storms over the *Szabad Nép* rebellion were still blowing when Miklós Gimes said to me one day, "Politics is not the thing for you. You would do better if you became a researcher; it would suit you better." I can still visualize the place where he gave me that advice. We were standing in front of the elevator after some unpleasant meeting.

I could not leave my job or change my occupation of my own accord. But when I and others were removed from our jobs by the leading body of the party, a chance to change my career arrived at last. I seized it. The Institute of Economics had been established not long before, and its director was István Friss, whom I had known for many years and who had earlier given me instructions when he was head of the economic policy department at party headquarters. I asked to be placed in his institute.

My career at the institute began with a spectacular demotion. Losing a high position in the newspaper office, I found myself on the lowest rung of the institute ladder: as an "assistant staff member," I received 40 percent of my previous salary.* I had had a spacious and attractive office before. Now I shared an office with two others.

However, my office mates, Péter Erdős and Róbert Hoch, were bright and inquiring people who were kind and friendly toward me. It was not easy to concentrate on work while I was in one room with them, because they were more interested in talking during those exceptional, troubled months.

Intellectual impulses

I had interesting, thought-provoking discussions with other institute colleagues beside the ones sharing my office.

At the beginning of 1956, the institute moved to 7 Nádor utca, a beautiful, neoclassical building designed by Mihály Pollack, a famous Hungarian architect (it now houses offices of the Hungarian Academy of Science). Tamás Nagy's department, where I belonged, had its rooms on the second floor. Also found there was the office of Antal Máriás, who became well known very young for his article on the efficiency of foreign trade written with Tibor Liska,[1] and who later became head of the

---

* To supplement my income, I wrote a few reviews of books and papers. It was through the helpfulness of editors that my writings appeared—but I could publish my work only anonymously or under a pseudonym.

department of economic policy at the university. Béla Csendes sat in the room next to mine, and a few rooms further down was Ferenc Vági. At the time, both were beginning their careers as agricultural economists. Béla later became a vice president of the National Planning Office and Feri ended up as head of the agricultural department at the economics university. András Nagy, too, was there with us. He had found his way into our institute after numerous jobs. He had held high positions in youth organizations, taught political economics, and then, after the Rajk trial, been reduced to being a laborer in the construction industry. In the end, when the new period started, he was able to return to an intellectual career. Róbert Hoch, Sándor Ausch, Ferenc Molnár, András Bródy—I could go on listing names that sound familiar to the ears of those who have kept track of the development of Hungarian economics in subsequent decades.

"Gyepsor"—the wrong end of the village—is what we called one of the corridors at the institute, or more specifically the group of young researchers who worked there.* In a way, it was a fairly heterogeneous group. There were some whose roots tied them to rural Hungary, while others had belonged to the city all their lives. Some had been doing academic work before, while others became researchers after radical changes in their careers. Still, we were similar in many respects. All of us had been disappointed in the Stalinist-Rákosi version of a communist regime, and would have liked to see a more humane and at the same time more efficient socialism. All of us detested the cold and empty patterns of earlier economic studies and wished to examine *reality*. None of us was, in the modern Western sense, a qualified economist. Even if we did not learn too much economics from each other, we were all inspired by each other's sincere reports of different experiences and by our honest political debates, always based on respect for one another. We had a lot of fun, teased each other—the atmosphere was friendlier than almost any I have experienced since.

The two biggest influences on the formation of my thinking on economics were not institute staff at all, however.

I had met György Péter, president of the Central Statistical Office, before, but at this stage I came closer to him, through Péter Kende. Initially, we all would meet;

---

* Before the war, the part of the village inhabited by the poorest people was called the Gyepsor, as Péter Veres writes in his work *Lunch at the Gyepsor*: "The Gyepsor is on the edge of the village. Beyond it lie the endless alkaline fields covered with the dung of geese, pigs, and cattle, instead of vegetation. Covered, that is, only as long as it takes the dung to dry enough for the inhabitants of the Gyepsor to gather it up for fuel" (Veres 1997 [1939], p. 32). I have taken this quotation from a study by György Péteri (1998, pp. 200–201), who gives a fine description of the people at the Nádor utca "Gyepsor" and their group life, supported by much interesting and instructive information (pp. 198–205).

later just the two of us got together regularly for confidential discussions. He came to our home a couple of times, but usually I would visit his beautiful, elegant apartment. His wife, Emmi Péter (Pikler), a well-known child psychologist and educator, would bring coffee and exchange a few words before leaving us to our talk.

György Péter was twenty-five years older than I was and a long-standing Communist. In the party, he was famous for spending ten years in prison under the Horthy regime, longer than anyone else except Mátyás Rákosi and another prominent party leader, Zoltán Vas. He was aptly described as a "Bolshevik *grand seigneur*" by András Hegedűs,[2] later his deputy at the Central Statistical Office for a time. He stood out among the many gray party bureaucrats for his colorful personality, refinement, generosity, and irony.

After one or two meetings, when he felt that he could trust me, he came forward with his ideas about economics. The market and only the market was the mechanism capable of effectively coordinating supply and demand. For the market to operate, prices had to be freed of their shackles.

Supply, demand, free prices, the market, efficiency—these were all concepts that students of economics at a Western university would encounter in their first lecture on microeconomics. György Péter was putting to us ideas that would seem unremarkable in another political setting—for example, in the Western academic world—but to me were almost revolutionary.

While still in prison, György Péter had obtained a textbook by Farkas Heller,[3] the best-known university teacher of economics in Budapest. Péter had a mathematics degree, but he taught himself from Heller's book the foundations of "bourgeois" (non-Marxist) economics. Though he did not pursue the subject any further, that intellectual experience in his youth influenced him for the rest of his life. What he had absorbed from Heller in theory was confirmed by his personal observations. He regularly took part in meetings of the UN European Economic Commission in Geneva, and he told me on several occasions what a revelation Switzerland was—a stable, consolidated country of wealth and plenty, compared with the penury and shortage found in Hungary and the other socialist countries. (György Péter was the second close friend of mine, after Miklós Gimes, to be astounded by his experiences of Switzerland.) He saw the elegance of Zurich's Bahnhofstrasse, with its incredible range of choice and supremely polite sales staff, as tangible evidence of the effectiveness of the market.

György Péter was not thinking of a "change of system" in the present-day sense. He was convinced he could retain his communist beliefs while rejecting the centralized command economy and substituting market coordination instead. At first, he advanced his ideas only in private conversations. Later, in 1954 and 1956, he published two articles outlining and defending his concept of reform,[4] the drafts having been discussed with one or two of his close colleagues and a couple of friends from outside the Central Statistical Office, of which I was one. I tried to contribute to the articles by making comments and formulating a few paragraphs, especially to the final version of the second study. I imagine others gave ideas and assistance as well. But the underlying idea certainly came from him.*

The almost mystic respect for the market that György Péter expressed in conversation and in his writings was quite alien to Marxist political economy. One pillar of Marx's intellectual structure was that markets make for anarchy. Economic progress demands that humanity be freed from the anarchy of the market and order established in its place. When György Péter (and Farkas Heller's textbook, which he recommended) taught me to concede the virtues of the market, they assisted me greatly in breaking with Marxism.

Apart from our intellectual relations, György Péter and I developed a sincere friendship.†

His critical remarks and heretical economic ideas made György Péter a thorn in the side of the conservative forces. In 1969, a police investigation was launched on flimsy grounds. He was placed under house arrest, not at home but in a hospital. He was killed by a knife in the heart. It was probably suicide; perhaps he could stand the humiliations no longer. But the possibility of murder cannot be ruled out.‡

To return to 1955–1956, an important part in the restructuring of my thinking about economics came from the intense dialogue I had with my closest friend, Péter Kende. As I related in chapter 2, we entered the realm of Marxism together, reading and annotating Marx's *Capital* with minute precision. The story is rounded off by the way we left that realm together (still crossing the intellectual border in secret). We had many, many discussions, and then we decided to put our thoughts in writing. First Kende set about writing what he thought of Marxism in a study called "Critical Remarks on the Economic Theories of Marxism."[5] After that, I wrote a

---

* György Péter's ideas bore a marked resemblance to Oskar Lange's "market socialism," but I am sure that he, like Kardelj (mentioned in the previous chapter) and other Yugoslav authors, was *unaware* of Lange's work. It was a case of concepts rediscovered by a self-taught man.

† After 1956 György Péter brought me economics books several times from the West and he mediated between me and my emigrant friends—to mention just some examples of his friendly and good-hearted assistance. I have written about György Péter in more detail elsewhere (1994c).

‡ At a meeting held in 1994 to commemorate the great reform economist, the lawyer Sándor Nyíri gave a presentation on the criminal proceedings against György Péter, revealing that serious professional mistakes were made while investigators were examining the place of death. The body was moved, numerous important details were not recorded, etc. It is thus impossible to establish today what the exact cause of his death was (Nyíri 1994, pp. 45–47).

paper titled "On 'Das Kapital' and the Economic Questions of Socialism." The two writings provided a framework for our further discussions.

When I was writing the Hungarian version of my memoirs I already had Péter's paper, which he had taken with him earlier to his exile and which then he handed to me again. At that time, I believed that my study was lost once and for all. But recently, after the publication of the Hungarian book but before the English version went to press, one copy of my paper turned up unexpectedly.*

It was an exciting experience to reread these works created fifty years earlier. Just their sheer volume is impressive.† Both of us had formulated our studies with great vigor. We presented our message in an elaborate and well-organized frame. Even though we showed them to only a few people, we nevertheless prepared them with the same care we would have used had we intended to submit them to a prestigious publisher.

As for the maturity of the messages, Péter was one important step ahead of me in the criticism of Marxism. He set forth his doubts about Marx's theory of value and the theory of surplus value while I at the time was still defending them, arguing against Péter. I cannot exactly reconstruct the rapid changes in my way of thinking at the time, but surely it could have taken several more months for me to change my opinion on this issue also.‡

We both sharply criticized Marx's theorems and methodology in many other respects as well. Péter briefly stated his opinion about the socialist economy; I devoted half of my paper to this issue. Here, in this study hidden from the public's eye, I wanted to tell those ideas that I could not publish in my candidacy dissertation.§ I wanted to clarify primarily for myself as well as for my closest intellectual associates the theoretical background of the book in the making.

---

* Pál Lőcsei preserved among his own files a copy of my paper that I had given him in 1955. He returned it in January 2006.

† Péter's paper is seventy-two typed pages, while mine is even longer.

‡ A later footnote mentions the discussions that Sándor Fekete and I carried on at the end of 1956 and at the beginning of 1957. By the time these conversations took place—so about six to eight months after writing the papers—I had already turned away from Marx's theory of value.

§ I am surprised to find that some of the ideas that I developed only later are appearing already in this paper. For example, I devoted several pages to the issue of the excessive pace of growth, which at the time I called "rush." One and a half decades later in a book published in English and dedicated to this issue, I used the same word to characterize these phenomena.

At the end of the 1955 study, I wrote the following: "It could make sense that a racing runner right before breaking the tape would push his chest forward, because by doing so he could perhaps gain the last inch needed to win. However, there is no point for a long distance runner to run with his chest pushed forward—as it will only cause him unnecessary fatigue." A nice metaphor—it is a pity that I forgot it and never used it in my published writings.

It turned out later that the two illegally distributed studies did not end up only in the hands of our few loyal friends. They had also left a mark in the archives of the political police. When Sándor Fekete was arrested in 1958, he included in the confession he wrote during the interrogations in his own hand a detailed report on me under eleven heads. Point 2, which reports on my work with Kende, mentions our writings that "overturned the principles of Marx's *Capital*."[6] Fekete puts this characterization of the study in quotation marks, then continues: "I first heard this from Gimes, who had really praised the study, then at the end of 1956 Kornai also showed it to me."*

When we reached that point in our estrangement from Marxism, we still knew precious little about the rival theories. It was not a question of rejecting one theory and adopting another. We pulled ourselves out from the bog of Marxism by our own hair, like Baron Munchausen. From the two studies a reader can discern that we were still using Marxian vocabulary (value versus use value, etc.) in our criticism of Marx's ideas. In our conversations and writings, we tried to establish why we had turned away from Marx's political economy and what we would expect of a truly scientific economic theory.

Breaking with Marxian political economy

I have emphasized several times already what a strong influence on my thinking was exerted by my oral and written dialogue with Péter Kende. Our economic and political views took new shape largely in parallel. But I must return here to the first-person singular. It is no easy matter to reconstruct where I stood in 1955–1956, at the beginning of my career as a researcher, engaged in a process of emotional and intellectual restructuring that lasted several years, and to avoid interjecting feelings and ideas that came only later. And if I find it difficult to do that in my own case, I certainly cannot undertake it in relation to anyone else, even someone as close to me as Kende.

Countless criticisms of Marx's teachings have appeared. A smaller but still significant number have approached the task with scientific objectivity and deep analy-

---

* In point 5 of this statement, Fekete describes showing me his "Hungaricus" study, which—and here I quote his written confession—"among other things included a remark about the 'young titans defeating Marx,' which was directed against him too. Kornai—at a meeting held in my flat—did not agree with the statement in 'Hungaricus' that Marx's theory of value and historical materialism qualify as much as an exact part of universal science as, let us say, Kepler's astronomical theses. Even more strongly than before, he professed that Marxist political economics were faulty right from the outset." Today, after fifty years have gone by, it feels strange to be reading how a conversation about Marx's theory of value became a criminal matter for the police. I will return to this statement by Sándor Fekete in the next chapter.

sis.* I do not have much to add to the latter. The lines that follow are not intended to refute Marxism in a few sentences. But my comments may still be instructive, less for the criticisms they contain than for their description of the process and course of disillusionment. What, in my case, was the logical structure behind the break with Marxism?

I reported in chapter 4 that the change in my ideas began on a meta-rational, not a rational, plane. My *faith* in communism was shaken as I recognized the lies and brutality around me. The collapse was in the moral foundations of my worldview.

If that, to use a geological metaphor, was the deepest layer, there was another above it, in the rational range: the *epistemological* basis of Marxism. Marxism calls itself the theory of *scientific* socialism. It dissociates itself from unscientific versions of socialist ideas, branding them naive and utopian. According to its own assertions, Marxism alone presents a scientific method for researching society and comprehending the body of knowledge about it.

I broke with Marxism because I became convinced that it lacked foundations in precisely this respect. I am aware that I am on shaky ground when I start expounding on scientific theory and methodology. There is no agreement among philosophers who specialize in the subject on what makes a statement "scientific" or even on when the truth of a statement can be deemed to be confirmed. Nor is it the purpose of this intellectual autobiography to try to decide such matters. All I am trying to do is to present my personal history.

Up until 1955, in my eyes the closed character of the Marxian intellectual edifice and its transparent logical structure offered sufficient evidence for saying it was not only closed and logical, but *true* as well. When I started to internally revise this theoretical conviction, full of disillusionment and suspicion as I was, I began with increasing decisiveness to take another approach—to compare the theory with reality. Its importance was enhanced by my bitter experience of being deceived. How did the "theory of value" relate to real prices? How did the theory of "pauperization" square with historical tendencies in living standards? How did the "theory of capitalist crises" reflect the changes in business cycles in real life? How did the theory of "classes" and "class warfare" compare with the actual stratification of society and social conflicts? The problem was not just that the theories performed badly in all these comparisons, that the Marxist dogmas failed to match reality. The main trouble was that Marx himself and his later disciples did not feel the primary intellectual duty to apply the elementary criterion of scholarship: testing their ideas against reality.

---

* About that time, for instance, I read the famous *Criticism of Marx* written in 1896 by the great Austrian economist Eugen von Böhm-Bawerk (1975 [1949]), which convincingly shows the contradiction between the first and third volumes of *Capital*.

Marxism is not the only school in the social sciences to commit this original sin, but in 1955–1956 I was calling on Marxism to meet the fundamental requirement of science and compare theory with the real world.

Of course, the social sciences are in a much more difficult position in this respect than the experimental sciences. The latter can confirm a theoretical supposition more easily and with greater statistical accuracy. But even if the scope for empirical confirmation of social phenomena is more limited, those doing research in this area must do *their utmost* to check their statements—that is, confront theory with experience as conscientiously as they can by the best means available to them. And if they see that reality departs in essential ways from theory, they have to alter the theory or, if such alteration is not possible, reject it.

To return to the earlier geological metaphor: a mass of false theoretical propositions have been deposited on the layer of false scientific theory and methodology. Such deposits of false theory could occur because the one who devised the theory did not call on himself or others to make comparisons with reality. The tenets of Marxism survived as obsolete doctrines, petrified like specimens of long-extinct species of animals. If Marx's admirers were obliged nonetheless to admit the falsehood of some dogma, they blamed poor students of the master for vulgarizing what they still held to be true. The real truth was that Marx had accustomed them (and us) to a bad algorithm of thinking.

To continue the geological metaphor:* believers in Marxist political economy saw the *theory of value* as the heart, the central idea of all Marxian economics. That is the next layer I would like to deal with briefly.

As my studies began, I started to see why the allocation of resources works badly in a socialist system. The function of prices in such an economy is almost impossible to explain. Marx certainly never undertook to say in advance quite what has to be done in a socialist system, but it should at least have been shown in his writings what happens under capitalism. Simply posing the question sufficed to make it clear to me that Marx had failed to provide the answer. His works contain frequent references to prices being set by "competition." But how? Volume 1 of *Capital* floats in the air. Its main contention, that work is the sole creator of value, epitomizes a

---

* I sense that my use of this metaphor has put me in a bizarre situation. While criticizing Marxism, I am employing one of the favorite formulas of Marxists, by contrasting the "deeper" essence with the superficial. Perhaps it is some consolation to remember that even psychologists who are far from being Marxists readily employ the metaphor of layers deeper and closer to the surface when describing the mind and thinking. One further observation: as I will show repeatedly, I still find many things associated with Marx and his followers workable and enlightening. So the fact that a metaphor is freely used by Marxists does not automatically put me off using it.

proposition that cannot be tested or refuted—in other words, that is nonscientific. Nor is there any way to derive by strict deduction from the main proposition in volume 1 the system of ideas in volume 3, where surplus value is "converted" into average profit proportionate to capital. Here some testable, refutable propositions appear, but they perform poorly when confronted with reality. What was putatively the explanatory theory of profit explains very poorly what factors actually generate profit in capitalist reality. In a word, I concluded that Marx's theory of value was inapplicable to reality.

The other Marxist economic propositions have been deposited onto the layers discussed so far. Let us take just one as an example: the assertion about *pauperization of the working class*. It does not follow in a deductive way from any previous statement. If one accepts Marx's theory of value, the theories about average profit and production price, and all other auxiliary propositions in *Capital*, it is equally consistent with them to say that the living standard of manual workers declines, stagnates, or rises relatively (compared to that of the other groups) or absolutely (considering changes over the long term). As for empirical verification, history has sharply refuted the Marxist tenet about pauperization as a long-term trend. Statistics clearly confirm that the material consumption of working people in all countries operating under a capitalist system rose substantially within one or two centuries and their living conditions improved.

Many members of the intelligentsia who have previously held Marxist convictions are incapable of making a radical intellectual break with them. They fight desperate rearguard actions, like a soon-to-be-defeated army retreating and abandoning its positions street by street, then house by house. They hold on to a theoretical proposition or a method of research and cognition for as long as they can. I myself used a different strategy when reshaping my ideas. At some point, around the end of 1955, I gave up Marxism. I announced, first to myself, that I was not a Marxist any longer. I would not reject every one of the theory's methods or statements (as I will explain further in later chapters of this book), but I would reject the "-ism" as such, the Marxian intellectual edifice. Sometimes among close friends I would describe my intellectual state by saying I had "written off" Marxism.* I would not accept anything merely because I was a loyal believer in a school of thought. Starting from that "write-off," I would have to overcome intellectual suspicions and uncertainties, understandable and justified in the light of earlier events, before convincing myself that if I found some Marxist proposition or mode of thinking to be usable after all, I should not necessarily reject it.

---

* I broke *radically* from Marxist theory and ideology. Yet I went on believing for quite a while that socialism could be reformed. I will say more later about how I gradually gave up on being a "naive reformer."

I saw that this strategy of making a clean break was valuable in my case. I became quite open to new ideas. I did not have to spend a long time contrasting every rival view with Marxist dogma, because I had cleared the latter away in advance. I found that this strategy gave me a big headstart over many of my contemporaries, who had become Marxists at the same time as I had but were spending much longer, even decades, freeing themselves of the shackles on their thinking. Many economists, philosophers, and historians in the Budapest intelligentsia of the 1960s and 1970s experimented with a "renaissance of Marxism" and went from one element of Marxist thought to another, deciding what to throw out and what to keep. I, on the other hand, had long gone beyond that phase of drudgery, which acts as a brake on one's thinking.*

I begin my research

I was not behind in terms of age when I started as a researcher. I began preparing for my dissertation at 27—about the typical age when American graduates do the same.

American Ph.D. students starting their dissertation already know much about how their professors go about their research work. Many will have had experience as an assistant to one of their teachers. Later they will officially request guidance from an adviser; these advisers pass on their research methods to their students, who in turn become teachers and bring up a new generation, just as master craftsmen and their former assistants once instructed apprentices in the guilds. I had no such chance to learn research techniques from my masters. My adviser, Tamás Nagy—who, as head of the General Theory Department, was also my boss at the institute—made many useful comments on my writing. He had good tactical sense and saw how far one could go amid all the political constraints of the time. But as he did not do research himself, he did not know the tricks of the trade and could not pass them on to me.

For several months, I did not have a subject. My officially assigned task was to work with Péter Erdős as his research assistant. I accompanied him on his journeys and we had many conversations. What really interested him was abstract theory, as his later work reflected. He had no experience in empirical research. He wanted to canvass opinion among economic leaders on problems of management and planning. But his manner and sharp, often arrogant interjections did not encourage

---

* Mihály Vajda, a well-known philosopher, gave the following account of this process (Pogonyi 2003, p. 14): "I remember saying this to my 'Lukácsist' friends in the mid-1970s: 'I don't believe I'm a Marxist any more.' Not because they did the whole beastly business in the name of Marxism, but because Marxism does not explain what is going on around me."

respondents to be frank. He was a witty and clever man, blessed with a deadly sense of irony. Woe to anyone whom he decided to criticize. There was much he grumbled about and disliked in the Stalinist political regime and the numbing state of Marxist ideology. He felt he had nothing to fear from me, an oppositionist freshly sacked from *Szabad Nép*, and so he opened up to me. But this openness was fairly one-sided. Despite all his criticism, he ultimately remained faithful and utterly loyal to the Communist Party and Marxist theory. I was cautious about showing him where I stood in rejecting Marxism and communist ideas. I contented myself with hemming and hawing as I listened to his critical outbursts. That proved enough for a friendly relationship to develop between us.

Neither Erdős nor Tamás Nagy objected when I asked after a few months to be allowed to work independently in the future. I had decided to confine my research to the single narrow field of light industry and try to see how economic management worked there. What did central planning mean in practice? I chose light industry as it would have been harder to obtain data for heavy industry, where the military connections meant that much information was classified. I was also interested in the relations of production and consumption, which could be explored more easily in a sector whose products were bought by the members of the public.

I had no prior positive hypothesis when I started researching. But my questions were influenced by an essential negative hypothesis: the assumption of the official textbooks and party propaganda—that the Planning Office prescribed plans, and the real processes in the economy followed the prescriptions—was not going to stand up.

I chose my research methods without hesitation or experiment. At the center stood a thorough questioning of those taking part in the economic management and planning process. I felt instinctively that they and only they really knew what was going on in the heads of managers and what they were doing. My questions were put to people in high-ranking, middle-ranking, and low-ranking positions. In most cases, the conversations were held one-on-one, but there were some group discussions as well. In several industries, the group came together repeatedly, because an exchange of views lasting several hours proved too brief to cover every subject on the agenda.

Almost without exception, people were glad to answer my questions. They were prepared to criticize the existing conditions boldly. I often wondered even at the time what made them so willing to do that. Perhaps one factor was that everyone likes to complain, especially Hungarians. But a more important stimulus may have been that they sensed my genuine interest in what they had to say. I was not running mechanically down a questionnaire devised in advance. They saw I listened to them wide-eyed and eager for information. I grumbled with them against the idiocy of the bureaucracy and raged with them against wastage, disregard for customer needs, and narrow-minded superiors. I built up genuine human relations with my interviewees. More than one tried to help me a few years later, even at risk to themselves, when I was sacked from the Institute of Economics and tried to find a job in light industry.

But let us not jump ahead. Let us stay with the research methods I applied in 1955–1956. Where did I get the idea of basing the empirical material for my study mainly on personal interviews? It must have been my experience in journalism. If I remember right, I was the one who introduced to *Szabad Nép* the genre we called an "analytical report"—which took up a page of the newspaper, not a couple of column centimeters like the usual reports. Two or three of us would spend days at a factory talking to people, asking workers what they thought of the work there. The relation I had with a manager respondent as a Communist journalist-interviewer certainly differed from the one I had as a researcher, but I had learned something of the technique as a journalist, and I sensed the scope it offered.

I was inspired also by the great literary tradition of Hungarian village research. I had found reading some works of that kind to be a great intellectual experience.* I sensed what a vast body of real knowledge lay in listening to people.

Of course, my empirical knowledge did not come entirely from my own interviews. I tried to complement what I heard by studying regulations and instructions and looking at numerical data, examining statistical tables on enterprises and industries. I realized early on how large the gap could be between an order and its execution, how the characterization of a phenomenon could differ depending on whether it was being described by someone higher in the hierarchy or lower. Circumstances like those lent great excitement to the research and the process of discovering the truth.†

No one taught me modern methods of analyzing quantitative data. I was unfamiliar with econometric techniques whose application these days is compulsory not

---

* I read Zoltán Szabó's *A tardi helyzet* (The Tard story; 1986 [1936]) and Imre Kovács's *A néma forradalom* (The silent revolution; 1989 [1937]) around this time. Besides what they told me about the life of the peasantry, I also found the methodological approach of the two writers and descriptive sociologists ("sociographers"), who belonged to the influential intellectual group of "people's writers," highly instructive: interviewing people, collecting data using questionnaires, and supplementing firsthand experience with a brief overview of statistics. At the time I became acquainted with these two studies, I had no idea about the methodology being applied in modern sociology.

† The validity of this approach remains. We would have better understood, for instance, what went on in the post-Communist transformation of Eastern Europe, the Soviet successor states, or China if analysts had followed not just sporadically but much more often a similar method of drawing on in-depth interviews.

only in a Ph.D. dissertation but for an undergraduate degree. I could be ashamed of my ignorance at that time. But perhaps I should rather be proud that I managed to find several important connections despite my lack of preparation. Now, fifty years later, I will chance an even more sweeping statement. There will be several references in the remainder of this book to the disadvantages of my not having had an economist's methodical training. But if that sounds like criticism from the mouth of a university professor enthusiastic about his field, let me say that my ignorance had some advantages too. I dared and managed to be original *precisely because* I did not have a professor in whose footsteps I should meekly follow. And precisely because I did not understand the modern techniques of economic research, I did not get lost in the formal, technical tasks, did not bother with whether my regressions fit well, and did not know and could ignore the strict technical requirements imposed by leading journals and publishers' anonymous referees. Nothing bothered me except understanding how the curious mechanism of running production in this country worked.

The historian György Péteri describes the approach at Friss's institute and my working method as "naive empiricism."[7] "Naive" is an apt word. My work had the naiveté of naive painters or instinctive artists. It was primitive and unsullied. I had yet to learn the finer points of my trade and so it was crude, but perhaps for that reason, it had "bloom," it was refreshing and sincere.

The "empiricism" label is only half the truth. I wrote a moment ago about the castles in the air of Marxist theory. It was a revolutionary act, in that intellectual climate, to disregard the distinction between "concrete" and "abstract" labor, reject the precept that "the sum of the values equals the sum of the prices" and similar empty theories, and make a 180-degree turn to learn from experience.

My work did not stop at charting reality and simply recording empirical facts. In that respect, I had gone further than the village research writers had. I had tried to incorporate my experiences into a strict intellectual structure and show what *regularities* appeared in the phenomena. I had attempted a causal analysis, but without arriving at a polished theory—thank goodness, as I was still far from having a thorough knowledge of the relations involved. But observant readers will have sensed the intention of drawing *general conclusions* from particular observations.

My approach to work also reflected a determined attempt to order my thoughts. I was not one to huddle over my notes all day. I developed a habit of taking long "working walks," rambling through woods or streets as I thought over material I had collected and a piece I was preparing to write. Carrying a pad and pencil in my pocket, I would stop now and then to note down an idea.*

---

* Much later, I was followed on such a walk by a suspicious passerby, who accosted me, demanding to know what I was writing. "Working for car thieves, writing down registration numbers, are you?" was his angry surmise.

At this time, I became accustomed to composing the study in progress not at work but at home or somewhere else, where I could concentrate without being disturbed. While most of my colleagues went to the institute every day, I spent quite a lot of time at home, writing. I started in this period to develop work-stimulating "rituals," characteristic of people in professions similar to mine: the ceremonial making and drinking of cups of coffee, music while I worked, leisurely walks as I took a break from the long hours spent stooping over a desk, and so on. My son Gábor was about 3 or 4 at the time. Often I took him to school (the way back counted as a "working walk"). He became used to it quite quickly, and later my other son, András, learned too that I was not to be disturbed while I was working at home. Naturally, the two intentions—spending as much time as possible with the children and as much as possible on my work—often clashed.* As far as I can remember, the conflict never became serious, although the whole situation may be recalled differently by the children or Teri.

I found great pleasure in research work. The conversations were absorbing. I gladly worked on my notes and found the writing enjoyable too. As for the flashes when I felt I had stumbled on something, found something out, they count among the happiest moments in my life. I had discovered the right place for myself at last.

The main conclusions in my dissertation

The first draft of my book was complete in just under a year. Bearing in mind the advice I received from colleagues, I altered it a little, but it was basically unchanged when I handed it over as my candidacy dissertation in the summer of 1956 and then submitted it to the Economics and Law Publishing House for publication in September 1956. It appeared under the title *Overcentralization in Economic Administration* (hereafter *Overcentralization*).

When, almost fifty years later, I picked it up again, reading it made me feel good. Some passages reflect my political naiveté at the time, but the rest I accept to this day, with the pride of an author.† (As will become clear, the same cannot be said of all my writings.)

---

* Like many parents, I can never forget the time spent together with my children reading books at bedtime. When the boys got a bit older, we read *Winnie the Pooh*, *Alice in Wonderland*, and a host of cheerful stories by Frigyes Karinthy. Perhaps it is no exaggeration to say that these early literary adventures and our monkeying around laid the foundations for my sons' sense of humor—clearly noticeable even in adult life.

† I am not alone in accepting it. It was reprinted in Hungary thirty-five years later by its original publisher, with a new introduction for the second edition. Oxford University Press similarly reissued the English translation after more than three decades.

I stated my program clearly in the foreword: "There are, of course, dozens of textbooks and collections of notes for use at universities which describe our methods of economic administration and planning, our pricing and wage systems, etc. However, all of these have a serious fault in common: instead of telling us how our economic mechanism works *in reality*, they merely describe how it would work if it worked as their authors would wish. . . . A coherent description of how the mechanism of our economy really does work represents a new task, not hitherto performed in the economic literature of our country."[8]

The book begins by describing the system of planning instructions. One would think a planned economy was primarily intended to enable people to think several years ahead. Not so. Even the annual plan was not taken entirely seriously at enterprises, mainly because there were no incentives attached to it. (Here *Overcentralization* brings up pointedly the problem area of incentives, which would become one of the main subjects of economics some decades later.) There were holdups in supplies of materials and semifinished products and unforeseen shifts in demand. These and repeated changes in the national economic plan produced constant uncertainty that undermined the reliability of the firms' annual targets. What most directly affected production was the quarterly plan. However, this was devised not by the enterprise itself but by its superior body, the directorate for the whole industry. The oft-mentioned enterprise independence was nowhere in evidence. But the goals set in the quarterly plan could not be fully achieved, either. An enterprise trying to strictly adhere to it ran up against the ever-changing conditions of operation. On the other hand, if its fulfillment was not strictly enforced, the quarterly plan ceased to command respect. "The nature of this contradiction is such that no regulation of plan modifications (whether strict or liberal) is able, in the present circumstances, to solve it, for its roots lie much deeper, in the contradictions of our planning methods."[9] (Such remarks as this enraged the command economy's apologists. I still remember an outburst at one debate: "It is no good to you this way and no good to you that way either. . . . So what do you want?")

The most important indicator proved to be "production value." Everyone in an enterprise soon learned that production value could be increased not only by "right and proper" methods but also by clever tricks. For instance, the product mix could be changed to include a higher proportion of material-intensive products whose price is higher. (Again, *Overcentralization* was pursuing a problem that even today greatly vexes those engaged in the theory and practice of incentives. Whatever quantitative indicator is linked to the bonus or penalty, the value of this indicator can be distorted. Whatever strategy the designer of the incentive turns to, those at whom it is directed will find an effective counterstrategy almost immediately.)

The book also discusses the other plan targets in detail. It demonstrates item by item over sixty-four pages how inconsistent the system of instructions was and what undesirable side effects it had.

A chapter is devoted to the useful and harmful effects of the incentives, including salaries, bonuses, and moral incentives. Also covered is the role of administrative controls and punishments (disciplinary proceedings, court prosecutions, prison sentences, etc.). "The less the reliance placed by the system on material incentives (and the less it is able to count on the enthusiasm of people), the more it will be driven to employ methods involving coercion."[10] The inconsistency of the system tempts the manager to break the rules that cannot be observed; and if he does so and is caught, he is punished for it.

One of the main conclusions in my book summing up the socialist system, written four decades later, was that partial reform or "loosening" of the socialist system undermined its viability. There could be no socialist system without repression. Now, rereading my first book, I came across an early forerunner of that idea. One outcome of the "New Course," according to *Overcentralization*, was that the superior bodies had been making much less use of administrative methods (various penalties and other forms of coercion) for tightening discipline. "But this relaxation was inaugurated at a time when a better and more comprehensive system of material incentives, replacing earlier measures, was not yet in existence. The previous economic mechanism continued in operation without modification. Yet this was a piece of machinery that could not work smoothly without the benefit of the type of 'lubrication' provided by a widespread application of administrative measures. In the absence of these, the gears of the mechanism failed to work satisfactorily. This ambiguous and ill-matched situation was one of the basic causes of the manifold troubles of that period."[11]

The instructions and incentives together generated some *regularities*, and the following were emphasized in *Overcentralization*:

1. A shift in the attention of managers to quantity. This is valuable insofar as an increase in the volume of production serves the public interest. Concurrently it is damaging, because the concentration on quantity becomes disproportionate.

2. A false order of importance among tasks. Cost reduction or technical development, for instance, is relegated to the background because neither is encouraged by the instructions or by the incentives.

3. The fetish of "100 percent." If the plan is taken seriously, a fulfillment rate of under 100 percent is a breach of instructions. This has the bizarre and often expressly harmful effect of making management want to squeeze out of their enterprise at all costs the performance increment needed to reach 100 percent.

4. "Speculation within the plan framework." I gave this label to activities in which managers adhered only to the letter of the law and their instructions when attaining the levels of production/consumption needed to ensure their bonus and recognition. Meanwhile they often ignored the question of the economy's best interests.

5. Battles over loosening and tightening plans. This aspect described and analyzed in *Overcentralization* was called in later Hungarian debates "plan bargaining" and by Western Sovietologists the "ratchet effect."* If an enterprise, in pursuit of a higher bonus and greater recognition, overfulfilled its plan by a large amount, that higher level would be incorporated into subsequent plans. The previous result of 105 or 110 percent was then made obligatory as the 100 percent for the following year. The enterprise therefore had an incentive to hold back its performance instead of allowing it to rise above 100 or 102 percent. Furthermore, managers might, during the debates before plans were finalized, present the capacity as lower than it really was and exaggerate their difficulties to obtain a "looser" plan.

6. Periodic unevenness of production. Production pulsated in a curious fashion, with alternations of "work spurts" and slack periods. There was a clear relationship between this fluctuation in production and the calendar rhythm of planning. As the plan period neared its end and fulfillment and bonuses seemed to be at risk, the rush got under way.†

7. Conflict between "today" and "tomorrow." This is a central problem of economics, especially in relation to today's consumption and tomorrow's investment and saving. *Overcentralization* presented this conflict from another angle, focusing on how the attention and energies of management centered on fulfilling short-term plans, while neglecting longer-term tasks (technical development, introduction of new products, modernization of work organization, and so on) that would make future production more efficient.

Overcentralization termed these regularities "tendencies that cannot be simply wished away; they can only be mitigated, not eradicated, by words designed to enlighten. In order to eliminate these tendencies, it is necessary that our planning and incentive systems, our methods of administering the economy, be themselves made the objects of comprehensive and far-reaching improvements."[12]

Let us compare this approach with the way the earlier literature of "political economy" followed Stalin in discussing "the law of planned proportionate development."

---

* A ratchet wheel with teeth to prevent backward but not forward motion provides a vivid metaphor for one characteristic of plan bargaining: once attained, a given performance level is thereafter required of a subordinate body by its superiors. There is no going back.

† András Bródy (1956) was the first to analyze the pulsation of production and its causes. I was convinced by and found instructive both his conclusions and his research methods.

Authors of such studies wanted the economy to develop in a planned, proportionate way. This normative requirement was then called a "law," a term that should be reserved exclusively for positive science. Science can term a law only what actually occurs. The regularities or "necessary tendencies" described in *Overcentralization* have actually transpired and thus refuted the proposition that there could be a law of "planned proportionate development."

The book devoted a chapter to a problem area later to become a central subject in my writings: *shortage*. Because I was analyzing production, shortage of materials was the central aspect of the investigation. I already sensed correctly the consequences of shortage: reduced efficiency and consumers left at the mercy of the producer. *Overcentralization* showed how close a relation there was between shortage and centralization, how shortage increased the tendency to centralize and centralization induced shortage.*

I was already keen to know why there was chronic shortage in a socialist economy. Some of the causes (and not the most important ones) are described in *Overcentralization*, but much more research was required before this causal analysis could be deepened.

The next chapter of the book went further in generalizing my conclusions. Enterprises were being influenced from two directions. They had horizontal relations with other enterprises and vertical relations with a superior authority. In the socialist planned economy, vertical relations are dominant, with relatively few horizontal relations. So far as I have been able to establish, this work was the first to apply that distinction, which has since become widespread.

The final chapter begins with a concise summary of one of the ideas underlying the whole book, the assertion that "excessive centralization is a coherent, unified mechanism, which has its own inner logic and several tendencies and regularities peculiar to itself."[13] However, that does not mean that this mechanism is harmonious. On the contrary, it involves deep inconsistencies. It seeks to regulate everything with instructions, a goal that is impossible. It sets out to centralize everything, an aim that is unattainable.

This idea presented clearly what I later came to call the "system paradigm." It is not enough to understand the details: the whole is greater than the sum of its parts. It is not enough, therefore, to change a detail or two—little alterations of detail cannot take the place of a comprehensive change.

* *Overcentralization* contains only one quotation from Marx, which refers to the problem of shortage. Marx very rarely alluded to how the socialist system would administer its economy. One such short excursus appears in volume 2 of *Capital* (1992 [1885]), pp. 544–545), where Marx advises that there should be persistent relative overproduction, thereby preventing fluctuations in production (i.e., by having inventories grow along with production).

The final chapter sought to clarify the origins of overcentralization, but it went only halfway in that effort. I still had not understood how deep the roots went, right through to the political structure and system of property relations. However, there is a notable passage about fear of spontaneity—a couple of paragraphs that thoroughly rattled the orthodox Marxist-Leninist readers of the book.*

Finally, *Overcentralization* shows how the timid experiments with reform so far had failed and warns of the conservative forces that stand in the way of reforms. The book dwells consistently on positive description and analysis, making no reform proposals of its own. Only the last few lines offer some encouragement to readers, with the claim that "the work of dismantling excessive centralization...will succeed in the end."[14]

In 2003, having gone through my *Szabad Nép* articles and *Overcentralization* in a matter of weeks, I was struck by a conspicuous change of style in the latter. I had found myself at last, replacing my earlier enthusiastic praises and loud exhortations to increase performance at work with a factual, objective style. Most of the book's 200-odd pages report *facts*.

The message of the book is conveyed not only in what the text contains but also in what it *does not* contain. It uses a "neutral" technical idiom and eschews the usual Marxist "politeconomy" jargon. What reformist economists debating the economic mechanism were then saying was not that we had to give more scope to the market, but that we had to "allow the law of value to apply more freely." Many years later in the Soviet Union, Leonid Kantorovich and his mathematician-economist associates were still employing Marxist jargon to talk about the so-called shadow prices that linear programming created.

The language used has great importance when thoughts are conveyed. I did not undertake an open critique of Marxian theory in *Overcentralization* or my subsequent publications. But I made a quite deliberate and conscious effort to avoid Marxist language, as readers familiar with it rapidly and clearly saw. (The *deliberate and conscious nature* of the effort is apparent from my remarks earlier in the chapter about my break with Marxism and my unpublished paper that complemented *Overcentralization*.) I wanted to demonstrate to my readers that it was possible to make meaningful statements about the economy if (and only if) the conceptual apparatus of Marxism was abandoned, because that apparatus laid intellectual traps. Some writers of Hungarian economic literature followed the course I had laid out, but use of the Marxian apparatus long continued to hinder the freeing of ideas in other socialist countries, as well as in most other disciplines of social science in Hungary.

---

* Unfortunately, these lines were excluded from the English edition. There will be some remarks about the circumstances surrounding the abridging of the text in the next chapter.

The initial reception of the book

The first readers of the dissertation—fellow economists and close friends—received it enthusiastically. It was a reaction I had not been expecting. Because I had entered on a research career with little self-confidence, the favorable reception gave me new strength.

There were plenty of appreciative remarks at the discussions in the institute as well. News soon spread by word of mouth, as it does in Budapest, that this was a "choice political morsel," different from the usual dissertation.

According to the regulations in Hungary, a candidacy dissertation had to be defended in public debate. The body entitled to award postgraduate degrees, the Scientific Qualifications Committee, would appoint both opponents and the committee that would decide after the debate whether the candidate was worthy of the degree.

Most candidacy debates attracted an audience of twenty or thirty: the friends and family of the candidate and a small number interested in the specific subject. The debate on *Overcentralization* was held on September 24, 1956, before a crowd.[15] Maybe my memory has embroidered the facts, but I think 200 or more people appeared.

The meeting was chaired by György Péter. Let me quote what he said: "I studied physics at one time. We learned that in physics, real science began with Galileo. What went before that was speculation, thinking things over. Galileo was the first to bring out rule, clock, and weights in physics and measure things. And that is where the history of the exact sciences really began. I am reminded of this by the objective discipline in this dissertation, the honest handling of things, uninfluenced by any inner emotion. This is like this, that is like that; he puts things under the microscope, dissects the phenomena, and writes down what he has seen."[16] The analogy with Galileo's achievements is, of course, an enormous exaggeration (and as far as Galileo's instruments are concerned, it is not even entirely precise with respect to the history of science). But it conveys keenly why Péter saw *Overcentralization* as a turning point in the socialist world, by comparison with the usual economic research. It was because speculation in a vacuum was replaced by objective observation of reality, measurement of phenomena, and exact description.

One opponent in the debate was Miklós Ajtai, state secretary at the Ministry of Light Industry. He expressed strong and appreciative agreement with the dissertation. (Ajtai later held a high position as deputy president of the National Planning Office under the Kádár regime. When *Overcentralization* was under crude attack, I asked him several times to publish his opinion as a review, but he sidestepped the request.)

The other opponent was Mária Augusztinovics, who also gave a very favorable opinion.[17] Her criticism was that the study did not contain enough theoretical analysis or use the abstraction method. When it was my turn to respond, I reacted irritably to her words. I did not doubt the importance of abstraction or "pure theory" in explaining the complex relations of reality, but Guszti, as she was known by everyone then and now, was requiring this of me at the wrong time and in the wrong place. The dire need at that point was for putting an end to empty abstraction that simply mimicked the Marxian style of thinking.

There were many interesting comments from the floor as well. The one that attracted the most attention at the time and was mentioned most frequently in later condemnatory articles was from Péter Mándi.[18] I had known him before. He had worked at the party headquarters for a time and then in the department headed by István Friss. His objection was that my dissertation did not go far enough in drawing conclusions. The source of the problems should not be sought simply in the specific economic mechanism. "If the system's bad," Mándi said, "the thing to do is not to weed out each of the mistakes, but to essentially change the whole system."

I do not know what Mándi understood by the system. All I can say is that with today's eyes, I certainly see things the same way. *Overcentralization* stops at a critical point in its causal analysis. It establishes correctly that among the causes of the problems are the command economy, an extreme degree of centralization, and exclusion of the market from coordination. But it goes no deeper. It does not recognize the basic contribution to dysfunctional operation of the economy made by political oppression, ideological monopoly, and state ownership squeezing out private property. Mándi may have understood these ideas by then. The maturation process took me longer. I still believed that the socialist economy could be reformed. I was still a *naive reformer*, as I described my 1956 state of mind in a later piece of writing.

I believed in the possibility of change so strongly that I had agreed in the spring of 1956 to direct a working group to summarize for the party and government the reform proposals devised in the institute. Several staff members and outsiders were given an opportunity to work on the proposals under my direction. Those assisting me were András Nagy, Péter Bod, and Aranka Rédey. In August, we put on the table 120 pages of material containing a proposal for introducing Hungarian "market socialism," phrased calmly and carefully, with plenty of specific detail.[19] The material, modestly, confined itself to light industry, but its message was broader than that. It can be seen as a first rough draft of the New Economic Mechanism eventually introduced in 1968. Standing behind the proposal for reform as sources of intellectual inspiration were the articles of György Péter and my book *Overcentralization*.

The proposal for reform became the subject of a substantive and objective debate sympathetic to its underlying ideas, held in the institute with outside experts included. Both my book and the institute proposal were read and commented on in detail by István Varga, formerly the leading economic policy figure in the Small-holders' Party, who was then invited by the Kádár regime in 1957 to head the Economic Reform Committee. Both were also studied thoroughly by Tamás Nagy, my adviser in my candidacy program and my superior at the institute, who was appointed by the party to be secretary of the committee preparing for the 1968 reform. Many of those influenced by the book or the summer proposal later served on the 1957 Varga committee and the committee headed by Nagy in the 1960s. I am sure my ideas of the mid-1950s had a strong and lasting effect on them. The influence on them and others continued and even strengthened after I myself had moved beyond being a naive reformer and had doubts about whether one could or should stop at partial reform of socialism.

I was approached by my old workplace, *Szabad Nép*, for an article summarizing the dissertation and the main ideas in the reform proposal. By chance and as an unexpected bonus, my piece appeared in the same issue, October 14,[20] as the news that Imre Nagy had been readmitted into the party.

I began my career at the Institute of Economics by being demoted to an assistant. Now my director, István Friss, publicly and emphatically underlined the great merits of my work, promoted me to research fellow, raised my salary, and gave me a bonus. Only a year and a half had passed since I had been sacked from *Szabad Nép*, but my career was rapidly advancing again.

Political background

If all this had happened in the United States, on Massachusetts Avenue in Cambridge, at Harvard or at MIT, you could say simply that Kornai had changed careers. He had been a journalist and turned to academic life, and was doing well.

But this was Budapest in Eastern Europe. I was not a graduate student in a quiet library in a peaceful university town, knuckling down to clarify a narrow problem recommended by my professor. Having concentrated so far in this chapter on the beginning of my own research career, it is high time for me to fill in the political background.

When I arrived at the institute, Rákosi and his clique were still at the helm of government, believing that they had consolidated their power again. Eight months later, the Communist countries were struck by the storm of the Twentieth Congress of the Communist Party of the Soviet Union, where Nikita Khrushchev delivered his famous speech on the sins of Stalin. Hungarian politics suddenly picked up again. The intelligentsia was soon in turmoil as ever more severe criticisms and charges were leveled at successive debates in the Petőfi Circle, the radical club of intellectuals. There were first timid, then progressively louder demands to return to the "New Course," dismiss Rákosi from his position, and recall Imre Nagy into the party and the political leadership.

That my writings appeared in such a political environment magnified their effect at home. I was not under any illusions that the large number who came to the debate had been drawn by any special academic merit in my dissertation. Many came because news had gone around that my book was strongly critical of the present conditions. It was September 24, 1956, only a month before the '56 Revolution broke out. There were clouds in the sky; the "cleansing storm" that Tibor Méray had called for at the rebellious *Szabad Nép* meeting was approaching.

Those conditions explain how reports on my dissertation debate came to appear in the daily papers. Normally, daily papers do not report on Ph.D. theses or candidacy dissertations in Hungary or anywhere else. They reported on my debate because it was more than a professional scholarly gathering: it was a political event.

Any author is flattered to receive special attention. I was delighted, too, but embarrassed as well. To describe my reactions, I have to go back in time and say what my view then was on the relation between professional research work and engagement in political and public life.

When it emerged that I would be on the staff of an institute attached to the Hungarian Academy of Sciences, I made a firm inner decision to devote all my attention in the future to scholarship. Even when I was working in it, I did not consider journalism a real vocation; I felt I had followed a *political* career from 1945 to 1955, and it was secondary whether my political role had been as a functionary in the youth movement or an editor on the central party daily. I now wanted to break once and for all with that political career. I was attracted to scholarship not only by intellectual interest but also by the hope that it would best allow my talents to develop. At least as important was the negative motive of getting away from politics.

I was disillusioned by politics and disgusted and deceived by it, as I wrote at the end of chapter 3. In addition, there was another aspect I should mention. The previous decade had been a long examination for me, and I saw that I had failed it. It takes two to be deceived, a cheat and someone who allows him- or herself to be cheated. I remember talking about the early 1950s to my son András once when he was a teenager, and his asking me, "Father, you are a clever man. How could you have been so dumb?"

I have tried in earlier chapters to give a faithful account and detailed explanation of how this process went. There are explanations and excuses, but the question András put is a fair one, however much it simplifies the matter.

Certain characteristics are indispensable for anyone seeking to be a successful politician. It is not enough to have mental capacity, which is required for many other professions as well. Apart from that, politicians have to *believe* very strongly in what they are doing and be able to convey this belief to others. I managed to be such a believer for a time, but in 1955 I decided I would never be such a believer again. I wanted to be free to doubt everything, and that is incompatible with succeeding in politics.

Successful politicians are motivated by a desire for power. That motive was weak in me even when I was working in the political sphere. Now that I had seen the crimes committed by people drunk with power, I decided finally that I was not going to strive for it. I would reject all positions in which even the temptation of power might appear.

Politicians cannot achieve much without possessing at least a modicum of mercilessness and unscrupulousness. They need thick skins to absorb insults and react to them with conscious political calculation, not haste. Service to political ideas and the party or movement stand higher in their system of values than joy in the family, friendship, art, or nature. I had never had much of a political temperament. Indeed, if I wanted to describe myself, I would say each of my characteristics was the opposite of those I just listed for a politician. I decided I would never want to have a mental disposition similar to that of a politician.

Nor did I want to try to somehow combine the roles of a politician and a researcher. I feared (I think rightly) that the two could not be pursued in equal measure. This difficulty arose not just because attempting such a dual role would ensure a competition for my time and energies between the two functions, forcing me to live in perpetual struggle with myself. In addition, both would affect my mentality. No one could be a passionately partial politician in the morning and objectively impartial in the afternoon. I could not believe unconditionally in my own rectitude on even days and then look skeptically on my own analysis on odd days.

I decided to choose scholarship. I do not say I have kept to that decision 100 percent ever since. Who can be entirely consistent? But I can say that with rare exceptions, I have remained true to my choice for almost half a century.

There remained a serious problem, of course. Where did the dividing line run between the two vocations? It never crossed my mind to choose a quite apolitical field within the world of science, although I could have done so. There are subjects in economics of a purely methodological, technical character, and these are held in high esteem. But they did not interest me particularly. I wanted most of all to understand and study what was around me. I was keen to know what the trouble with the socialist system was. I never felt for a moment that turning to science would end my responsibility to the country or humanity. I wanted to practice "committed" science.

So turning to the question again, where does the border between "politics" and "science" run in my case? While I was firm in my basic decision (science, not politics), I had no clear prior idea of their boundary. I soon found that between them lay not a sharp line, like the border on a map, but a wide no-man's-land. I tried (and still try) to inch toward every choice case by case, making mistakes on the way, as I decided what I could take on and what I would rule out.

I had a few points of reference to go by. Anyone wanting to contribute to science and scholarship needs to publish his or her findings. I had no idea then how an academic career and publication in the West are connected. It never occurred to me that my writings might earn me a university chair. But I knew from scientific history that a work that remained in a drawer might astonish a couple of later scholars, but it would not have influence. If I was working in a country without freedom of speech and with political constraints on legal publication, I had to reckon with those circumstances realistically. I will return later in detail to that extremely important question (legal versus illegal publication), but I have to say in advance here why I confronted this tough dilemma at that time.

When I had finished the long study reacting to the piece by Péter Kende and setting forth my views on Marxism, it was read by Miklós Gimes, who was highly appreciative and offered to distribute it in duplicated form. I rejected that offer, not wanting to jeopardize the legal publication of my dissertation. For me, that piece on Marxism had served its sole purpose—to clarify my ideas. The main thing for me was to have things clear in my head as I wrote my dissertation, so that I could gauge point by point what I knew and would publish, and what I likewise knew but would not publish. It meant some of my message remained inside me, and that forced silence was very painful. The few dozen, even few hundred people who might have read an illegally distributed study were robbed of stimulating ideas. But the book published legally reached thousands of readers in Hungary and abroad and had a lasting influence.

I felt great intellectual and political excitement at the meetings of the Petőfi Circle. I attended all of them, with perhaps one exception. Yet I spoke only once, when I could not stop myself from posing a question in the economics debate. Although I had written many papers on the questions at issue, I did not attempt to give a talk. As a listener, I was drawn as if magnetically by the atmosphere of the meetings. As a potential *lecturer*, I felt that the setting did not really suit me. The meetings were curious combinations of expert debates among intellectuals and political rallies. Speakers had to use not just objective argumentation but also the instruments of mass psychology. I sensed that the debates in the Petőfi Circle were promoting important and desirable changes. But having sized up my own abilities soberly, I decided it was not my genre. I enjoy the question-and-answer periods after a university lecture. That fits into a scholarly role; it is enough to be professionally prepared and intellectually on the ball. Meetings with a strongly political content require one to inspire enthusiasm, or arouse indignation toward opponents—and I do not feel I have any talent for that.

It was one thing or the other. For some, the choice I made was too absolute, but others accepted it with understanding and tact. Whatever the reaction was, I had decided I wanted to stay in the world of science and scholarship entirely, not divide my commitment.

6

Revolution and After—October 23, 1956–1959

The Hungarian Revolution of October 1956 was not altogether unexpected. I remember two friends of mine—Miklós Gimes and Péter Kende—commenting (independently, I think) on different signs that political tensions were mounting and discontent could well break out in some form in the autumn. By September and October, events were obviously speeding up. But perhaps no one—certainly not I— could have forecast just when or how the explosion would occur.

The new government program of Imre Nagy

In the early afternoon of October 23, I was speaking to Ferenc Donáth and it came up that we would both be taking part in a discussion in the office of Zoltán Vas. Donáth was a long-standing, respected Communist who had been state secretary when Imre Nagy was agriculture minister. Later he had run Mátyás Rákosi's secretariat, but he had been arrested during the preparations for the trial of János Kádár and kept in prison for several years. On his release in 1954, he was appointed deputy director of the Institute of Economics under István Friss. He was seen as a leading figure among the "right-wingers" sidelined at that time. I had great respect for him and he also esteemed me. Later, when he had been released from the imprisonment he suffered under the Kádár regime as well, we became friends.

Zoltán Vas, whose office we were going to, was also an old Communist. He had spent more than fifteen years in Szeged Csillag Prison with Mátyás Rákosi. In 1945, he had won legendary fame as mayor of Budapest. During a checkered career, he had chaired the Economic High Council and the National Planning Office (where I had met him), being promoted and demoted by turns at Rákosi's whim. In 1956, he was serving as president of the National Council of Cooperatives.

Vas now supported the Imre Nagy group. As we talked in his office, the telephone kept ringing and Vas received reports on the crowd that had gathered in Bem tér and moved off toward the Technical University. Donáth predicted that Imre Nagy would certainly be the new prime minister. We had to prepare the speech he would deliver in Parliament outlining his program. First, we had to agree who would prepare the first draft. Someone (Tamás Nagy, I think) suggested I should write the economic part of it. Béla Csikós-Nagy volunteered, saying he would be glad to undertake it. But Donáth decided on me instead. Imre Karczag, who earlier had served as the state secretary for industry, handed over to me a summary of his proposals. Júlia Zala, a close associate of György Péter, said she would give me a hand if I needed data, and suggested we go over to the Central Statistical Office to work. György Péter was abroad and we could use his room, where the secretariat would be at my disposal. I accepted the task.[1]

There was no knowing that afternoon what October 23, 1956, would come to mean, but like the others at the meeting, I sensed we were experiencing remarkable, indeed historic hours. At that dramatic moment, I cast aside my determination to deal with science, not politics.

There were long arguments at the meeting about the content of the program. When I arrived home late that night, I heard from friends over the telephone about the developments, including the events at the Radio, the radio station where the ÁVH (State Security Police) had shot unarmed demonstrators. On the next morning I went into the Central Statistical Office, sat down at György Péter's desk, and started to work on the draft.

Unfortunately, the text I drew up was lost. After November 4, I asked my sister Lilly to hide it for me, as I was afraid my apartment would be searched and the police would find it. That was all very well, but not long after, I asked Lilly and my mother to hide Miklós Gimes for a few days. He was arrested the day after he left my mother's apartment, and now Lilly had good reason to fear there would be a search of her apartment as well. She therefore burned the papers of mine she was hiding, including the draft program for the government I had drawn up in October, so I will have to rely on memory to reconstruct it.

I usually write quickly and easily, if I know what I want to say. I do not know how many times I must have started on this text, only to start again. A rough draft emerged after two or three days. My assignment was to outline an *economic* program and the social and political measures for implementing it. I was not supposed to articulate any party/political, legal, or foreign policy plans.

As I have mentioned, we had discussed some aspects of the economic policy to be drafted when we met in Zoltán Vas's office on October 23, but I thought I had a free enough hand to simply write down what I thought was correct. Imre Nagy and his immediate associates would look over my draft and decide what to keep of it and what to change.

Had the draft been adopted, the prime minister would have announced an intention to dismantle the system of planning instructions, after due preparation, and to develop a market economy instead of the command economy. In conjunction with this change, he would have allowed the workers a say in decisions on enterprise management, thereby institutionalizing workplace democracy. (I had been working for two or three days when news started to arrive about the formation of workers' councils. This confirmed me in my opinion that some kind of worker self-management would have to be built into the program.)

The draft encouraged private craftsworkers and traders to go into business again, but the idea of privatizing state-owned enterprises was not broached. On the contrary, it was emphasized that state property had to be protected.

In agriculture, cooperatives (collective farms) that had been forcibly organized could be dissolved and private peasant ownership restored, where that was what the members wished. On the other hand, support was promised for cooperatives that decided to stay together.

The program proposed building up broader foreign trade relations in all directions, but without taking Hungary out of COMECON* or completely liberalizing trade.

Mention was made of the macroeconomic tensions. It was stressed that the living standards attained should not be jeopardized, but further rapid improvements were not promised.†

The draft I wrote was a direct continuation of the "New Course" of 1953, in the context of the specific economic situation three years later. Where it went beyond the earlier movement was in building "market socialism" and "workplace democracy" into the program. These had not featured in June 1953. Obviously, I promoted them because my ideas had been pushed in that direction both by my research in the last ten or twelve months and by our reform proposal, which had been received favorably by experts.

Let us turn back to 1954. If Imre Nagy had been addressing Parliament in October 1954, a couple of weeks after his temporary victory in the Central Leadership of the party, my draft would have been a good starting point for a program. It was

---

* The Council for Mutual Economic Assistance was the organization coordinating economic relations between the Soviet Union and the East European Communist countries. It was commonly known as COMECON in the West.

† There had been debate on this point at the October 23 preparatory meeting. Some wanted to compile as popular a program as possible for Imre Nagy. Others said only realistic, feasible promises should be made. The same dilemma seems to have arisen then that puzzles and divides politicians repeatedly today. I was a believer then as now in sober, responsible promises.

indeed tailored for Imre Nagy. That was as much as could be fitted into his radical, reform communist frame of thinking.

But of course, history had not stood still since October 1954. What started on October 23, 1956, went far beyond any such framework. For the first couple of days, it might still have been conceivable for a one-party system to remain in a reformed, "democratized" shape. But it was soon clear that change was accelerating. A coalition government was being formed, for the time being with the old coalition partners of 1945. More than twenty political parties were reconstituted in a matter of days, and the political scene was careering toward pluralism. By the third or fourth day, I was of the view that my draft was no longer in touch with political reality. And drafting an economic program for a multiparty coalition was a task for which I was unprepared.

It is impossible to describe in counterfactual terms what the economic program of Imre Nagy's coalition government would have been if the situation had stabilized enough to allow its presentation to the public. On November 3, 1956— a day before the Soviet intervention—Géza Losonczy held a press conference and said in response to a question, "The government is unanimous in adhering to the achievements of the past twelve years; it will not abandon the land reform, nor the nationalization of factories, nor its welfare reform.... The government is determined—unanimously—not to tolerate a restoration of capitalism under any circumstances."[2] My own agony over the government's economic program had taken place a few truly momentous days before that press conference of Losonczy's. I confess I felt very dubious about the country's political future. I did not exclude at all the possibility of Hungary going radically beyond the stage of socialist reform and establishing a Western-type economic system.

A lot of things worried me: the heated atmosphere, news that reached me of signs of extremism, and so on. It was not that I felt antagonism, in terms of politics or worldview, to the direction events were taking. On the contrary, I was delighted that Hungary seemed to be heading for true democracy. But I did not have the expertise or information on which to base a program to fit the new political realities. I saw that although Ferenc Donáth, Zoltán Vas, or Tamás Nagy might think me a knowledgeable economist, in fact I knew very little about how to move from a one-party to a multiparty system and from a socialist system to a true market economy, a capitalist system.*

---

* Thirty-three years later, the case was different. I had a mature and well-considered message to deliver on these matters, based on a body of knowledge. In 1989, when I was writing my "passionate pamphlet" (the Hungarian antecedant of *Road to a Free Economy*), I felt I could express what I thought the tasks were and convey them to those who could undertake them, if they wished.

After several days of painful struggle, I drew the final conclusion and stopped composing the program. I informed Donáth of this decision and he took understanding note of what I said. Through his secretary, I passed him the text I had put together. I assume that that copy, too, has been lost.

It was a bitter feeling to abandon the task—a professional and political failure. The storms of history were raging around me and I, with my narrow, superficial stock of knowledge, had been sitting over the papers unprepared and unable to proceed.

Magyar Szabadság—A new newspaper

After days spent motionless at my desk or dictating to kind and willing secretaries in Péter's office, I wanted to get out and look around the city. On the morning of October 29, I walked across to Péter Kende's flat, who lived close by, and we went on together to Pál Lőcsei's. I remember the amusing moment as he received us there in a pink nightshirt. He quickly dressed and the three of us set off toward the intersection of Nagykörút and Rákóczi út, where more daily newspapers' editorial offices were located.

I have read Kende's recollections of that day.* We all remember the *facts* in the same way. All I can add is what was going on in my mind and what my feelings were.

We first went to the New York Palace, the office building where the daily *Magyar Nemzet* had had its offices before the revolution. There we met Gyula Obersovszky, who had been editing a new paper called *Igazság (Truth)* for the last couple of days. (Obersovszky was condemned to death under the Kádár regime and reprieved only because of the strong protests against the sentence.) He spoke inspiringly of how his paper sought to be the mouthpiece of those who had taken up arms with a bravery oblivious to death. He invited us to join and take part in the work. Pál and Péter spoke during the meeting, but I kept silent. I too recognized and marveled at their bravery and felt that their armed actions had brought a turning point in events. But what kind of people were they? I did not know one of them. Were they fighting consciously for noble ideas? Were they young adventurers whose eyes lit up as they took hold of a rifle? Who had put guns in their hands? And was I at all glad that the guns were firing? Could not there be progress toward democracy without bloodshed? One thing was certain: I felt no moral or political right or inclination to be a

---

* Kende published his recollections in an interview for the Oral History Archives (OHA Interview no. 84, conducted on September 5–20, 1987, pp. 358, 359, 372). Sándor Révész gives a detailed account of the foundation of *Magyar Szabadság* in his book on Miklós Gimes (1999, pp. 317–322).

mouthpiece for the insurgents. I was not passing any kind of judgment on the uprising: I was enthusiastic about the victory of the revolution. But I was disturbed and
unable to orient myself among the events and the forces at work in them.

We left Obersovszky and his team on friendly terms and went over to the *Szabad
Nép* building. I had not been there for more than two years. Meanwhile, the three of
us had agreed that we would not join any other paper, but start one ourselves.

The building had been taken over by a new political force consisting of insurgent
groups of many kinds, headed by István Dudás. (Dudás was condemned to death
during the reprisals under the Kádár regime, and the sentence was carried out forth-
with.) Lőcsei negotiated with them and returned to say that Dudás and his group
would not put any obstacles in our way if we produced a paper.

Meanwhile Miklós Gimes arrived and agreed to write the editorial for the first
issue, under the title "Magyar Szabadság" ("Hungarian Freedom"), which was to
be the name of the paper as well.[3] Lőcsei and Kende also began writing articles
straightaway, Lőcsei on domestic policy and Kende on foreign policy. The assignment for me was obviously to write about the economic situation and the challenges
that it presented.

When I had been working on the government program, I had spent days trying to
complete the task. I began again now, but I gave up much sooner. I did not want to
withdraw from the common venture, however, and so I took the job that had occupied me in my last few weeks at *Szabad Nép*: putting the paper together and doing
the technical editing. I was performing a good service, I presume, by helping to get
the machinery of a daily paper operating.

Other staff appeared later the same day—Gábor Lénárt, Erzsi Kovács, and László
Horváth, among others. All old colleagues, if I remember rightly. A team of journalists gathered, burdened by their *Szabad Nép* past and headed by those who had
been intellectual leaders and bold participants in the erstwhile "rebellion" there.
We were bound by our common past and by some common ideas: democracy, independence, and freedom. We had faith in some kind of socialism, but knew only that
it had to be very different from the Communist system under Rákosi's dictatorship.

I suffered a complete writer's block because my political ideas were unclear. The
clever people with pure intentions who gathered there were certain only of what
they did not want. There was no chance for them to discuss thoroughly what they
would like to see instead of the past that had to be erased. Whom would they want
as tactical or lasting allies? Whom would they not be prepared to ally with at all?
What means did they deem permissible for attaining their political goals, and what
means would they exclude?

Decades later, having faced many difficult decisions over the years, I am better
placed to assess my abilities and shortcomings objectively. My judgment has proved
fairly reliable when it rested on firm and confident intellectual and moral founda-

tions. Another requirement is that I have time to weigh things carefully and subject my first, improvised reactions to repeated reexamination. None of those conditions applied there in the former offices of *Szabad Nép*, on that dramatic day, October 29. My old Communist view of the world had collapsed, and I had only just started to assemble a new one for myself. It was still only half-ready in my mind. How could I have drawn conclusions for day-to-day politics from those still half-formed premises? Some have political instincts to guide them on such occasions. My instincts were silent.

Earlier, I described myself as a *sleepwalker*, boldly stepping out while unconscious onto a balcony rail or the edge of a roof. Now I had awakened. The past two years and October 23 in particular had roused me thoroughly, but had dispelled my self-confidence as well.

Many years later, I was talking to Alíz Halda, Miklós Gimes's partner, about that afternoon. We compared how Miklós had thought and acted and what I had gone through. Let me quote our conversation, as reproduced in her book. (Alíz's comments are in roman and mine in italics.)

I could not write a line. I just did not know how to advise the Hungarian people in that situation. Then I understood for sure, that this was not for me....
Ultimately, that is no great problem. People each have their function in a society and someone could hardly have been more useful than you were.
It is not so simple. As you can imagine, I thought this over a thousand times over the decades, often opposing my own actions to Miklós's self-sacrifice. He obviously felt an ability in himself to decide in such a situation.
...I think your actions were also motivated by pangs of conscience.
I had pangs of conscience as well. How could I not? But that, unfortunately, did not mean I knew what to do. To make a comparison, if I run someone over and there is no doctor nearby, I will not start operating myself. The fact that I ran the victim over does not turn me into a surgeon.[4]

I did not stay on *Magyar Szabadság*. In the days that followed, I went into the institute, walked around the city, and met friends. Lajos Fehér, a former "companion in rebellion," called a meeting to recruit staff for the paper *Népszabadság* (*People's Freedom*), which was being planned at the time. I said no. István Friss rang me at home urging me to go to the Radio, so that a sober voice would be heard. I declined again. I tried to understand what was going on around me. I rejoiced at good news and worried that things might take a bad turn. And that brought me up to November 4. The Soviet tanks appeared.

Troubled days, troubled years

Here I am going to break off my chronological account. The two or three years that followed were the most troubled period in my life, as they were for many other

Hungarians. If I were a film director trying to convey how my life went, I would flash a succession of shots. There I would be full of anxiety, preparing for an interrogation in the Gyorskocsi utca prison.* There I would be sitting at a desk, industriously taking notes on Paul Samuelson's *Foundations of Economic Analysis*. I am anxiously waiting in the hospital corridor for our second child to be born; the nurse appears to tell me the good news: it is a healthy boy!† I would be seen whispering with friends in the institute: a committee of delegates from the Communist Party was reviewing the staff, with a purge due to follow. There would be a moment of joy as the galleys for the English edition of *Overcentralization* arrived. There would be horrifying news: arrests of close friends. There would be a businesslike talk with the manager of a textile mill. And so on: a series of shots, fearful and reassuring, happy and embittered, instructive and grotesque.

I am not a film director. I have to renounce any attempt to impart the mood of that oppressive period or the nervous ups and downs in my thoughts and emotions. My memoirs require *analysis* if they are to fulfill their purpose. I have to separate the strands. I will be discussing in this and the next chapter various dimensions of my life, but I have resigned any ambition to adequately convey what an excited,

---

* Interrogations into matters on which I was among those subpoenaed were held in the Interior Ministry's premises at 31 Gyorskocsi utca, in the Second District of Budapest. The official name of the body conducting the investigation was the "Investigation Department, Political Inquiry Section, National Police Headquarters, Interior Ministry."

The Investigation Department was housed in the rear of the immense block, which looks onto Gyorskocsi utca at the back and Fő utca at the front. There officials remanded in custody for the period of the investigation everyone whom they wanted to subject to a political trial, including friends of mine of whom I will speak in this chapter. Imre Nagy was also locked up there after he was brought back from Romania, as were the others accused in the Imre Nagy trial.

Under normal conditions, the Fő utca front of the block housed the Military Court and the Military Prosecutor's Office. One of the rooms there was chosen for Nagy's secret trial. This was very convenient for the prosecution. The accused did not have to be driven across Budapest by car for the hearings. They were taken from the place of investigation to the place of sentencing within the same block. The arrangement also made it easier to keep everything secret. Imre Nagy, Pál Maléter, and Miklós Gimes were sentenced to death there, at 70 Fő utca.

The square with the leafy park that flanks one side of the block is today called Nagy Imre tér.

The name "Gyorskocsi utca" has become identified among us with the place where the political police interrogators operated.

† Things were much different in June 1957, when András was born, from what they had been in 1952, at Gábor's birth. Then his lunatic father had still been convinced the world and the newspaper offices would fall down, or at least that he would be committing a heinous moral crime, if he abandoned his post on a private matter and asked someone to take over while his child was being born. This time I behaved like a normal person.

combative, or often alarmed state the mutual effects of these simultaneous occurrences induced in me.

Overcentralization continues its career

Not long before the revolution, I had submitted the manuscript of *Overcentralization* to KJK (Közgazdasági és Jogi Könyvkiadó), the Economic and Legal Publishing House. I went to their offices again in the early days of November and asked for the manuscript back. Who knew what would happen? It would be better to have it with me.

When the situation calmed a little after November 4, I appeared at the publishers again. The original preface to the Hungarian edition, dated January 1957, notes that I had submitted the manuscript in October 1956, and goes on:

Its appearance has only now become possible. I naturally returned to it and read it through—but I felt it would not be proper to make changes to it now. The proof of this work prepared with scientific intent is whether it stands the test of time. Events that will have importance for decades have been taking place in this country in the past few months. Many people felt it necessary to change their position on many basic political and economic questions in the span of a few months, perhaps more than once. I, however, think that what was true on October 22 remained true on October 24 and in January 1957. The question remains whether it was true originally. And since I am convinced that I wrote the truth about the situation in 1955–1956 (whether rightly is for my critics to establish), I have not reworked the study.[5]

These insolent remarks infuriated those who later attacked the book. But let us not run ahead. We are still in 1957. The regime was headed by János Kádár and Ferenc Münnich, who were concentrating all their efforts on subduing the remnants of the rebellion, soothing the striking workers, and beginning the campaign of reprisals. They had no energy left for book publishing. Luckily for me, the manager of KJK, Tibor Keresztes, and the editor of the manuscript, Margit Siklós, were prepared to take a risk and sent the book to the printers. It appeared a few months later and soon sold out.

A few months earlier, at the end of 1956, the journal *Közgazdasági Szemle* had carried an excellent account of the debate on my dissertation, written by Zsuzsa Esze.[6] This drew many people's attention to the book. Then, as a continuation of the praises at the dissertation debate, came one or two favorable reviews. Of these, let me single out that by György Péter, which he intentionally placed in the weekly paper of the regrouping Rákosi faction and which came out entirely in favor of *Overcentralization*.[7]

But times had changed and words of praise were growing scarcer. A succession of attacks on the book began to appear in the spring of 1957—in economics journals, in the economics weekly, in the daily *Népszabadság*, and in duplicated university teaching materials—describing it as a prime example of "revisionism."* It was accused of rejecting the fundamental principles of a planned economy and seeking to unleash the spontaneous forces of the market. In the words of Géza Ripp, "The revisionist views that appeared in economics . . . were connected with the ideological preparations for the counterrevolution and provided a kind of economic foundation for these."[8] Endre Molnár remarked, "It is not true that economics in the strict sense has nothing to do with the counterrevolution. . . . The lesson is not to be lenient even with the first shoots of revisionism," and he went on to cite my book as a blatant example.[9] "Kornai's dissertation," wrote Emil Gulyás,[10] in teaching material distributed at the party college, "fitted perfectly into the political and ideological campaign that constituted intellectual preparation for the counterrevolution."†

In September 1957, I innocently went to a lecture given by István Friss, the director of the institute, delivered at the Political Academy of the reorganized Communist Party. The second half took on the "revisionist" economists one by one. György Péter was let off lightly, but Tamás Nagy and Péter Erdős were rebuked more severely. I came last. I will never forget the shock and agitation that filled me as I sat there in the audience. I listened in astonishment as István Friss, having a year earlier praised my book, given me a bonus, and promoted me, tore into the same book. My message was to be understood as a rejection of the socialist system, he said. If that is what Kornai thought, he did not just hold anti-Marxist views, he rejected Marxism.

I had mixed feelings, reading the attacks at the time and rereading them recently. Thinking through what was actually said led me to the conclusion that the attackers were actually right. *Overcentralization* had gone beyond pointing to one or two mistakes and criticizing a narrow field of economic administration. The book showed that the command economy worked badly as a system. *Overcentralization* was indeed part of the intellectual current that questioned the foundations of the socialist system and thereby prepared ideologically for the October 23 revolution. Its author had indeed broken with Marxism. I accept the accusations.

But that is only half of the story. The other half was decided not by the truth contained in the arguments and counterarguments, but by the context in which the attacks were heard. This was not an intellectual duel between contestants with equal chances—János Kornai saying this and Géza Ripp, Endre Molnár, Emil Gulyás, and

---

* The label "revisionist" was applied in Communist Party jargon to those who called themselves Marxist but sought to revise one or two of Marx's tenets. The epithet did not fit me, as I was not aiming to revise Marxism. I had broken with it.

† József Révai also fulminated in an article, written in 1957, on the ideologists preparing for the counterrevolution and spoke strongly about the indolence shown in the intellectual battle. My former editor in chief had a few words of denunciation for me as well. His article was found too strident even by Kádár's party leadership and it was withheld from publication (PIL 793. f. 2/116. ő.e., p. 14).

István Friss saying that. They were free to attack, but I could not defend my position publicly and sincerely or express all my arguments. It was 1957. By this time, some of my closest friends were in prison and others had been dismissed from their jobs. All those who had taken the side of the revolution were being persecuted. In that situation, labels like "revisionist" and "rejecting the socialist economy" embodied serious threats. Indeed, Endre Molnár had warned readers "not to be lenient even with the first shoots of revisionism."

I will leave until later my account of how the threats materialized, because I would like first to follow the career of the book. As the attacks continued in Hungary, another strand in the history of *Overcentralization* began. András Nagy had encouraged a young economist, István Zádor, to take a short abstract of the book prepared here with him when he defected to Britain and to show it to British economists. He did so, and eventually the account reached John Hicks, an Oxford professor and one of the most important figures in modern economics (he later received the Nobel Prize). At the same time, Anthony de Jasay (Antal Jászay), an English economist of Hungarian origin, read the book, and he, too, called Hicks's attention to my work.* Hicks suggested to Oxford University Press that they publish the book. Not long after, I was offered a contract.

I naturally wanted to seize this unexpected opportunity, but the regulations required me to get permission from the director of the institute, István Friss. Friss had two, indeed several sides to him. Having praised me to the skies and then crushed me for writing the book, he now gave permission for the English edition.† The translating work began. As luck would have it, a former classmate of mine at the German school, Mária Knapp, had an older brother, János (John), who was an

---

* Zádor later committed suicide, and we never had the opportunity to discuss the story of the book. Many years later Professor Jasay and I exchanged letters, but I still cannot quite recall whether Zádor's and his actions ran parallel or were somehow connected. I am greatly indebted to all three of them—Hicks, Jasay, and Zádor—for making the English edition possible. Let me quote a passage from the letter Professor Jasay wrote to me in 1990, which I have kept in my private archives: "There is no question of your owing me any gratitude, belated or not; if I recommended your book for publication by OUP back in 1957, it was because it seemed to me highly original and worth publishing. My only merit was that I read Hungarian and was able to spot it, and John Hicks was prepared to believe me."

† Friss attached conditions to the publication of the book. He wished to omit the original preface. I wanted to keep it but I agreed to omit the cheeky sentence quoted above. I wrote, in addition, a foreword to the English edition, which established that the book was not a general description of the socialist planned economy but an account tied to a particular space and time, and that since its publication, some progress had been made toward reform. I also had to omit a few passages from the text that particularly annoyed Friss and other people around him. I made concessions, but in retrospect I think they were worth it, for the sake of having the book published abroad.

economist living in England. He took on the task and did an unbelievably conscientious job. I have just leafed again through our long correspondence, where we clarified all the terminology and problematic expressions. It was no easy task to attend to the comments of a translator respectfully faithful to my text and, beyond that, to risk publication in the West, while the Hungarian press reviled and classed it as a dangerous counterrevolutionary work.

When the English edition appeared in 1959,[11] it soon attracted attention in the West as well. Articles praising it appeared in three leading British newspapers, the *Financial Times*, the *Times Literary Supplement*, and the *Guardian*,[12] and it was conscientiously and favorably reviewed in the leading economics journals. The *American Economic Review* wrote, "This is definitely an important book—candid in tone, rich in insights, abundant in valid analyses."[13] The London journal *Economica* remarked, "Mr Kornai has put us all in his debt by providing a logically argued and coherent picture[;]...his work is so far unique. Nowhere else in the Communist world has such a study appeared."[14]

Several years later, I met personally with Alec Nove, Joseph Berliner, David Granick, Nicolas Spulber, and others who had written reviews. They told me what a stir the volume had caused at the time. They were trying to guess who it could be who would speak from behind the Iron Curtain and dare to say what the book was putting before the world in English.

Dismissed from the institute

Several decisive events in my life have been linked with Nádor utca in Budapest. My father had his lawyer's office there before the war. As I have mentioned, the Institute of Economics moved there.* At the end of November 1956, I bumped into a young woman on the corner of Nádor utca and Mérleg utca. She was the Fifth District secretary of the Hungarian Socialist Workers' Party, the reorganized Communist Party. I knew her well, having spent a holiday in the same guest house with her. We started talking, mainly about the past few days and the political conditions. I told her in this conversation that I was not a Marxist. Let me stress that this was not said in confidence. I was asking her to take note of the fact in her capacity as district secretary.

Why did I say this to that friendly, well-disposed woman? Out of anger and defiance. I wanted to dissociate myself from those who were hastily repositioning themselves and shrugging off the revolution. I also dissociated myself from Marxism in front of several people in the institute, where reorganization of the party branch was

---

* Later the National Planning Office was also on Nádor utca. I often went there to work on our mathematical planning models, and there I became close to my future second wife, Zsuzsa Dániel, who was on the Planning Office staff.

just beginning—reorganization meant that all memberships automatically ceased and those who wanted to join again had to apply. The work was started by my old office mates Péter Erdős and Róbert Hoch. I announced I was not going to join and my remark to the district secretary soon reached the institute, where it was inscribed indelibly on my cadre record: János Kornai had declared he was not a Marxist. Rejecting Marxism was no special crime for István Varga, Ede Theiss, or Jenő Rácz, who were seen in any case as "bourgeois" economists. I was not a "pagan," however, but first a "heretic" and then an "apostate." I had once possessed the truth and then betrayed it. To be a long-standing non-member of the party was an acceptable status. Communists even took silence as a friendly gesture from non-party people. But those who left the party and gave up Marxism were renegades and traitors.

Most of my colleagues at the institute decided, after a longer or shorter period of hesitation, to join the new party. Quite a number of them thought it important to come to my room first and explain their action. It was a grotesque situation, as if they were asking for permission or spiritual dispensation.

Two of us, András Nagy and myself, remained adamant; we held aloof even from the idea of joining. I do not want in 2004 to judge people according to whether or not they were party members under the Kádár regime. I know there were plenty of upright, well-intentioned people within the party, and many dishonest and ill-intentioned ones outside it. At this point in my memoirs I am talking of 1956–1957 and a workshop of intellectuals where all but a couple of people had been party members up to October 23. During the days of the revolution, almost everyone in that workplace had expressed sympathy with the changes and hardly anyone had said a word against them. Then the revolution had been defeated by Soviet tanks. To slink back to the party *after that* had special significance in my eyes. That rapid metamorphosis has left me to this day with insuperable doubts and uncertainties about people's resolution and consistency.

Perhaps my judgments at that time were too strict and rigid. Many people certainly remained sincere believers in socialism. Among them were those who genuinely thought they could exert more of a positive influence by joining the new party than by staying out. I also admit that not a few kept to their resolve and worked as party members for reforms and the good of the country. But at the time, I was not open to such ideas.

A few weeks after the process of restoration began, I received a telephone call from the party headquarters from Jenő Fock, a future prime minister. I had met him before, when he was minister of metallurgy and engineering. The party wanted to deal with reform of the economic mechanism. He had heard of my work and asked me to cooperate. I declined.

István Varga got in touch with me. Despite his great knowledge of economics and professional reputation, he had been sidelined and overlooked during the Rákosi period. Now the Kádár–Münnich government was asking him to head a committee of experts to draw up detailed proposals for reform. I had spoken to Varga several times in recent months. As I noted above, he had carefully studied my book and the proposal for reform drawn up under my leadership in the summer of 1956. He tried to persuade me to join in the work that was starting. I declined.

Why did I decline? The reason was not a theoretical conviction *at that time* that the socialist system could not be reformed. Nor could I say I was rooting for the other side. I had never accepted the Machiavellian principle, "the worse, the better." I felt it would be pure gain if the bureaucratic centralization eased a little.

I was not against the task of reform as an economist. My reasons were political. I had been utterly revolted by the Soviet intervention. I felt anger and contempt for János Kádár and his accomplices, who had first supported the revolution and then betrayed it. I saw the forcible exile of Imre Nagy and his associates as a monstrous breach of faith. I mentioned a few pages earlier the confusion I felt within me during the *victorious* days of revolution. I could not decide what to do. My instincts were not prompting me. The situation changed completely once the revolution suffered *defeat*. I felt instinctively that I had to say no.

At the end of 1957, the party headquarters sent out a committee to investigate how the institute had performed before, during, and after the "counterrevolution."* It was headed by László Háy, rector of the Karl Marx University of Economics. (He had declared, incidentally: "As long as I am the rector, Kornai will not teach at the university.") The committee's secretary was the Endre Molnár who had written the most vitriolic articles against me. There was a tussle behind the scenes.†

---

* An article was published in *Közgazdasági Szemle* in 1958 about the party investigation at the institute—under the initials I. K., not the author's full name.

† In spring 1958, the party leadership of the institute expressly suggested that colleagues who had been active in October 1956—including András Nagy and myself—should employ the June staff meeting to exercise some sincere self-criticism. They should dissociate themselves from the "counterrevolution" and Imre Nagy, and declare their loyalty to the new leadership under Kádár and their adherence to Marxism and Leninism.

The meeting was held on June 23, 1958, just a few days after the verdict in the Imre Nagy trial had been made public. Many colleagues went out of their way to recant their former views and condemn their acts. András and I, however, again refused to do so, despite repeated warnings. Both of us decided that if our well-meaning colleagues insisted on our speaking up, we would acknowledge "errors" in politically irrelevant economic questions. I said, in my remarks, a few words about the significance of centralized planning and economic leadership in general, admitting I had perhaps not stressed this enough in my works. However, I made no political self-criticism, no condemnation of the October revolution or Imre Nagy, nor any declaration of political and ideological loyalty. It was the same with András. This behavior (or as some colleagues who remained in the institute put it, "this obstinacy") no doubt influenced the decision to dismiss the two of us from the institute.

One view was that the institute was a hotbed of revisionism that should be disbanded. István Friss and the party organization in the institute, especially Erdős and Hoch, fought for its survival. Two of us, András Nagy and I, were fed to the wolves.*

István Friss felt it would be embarrassing to convey the decision to us himself and told Tamás Nagy to do it. We were not surprised by the decision. We were left to find jobs for ourselves. András, who was an acknowledged expert in foreign trade, went in that direction. I looked for a position in light industry.

I think back gratefully to my colleagues in light industry—György Sík, Miklós Simán, Sándor Fülöp, and György Schiller—for their help in finding me a job. I found not just a source of income but a post where I could carry on surreptitiously with my research, first in the Light Industry Planning Bureau and later at the Textile Industry Research Institute.

The search was made easier by support from the Institute of Economics. I have heard many stories of how former workplaces went after dismissed employees and made it as difficult as possible for them to find new jobs. I do not know what telephone calls were made behind my back, but I have the impression that István Friss showed his benevolent side again. Although he was prepared to sacrifice us, not on his own initiative but at the behest of Háy and Molnár, he still wanted to help us continue our careers as economists.

I left the Institute of Economics with a heavy heart, on September 15, 1958. Formally, I became an employee of the institutions I just mentioned, but in fact, my time was my own. I did some of my work at the Ministry of Light Industry (opposite the dark block of the Fő utca–Gyorskocsi utca prison, where friends of mine were kept and occasionally hauled out for interrogation). I spent a lot of time at home. Many of my working discussions took place in the Gresham Café or the Gerbeaud, not offices.

Even then, I felt I had no reason to feel sorry for myself or be pitied. Although I had lost the prestige of working for an institute attached to the Hungarian Academy of Sciences, I had been left to myself. And beneath me, I had a safety net of friends and colleagues.

At large, but under threat of imprisonment

On December 6, 1956, I met at my mother's apartment with Alíz Halda, Miklós Gimes's brave companion. Miklós had spent the night there two days before and

---

* Tamás Nagy recalled the party investigation in an autobiographical interview submitted to the Oral History Archives: "The institute was described as a pustule and a number of people were thrown out. Friss tried, I think to his credit, to find tolerable jobs for these people . . . but he did not really defend them" (OHA 1986, interview no. 26, p. 133).

the night after somewhere else. I now discovered that he had been arrested. That was when I first felt the shadow of prison looming over me. After that, I would often wake up at some noise in the night, then rush out to the kitchen and look into the street to see if a car had come to take me away. I mentioned earlier that I had no fear of arrest in the Rákosi period, because I was a sleepwalker boldly stepping on to the balustrade of the balcony with no fear of falling. Now I knew more than enough about the system and I was afraid.

Despite my fears, I did not leave the country. The Iron Curtain was more or less lifted for several weeks after the defeat of the revolution, making it far less risky than usual to cross the frontier illegally. Some 200,000 to 250,000 people fled, among them a good many of my close friends—including Péter Kende, who was closest to me of all. We had no way of telling if we would ever meet again. Would there be an opportunity for me to travel abroad or for him to return home? My wife and I decided we would stay. I will have more to say about the "stay or emigrate" dilemma in a later chapter.

The period I gave in the chapter title ends in 1959. That marks a boundary in my personal history, not in Hungarian history. Looking back, I can say that the repeated police harassment and the depressing series of interrogations to which I was subjected ended in 1959.

I had several conversations with Sándor Fekete, one of the *Szabad Nép* rebels, about how we would behave if arrested and called on to confess.* He declared boldly he would not confess. I doubted him (rightly, as we will see). I had formed my own opinion much earlier, after talking to those who had suffered in the torture chambers of Rákosi and Gábor Péter, and I had read a lot about what went on to elicit Soviet, Yugoslav, or Hungarian confessions. I clearly had to conclude that no one was able to resist forever. The time of capitulation depended on the physical and mental strength of the tortured prisoner. If interrogators are prepared to go far

---

* One such conversation took place at Fekete's flat. It has recently emerged from police records that the flat had been bugged by that time (ÁBTL 0-10986/1, pp. 187–196. Report on wiretapping Sándor Fekete's apartment. Date: July 4, 1958). I paid him a visit on July 4, 1958. As always, we discussed a variety of subjects—some lofty (Giordano Bruno and other heretics' martyrdom, the future of China), and some not so lofty (the forgetfulness of the Kornais' household help, or the recent order on house rents). The police assigned to tap and interpret our conversation were unable to properly follow our discussion of how much moral strength we would have to resist persecution. Reading this report—full of dotted passages and question marks—today, forty-six years later, I have mixed feelings. I would really like to laugh off the coarseness and ignorance of the police and the crazy misunderstandings that the report brims with, if only—even after so many years—I was not still appalled by the tyrannical control over free thought, the contemptible intrusion into personal conversations.

enough with their torture, a stage is reached at which the prisoner will do anything.* I suffered from chronic dislocation of the shoulder and every dislocation caused me agony until it was set. I have the painful habit of going through bad things in my imagination that may, perhaps, happen. I thought over what I would do if they intentionally dislocated my shoulder and told me they would not set it right again until . . .

I decided I would determine my political actions in a way that would avoid my being tortured. The Communist restoration took place in the shadow of Soviet tanks. Who could know in advance what means would be used in the new repression—what methods Kádár's political police would take over from the Soviet Cheka or NKVD (Narodnyĭ Kommisariat Vnutrennikh Del, or the People's Commissariat of Internal Affairs), or Rákosi's ÁVH? I feared being tortured. But I feared at least as much that if they tortured me, I would not withstand it—I would betray not only myself but others. I wanted to protect myself from the shame of that when I decided to avoid doing illegal acts. One reason was a bitter, sober recognition of my own limitations.

It is worth turning at this point to the story of Sándor Fekete, my conversation partner. He took part in several brave illegal actions. He was arrested. He was not subjected to physical torture, but he was threatened with the gallows. In his alarm, he confessed to his own deeds and also told everything he knew about his friends and companions.† (I have already mentioned the confession he made about me, and I will come back to that later.)

So I came to a firm resolve, but it was not possible to say accurately where the boundary between legality and illegality ran. Such bounds are not always clear even in a legally constituted state, let alone under a Communist autocracy. In such cases,

---

* George Orwell (1966 [1949], pp. 196–202) illustrated this point vividly with his torture machine and its quantitative scale. Just move a lever and the pain would increase. It varied from prisoner to prisoner whether confession to false charges or betrayal of one's lover ensued at Mark 50 or 70. I had lent the book to Fekete at just that time, not long before he was arrested. (ÁBTL V-145-288/document 2, p. 326. Date: December 18, 1958. Sándor Fekete's confession in his own hand, point 6.)

† I quote György Litván, who at a roundtable discussion in 1981 described Sándor Fekete's behavior as follows: "They showed him a photo of Gimes swinging from the gallows—he disclosed this very confidentially. They tried to influence him with things like that. He came to the point at which he realized that denial would make his situation a lot worse. It is true that he confessed everything, but it is also a fact that nobody was locked up because of him, although that was not entirely his doing anyway, as they were trying to close these investigations by then." The roundtable discussion was moderated by Zsolt Csalog, Gyula Kozák, and Miklós Szabó; the report is kept at the Oral History Archives (OHA 1981, interview no. 800, p. 953).

the text of a legal stipulation would leave wide scope for interpretation, within which criminal investigators or courts could decide what to class as an illegal act and when. My resolve to confine myself to legal activities reduced the chances of my being arrested or convicted, but it did not eliminate them.*

Nor did I consistently keep to my decision. Sometimes I was careless or incautious and sometimes I overstepped the bounds of law deliberately, leaving an opening for me to be "legally" brought to account. One of the curiosities in my story, it emerges later, was the way events would sometimes push me toward the criminal trials when I had said no to taking part in an illegal action and abided by my decision.

I was interrogated several times, and after a while, I almost had a routine. But in fact, it was a nightmarish experience that I could not get used to. If I remember rightly, I received a summons each time, which gave me a chance to prepare myself to some extent.† The summons never stated what they wanted to question one about. I would run with utmost concentration through a number of possibilities and dialogues in my mind, working out how I would respond to various potential questions. Sometimes there would be a clue in what some friend or close acquaintance of mine had been questioned about before me, so I could guess what was on the agenda. This kind of preparation was an *intellectual* task, in fact, a mental duel between the interrogating officer and the interrogated person. But it was an extremely difficult contest. More than once I had the surprise of finding that the interrogator knew exactly what I wanted to conceal from him. First he would hear out my statement, partly true and partly false, and *then* he would say what information he possessed.

But the real difficulty was not the battle of intelligence and information between the interrogator and the interrogated. The real dilemma was a *moral* one. We who were still at large tried to agree among ourselves how we would handle each piece of information. That agreement included those who were later arrested. (The exercise was sometimes futile, because someone at large or under arrest would breach our agreement.) The problem turned almost unbearably serious with the uncertainty over how persons being interrogated were damaging themselves and damaging others with their statements. If you were questioned as a witness and refused to say anything, you would certainly be kept inside. If you wanted to avoid being put in

* A Budapest joke of 1957: Two people are talking about friends who were convicted. "I understand how 'A' got eight years, but how come 'B' got four? He had not done anything." "No, I don't get it either. They usually give two years for nothing."

† Once I was seriously ill in bed, and then a police officer came to my apartment and sat by my bedside to question me. I can remember the relief when he went and our home help, Magdi, appeared in the door with a cup of coffee.

the cells as a suspect, you had to say something. But what to say? There was no prior agreement on that. We had not decided on any "moral code" for the period of interrogation.

I tried to devise moral rules and prescriptions for myself. I would not be a stubborn witness who would not say anything. I was ready to say what I assumed the interrogator already knew. I was ready to divulge facts that I assumed would do no harm to those in custody. I am not sure that I always managed to observe those self-imposed rules to the letter in the cat-and-mouse game between interrogator and interrogated. But I certainly do not know of a case where I broke them. I know these rules are no exalted postulates of heroism. I did not undertake to be a political hero, turning his defense into a speech of accusation. I set myself a more modest standard of observing elementary requirements of human decency and tried to keep to it as far as I could.

Let me turn now to some specific instances, in the order not of the interrogations but of the events on which my interrogations focused.

The case against Pál Lőcsei included the events of October 29, when the paper *Magyar Szabadság* had been founded. (This is an example of what I was just talking about in general. I did not undertake to write for the paper and I left the editorial offices after one night. But that did not prevent the police from pestering me about it.)

Several of us attempted in Lőcsei's case to agree on a statement that we would make to the police, and we also spoke to his defense lawyer (in vain, I think). I was called as a witness during the investigation and at the trial.[15] The interrogations came up in conversation several times after his release. Lőcsei spoke at a small gathering of close friends for my seventy-fifth birthday, and I must say I was touched and morally reassured to hear his kind words. He recalled my cross-examination at his trial, my nervous tone and frightened look, reflecting my thoughts: "Oh dear, if only I can avoid doing Pali any harm." It also emerged from his remarks that what had most cheered him as he sat alone in the dock was the way I had given him an encouraging, affectionate look as I left.

During the first half of November, Miklós Gimes called me and several other former journalists to his office at the Corvina publishers and proposed continuing the struggle by editing and producing an illegal duplicated paper or journal. I did not agree to take part. Aside from my personal intentions, which I have mentioned, I was also against the idea because I saw no sense in it under the current circumstances. With the revolution having been crushed by brutal military force and Communist power restored, whom could a little duplicated paper recruit and how could it mobilize its readers? As I saw it, the risk was out of proportion to the likely political effect.

Was my argument correct? I am still not sure to this day. If a "risk-benefit" calculation is done, then I was right, except that that was not the only possible measure. In historical terms, there is enormous moral value for the Hungarian nation in the presence of heroes like Miklós, ready to risk any danger. The newspaper *Október 23* appeared, and that very fact showed that the regime could not entirely crush the spirit of revolution.

On April 16, 1957, they began to ask me in Gyorskocsi utca who had been at that meeting in the Corvina offices.[16] I stalled, saying I could not remember. Whereupon the investigating officer began to read out the April 10 confession of one of the participants, P. P., who was already in custody, describing the meeting in faithful detail.[17] I was stunned at what I heard. I decided I could do nothing other than confirm P. P.'s list of the participants.

The investigating officer also asked me to confirm that at the meeting held in the Corvina, Miklós Gimes suggested the launch of an illegal paper. I present an excerpt from the interrogation report:

Question: What sort of things did Gimes ask during the conversation?
Answer: I cannot recall, since we discussed a number of different topical issues.
Question: According to information in our possession Gimes has clearly suggested that he launched an illegal paper. Let me quote the relevant part of P. P.'s confession. Gimes said he launched an illegal mimeographed paper, which he sought to bring out on a regular basis. We want your evidence on this.
Answer: I don't remember this, nor can I say anything about the paper because I declared that I had no wish to participate in any kind of political activity. I have nothing else to say.[18]

I think my interrogation was a fairly minor event in the investigation. It did not matter much to Gimes's "list of crimes" to say who had been at the Corvina offices in November. What counted if anything was the paper's appearance, which Gimes himself admitted later under the horrible pressure of interrogation.*

That interrogation shook me deeply. I faced for the first time a case in which an arrested man, in this case P. P., had given crucial evidence against his arrested associate and against his former comrades-in-arms who were still free. Doing research for my memoirs forty-seven years later, I read through a number of documents in P. P.'s file, and it became clear that soon after his arrest, he had revealed much about a lot of people in his reports.[19]

The discussion at the Corvina offices was the second time I had declined to take part in an action, but it did not save me from being summoned to Gyorskocsi utca again.

---

* Sándor Révész describes in his book (1999) the terrible pressure and threat Miklós Gimes was under between his arrest and his trial, where he was sentenced to death.

The case of Sándor Fekete was different, in my view. That may exemplify how I was not consistent in my refusal to take part in illegal, conspiratorial actions.

At the turn of 1956–1957 Fekete, under the pseudonym Hungaricus, wrote a study that sought to assess the revolution—its causes, course, successes, and failures.[20] He showed it to several friends, including me. Then, in making his confession to the police, he quoted accurately what I had said in a confidential conversation: to my mind, his paper was "too Marxist," as I mentioned in the previous chapter.

Returning to the Hungaricus paper, I was willing, despite my political and ideological reservations about its contents, to get it to the West illegally for publication. I had introduced Fekete to a leading young Greek Cypriot Communist, Jorgos Vassiliou.* Jorgos was a charming, bright young man, studying for a candidate's degree under István Friss. In that capacity he came to the institute, where he made friends with András Nagy and myself. He dropped in several times. He was off to France and Britain quite legally and agreed to take Fekete's paper with him and hand it over to Ferenc Fejtő, the legendary historian and political journalist who was living in Paris,† and to Péter Kende. I was not the one who asked him to do this, but I knew what was going on. It emerged from the police confession made by Jorgos that it was important to Fejtő and his group that Jorgos could also cite my name. Doing so helped to convince the Parisians that the article was not a provocation. The paper appeared in leading French intellectual forums and caused a stir.[21] Jorgos had agreed with me on a secret message to confirm that he had passed the paper to its addressees.

Jorgos was harassed by the police.[22] He was a party member and expelled for this affair. Shortly afterward, he left Hungary for good.

Thirty years later, in 1988, Jorgos Vassiliou became president of the Republic of Cyprus.‡

But let us get back to Gyorskocsi utca in 1958–1959. It emerged that I kept up with Péter Kende and would know about the essay by Hungaricus being smuggled

* András B. Hegedűs conducted an interview with him in 1991, which came out in book form in Hungarian; there the Greek name appears as Georgios Vassiliou. We, the Greek boy's Hungarian friends, called him Jorgos. In recalling these events I will stick to this name.

† Before he emigrated, Ferenc Fejtő was an editor of *Szép Szó*, along with the poet Attila József. He has earned acclaim in France as an authority on Eastern Europe. More or less as I write this, he is celebrating his ninety-fifth birthday with Hungarian friends.

‡ In 1990, Árpád Göncz, president of the Hungarian Republic, attended a reception in Japan, where someone standing next to him said in a rather strange accent, but in fluent Hungarian, "I'm also a Hungarian president." It was Jorgos, who by then held the title of president of Cyprus.

out.[23] There was no denying it after Fekete and Vassiliou had confessed. So it could be clearly proved that I had "neglected my responsibility to report."*

In helping to get the Hungaricus article out, I had clearly broken my resolution not to undertake political activity and to refrain from taking part in illegal actions. I cannot give a clear explanation why I was inconsistent. Perhaps it was because it was hard to keep saying no when I was bound by a web of friendly ties. Owing to my self-imposed ban, I refused a succession of invitations from close friends to take part in political acts. Sándor Fekete was a friend of mine, although not such a close one as Kende, Lőcsei, or Gimes. When the idea of sending out the Hungaricus article was broached, Kende was already in Paris and Lőcsei and Gimes were in prison. Perhaps I was afraid that if I declined to help I would also lose the friendship of Fekete—the only person who was still available from our former close company of friends.

The friendship was lost in any case.

Friendship and solidarity

I felt it was most important to show solidarity with those whom the Kádár regime was persecuting. I remembered how people who had been released from Rákosi's prisons would complain that former friends had abandoned them and their dependents.

One close, much-loved friend of mine was Sándor Novobáczky, one of the *Szabad Nép* rebels. He had written a much-discussed article, which appeared in the *Irodalmi Újság* (*Literary News*) before the revolution, about Communist arrogance, using words of Stalin's: "We Communists are people of a special mold..."[24] The authorities still could not forgive his mockery. When Sándor was taken away, I had no idea what the reason for his arrest could be. I wanted to talk to Lajos Fehér, a mutual friend, whom I met more than once at the Novobáczkys' apartment when we were preparing for the rebellious party meeting. Once one of Imre Nagy's closest associates, Fehér now belonged to the innermost circle around Kádár. I, naive as I was, wanted to ask him to intervene to get Sándor released. His office was in Parliament. I got as far as his secretary, whom I had known from my newspaper days, and whom I had told in advance why I wanted to see her boss. Lajos Fehér sent a mes-

---

* All this was added to my criminal record, which was checked every time my name came up in some context or another. "He had knowledge of sending the counterrevolutionary publication 'Hungaricus' to the West. In 1957, he had contact with a defected member of an illegal counterrevolutionary group. On February 9, 1959, he received a police warning," is what the file says (ÁBTL C-R-N 0082-479-2. Date: December 21, 1966).

sage back through her saying he was not prepared to receive me. He did not want to do anything about the Novobáczky case.

Several friends of mine and I made regular collections for the dependents of those arrested.[25] I felt that doing so lay within the restrictions I had made for myself and saw it as humanitarian work, not political. I could not stand idly by while the dependents of friends of mine were in want. In some cases, they were not merely "dependents of friends" but friends in their own right, such as Gizi Lőcsei or Éva Novobáczky. But apart from that, we felt that in collecting the money we were fulfilling a moral obligation and that we should also help the wives and children of prisoners not known to us personally.

Again, my initial idea—that politics would stay out of "humanitarian" activity—proved illusory. During the police investigation into the Mérei–Litván–Fekete case, the authorities treated the collections as part of the political conspiracy. I assume the police chiefs must have remembered that Red Aid, an illegal organization of the Communists that helped the families of their imprisoned comrades during the Horthy regime, was a curious "mass movement," through which the isolated party members could make contact with broader circles of sympathizers. They must have thought that this collecting work was a similar cover for an organization. They could not imagine it was motivated simply by humanity and solidarity with people in trouble, not by any political intentions.

This was a sad story, but there was another one that was utterly ridiculous. We tried to keep our good humor as the arrests were going on around us. We decided to hold a New Year's Eve party at the end of 1957. It took place in Péter Hanák's flat, attended by ten to twenty people. Péter and I were the main organizers of the "show." Most of us presented carefully edited cabaret numbers, and the most successful of them has remained clear in my memory. Sándor Fekete and György Litván pulled their shirts out of their trousers, tied their belts over them, and wore flat caps, like real Russian peasants. The scene was set in Siberia. Litván was supposed to have been deported there, and a freshly arrived Fekete was telling him what had been going on back in Budapest: one blustering revolutionary had just joined the party, another had just been imprisoned, and so on. The scene was met with loud laughter, but it proved to be a prophetic vision in many respects.

The celebrations continued in Gyorskocsi utca.[26] Our New Year's Eve gallows humor was taken quite seriously and classed as conspiratorial. It was taken as a test by which this putative organization tried to find out how it could recruit people and create a counterrevolutionary atmosphere.

Meanwhile it became clear—sometimes at the time, and sometimes years later, when police documents and informers' reports became known—that not every friendship would survive the difficult years, though the ones that survived were strengthened. It meant a lot to me that I had people I could talk to sincerely and confidentially and could rely on at the worst moments. The first I have to mention here is Teri, my first wife. We lived through difficult times together. Teri stood by me and I could always count on her understanding, advice, and assistance.

During the same period, I became very close to Péter and Kati Hanák, Gizi Lőcsei, Duci Fónyi, Éva Csató, Gyuri and Éva Litván, András Nagy, and Ági Losonczy. There were many strands binding us, from exchanges of the latest political news to long theoretical debates, from joking to jointly helping those in trouble. These friendships were made for a lifetime.

Later, when I was spending a lot of my time in America, I noticed how easily people there used the term "friends." Friends might be people they had had a good time with at a party or met once or twice on a university committee. In our time, the word was not used so lightly; it had weight. Life under a dictatorship would have been unbearable without friends.

7

My Universities—1957–1959

"My universities" was a name Gorky gave to the period when life, rather than university teachers, taught him a great many things. I readily use the same expression for the story of my development. What I learned before 1955, as usable experience and sobering, disillusioning lessons, can be called "preparatory training." Even thereafter, when I became a professional scientific researcher, I was still in fact teaching myself, though much more methodically than before.

Self-instruction

After the revolution had been defeated, I resolved that I would not leave the country. Nonetheless, I decided I wanted to be part of the economic profession in the West. One strong impetus behind such a consciously "Western" orientation came from the fury I felt over the entry of the Soviet tanks.

I could still read German fluently, but my secondary school English had grown rusty. So one of my first tasks in 1957 was to learn it properly. My spoken English was shaky, but I could soon read economic literature in English effortlessly.

It would be misleading to say I "devoured books." (That is what I had done with literature in my teens.) I read a lot, systematically. Perhaps I had good advice from someone or perhaps I just had good luck, but I was fortunate in my choice of basic works. I started with Paul Samuelson's famous textbook,[1] in a German translation. For an "intermediate" survey, I studied very thoroughly the didactically first-rate three-volume textbook by the West German economist Erich Schneider.

That ended my study of general textbooks. Thereafter I read various monographs, volumes of studies, and articles in journals. I still have many of the notes I took of my reading in that period. As illustrations, here are some of the authors (in alphabetical order, not the order in which I read them): Kenneth Arrow;[2] Arrow, Samuel Karlin, and Herbert Scarf; Kenneth Boulding; Walter Eucken; Ragnar Frisch; Gottfried von Haberler; Friedrich von Hayek;[3] John Hicks;[4] Michał Kalecki; Arthur

Pigou; Samuelson;[5] Heinrich von Stackelberg;* and Jan Tinbergen.[6] I have mentioned only writers whom later, on the basis of my experiences abroad, I found to
be great names.† Meanwhile I also read many works that I concluded later had not
been good choices. The time and energy they took to read could have been devoted
to studying more important writings. Unfortunately, I lacked a teacher with up-to-
date knowledge of the current literature to guide me.

I studied very intensely, not just running over the text but taking notes of the
main points, partly as an aid to memory, and solving problems. Whenever a work
prompted me to do so, I would think over what might follow for a socialist economy from what I had read. Could the same apparatus be applied to understanding
the operation of a Hungarian enterprise, a branch of Hungarian industry, or the
whole economy? It was an intellectual approach valid for a lifetime, as I became
acquainted not just with the findings in the works I was reading but with the
method and *style* employed. The conclusions were drawn from logical argumentation—sometimes difficult but always possible to discern and follow—not from
empty, doctrinaire speculation. Authors did not try to refer to authorities as a substitute for argument. (The perceived need for genuine argument would have been
self-evident to a Western student, but to me, it came as a refreshing change after
writings stuffed with quotations from Marx, Engels, Lenin, Stalin, and Rákosi.)

I was interested mainly in microeconomics and allied subjects, especially welfare
economics and the theory of rational choice. (An acquaintance with John Maynard
Keynes followed later.) Expunging from my mind Marxist prejudices against "bourgeois economics," I became receptive to the "mainstream" of economic thinking.
Such receptivity was not the same as uncritical self-immersion in an "-ism," as I
had done ten or twelve years earlier when I studied Marxism. The explanation of
economic phenomena that I found in these books seemed convincing. I was already
familiar with the meaning of the term "neoclassical" from Samuelson's book. In
fact, I was not far short of describing myself as an adherent of neoclassical thought
by the end of my private course of study. What held me back were not real doubts
or counterarguments but a resistance born of earlier disillusionment and a determination to stay intellectually independent.

There was no one behind me to goad me to study, no one to award me a certificate that would launch me on my subsequent career. On some days I was interro-

---

* Eucken and von Stackelberg were German economists who contributed important ideas to
economics. They were available to me in German in 1957, which meant I could more readily
imbibe their ideas than those of writers in English.

† György Péter and the composer András Mihály, later director of the Budapest Opera, traveled in the West and were willing to bring me books. Others were available in Budapest university libraries and the libraries of academic institutes.

gated by the police in the morning and still sat down to my books again in the afternoon. On Monday would come terrifyingly bad news, but on Tuesday and Wednesday I would, just the same, get through the quantity of study I had set myself. Then (and later, when I had serious problems to cope with) I used study and work as therapy, a way of treating spiritual wounds.

Let me now jump forward for a moment. When I was teaching regularly at an American university, it never crossed the minds of my teaching colleagues or my students to wonder where I had gained my knowledge of economics. The answer seemed obvious to them. But it was not, and not just because I had not attended Budapest's Karl Marx University of Economics. If I had done the course (as I might have in the late 1940s and early 1950s—that is, in the period when Marxist ideology was taking over and gaining a monopoly on power), I still would not have learned modern Western economics.

The Lange–Hayek debate

It is worth recalling here the intellectual excitement I experienced when I studied an earlier debate about socialism among Western economists in the 1930s. The first economics text I read in English was in fact a classic paper on socialism by Oskar Lange, the great Polish economist, who was living in the United States at the time he wrote it. Later I read the main contributions to this debate on socialism, including the volume edited by F. A. Hayek[7] that fired a broadside at planning and Abba Lerner's famous *Economics of Control*. In choosing what to read I was greatly helped by a wise survey of the literature by Abram Bergson. I never imagined as I read those works that I would ever meet Lange, Lerner, or Maurice Dobb personally, or that my office at Harvard would be next to Bergson's. (Later we also lived in adjacent apartments in Cambridge.)

Remarks and writings by György Péter and descriptions of the Yugoslav system had introduced me to the idea that allocation of resources in a socialist economy should be left to the market. My own book was directed against "overcentralization." I now found that twenty years earlier, economists in Chicago, London, and Cambridge (both in the United Kingdom and in Massachusetts) had been debating on a high theoretical plane how far an economy in which factories are state-owned could go with decentralization. Lange built a theoretical model in which production occurs in publicly owned enterprises interested in the single economic objective of profitability.* Instead of being free, prices are set by a central planning authority according to a very simple rule. If demand for a product exceeds supply, its price is

---

* Lange originally wrote "cost minimization," but that was corrected in later articles.

raised; and if supply exceeds demand, its price is lowered. The central planners have nothing else to do beyond observing the relations of supply and demand and altering prices accordingly. Lange, in line with the conventional assumptions about the market and prices in neoclassical microeconomics, confirmed that the state of the market would converge to an equilibrium. There, in Lange's study, I first came across the English idiom "trial and error."[8] An "equilibrium price" was reached after repeated attempts and frequent failures. The founder of the theory of general equilibrium had been the French Swiss Léon Walras, one of the giants in the history of economics. Every line in Lange's study is imbued with the inspiration of Walrasian economics.

Lange's paper took the right form and came at the right time to meet the intellectual and ideological requirements of many Western economists with left-wing ideas. Their *political* sympathies tended toward some kind of socialist system, but, on the other hand, they rejected Marxism's antagonism toward the market. They were pro-market on practical grounds and out of theoretical conviction. They stood a long way from Marxism and took sides with Walras and neoclassical theory, which is why they were enthusiastic about the synthesis that Lange was offering. It was extremely congenial to me as well, for similar reasons. I found its economic content convincing and I was impressed by the line of argument, or perhaps it is more apt to say its "aesthetics"—the simple, clear harmony in his theoretical edifice.

But I also found Hayek's critique thought provoking. He drew his main arguments from practical considerations rather than theory. How will central planners be able to trace the supply and demand of a million types of product at once? His arguments pushed my nose into something that I knew well enough: the limitations of centralized knowledge. Hayek rightly pointed out that the market was not simply a balancing mechanism. Knowledge in society is decentralized. Only a decentralized market and private ownership can make it possible for anyone receiving a direct incentive to make the best use of the knowledge in his or her possession. Reading Hayek directed my attention to the close tie between knowledge, incentives, and property. The structure of the relations between them was still unclear to me at the time, but at least I began to think about it more methodically.

I do not want to project back onto 1957 a position I expressed in several writings much later, which formed the basis on which I rejected Lange's proposal. My later counterargument rests on the inseparability of the political structure from property relations and from market coordination. I had not yet seen those connections clearly in 1957. I would say my reaction to the debate was one of inability to adjudicate. The reasoning of Lange and Lerner seemed clever and consistent, but Hayek's critique was also striking.

I may have been affected as much by the style of the debate as its subject matter. A debate was then going on in Hungary on what was really a related theme. György Péter and I were advancing ideas similar to those of Lange and Lerner in the West. We were disparaged and threatened. There the discourse went on in civilized tones, with arguments answered by arguments, not anger and aspersions. It was clear to me that our mode of combat had not started with Endre Molnár or Géza Ripp. Insulting enemies and showing disdain and arrogance for those with other views fell into a tradition that went back to Marx, was continued by Lenin, and culminated with Stalin. Stalin did not just affront his opponents, he had them shot as well.

Continued research into light industry

While I was studying, I also wanted to continue the research begun in *Overcentralization* and extend it in two ways. For one thing, I wanted to extend it to subjects that I had not had the energy to pursue earlier, such as prices, investment, and the taxation and credit systems. For another, I wanted to trace what changes were occurring in the methods of economic administration. Had the proposals made before the revolution and those advanced by the Varga Committee (mentioned in chapter 5) had any effect? For the two pointed in similar directions—if not to abolition of the command economy, then at least to its containment and the concomitant expansion of the range of the market mechanism.

I continued the research intensely. I renewed my old contacts in light industry and made the acquaintance of many new people as well. This time I was more systematic, using questionnaires prepared in advance. I also sought to apply the new knowledge I had gained from Western literature. After I learned about the firm's cost function, I used that concept in my next factory visits, trying to determine the real cost function of a textile mill while bearing in mind that it was a case of vertical production in several steps and of a great many products produced side by side. Once I had encountered the conceptual apparatus of substitution and the marginal rate of substitution, I tried to clarify how the prices of the imported and domestic materials that substituted for each other in Hungary were set. If the Hungarian practice was not rational enough (i.e., did not conform to the normative model I knew from Western literature), how could the price-setting procedures be altered?

It was a healthy way to link study and research. It is didactically useful for a student to be able to compare a written model with actual practice. Such an approach also helps greatly with memorization. More importantly still, it trains one to check the workability of theories. These were not great theoretical propositions, just little pieces of the comprehensive neoclassical theory, but at least they lent themselves to what I had found lacking in works of Marxist theory: repeated comparison of theory with practice.

Apart from practical verification and application of the newly learned theory in my head and notes, I tried to work it up in articles of various lengths. The result was a succession of publications in small-circulation journals in technical and commercial fields.* I was prompted to publish them by several factors. For one thing, they were exercises. I am a "graphomaniac" who cannot go for long without writing. I was also urged on by a desire to clarify my ideas. Whatever the problem occupying me, then or now, I need to write my various ideas down to get them in order—in an article, or a letter to someone (even if it is never posted), or just a note to myself. For me, the act of clarification calls for writing things down.

I was also motivated by a desire to share my information with others. Once I had finally understood something or other, let others read and understand it as well.

None of these short articles contributed to the development of economic ideas. They did not add to scholarship, but they did help my growth as an economist. Looking back on them, I would equate them with the training an athlete does.

Dissociation

The structure of these memoirs induces me to separately discuss stories which were, in fact, closely intertwined. The previous chapter dealt with political storms around and within me. This chapter has so far been about quiet intellectual activity—reading, talking to colleagues, taking notes, and writing articles like any young researcher at Oxford, Princeton, or Kiel. But let me repeat that my situation in this period was different from theirs. My thoughts and feelings and free associations of mind were influenced, in ways that cannot be teased apart, by experiences of economic readings and police interrogations, article writing and baneful political events alike.

The police investigation into Sándor Fekete's Hungaricus study was still going on when I was approached by an old colleague from the Institute of Economics. He was an active party member with sincere convictions. He had always behaved

---

* I wrote articles on other subjects, too, not only issues closely related to my studies. I gratefully remember the editors of the periodicals *Élet és Tudomány* (Life and Science), *Figyelő* (Observer), *Közgazdasági Szemle* (Economic Review), and *Statisztikai Szemle* (Statistical Review), who were well aware that those in power were far from pleased to see my writings in print, but published them nonetheless—in part to allow me to make some extra money. Sometimes they were forced to publish my articles anonymously or under my initials (or false ones).

benevolently to me and we had been quite close, so he knew a lot about my views and circle of friends. We began to talk of this and that. Then it emerged that he had brought a message. "The comrades would take it well if you could dissociate your-self in some form from Péter Kende, who is attacking the country from Paris and citing your book." Such references to anonymous "comrades" were common at the time. Neither then nor later did I ask who had sent him, and because he is no longer alive, I cannot question him as I write. I suspect that the message came from István Friss. The investigators would have asked him what he thought of me and told him about the Hungaricus business. Jorgos Vassiliou had been studying under him, and the incident would have been unpleasant for him. It is also worth noting that he was the one who read my article for the journal *Közgazdasági Szemle*, about which I will speak in a moment. But that is all supposition. The source could have been someone at the party headquarters or at the police. Friendly though the tone was in which my former colleague imparted the message, I felt a strong threat implied by those send-ing it.

Péter Kende wrote an interesting and clever article for a French periodical on the Hungarian planned economy, citing *Overcentralization* several times.[9] He clearly thought it was important to indicate correctly the source of specific ideas and infor-mation, as is customary in scholarly publications. He also had a right to feel some extent of involvement in *Overcentralization*, as my frequent dialogues with him had strongly influenced me as I wrote it. Then, too, he may have thought that authors, on the whole, are gratified to be quoted. And I *am* gratified—unless the quotations are made by Péter Kende and appear around 1957. It was awkward indeed, as Fekete and Vassiliou had been interrogated in Gyorskocsi utca about, among other things, what role the Kornai–Kende link had played in the publication of the Hun-garicus study. I had been shown the minutes of their interrogations while I was being questioned. (As I mentioned earlier, the Kende–Kornai link was on the police register of my ostensible crimes.)

I decided to do as I was "advised." I was working on an article based on my re-search in light industry, which explored the extent to which manager behavior was affected by a "quantitative outlook" and an "economic-efficiency outlook."[10] In a somewhat far-fetched manner, therefore, I included language distancing myself from Péter Kende in the article. It protested against the way he was reading the fail-ure of socialism into my book, adding self-critically that faulty wording in *Overcen-tralization* made it possible to draw such a conclusion.

It was an oppressive and degrading feeling to yield to the pressure. I was ashamed especially because I did it against Péter. I could console myself by saying that he, liv-ing safely in Paris, was unharmed, while my situation had been eased. Cool-headed economists are wont to call this a "Pareto-efficient solution."* Such action may be justified as a survival strategy, but I feel that this "dissociation" breached those norms that I consider valid in regard to friendship.

We met in 1964 for the first time since Péter had emigrated. The affair with the article came up, but Péter reproached me for only one thing: Why had I not sent him a message, saying "I was forced to write that, but of course I do not mean it"? I admitted that shortcoming and we agreed never to return to the matter again.

Although we met several times during the decades he spent living outside Hungary, in various parts of the world—Paris, Venice, Belgium, Holland, Britain, Switzerland, and Germany, and since the end of the 1980s in Budapest, too—we have never said a word about this touchy subject, as we agreed in 1964. I expect Péter's reactions were an amalgam of many feelings, but perhaps his humor and irony were dominant. When a book of his studies including this article of his appeared in France five years later, he sent me a copy with a dedication inside:[11] "I can cope with the works of my enemies, but God save me from my friends! An Author."

A blind alley

Not long ago, I was looking over my publications born out of the research into light industry and found one that caught my eye: "Should the Profit-Sharing [System] Be Corrected?"[12] This dull title masks a subject that is still exciting today. In 1957, a scheme was devised to give managers and workers in state-owned enterprises an incentive to increase profits. At first sight, this seems a promising idea. State-owned enterprises were moving away from "quantity-maximizing" incentives toward the "profit-maximizing" ones typical of a market economy based on private ownership. So far, so good; but it turned out that the distribution of profit shares among enterprises was "unfair." One enterprise was left with only a small profit because of external economic conditions beyond its control—demand for export products had declined, for instance. Another made a low profit because of a superior body's intervention, which forced it to produce less profitable lines. A third could explain its relatively disappointing profits by pointing to its lack of technically sophisticated equipment—which was not its fault. The responsibility lay with those who made the decisions on investment and technical development on the enterprises' behalf. Firms were demanding that their profit shares be "corrected." They should be com-

---

* A change is called a Pareto-improvement if it improves the position of an individual or group without hurting that of others. The state of the economy is Pareto-efficient if further Pareto-improvements cannot be applied. (These concepts were introduced into economics by the Italian Vilfredo Pareto.)

pensated for all shortfalls due to causes outside their control. Profits, therefore, should be not a market category determined by exogenous supply and demand or differences between prices obtained and costs incurred, but a fair reward that depends solely on the enterprise's endogenous merits, whether it has done "well" or "badly."

In writing that article in 1958, I was approaching problems that I termed twenty years later the syndrome of a "soft budget constraint." Enterprises try to get superior bodies to compensate them for losses they "cannot do anything about." In fact, real profit incentives work fully only if the enterprise is not going to be extricated from financial woes, regardless of whether they are self-caused or result from unlucky outside circumstances. This may not be "fair," but it compels economic actors to address difficulties, adapt to unfavorable conditions, and go for big profits by pursuing technical and commercial innovations, even in times of trouble. Compensating firms for unfavorable conditions, in contrast, makes them passive and wont to cry for state aid instead of struggling on.*

The appearance of this article suggests that I would probably have arrived at the later discoveries much earlier if I had been able to continue my research in a freer atmosphere. Sadly, that was not to be. Answering one of the prime questions raised by the light industry research I began in 1957 proved particularly difficult. Did anything change about the economic mechanism after 1956? Did the government keep its promises not to return to the bureaucratic overcentralization of old? Actually, precious few favorable changes toward decentralization had been made (profit sharing was supposed to be one), and many that did occur were soon reversed.

To have said that openly or published it as a research finding would have been politically impossible at the time. On the other hand, I saw no sense in writing something just to stick it away in a drawer. If the far-reaching conclusions of the research and the rich factual evidence for it could not be described or published, I had to acknowledge that the research had run up against a political constraint. I felt I was down a blind alley. Now that I am writing my memoirs I wonder, of course, whether my assessment of the situation was correct. Should I not have carried on working on a sequel to *Overcentralization*—would it not have been worth it? One thing is certain: *at that time* I thought that the answer to both question was no.

I came to believe that it would not be enough to slightly modify the subject matter. I had to choose a new line of research: *economic applications of mathematical methods*, which is the subject of the next chapter.

---

* Published in 1958, these reflections above foreshadowed a train of thought that was later developed by economics in connection with the problem of moral hazards.

The period denoted in the title of this chapter ends in 1959. I did not turn from one subject to the next overnight, of course. But by the end of 1959, I had completely and irreparably abandoned my investigations of the post-1956 methods of economic administration in light industry. I had put a lot of work into this study. Despite all the efforts, I only gained some training experience in my own professional development; otherwise it was basically wasted, fruitless work. I have thousands of notes in my archives, carefully filed away. As I handled them again while writing these memoirs, even after all those years, my heart was heavy.

Decisions for a lifetime

"That is not by chance, Comrades," was the trite phrase that often began a statement in those days. Those conversant with Marxian philosophy would say that Marx's works never reflected extreme fatalism or a belief that events were predestined. But in daily life under the socialist system, party secretaries and journalists, history teachers and planning office department heads liked to imply there was *no alternative*. The only thing to do was what the historic forces of progress dictated. And those dictates normally coincided with their instructions. There was no other option but to collectivize agriculture. The economic plan was drawn up in a single "version" that every organization, though formally entitled to accept it or reject it, had to endorse. There was only one party, and that one had to be elected.

During the second half of the 1950s, the opposite idea came at me in many forms and from many sources: there *was* a choice.

I read the plays of László Németh, the great Hungarian writer, at that time. It was a staggering experience to take them one by one and see the alternative answers they gave to truly great problems of choice. They treated Jan Hus, the most important fifteenth-century Czech religious reformer, who unhesitatingly rejected all concessions—and was burned; Galileo, who made a concession at the toughest moment—and could never be at peace with himself again; Miklós Misztóthfalusi Kis, a seventeenth-century Hungarian typographer and theologian, who withdrew his words—and was left spiritually crippled by his unprincipled concession; István Széchenyi, initially unenthusiastic about the 1848 revolution, who could not come to terms with its collapse—and committed suicide; and Sándor Petőfi, who went into battle not of his own accord but yielding to the expectations of those around him—and died a martyr's death. László Németh's plays as a whole do not give guidance on what is a good decision. They show the alternative solutions to great tragic dilemmas and the pain of having to choose.

About that time, I came across the existentialist philosophers. The first work I read was a short piece by Sartre. Then I studied others. My reading of these too (perhaps because that was what I wanted to read into them) was that if there is no God, people are free and obliged to choose. There are no desperate situations in which no choice remains and the responsibility for deciding can be avoided. For me, having had it drummed into me that "the party will decide," it was vital to understand that I was responsible for my decisions and I could not blame circumstances.

By then, the model of rational choice had become the main conceptual framework of my thinking as an economist as well. A later chapter deals in detail with criticism of the theory. At this point, however, I want to emphasize one great virtue the model has. Its underlying structure suggests that there *is* a choice. When it is used for purposes of positive analysis, we must establish retrospectively, even against the facts, what possible but rejected alternatives we had in the past. When it is put to normative use, we must determine just what restrictions independent of ourselves are on our choices. There is freedom of choice within this restricted set of alternatives.

Let me try to sum up where I stood in my choices around 1959. Some people may switch to a new career in a single dramatic turn. It took me some five years, from 1954 to 1959, to work out how I wanted to live in the future. My basic decisions had been taking shape through a series of conscious deliberations and improvisations, intertwined with each other. At every moment the room for potential choices was narrowed by pressures from the outside world. There was choice available in each moment. Nevertheless—in retrospect—it could be stated that by 1959 some of my basic decisions had already emerged. I emphasize five of them here.

1. I would break with the Communist Party.

2. I would not emigrate.

3. My vocation would be research, not politics. I would not indulge in heroic, illegal forms of struggle against the Communist system. I wanted to contribute to renewal through my scholarly activity.

4. I would break with Marxism.

5. I would learn the basics of modern economics. I wanted my studies and researches to be part of the Western profession of economics.

I mentioned each of these decisions separately in earlier chapters, but this is where I would like to range them side by side and review my decisions overall. None is self-evident; none was predetermined. I could give countless examples of people around me—acquaintances and friends—who made a different choice regarding one or another or all of these five areas.

By 1959, these few decisions were no vague or loose clusters of intentions but a *conscious*, considered strategy in life. I spoke of these principles to those closest to me.

Forty-five years have passed since then. It is long enough for me to say that these five decisions held for the rest of my life. I do not claim that I have followed them all without exception in all instances. People are frail. But I certainly tried to keep to my strategy in life as far as possible. If I erred against one of my principles, I would reproach myself later. I attach great value to the moral imperative of being true to oneself.

The Economic Application of Mathematical Methods—1957–1968

Two-Level Planning

As I progressed with my studies, it became clear to me what an important part mathematics plays in modern economics. I would not be able to follow what I was reading without understanding the language of mathematics. I would have to study the application of mathematical methods if I wanted to do economic research that matched the standards of the period. An important part of that undertaking was the study of the application of mathematical methods, which required progressively altering my research profile.

Making the acquaintance of Tamás Lipták

My plans were made easier by my attraction to logical clarity. I always received top marks for mathematics and physics at school, and I began to refresh my knowledge of mathematics and to develop it further. I learned from books at home and I took various courses, concentrating on the sides of mathematics that economists were using most at the time: calculus (differential and integral) and linear algebra.

I would also have liked to use mathematical methods as a researcher. As part of the empirical work described in the previous chapter, on the post-1957 transformation in the methods of economic administration in light industry, I began to be interested in the role of enterprise profits. Western writers considered it self-evident that the motivation of the decision makers in a firm were linked to the firm's maximizing its profits. Well, attempts were made in Hungary after 1957 to give a profit incentive to managers, and even to all workers in light industrial enterprises. Various bonuses were attached to profits, but in a curious way. Profit distributions depended on whether profitability (as a proportion of sales) had improved over a specific level. Managers were encouraged to maximize (in mathematical terms) not an *absolute sum*—the enterprise's profits—but a *quotient*, the ratio between profits and sales. Although many thought that the two kinds of incentive came to the same thing, I saw that they would have different economic effects.

I began to formulate in mathematical form the two types of maximum criteria and the programming tasks associated with them. I cobbled together a model, but I was not satisfied with it. That is how far I had gotten when I spoke to András Bródy, a former colleague at the Institute of Economics, who was far ahead of me in applying mathematical methods to economics. He offered to introduce me to a young mathematician at the Institute of Mathematics of the Hungarian Academy of Sciences. Bródy was on good terms with its director, the world-famous mathematician Alfréd Rényi, and had done research with him. He had heard from Rényi of a pupil of his who was interested in economic applications: Tamás Lipták.

That is when I came to know Tamás. Our working relations became ever closer and were augmented by personal ties. It soon emerged that we shared political views as well. Let us not forget it was 1957. Members of the intelligentsia could not keep up an intimate friendship with anyone whom they had political cause to fear.

He was an implausibly thin young man (and remained thin later in life). He had a handsome face, a kind voice, and a bright way of speaking that won people over in seconds. His appearance was far from an advantage to him, but women adored him.

Lipták had an exceptional talent for mathematics. Perhaps it is no exaggeration to say he had genius. Not only did he make use of his huge accumulated knowledge with absolute certainty, but he could bring up unexpectedly some theorem or method he had previously read, just when it was needed. He was an original, innovative thinker.

I learned much from Lipták, who was my private tutor in mathematics for several years. Rather than following a methodical course, he would bring up a subject that was apposite at that juncture. He would recommend reading matter and give me help in following it. And apart from the knowledge I gained with his assistance, I learned a lot from him about how to address a problem. He never tried to hide what abstract assumptions a model was based on or what simplifications of reality it employed. On the contrary, he wanted to present the simplifications in the model with maximum intellectual sincerity.

Absolute precision was required. In his case, this admirable, scientifically justified aim was taken to extremes that may have been the first symptoms of his later mental problems. We were in the period before computers. Tamás wrote each work of his by hand, with calligraphic precision. If he found a little mistake on the twentieth page of a text full of equations, he would rather throw it out and start again than correct it. A manuscript had to be flawless!

I never attained his absolute level of precision, but I developed greatly in this respect owing to his example. Even now, if I notice that something in a text I am writing is not quite accurate, a vision of the Don Quixote of mathematical precision appears before me: Tamás would now jettison the text and start all over again.

I do not want to present an idealized picture of Lipták. That brilliant mind and infinitely kind man could sometimes be difficult to tolerate. I discipline myself to be utterly punctual and arrive wherever I go well before the time arranged. I am irritated, even annoyed if others are late.* I strive to keep to the agreed time and feel dreadful if I fail, or at least try to minimize my lateness. Tamás was my opposite in this respect. He would hardly ever turn up for our meetings on time and never met a deadline. Then he would give childish excuses for being late, missing a meeting, or omitting to do what he had agreed, or would fail to mention that he had been remiss. This difference in temperament caused friction on many occasions.

A mathematical investigation of profit sharing

Let us turn to the economic issue that prompted me to seek out Lipták in 1957. It soon emerged that the problem was hard to handle mathematically if accuracy was insisted on, rather than simplifying matters until the complications caused by reality disappeared. We had to analyze a specific type of nonlinear programming task. We went at it repeatedly. The chapters of the study were written in a dozen versions, each after protracted head-scratching and numerous joint sessions of many hours. Finally, a text of some 250 pages was ready and seemed acceptable to us both.

Then our work was broken off. Tamás was arrested. He had cooperated as a volunteer in an action covered at length in the previous chapter. Sándor Fekete's Hungaricus study, whose journey abroad I had aided, was previously distributed in duplicated form in intellectual circles in Hungary. Tamás had helped by working the duplicator. We had not yet known each other when we both did our bit in that action. Later, as we began our struggle on the scholarly and not the political front, this political past was something that we found we shared. Tamás's arrest did not come as a surprise to us.

He was well down on the list of the accused. He spent about a year in pretrial detention and then in prison. Once, I wrote out a couple of mathematical problems having to do with our joint research and gave them to his wife, Manyi, to see if she could hand them over to Tamás, for him to think about in his cell. I did not think the problems themselves were urgent, but I thought they might help Tamás,

---

* I was still a beginning journalist when Ernő Gerő, the "czar" of economic policy in the Communist Party, summoned me to his office at a specific time. I waited for a while and then told the secretary in an irritated tone that twenty minutes had gone by since the time set for the appointment and I was off. People could hardly fathom my audacity. Gerő, however, seems to have been impressed by my insistence on the time we had arranged and made no remark on the unusual step I had taken.

by diverting his attention from prison life.* Poor Tamás, far from thinking of mathematical or economics problems, attempted suicide. It was a catastrophic sign of depression, which would overcome him later. Luckily, his life was saved.

Tamás was still in prison when I was dismissed from the Institute of Economics. I sought help from the Ministry of Light Industry in publishing our book-length manuscript. The ministry was prepared to shoulder the printing costs, but insisted the name of the imprisoned Tamás Lipták could not appear on it. I sought the advice of Alfréd Rényi, Tamás's superior and fatherly friend, and agreed with him that the formula "With the cooperation of the Institute of Mathematics of the Hungarian Academy of Sciences" should appear on the title page instead of Tamás's name. In the end, the study came out in 1959 as a book with a primitive appearance, using duplication.[1]

The bibliography included, apart from empirical works on Hungarian light industry, a few Western works of economics that I had been studying at the time. Chapter 5, for instance, cited Erich Schneider and Jan Tinbergen. There does not seem anything strange in that today, but in Hungary in 1957, it was not usual to allow the names of "bourgeois" economists a positive ring.

Once Tamás was out of prison, we decided to publish our results in the West. We prepared an article of journal length in English.† Tamás was in his element. I had just started to get to know the style and formal requirements of mathematical and economics journals in the West, but Tamás had been reading them for some years.

---

* The idea was not completely stupid. It turned out later that some of the 1956 convicts learned foreign languages and did translations or were writers and tried to compose literary works.

† The Hungarian text was translated, as "A Mathematical Investigation of Some Economic Effects of Profit Sharing in Socialist Firms," by (Baron) József Hatvany, whose earlier life deserves a whole novel, not just a footnote. A member of the extremely wealthy, celebrated Hatvany family, he was a nephew of Lajos Hatvany, one of those who had discovered the superlative poets Endre Ady and Attila József; his uncle gave generous support to these two literary giants and many other writers and was an enthusiastic organizing force in Hungarian literature.

József Hatvany had read physics at Cambridge and learned to speak and write English like a native. He had become a Communist in England, and after the war, he felt obliged to return to socialist Hungary, only to be imprisoned as an ostensible British spy. For what else, it was argued, could have induced this enthusiastic young Communist to leave the comforts of academic life in England and a rich, noble family to return home? He was among those released in 1954, but imprisoned again after 1956. After his second release, he earned his living as a translator for a time, seeking worthwhile work that would interest him as well as earn him money. That is how I came to ask him to translate several works of mine. Hatvany later went back to academic life and became one of the intellectual forces behind computer technology research in Hungary, gaining international fame and appreciation in that field.

The *content* of the article was our joint intellectual product, but its mathematical precision and its Western structure and style were all to Tamás's credit.

At this time and for a long time afterward, no writer of a scientific or scholarly work was supposed to send it to the West without first obtaining permission. The usual procedure was for the researcher, who in most cases would be an employee of a research institute or a university, to present the article to his or her official superior. It would then be passed to that person's superior. If it was politically problematic, it would be sent to the party headquarters as well.* The decision would then be made at one level or another whether it could be submitted for publication in the West.

Lipták and I decided not to apply for any such permit. We simply put the article in an envelope and mailed it. Those who had been accused, among other things, of sending the work of a Hungarian writer (Sándor Fekete) abroad illegally were still in prison at the time. Both Lipták and I were embroiled in that affair. Even if the article we were now sending was free of politics, we were doing something illegal. We both felt it was important *not* to submit ourselves to a prescribed official procedure. For me, the move was a precedent that I followed thereafter with all my publications abroad. I did not ask for my superiors' permission but simply sent the work straight to a journal or publisher. In this, I did something different from many colleagues in Hungary and other socialist countries, who later complained they had not received authorization to publish abroad. I followed the example of Hašek's Good Soldier Švejk under the Austro-Hungarian Empire: do not ask, for if you do, the answer is going to be no.

We submitted our article to *Econometrica*, the leading journal of mathematical economics. Several years later, I heard that it had come into the hands of Edmond Malinvaud, the journal's French co-editor, who immediately accepted it without changing a word or a comma.† It appeared in January 1962.[2]

The article dealt with a very specific problem, since it analyzed incentives for firms that were used exclusively in Hungary. It underlined that we were examining a *socialist* economy. Even posing the question was an intellectual challenge:

---

* I have a book containing politically sensitive statements going through the publication process in China as I write (in 2004 and 2005). The first publisher to accept it found the work problematic and sent it to Chinese party headquarters for approval. Publication was not permitted the first time. A second publisher has taken up the task, and permission has been refused again.

† Much later, when I became familiar with the editing and reviewing practices of leading Western journals—such as rejecting most manuscripts and sending others back for repeated revision—I appreciated better what a tribute that immediate acceptance without changes had been.

• The incentive is not determined in advance. Rather than arising naturally or spontaneously out of property relations or institutional conditions, it is decided on a case-by-case basis. This approach was in fact a forerunner of a later line of research—the major body of literature on incentives and the relation between principal and agent.

• The prices are not determined in advance either. Rather than their being set by the market, there is central price control. The article analyzes the rich system of relations between enterprise incentives and prices on the one hand and quantity and composition of production on the other. Which incentive leads to production that is under or over capacity? In which direction does it push the range of output?

I often used to hear Eastern European economists say that they have not published in Western journals because the editors were not interested in their economy. My experience was the opposite, with that study in *Econometrica* and with my later publications. They attracted interest *precisely because* they had been written by an author living in a socialist country and were reporting on a world distant from that of the editors—but in their idiom, the language of modern economics.

Programming of the textile industry

Tamás Lipták and I had done a *theoretical* analysis. Concurrently with that, I had undertaken research in another direction. I wanted to apply mathematical methods to the purposes of economic planning. Here the goal was not theoretical findings but computations from factual quantitative data reflecting the real economy, used to prepare for making real decisions. In other words, *applied* economics.

I immersed myself in the literature. I had to learn and digest the contiguous, overlapping parts of the accumulated knowledge of microeconomics, decision theory, operations research, and cost-benefit analysis to discover how they could be applied to the conditions of a centralized socialist economy. The mathematical apparatus for the computations was supplied by *linear programming*. I learned the conceptual system of this method, the structure of the linear programming model, and the techniques of thinking that enabled problems of practical choice to be translated into its language.

One work that had a big influence on me at this time was *Linear Programming and Activity Analysis* by Robert Dorfman, Paul Samuelson, and Robert Solow. This text and *Three Essays* by T. C. Koopmans helped me greatly in understanding how the relations I knew from microeconomics were reflected in linear programming. After a while, I felt conversant with two types of thinking: theoretical microeconomics and the practice of numerical decision-preparing computations.*

---

* It was a great experience to later meet these four heroes of my period as a novice researcher and become friendly with them.

My first linear programming model sought to answer the following question. Planners faced several alternative courses of technical development in the cotton industry. They could conserve the existing technological conditions, carry out a modest amount of technical development at relatively small cost, or increase productivity more rapidly through greater expenditure on investment and costlier imports. The computations did not intend to offer a single, simple answer. They were meant to show how the best choice depended numerically on various factors, such as the interest rate, the exchange rate, and future export and import prices.

Planners, technical people, foreign traders, and computer experts in light industry took part in the work, inspired by the novelty of the approach. The electronic computer was going through its pioneering period in Hungary at the time. We were behind the West in that field as well. It was a thrill simply to see our first computer, still operating with vacuum tubes and taking up a whole room. That huge contraption operated by the Computing Center of the Hungarian Academy of Sciences had a tiny fraction of the power of a present-day laptop.

An enthusiastic team of mathematicians and engineers worked for weeks on solving a system of twenty-four equations with the machine.* (These days, models a hundred times that size can be easily solved in seconds.) We rejoiced in the knowledge that we were pioneers on two promising trails at once: linear programming and the practical economic application in Hungary of electronic computers.

Thought-provoking cooperation and rivalry grew up between two groups applying mathematical methods: those employing linear programming and those engaged in the input-output analysis devised by Wassily Leontief, a Russian-born U.S. economist. The latter approach, pioneered by András Bródy and later Mária Augusztinovics, had many advantages. These leading figures had begun earlier, so they were conversant with the literature on input-output analysis at a time when I was just beginning to inquire into linear programming. The Central Statistical Office invested great resources into compiling large input-output tables based on statistical surveys. These data gave a strong empirical background to the calculations. The parameters of our linear programming models were based mainly on the estimates of experts—in other words, on intuitive feelings about the true numbers representing reality.

We talked and argued a lot about the two approaches, at private meetings and later at conferences as well. I was induced mainly by theoretical considerations to stick with the programming approach. I saw a *deterministic* philosophy behind input-output analysis. If the vector of final use is given (and planners tried hard to present it as such), then the production and all input-output combinations compatible with this vector are given as well. Linear programming, on the other hand,

---

* More precisely, what appear in linear programming are inequalities—that is, upper and lower constraints on the decisions.

suggests the possibility of choice. I have spoken already about the importance this had for the new view of the world that had been forming inside of me.

András Bródy gave a masterly demonstration of how, using Leontief models, one might describe the famous "reproduction schemes" in the second volume of Marx's *Capital*.[3] Marx devotes a central part of his work to *average* production cost and *average* profit, and this emphasis fits in well with input-output analysis, because each coefficient is designed to represent just such a social average. I then recognized (as I do now) the pioneering part Marx played in what Marxists call *analysis of reproduction*; economists in our time, *dynamic models*. Nonetheless, its compatibility with Marxist political economy did not attract me to input-output analysis. Instead, it left me with doubts. I saw correctly that something was being lost here: the choice about technology, the decision. I sympathized with neoclassical economics, to which linear programming was akin. (See the book I mentioned by Dorfman, Samuelson, and Solow.) The "marginal" categories that play an important part in Western theory (marginal cost, marginal rate of substitution, marginal revenue, marginal product, etc.) cannot be calculated by input-output analysis, while linear programming produces these indicators automatically.*

There appeared to be two "empty" mathematical frameworks opposing each other, two mathematical methods free of politics or ideology. But the levels of theoretical disagreement lent a particular coloring to this debate. Though unspoken, intruding into the intellectual background of the debate was the question of whether Marxism should be renewed through modern mathematical techniques of thinking or—as was my strong personal conviction—should be abandoned.

Two-level planning

The programming for the cotton industry, which was successful and won professional acclaim, was followed by computations for other sectors of industry. I then asked myself whether these sectoral data could not be linked. My real interest had long been in the country's comprehensive economic problems. How could linear programming be applied to planning for the whole economy?

Writing the whole economy into a single model in the same degree of detail as the sectoral models would call for a system of equations twenty or even fifty times as extensive. Such an undertaking was precluded by the primitive state of computing

---

* In each case we talk about the first derivative of a variable: that is, about a differential magnitude. Here is a somewhat simplified example: if we increase production by one unit, how much do the costs increase? That is the meaning of "marginal costs." Or another example: if the available resource increases by one unit, how much does the return increase? That is the meaning of "marginal return."

at the time. So the idea arose of breaking the single large-sized economic model into smaller parts. By systematically harmonizing these partial computations with each other, we could arrive at the "great" common solution. So-called decomposition algorithms of linear programming designed to do this task had already been published. This was the field in which to look for the appropriate procedure.

I thought about how the National Planning Office worked. First it prepared economy-wide targets and then broke them down by sector. These breakdowns were passed to the ministries directing the sectors, where the Planning Office figures were studied. Then began negotiations with the central planners, who might modify the sector targets. A national plan and a breakdown by sector were agreed on after repeated bargaining.

Finally, there was a third inspiration, found in Samuelson's theoretical work.[4] Even if at any one time transactions in a certain product were carried out at several different prices, *equalization of prices* occurred by the time the market reached an optimal state of equilibrium. One product—one price.

These ideas led me to the basic notion for an algorithm of two-level planning. I began outlining a model. The center would allocate quantities (input quotas and output targets) for the sectors, which would devise optimal plans to satisfy the center's demands—as we had done so far with our sectoral linear programming—and then report back shadow prices for their resources and targets.* This was a kind of economic efficiency report. The center would apply the price equalization principle to perform the allocation again, withdrawing resources from places where the marginal return was lower and transferring them to where the marginal return would be greater. The production requirements would be reallocated similarly. The sectors would do their computations again, and the process would be repeated until the optimum allocation was approached.

The idea was there, but I could not express it precisely. I could only point to an analogy: if Samuelson could prove his factor-price equalization theorem, then the reallocation rule just outlined should lead to equilibrium and an optimal solution as well. But pointing to an analogy is not enough. A proposition has to be *proved*, and that was beyond me.

What I could not do, Tamás Lipták could. He had the brilliant idea of expressing the problem as a game theory model—in 1963, many years before game theory had its great renaissance in economics. One player is the center and the other the ensemble of sectors. This formulation yields a rigorous mathematical proposition

---

* Actual prices are determined by the market. Shadow prices are artificially calculated and used for certain analyses, e.g., a cost-benefit analysis of investment projects, and there are different approaches to calculating them. A linear programming computation automatically generates a set of shadow prices.

proving that the procedure just outlined will tend to converge to the optimal solution.

The study "Two-Level Planning" was completed.[5] The basic *economic* ideas in the model and the computation algorithm came from me, and I interpreted the mathematical model and algorithm. Credit for the imposing precision and elegance of the description goes to Tamás Lipták. And he came up with the trick (reformulating the task as a game theory problem) that rendered this difficult problem amenable to mathematical treatment and our suppositions susceptible to proof.

We turned to *Econometrica* again with similar results: the paper was accepted immediately without alteration and published in 1965.[6] It almost instantly made its authors' names known in the world of mathematical economics. It was cited several hundred times, translated into many languages, and incorporated into university syllabuses. In 1971, when Arrow compiled a volume of the most important and most influential twenty-two theoretical studies ever published in *Econometrica*,[7] he included our paper "Two-Level Planning."

The article linked two aims of mine. I wanted to turn from branch-level models to programming on a national level, with an algorithm that allowed sectoral models to be combined. I will return shortly to that intention and its implementation, but first I have to say a few words about my other purpose: a *theoretical* examination of central planning.

An idealized model of central planning

Two-level planning could be seen as an idealized model of central planning. It showed a procedure by which central and sectoral planners, by their common efforts, could arrive at a plan that could satisfy the following requirements:

• The sector plans would fit accurately into the compass of the central plan. There was full accord between the central plan and the sectoral plans.

• The plan was feasible: it fitted the resource constraints at the national and at the sectoral level.

• The plan was the very best of the feasible versions. It best satisfied the objective set by the center.

• The plan was not just imposed from the center. It did not require that the center possess all information. It rested largely on the decentralized accumulation of information (at the sectoral level, in our model).

Western mathematical economists were enthusiastic about the theoretical model of two-level planning because it provided neat and clear opposition to the model of Oskar Lange discussed in the previous chapter. Though Lange had not used a mathematical model to present his ideas, they were later transformed into mathematical terms, the theoretical construction coming from the great French economist Edmond Malinvaud.[8] His model, like ours, had an upper level and a lower—in his case, the center and the firms. But the flow of economic information in the Lange–Malinvaud model* was the reverse of the flows in the Kornai–Lipták model. In the former, central prices were set to which the firms adjusted, reporting the quantities of output and inputs back to the center. Drawing on those reports, the center established where there was excess demand or supply and therefore where and in what direction the prices had to be centrally adjusted. That was the idealized picture of market socialism. In our case, the flows were switched. Flowing from top to bottom was not price information but quantitative information: resource quotas and production targets. Here reports on the economic efficiency in the use of resources and the output tasks assigned to the sectors flowed upward. That was the idealized picture of central planning.

The comparison can be taken further. The Kornai–Lipták model features "perfect planning." The contrast here is with the "perfect market" of the Walrasian model, the general equilibrium theory. The former confirms the theoretical possibility of a system in which full centralization works perfectly, while the latter shows the opposite: a theoretically conceivable system in which full decentralization works perfectly.

Let me add a few notes to what has already been said. I am not describing here what I thought when the study was completed, but what I think now, in 2004 and 2005. I am not trying here to use a relative measure to gauge what this achievement by two Eastern European researchers isolated from the world meant. What I would like to establish is whether our articles have a *theoretical message of lasting validity*.

I think they have. The great strength of mathematical modeling lies precisely in its being able to clarify *under what conditions* the derived statements hold. Those who know how to correctly interpret a theoretical work of mathematical economics will be able to think far more clearly about those assumptions.

The algorithm of two-level planning operates under (and only under) the following conditions:

1. The central planners in the model have clear, explicit goals. (These goals are expressed by the objective function.) The actual situation in the socialist economy is different. The central leadership is not consistent, modifies its policies unexpectedly, improvises, moves forward and then back, hesitates, and suffers from internal

---

* Lipták and I had not encountered Malinvaud's model when we were working on the model of two-level planning. When Malinvaud received our manuscript, as an editor of *Econometrica*, he acted with enthusiasm and commitment in helping us to publish it. He took every later opportunity to assist me in my work as well.

conflicts. Its economic policy fails to consistently reconcile its various aims. It is unable to give relative weights to them and does not attempt to do so.

2. The sectors in the model have no distinct purposes of their own. They subordinate their aims to the central goals. In reality, all actors at all levels of the hierarchy in a socialist economy have their own interests that they want to promote.

3. In the model a plan can qualify for acceptance only if it satisfies various upper and lower constraints reflecting the actual conditions. In real life, unrealistic (usually overly ambitious) plans are adopted despite the knowledge that they will come up against various constraints.

4. All the information in the model is accurate, whether it is flowing upward or downward. The reality of the socialist economy is that all items of information are uncertain. Moreover, economic actors lie to further their own interests, distorting their figures upward or downward depending on which inaccuracy favors their position.

5. There is perfect discipline in the model. Central figures go out on time and sectoral responses come back on time and in the same rhythm. In fact, lateness and unreliability are rife in the socialist economy—it has people working in it, not machines.

6. The planning apparatus in the model is patient, as repeated iterative adjustments take place between center and sectors in order to approach the optimal solution. In the real socialist system, plans are drawn up under deadline pressure. Even if there were a desire to repeatedly correct the target figures, there would not be time to do so.

So the following line of argument has to be followed:

First, understand the proposition in the theoretical model: central planning operates perfectly if . . .

Second, consider these "ifs" thoroughly and compare the theoretical assumptions with reality.

Third, establish that the conditions are not fulfilled. Indeed, it is *impossible* for them to be fulfilled.

Fourth and last, draw the conclusions from the previous observations. It is impossible for central planning to work perfectly.

One purpose of the theoretical model is to provide a way of following this line of thought strictly. In that respect, the model of two-level planning remains a valid and useful intellectual tool to this day.

It is worth adding a personal comment. It will become clear in later chapters that in a later period, I became very critical of neoclassical thinking and its theoretical kernel, Walrasian equilibrium theory. One of the factors reinforcing my criticism of mainstream economic thought was precisely the line of argument I have just presented: the verification of the model's assumptions and their comparison with reality. But at the time we were designing the model of two-level planning, that critical stance was not yet present in me at all—it was then that my identification with the neoclassical mainstream was most complete. Its intellectual leaders could rightly feel we were on the same wavelength. That intellectual sympathy enhanced their interest in my work and in me personally.

Programming the national economy: Some initial principles

Tamás was interested mainly in theoretical aspects when we were writing the study on two-level planning. He as a mathematician was drawn to the challenge of formulating the problem, while I was equally concerned about the application of the theoretical analysis in practice.

It had to be clarified what should be the relation between official plans compiled in the National Planning Office and the ministries and a plan devised by researchers with the aid of the mathematical model. The mainstream of economic theory suggested that researchers should formulate a "welfare function" designed to express the common interests of society. This would serve as the model's objective function. A plan would be optimal if it maximized the welfare of the members of society while observing the constraints describing objective conditions. Enlightened research economists will tread carefully in determining and interpreting the welfare function. They will interpret it according to their preconceptions of what welfare is, bearing in mind material and nonmaterial (cultural, strategic, geopolitical) aspects. They also consider the welfare not only of the present but of future generations. Once such a welfare function is obtained, mathematical planners can make their calculations and submit the plan with the comment that *this* is the optimal plan for political decision makers to accept, not the one fashioned by the planning staff using traditional methods.*

Faced with this task, I wanted to take a different approach. I was motivated by a number of factors when I drew up the initial principles for my research.

I was influenced by tactical considerations. I did not want planners to see those working with models and computers as rivals who were out to replace them. I wanted amicable cooperation between the nonmathematical (traditional) and the mathematical planners. That was achieved, for the most part. The heads of

---

* In our debates, the idea arose that mathematical planners should question top economic policy makers on their preferences, which would then be expressed in the objective function of the model. Thus the model would reflect judgments of politicians, not the public's wishes.

long-term planning at the National Planning Office, István Hetényi in particular, showed great interest in our work and supported it.*

I had strong theoretical objections as well. I could not accept either then or later that a single aggregate all-encompassing welfare function can be determined. In other words, there is no way of establishing unambiguously what the presumed interests of society are. Society is not a homogeneous unit. Groups and individuals differ strongly in what they see as their interest, how they define welfare, how they want costs and benefits to be distributed between present and future generations, and so on. Conflicts of interest are decided in the political arena, where the decisions on the budget, economic legislation, and economic plans are made. A mathematical economist cannot undertake to make such decisions. I expressed this objection in print as well.[†]

When raising theoretical doubts about the welfare function in the 1960s, I was quite unaware of seminal work then under way; the most significant and fertile idea emerging from these studies was put forward by Kenneth Arrow in his famous "Impossibility Theory,"[9] which has since developed into an important and successful research trend.[‡] It is possible to prove rigorously the following statement: There is no democratic decision-making procedure that can unite distinctly different, individual preferences into a common welfare function.[§] Having studied the relevant literature, I was reassured that I had been right in rejecting the idea of determining a single quantitative "optimum criterion of socialist economy," which supposedly expressed the interests of society.

---

* Readers may wonder why I cooperated so readily with the National Planning Office while I refused to become involved in the "reform committees" set up by the party. I will return to this question in the discussion of the 1968 reform in chapter 15.

† Professor Tinbergen also joined in the debate, agreeing with Abram Bergson and Ragnar Frisch that it would be possible and desirable to devise a "welfare function." It was a great honor for me that Tinbergen mentioned the debate between us in his acceptance speech for the Nobel Prize, proposing "that both East and West try to specify their social welfare function so as to see whether the ultimate aims are very different or not" (1981 [1969], p. 21). This proposal of Tinbergen's shows his deeply felt desire for peaceful coexistence and cooperation, and it reveals as well that his good intentions were unfortunately joined with political naiveté.

‡ The work of Amartya Sen (1997 [1982]) has played an outstanding role in expanding and broadening the theory of social choice. I happened to be fortunate enough, two decades after the events described here, to have Amartya Sen as a colleague and friend at Harvard University. We had frequent opportunities to discuss the problems of social choice.

§ As early as the 1940s, a debate had developed between economic theorists about the interpretation of the welfare function, examining among others the approach applied by Abram Bergson and Paul Samuelson. To clarify how the various theoretical constructs compare with each other is beyond the scope of this memoir.

Connected with that rejection were political and ideological considerations as well. These I thought through carefully, although I did not publish them. I had to accept that like it or not, the fundamental decisions under a regime such as Hungary's are made at the top of the party hierarchy. The planners in the National Planning Office and the ministries then adjust to these. Their sense of duty may induce them to say a cautious word, if the basic targets dictated to them appear unrealistic, but ultimately they can only follow their orders.

Surrounded by planners using traditional methods, I began to make plan computations using mathematical tools. I wanted to do so while maintaining a distance from the decision makers. Instead of beginning to argue with them about what welfare function to employ, we used a simple formula. Taking the "official" plan as *given*, we prescribed its quantitative data as constraints of our model. We would then assign as the objective function an indicator whose improvement would be indisputably useful. In our case, this could, for instance, be an improvement in the current account balance in convertible currency. The model would provide a plan that produced everything the plan devised by traditional methods would do, and then—as *a bonus*—leave Hungary less indebted than before. The planners, irrespective of the mathematical programmers, could elaborate a plan for the country. We would take cognizance of it and then try to further improve the country's economic situation relative to it. However one viewed the political conditions and the future, all could agree it was pure gain for the country to be less indebted.*

The idea of using mathematical methods for planning also arose in the Soviet Union in those years. Leonid V. Kantorovich, who discovered and elaborated the mathematical foundation of linear programming, was the leading intellect in a group in Moscow and Novosibirsk working on plan models. The rhetoric of the Soviet school differed sharply from what I was recommending in Budapest. They claimed to be able to supply "optimal plans," which sounded to me like a false promise likely to mislead and foster illusions.

I repeatedly disputed this view, which had its followers in Hungary as well. I stayed with a much more modest undertaking: that our computations, all being well, would lead to recommendations that could bring a tangible improvement over the official plan being prepared.

I never toyed for a moment with applying linear programming to the operative planning of the economy—that is, to support the elaboration of annual economic

---

* We used various types of objective function in our calculations, such as maximizing personal consumption—while fulfilling the other targets of the official plan. These translated into several plan variants that increased choice. Again, we were trying to contribute to overcoming the dogma that only one plan was possible and that only one path could and had to be followed.

plans. To me, day-to-day coordination of production and consumption was clearly a task for the market, not for a mathematical model. I wanted to contribute only to medium- and long-term planning. Already the programming projects at the sectoral level had dealt with choosing between investment alternatives, and I wanted to continue that trend on a national level.

The computations

It is worth saying a few words on the practical application of our ideas.

The merciless repression after 1956 was beginning to ease at that time, in 1962–1963. My imprisoned friends had benefited from a general amnesty, and there were signs I was going to be brought out of my light industry exile as well: During my research into the textile industry, I cooperated with those running Hungary's first computer, the staff of the Computing Center of the Hungarian Academy of Sciences, and they invited me to go and work there. I was delighted to accept.

I also had working relations with the Institute of Economic Planning of the National Planning Office, which agreed to pioneer the application of mathematical modeling to planning.* Programming for national-level economic planning began with several colleagues actively involved there and strong support from some directors in the office.

---

* The heads of the Institute of Economic Planning wanted me to work there full-time, but the idea ran up against a veto from the personnel officer at the National Planning Office. Now that I am able to look into the contemporary police documents, I can reconstruct what had happened before that veto. The personnel department at the National Planning Office made inquiries of the personnel officers at my previous workplaces. My two workplaces in light industry did not wish to stand in my way and gave fairly neutral opinions. The assessment from the Institute of Economics of the Hungarian Academy of Sciences was a *comme ci, comme ça*—highlighting my professional merits, but not hiding my involvement in 1956 and its aftermath—and stated clearly that I had been dismissed on political grounds. That information gave the National Planning Office little encouragement to employ me. They also contacted the Interior Ministry for an assessment. The Interior Ministry's III/III department (interior intelligence) and III/II department (foreign intelligence) consulted each other at the level of police colonel. They looked into my files and established that "the above-named appears in our records for his activities during the counterrevolution" (ÁBTL V-145-288-a, pp. 502–505. The instruction to the III/III department to launch an investigation is dated December 27, 1962). Clearly, it was the Interior Ministry's refusal of permission that prompted the National Planning Office to change its mind about employing me in their own institute. Kornai's return under the aegis of the Hungarian Academy of Sciences was one thing, but for him to join the National Planning Office would be going too far. This incident exemplifies well the parallel dimensions of my life. The visible dimension was the effort I put into researching the mathematical methods of planning. The invisible was the network of personnel departments and political police, shadowing me and interfering in my life.

We began compiling a network of models according to the structure described in the Kornai–Lipták study: a central model and (for the first experimental calculations) eighteen sector models. To build each of the sector models, I recruited several economists from various central and sectoral institutes and ministries. Meanwhile I assembled a core team of a few people who would work on the computations full-time and others to help with advice or specific problems. At the height of the work, we had a little army of 150 to 200 staff members enthusiastically engaged in compiling the model, gathering data, and making computations. Many of these "two-level planning" people were near the start of their careers when they joined but later made a name for themselves as economic policy makers, leading executives, or research economists (Gusztáv Báger, Pál Benedek, Anna Jónás, András Nagy, Ferenc Rabár, Judit Rimler, György Simon, József Sivák, Márton Tardos, and many others). It was a team of first-class minds.

It was also essential to get funding. I went to several government offices seeking financial support for the sector modelers. A series of pamphlets was prepared for the people and organizations involved—the leading officials supporting the project and others who showed interest. Some of these gave detailed instructions on how to construct the models and on what computations to do, or provided theoretical explanations. Others reported the findings. Most of the pamphlets I wrote myself. During the project I turned out no less than 2,000 pages of writing, for distribution in duplicated form to Hungarian economists.

The work's first phase, which I directed, started in 1963 and took five years.* Most of the sectoral computations were done and some notable results obtained. We struggled a lot with the central computations. It turned out that given the computers of the time, the Kornai–Lipták algorithm was very slow and called for too many calculations. Elegant though it was, it was not efficient enough and had to be replaced by much cruder, less exact methods.

In the meantime, we put together another, smaller-scale, aggregate economy-wide planning model and used it for a number of calculations. The idea was that as the computations of the large two-level model would take a long time, we should at least have a small-scale model to prove to the planners that linear programming was useful.†

---

* The last duplicated bulletin on programming the economy appeared in 1968 and gave the final results of the calculations. I did not take part directly after the first experimental programming was concluded. The project was taken on by other economists and former colleagues of mine.

† Zsuzsa Dániel (then Zsuzsa Újlaki and later my second wife) and I developed a model together and published our results in a joint paper. It was then that we formed a close relationship. Even if the years I devoted to mathematical planning had had no other reward, they were well worth it for that single reason.

As years passed and successive new obstacles appeared in data collection and computer processing, the initial enthusiasm died down. A once-spirited team began to dwindle and tire. Some felt they should not leave the project in the lurch and should see it through to some conclusion, but the ultimate results of the computations had no impressive and decisive presentation. We could not and did not say that here we have finally arrived at a national economic plan that is scientifically confirmed by a mathematical model and is based on computer calculations.

Emotions became complex toward the end of the project, a mixture of feelings of success and of failure at the same time. The team working on the project never got together to assess their experiences. Some of the results of the vast project were simply published by people in their own studies. I wrote several articles, too. Some of my observations and conclusions were incorporated into my book *Mathematical Planning of Structural Decisions*, the second edition of which included a detailed report on the model for national economic programming, the computations made, and some economic lessons to be drawn from them.*

Was it worth it?

How can I assess today that gigantic undertaking, which demanded huge amounts of time and labor from me and from my colleagues on the project? Let me compare, item by item, what I had expected of it when I began and how far my expectations were met. This analysis is concerned mainly with modeling on the national economic plan, but some of what I say refers to other research projects dealing with mathematical planning as well.

One expectation concerned the political environment around me. I described at the end of the previous chapter my feeling toward the end of the 1950s that the empirical research program I had started with *Overcentralization* had reached a blind alley.

If further explorations led (as they would have) to strong criticism of the existing regime of economic administration, it would have been impossible to publish them. Applying mathematical methods seemed to resolve the quandary. Mathematical language was incomprehensible to commissars, party officials, and all who kept watch on institutes, publishers, and journals. Having seen a few equations in a manuscript, they put it down with a shiver. So the language itself gave some cover from the sharp eyes of politicians and the *polgazdosok*, the political economy vigilantes who

---

* The second, enlarged edition appeared in 1972 in Hungarian and 1975 in English. If the additions made there are seen as part of the research into national economic planning, the task took up most of my time for about a decade.

assisted and advised them. Mathematical formalism gave an impression of political neutrality—rightly, to some extent, as a formula, equation, or geometrical figure has no inherent party allegiance. The field thus promised to be a quieter one, relatively speaking.

That expectation was met. No one ever objected on political grounds to research of mine that used mathematical methods. I can say that watchful as the commissars were, I outwitted them with this choice of subject. That success is still gratifying today.

I thought that the application of mathematical methods in my research would advance my self-education and increase my grasp of modern economics. That expectation was met to the full as well.

I imagined that I would be able not only to learn during these tasks but also teach. In that respect, events exceeded all my expectations. I was excluded from university teaching; formally, I was not licensed to have pupils. But in the course of directing the great research team (much greater than envisaged beforehand), I was able to teach after all. Not in a formal teacher–student relationship, of course, for some of my colleagues were the same age or older than I, and I was not officially their superior. They all accepted voluntarily that I would direct their work within the framework of the project. I am sure there were many ideas that I conveyed to them, and they, like me, found that economic programming helped them to explore and grasp modern microeconomics.

The application of mathematical methods in economic calculations and research did not remain, in the strict sense, a "methodological" effort. It developed into a real intellectual movement. In that rather special movement, we "two-levelers" formed one faction, but other groups emerged as well, such as the "input-outputters," the econometricians, and the operations researchers. They often overlapped. What we had in common was estrangement from the blind alley of the so-called political economy of the 1950s, a determination to be exact, and an intention to study and adopt the results of modern (Western) economics. We would organize conferences. A few of us got together to set up the Section of Mathematical Economics of the Hungarian Economic Association.*

* By that time, I was acquainted with the statutes of the Econometric Society; accordingly, I suggested that instead of having a permanent chairman, we should elect a new one every year. And so it happened, but only in our section. The first chairmen, including myself, served only a year each. But the procedure, based on rotation and election by members, irritated our superior authority, the heads of the Hungarian Economic Association. The chairmanship there was, so to speak, a position for life. The chairman could hold onto the position as long as the higher political authorities allowed. A few years later, the Section of Mathematical Economics was obliged to follow suit.

I have already explained emphatically my conscious desire to become part of the Western economists' profession. In this respect, events far exceeded my expectations. I felt increasingly, as time went on, that I had joined a strong Western current of thinking. This was the time when institutions for national economic planning were being established in France, the Netherlands, several Scandinavian countries, and elsewhere in the developed world, and they all were using mathematical models. Economists specializing in developing countries were devising planning models for India, Mexico, and Turkey, in conjunction with local economists. India established a state planning commission, in which mathematical economists exerted great influence.

The plan modeling undertaken in Hungary attracted keen interest from Western colleagues. It was not just a question of the Lange–Malinvaud and Kornai–Lipták models being compared theoretically. Practitioners also compared the structures of the computational models as well as data collection and model application promoted by French, Dutch, and Indian state planning institutions with what was going on in Hungary, with the assistance of the National Planning Office. Our work gained esteem abroad and was seen as a significant intellectual achievement.

It has to be asked, when comparing expectations with accomplishments, whether the methodology we introduced found its way into the practice of planning. Here the answer is less clear. On the one hand, the methods—the earlier input-output computations and the technique of linear programming—were adopted by the National Planning Office and the ministries. They charged departments and smaller groups with applying these methods and regularly submitting results of their computations to the planning apparatus, where officials presumably thought about them. But I cannot say to what extent these results were accepted.*

On the other hand, my impression—while I was able to observe the situation from the inside—was that mathematical planning remained alien to the bureaucratic organism of traditional planning and was not really built into it. Several senior people in the National Planning Office and ministries sympathized with our work. It had a certain aura, giving the impression that planning had been made scientific and modern, because it used mathematics and an electronic computer. So what was the problem?

All the problems concerned the six questions that I discussed earlier in connection with the *theoretical* model of two-level planning. Not only did the theoretical model

---

* My work took a different turn at the end of the 1960s, and I had little direct experience of later decades in state planning. The methodology may have been used more extensively than I suggest. Furthermore, the spread and increasing power of personal computers may have strengthened the role of mathematical planning. No definitive assessment can be made, as the apparatus of central planning was dispersed after the change of system in 1989.

differ in essential respects from practice, but the *application* of the model did not match the actual daily practice of real socialist planning. If planning were to be based on the mathematical model, then it would be essential to address the following problems:

1. Economic policy intentions have to be plainly stated and the planning begun over each time those intentions and objectives changed, but what politicians are prepared to do this? Politicians favor ambiguity. They do not care if there are contradictions in their declared aims. They like to express themselves in generalities. They are not prepared to give in numerical form the relative weights of policy endeavors and intentions stated at the same time, to establish an order of priorities—that is, to give all the information that appears in quantified form in the objective function of a programming model. They shrink from doing so because such numbers could be grounds for calling them to account later.

2. When we gathered the material for national economic programming and presented interim results, we found that everybody and every organization received them differently. If our calculations happened to support what they wanted to do in any case, they gave them a warm welcome. If they did not, they would wince, saying (rightly) that the model simplified reality, neglected this and that, rested on uncertain data (again rightly), and so on.

3. It was often hard to make economic policy makers and their planners understand that they had to distinguish the goal—the direction of policy-making intentions—from the constraints, which placed limits on their decisions. As mentioned in point 1, politicians dealing with economics do not like saying whether growth is more important than curbing inflation or vice versa. They prefer to set a target for each. Doing so creates no problem for the mathematical structure of the model, where such macro intentions might also feature in a mathematical sense as constraints. But it is not certain that these arbitrary, *subjective* constraints that represent economic policy intentions are in accord with each other and can be accomplished together, or whether they match the *objective* constraints that reflect external conditions (such as natural resources, production capacities, supplies of labor, or import restrictions).

4. Nor could we take very seriously the data we were feeding into the computer. The planners tried to feed these numbers to us. They were reluctant to say what calculations they had used for their own estimates. They scribbled the figures on slips of paper and hid them away if they could. For these figures constituted the weapons each planner possessed in the battle to obtain scarce resources and ward off targets set too high.

5. and 6. We might, with twenty-first-century computers, have been able to keep pace with the rhythm of plan preparations. We were incapable of it at the time.

Our computations came too late. It was easier to just look at the figures and rely on a practiced eye to guess at the balances in the plan than to calculate them with a rigorous system of equations.

All these difficulties had a common root. Socialist planning was a kitchen whose chefs were not going to let strangers see their tricks of the trade. They could not stand publicity and transparency. The mathematical model would have imposed discipline on them, making them add up what had to be added up and subtract what had to be subtracted. That was unacceptable to them.

To return to the problem today, we find ourselves led to Hayek's line of argument, mentioned earlier. It is impossible to gather all knowledge and all information in one central place or in a center and a few auxiliary subcenters. Knowledge is necessarily decentralized. If it is to be used fully and efficiently, those in possession of the information must be able to use it (or at least a significant part of it) for their own benefit. Decentralized information must be coupled with free enterprise and private ownership. Not every bit of information but as much as possible needs to be used in a decentralized way.

That observation takes us from a narrow question (why mathematical planning could not embed itself in the normal operation of socialist central planning) to a much more general one: why central planning could not operate with efficiency and up-to-dateness in that socialist politico-socioeconomic environment.

Ultimately, many years of working inside institutions engaged in planning did not reconcile me to the idea of central planning. On the contrary, it alienated me from it further still. I had turned sharply away from bureaucratic centralism in 1956. Then I had been studying the problem on a level of enterprises "below" and lower-level authorities directly managing them. Now, between 1963 and 1968, I found out what went on higher up in the bureaucracy. I became all the more firmly convinced that socialist planning, however modern the techniques tried, would never be able to fulfill the hopes socialists placed in it.

To conclude this comparison of expectations with their fulfillment, I would like to add a few words on the faith placed in the promise of planning. Many people were drawn to socialism by its supposed ability to make planning forward-looking and conscious. It is a marvelous idea to have human intellect instead of spontaneous blind market forces regulating what happens in the economy. Success in planning on a national scale would justify confidence in human rationality. We could say even more: national planning in the socialist countries was a daring attempt, unmatched in human history, to turn this faith and hope into reality.

I am trying to relate in these memoirs how I came to break with communist ideas and Marxist theory, in several stages. My political opposition was total and I had moved far from Marxist political economy. But I still believed that central planning might play an effective and progressive part in allocating investment resources and determining how different sectors of the economy would develop over the long term, especially if it was done using up-to-date methods (mathematical models and computers). It was a dismal feeling to be disappointed in that hope as well.

Yet the disillusionment was mingled with a knowledge that I had learned much from the time I had spent among planners. It was a bit like an anthropologist spending months among the people being studied. I can call my own work *authentic* because I got to know the socialist system from the inside. From that point of view, the great task of programming the national economy had been invaluable to me.

Let me suspend my autobiographical account for a moment to consider what might be the prospects for planning now, in 2004–2005. I think it is regrettable that the failure of the communist system should have discredited the idea of planning. Not just Hungary's National Planning Office but the Soviet Gosplan and the central planning apparatus in every former socialist country were dissolved. The ranks of planners have thinned and planning institutes have lost influence outside the former Soviet bloc as well. You do not need to be a Communist or accept Marxist thinking still to see possibilities in planning on a national economic level. The undertaking would require computations that went beyond the bounds of one or two fiscal years and tried to survey consistently the development alternatives before a country. Such planning need not lead to a document full of instructions for the actors in the economy. It would be enough to compute alternative development paths for politicians and for other decision makers to think about and use as background in their discussions—rather as Ragnar Frisch, Jan Tinbergen, and the French planners of the 1960s envisaged when they recommended *indicative* planning (compatible with the market economy) instead of the *imperative* planning of a communist economy. Perhaps one day, when the dire memories of old-style planning under a communist system have vanished, the idea of planning may enjoy a renaissance. And then, perhaps, the experience that we former mathematical planners amassed may come in useful after all.

Cooperating with mathematicians

Let me return to my personal history. Tamás Lipták and I made several attempts to continue our joint work after the 1965 article appeared, but unfortunately, we could not. Tamás's mounting mental problems steadily undermined his ability to do research. Never again after the "Two-Level Planning" article did he do truly significant work with me, with any other coauthor, or by himself. I tried while he was still in Hungary to supply him with work (or at least sinecures that would earn him a living) and so did other friends. Then he left for England. There, too, people initially trusted that he would do research to match his reputation. Later people had to resign themselves to accepting that this man with a mind that had begun so brilliantly was incapable of any more productive activity and would have to live off the British welfare state. He died in 1998 as a consequence of an accident he suffered while on a visit to Budapest.

When I first set about mathematical modeling, it seemed self-evident that such tasks should be done jointly by an economist and a mathematician. Tamás and I brought from our two disciplines different approaches, which proved complementary. Mathematicians are trained to the utmost degree of abstraction, while economists are drilled to keep returning to the practical world. The ideal, of course, would be for one mind to possess maximum ability in abstraction and a maximum sense of reality, but that can hardly be expected.

After my collaboration with Tamás Lipták was over, I worked on several research topics and coauthored studies with other mathematicians or economists who had trained as mathematicians. I cooperated with Péter Wellisch, Bálint Dömölki, Béla Martos, Jörgen Weibull, and András Simonovits, and a useful complementarity of outlook and knowledge asserted itself in each case.

Later, when I became better acquainted with economics research in the West, I realized that this type of cooperation, which I had thought so obviously desirable, hardly ever occurred. An aspiring economist simply had to acquire the mathematical skills needed to supply a developed mathematical apparatus for his or her work. Coauthors likewise tended to be economists employing mathematical methods to a high standard.

Such self-reliance certainly has several advantages. I do not want to make a virtue of weakness; I have often felt bitter that I did not get the regular graduate training that would have given me confidence in employing sophisticated mathematical methods. But perhaps there are drawbacks as well to economists confining themselves to "do it yourself" mathematics. They have to confine their research within the limits of their mathematical knowledge, which professional mathematicians consider limited indeed. In many cases, the *technical* limits of mathematical economics have been vastly expanded by scholars whose original field was mathematics—John von Neumann and John F. Nash, for instance. There are indeed problems whose mathematical implications are too difficult to be grasped by a mere economist conversant with mathematics, though a real mathematician could tackle them.

There is much discussion these days about the importance of interdisciplinary research. It would be worth considering whether there is not a place in the wide range of future economics research for economist–mathematician cooperation of the Kornai–Lipták kind.

9

Traveling to the West—1963 Onward

A long-standing desire and hope of mine was fulfilled in the summer of 1963, when I managed to travel to a conference in Cambridge, England. A long chain of events led up to that journey.

Previous events

When my book *Overcentralization* appeared in English in 1959, the *Guardian* carried a full-page review by Professor Ely Devons, head of the economics department at the world-famous London School of Economics (LSE). Already in 1958, Professor Devons had invited me to visit the LSE to give lectures and conduct a seminar. Those would be my sole responsibilities. Otherwise my time would be my own.

The invitation, my first to a Western institution, had an electrifying effect on me. I immediately sent in a passport application, which was rejected after a long delay. After that, I reapplied and was rejected repeatedly.

I was allowed to travel in 1962, one sign that the repression was lifting—but only to other socialist countries, not to the West. I had friends in light industry to thank for chances to attend conferences and give lectures in East Germany, Poland, and Czechoslovakia. These were my first academic appearances abroad.

Also in 1962, I received an invitation to the 1963 Round-Table Conference of the International Economic Association (IEA) held in England at the University of Cambridge. The subject was "Activity Analysis in Long-Term Growth and Planning." (Applying mathematical programming and similar mathematical techniques to economics was known in those days as "activity analysis.") One of the chief organizers of the conference was Edmond Malinvaud, an editor of *Econometrica*, who had encountered the studies I had written with Tamás Lipták, as I related in the previous chapter. They would have liked to invite Lipták as well, but given his "criminal" record, he did not even try for a passport. I made yet another application to travel, based on an IEA invitation instead of an LSE one, and succeeded at last.

Cambridge, England

The barrier was going down after a five-year wait. I was especially glad that my friend András Nagy was invited as well. We had been dismissed together from the Institute of Economics, and now we were being allowed to visit England together.

Arriving in London by air in July 1963, we traveled to Cambridge the next day. The conference was in Clare College, where we also were staying. I felt that Cambridge was paradise for young people eager for knowledge. We strolled through the calm, harmonious buildings of Clare and visited other colleges as well—King's, Trinity, and others—admiring also the famous English lawns of the rectangular courtyards. I have been to many places since, but I still feel that Cambridge, England, with its countless beautiful buildings and parks, is one of the loveliest places in the world, a place of peace and calm to which I had traveled from the hectic life of Budapest.

The IEA Round-Table Conferences are select events, designed to gather the best experts in a specific subject. Those attending and speaking on that occasion included Maurice Allais, Sukhamoy Chakravarty, Robert Dorfman, Terence Gorman, Frank Hahn, Leonid Hurwicz, Tjalling Koopmans, Lionel MacKenzie, Roy Radner, and Richard Stone. (Allais, Koopmans, and Stone would all later be Nobel Prize winners.) More familiar with the literature by then, I recognized most of the names and it was a great treat to put faces to them. I learned later how well known some of the other economists were as well.

The lectures and discussions were of a very high standard—immeasurably higher than what I was used to in Budapest. Although everyone was friendly, I sat anxiously through the sessions, feeling I could never reach the stature of those in that company.*

I still did not dare then to lecture in English. I spoke in German with a professional interpreter, or sometimes Koopmans or Hurwicz, translating for me. I was terribly nervous before delivering my lecture.[1] (Nervousness and fear before lectures have remained with me throughout my career. However, it is a great pleasure to express my ideas orally, even at the price of stage fright.)

The lectures were on interesting and thought-provoking subjects (the full proceedings were later published in a volume).[2] I heard for the first time in detail about Edmond Malinvaud's planning model, mentioned in the previous chapter, which was compared at the conference with our two-level model.

We were housed in undergraduates' rooms, which struck me as pleasantly furnished studio apartments, especially in comparison with the crowded rooms of the

---

* It is pleasant to realize that as I write these memoirs, I happen to be president of IEA, which organized that 1963 Cambridge conference.

dormitories at home. One morning, Tjalling Koopmans and Leonid Hurwicz knocked on the door for a little chat. They asked many things about my research and the situation in Hungary. It was my first personal meeting with Koopmans, who adopted me as a friend and later helped me in my work in hundreds of ways. He was not a jovial, witty, or intimate man, but he was open, straightforward, serious, and humane, qualities displayed not in emotional statements but in his manner of thinking. He attached importance not to his own words but to what others were saying, which he would follow quite attentively and with an open mind. It was the same on that occasion.

In a sense, the conversation was a kind of oral exam. I could not have chosen better teachers for it. At the same time, we got to know each other. On one side were two scholars from the West, Koopmans, born in the Netherlands, who had started his economics studies under Jan Tinbergen, and Hurwicz, born in Poland, once an assistant to Oskar Lange. Both had lived in the United States for many years, and this may have been the first time they had met someone from behind the Iron Curtain, who although he spoke broken English yet spoke the same language as they. The meeting must have been interesting for them too.

That evening, my fellow countryman Nicholas Kaldor gave a reception at his house for the conference delegates. (I have already introduced him in chapter 1.) There Joan Robinson appeared, dressed in an Indian sari. Robinson was one of the outstanding personalities of twentieth-century economics, one of the pioneers of the theory of imperfect competition, and I already knew her name from my readings.* Again a legend was present in the flesh.

I went up to London after the conference and called at the LSE. Professor Devons, who had initiated my invitation, took me to see the school's director, Sir Sidney Caine. He was in shirtsleeves, and his shirt was hanging out at the front, which often happens to me as well. If I notice or I am told, I do something about it, but I am reminded of Sir Sidney and I am not abashed.

---

* Joan Robinson went about stirring up professional and political storms. She became an enthusiastic and partisan Maoist in her old age. In 1977, a small group of Hungarians met at Kaldor's house: Tibor Scitovsky and his wife Erzsébet, Zsuzsa, and I. We were speaking Hungarian, when Joan Robinson turned up unexpectedly—she often visited the Kaldors. We did not immediately switch languages. Joan Robinson silently put up with this for a while and then said in a voice of command, "Kornai's coming with me." She drew me out of the circle of Hungarians, took me to her house nearby, and started a conversation about China. She went to great lengths to persuade me that they had found the real road to communism, because the functionaries of the party and the state—I quote Joan Robinson word for word—"served the people voluntarily" and not for mercenary motives, as in the Soviet Union. She would not listen to any counterarguments or hear about any experiences in Eastern Europe.

It was agreed that if no obstacles arose, I would return to London the following year.

At the London School of Economics

The plan succeeded. I arrived in London by train in April 1964. I managed to leave my briefcase at Victoria Station in my excitement and not notice for two or three hours. I rushed back and found the briefcase just where I had left it. That experience reinforced my confidence in English people.*

I was at the LSE the next day and soon began to teach, giving a course of lectures on economic planning and related mathematical methods. I had the impression that my message and English were understood, if with difficulty, as the group of ten to fifteen graduate students were attentive. Some of them came to my office to discuss problems arising from the course. There was great interest, especially on the part of Michael Ellman, who already stood out for his interesting ideas. Later a professor at Amsterdam University, he and I have maintained our friendly professional relationship.

Starting to teach does not pose any special problem for young researchers in the West. They have experienced as students how teaching is carried out in universities there. But I had never been an economics student, either in Hungary or abroad, and now I was jumping into teaching in London. It was a hard task, I found. I had to develop teaching methods for myself.

I had plenty of interesting intellectual experiences. I heard several lectures by LSE staff or visitors. One of the faculty was A. W. Phillips (who introduced and gave his name to the Phillips curve, a theoretical construct often cited in macroeconomics). Two great American economists, Lawrence Klein and Robert Solow, both spoke to packed lecture halls. That couple of months gave me my first information on how economics was taught in that part of the world.

I learned much, but to be frank, I felt lonely. I was too old to socialize with the students. As for the faculty, they did not really make friends with me. It may be that the ties among the lecturers were loose in any case. The only one who showed genuine friendship was the LSE's expert on the Soviet Union, Professor Alfred Zauberman, an émigré from Poland. I made another lasting friendship during a visit to Scotland, where I met Alec Nove, the world-famous expert on the history and economy of the Soviet Union. More important still, he was a kind, warmhearted, good-humored man. We met and debated on several later occasions as well. He kept an unshakable belief not in "existing socialism"—that is, in the system prevailing in the

---

* I have left things behind frequently since. It is good to know that in my case this is a personal trait, not a sign of old age.

Soviet Union and Eastern Europe—but in "feasible socialism," a better, more desirable form of socialism, at a time when most of us Eastern Europeans had long become disillusioned with the idea.

There was another Hungarian teaching at the LSE, Imre Lakatos, a man with a remarkable intellect that many were already noticing at the University of London as well. He later became world famous as an authority on the philosophy of science; his work continues to be cited. I had known him briefly in Budapest. Although our mutual acquaintances in Budapest had acknowledged his exceptional intellectual abilities, he had a bad reputation among them because of his political past. He may have sensed that I knew this and that about his past, or may simply not have found me congenial. We met only once or twice for a couple of minutes; otherwise he showed no sign of wanting to know me.

Luckily, Imre Lakatos's distant attitude proved to be the exception. Countless times on many visits abroad, I have been the object of solicitous attention from émigré colleagues from Hungary, who have helped me in my work and my daily life. The simple fact that I came from Hungary was enough to elicit solidarity and helpfulness from them. I had heartwarming experiences of friendship with Béla Balassa, Thomas Balogh, William Fellner, János Harsányi, Nicholas Kaldor, Richard Quandt, Tibor Scitovsky, and Thomas Vietorisz.

My stay in Britain meant much more than getting to know the LSE in a professional sense. I had long wanted to travel to London. A book called *Hallo, It's London!* had been one of my favorites as a child.[3] I knew the names of all the famous streets, squares, historic buildings, and monuments. Now here it all was before my eyes.

After so many years in a shortage economy, I was struck, as György Péter and Miklós Gimes had been, by the plenty, the wealth, and the peace. My short trip to Cambridge in 1963 had given me a glimpse into English life. Now I was in London for several months. Intellectually, of course, I knew before I went what the difference was between British and Hungarian life; but it is one thing to read a book about it, or hear about it from others, and another to see for yourself, day after day. This, in a way, was my real start with the "comparative economic" approach that was to be a mark of my work. I could compare the two systems theoretically and statistically, but behind the ideas, stimulating and confirming them, lay direct, personal experience of both.

The same, through the eyes of spies and informers

Forty years after the events I have just described, I gained access to secret documents that told me a lot about what had happened concerning my travels behind the scenes, without my knowledge, in the offices of the political police.

The economist Tamás Bácskai served the political police as an informer. One of his handwritten reports is about me:[4] "I spoke to János Kornai about a month ago. He stated that he is not a Marxist.... For instance, he does not accept the absolute pauperization of the working class, he does not accept the leading role of the working class.... [H]e does not accept the leading economic role of the state."

Having read several informers' reports in the documentation of my life that I obtained, I see that they took a standard form. The report was evaluated by the police officer in charge of the case, who appended further instructions to the agent. Let me quote from the comment made on the report just cited by the police major assessing it:

Note. Kornai wants to travel to Britain in the autumn.

Assessment. The report is valuable, because it reveals how Kornai has not abandoned his earlier revisionist position. If that is the case, it is not good for us at all that he should travel to Britain, because [the imperialist enemy] may easily exercise its influence on Kornai, or even recruit him.

Order. Speak to Kornai and return to the questions on which Kornai does not agree with Marxism.

The reports of Tamás Bácskai fill a thick file.* His colleagues, friends, and relatives included mainly economists, men of letters, and film people; he wrote reports on many of them. He also used information gained in conversations with his own father and younger sister. Bácskai cannot be counted among those I called a friend in the strict sense, but we had several years of friendly relations behind us.

Let me add to the text of the police document my own hypothesis about why I received permission to travel to Britain. The position of the political police prevailed during the darkest, most repressive years of the Kádár regime, up to the 1962–1963 amnesty, and in cases like mine, applications for a passport were refused. As the machinery of oppression loosened somewhat and the regime tried to show a friendlier face to the West, considerations of cultural and foreign policy came to prevail over the police position. I was allowed to travel, but the secret police, as we will see in a moment, continued to keep an eye on me.

One person I met in London was R. R., a former colleague of mine, a journalist. By the time of my visit to London, we had been close friends for seventeen years. That we did not see eye to eye politically on many things was obvious, as he was

---

* Tamás Bácskai's activities as an informer were revealed in an article by Erika Laczik (2005). He served in this capacity for almost five years, from November 29, 1956, to August 16, 1961. The article discusses in detail the spheres in which Bácskai gathered his information and those on whom he reported; he made a public admission shortly after the article appeared. I will return later to this point and explain why I disclose Tamás Bácskai's name, while I do not reveal the names of other informers.

working as the London correspondent of a Hungarian Communist newspaper. Nonetheless, I felt we were friends. Before the action was uncovered by the police, I had sought him out several times and collected money from him regularly to help the relatives of '56 prisoners.

We had several long conversations in London. He took me out for an excursion in his car. He went with me to buy an African carving—he was a passionate art collector and knew where to find good pieces more cheaply.

I recently received copies of the police and intelligence files kept on me in those days. I was astonished and upset to find that R. R. had sent a detailed report on my political views and of our conversations to his superiors at the secret police.[5] The report was written in 1965. At that time, the secret police were out to collect information about me and had discovered that R. R., one of their permanent agents in London, knew me quite well. This agent received orders to write a full report on me. He immediately obeyed, and for the purpose of his report, recalled the discussions we had previously had in London.

R. R. reported not just about me but about others as well. He had a regular code name. His reports on my views were accurate, neither embellishing (from the Kádár regime's angle) nor exaggerating my opposition to conditions at the time. He told his superiors just what I had said in an intimate conversation between friends.

Let me quote from the report: Kornai "does not see himself as a communist. . . . He wants to turn his back on politics. . . . He asked me to help Pál Lőcsei's wife. . . . He does not approve of the economic aspects of the party's policy. . . . He considers that unscientific and discredited."

Should I not have spoken to R. R. sincerely? Who is a person supposed to trust in if not friends? Or was I naive, obstinately unsuspecting to think that friendship was stronger than loyalty to the Communist Party? Despite the differences in our political views, I thought we were friends. Yet in his account of me, he reported to his superiors, "We used to be good, close friends until 1953–54. After that, differences arose in our views and the intimate friendship ended."

I know exactly who R. R. was, based on documents that I checked thoroughly. The same goes for all the other informers, traitors, and secret agents designated in this book by pairs of arbitrarily chosen initials (not their true initials) who appear later in my story. Readers will obviously wonder why I have not given their real names, if I know them.

Under Hungarian law valid at the time of my writing this autobiography, citizens have a right to know who betrayed them and who wrote reports on them,* but not to make that information public.

---

* That the right cannot always be exercised is another matter—it is not always possible to obtain the desired information.

There were sharp debates all over Eastern Europe, after the Communist regimes fell, about what should happen to the records of the former secret services. Many people backed Germany's radical solution of making records of the former Stasi (Staatssicherheitsdienst, or [Ministry for] State Security) available to all. That approach had its supporters in Hungary, too, but it ran up against resistance from the political authorities entitled to decide the matter. Legal, security, and ethical arguments against it also came up in public debate. It may well be that considerations of party politics had some impact as well. Perhaps some party politicians—though untouched themselves—were worried about their party's prestige if it should turn out that it had former spies and informers in its ranks. Time and again, arguments flared up on whether to amend the legislation and reveal the names of agents, informers, and spies, as well as other members of this secret network. At the beginning of February 2005, as I was finishing this autobiography, the debate gained new impetus behind the scenes and in public over what should, could, and could not be published from the records about informers, their principals, and their victims and those they observed. The matter was still unsettled when I submitted the manuscript to the Hungarian publisher.

I asked myself whether I would publish the names even if Hungarian law did not prevent it. I do not want to sidestep the question by referring to legal stipulations. I want to face what is an ethical and emotional dilemma.

Since such cases appear in this book on numerous occasions, I was forced to think about the problem repeatedly. Every story is different. There were informers—or persons serving up their friends and acquaintances to the secret services in some other ways—with whom I had only loose or superficial relations, although they were not altogether unknown to me. But others I had counted among my closest five to ten friends. I recalled the discussions we had had over fifteen or more years, about work, public life, family, and children. How could a former friend have betrayed me? What made them engage in that hideous game, which they presumably played with other friends as well?

I do not know. One important concept that embedded itself in my mind during the long years I spent in the Western world, especially America, is called due process—the right to a fair and honest procedure. All who are suspected or accused of something should be given the chance to defend themselves. If they feel the suspicion or charge against them is false, they should have the chance to refute it. If there are extenuating circumstances, they should be given the opportunity to point them out. Those bringing up the suspicion or accusation—irrespective of any confession by the suspect or accused—should be able to prove their allegations. If they know of any aggravating or extenuating circumstances, they should be bound to reveal them. Witnesses must be heard. Once judgment is reached, there should be a way to appeal it, and so on. Who, in this case, can enforce such due process today, thirty or forty years later? Some of the presumed betrayers are already dead.

However, that is not even the most important of the reasons that make me decide against making the names public. I am not entitled to make moral judgments. Perhaps these people were forced into playing their deceitful role by methods it would also have been difficult for others to resist.

I am not acquitting them unexamined or saying that informers are victims too, forced to play that role by a horrible, oppressive system. Although the system is primarily what needs to be condemned, that does not overrule my conviction that each of these individuals is responsible for his or her own actions. There were some who dared to say no. There were others who were not even approached, because the secret police knew too well that they could not be trusted. But I make no generalizations in the opposite direction either. I do not want to condemn an informer's sins unseen, because I am not in the position to weigh the arguments on each side.

I do not pass judgment. Even the thought of revenge is alien to me. If I revealed the informer's name, that in itself would be a punishment. I do not claim the right to punish R. R., or the others, or, perhaps indirectly, their family members as well.

Tamás Bácskai's name did not appear in the earlier draft of my autobiography other than as a pair of initials. But while revising the manuscript, the article exposing him appeared in the press, mentioning that I was among those on whom Bácskai had reported. Bácskai admitted that the accusation is true. Under such circumstances, I do not see any reason to keep him anonymous here.

The number of articles exposing informers has grown in the past few months. I do not aim here to assess this process in legal or ethical terms. I would like just to assert that I do not intend to take part in the campaign of exposure. I have thought over again the principles just mentioned and I wish to uphold them even in the light of recent developments. Yet I am convinced that my action of writing down the name of an informer who has already been exposed and already acknowledged his fault does not run counter to those principles.

After that detour, let me return to the main train of thought in this report and analysis.

As I looked at the documents of that period, I saw again that there had been two parallel stories. In one I was directly involved: I applied for a permit to travel, was refused, then permitted, then traveled and ultimately returned to Budapest, always anxious that the authorities would not let me travel next time, and so on. Meanwhile the other, secret story was unfolding without my knowledge. Reports were being written about me, my remarks were being assessed. They analyzed what "thought crimes," to use Orwell's expression, I had committed.

When the political secret police with its network of domestic informers and the intelligence service (they worked closely together in the same division) decided to lift their veto on my proposed travels, they wondered about recruiting me as well. One secret agent in London, X. X., a member of the embassy staff, submitted a proposal to his principals after my first visit to England. I remember clearly that X. X. was extremely obliging and friendly. I was so naive at the time that I did not even suspect him of being one of the Hungarian secret agents in London.[6] I remember that he took me to a fabric store where I could purchase some excellent English tweed at a good discount.*

X. X.'s proposal was seriously considered and they looked thoroughly into who I was and what my views were. I quote the document of March 26, 1964, recording the decision: "Based on Comrade X. X.'s earlier suggestion, we assessed the operative usability [of János Kornai]. During the assessment, however, that person was not found suitable for recruitment. In view of the wavering political behavior he has exhibited in the last ten years, we do not brief him before his trip abroad, either in the name of the Foreign Ministry or in our own name.... Following his trip abroad and depending on his behavior, Comrade X. X. can use him in dark ways, but only in questions connected with his legal activities at the embassy."[7]

A little explanation is necessary here to clarify what the expressions "briefing" and "use it in dark ways" mean in this context, in the jargon of the Hungarian intelligence services.

People traveling to the West who might be useful for gathering political intelligence and were loyal to the political regime were "briefed" before their departure. That briefing would take place in the personnel office at their place of work, or they might be called in to the Foreign Ministry or the police. It would be explained how they had to behave abroad, whom they might have contact with, whom they should keep a distance from, and what information they should inquire about. The authorities expressed their wish that the traveler should give a detailed report on his or her experiences abroad. This briefing did not yet mean that individuals were formally recruited, simply that contact with them had been made and the prospect of strengthening the tie in the future remained open. The political police and the intelligence service would risk establishing such loose contacts only with travelers of whose loyalty they were convinced. It would have been embarrassing for the police if the traveler had gone to the West and there revealed how such "instructions" had been given. In my case, it was clear to the secret police from my declarations and from informers' reports not only that they would have to refrain from formally rop-

---

* He seemed so friendly that after my first trip to England in 1963, and before my visit in 1964, I wrote him a letter from Budapest saying I was coming to London again and I would like to spend some of my time learning English. I asked him to recommend a good language course. I was rather taken aback to discover this friendly, personal letter in secret agent X. X.'s files. He himself had attached it to the report.

ing me into their ranks but also that they could not trust in me even to the extent of a "briefing." My thinking—the way I had turned my back on the ideas underlying the Communist Party—protected me from attempts to recruit me.

To explain the other secret service jargon, let me quote from a word list compiled by János Kenedi: "'Dark' intelligence: the informer or agent collects valuable data or information in the course of a discussion, while the partner is unaware that he/she is talking to an opponent and communicating information important to the other side. He/she does not know of the opponent's 'dark' intentions. The conversation is designed and prepared for by the informer or agent."[8] In this light, X. X. intentionally tried to get information out of me that was important to his principals, while we were walking toward the fabric store in Regent Street and talking of all sorts of things. One thing is sure—even if I had no suspicion that he was a secret agent, they would not get anything out of me that could be of use for them.

Let me recall one more document from the period. When I subsequently applied to travel after receiving further invitations, an application of mine reached the political police again. The person reporting on me—as the document's wording makes clear—was quite well informed about my activity. Whether the person was an employee of the secret police or just an outside expert, the expertise shown reveals that a *fellow economist* evaluated my work. He or she remarked that Kornai "did pioneering work in domestic terms on economic applications of electronic computers (mathematical programming). He based all this almost exclusively on Western sources; he did not introduce anything not known in the West. His research work at home does not warrant his successive invitations from the West. Kornai cannot give the West anything new."[9]

General remarks on my travels and publications abroad

One piece of information expressed by the expert reporting to the secret police on my work was certainly true, namely that I was getting successive invitations from the West. He or she was right in saying that those in the West did not want to learn from me what good things electronic computers were. Theirs were far more modern than our vast, Soviet-made Ural machine, a decade or two out of date. It is also correct that I learned about the economic applications of linear programming from Western books, not they from me. Nonetheless, I seemed to be able to convey to Western audiences something new, because they wanted to see and hear me.

The invitations I was receiving were not a subject of comment just at the secret police. They were discussed among economists too. It is common enough in Budapest to retail to people things that have been said behind their back. So I knew there were those who thought my invitations showed that Kornai was being "smart." He built up his connections and managed to get acquaintances to invite him places.

I would like to face these sarcastic remarks, especially as a series of invitations followed my Western trips of 1963 and 1964. I was invited to ever more places, and my Western travels became ever more frequent and regular. I do not want to deal *in general* with the grounds on which researchers travel abroad, as I have not studied the experiences of other such travelers. I would like to write exclusively about my own travels.

In each case, the spur to invite me was a favorable assessment of my work. As I have related already, I was asked to the 1963 Cambridge conference because Professor Malinvaud, its French organizer, had gained good impressions from two articles in *Econometrica*. I had been invited to the LSE because Devons, the head of a department there, had liked my book published by Oxford. I was invited in 1966 to a Rome conference of the Econometric Society because Koopmans, heading the section on planning, had gotten to know me in Cambridge and thought I had made a remarkable contribution there. I then took part in a seminar in Venice, at which I met Eastern and Western economists, because the organizers' attention had been drawn by my book *Overcentralization*.*

I could continue, but it is not necessary. I managed to go to many places without ever asking anyone to arrange an invitation for me. If the subject came up, I always advised younger colleagues to publish in journals to which attention is paid internationally. This effort would bear fruit eventually and draw attention to their work. Some took my advice and some did not.

There is much talk nowadays about the importance of *networks* in political, business, cultural, scholarly, and scientific life. Some people make "networking" their primary strategy in life; they see having manifold useful connections as a success in itself. I do not want to start arguing here about the right strategy or evaluating approaches for their expediency or morality. For me, however, making a connection was never an intrinsic achievement; it was simply a by-product of my researching, teaching, and lecturing activity. I made connections with people primarily through their reactions to my articles, books, and lectures. Some remained at a level of professional fellow feeling or teacher–pupil relations. Other relationships burgeoned into friendships. My "network" has grown to huge dimensions, with thousands rather than hundreds of strands. The primary ties produce secondary ones; after a while, acquaintance and reputation create connections by a self-generating process.

---

* Western economists initially knew two Kornais. To specialists in the Soviet Union and Eastern Europe, Sovietologists, and comparative economists, I was the author of *Overcentralization*. To mathematical economists, I was one of the authors of the Kornai–Lipták model. With only a few exceptions, Sovietologists did not read *Econometrica* in those days, and theoretical economists were not abreast of the literature on the Communist economy. The invitations came now from one camp, now from the other. It took time for these images generated by two different aspects of my work to merge into one.

What I would like to emphasize is the origin of the primary connections; and in my case, that was first and foremost academic achievement.

Let me return to my travels, in line with the title of the chapter. I promise not to burden readers with lists of the journeys I made or to give a tourist's account of the places visited. (I have no particular talent for that. When I return from abroad, I seldom manage to give a colorful or entertaining description of where I have been even to family and friends.) Let me instead make some comments that applied to all my journeys, and introduce some rules I made for myself when traveling and appearing abroad—and in publishing there, a closely related activity.

Once I had had my first chances of traveling to the West, in 1963–1964, my applications to travel were generally accepted. Western readers and younger people may not realize that in those days, possessing a valid passport did not suffice to allow Hungarians to leave the country. You needed a "window"—an exit stamp—for each occasion. For each window you made a specific application, which had to be signed at work by your superior, the personnel officer, and the party secretary. It was a demeaning process even if you could count on the signatories' goodwill. Even when I was regularly receiving permission, I was still anxious that I might be refused one day.*

The change of system brought a real feeling of liberation when it ended this degrading process and everyone gained the right to travel abroad at last.

Returning from an official trip, travelers had to write a report for their superiors. I fulfilled that obligation after my early trips to the West, although my reports were already something of a meaningless formality. But I stopped once my professional reputation in Hungary had grown a little more substantial. There were one or two reminders before those involved resigned themselves to not receiving such reports from me. I balked not because they would have made any of the intelligence-gathering organizations wiser at all; I simply did not want to perform a chore that I found demeaning.

I would accept invitations from abroad only if the host covered all the expenses.†
Whatever organization I was employed by at the time, it was ultimately funded by

---

* In 1970, I was invited to Bulgaria, to an international conference organized by the UN European Economic Commission. I remember the depressing anxiety I felt over a delay in obtaining my permit to leave Hungary. I received the stamp in my passport literally at the last moment, a few hours before my departure.

† The exceptions were trips that depended not on my being invited, but on my being sent by an official body of the Hungarian state. The Soviet and Hungarian academies of sciences, for instance, agreed that each would choose its own delegates to go to the other's country and would finance the visit. Soviet colleagues who wanted to meet me could not just send me a direct invitation. They had to persuade the Soviet Academy of Sciences to recommend to its Hungarian counterpart that I be sent.

the Hungarian state; but I was not motivated in my policy by a desire as a citizen to save the public money. I was thinking of the fact that institutions' very small allocations for financing travel by academics led to bitter fighting over the privilege. It was quite understandable in human terms that many wanted a chance to go abroad, but I decided to avoid the whole tussle.

I tried not to be two-faced, not to show one face at home (and in other socialist countries) while presenting another in the West. That was no easy task, because the free atmosphere of the West was a constant encouragement to speak out more plainly than one would at home in the oppressive atmosphere of threats, denunciations, informers' reports, censorship, and accusations. I set myself that rule in self-defense, delivering my lectures in the West in the knowledge that informers from the Hungarian secret police could be sitting in the audience at any time. (I was right to think that. The secret documents I recently reviewed on myself included an agent's report on a lecture that I gave in New York in 1985. I will say more about that in detail in a later chapter.) But apart from the defensive reason, I had moral qualms about inconsistent behavior. The boundaries were blurred between speaking and writing selectively in sober self-defense and being two-faced. Where would I end if I became used to speaking and writing one way here and another way there?

I let myself be more relaxed in private, among intimate friends, than I was in public. (That applied in the East as well as the West.) But I did not allow the message of my public lectures or articles in Eastern Europe to differ from the one I gave in my appearances in Western Europe or the United States.

The same determination to present one face meant that I went out of my way to arrange for all my writings to appear in parallel in Hungarian and in English (or another Western world language). There is no major writing of mine aimed exclusively to the east of the Iron Curtain or the west of it.

That decision, which I have summed up here briefly, objectively and in dry words, was one of the most troubling problems I faced in the period between 1964 and 1989. The change of system took a huge load off my mind.

A blighted attempt at a "fabricated trial"

There is another story that belongs in this chapter, in which I have often talked about the activities of the intelligence services. As I write this, I have at hand a photocopy of a letter written to me on October 14, 1964, by John Michael Montias, an American economics professor at Yale University. He was planning to come to Hungary on a scholarship and requested some advice on his work. He also mentioned that he had begun to learn Hungarian.

The letter had a short history behind it. I first learned about Montias's work from his writings, and then met him in person in Budapest in 1963, where he was taking part in a conference on mathematical economics. Montias attracted the attention of all the participants at the conference when he volunteered to do a simultaneous translation from Russian into English of a presentation by Leonid Kantorovich. He also interpreted the ensuing debate in both directions. He was obviously both a good economist and someone with an exceptional gift for languages. We afterward met once more in Venice in 1965 at a conference of Western and Eastern economists specializing in the study of the Soviet Union and Eastern Europe.

Let us come back to the letter addressed to me. I found it not in my own collection of letters but in the secret service archives.[10] An American professor's personal letter to me had been opened and photocopied in Budapest, then sealed again and delivered to me by the Hungarian post office. Everybody suspected that things like that often happened, but it was still a strange feeling to have firsthand evidence of it.

At the time, I only saw bits of the "Montias case." But I have managed now to reconstruct more or less the full story from the police records.

Montias was an outstanding figure among American Sovietologists. Most of his colleagues knew only one of the many languages spoken in the Soviet region, whereas Montias spoke several and was able to read even more. Although most Sovietologists in those days were qualified economists and had extensive knowledge of the political and economic situation in the Soviet Union or certain Eastern European countries, they were not skilled in the theories of modern economics written in formal mathematical language. Montias, in contrast, belonged to a new generation that handled such modern tools with great skill. (On one occasion, he was a coauthor with Koopmans, the great mathematical economist often mentioned in this book.)[11]

I was happy to help Montias prepare for his trip to Budapest. I gave him some advice on his choice of topic and offered to introduce him to Hungarian colleagues. We exchanged letters several times. Montias handed in a regular application, in which he described his scientific program and Hungarian connections. My name was among those in the relevant part of the application form.[12]

While in the foreground everything was proceeding according to the rules and practice of international scientific relations, and Montias and his Hungarian colleagues were preparing for the visit, behind the scenes the secret police continued to work at full throttle. The first warning came from Czechoslovakia: there was reason to believe that Montias was a CIA agent.* Counterespionage officials must have thought they were going to make a big catch!

---

* Documents recently obtained reveal just how closely the secret services of the Communist countries cooperated. The Czechoslovak state security bureau conducted a secret house search in 1963 in Montias's apartment in Czechoslovakia, and found in his coat a slip of paper with my name and home telephone number on it. This they reported to their Hungarian colleagues (IH 1656. 2/2-2358, p. 3. Date: May 8, 1964. Also IH 34-4-797/1965, p. 4. Date: April 23, 1965).

As the date of the visit approached, more and more people became involved in the case. They fished out the "material" they had on the Hungarian scholars whom Montias had named in his application. There were some other names in the files as well, but what I managed to find out from the archives was what actions were taken concerning me.

My files in the various branch offices of the III/III department for the period between 1956 and 1959 were retrieved, as well as those for my trips to England in 1963 and 1964. Then Captain Z. Z. wrote a summary report taking stock of everything they had against me.[13]

While studying the written documents of the secret service, I came across transcripts of tapped telephone conversations dating from 1963. A list was drawn up with the names of everyone I had contacts with. This produced nothing of interest for them. The list contained the names of friends in Budapest, relatives, and economist colleagues, including the foreign economists Ely Devons and Tjalling Koopmans. Here is a quote from one of the scripts: "Helga? Olga? Paid Kornai money." Here the police agents used a Hungarian slang term, applied when, for example, a man is paying money to his mistress for her services. Very suspicious. Kornai is being paid by a woman.... As a matter of fact, it was a dear acquaintance of long standing named Elga, to whom I had lent some money during the summer vacation. We had been discussing how she would pay it back. One might laugh at the stupidity of these people if one could only find such a dark story amusing.[14]

There is a comment on Captain Z. Z.'s report, handwritten by his boss, advising him not to use me for "throwing under."[15] I have consulted experts to find out what exactly that meant. The secret service had to find an agent who was, in secret service terms, reliable and obedient, and who could gain the confidence of the person under surveillance. Such an agent was said to be "thrown under" the person under surveillance, and would in turn provide the secret service with useful information.

Let us return to the visible surface. Montias's application was accepted by the Hungarian cultural relations bodies and he was granted a visa. So Montias arrived. He met and talked to several Hungarian economists. He started to learn Hungarian. I recommended a friend, Kati Hanák, as a Hungarian teacher, and she accepted. Montias progressed fast. He lived the usual life of foreign visitors, went to the opera with his wife, and sometimes ate out with Hungarian colleagues. We wined and dined them, too.

It transpires from the files that he was shadowed all along. His phone was tapped and he was followed about in the streets. I read the observers' reports: absolutely nothing comes out of the piles of pages. I can only repeat what I have just said: one might laugh at the report if one did not realize what evil forces lay behind those leading the investigation. I have not read much spy literature. Perhaps there is some rule or tradition that says that persons under surveillance cannot be referred to by their real names, even in internal reports. We lived on Pusztaszeri út, and so instead of referring to us as Kornai and Laky (my wife), the report called us "Mr. and Mrs. Puszta." The Hanáks used to live on Garas utca. So they were given the names "Mr. and Mrs. Garas."[16] Montias could certainly not appear in the confidential internal reports as Montias. Instead, he was given the name "Zimelio" (and in the street observation reports, he features as "Master," for a change).

The plan took shape. Montias would be accused of obtaining—by misusing his position as a visiting research scholar—classified information about the Hungarian economy and COMECON (the Council for Mutual Economic Assistance). The Hungarian economists with whom Montias was in touch were interrogated.

I was interrogated too. I have recently reread the reports. None of the witnesses made any accusations against Montias. None of them confirmed the suspicion that Montias had collected classified information.[17]

Before long, Montias was expelled from Hungary, effective immediately. An article was published in a newspaper explaining Montias's expulsion.[18] He was accused of gathering secret information, of spying. This accusation, however, could not be supported by facts, testimony, or any other evidence. There was not going to be a spectacular espionage trial.

The story is remarkable in many ways. It is a case that illustrates what I have discussed in this book many times (and will discuss further): the world of scholarship was not a privileged or protected area. The tentacles of the totalitarian state reached deep into it, and it was observed and terrorized.

While there was continuity between the Rákosi and Kádár eras, there were some essential changes as well. In the days of the old ÁVH, all the players would have been arrested—the American professor and his Hungarian friends—and tortured until they confessed and it could be confirmed in court that they had been spying for the CIA all along. Even then, in 1965, the interrogations were depressing and very trying for the Hungarian witnesses. But we did have the chance to refute the false accusations.*

At the time of the Montias case, there were two opposite political trends on the Hungarian political scene. The "soft-liner" or reform-oriented forces were out to

---

* I have written in an earlier chapter that after 1956, I resolved to become a member of the Western economic profession. I was well aware of the risks involved. Still fresh in our memory were the times when the mere fact of having a "Western connection" was enough to make one suspect, and when innocent professional interaction would be classified as "spying" in trumped-up criminal proceedings. This nightmare haunted us for as long as the Communist system existed. We know now, *in retrospect*, of course, that there was no Stalinist restoration. But nobody then, *in advance*, could say for sure that such an attempt at restoration would necessarily fail.

establish friendly relations with the West, especially in culture and science; the "hard-liner" or anti-reform forces, however, tried to seize every opportunity to blight East–West relations. Uncovering an American agent would have come in handy to the hard-liners, but the plan turned out to be a failure in the end.

Two postscripts need to be added to the story.

One is about how my relationship with Professor John Michael Montias continued afterward. In 1970, I spent six months at Yale University. There Mike and I met and talked a lot. We did not discuss the story of his expulsion. He—rightly—felt it proper not to bring it up, as he was aware that I would be returning to Hungary. Later, we would meet each time I visited Yale. I even gave a talk at the institute he headed. When he brought out a book on comparative system theory in 1976, I wrote an appreciative review,[19] not only because I thought it was a good book, but because I wished to make a statement: I held him to be a *scholar*. Montias was a founding editor of the *Journal of Comparative Economics*, which became the leading journal for researchers comparing economic systems. It frequently published articles by economists from Eastern-bloc countries. I myself published several articles there.

Montias would have liked to visit Hungary again in the 1970s, but the Hungarian authorities did not grant him permission to enter the country.[20] His name was not removed from Hungary's persona non grata list until the final hours of the old regime in 1989.[21]

Unfortunately, his Hungarian adventure rather dampened Montias's enthusiasm for "Sovietology." This was a real loss to the profession. He gradually turned to art history. His books on seventeenth-century Dutch painting are widely regarded by art historians as classics in the subject.[22]

I have to finish this story with a sad report: Mike died recently, in 2005.

The other postscript relates to a Budapest experience of mine. When I first asked to look into the files of the Montias case in 1998, I was granted permission—with a number of restrictions, however. I was not allowed then to make photocopies of the documents. While reading the files, someone from the office was to be present. Perhaps he was told to keep an eye on me, lest I try to sneak out one of the files secretly. He was a pleasant man. After I had finished reading, he started to chat, saying, among others things, something to the effect of "Well, yes, we never managed to catch the man." I could not quote him word for word. I did not tape the conversation so as to be able to report his words verbatim. This much is certain: he made this remark as someone who fully identified with the counterintelligence people working on the case, in the first-person plural, ironically and with some tone of regret in his voice. A weird continuity.

Against the Current—1967–1970
Anti-Equilibrium

While half my energies were being spent on the computations of mathematical planning, the other half were taken up with a new research program: a critique of the
neoclassical theory of economics, especially the general equilibrium theory. The outcome of this I published in my *Anti-Equilibrium*.

The antecedents of the book

The manuscript of a shorter version of the book, finished in 1967,[1] was subtitled
"Essay on Theories of the Economic Mechanism and Tasks for the Researcher."* I
also had the "Essay" (as I will refer to it hereafter) translated into English.[2]

Then came an invitation from Kenneth J. Arrow to spend a few months at his institute at Stanford University. Arrow was to receive a Nobel Prize in 1972, and it
was generally agreed in the profession that he was one of the top figures in mathematical economic theory. I took the "Essay" with me and continued to work on it at
Stanford. I felt that the situation was somewhat embarrassing, as the book centered
on a critique of a theory that had been put in its modern form by Arrow and a
French-born American economist, Gérard Debreu. I could not bring myself to tell

---

* By the time I started work on that manuscript, I had developed the habit of "escaping" for
the period in which I was engaged on something that demanded great concentration. Instead
of working in the comfort of my home or my room at the institute, I prefer to pack up and
hide in a holiday resort or hotel, unavailable to family, colleagues, or anyone else. I work very
intensely for a week or even two, and talk to no one except waiters and cleaning ladies, until
my wrists ache from typing and I am finally forced to give up banging away at the typewriter
(or, later, computer keyboard). This habit has become something of an addiction: I feel something is wanting if I am unable to create such conditions while writing a major paper or a
book. I began the first version of *Anti-Equilibrium* at Siófok, continued with it at Visegrád,
and eventually finished it at my favorite place, the Academy's holiday home at Mátraháza.

I think with gratitude on the place and its kind staff, for providing a peaceful paradise for
concentrated work.

Arrow what I had in my drawer. Then he heard from others about the manuscript, which I had shown to several colleagues. He asked to see it and read it carefully. (Arrow was astonishingly fast in his ability to grasp ideas and react intellectually. He also spoke very rapidly, a trait that made him hard to follow. His ideas raced ahead so fast that ordinary mortals could hardly catch up with him.) Far from being offended, he welcomed enthusiastically the intellectual challenge in an environment where everyone had accepted his theory without hesitation. We went right through the manuscript during several discussions. He appreciated the way the critique rested on an accurate knowledge of the Arrow–Debreu theory, first presenting its content in objective detail and only then criticizing it, and he made several constructive suggestions to improve the text. "It will make a fine obelisk on the burial mound of the general equilibrium theory," he remarked with a smile.

When I returned home to Budapest, I finished revising the "Essay," which had swollen, unfortunately, into a much larger book. By the time the Hungarian text and the new English translation were ready, I had received a new invitation, initiated by Tjalling Koopmans, to go to the Cowles Commission, a research body at Yale. In American mathematical economics, this was a legendary institution; it was where Debreu, for instance, had written his classic *Theory of Value*, which *Anti-Equilibrium* was intended to dismember. Koopmans, himself among the great masters of modern mathematical equilibrium theory, received the criticism openly. He asked me to address a seminar of his and made several suggestions for improving the expanded version.* He and another outstanding senior figure at Cowles, Professor James Tobin, entrusted two of their students with the task of looking over the Budapest translation.

I will never forget the generosity and scientific magnanimity of those two great economists, Arrow and Koopmans, in putting every facility at my disposal to enable my critique of their intellectual creation to be as effective and precise as possible.†

My book appeared in 1971, in both Hungarian and English editions. It was later translated into several other languages.

---

* When I was looking through the documents gathered while I was writing *Anti-Equilibrium*, I was moved to find again the twenty-one-page memorandum that Koopmans typed for me himself, giving his observations page by page. It is rare for a scholar as great and as busy as he was to devote so much effort to helping a younger colleague in his work.

† One story that illustrates Koopmans's greatness as a man concerns his Nobel Prize. He shared it, for developing linear programming, with the Soviet mathematical economist Leonid Vitaliyevich Kantorovich; but in Koopmans's view, it should also have been shared with George Dantzig, who devised the algorithm that allowed linear programming to be put to practical use. Indeed, he himself should have received a third, not half of the prize, Koopmans felt. So he donated the difference between half and a third of the sizable award to an international research institute.

1. Sitting in the lap of my brother Bandi, with my sister Lilly and brother Tomi beside us (1929).
2. With my parents, brothers, and sister (1930).
3. The first grade of the Imperial German School. I am sitting in the front row on the extreme right, next to my friend Péter Kende. In the row above us, right above Péter, is Éva Székely, who later became an Olympic champion swimmer (1933).
4. A portrait from my teenage years.
5. Number 18 on Akadémia utca in Budapest's Fifth District. Our apartment and my father's office were on the third floor (the second floor, as Europeans count). The whole house is now taken over by the Prime Minister's Office.
6. With my brothers Bandi and Tomi (1943).

7. Miklós Gimes, my first boss at the newspaper *Szabad Nép*, who died a martyr's death in the 1956 Revolution (about 1950).

8. With confident faith (about 1948).

9. In the woods on Galyatető during the winter break (1949).

10. Covering a meeting in Vienna for the newspaper (1950).

11. My sons Gabi and Andris (1964).

12. My first wife Teri with our sons Gabi and Andris (1966).

13

14

15

13. With Tamás Lipták in Cambridge, England, thirty years after we wrote our study "Two-Level Planning" (1992).
14. The "Kornai Group" at the Institute of Economics, at a gathering to mark the fiftieth anniversary of the institute's foundation. Left to right: Mihály Laki, Zsuzsa Kapitány, András Simonovits, Mária Lackó, and Judit Szabó.
15. With András Bródy (2004).

16

0000 8.

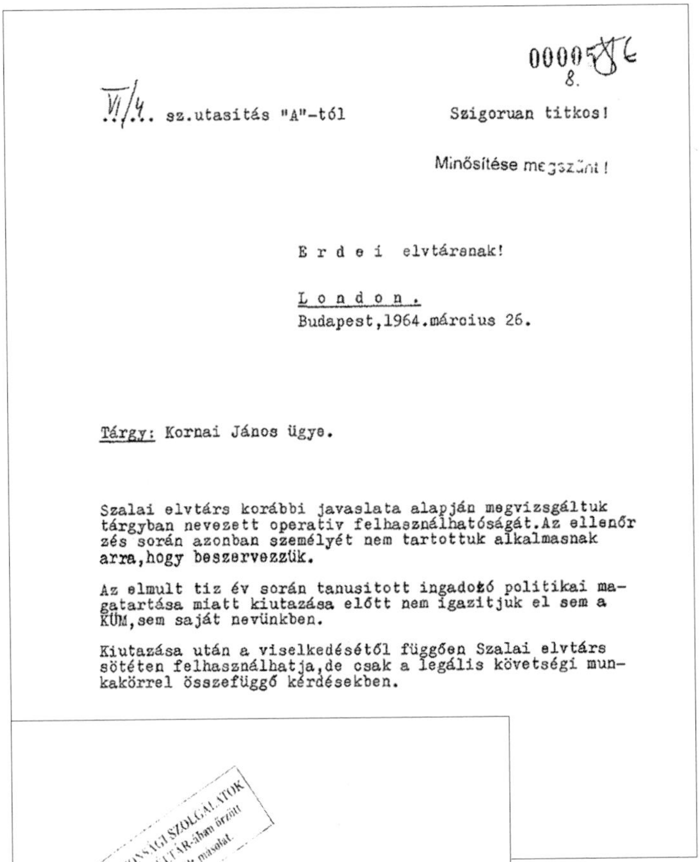

..?./.4. sz.utasitás "A"-tól   Szigoruan titkos!

Minősítése me;szünt!

E r d e i elvtársnak!

L o n d o n.
Budapest,1964.március 26.

Tárgy: Kornai János ügye.

Szalai elvtárs korábbi javaslata alapján megvizsgáltuk
tárgyban nevezett operativ felhasználhatóságát.Az ellenőr
zés során azonban személyét nem tartottuk alkalmasnak
arra,hogy beszervezzük.

Az elmult tiz év során tanusitott ingadozó politikai ma-
gatartása miatt kiutazása előtt nem igazitjuk el sem a
KÜM,sem saját nevünkben.

Kiutazása után a viselkedésétől függően Szalai elvtárs
sötéten felhasználhatja,de csak a legális követségi mun-
kakörrel összefüggő kérdésekben.

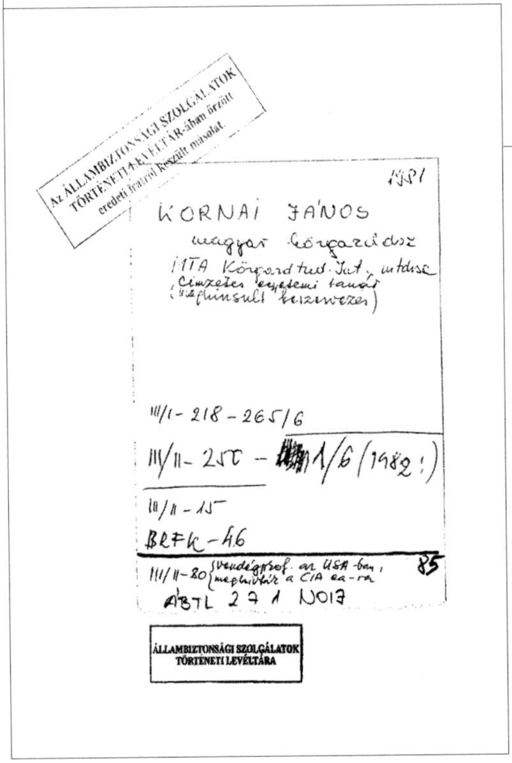

17

AZ ÁLLAMBIZTONSÁGI SZOLGÁLATOK
TÖRTÉNETI LEVÉLTÁR-ában őrzött
eredeti iratról készült másolat.

1981

KORNAI JÁNOS
magyar közgazdász
MTA Közgazd.tud. Int. mtársa
Cimzetes egyetemi tanár
(sz.pénzult beszervezés)

III/1- 218 - 265/6
III/11- 250 - 1/6 (1982)
III/11- 15
BRFK -46
III/11-20 {vendégprof. an USA-ban;
meghivur a CIA ea-ra}   85
ÁBTL 2 9 1 NO17

ÁLLAMBIZTONSÁGI SZOLGÁLATOK
TÖRTÉNETI LEVÉLTÁRA

18

16–17. A decision in 1964 by the secret
service: János Kornai was "not found suitable for recruitment" as an informer. The
index card dated 1985 refers to this decision: "failed recruitment."
18. Clare College, Cambridge, England,
venue of the 1963 Round-Table Conference
of the International Economics Association.
There I delivered my first lecture before an
international academic forum.

19

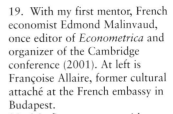

19. With my first mentor, French economist Edmond Malinvaud, once editor of *Econometrica* and organizer of the Cambridge conference (2001). At left is Françoise Allaire, former cultural attaché at the French embassy in Budapest.

20. My first encounter with Western Sovietologists at a 1965 conference in Venice. Left to right: Alfred Zauberman (London School of Economics), myself, David Granick (Wisconsin), John Michael Montias (Yale), and Hans Raupach (Munich).

20

21

22

23

21. In the middle is Kenneth Arrow, one of the great economists of our time, at whose invitation I arrived at Stanford in 1968. At lower right sits Arrow's wife, Selma. The other couple are our dear Stanford friends, Alan and Jackie Manne. In the center is my wife Zsuzsa. The picture was taken in 2002, when we visited California before leaving America.

22. Seated at my desk after my first shoulder operation, in plaster down to my waist (1972).

23. Before the famous fountain at Stanford.

24. With Gabi, Judit, and Andris at Tihany (1972)

25. With my mother, Munyó (1964).

26–27. Munyó on her eightieth birthday, with her three surviving children, Tomi, myself (my posture is strange, as my arm is in plaster after a second shoulder operation), and Lilly (1972). Munyó on the same occasion surrounded by grandchildren and a great-grandchild.

28. With Zsuzsa (1972).

29. With Judit on the beach in New Jersey (1972).

30

30. At the Geneva meeting of UNCTAD, the UN trade organization (1974).

31. With my students while giving a series of university lectures in Calcutta, India (1975).

32. View from our window in Lidingö, a suburb of Stockholm, where I wrote *Economics of Shortage* (1976–1977).

33. At the 1978 annual conference of the Econometric Society, a few minutes before delivering the presidential address. I was introduced at the session by my mentor Tjalling Koopmans.

31

32

33

34

34. The rector of the Sorbonne presents me with an honorary doctoral degree (1978).

35. *The King Is Naked*, an amusing drawing done in the technical department at the Hungarian publishers of *Economics of Shortage* (1980).

36. János Kass, a celebrated artist, was inspired by the manuscript of *Economics of Shortage* in 1978 to do a series of drawings. This one is titled *Paternalism*.

35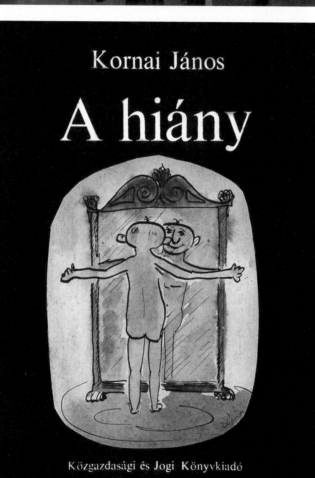

Kornai János

A hiány

Közgazdasági és Jogi Könyvkiadó

36

37. Harvard's Littauer Center, where my
university office was from 1984 onward.
38–39. During a lecture: the professor
explains and the students take notes.
40. In my office at Harvard, sitting at my
desk with a poster of Bartók behind me.
41. Harvard Hall, one of the university's
fine old buildings, where I had given my
lectures since 1990.

37

38

39

40

41

42. My best Chinese students. Left to right: Chenggang Xu (London School of Economics), Yijiang Wang (University of Michigan), Yingyi Qian (University of California at Berkeley), and David Li (University of Hong Kong). I had met each of them separately since they completed their studies at Harvard, but here we were all present at a conference in Hong Kong in January 2005.

43. At a commencement ceremony at Harvard University.
44. On my left, Karen Eggleston, a student of mine and later a coauthor, and on the right, John McHale, a student of mine and later a partner in writing articles and holding seminars, with his wife Liza, seen in our apartment in Cambridge (2001).
45. With Yingyi Qian and Zsuzsa in Beijing (1999).

46. Portrait with a characteristic Harvard tower in the background (1996).
47–49. Unpacking on arrival; packing for the following journey.

46

47

48

49

50–54. The 1985 "boat conference" in China.
50. One of the discussions.
51. Shaking hands with Prime Minister Zhao Ziyang, one of the architects of the Chinese reform. (Later, for making a gesture of sympathy toward the rebel students of Tiananmen Square, he was placed under house arrest, where he died.) In the middle is Ed Lim, the main organizer of the conference.
52. Group picture on board the vessel. In the front row are the main Chinese organizers and the seven invited foreign economists.

50

51

52

53

54

53. A little relaxation: being shown how to make the famous Peking duck.
54. A motorboat excursion to the Three Gorges—now no longer visible in that form, having been flooded by the reservoir above the dam built across the River Yangzi.

55

55. Talking to my visitors Péter Kende and Pál Lőcsei about my *Passionate Pamphlet*, which I had written while lying ill in bed (1989).
56. Seated at the desk in our Cambridge apartment (2002).
57–58. Enjoyable moments in the life of an author.
57. The proof of the English edition of *The Socialist System* arrives (1991).
58. The first complimentary copy in my hands.

56

57

58

59

59–63. An author's great reward: signing copies of my books for interested readers.
59. For university students in Hanoi, Vietnam (2002).
60. For Yelena Kaluzhnova, a Russian economist, in my room at Harvard (1998).
61. In Shanghai, China (1999).
62. For a student in Hong Kong (2005).
63. For staff at the publisher in Taiwan (1994).

60

61

62

63

64

65

64. In Bratislava, before the launch of my volume of studies translated into Slovak, with the editor, Ivan Miklos, who became his country's deputy prime minister and finance minister a few years later (1998).

65. Talking to students after one of my lectures at Shanghai University (1999).

66. A lecture at the New University in Moscow. I am introduced by one of the founders of the university and a recurrent guest professor, the Israeli economist Gur Ofer (2003).

67. In Paris, at the launch of a French volume of my studies. Beside me is one of the editors, Bernard Chavance (2001).

68. One of my passions is photography, and more recently video. Here I am capturing the Wailing Wall and al-Aqsa Mosque (1995).

69. Receiving an honorary doctorate from the Lajos Kossuth University of Sciences in Debrecen (2001).
70. Princess Anne, in her capacity as chancellor the University of London, places over my head the hood, one of the symbols of an honorary doctorate (1990).
71. The award of the Seidman Prize in Memphis, Tennessee (1982).
72. Trying on formal evening dress in Stockholm, before the award of an honorary doctorate at the Stockholm School of Economics (2001).

73. My sister Lilly, ill in bed, as I show her an award I have received (2000).
74. One of my favorite photographs, with Zsuzsa, when I was receiving the French Legion of Honor (1997).
75. An honorary doctorate in Turin (1994).

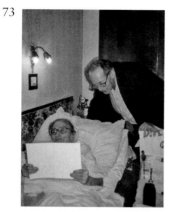

76. With Gabi and his wife Tünde (1990).
77. With Judit on the terrace of our apartment (1984).
78. With Andris on the Esplanade in Boston (1990).
79. Teaching my Swedish grandchildren, Zsófi and Anna, to swim (1990).
80. The Kornai clan at the Hungarian Academy of Sciences holiday resort at Balatonvilágos.

81

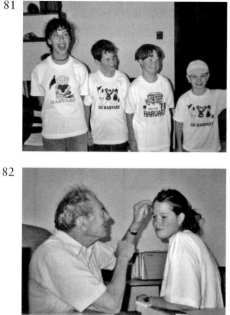

81. Four grandchildren, Julcsi, Zsófi, Anna, and Tomi, in Harvard T-shirts (1994).
82. It became a family tradition to count freckles at the end of the summer, with proper comparative statistics, a time series, and a graph of the results (1999). Right here, it is Anna who offers her face for the counting of freckles.
83. With Zsófi (2000).

84

82

83

84. Excursion to the Buda Hills: Julcsi, Tomi, Zsuzsa, and Gabi (2001).
85. Deep in our books. My grandson Tomi and I at Lake Balaton (1994).

85

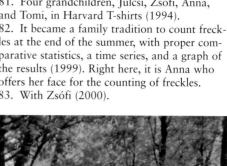

86

86–87. The two little American grandchildren, Dani and Nóri, with us and with their mother, Ági.

88. Our oldest American grandchild, Mishka, enthusiastic about the *palacsinta* (crêpes) Zsuzsa has made (2000).

89. A special occasion—I cook "Jancsi's lecsó," a favorite with my grandchildren, using a recipe of my own (1996).

87

88

89

90

90–93. With
Hungarian friends.
90. Left to right:
András Nagy,
Hanna B. Kende,
Ágnes Losonczi,
and Péter Kende
(2003).
91. Péter Kende
and György Litván
(1996).
92. Dinner with
the Lőcsei family:
Pali Lőcsei and
Kati and Péter
Hanák (1992).

91

92

93

93. Walking in
the Buda Hills:
György and Éva
Litván, Zsuzsa,
and beside me,
Zsuzsa's sister
Mari (2003).

94

95

96

97

98

100

99

94–100. Friends abroad.
94. Robert and Bobby Solow.
95. Mimi and Gerry Berlin.
96. Helen and Herbert Levine.
97. My Vietnamese friend and translator, A Nguyen.
98. Francis Bator on the terrace of our apartment.
99. Tibor and Erzsébet Scitovsky.
100. Zsuzsa with Tjalling and Truus Koopmans.

101

103

102

101. Friends present me with a *Festschrift* in my honor on my seventieth birthday. The picture shows Jenő Koltay, director of the Institute of Economics, and János Gács, one of the editors of the volume.

102. Celebrating my seventy-fifth birthday at Collegium Budapest. On my left is Imre Kondor, rector of the Collegium, and on my right, my assistant Kati

Szabó. The bearded man behind is
Brian McLean, who has been translating my work into English for two
decades (2003).

103. Birthday celebration at home:
on the table before me is my favorite
marzipan cake, before the candles are
blown out (1999).

104. In our apartment with our
American friend Dale Jorgenson, eating fishermen's soup. An apron is a
good idea on such occasions.

105–107. We leave America (2002).

105. Taking my bag at the end of my
last university lecture.

106. On Brooklyn Bridge with
Zsuzsa.

105

104

106

107

107. Bidding farewell to the port at Boston.
108–109. The farewell dinner given by Harvard University.
108. Kenneth Galbraith and his wife.
109. Behind: Jeffrey Williamson and Jeffrey Sachs. In the foreground: Sachs's wife Sonia Erlich with Eric Maskin.

108

109

110

111

110–111. Loading up the furniture of our Cambridge apartment into a shipping container in front of the house.
112. The old Budapest flat is already half empty. I am sitting in a provisional study made up of garden furniture and do my work with packed boxes beside me. Zsuzsa calls me the "steadfast tin soldier" on such occasions.

112

113

113–114. The inaugura-
tion of Collegium Budapest
in 1993; with Hungarian
President Árpád Göncz;
Professor Viktor Karády;
and Richard von
Weizsäcker, president of the
Federal Republic of
Germany (in profile).
115. Talking to Domokos
Kosáry, president of the
Hungarian Academy of
Sciences, and the writer
Péter Esterházy, during the
break of an event in the
Collegium.

114

115

116

116. Before the famous statue of Pallas Athene on the Szentháromság tér corner of the Collegium.

117. The Úri utca side of the Collegium Budapest building. I worked in the upstairs room with the loggia from the institution's foundation until 2003.

118. The three editors of the two volumes of studies written by the members of the "Honesty and Trust" international research group. Left to right: Susan Rose-Ackerman (Yale), myself, Bo Rothstein (Gothenburg), and Karen Cook (Stanford), a member of the group who was present at this meeting.

118

117

119

119. Lecturing in Beijing. I was introduced by my former student at Harvard, Professor David Li of the University of Hong Kong.

120. Professor Wu Jinglian, one of the leading intellects behind the Chinese reform, with whom I have been friends for two decades. We have birthdays within a few days of each other, and our Beijing hosts treated us to a celebratory dinner in January 2005.

121. At my desk in our new Budapest apartment.

120

121

Photo credits:
Figure 20
Gregory Grossman
Figure 30
L. Bianco, Geneva
Figure 34
Studio Orop, Paris
Figures 46 and 117
Éva Kigyóssy-Schmidt
Figure 70
Rod Phillips, Memphis, Tennessee
Figure 74
Judit Müller, Budapest
Figures 114 and 115
Mrs. György Nagy, Budapest

What prompted me to write the book

Ever since I had started to look critically at the command-based socialist economic mechanism and study modern economics, I had been pondering a number of essential questions.

What kind of price system would give better guidance to decision makers? Could price setting be left to the free play of supply and demand? Was there not a need for state intervention, at least at certain junctures?

Could a market economy be created *within* a socialist economy? Would it fit in with state ownership and the political structure of the communist system? Or was the cohesion between the political and economic spheres too tight for that?

When the two "great" systems were compared, why did capitalism turn out to be more efficient than socialism? Because it is more able to calibrate the prices that provide incentives to create market equilibrium and efficient input–output combination? Or was there another, more important explanation for capitalism's imposing economic achievements?

By that time, I possessed knowledge beyond what I had gained from theoretical books. I had spent several months in London and visited several other Western cities. The expression "market supply" would make me think of Selfridge's department store on London's Oxford Street or the shops on Bahnhofstrasse in Zurich. What encouraged sellers to keep such an incredible range in stock? Each time I traveled, there were new products about. (Pocket calculators appeared, for instance, and then the first personal computers.) What induced producers to keep bringing out something new?

Sticking to theoretical convictions is rather like being in love. I had been blindly and passionately attached to Marxism, and abandoning it was traumatic. Then I developed a slight affection for neoclassical theory and was rather partial in my outlook initially. You tend to be lenient with a lover's faults, while the love affair lasts... But that was not by any means so strong a passion as I had had for Marxism. My eyes were soon opened and I began to be annoyed, and later furious, that neoclassical theory was not giving satisfactory answers to the questions that were torturing me—or, worse still, that I sensed the answers were wrong.

As I said earlier, I turned away from Marxist theory because, among other reasons, it did not compare its theories with reality. I now had similar feelings about neoclassical theory, although the problem arose in a less annoying and acute way. Researchers contrived several partial theories that they tried assiduously to verify in practice. Econometrics, the science of analyzing economic measurements, had led to the development of some first-rate methods, and those techniques were taught to all economics students in Western universities. It was in dealing not with the parts but with the whole that I felt theory was failing to confront practice. This kind of comparison was especially missing from the comprehensive theories covering the whole systems of capitalism and socialism. That line of thought led me to place the so-called general equilibrium theory at the center of my critical investigation.

What economists call neoclassical theory consists of several partial theories. Popular Western textbooks offer a good survey of what can be included here, what its main concepts are, what questions it seeks to answer, and what methods it uses to confirm them. Neoclassical theory counts these days as the mainstream of the economics profession.* The theoretical kernel in this body of ideas is the general equilibrium theory devised in the latter half of the nineteenth century by the French Swiss economist Léon Walras. The simplified world of his model consists of firms intent on maximizing profits. Furthermore, the system includes households intent on obtaining maximum utility for their money. The theory demonstrates the existence of prices that balance the supply and demand of firms and households, so that under certain conditions an efficient equilibrium appears. Equilibrium, harmony, the best state possible under the given conditions—that is the image of society projected by this theory.

The Walrasian model alone of many neoclassical models tries to encompass the entirety of economic activity—not in condensed form, as macroeconomic theories do, but broken down into constituent parts. The actors in the economy appear along with the flows occurring between them. It is the one model that describes the market economy as a *system*. It was reasonable to think, therefore, that if I had trouble with the answers obtained from neoclassical theory, my critical analysis should focus on the general equilibrium theory.

Walras himself expressed the theory in mathematical form. Later Arrow, Debreu, Koopmans, Lionel McKenzie, and others helped create a much more appropriate mathematical armory for proving the theory. The theory is strictly logical and I might say beautiful in its conciseness and crystal clarity. It captivates all who come to know it thoroughly. It captivated me, too, until I woke up to some of my critical objections.

My main objection was that the theory, the multiplicity of research it instigated, and the comprehensive scientific program of mainstream economics failed to answer

---

* No consensus has emerged on what should be understood by "neoclassical theory" or the "mainstream" of the economics profession. The situation is complicated further because the interpretations vary over time; thus, for many people, the terms cover something different from what they did a few decades ago. Clarifying them is a task for thorough, objective works on the history of economic thought. I feel it is permissible when writing an autobiography to stay out of the debates and use these terms simply to give some impression of the groupings within the profession.

the *big* questions, to assist in a deeper understanding of capitalism and socialism, or to indicate how the world might be "improved." This (if not in exactly the same words) I explained in the preface and introduction to my book.

Some thought-provoking similarities

The Walras–Arrow–Debreu model can be compared with the Kornai–Lipták model discussed in chapter 8. They depict two diametrically opposite economies, the former a perfectly decentralized one and the latter perfectly centralized. The prices in the former carry information between decentralized units independent of each other and equal in rank. The latter has quantitative targets prescribed by the center for units subordinate to it and bound to obey.

And now comes an astonishing inference. Equilibrium is reached by both systems so long as certain rules are adhered to. Indeed, under a given optimum criterion and other conditions, both systems may arrive at an optimal state. This statement can be demonstrated and proven mathematically.

The similarity perplexed me. Was it then immaterial whether we lived in a centralized or a decentralized economy, under capitalism or communism? Or had the perplexing similarity arisen because both models overlooked the very attributes of real, living economic systems to explain the difference between actual capitalism and actual socialism—a living market economy and a living command economy?

I pointed earlier to some assumptions in the two models that disregard just such essential attributes of reality. Though they were mentioned in chapter 8's treatment of mathematical planning, let me recapitulate.

Both general models assume that decision makers possess accurate information. In fact, the information in both worlds is full of distortions, both spontaneous and intentional. But there the similarity ends and the essential difference begins. In capitalism, a system based on free enterprise and private ownership, there is a connection between information and incentive. Anyone may try to profit from knowledge that he or she possesses or may purchase it from others. Those doing so have an interest in ensuring that the information supplied is accurate. Under socialism, on the other hand, the scattered information has to be supplied willy-nilly to the center, like grain from the collective farm. Those who have the information, who discovered it or collected it first, cannot make a business out of it, buy more information, or trade in it. It has to be handed in to the center. Capitalism receives an enormous boost from its combination of decentralized information and decentralized incentive, and this blend is absent from socialism.

All processes in the Walrasian and the two-level planning models are assumed to take place without friction: adaptation is perfect. In fact, the mechanism of adaptation in both systems creaks and grinds, but to different degrees. The socialist system, for several reasons, is far more rigid than capitalism. Decisions in a decentralized economy can be taken at the lowest level. In a central economy, any evidence of an obstacle has to be passed up several steps in the hierarchy to the level competent to decide how to address it, and the answer then makes its way down again to the level able to implement the friction-eliminating decision. That is a much longer route. Then there is another factor: planning targets that cause strain prevent actors from accumulating reserves at all points of utilization, although doing so would be the one way to ensure rapid adjustment to demand.

That failure ties in with another problem. Both models have the decision makers acting in a strictly rational way, in the sense that neoclassical theory defines the word "rationality." Their preferences are constant and applied consistently when choosing between available alternatives. Here too I sense serious problems. Let me mention just one of them. The Kornai–Lipták model assumes that the planning center is strictly rational and perfectly consistent in its decisions. I visited the planning office in Budapest countless times and I heard much about the kind of instructions that the planners received from the party center. Rational? Consistent? No, they embodied impractical desires divorced from reality. Pressure on the planning apparatus came from various political forces and from trade or regional lobbies. The changeable power relations were accompanied by changing priorities. Sometimes a hasty switch would overturn all previous preferences. (The rationality and consistency of individual decisions will be returned to later.)

The two general system models also resemble each other in being static. Yet one of the essential differences between them lies in their dynamics. The competition in capitalism provides an impetus that pushes producers into continuous technical renewal. Socialism, in contrast, lacks the spontaneous force of competition: new products arise fitfully and reluctantly from the bureaucratic orders of central planners.*

What can and cannot be expected from general theory

I tried to explain why I developed an antipathy to *both* models. While I had trouble with both, the reactions they prompted in me were different. Let us first take the two-level planning model. I was reluctant to deal with theoretical interpretation of

---

* There is another important difference between the two systems that both models abstract away. When working on my critique of the equilibrium theory, I had rejected firmly the repressive political structure and official ideology of the communist system, but I had not yet grasped the complex ties between democracy and economic decentralization, between dictatorship and economic centralization. That argument was still absent from my writings and my thoughts at the time.

it in more detail. On a first approach, as discussed in chapter 8 and above, the model can be perceived as one of "perfect central planning." Now if perfect planning were possible, at least on a level of abstract theory, superficial or biased readers might, contrary to my intentions, think of this as a glorification of the socialist system.

Such considerations did not keep me from criticizing the Walras–Arrow–Debreu model.

Today I see serious errors in the theoretical starting points of my critique, within the philosophy of science.* The essential question was to clarify what can be expected of an abstract model.

Modelers can be accused of many mistakes, but not of abstracting from reality. That is the essence of building models. The easy way to criticize is to say, look, the model assumes this thing, but in reality everyone sees something else instead.

A theoretical model can be used for various tasks. Let me highlight here two connected ones.

A theoretical model helps to clarify the conditions under which a statement is true. In constructing a theory, a model builder will usually start by thinking not of the premises but of a predicted conclusion, and then work backward. What needs to be assumed for that conclusion to hold? The model builder wants to erect the model as parsimoniously as possible. So what are the necessary and sufficient conditions for proving the statement? Once this line of argument has been constructed, it can be a starting point for refuting or at least casting doubt on several other statements.

The Arrow–Debreu theory, for instance, states that equilibrium might occur and (according to certain criteria) an optimal state might be attained if and only if the information flowing into the economy is accurate. That does not mean that Arrow or Debreu did not know how much uncertainty and inaccuracy were concealed in the information.† Those who interpret the model correctly recognize a warning in the argument: if the information is uncertain and distorted, one should not imagine that the market mechanism is certain to bring the economy to an optimal state. Such optimization would happen (in the conditional mood) only if the information were accurate.

If this approach is used with each one of the assumptions in the Walras–Arrow–Debreu model, it ultimately becomes a very precise list of warnings, not an apology

* Frank Hahn pointed to this mistake in *Anti-Equilibrium* in a very thorough, article-length review that appeared in 1973, titled after Shakespeare, "The Winter of Our Discontent"—a reference to dissatisfaction both on my part and on his.

† Arrow was among the first to write major studies on the effects of uncertainty and on market failures. He was a pioneer, for instance, of theories proving that health care could not operate purposefully under a *pure* market mechanism.

for the market. If this abstraction or that fails to hold, then the final conclusion of the theory would not be valid and the market would no longer qualify as a perfect regulator.*

Related to this feature is another function of "pure," strongly generalizing, very abstract models: they can be used as a measure or a standard of comparison. The market economy that actually operates under capitalism is far from the Walrasian ideal, but the ideal makes a useful gauge of *how far* reality lies from it. For instance, it can be said of factual information exactly how it departs from the absolute precision of the Walrasian model. Similarly, it can be said how far the friction of reality differs from the friction-free state of the Walrasian model. I have to add that I made good use of the Walrasian model in my book *Economics of Shortage* for such comparisons.

The Kornai–Lipták model can be used in the same way, as I pointed out in chapter 8. The pure model of "perfect planning" compares well with the not at all pure, far from ideal reality of planning.

The trouble is not that the pure model shows an ideal, extreme world but that many misinterpret it and draw false conclusions from it.

Many readers of theoretical works tend to skip ahead in their thinking, forgetting all the strict assumptions behind a model and thereby misunderstanding a proposition that applies only *within* the model. For example, the Walras–Arrow–Debreu model is read as praise for a market left to itself, free of all state intervention, although that does not follow from the theory, provided it is grasped thoroughly. That misunderstanding or even misinterpretation deserves stern criticism.

The theory cannot be blamed for departing from reality, but those incorporating it into their thinking should be warned more emphatically about what has been disregarded and how there has been a departure from reality. Practicing economists should be trained to always keep in mind that they have to be very cautious when inferring practical conclusions from pure theory and talking about a theory's "economic policy implications." It is imperative for every single assumption to be weighed. Abstracting away from reality, necessary when formulating theories, can cause trouble for those taking action, when real conditions can no longer be disregarded.

I began the section by pointing to an essential mistake in the domain of the philosophy of science in *Anti-Equilibrium*. I should have attacked not the purity of the theory (the abstract, unreal nature of its assumptions), but the wrong use of it in mainstream economics. The real addressee of the critique should have been *main-*

---

* The argument applied here to the Walras–Arrow–Debreu model also surfaced in chapter 8, when the Kornai–Lipták two-level model was interpreted. I did not point out there, however, that this approach is linked to some especially difficult problems of the philosophy of science.

stream teaching practices and research programs. The creator of a pure theory cannot be obliged to include such a warning in his or her work. However, anyone who interprets and teaches the theory later can be called to account for failing to give that additional explanation. Do they teach theory well? What do they explain and what do they fail to show about how to correctly interpret theory? What warnings are required but commonly omitted by theorists in their articles and by teachers of theory? It would have been better to concentrate the book's criticisms on these questions.* The error in the underlying philosophy-of-science foundations that runs through *Anti-Equilibrium* weakens its persuasive force, even when the criticisms expressed stand out and provoke thought.

Rational decision makers

Let me turn to some strong points in the book that even today I consider valid.

Assumptions about the rationality of the behavior of decision makers are not confined to the Walras–Arrow–Debreu model. They are prominent in the whole mode of thinking of the neoclassical school. Economists traditionally interpret "rationality" in a specific and different way from other professions or from common parlance.

For a mainstream economist, rationality largely coincides with the requirements both of freedom from contradiction and of temporal consistency.†

Given the line of argument just expressed, the extreme model that assumes a rigorously consistent decision maker can do useful service. It can serve as a standard for establishing what inconsistencies are apparent in a real decision maker's behavior—in what decisions, in what direction, to what degree, and with what frequency it departs from that of an ideally consistent decision maker. It is regrettable that *Anti-Equilibrium* did not appreciate that valuable role sufficiently.

---

* Among the readers of the Hungarian edition of this book, I found some who thought that my criticism here of the mainstream in teaching and research applied far more to the *present* state of affairs, the period after the theories related to "rational expectations" became very influential, than to that of thirty-five years ago, when I was writing *Anti-Equilibrium*. Thus in a way *Anti-Equilibrium* received later recognition for pointing ahead to likely problems.

† For those not conversant in the subject, let me sum up the idea briefly. Decision makers can be called rational if they have preferences to which they adhere. They prefer alternative A to alternative B or vice versa, or they are indifferent. But if they now have a preference for A, they will not choose B as their next selection. Most works of the neoclassical school assume that decision makers have a "utility function." Their behavior can be interpreted as maximizing or "optimizing" that utility. It can be shown that with certain assumptions, the two types of formalism—preference ordering and maximization of the utility function—are equivalent. Amartya Sen (1977) aptly parodied this equivalence when he wrote that "rational fools" also fit the model's picture of rational decision makers. Even if they follow crazy ideas, they still count as rational if they do so consistently.

Unfortunately, the concept of a consistent, rational decision maker is not applied in many of the mainstream models in that subtle sense. Instead, it is assumed that strict consistency, utility maximization, and optimization more or less approximate typical behavior. Exponents claim to have a *universal* explanatory model of human behavior on their hands, able to describe anything—not just narrowly economic decisions but all problems of choice, from divorce and family size up to parliamentary votes. The book rightly spoke out against that simplistic approach. What I have just said in general terms about the mistakes in interpreting and teaching neoclassical models is especially pertinent to theories of optimization, utility functions, and preference ordering. Economists become accustomed to regarding this approach as a universally valid model and think in its terms even when it is wrong to do so.

Anti-Equilibrium devotes two long chapters to the problem, but here I would like to pick out only a single theme. The book discussed important distinctions between recurring and nonrecurring decisions and between comparable and noncomparable decisions.

I can choose each day what liquid to drink with my meals. Even if the specific choice depends on the menu or my inclinations, a definite pattern can probably be discerned in my consumer behavior, with a degree of permanence appearing in my preferences and dispreferences for drinks. The choice of liquid is a recurring decision, and the decision-making problem today is comparable in every respect to that of yesterday.

Let us contrast that with another decision-making dilemma. In 1956–1957, Hungary's borders opened up and it was possible to crawl under the Iron Curtain without risk. It had been closed, and everyone presumed (rightly, it turned out) that it would soon close again. Should one stay or should one go? That was a nonrecurring decision-making problem. Many people "defected" later, but under different circumstances, running different risks and encountering a different reception abroad. For us the later problem of staying or going was not comparable with the dilemma experienced in 1956–1957.

I would like to add two comments to that.

The neoclassical model of preference is appropriate for analyzing recurring and comparable decision-making problems. It can help to measure inconsistency, for instance. But the model of rational choice simply cannot be interpreted as operating and does not operate with nonrecurring and noncomparable decisions.

The first, recurring little decisions, are of interest, of course, especially for economists. They make it possible, for example, to estimate demand functions by drawing on regular observations of consumer behavior, or to produce functions describing the behavior of firms with respect to the recurring decisions of management.

But the great, important decisions in life are usually unique and nonrecurring. There are turning points and nonreturning events in the history of individuals and peoples. Woe to social scientists who seek to explain with ready-made preference orders how people will behave in making the big decisions. When I formulated my view on the matter in 1967–1970 and introduced this distinction, I was resorting to introspection. I could not see into the souls or decision-making processes of others, only into my own. I know I do not have preconceived preferences at such crucial dramatic moments—when I decided against emigrating during the great emigration wave following 1956 or against rejoining the Communist Party, chose what to do at certain junctures in the revolution, and so on.* Reciprocal effects develop between values (preferences) and conditions or choice possibilities. "Constraints" and "preferences" cannot be separated. Nor can the question of strict temporal consistency really be raised, because the great challenges and the circumstances of major decisions at one time might differ radically from those associated with earlier ones.

I still consider now that I was groping in the right direction with that distinction and other critical remarks I made in the book.

It is not possible to assess clearly in this respect how science and scholarship have developed in the period since *Anti-Equilibrium* was written. There have been some gains, pointing in the direction identified as desirable in *Anti-Equilibrium*. The most important is the cooperation that has developed between psychologists and theoretical economists in studying decision-making processes and reassessing the idealized model of a "consistent decision maker." Several valuable findings have been made. The research program that calls itself *behavioral economics* has developed into a school of thought. It seeks to emulate human behavior with fresh eyes and intends to describe it using models truer to reality. Particularly prominent in that school is the work of Amos Tversky and Daniel Kahneman, which revealed several anomalies in the theory—in other words, well-observable systematic deviations from what the standard model of rational decision making predicts should happen. Kahneman's Nobel Prize in 2002 was an expression of general appreciation by the economics profession. (Unfortunately, Tversky did not live long enough to share that honor with him.)[†]

---

* I have described in chapter 2 the decision-making process that led in my case to joining the Communist Party. I had had no special preferences beforehand. There were several motivations behind it. And after the great, far-reaching decision had been made, that choice later shaped my preferences in many less significant, recurrent problems calling for decisions.

† The findings of Tversky and Kahneman are customarily acknowledged—say, in a footnote. Yet most mainstream economists have continued their work as if the new theory had never appeared.

Other trends are more disquieting, however. The rational choice model has begun to be widely employed in sociology and political science, and even in history: that is, exactly in the discipline that has the most distinguished role in examining nonrecurring events. Unfortunately, in these disciplines the theory of rational choice is not used in the subtle way suggested above. Because its interpretations are often quite crude and oversimplified, the warnings and criticism of several decades ago have not lost their immediacy.

Non-price indicators

According to the theory criticized, only one type of information flows between the units of the system: price. That decision to assign price an exclusive role bothered me.

Prices have little influence on production and consumption in relations between enterprises under socialism. In contrast, great influence is exerted by other types of information: planning instructions, indications of rising or falling inventories, length of customer waiting lists, size of orders received, and so on. If all these were omitted from the analysis, there would be no way to explain what special advantages price signals would have if the market mechanism were restored.

Prices are not the only information vehicle in a capitalist market economy either. Non-price indicators play an important role there as well.

Anti-Equilibrium was feeling its way in the right direction on that issue. There has been a huge, welcome development in research into signals and the role of information in the decades since.

Equilibrium and buyers' and sellers' markets

"What seems to be extremely difficult in economics is the definition of categories.... It is always in the conceptual area that the lack of exactness lies."[3] I used that quotation from John von Neumann in the book. There was (and remains) confusion about the concept of equilibrium.

Physics and the exact sciences in general take it as a *positive* category. The word (in Latin, English, or German) derives from the notion of scales with equal weights on each side. Touch the scales, and the balance soon returns to equilibrium. It will not tip of its own accord—there is a stable, *static equilibrium*. It is possible similarly to talk of a path of *dynamic equilibrium*. The system moves, but any still shot taken from a film of it would show a system in equilibrium.

The neoclassical school of economic theory uses the concept of market equilibrium in that positive sense. In static theory, the market is in equilibrium if supply and demand for all products are equal—a definition that suffices for many analytical purposes. As economic knowledge spread, this definition passed into general parlance among economic policy makers and journalists.

The notion was joined by a *normative* approach to the problem. It is desirable for the market to be in equilibrium. It is not good for demand to exceed supply, thereby producing a shortage, or for unsold inventories to keep increasing.

Although I concede that this usage has clarifying power and it has won over economists and the public with its simplicity, I thought it was inadequate when I was writing *Anti-Equilibrium* and I hold that opinion to this day.

Let us look first at capitalism. Sellers always want to sell more than can actually be sold at prevailing prices, given all buyers and all sellers. Each is prepared, if successful, to sell more than before and has spare capacity and inventory for the purpose. In *that* sense, supply exceeds demand. And when supply does not precisely equal demand, it is always the smaller quantity that determines actual sales and purchases. Using the word "equilibrium" as one might in physics, *this* is the state of equilibrium, not one in which supply equals demand. This is the state to which the market returns, even if displaced by the trade cycle. (A boom will absorb or strongly reduce excess capacity and drop inventories to abnormally low levels.) And there is no need for concern about it, because that asymmetry is one of the great forces behind true capitalism, driving competition and whipping up rivalries. It gives supremacy to buyers: they can pick among sellers, instead of sellers picking among buyers. Most important of all, competition and rivalry propel technical development and the marketing of new products.

I felt this asymmetry even more strongly as I was living under the reverse conditions, where sellers had supremacy and picked among buyers. This was no momentary tip of the balance. The excess demand was persistent and the shortage continually reproduced by specific political and economic conditions. The shortage economy was the real state of equilibrium under the socialist system, not one of supply equaling demand.

I gave new, unaccustomed names in *Anti-Equilibrium* to these two states of equilibrium: *pressure* and *suction*. In the former, sellers press products on buyers, while in the latter, buyers thirstily absorb them from sellers. I have to say that the two names were not accepted by economists or in general speech and I abandoned them in later writings, turning to the expressions "buyers' market" and "sellers' market," which had earlier become current among economists.

Unfortunately, I have to conclude that the main problem preventing acceptance was not my terminology. The underlying idea of a skewed, asymmetrical state subsisting under both systems—superiority *either* of buyers *or* of sellers—made little headway. I still hold to that proposition, and I am sorry I have not persuaded my colleagues to do likewise.

The Walras–Arrow–Debreu theory brings in the concept of "competitive equilibrium," a state in which supply and demand are equal in each part of the market. I recognize that this theoretical category can also be used, owing to its precision, as a standard. Describing a real system becomes an easier task if it can be said to depart from the Walrasian competitive equilibrium in such and such a way. But the term "competitive" is out of place here. Real competition is just what would be lost if capitalism reached this Walrasian point of rest.* There is no further reason to strive or innovate. Every Jack has found his Jill. Every producer's or seller's production has found a buyer. This, luckily, is not the normal, lasting state of equilibrium under real capitalism, where producers and sellers compete strongly and are constantly renewing the composition of their production.

I can now explain the title of the book, with its double meaning. On the one hand, it was intended as a critique of the general equilibrium theory. On the other, it took issue with those desiring the calm, non-innovative state of competitive equilibrium.

The interpretation of the general equilibrium theory from the political point of view

Radical critics of capitalism accuse proponents of the neoclassical school of economics of defending and lauding the system in their theories. That is a false generalization.

Neoclassical theory, like the general equilibrium theory at its heart, is politically neutral. Neither in its axioms nor its conceptual framework is it "biased" politically. Its adherents and users include conservatives, liberals, and socialists. This point was underlined in *Anti-Equilibrium*, in opposition to those at the time who spoke of the neoclassical school simply as "bourgeois economists" and "apologists for capitalism."

I found two typical errors in the Western economics of the time, from the angle of a researcher seeking to compare systems and change the prevailing order. One was its tendency to idealize the market without impressing on economists sufficiently the need for state action and other auxiliary regulatory mechanisms. The other was its failure to point to the true advantage of the real market and the true forces propelling capitalism, which have just been discussed. Its picture of the market was at the same time too rosy and not rosy enough.

---

* As mentioned before, the publication of *Anti-Equilibrium* was preceded by the shorter "Essay," where I compared the pale category of competitive equilibrium to relations between a frigid woman and an impotent man. Later I seem to have thought a more modest style more expedient, as the comparison was left out of the book.

I tried to chart carefully where similarity to the Walras–Arrow–Debreu model and more generally to neoclassical thinking could be found in radical socialist works.

An example was the writings of Oskar Lange, who has been mentioned already. He applied the intellectual machinery of Walrasian theory to create his famous theory of socialism.

A more recent case was the Soviet Kantorovich school, which seriously suggested regulating the economy with shadow prices gained from linear programming, as proxies for the prices on a real market. It is easy to see why Western economists saw a kindred spirit in Kantorovich, for his system of equations was, in a slightly modified mathematical form, a variant of the Walrasian system.

Anti-Equilibrium also found features similar to general equilibrium theory in the equation system of the second volume of Marx's *Capital*. This discovery irritated my Marxist readers.

Nonetheless, those on the radical socialist side were more inclined to greet *Anti-Equilibrium* as an ally than to dismiss it. They rejoiced that we had a "common enemy." They did not conclude that it was a much stronger apology for capitalism than any simple praise of bland "competitive equilibrium." My book underscores, as one virtue of capitalism, something acknowledged in Marx and Engels's *Communist Manifesto* and central to Schumpeter's theory: technical advance and continual innovation are the driving forces constantly generated by the intrinsic attributes of the capitalist system.*

Reform or revolution in science

Looking over the state of economics at that time, I recognized there was much effective research going on that pointed in a direction I thought desirable and that was beginning to plug the gaps between Walrasian theory and reality. But I thought change was occurring too slowly. I wanted a scientific revolution, not mere reform of current scientific thinking. I was not immodest and did not claim for a moment that my book amounted to such a revolution.

I called my work a semifinished product, a work that did no more than express the *desire* for a revolution. I expressed myself forcefully. Adopting a phrase from Werner Heisenberg, I called the general equilibrium theory a "mathematical crystal," a closed system that cannot be corrected.[4]

---

* The book includes a detailed table of when and in what country the main new products that truly revolutionized production, consumption, and ways of life were created. It emerged that the socialist economies, during the historical period since their establishment, had created hardly any "revolutionary" products at all. The vast majority had been developed in capitalist economies. This comparison was in itself an indictment of the socialist economy.

Looking back today, I consider that revolutionary approach to have been mistaken.*

Since the 1962 publication of Thomas Kuhn's classic work on the philosophy and history of science, the question of whether revolutions take place in the history of natural sciences in a real sense has been a matter of debate. But this much seems certain: a high degree of continuity exists in the development of social sciences, despite turning points, sudden advances, and replacement of early subsystems of thinking by new ones. Elements of reform and revolution are constantly intertwined.

When writing *Anti-Equilibrium*, I undervalued the willingness and ability of mainstream economics to renew itself. The many new advances noted in this brief discussion and many not mentioned confirm that the school has moved far ahead of where it typically stood in the 1960s, and done so without a spectacular revolution.

But I have to add that my impatience at the time was understandable and has not subsided since. The ability to renew is apparent, but so is a trait of obstinacy, an almost stubborn insistence on keeping its tried and comfortable schemes of thought, even when legitimate doubts about them have arisen.

Initial reception and influence in the longer term

Initially, there were strong reactions to *Anti-Equilibrium*. In their Nobel lectures, Kenneth Arrow and Herbert Simon mentioned with agreement certain statements in the book.[5] Many other citations appeared in articles and books. In the early years after its appearance it received a huge number of reviews internationally. It was discussed in many places by economics students. The simple fact that a book had extensively criticized an almost ubiquitous school of economics caused an intellectual stir and pleased many people.

There were hardly more than a couple of strong rejections of the book. I thought my work would initiate ferment, bear fruit, and have a lasting influence. That was not to be the case. The early rejections were not followed by others, but neither were the early positive references. The debate stalled. The initial interest that the book excited died down.[†]

---

* When I broke with Marxism, radicalism stood me in good stead. Having written off all the intellectual capital taken over from Marxism, I rejected it entirely and restored tenets or methods only singly, after thinking them over again and being convinced of their usefulness. The same radicalism (for which I seem to have a penchant) did not serve me as well in my grappling with the neoclassical mainstream. The latter, to borrow Imre Lakatos's phrase, is not a degenerating scientific program but one that remains viable.

† When Olivier Blanchard, the famous Franco-American macroeconomist, interviewed me for a journal, I mentioned that *Anti-Equilibrium* had vanished, so to speak, after a couple of

I have related how fruitful research was being carried on in several fields along lines indicated by *Anti-Equilibrium*. This gave me a good feeling. To be honest, though, I have to confess that I was disgruntled over the fact that publications failed to mention *Anti-Equilibrium* as one of the theoretical-historical precursors to newer developments.*

I had expected *Anti-Equilibrium* to be highly influential. Why was it not more so? Some of my works have met or surpassed my expectations in that regard. Why did this one fall short?

One problem is the style or "genre" in which it is written. It is packed with mathematical symbols, but it does not use these for mathematical analysis. There are too many pedantic definitions, laboriously clarified and then not incorporated into the treatment. The book is replete with new terms for old categories. That approach seldom succeeds and certainly backfired here. Readers were repelled by the many new concepts.

The "Essay," the earlier, more concise, equation-less version, made a better impression on the reader. I misunderstood the situation. Seeing the many works that use a mathematical apparatus, I thought I would incorporate mine into the same genre. It would have been better to stick to the style of an essay.

The tone of my critique was polite, civilized, and free of the arrogant rebukes found in Marxist-Leninist discourse. Nonetheless, it was still too radical. I was struck when I read a piece by David Laibson and Richard Zeckhauser on Amos Tversky, the great Israeli psychologist and economist who had contributed so much with Daniel Kahneman to a better understanding of decision making. Tversky committed none of the "undiplomatic" mistakes that I had made in *Anti-Equilibrium*. He had not said, "Start from scratch!" He had recognized the merits of the model used hitherto. Let us start from that and build on it, he had advised. That approach was much more palatable to the colleagues he set out to convince of the need for change.

---

years. His reaction was this: "It was a very influential book. In France, where I come from, it was one of the books we all read. It became part of the common knowledge and as such, it is hardly ever mentioned. The same seems to have happened to many other ideas. Maybe it is a mark of success" (1999, p. 433).

* Some famous economists who advanced comprehensive critiques of neoclassical theory repeated in several places problems I had treated in my book in 1970, but did not refer back to it.

Why no references? The researchers concerned may have been unaware of *Anti-Equilibrium* and reached their conclusions independently. Or if they had read the book at some point, they may not have remembered it consciously as they wrote or lectured. Nor is it inconceivable that they remembered it but felt no obligation to share their memory with their readers or audience.

Analyzing the reasons for the failure (or, more precisely, semifailure) of the book brings me to some reasons of content more important than those of style or genre.

In itself, criticism at most weakens the existing respect for a theory and blunts the intellectual resistance to a new one, but it does not overturn an accepted, generally applied theory. There cannot be a vacuum. A new theory can oust an old only if economists are convinced that it is more viable.*

Anti-Equilibrium did not offer a new theory. That is why it could not break through.

Let me mention one example. The book points out how the Walras–Arrow–Debreu model projects an image of harmony—everyone nicely and peacefully finds a place in the equilibrium. It was time to pay much more heed to modeling conflicts. The book gives examples of conflict among branches of the state bureaucracy or within firms. Its proposal that such conflicts should be researched came well before the renaissance of game theory.

That is just the problem. Examination of conflicts gained fantastic impetus once John Nash and his associates had devised new theoretical means to undertake such inquiry and set about applying them in new theoretical constructs.

There is hardly any example of a plain *suggestion* of a big and important subject instigating a fruitful research program. Truly productive research programs start with a stimulating *constructive creation*. Such works are customarily called seminal.

Do it yourself if you have no servant, as the Hungarian saying goes. I tried several of the research tasks recommended in *Anti-Equilibrium* (alone or with associates), and some led to new theoretical findings. (I will return to these in later chapters.)

This problem actually brings me to ponder my lifetime scientific achievement. There is one type of researcher who once has a great idea, a truly original and important thought, and devotes his or her whole life to working on it, developing it, applying it, promoting it, and forming a school of thought around it. Some manage to do the same with two or even three significant ideas. The history of theory shows that a concentrated research strategy of this kind can yield very great results. I had to accept that my own inclinations pointed me toward a different strategy. I was struck by successive new ideas. Unfortunately, I seldom had the patience to stay

---

* This dynamic became obvious to me before the criticism after the book's publication. It had been drawn to my attention during discussions of the manuscript. I have kept a copy of a letter concerning the matter. I was at Yale University when I sent it to a colleague in Budapest in 1970. In it, I recounted the reception of the five talks I gave on the subject area that *Anti-Equilibrium* analyzed. I first reported the appreciation I had received and then continued, "The other group of opinions is a mixture of acclaim and dissatisfaction. One colleague called this, with self-deprecating irony, schizophrenic behavior: one segment of one's conscience tells us that what we do is not right, yet we go on doing it. They will stop this only when someone puts a better approach into their hands."

with one in particular and work on it, develop it, apply it, promote it, or form a school of thought around it myself. By the time all this had started (and start it certainly did in some cases), I had already gone on to the next exciting idea. This pattern did not recur in every case, but I could give several examples of it from my work. Such galloping ahead is well demonstrated by the content and subsequent history of *Anti-Equilibrium*. Despite all the editing it underwent, it charges from one half-digested idea to the next.

Worth writing?

I certainly caused several difficulties in my later career by writing and publishing *Anti-Equilibrium*. It was seen as unforgivable by some diehard, blinkered members of the neoclassical school. Furthermore, although I now see many faults and weaknesses in the book, I still consider many of its ideas valid. Even today I look on the neoclassical school critically, and not as a blind believer in it. Nowadays, I like to characterize myself as having one foot in and one foot out of the mainstream. On some questions I go with the stream, and in other cases I try to swim up the stream. This half-in, half-out situation sometimes causes conflicts. My writings often fail to appeal to editors and readers not sufficiently open to such oddities.

How did I gather the courage to write it? I had no doubts even before I wrote the book that its strong criticism would cause a fierce backlash. My ever stronger inclination to doubt and rethink things, developed after I lost faith in Marxism, must have contributed to that determination. Having been blind and uncritical once, about Marxism, I did not want to be blind or uncritical again.

I have described in earlier chapters the disadvantages of not having been to a good university and of having to teach and train myself. But being self-taught has advantages as well. I learned the theory of the mainstream, but I did not have it so deeply drummed into me, in lectures or seminars or while preparing for exams, that the conventional neoclassical answer to every question became automatic, even in my sleep. Far be it from me to compare myself to Haydn, but I feel some similarity in my *situation*. For Haydn, having spent long years away from the centers of world music (indeed, he was in Hungary, at the Esterházy Palace), once wrote, "I was cut off from the world, so that I had a chance to develop and take risks. There was no one at Eszterháza to distract my attention or sow doubts in me. That is how I became original."[6]

If I had spent my entire academic career in American universities, I would have been writing *Anti-Equilibrium* at about the age when academics are normally appointed to a full professorship. My manuscripts would have been rejected by leading journals because they contained half-formed messages and, furthermore, unorthodox ideas that criticized fundamental dogmas. Keep in mind that professorial appointments depend on how much the junior faculty member publishes in leading journals. At a time when decisions were being made about me, I might have sheered away from annoying colleagues whose opinions could have influenced my promotion. In that respect, living in faraway Hungary did me good. Strange as it may sound, it made it easier for me to retain my autonomy. I was not "broken" to accepting the conventions of Western academic life in the way that young academics there are, by the system of graduate education, the first job, and, later, the process of promotion.

So was the book worth writing? Did I regret writing it? Here I can use myself as an example to illustrate the many inconsistencies of human behavior. Sometimes I think, "If only I had not written it." Sometimes I think differently, not wanting to remove from my works my critique of neoclassical theory. Yet it would be good if by some Orwellian trick I could excise the 1971 version and instead write a new one that reflected my present view and knowledge. It would be good to substitute that revised version for the one that is gathering dust on library shelves. However, as Kálmán Mikszáth, the great Hungarian writer, said, "Once someone has written something, he cannot cut it out again, even with an axe."*

But overall I do not regret that *Anti-Equilibrium* appeared. The sharpest and most thorough critic of it, Frank Hahn, whom I have quoted already, concluded his review: "I would much rather have this book than not have it. Kornai is so patently honest and so clearly a scholar of integrity that one is always drawn away from the bad to the good things he has to say. And among the good things some are very good indeed."[7] I feel some pride in the achievement. As Hahn wrote, "That book sufficed for me at that time." Perhaps it was also useful that I learned from writing it and from the debates about it. Whatever the case, it has certainly been part of my life.

Some subjective closing comments

Finally, I would like to leave behind the world of economics and scientific theory for a moment, and make a few personal comments about *Anti-Equilibrium*. One of the readers of the first draft of these memoirs commented on this chapter, "Why go into the reasons for failure in such detail? Try and get over it." Another reader remarked, "People don't like resentment.... What you write about references is dictated by vanity. Not everyone thinks it is so important."

I admit, it would be more graceful to wave aside the problems that the history of the book caused me. But I am not the kind of person who can casually wave things

---

* Péter Esterházy quoted this saying with reference to a book by András Nyerges.

aside. I envy people who feel, like Edith Piaf, "Non, je ne regrette rien" (No, I do not regret anything). I cannot say the same for myself. There are things I have regretted and others I have not. There is more than one thing I have done about which I still cannot form an unambiguous judgment, even in hindsight. I frequently find myself ruminating about old dilemmas. Should I not have chosen the other course instead? No doubt I experience failure more intensely than success.

Anti-Equilibrium is not merely an item on my list of publications. It was the most ambitious enterprise of my career as a researcher. I had undertaken something bigger and more difficult than what I was able to accomplish. I am aware of that, but it still does not make its failures easy to come to terms with.

I am indifferent to neither success nor failure. I am convinced that most scholars feel the same, though very few will admit it. They are afraid that the public will take their concern the wrong way. It looks better if a scholar, unaffected by the subsequent assessment of his or her work, gives the impression of caring about nothing except the progress of science and finding the truth. If that is the case, then why is there—in the world of science, just as in literature, arts, sports, production, and business—such a colorful array of awards, honors, and marks of status and recognition, and on the other side, signs of disapproval ranging from silence to public attacks and humiliation? There may be fanatics and saints out there, completely unaffected by such things. But most fallible humans feel an intimate positive relation between their very intense experience of success and failure and the drive to create something. No doubt the joy derived from knowledge and the desire to search for truth *are* the main driving forces in research. However, there are some auxiliary motivations that further boost that drive. Those indifferent to what others think about their performance (not just hypocritically feigning indifference) will usually make less effort.

In this chapter—as in other parts of the book—I have striven for honest introspection. I have tried to find out how much responsibility I bore for *Anti-Equilibrium*'s not achieving the effect I had expected it would. Among others things, this honesty gives me the moral basis to ask, "Can the lack of success be attributed *only* to me?" It is not ill-feeling that makes me seek an answer to this question. I am speaking for many researchers when I broach the issues of the profession's refusal to accept heavy criticism and of its shortness of memory; that memory ought to honor the first appearance of important—primitive, clumsy, but nevertheless pioneering—new ideas.

I could easily have listened to my two readers' advice. I could have deleted a few paragraphs here in chapter 10 and perhaps from other places in the book. Doing so would have instantly removed the possibility of creating such dubious impressions of me. There is a chance that the resulting image would more closely resemble the ideal formed of a "scholar"—but it would not show a picture of me.

11

Institute, University, and Academy—1967 Onward

Let us turn back from pure theory to the far from pure social milieu of Budapest. My main employer as I was writing the "Essay"—the first draft of *Anti-Equilibrium*—was the Computing Center of the Hungarian Academy of Sciences, where I was still engaged to some extent in mathematical planning. But concurrently, I had returned part-time to the Academy's Institute of Economics, from which I had been dismissed in 1958. Then its director, István Friss, telephoned in 1967 to ask me to return full-time, which I did. After that, the Institute of Economics was my workplace in Hungary for more than twenty-five years.

The economics supremo

It is time to say a little about István Friss, the man who called me back to the Institute of Economics. The Hungarian Academy of Sciences and its research institutes had a complex hierarchy; Friss headed Department IX, covering research into economics, law, and some other social sciences. Within Department IX, he chaired the Academy Committee for Economic Sciences, which made him responsible for the discipline. Finally, he was director of the Institute of Economics. It was rare for one man to hold positions on three levels of the hierarchy, so that theoretically he was his own boss and supervisor twice over, under a political structure in which these offices brought considerable power.

Friss showed inconsistency in his personality. His outlook was a compound of several conflicting values, and his behavior reflected in turn several patterns, traditions, and reflexes. Above all, he was a Communist. He had left a prosperous, middle-class background at an early age and joined the illegal Communist Party, despite the persecution that such an act would entail. He remained firmly faithful to his Leninist convictions until he died. His behavior showed some marks of the period he had spent in exile in Moscow—a distant manner and suspicion of colleagues. But he took no pleasure in acting the boss, pulling rank, or throwing his weight about. He had done some of his studies in Germany and England, and something of the quiet-spoken, well-mannered gentleman stayed with him for the rest of his life. He produced little as a scholar and researcher and came up with no original ideas of any importance, but he earned much merit as an organizer. Wherever he could (and the stipulation is grotesque in itself, of course), he respected his subordinates' freedom of expression. He did not require them to toe the party line, as many others in similar positions did in the Soviet Union and Eastern Europe. He was especially keen to encourage empirical research and the observation of reality.

Friss and I developed an ambivalent relationship. He was twenty-five years older than I was, so elements of the patriarchal and paternalistic were involved. We used the familiar second person together, but he called me Jancsi, while I, like everyone else, called him Comrade Friss.

At a risk of repeating myself, let me gather together here some events I have touched on in earlier chapters. Friss had given me information and instructions on party economic policy in the days when I worked for the newspaper *Szabad Nép*. When I was sacked from my position there, he took me in but cut my pay to a minimum. As my work began to shine again, he promoted me and presented me as an example for the others at the institute to follow. He phoned me at the time of the 1956 Revolution, wanting me to speak up for the Communist cause on the radio, which I declined to do. After the revolution was defeated, he spoke of me from the party rostrum as a traitor to Marxism. He did not initiate my dismissal from his institute, but he did not impede it. He carried out the decision to remove me like a disciplined party warrior. On the other hand, he helped me to find a job and to publish my book in England.

Now he was inviting me back to the institute. And what followed? He expressed in several forms how much he appreciated and respected my work. When I was sick at home after an operation, he visited me and asked whether I would not like to be his successor as director of the institute. (I would not.)

As if nothing had happened

My removal from the Institute of Economics was one of the great crises in my life. My return took place calmly and unspectacularly, as if nothing had happened. István Friss did not refer to the past. Nor did any other of my colleagues or I.

I had a great many ideas and feelings churning together inside me at that time. Preparations for the so-called New Economic Mechanism of 1968 were being made at full speed. A few years before I returned to the institute, I had briefly met Rezső Nyers, who at the time was the secretary of the party's Central Committee and was running the reform work. He made a comment in passing: "You know you have been rehabilitated, don't you?" To which I replied, "Where would I know this from? No one told me." Many of those who had read my book in 1956–1957 or who had taken part in the debate on our 1956 reform proposal or with whom I had discussed the subject a decade ago were now participating in preparing the reform. I was sure that I had influenced their thinking. Yet no one ever mentioned that influence, in speech or writing. Friss never returned to the fact that he now, in accordance with the party line of the day, was giving support to a reform initiated by those people (particularly me) whom he had denounced in the party's name only a couple of years before.

But it would have embarrassed me if anyone had begun to probe then into what my relationship was to the economic reform. I was over the "naive reformer" phase of my life and ever more strongly convinced that the changes planned did not go far enough.

My differences with the existing regime were primarily political in nature. I recalled the charges made against me by the commissars dispatched to the institute in 1958. They had been *right* to think of me as their ideological foe. My writings had indeed helped to erode the Communist worldview, and I had played a part in the intellectual side of the 1956 Revolution. They had been *right* to consider me unreliable. Many of my friends were in prison or exile, or had lost their jobs. I had renounced Marxism. I had not joined the new party. I had been dismissed from the institute not simply because I wrote an objectionable book but because I had turned against the party. There was nothing to warrant their suddenly taking it all back. In the *political* sense, Communist Party practice allowed the "rehabilitation" only of those who had stayed Communists, even when their own comrades denied them the label.*

Those who had decided to take me back would not have been willing to abandon the views they held then. As far as I was concerned, I did not want to give the impression that there was now an understanding between me and the ones who had first dismissed me and then invited me to return. The one solution acceptable to all sides was *not* to explain anything. It was a prescription applied widely under the Kádár regime.

Nonetheless, this glossing or stepping over the past still bothered me. I had to concede, as a temporary loser in an earlier political battle, that it was the least awkward solution for me at the time. Those entering the political arena should not

---

* Consider a joke current in the 1950s: Kohn has been expelled from the party, but dreams that night of U.S. troops occupying Hungary. President Eisenhower arrives in Budapest on a white horse, like Miklós Horthy in 1919. A kneeling Mátyás Rákosi hands him the keys of the city. Eisenhower then speaks in a commanding voice: "Rákosi! Take Kohn back into the party!" By 1967, I was far from sharing that comical desire of poor Kohn.

spend time licking their wounds. But as a researcher and a man of science, I saw that a grave blow had been dealt in 1958 to research freedom and that Friss had lacked the moral courage to at least say something about that aspect of the affair.

Trust and tolerance

Let me now try to say how much trust I felt for my colleagues. I will omit close friends from before 1967: András Nagy (removed from the institute at the same time as I and invited back in 1973), Judit Rimler (I proposed hiring her),* and Márton Tardos (a close friend since about 1956, who joined the institute at the end of the 1970s). I want to discuss here my relations with the other institute staff.

When I returned to the Institute of Economics, I felt an oppressive distrust of conversations with any direct political bearing. I vividly recalled the interrogations I had undergone, where it had emerged that a close friend had recounted to his questioners my ideologically charged comments on his study. It was hard to repress the thought that anyone I talked to now might do the same.

My colleagues also sensed this distance and coldness. I had worked for a couple of years with Kati Farkas, who later died young. We built up a good relationship. Once she looked at me with her kind face and asked me, a little reproachfully, "Tell me, János, why are you so distrustful of us?" We talked about it and I tried to explain what was causing my feelings. What is important here is not so much what was said in our discussion but rather the effect on me of the mood it created. I began to relax a little with those I felt would never abuse my trust in them. But that easing up was a slow and gradual process, and in most cases it only went part of the way.

Even later, I would never let myself go and speak spontaneously and frankly about an important political development without first thinking about whom I was addressing. I maintained strong self-control. I assessed everyone according to their personality, writings, comments, and actions. Then I would apportion my trust, meagerly or liberally as the case might be. "Do not squander your trust," the poet Attila József remarked,[1] and I certainly did not.

If I did influence colleagues around me, especially younger ones, it was not by expressing my political views but in other ways. They saw how I worked, came to know in conversation my professional standards, and learned my intellectual orien-

---

* I had the chance to take on an associate in 1959, during my "exile" in light industry, and asked friends at the university to recommend their best student. That is how I came across Judit Rimler, my first research assistant, who later became a reputable researcher herself. When I changed jobs, I insisted she join me in my new workplace.

tation from my writings. Those open to such impressions were able to accept a great deal of them.

As time went by, the number of people I would gladly converse with increased. It became possible after a couple of years to bring one or two people into the institute. Later, I was appointed head of a group and had a few young researchers working directly under me. I taught the married couple János Gács and Mária Lackó at the university, and suggested that one of them should come to the Institute of Economics to work—I could not offer two positions at the time. They decided that Mari should be the one to work with me. Another university student of mine was Judit Szabó. András Simonovits, a recent graduate in mathematics, was recommended by Tamás Lipták. Later, Mihály Laki became a member of the team. Zsuzsa Kapitány, originally a secondary school teacher of mathematics, was a computer operator aiding another colleague and then came over to me, initially in the same capacity, before steadily retraining herself as an economic researcher. All those mentioned were younger than I was. There was someone of my generation working alongside us, although he was not a member of the group, and that was Béla Martos, originally a mathematician.

Members of the Kornai Group were bound mainly by their work and similar professional approach, of course.* (I will talk about that in the next chapter.) At the same time we shared sympathy and friendship. As I have mentioned before, I have never been content with a purely working relationship with those around me. That was true at *Szabad Nép* and that is how things developed at the Institute of Economics and later at Harvard as well. It may not be the most efficient and professional method of organizing work. It may prevent the building of a hierarchical relationship based exclusively on the demands of the job. But I do not regret my habits and requirements. For me the warmth of human relations, friendship, and trust are valuable beyond measure.

It became a tradition that the Kornai Group would go for lunch together at precisely 11:30 A.M. To be frank, I was the one who set the early time, because I like to eat early, I do not like to wait in a restaurant, and I wanted us to be among the first to be served. We were always joined by several colleagues. The lunch itself was not usually anything special, but we took pleasure in each other's company and lively conversation.

That special admixture of friendship in my relations with colleagues was not confined to the young people working in my research group. It extended to others who arrived at the institute during those years: Tamás Bauer, Aladár Madarász, Károly

---

* The institute was divided at the time into parallel groups, each headed by a more experienced member of staff. The word "group" is used here in the *organizational* sense.

Attila Soós, Iván Major, János Köllő, Péter Pete, Gábor Kertesi, and Péter Mihályi, to mention just a few. They have all had notable academic careers since then, almost all of them becoming full professors at various universities. Some of those mentioned also filled high political positions for a while after the change of system. I first met them at a formative stage in the development of their thinking. With some, I had a series of long discussions; with others, my relations were less intense. A few of them I had taught at the university. Apart from reading carefully and commenting on their studies for the institute (I still have the notes I made), I also talked with them about research and economic reform, as well as many general intellectual and ethical questions.

My discussions with members of my group and others, as well as their studies that I read, were very instructive. I learned much about the operation of the Hungarian economy, debates among economists, the mood of the country, and alternatives for the future. It was a refreshing intellectual environment, and I was glad to be in it. I know less about the effect in the opposite direction. It is for them to say how strong an influence my work and our personal contacts had on them. I meet them all from time to time, some quite regularly, but that is a subject, understandably, that does not come up in our discussions.

A sociologist could professionally plot the networks of relations in the institute, with centers, arrows pointing from one person to another, and numerical indicators of how intense the relations were. The chart would certainly show what clusters grew under the influence of various factors.

One factor helping or hindering the formation of connections was the opinion people held of mathematical methods. In that respect, the situation in Hungary resembled the one found in economics departments of American universities some decades earlier: most researchers were averse to applying mathematical models and econometric analysis. There were some in the institute with almost a phobia against the advance of mathematics, which they saw as intellectual sleight of hand. Conversely, a special solidarity was felt among the users of mathematical methods, irrespective of whether they were Marxists or had sympathy or antipathy for the Kádár system.

As in all fairly large organizations, there were a few strong personalities who produced groupings by attracting or repelling people.

The main determinant of attraction or repulsion was worldview or political stance.* People did not make political declarations in the institute, but it was apparent where everyone's heart lay. I think political agreement was a stronger binding force than it is among intellectuals in the Western world.

---

* The networks formed by various criteria partly overlapped. Any member might be associated, loosely or closely, with several groupings.

The political views prevalent among the institute's researchers at any time spread over a wide political spectrum. We had no die-hard Stalinists, but there were a few dogmatic, conservative Communists of the old school. Many were "reform communist" in type, gradually awakening, anxious for change. They hoped to inject a larger or smaller dose of the market into the economy, to see greater opportunities for criticism, and to attain a measure of "democratization," while still feeling a basic affinity with the Kádár system. Then there were those who had broken with the Communist Party or never been close to it and were strongly critical of the regime in power.

The political composition of the institute staff would shift as some left, others arrived, and many changed their views, in certain cases radically. Such shifts altered the sizes of the informal groupings or clusters. At any point of time in the dynamic process, informal groupings based on political convictions would always be present. Observed closely, people who took similar positions had greater political trust in each other than in those with other convictions. I too tended to confine my personal relations to those with whom I did not feel constrained by political differences.*

There were groupings, but no trench warfare. The older ones and the middle-aged (such as I was at that time) had borne on all of their nerves the trauma of 1956. Since then, we had digested the experience, each according to his or her view of the world. What was common in these generations of the intelligentsia was that they were not spoiling for ideological or political warfare against each other. There was *treuga dei*, a strange "truce of God" among us: we will not harm you, but we expect that you will not pick on us either. Live and let live. There were no sharp, open political clashes.

How can the situation be described? We all retained our principles without making shameful concessions to one another.† Individually, people fought their battles outside the institute walls, if they happened to be the battling kind. Individually, they advanced and expressed their views in their academic work, if they had timely things to say in the public interest. But within the walls, there was a kind of *tolerance* of each other, for fear of upsetting the applecart and attracting much greater harm from those outside, who were prepared to exert much crueler forms of

---

* That did not, in my case, mean that I observed the boundaries of these clusters strictly in the later, softer period of the Kádár regime. A couple of my colleagues obviously had different convictions from mine; nevertheless, we became friends.

† I am aware that not everyone would share that assessment. Some radicals regard such local "peace pacts" in the Kádár period as unacceptable compromises that helped to prolong the life of the regime. Perhaps they did prolong it, but they made people's lives more bearable. That verdict leads ultimately to the underlying question of whether people can be expected to put a great communal goal—in this case, the goal of ousting the regime as soon as possible—before their personal betterment.

control. Maybe that sense of common danger and a common enemy generated among us a tolerance all too rare in intellectual circles these days. The power relations in the institute at that time gave the advantage to those who made open gestures toward the Kádár regime and proclaimed Marxist theories. It is good to be able to say that they did not use that power to provoke political arguments or "expose" anti-Marxist views. They left those who thought otherwise in peace.*

I am satisfied even in hindsight to remember the institute as an island of peace in the stormy sea. Research was the most important thing for me, calling on all my energies and demanding maximum concentration. For that, I needed peace.†

An aborted reform of the institute

I often traveled abroad in that period, not just to attend a conference or deliver a lecture but for longer stretches as well. I began to know from within what life was like there and how research and teaching went in the famous Western centers of scholarship. Some aspects of this I would have liked to transfer to our Institute of Economics. In 1971, I joined with two colleagues, Ádám Schmidt and János Kovács, to put up a proposal for reform.² Although the ideas of all three appeared in the document, the most delicate and controversial proposals came from me.

I was suggesting closer connections between promotion at the institute and publication. Publications should be weighted. Greater emphasis should be given to publication abroad, while bearing in mind the scholarly reputation of the book publishers or journals concerned.

These were self-evident criteria in the West.‡ Not so in Hungary. The bar for publication in Hungary was not set high enough. Studies of high quality and rich content appeared, but alongside them works of little professional significance also found a forum relatively easily. Very few economists published in the West, and it was even rarer for them to approach the prestigious journals. While the infant system of "market socialism" recognized that the real test of product quality

---

* Certainly one key factor was that successive directors of the institute, István Friss, Rezső Nyers, and Aladár Sipos, did not initiate political purges. On the contrary, when political attacks began on Tamás Bauer, for instance, and his dismissal was demanded from above, Nyers, then the director, defended him.

† The calm atmosphere of the workplace helped me a great deal at a time when I was going through a period of crisis in my private life. My marriage with Teréz Laky broke up. Soon after I returned to Hungary in 1970 after half a year at Yale University, I moved into a new apartment with my second wife, Zsuzsa Dániel.

‡ There the problem has been the opposite extreme: pressure to publish so great that it may even prove harmful. I will return to this point in a later chapter.

was whether it could compete in Western export markets, no such export test was applied to the products of research.

Nor was it only in publications that the strict international quality test was lacking. People were able to vegetate at the institute for years, publishing little or nothing. Once you were in, you could stay for a lifetime, even if more talented and productive researchers were beating at the door, ready to take your place.

Another problem was that many who did publish were working at a very low level of efficiency by Western standards. Although they did not have part of their time consumed by teaching, as did their counterparts in Western universities, the volume of their publications was only a fraction of those produced by their Western colleagues in leading universities (to look only at a quantitative measure).

My experience abroad was not the only influence on me as I formulated the demands I have outlined. I was trying to pass on my own work ethic and professional ambitions to others, to judge others as I judge myself. I gladly spend some of my working day in conversation, but I like to spend most of it in productive research. I was irritated to see many people spend hours and days just talking. I have to admit that dialogue and debate behind closed doors went part of the way toward offsetting the lack of openness and freedom of discourse in public life, helped people to clarify their thoughts, and stimulated ideas and spread knowledge. But the forward-looking aspects of those conversations inevitably combined with redundant chatter that took valuable time from research.

The management of the institute tried to implant some working discipline by having us clock in and out. That grotesque administrative measure was worth nothing, of course. The drive had to come from *within*. Drawing on my Western experience, I believed that the motives of many researchers were not separate from outward incentives or conditions for admission to the institute, remaining in the job, advancing up the ladder, and formal and informal workplace recognition. The proposed reform therefore recommended substantial changes in incentives, assessment, and promotion.

The proposal had a mixed reception. Despite some approving murmurs, most of my colleagues did not in fact like the idea. Some argued that Western journals and publishers were rejecting work simply because it was written by Marxists. (That was not true; several counterexamples could be given.) Others said that the West was indifferent to events in the East. (That was not true either; a piece's chances of being published depended largely on whether it met professional standards.) Yet others (especially in private) argued that they had come a long way in their critique of the system, but they could not publish their findings legally. (That was a more serious argument, which I will consider in detail in a later chapter.) Even then, I did not believe that the selection mechanism of Western periodicals worked perfectly, and now I look on their editorial practice with a still more critical eye. Sometimes they are unjustified in discarding pioneering articles whose ideas are unusual, thereby impeding the dissemination of important results. The converse error also occurs frequently. Works of little value slip through the filters—even though they have nothing really important or new to say—because they conform with and accommodate to the intellectual world of the mainstream, and adopt its style and methodology. However, in spite of such weaknesses and errors, the positive correlation between the true scholarly value of works and their publication in an internationally acclaimed periodical is rather strong. So even in retrospect, I believe it was right to try to encourage my colleagues to publish in prestigious journals.

One more argument in the discussion was raised against our suggestions. Why should so much emphasis be placed on publication? It was at least as important or more so to measure the extent to which colleagues were influencing economic policy making and to gauge what role they were playing as experts and advisers—whose names would not appear, of course, in published state documents, party resolutions, or legislation. We contested that argument, too. Such economic political activity is also praiseworthy and admirable, but not sufficient to demonstrate *scientific* progress.

I mentioned in the previous section that groupings distinguished by political criteria and worldview existed at the institute. The reform proposal cut across them to produce different combinations among the researchers. Many agreed with the changes proposed, as they had already managed to publish in prestigious journals or they sympathized with the spirit of the proposal and aimed to bring their work before an international public in the future.* But the proposal was opposed by all (irrespective of politics) who lacked the talent, industry, or ambition to adopt Western professional norms—who did not want to join the competitive arena of publication, a not entirely reliable but still useful yardstick of academic achievement.

In practice, the proposal was dropped. The institute did not alter its operative norms and procedures in the spirit we had recommended. Everything stayed as it was.

It is another matter to say how staff members decided individually on their professional strategies in life. Some (relatively few, in fact) took up the challenge of Western-style professional measurement seriously and consistently, trying, sometimes successfully and sometimes not, to publish abroad and present themselves to Western economists through their lectures. Most of them did not enter the contest.

* Many Hungarian economists, including several at the institute, had impressive publication lists before the reform was proposed. Later their number grew, but not for many years after the debate were publications gradually added to the main criteria for professional assessment and promotion.

After the change of system, I spoke to several of my colleagues of that period who realized what a big mistake they had made. They could never make up for the years or decades they had lost.

Banned, but teaching nonetheless

I related in chapter 6 how the Institute of Economics was investigated in 1958 by a board of party commissars, whose head, László Háy, swore, "As long as I am the rector, Kornai will not teach at the university." He kept his word, and his successors kept to the decision as well. Many famous universities abroad would have welcomed me to their faculty, but for decades, the one with a monopoly of economics teaching in higher education in Hungary, the Karl Marx University of Economics (Marx Károly Közgazdaságtudományi Egyetem, or MKKE), never offered me a teaching post. I suppose high circles in the party must have reached or at least confirmed the decision that Kornai might do research, but he had to be kept away from young people.*

Disintegration of the Kádár system was proceeding apace when I had my first offer of a Hungarian university post; it came from the rector of the day, Csaba Csáki. Let me quote from my reply:

Your initiative came...after I had accepted an offer from Harvard University. I am grateful for your attention, but have to say it has come too late. One can only live once; I do not know how my life would have gone if the MKKE had sought my involvement earlier. I can state that at any time in the three decades before I accepted the offer from Harvard, I would have been ready to expend a high proportion of my energies in the service of the MKKE....It has caused me bitter and painful feelings throughout my academic career that [the institution] where Hungary's young economists are trained has not invited me to be a teacher—has not wished either to accord me the rights and intellectual influence of teaching or to give me the opportunity of a close relationship with young people. This is an irremediable loss to me, for which other achievements in teaching and research cannot compensate.[3]

Although I did not receive a teaching post, I did manage to teach at the MKKE in one form or another, and in 1968, I was given the rank of titular university professor. That did not give me the rights and the influence on university affairs that a full professorship would have done, but it allowed me to hold occasional seminars or series of lectures. I led what was called a "special seminar" for three years. Not knowing any pattern to follow, I tried to work out for myself what to teach and how. Each year was spent dealing intensely with a set of problems, mainly ones I

---

* Party leaders remembered how university students had helped to foment revolution in October 1956 and tried to isolate them from intellectuals whose influence they felt would be risky. Many of those prosecuted after 1956 were allowed to do research in institutes of the Hungarian Academy of Sciences, but none received a university appointment.

had encountered in my work. I thoroughly enjoyed this work, and to this day retain fond memories and warm feelings toward the members of those seminars. I hoped the courses served as an intellectual antidote to the official syllabus, which was often presented mechanically, and I believed it benefited the students to hear a researcher's ideas at first hand and get familiar with some unorthodox, extracurricular thoughts. My intention was less to impart knowledge as such than to inspire critical thinking. Several of those who attended my seminars went on to become excellent research economists, professors, and business executives.

I rate particularly highly the ties that bound me to Rajk László College, founded in 1970 and attached to the Karl Marx University of Economics. Its founder and principal, Attila Chikán, turned it into an intellectual workshop unlike any other in Hungary. In its mode of operation, it borrowed much from the traditions of the "people's colleges" disbanded in the Rákosi period, from Eötvös College at Eötvös Loránd University, from the grandes écoles of Paris, and from the colleges of Oxford and Cambridge, England. These models it adapted and augmented with innovations of its own. The students of Rajk College were carefully selected from the best at the university and received instruction in modern fields not covered by the standard university course. They were trained to think independently in ways that broke with doctrine. This independence was expressed, for instance, in whom they invited to lecture. The list included well-known intellectuals who had been in prison a few years earlier, as well as leaders of the "democratic opposition" to the Communist system that arose in the 1970s.

I lectured at Rajk several times. If I was working on a study, I would gladly try it out first on the attentive, well-informed audience I found there.

The graduate training required for a doctoral degree is provided in most Western countries by universities. Discussing my own education in chapter 5, I explained that the procedure was different in countries adopting the Soviet pattern. In Hungary, the training for the Ph.D. equivalent—the candidacy degree—was obtained by the "aspirant" not at a university but through a special central Scientific Qualifications Committee (Tudományos Minősítő Bizottság, or TMB). This nominated a director of studies or an "aspirant leader," rather like the dissertation adviser found in the West. Another important difference was that instead of the graduate student picking an adviser, the adviser in the East was assigned by the TMB in accordance with several criteria, not least political ones.*

I later helped a number of Harvard graduate students as their adviser. Not so in Hungary. I had received a candidacy degree in 1956, which qualified me to be an

---

* Each system involves consent, as both adviser and the aspirant leader have to accept the task.

aspirant leader under the regulations at the time, but never once in almost half a century of existence did the TMB invite me to be one. To translate that into Western language, I was never entrusted with a single graduate student.

It is heartbreaking to think of it. Professors at Western universities often remark that someone "was a student of mine," if they acted as that student's adviser in a Ph.D. program. In that sense, I cannot say anyone in Hungary was a student of mine. It is some compensation to hear certain economists say that they nonetheless consider themselves my students.

How I became an academician

The Hungarian Academy of Sciences, following the Soviet pattern, had several functions. I was its paid employee, since I worked at one of its institutes. It employed several tens of thousands of people.

At the same time, the Hungarian Academy of Sciences also had the traditional function of a national academy, declaring itself the body of the best scholars in the country. But how were they measured to be the best? The qualifying procedure prescribed by the statutes of the Academy resembled that of the great Western academies. After careful prior assessment the members of the Academy would elect new members by majority decision in a secret ballot.[*] But it is worth considering more closely how the election process went in practice. This can be followed through my own example.

Scrutiny of the Academy's charter at that time reveals that its members were expected to have "the most progressive worldview";[†] in other words, a member must be a Marxist-Leninist. That was a troublesome criterion for those recommending me as an academician.[‡] My own declarations, documented in my "cadre sheets," made it absolutely clear that I was not a Marxist-Leninist, and any attentive reader of my works would come to the same conclusion.

---

[*] Membership has two grades: corresponding membership and full membership. Obtaining the lower grade was the big hurdle; a strong argument for the nomination had to be made by a full member. The next step was easy. Corresponding members became full members almost automatically after a time.

[†] Section (1) of paragraph 1 of the statutes of the Hungarian Academy of Sciences prescribed that the Academy should pursue its activity "on the basis of the scientific worldview of dialectic materialism."

[‡] Some individuals "volunteered" for membership, lobbying academicians for recommendations and trying to persuade other academicians to vote for them. Others felt such self-advertisement to be unworthy and trusted the choice to their colleagues' professional conscience. I was among the latter, in this case and with other honors too. Those proposing me as a member in the 1970s did so on their own initiative, according to their own judgment.

When the question of my membership was first raised among academicians in the early 1970s, I had already gained a reputation at home and even abroad. Perhaps more awkward still, the American Academy of Arts and Sciences had elected me an honorary foreign member and I had had other marks of international recognition as well. The Kádár regime, at that time, was anxious to demonstrate how civilized, cultured, and Western intellectual life in Hungary was. How did it look if a Hungarian researcher was a member of the American Academy but not of the Hungarian Academy? Consideration of my membership could not be postponed any longer.

I will have to describe the election process in some detail to make clear what occurred. The de jure process occurred in two stages. First, the Academy section covering the discipline concerned (in my case, Section IX, responsible for economics, law, and other social sciences) had to decide by secret vote whom to put forward to the General Assembly. A simple majority sufficed. Then the General Assembly of all the Academy members would vote in new members from the sections' candidates, again by secret ballot. The General Assembly voting was a formality; the candidates normally received an overwhelming majority. The real battle went on in the sections over whom to put forward.

Most of the academicians were party members. It was generally known that the "official" nomination meetings of the sections were preceded by the meetings of their party members; there they agreed on which of the possible candidates to vote for and against. Since the party members formed a majority of the committee, they ultimately decided who was going to be a member.

My nomination was defeated at the first attempt, during the preparation for the election of members in 1973, right at the first phase—the meeting of the Academy's party members. From what I have gathered from the archival material now available, the relevant department of the party headquarters prepared a report for the Politburo, the supreme decision-making body of the party, on the preparations for the 1973 General Assembly of the Academy.[4] This contained an account of whose nominations the party members supported and whose they rejected. My nomination was supported by István Friss, but the majority of the Communist Party members (including László Háy, who after 1956 was banned from teaching at the university), opposed it.* The Political Committee considered my nomination and "did not support" (i.e., forbade) it.[5]

---

* When my nomination was tendered again in 1975, Mihály Kornidesz, head of the relevant department of the party headquarters, recalled the opinions of my work that had reached them at the time of my first nomination in 1972. I quote what he said before the Political Committee: "When his name was first put forward, we heard conflicting opinions about him. Some said he was professionally weak, that he was not up to the standard, that he was an armchair scholar divorced from practice, and they considered him politically unreliable" (MOL M-KS 288. f. 5/682. ő.e. p. 3: minutes of the meeting).

The following election was scheduled at the 1976 General Assembly. The usual preparatory procedure took place. This time only a thin majority opposed my Academy membership at the party members' meeting. But it was sufficient for the Communist Party members' meeting to reject my nomination.

As usual, the relevant department of the party headquarters submitted its report on the preparations for the Academy's 1976 General Assembly in October 1975, dealing, among other things, with my case. The report refers to the Politburo's negative decision two years before and adds the following comment: "The situation has, in essence, not changed."[6] This time the Politburo did not decide immediately on the nominations to the Academy, but resolved to return to the question later.

After that, the story took an unexpected turn. Not much later, the meeting of the Academy's section of economics and law (Section IX of the Academy of Sciences) was held; there all the members of the section, not just the party members, took part. As I have mentioned, this body "decides" de jure on the nominations. On paper, I could not have attained a majority in the secret ballot if every party member academician had voted in accordance with their previous decision—that is, if each had voted against me. To general surprise, my candidacy was approved by a large majority. Clearly, party members who had not spoken up in support of my candidacy at their own meeting nevertheless had flouted party discipline under cover of the secret ballot and voted for me after all. Apart from me, another economist (with whom the party had no political problem) received the necessary majority.

The situation was complicated, however: two more economists, whose candidacy the party headquarters had been promoting, received exactly 50 percent in the secret ballot. According to the letter of the Academy statutes, their names could not go forward, as they had not received a majority.

The functionaries responsible for Academy affairs found this outcome an embarrassment. There was Kornai, politically suspect, gaining a majority, while two reliable people of theirs did not. It was too grave a problem to resolve in the formal venue of the Academy or even at the middle level of party management. The matter had to go up to the country's supreme political body, the Politburo of the Communist Party.

In January 1976, the Politburo again discussed the issue of nominations. A new submission was prepared, and in the debate, the submitter of the report stated that they had inquired widely about my work; this time, the opinions had been favorable.[7] Finally, János Kádár took the following view (quoted word for word from the minutes): "As far as these changes are concerned, I believe Kornai is acceptable, because the political aspect is not so relevant. It is difficult to compare, but we are not dealing with party functions or party membership, but with the Academy of Sciences, where it is possible that some people with minor political problems will, if their scholarly work is otherwise positive, become productive and useful members of the Academy. So his not meeting the ideological rigor of old party members is not a reason to exclude him."[8]

With that, the issue was decided. My membership in the Academy could now follow the regular course.

Yet a need for balance was still felt at party headquarters. The Academy statutes were bent and the two names with precisely 50 percent approval were also put forward at the General Assembly. With three reliable new people joining the Academy along with Kornai, the required balance would be ensured. And that is what happened: four new economists became corresponding members in 1976.

That is how the autonomy of the Academy was maintained in the 1970s, with sovereign secret voting and valid statutes. In the course of selection, the assessment of genuine scholarly performance was mixed, as in every sphere of life, with the Communist Party's desire to wield power. Selection according to political criteria left a marked impression on the composition of the body of the Academy, with consequences that are felt to this day.

What happened in my case was as if the U.S. cabinet were to debate and the president decide whether Professor X could become a member of the National Academy of Sciences or the American Academy of Arts and Sciences—that is how absurd the procedure was.

As well as whittling down the Academy's independence, the incident also illustrates another important phenomenon: the willingness to make concessions typical of the cultural policy of Kádár. He and his men did not recoil from making occasional compromises. My "admission" to the Academy was one such compromise, if some recalcitrant party members, taking refuge behind the secret ballot, so wished. At the same time, they wanted to ensure that the leading positions remained in their hands; if such compromise was the formal condition of their exercising their political will within an "autonomous" organization, theirs should be the majority faithfully following the party line.

The privileges of an academician

Members of a national academy of sciences under the Communist system were advantaged people. They received enhanced salaries and many other privileges.

The rank and relative prestige of the title of academician was still greater in the Soviet Union than it was in Hungary. Not long after my election, I received an invitation from the Academy of Sciences of the Soviet Union to visit Moscow, after a recommendation from Soviet friends of mine who knew my work and wanted to have a personal meeting. When I arrived, there was no one waiting at the airport, but I managed somehow the none-too-easy task of finding my way to where I was staying. The next morning, the phone rang and there were deep apologies from the international department of the Soviet Academy. Yesterday they had thought I was just a "doctor of sciences." Only today had they heard I had been elected an academician. They asked my pardon for not sending a car to the airport as they should have. Thereafter, I had an official car and chauffeur at my disposal in Moscow.

The title of academician was worth a lot in Hungary as well. A few years before my election, my family and I had moved from a smaller apartment to a more spacious one, with many advantages but no telephone. Younger people who hardly ever put down their mobile phones and have rival telephone companies trying to persuade them to make more calls may have trouble imagining what it meant in those days to spend years on the waiting list for a phone line. Sometimes personal connections helped. In 1975, after the move, I asked the new director of our institute, Rezső Nyers, if he could try to get me a phone. He had been a powerful party secretary not long before, with everyone in the economy hanging on his words. He spoke to those knowledgeable about the matter, and on advice from his acquaintances in the post office, he passed on to me the following message. The time was not ripe for me to jump the queue for a telephone. I should wait until I was one step further up the ladder and a member of the Hungarian Academy of Sciences, and then apply again. That is what happened. I became an academician, Rezső Nyers made another call, and behold, a few days later the technicians appeared to install the phone.

Being privileged poses moral dilemmas. I had mixed feelings inside me. It was disquieting to know I was receiving benefits denied to many other worthy researchers and members of the intelligentsia.* I do not think the benefits I received were obtained in unworthy ways. The colleagues who strove to have me elected sincerely appreciated my work. I felt I could accept with a clear conscience the privileges that accompanied membership in the Hungarian Academy of Sciences.

---

* Speaking with Western colleagues, I found repeatedly that they had serious misconceptions about the material privileges of academicians. Many of them believed that they had an especially high standard of living, measured by Western standards. This of course is far from the truth. Even after its enhancement, an academician's salary was a fraction of theirs. The guesthouses for scholars and scientists, where I gladly went for periods of study, reached the standard, perhaps, of a Western two- or three-star hotel, whereas a Western professor could afford much more lavish accommodation. Although official cars were not sent to the airport to meet them, they could find and pay for a taxi without any trouble. Nor did they have to pull strings to avoid waiting several years for a domestic telephone.

The same was true of academicians as of other privileged groups in the socialist system: the material privileges they enjoyed were privileges compared only to the low average standard of living of researchers. For my part, I felt that the most important advantage of the academic status was that it relaxed somewhat the restrictions and limitations placed on travel (although it did not completely lift them).

Pathfinding and Preparation—1971–1976

Rush versus Harmonic Growth
Non-Price Control

My book *Anti-Equilibrium* appeared in 1971. Over the next six or seven years, I was affected by many intellectual impulses: reading matter, debates, my own research along various lines, travels, and direct observations as consumer and builder of our home. Looking back on that period today, I can say that all those influences helped me to prepare for the comprehensive analysis of the socialist economy that I began in 1976. I had many experiences that would affect me for the rest of my life and make their mark on much later work of mine. But it is only in hindsight that I can call this a period of preparation for a book I would write many years later. It had not even occurred to me in 1971 that I would write a monograph devoted to the shortage economy. One of my purposes in these memoirs is to show introspectively, drawing on my own experiences, how the creative process developed during my economic research, how recognition and understanding went forward or came to a halt in a blind alley. To that end, I will refer periodically to links between intellectual events and later works.

Unlike in other parts of the book, what I mean to tell in this chapter cannot be arranged in a logical order. The cohesive force behind the manifold experiences following or running parallel to each other was the end result: the book that I completed in 1980. Several important events occurred in the Hungarian economy during these years. The reform was begun with great energy in 1968, only to stall in the early 1970s, as the political balance tipped back toward anti-reform forces for a time; in some respects the changes went into reverse. There were similar moves to revive earlier restrictions in intellectual and ideological life as well. While I was influenced, of course, by my immediate environment, I was also affected by other impulses that had a lasting impact on my thoughts.

Growth: Forced or harmonic

Jan Tinbergen, the Dutch professor who shared the first Nobel Prize for Economics with Ragnar Frisch of Norway, asked me to deliver the 1971 De Vries Lecture at the

University of Rotterdam. Tinbergen was among the finest men I have ever met. His exceptional knowledge and original cast of mind were combined with infinite simplicity, modesty, and heartfelt goodwill. Perhaps the one human weakness I discerned in him was a belief, almost to naiveté, that others were like him—as rational, honest, and unselfish as he was.

As always, I was tense about fulfilling an engagement that was such an honor, and as on other occasions, I felt I should come up with a new subject. By then I had long been dealing with the possibilities of long-term planning and had taken part in several debates on various growth strategies. So I chose the subject of my lecture to be held in Holland from the area of growth theory.[1]

I began with an analogy: "A man who wears a shirt made of fine material, a beautiful tie, an elegant jacket, but worn, though acceptable trousers, and, in addition a pair of shoes with holes in their soles, makes a disharmonic impression."[2] A similarly disharmonic impression is given by a country that shows uneven rates of development in the various sectors of its economy. My lecture was a critique of the theory of "socialist industrialization," which sought to make a virtue out of a grave problem: the disproportions and disharmony generated by forced growth. The English word "rush" that I used in the title of the lecture was perhaps more expressive than "forced growth." Hungarian industry was rushing ahead to make its growth rate as high as possible, especially in heavy industry. This rush was being undertaken even at the expense of living standards; maintenance of national assets such as buildings, machinery, equipment, and roads; the health service and education system; environmental protection; and the accumulation of adequate reserves for hard times.

The lecture, given the title *Rush versus Harmonic Growth* when it appeared in book form, took issue with Albert Hirschman and Paul Streeten's theory advocating unbalanced growth, which was attracting wide notice about that time.[3] They argued that it was expressly advantageous for developing countries to have bottlenecks, shortages, and conditions of disequilibrium, as these urged a slothful society toward restoring proportionality and equilibrium. My bitter experiences of the socialist economy, however, showed me that such disproportions caused much more harm than good.* The problem with the plans in a socialist economy was not that they led to inertia but, on the contrary, that they caused hyperactivity at the macroeconomic level—investment at a forced, hastened pace. The study touched on the link

---

* My book has been translated into several languages, including Chinese. Not long ago I visited China again and the analysis it contains came up again in my conversations. There the dark side and social losses associated with extremely fast, heated growth and the accompanying one-sided "growth mania" are strikingly apparent; and emphasizing the requirements of harmonic growth is more timely than ever.

between distorted, rushed growth and widespread shortages, although my causal analysis of the two phenomena was not yet developed.

Together with the theoretical study of forced growth, using Hungarian statistical data I built and applied dynamic simulation models, in cooperation with several coauthors. I was just getting to know computer simulation techniques as a flexible method eminently suitable for analysis. One calculation, which we termed "plan sounding," gave an instructive picture of the harm done by disharmonic growth—notably, neglect of the infrastructure.*

An invitation to Cambridge

Attending a conference in Geneva in 1971, I met again with the great British economist Richard Stone, whose acquaintance I had made on my first trip to England in 1963.† He asked me to speak to him privately and told me he would be glad to invite me permanently to Cambridge University. There was tension mounting there between two groups, one of mathematical economists, headed intellectually by Frank Hahn, and the other of opponents of such methods, centering around Joan Robinson and my fellow countryman Nicholas (later Lord) Kaldor. His probings of opinion so far suggested to him that both sides would be pleased to see me given a chair, a development that might even help to ease the tension. He offered the professorship not on his own initiative, but on behalf of his colleagues.

Cambridge! It was the bastion of economics where Keynes had worked and taught and the place where I had first sampled the Western academic world. Lovely colleges hundreds of years old, flower-filled parks, and intimate, peaceful riverbanks! This was my second chance to emigrate, but now under circumstances far removed from the uncertainties of 1956–1957 and its flood of refugees. Fifteen years had passed, and I was being offered a tenured professorship in one of the foremost universities in the world.

I asked for a short period to consider and consulted my wife, who was also at the conference. Then I expressed gratitude for the great honor, but declined. I will return

* My coauthors in this work were my wife Zsuzsa Dániel, Anna Jónás, and Béla Martos.

† Stone was no ivory-tower scholar cultivating abstract theories; rather, he was interested in research that directly assisted practice.

He headed the team devising the UN-approved system of accounting and statistics that ensures uniformity and comparability in international economic statistics. Stone won the Nobel Prize a few years later. His character easily encompassed both dedication to scholarly work and the enjoyment of the pleasures of daily life. He dressed with unusual elegance, and he loved good food and drink. He occupied many social positions, the one he was especially proud of being the presidency of the "Wine Committee" of King's College. This committee was entrusted with deciding what wines to buy for the college cellars.

in more detail later in the book to the great dilemma of whether to emigrate or stay behind in Hungary. I mention the event here only to position it chronologically.

In a cast to the waist—Keynes and Hirschman

I had surgery twice early in 1972, after suffering dislocations of both my shoulders with increasing frequency. This very painful disorder had to be surgically corrected. The operations were followed by several weeks with my trunk in a cast, which much restricted me in my movements.* It was a perfect opportunity to read. I was in a crowded ten-bed hospital ward, with no room for even a chair. When the staff let me get up, I spent most of my time sitting about in the corridor. Later they sent me home to convalesce. Friends visiting me in the hospital and later at home were surprised to see Keynes's basic work *The General Theory of Employment, Interest and Money* in my hand, not an entertaining crime story.

Many years earlier, during my period of self-taught "university studies" in 1957–1958, I had acquired a knowledge of macroeconomics, but then I had relegated it to some distant part of my memory. As I reread Keynes, I realized that Hungary's shortage economy was in some sense a mirror image of Keynesian disequilibrium. For Keynes, *unemployment* was the obvious phenomenon through which to present and examine the problems of capitalism. The *shortage* syndrome, with an opposite sign, could play a similar part in my analysis. Keynes described an economic situation in which transactions between buyers and sellers are constrained by *demand*. Producers would make more at a given price, but the demand is insufficient. I was trying to convey and explain the mirror image of that circumstance, where transactions between buyers and sellers encounter a *supply* constraint. Consumers would buy more at a given price, but the supply is short.

Another work that left a deep impression on me at that time was a brilliant little book titled *Exit, Voice, and Loyalty* by Albert Hirschman. The basic idea behind it can be understood through a simple example. A regular customer at a restaurant is repeatedly dissatisfied with what he has been served. What can he do? Either he can complain to the manager (*voice*), or he can choose another restaurant (*exit*). If he is tempted by the latter course, a long-standing relation with his favorite restaurant (*loyalty*) may perhaps hold him back.

There are many similar situations. Customers find themselves dissatisfied with an accustomed shop, shareholders with certain stocks, or a student and family with

---

* I was a grotesque sight. As I came home, a child who saw me in the elevator burst into tears. I had one arm stuck out horizontally to the front, bent at the elbow. My son Gábor, known for his sense of humor, said my protruding arm would make a perfect hanger for trousers and hung a pair on it to see how the ensemble looked.

a school. Will anyone listen if they complain and do something about the problem? Is there a risk in using one's voice? What will exit achieve? Is it possible? It was exactly those thought-provoking questions of Hirschman's that led me to the problems of the shortage economy. The management of Fiat or Citroën would be concerned if car owners in large numbers began to complain about quality, and consternation at the company would be greater still if they turned without a word to Toyota or Volkswagen. But what does the Trabant or Skoda factory care about the voice of owners? It has no fear of exit if its buyers are prepared to queue for years. There is no effective voice or threat of exit in a chronic shortage economy. If you don't like it, you can lump it.

Hirschman emphasizes that both voice and exit serve as signals and—under fortunate circumstances—are associated with feedback. If that mechanism works well, the signals will change the situation for the better. A system or subsystem works efficiently only if both signals operate freely and effectively.

Hirschman's ideas have relevance beyond the economy. He himself mentions the grave situation of members of a Stalinist party. They cannot express a view on essential questions, nor can they voluntarily quit the party for fear of serious reprisals. That stifling of feedback brings about ossification and chronic degeneration of the party. Another line in the argument leads to the dilemma of emigration. Should people stay at home and voice their dissatisfaction, or should they exit—choose to leave the country and protest in that way?

At that time, I knew Albert Hirschman only through his writings. We first met ten years later, when he invited me to the Princeton Institute for Advanced Study. It was a great intellectual experience for me to encounter his original way of thinking, his distance from fashionable trends, his dazzlingly broad knowledge, and his familiarity with the literature.

I returned home from hospital after my operations, still in plaster down to the waist, to take part in the family celebrations for my mother's eightieth birthday. Munyó awaited this day with great excitement and was a little anxious about whether she would last until the event. Photos were taken showing all the members of the family surrounding her with adoring love. A few months later she fell asleep peacefully and never woke up again. In the last years of her life we met a great many times and spoke on the phone every day. It is an unspeakable loss that I can no longer hear her cheerful voice. I remember the special respect with which she spoke of the professors of medical science who were treating one or other of the family's members, and whom she referred to as "famous professors." She considered this a far higher rank than anything that fortune or a high position in the state apparatus could give to people. What a pity that she did not live to see the day her son too became a professor! What a pity she was not able to visit us in America! How proudly she would have recounted that experience to her elderly friends while sipping coffee in her favorite coffee shop, next door to the house where she was living.

Teaching at Princeton

After I had recovered from my operations, my wife and I traveled to the United States for a whole year.* The first stop was Princeton University, where I spent the first half of the academic year.† It was interesting to observe the different types of young economics student there. Several European students in my course had thought much about the various drawbacks of the capitalist economy and would have welcomed an improved version that moved in the direction of the welfare state. That set of ideas aroused their interest in planning, and especially in the impressions of someone who had studied the planned economy from the inside. I am very glad that two of the students with whom I became personally friendly have done very well later in life. Louka Katseli became president of the Greek planning office in the early 1980s, under Andreas Papandreou's socialist administration, and is now director of the OECD (Organization for Economic Cooperation and Development) Development Center. The other, Kemal Dervis, became a deputy chairman of the World Bank before being recalled to Turkey to handle a grave economic crisis; he served as a social democratic finance minister through very difficult years. He is now head of the UN Development Program, the largest UN agency fighting poverty. The conflict between the Greeks and the Turks has a long history that flares up again and again for various reasons. It was reassuring to see that in the supranational intellectual world, friendship could form between a Greek and a Turkish student and their wives.

Katseli, Dervis, and many other like-minded students sympathized with economic *reform* of modern capitalism introduced by the left, but they did not want to do away with the system or put a socialist one in its place. One deterrent to adopting revolutionary ideas was the grave problems experienced in the communist system. However, there was another group of students at Princeton, calling themselves the "radical economists." They read *Capital* diligently—if not perhaps so thoroughly as I had twenty-five years earlier. They knew who I was and where I came from,

---

* I promised readers earlier not to trouble them with accounts of my travels and I will keep my word. While mentioning here and elsewhere in the book foreign parts that I visited, I will not append any tourist's impressions, confining myself to intellectual and political experiences in one place or another.

† I look back with gratitude and affection on the many courtesies and warm friendly assistance we received there from my fellow countryman Professor Richard Quandt, the author of many well-known works on microeconomics.

and that the problems of *existing* socialism were discussed in my classes.* Nonetheless, or perhaps precisely for that reason, none of them joined the course. However, they invited me on one occasion to an extracurricular gathering for self-improvement. They seemed to be naive, well-intentioned young people with sincere beliefs.

I was not armed only with Eastern European experiences. During my stay in the United States in 1968, in California, at one of the birthplaces of the New Left, I became acquainted with its ideas. We had been through the 1968 student uprising in Paris, and I had encountered "new leftists" in many European cities, including Budapest. I would argue with them, again and again, sometimes with patience and sometimes with annoyance. I was disturbed by their protest against "refrigerator socialism," while in Hungary the slight relaxation of the shortage economy had brought a little improvement in people's circumstances, enabling the consumer at last to lay hands on goods previously impossible to get. The steps toward a spreading market economy were, in my view, not the betrayal of elevated principles but the triumph of common sense, in the interest of improving people's lives.

About that time, I came across a recent book by the Swedish economist Assar Lindbeck: *The Political Economy of the New Left: An Outsider's View*. This concisely and wittily summarizes New Left views and the opposing liberal line of argument.

I tried to muster arguments against the views of the Princeton young "radicals" before I met them, but unsuccessfully. The problem was not with socialism, they stressed, it was simply that it was *badly applied* in the Soviet Union and the other Eastern European countries. It needs to be done properly. That meeting in Princeton and many others with members of the New Left in developed countries confirmed what I deduced from introspection in earlier chapters of this book: faith can be stronger than rational argument. People with a deep, strong faith usually need a strong experience to produce a turning point in their ideas, a kind of shock that shatters the fundaments of their previous beliefs.

During our time in Princeton our three children, Gábor, Judit, and András, each spent two months with us. While as a teacher I learned what American, Greek, or Turkish students thought of socialism, as parents we were able to see what the first encounter with America was like for three Hungarian teenagers. Naturally, all the children experienced things differently, in their own ways. But there were similarities, too. It goes without saying that like all tourists, they marveled at the

---

* Many intellectuals in Eastern Europe use the adjective "existing" derisively. I think it is an apt description and willingly apply it without quotation marks. Socialism existed and that is what it was like, not what the advocates of the idea of socialism supposed it would be like.

skyscrapers of New York, the galleries, and the fine campus of Princeton University. I will mention here only the reactions that I, as a researcher into the shortage economy and the socialist system, felt to be particularly characteristic. At least in the first few days, they practically wolfed down the foods and soft drinks that Hungarian children could not get back home. One could not resist ice cream or the drink known as Dr. Pepper, while another gorged on cornflakes. One of them was astounded at the infinite offerings of the countless television channels and sat glued to the screen. Another was amazed by rock music and the famous musicians, a couple of whom they were able to hear live in concert. For a couple of weeks, András and Judit attended a high school in Princeton, while Gábor spent a few weeks in one of the colleges of Yale University. What they most valued of their school experiences was perhaps the broader choices offered to students, far more extensive than their Hungarian counterparts enjoyed. The experience of their first exposure to the American lifestyle had a strong effect on all three, and when they returned home, it took some time for them to adjust to conditions in Hungary again. Later, as they matured, the positive intellectual effect of the encounter became stronger. Today, they and we, their parents, believe that the first trip to America contributed to the openness of their thinking and the formation of their freedom-loving system of values.

An epilogue has yet to be added to the 1972 Princeton period. In 1974, I received an invitation from Princeton for a full professorship, similar to the one I had received from Cambridge.[4] Even the environment would have been rather similar, as the Princeton campus has buildings and fine gardens reminiscent of Oxford and Cambridge colleges. It was again tempting, but I again declined.

Continuation in Stanford and Washington

We spent the second part of the 1972–1973 academic year at Stanford University. I had a wealth of experiences during those months. We became close not only to Kenneth Arrow and to Alan and Jackie Manne, but also to Tibor Scitovsky and his wife Erzsébet, whom I had met at Yale in 1970. Our relations developed in this period into warm, strong friendships.

Tibor was born and bred in Hungary. His father had been a prominent figure in public life and in business, serving among other things as foreign minister and as chairman of the largest Hungarian commercial bank. He had a conservative cast of mind, but Tibor, while remaining respectful in his relations to his parents, soon departed from them in his outlook on the world. In his thinking, he became a liberal who invariably felt compassion for the poor and disadvantaged, and was particularly concerned about the development of the most backward countries. He championed economic policies that would improve the situation for those strata and countries.

He had been living in the United States for several decades by the time we became close. He was a refined, quiet-spoken, always cheerful man, and a blend of the best in European and American culture. At the time, we only touched in conversation on the way many Americans, while living well, were unable really to enjoy life: they did not go to the theater or concerts enough, and they ate "fast food" rather than tasty or healthier fare. Some years later, these critical observations appeared with scientific, statistical grounding in a splendid book titled *The Joyless Economy.**

Unfortunately, in 1973 our conversations did not yet cover analysis of market operations. It emerged years later, after I had written *The Economics of Shortage,* that there was an important point of contact between our ideas. Both of us were dealing with *asymmetries* in the situation of buyer and seller. (This contrasted with the normal approach, which is inclined to see the two parties to transaction as symmetrical mirror images of each other.) Scitovsky had clarified in a much earlier study an important aspect of this buyer–seller asymmetry by distinguishing the roles and behavior of a *price-taker* from those of a *price-maker.* I was unaware in 1973 that Tibor had introduced this distinction into economics and he modestly did not mention it, which may be why it did not come up in our discussions.

My wife and I traveled to Washington for a month at the end of the academic year. It was long before the period when Eastern Europeans succeeded each other in high positions at the city's international financial institutions. As far as I know, I was the only Eastern European research economist who had been working with the research section of the World Bank as early as 1968. That work entailed open cooperation with an institution branded an agency of imperialism by Communist regimes. I wrote two studies for the Bank, both of which appeared, and I made it public that they had been commissioned by the World Bank.

Watergate broke while we were in Washington. By that time, I was reasonably familiar with U.S. affairs. Even earlier, I had been strongly affected by reading the *New York Times* and the *Washington Post*, where the anonymous editorials expressed, concisely and with crystal-clear logic, a liberal viewpoint that was congenial to me and was based on reliable information. I was no less impressed by the opinion and editorial pages of open debate and conflicting views. I was similarly awed by the evening news on the Public Broadcasting System television station financed mainly by private donations—the famous MacNeil/Lehrer News Hour, which usually combined objective news coverage with a debate. If the subject was

---

* There seems to have been some advance, in the decades since the book appeared in 1976, in overcoming the distortions in consumption found at that time in the United States.

domestic politics, Democrats and Republicans would sit side by side and express their opinions. If it was the India–Pakistan conflict, there would be the Indian and Pakistani ambassadors. Each of the opposing views was heard and the approach to opponents was civilized. The person moderating the debate would not take a position but would pose all the sensitive questions. I learned from these comments on daily events what freedom of speech and the culture of debate mean. For me, it was all schooling in democracy.*

So I already had an idea of how a free press worked when the Watergate affair began. But it is unusual, even where a free press has been integral to civil society for centuries, for a daily paper to find the Achilles' heel of an unpopular president who trifles with rights and freedoms. The *Post* went on to follow the trails like a bloodhound and to come up with successive revelations. Back in Hungary, it was claimed by official commentators and ill-informed independent members of the intelligentsia alike that Nixon was being attacked by ultra-reactionaries for giving some flexibility to the rigid American stance toward China and the Soviet Union. I, on the other hand, was capable to some extent of seeing things from the inside and grasping what was happening in the United States. For the attack had come from the opposite direction. Those out to topple Nixon were those anxious to save democracy and human rights from a hard-handed, power-crazed president suspicious of everyone and using methods that were on the fringes of legality or were downright illegal. They attacked him not only because of the illegal actions before the elections but because of the later attempts to hide evidence and have the crimes covered up by encouraging participants or witnesses to deny them. We sat flabbergasted in front of the television as if the congressional investigations and the testimony of the witnesses were part of a thriller.

We left the United States long before the Watergate affair reached its conclusion. Back home, we were satisfied to hear that Nixon had resigned at last.

Autonomous control

At the beginning of the 1970s, after the appearance of *Anti-Equilibrium*, I started, with my colleagues Béla Martos, András Simonovits, and Zsuzsa Kapitány, to con-

---

* I did not read the tabloids or watch the vast quantities of worthless television programs. I was open, however, to the best of the American press and television and the highest standard of journalism. I soon saw that the two extremes of the media went together. Freedom of the press allows high-standard speech and strong criticism of the government of the day, but it opens the floodgates to cultural trash as well. They are, unfortunately, twin products. Freedom of the press is associated with the market economy and the freedom to do business, and the production and sale of trashy cultural products undoubtedly offer enormous business opportunities.

struct mathematical models of some of the ideas contained in the book.* My first joint publication on the subject with Béla Martos appeared in 1973, under the title "Autonomous Control of the Economic System." It was published in English by *Econometrica* in 1973.[5]

The idea of autonomous control in the economy relies on a metaphor taken from the human nervous system. The higher tasks of control are the province of the central nervous system, but simpler tasks such as breathing, digestion, and the circulation of the blood result from the automatic operation of the heart, lungs, stomach, intestines, and kidneys and are controlled by the autonomous nervous system (aptly termed the "vegetative nervous system" in Hungarian and some other languages). There is a similar division of labor in the economic system, where many repetitive, almost autonomous tasks of control are performed by very simple mechanisms.

The article expresses this idea in a general form before presenting an example in detail, in mathematical form: control based on inventory-level signals. Think of a supermarket, for instance. It is not worth waiting for excess demand or excess supply to raise or lower the price of a product, or the profit margin to widen or narrow before ordering replacement stocks. It is enough to monitor inventory. If the stock of a product falls, it is worth reordering it. If the inventory rises above a normal level, there is a wait while it decreases before new stock is ordered, and so on. Customary commercial practice enables customers to be supplied smoothly without price signals, simply by observing how inventories rise and fall.

We dealt with various types of signal. Another important non-price signal is the stock of orders, or related information: the length of the queue for goods. Every category of queue has a mean value or "normal" length. If the queue is longer than usual, more of the product or service needs to be offered. If there are too few in the line, it is worth reallocating resources to produce those goods for which the queue is longer than usual.[†]

There are various conclusions to be drawn from these observations.

Many authors describe the socialist economy as if all regulation and control were concentrated at the center. This is an untenable assumption. Extremely centralized though a system may be, many processes are still controlled in a decentralized way through autonomous control mechanisms of the kind just outlined.

---

* I deliberately use the first-person plural in this account, because I am sketching the common ideas of the group carrying out the research. András Simonovits, in an article written in 2003, called the research trend described here the "Hungarian school of control theory."

† A notable type of non-price information is mentioned in *The Economics of Shortage*: the "catastrophe" signal. Some decisions are postponed until serious trouble occurs, and moves are made only after a catastrophe has ensued.

This kind of autonomous decentralization cannot ensure that resources are allocated *efficiently*, however. It is not capable of driving technical development or adapting to demands for new products. The elements essential for this latter kind of control function are prices reflective of relative scarcity and incentives to react to prices, costs, and profit. Autonomous control can provide coordination only for accustomed technology and existing input-output and supply-and-demand combinations. You might say it can provide only elementary coordination of production. It does so in a conservative way, ensuring nothing else but the repetition and reproduction of earlier patterns. That is to say, it is in a limited way capable of operating the economy.

One of the central concepts in the research was "viability."* The purpose was to understand how it was possible for the socialist system to survive from one day to the next despite its distorted prices and faulty incentives. (To jump ahead, it became common after the change of system for ordinary people, and even for experts, to say that socialism collapsed because it "did not work." That sounds good, but it will not stand up. The system's elementary processes always "worked." People turned up at their jobs, shops served customers, schools taught children, hospitals treated patients, and so on. But the system did not work *well*. It was weakened by dysfunctional features, its advocates lost confidence, it became unable to resist outside pressure, and many other things could be cited in a genuine analysis of what caused the collapse. But the system met the elementary requirements for viability to the end.) Why was this? It is not enough to look to central planning commands or the disciplinary force of repression. Autonomous control provides an important part of the answer.

Although attention has been focused here on the socialist economy, the argument points beyond it. There is autonomous control in *all* economic systems: it is what provides in all of them most of the primitive, elementary functions of control.

The starting point for designing some of our models was that the control of certain elementary processes in the economy somewhat resembled the mechanism for regulating the central heating in a home. The desired mean temperature can be set with a thermostat. Let us call this temperature the *norm*. If the actual temperature is higher than the norm, the heating switches off and the temperature decreases; and if it is lower, the heating switches on and the temperature increases. This operation can be called control by norm. We saw that many processes of this kind in the economy (and indeed in the noneconomic spheres of society as well) were controlled by mechanisms of this type. We did not deal with the question of how the norms are set—but once they were, control by norm became *viable*.

---

* Efficiency and optimality are conditional on viability, but the statement cannot be reversed. A system that is neither efficient nor optimal may also be viable.

There is plenty of experience to show that norms exist and that society uses various techniques to bring aberrant individuals and organizations back to or near to its norms. It could be seen that socialism was intolerant toward people who stepped out of line and behaved other than normally. But we were convinced that this was a more general phenomenon, with various manifestations under other systems as well.*

The findings were published first in journal contributions and then in book form in 1981 under the title *Non-Price Control*.[6] On that account, it is worth summing up my reflections on that research, which lasted for about ten years. We had no need for dissatisfaction in terms of the reputation of the academic publications in which our findings appeared. They appeared in high-ranking journals and in the famous "green series"† of the prestigious publisher North-Holland.[7] Nonetheless, I have to say that when this line of research began, I had been expecting a bigger reaction.‡

I suspect there were several reasons why the hoped-for response did not materialize. One was that economists dealing with comparative politico-socioeconomic systems were more interested in research that had some ideological or political content, or at least the flavor of such content. Market versus central planning, prices versus commands, centralization versus decentralization—those were the truly exciting subjects, on whichever side a researcher stood politically. Phenomena that occurred in all systems were less exciting to Sovietologists or economists specializing in Eastern Europe or China.§ That explanation applies especially to those within or outside the socialist countries who opposed the communist system. They wanted to see models (which I produced in other works) that demonstrated the shortcomings of the socialist economy, rather than ones showing why the socialist economy was able to vegetate on despite its blatantly dysfunctional features.

---

* There is another autonomous control mechanism, in which an observed variable moves only within upper and lower limits constituting the system's *limits of tolerance*. Mathematical models of mechanisms operating with limits of tolerance were devised by the Polish French researcher Irina Grosfeld. The mechanism is very widespread not only in the economic sphere but in politics and in control of social behavior as well.

† The book was number 133 in the series Contribution to Economic Analysis.

‡ I must return to the first-person singular when talking of expectations and how far they were fulfilled. I do not know whether other team members shared my opinion.

§ Many economists among them may have been scared off from the start by the mathematical apparatus employed in our studies. In contrast, there were other economists glad to read work written in terms of mathematical models; nevertheless they too felt aversion. I will return shortly to the way this group was put off by the *special* mathematical approach we took.

Let us now look at another group of economists: the theorists. I can easily under-stand how our research was received in the touchy atmosphere of the Institute of Economics by theoretical economists antagonistic to mathematical methods. But why was there not more of a response in Hungary and abroad among those who believed in formalized theoretical analysis? It could hardly have been an oversight, for *Econometrica* and the "green series" were regular reading for them. The recep-tion of some of my works in the West was impeded by their lack of mathematical formulation, but that cannot have been the case here, where all our ideas appeared in the language of mathematical models, indeed expressed with an up-to-date or even elegant formalism.

I think the explanation lies primarily in the *theoretical apparatus*. Our studies did not feature "optimum criteria." We did not discuss whether there are utility func-tions for the actors in the economy or whether they have aims they want to achieve. We predicted the behavior of actors in the economic system in models of a simpler, more elementary nature (and therefore with general validity in many respects). A de-cision maker is touched by an impulse, whereupon he or she reacts in accordance with some set of rules. This simple formula (impulse → reaction) is encompassed in the mathematical apparatus applied: difference or differential equations.* We were not seeking optimal solutions. We wanted to know whether, under the existing con-trol mechanism, the system had sustainable dynamic paths, and if so, what their characteristics were. Our models sought to present the simple laws of motion in the economic system or subsystem. In fact, they showed great similarity to the approach taken in many of the natural sciences.

The idea that there cannot be a model without optimization is deeply fixed in the minds of mainstream economists, especially theoretical economists employing math-ematical methods. Meaningful microeconomics requires that one say what the utility function of the decision makers is. It is mandatory to prove that some macro regu-larity fits in well with its "micro foundation"—that is, the neoclassical conditions applying to a "rational," utility-maximizing decision maker. The enforcement of this requirement, far from relaxing in the past few decades, has become more ag-gressive. The easy times have passed when, inspired by Keynes, one could say on the basis of empirical observation that an impulse (an interest rate increase, for instance) elicits some response. One is called on to show whether the regularity observed is compatible with the neoclassical theoretical micro foundations! The set of models presented by us stood out against the background of this strict discipline, and from the world of orthodox decision theory.

---

* Economics had applied difference and differential equation systems before, but mostly for the purposes of macroeconomic models. Our studies utilized this apparatus for modeling microeconomic processes.

The situation is bleak, but perhaps not hopeless. I am not alone in thinking that a monopoly held by one narrow theory of limited validity will become one day an impediment to the process of understanding and recognition. A doctrinaire micro basis can be a starting point for explaining many things. But for dealing with many other things in the economy and society, it proves unnecessarily strict (e.g., leaving no scope for autonomous control) or plainly misleading (as in examining the political sphere, for instance, and the relations between politics and the economy). And if many people think that way, research will eventually break the shackles.

Creaking machinery of adaptation

In 1974 I wrote a study titled "The Creaking Machinery of Adaptation,"[8] in which I anticipated many of the ideas in *Economics of Shortage*. The title was apt, but there were many clumsy passages in it, the line of argument was still unsettled, and the conceptual apparatus only half complete. Some people discerned inherent worth in "Creaking Machinery" when it was debated in the Institute of Economics, but it received some crude and ill-tempered criticism as well, above all from my colleague Péter Erdős.

I have already mentioned that name several times. He was an interesting partner in conversation when I arrived at the institute in 1955 and we shared a room. I was assigned to be his assistant for a while. We later grew apart from each other, especially after he was one of the first to join the new Communist Party in 1957 and I refrained from doing so. Nonetheless, we had remained on friendly terms.

Péter had a razor-sharp mind. His Marxist training was coupled with a thorough knowledge of Western writing, especially Keynes. He was a curious combination of an open mind, a critical view of existing political and economic conditions, and unconditional adherence to the ideas of communism. He was sidelined more than once and even expelled from the party, but he stood by it obstinately until his death.

If he did not like a study, he would not just criticize it, he would rip it to shreds, employing not only rational argument but arrogant scorn as well. There were plenty of writers from whom he could have learned that style, from Marx to Lenin, but he outdid his masters. Incidentally, I have discovered this kind of intellectual sadism in others besides Marxists. Some seem to get positive enjoyment out of mincing up another person's work and humiliating the author intellectually. I felt aversion for these attacks by Erdős even when they were aimed at others. Now it was the turn of my "Creaking Machinery" and of myself.

I survived. I could even be glad of the criticism. It was better not to have sent this semifinished product to a publisher and to have published the more mature

Economics of Shortage later instead. But there is no need to humiliate a researcher intellectually to motivate him or her to undertake a thorough revision.* That outcome can also be achieved if, together with analyzing the mistakes, the critic recognizes and identifies some of the study's achievements and virtues and, above all, its promise (if it is indeed promising) and encourages the researcher to think further and rewrite the study.

After such brutal criticism, a researcher has to grit his or her teeth and be firm, or risk losing the will to continue the work. I am glad I had the necessary commitment and faith in the direction of my research.

I was directing another line of research besides "Creaking Machinery," an overly ambitious attempt to build a gigantic macro-simulation model based on Hungarian data. This project became bogged down and could not be completed. I regret all the work I put into it and, perhaps even more, the energy that my young associates, above all János Gács and Mária Lackó, expended.

If my "behavior pattern" as a researcher were to be described, the 1971–1976 period could provide a typical example. Many Western researchers had an easier time of it when they examined some problem or other in a capitalist economy, because they had a ready-made intellectual construct to which they could add. There was no such ready-made construct available for explaining the socialist system. Those seeking a true understanding had to follow unmarked paths and almost inevitably arrived at a dead end, forcing them to turn back and seek another way forward.

I think I can say I sought new paths without becoming discouraged. I would set about several simultaneous projects, any of which could have employed a researcher full-time. The problem with my approach was the breadth of the front line across which I wanted to progress. I have no reason to be ashamed of the quantity or quality of my research output, but looking back, the ratio of input to output is alarming. I published a great deal, but many projects became stuck before they matured to the publication stage. I had big projects involving several colleagues that came to an abrupt end. Many of the results of these simultaneous undertakings came to be integrated into *Economics of Shortage*, but some were irrevocably lost. It was as if a

---

* The question may arise as to why I do not shrug off this old experience, or laugh at myself a little as I look back on it. I would not be honest with the reader if I did so. Not long ago, I read Douwe Draaisma's illuminating book on the nature of memory. It can be shown that the human memory records with extreme clarity experiences of humiliation, usually in far more detail and with more precision than moments of success and pleasure. It seems as if these humiliations held in the memory have an "exceptional place—or rather, could not be condensed like the rest. They retain their original impact, but also their color, taste and acuity. In old age, they still seem to have the vividness that one would rather reserve for other memories" (Draaisma 2004, p. 185).

sculptor had tackled a block of marble larger than the task required, thus wasting too much valuable material and time before finishing the sculpture.

I have not just seen that problem. I have known about it for a long time. But I cannot seem to remedy it. Even now, I repeatedly notice myself wasting energy in just the same way.

Building a new home

While I was busy on my research, a good deal of my energy was being poured into another kind of enterprise: house building. In 1974 a condominium for ourselves and four other families was completed. Legally, this type of undertaking was known as "self-built construction," which meant that there was no outside contractor to co-ordinate all the necessary activities. The future occupants themselves hired the people to do each task, either tradesmen with official permits or moonlighters from the "gray" economy. They also had to procure most of the materials and equipment for themselves.

As the work ground on, my wife and I had increasingly become the unwitting managers of the work. We found ourselves up against the reality that it was nearly impossible to obtain the building materials required. Finding clinker bricks or bathroom tiles meant long searches and, if need be, painful reductions in our quality requirements.* We passed all the Stations of the Cross endured by consumers in a shortage economy, which I later put into a systematic order in *Economics of Shortage*. In each case, we had to choose between searching, waiting, making forced substitutions imposed by chronic shortages, or giving up our buying intentions. Apart from the product shortages, we came up against labor shortages as now one and now another skilled tradesman failed to turn up and thereby stalled the whole operation. We had to realize that shortage leads to corruption. We learned how much to give to the warehouseman at each factory to obtain the missing material and what brand of cognac it was appropriate to present to the official at the district council who issued the permits.†

I visited the West quite often in those years, and on each occasion, I took a shopping list with me. Not a list of things that were cheaper in the West than in

---

* I had to draw on the connections of my mother-in-law in Szolnok to obtain a bathtub. The one she found was slightly faulty; we brought it from 100 km away to Budapest.

† János Kenedi published a little diary-like book about his similar experiences of building privately. He wittily chose as his title an old slogan of Mátyás Rákosi's: "The country is yours, you build it for yourself." The book was printed in the series Magyar Füzetek Könyvei (Hungarian Pamphlet Books) published by a group of Hungarian émigrés in Paris.

Hungary, or of what local specialties were worth buying, but a list of what could not be had at home and could be found in a normally functioning market economy.

An experience I had in Moscow seemed to emblematize the East–West difference in buyer–seller relations. Taxis stand in lines outside airports in the West. Passengers hop in and say where they want to go. Taxis pulled up intermittently in Moscow, to be besieged by passengers asking where the taxi was going. Those wanting to go where the taxi driver fancied going got in. Who should choose the destination: passenger or taxi driver?

Everyone constantly had similar experiences. Whomever I spoke to, from research workers to cleaners, from company managers to drivers, would be full of tales of annoyances and trials related to the shortage economy. All of these had settled in me, and they emerged when I set about writing a book about shortage.

Market-oriented reform, through the eyes of Maoists in Calcutta

My wife and I set off in 1975 for a two-month study and lecture tour of India, initiated by some Indian economists. I could devote an entire chapter to the trip, but I will confine myself to one episode.

Before my arrival, I was aware from statistics of where India, this large country of glittering cultural traditions, stood in its economic development. I had come to know splendid Indian economists before. Sukhamoy Chakravarty, later president of the Planning Office, I had met in 1963 on my visit to England, and T. N. Shrinivasan (or TN, as his friends called him) I had befriended at Stanford in 1968. They explained many things before guiding me around India. But the spoken or written word is different from what one sees for oneself. It was a real trauma to see whole families living in tents on the Calcutta pavements. I saw women washing pots in dirty drain water. I saw half-dead people lying in the street. Experts say Calcutta (now officially called Kolkata) is the most crowded city in India, where misery is seen in the greatest concentration.

The Indian Communist Party had split into two parts. The pro-Moscow wing sympathized with the sluggishly reforming Soviet Union, while the radical, revolutionary, Maoist wing was friendly to Beijing. The latter included groups that did not shrink from methods of terrorism. Calcutta was the intellectual center for Indian Maoists.

I gave a series of lectures, but one I remember especially clearly for the debate it provoked.* I talked of the 1968 Hungarian reform and dilemmas caused by

---

* I was making a preliminary attempt to express the line of argument I would use in a later article, "Efficiency and the Principles of Socialist Ethics" (1986b [1980]).

the ensuing changes. Several speakers in the debate rejected sharply—or rather, indignantly—any idea that would shift socialism toward a market economy. They would rather have a rationing system, small rations, and shortage—but with their coupons, everyone should receive the same provisions! They protested against the anarchy of the market. They did not plead the organizational benefits of a planned economy. They were ready to admit its large drawbacks. It was immaterial to them what macroeconomic policy or microeconomic incentives were used to raise production and supply. Their only concern, intellectually and emotionally, was fairness in distribution. I could understand someone—even a university professor—thinking like that amid the misery of Calcutta. I could understand it, but I could not agree. Then as now, I see that the lasting solution to misery lies in reforming production, not distribution. Rationing systems that spread misery equally may assuage feelings of injustice for a while, but they will not solve anything.

The debate continued later among a few people in the home of a professor, but on a political plane. India at the time was one of very few developing countries with a working parliamentary democracy. There was a legal opposition to the government, the ruling party could be turned out in elections, the papers were free to criticize those in power, and the judiciary was independent of the ruling party and the government. But the radical opponents of capitalism belittled all these things. What were the empty frameworks of formal democracy worth if millions were starving? Let there rather be a dictatorship if that meant fair distribution and thus less hunger, rather than bourgeois democracy and the associated mass poverty and famine.

Many years later it emerged that millions had starved to death in Mao's China. Socialist ownership and the planned economy had failed to prevent the dreadful toll. All dictatorship could manage was to conceal the ghastly events from the Chinese and international public and thereby forestall efforts to relieve it.

Nothing about the disastrous consequences of the Great Leap Forward had come out when I paid my visit to India, although it would have been a cogent argument. So we debated without managing to persuade one another.

13

Pieces Falling into Place—1971–1980
Economics of Shortage

My wife and I arrived in Stockholm in early 1976 at the invitation of Professor Assar Lindbeck, for an extended stay while I worked as a guest researcher in the Institute for International Economic Studies. Things did not augur well at first. We could not find suitable housing for a time, and hotel life was unpleasant. Then I left behind on the subway some fat files of notes I had taken on writings I had read, compiled over several years. The autumn weather can be gloomy in Scandinavia. One wet, windy morning on my way to the university, I felt like packing up, leaving, and returning home.

Doing that would have been a shame.* The very helpful secretary at the institute, Birgitta Eliason, was indefatigable in finding us a congenial apartment. My notes turned up again in good order. Ideal working conditions in Stockholm led to what I see as the most successful period in my career, when my book *Economics of Shortage* was written.

Inspiring surroundings

There is much debate these days in the academic world about the funding of research. Where state or supranational organizations control how funds are distributed, the bureaucracy usually requires applicants to submit a plan in advance, saying what they aim to accomplish in their project and accepting deadlines for delivering the "product." Increasing numbers of public and private foundations make similar stipulations.

If I had been asked to fit my work in Stockholm into such a Procrustean bed, I would have failed. I would not have been able to formulate a precise topic before I arrived. I had in mind a general idea like "Anti-Equilibrium Revisited." Not until we

---

* If we had turned back then, our daughter would not have married in Sweden and our two Swedish Hungarian grandchildren, Zsófi and Anna, would not have been born. Luckily, we did not give way to our first depressing experiences.

had passed a few quiet weeks and settled down in Stockholm could I clarify the subject for myself. My hosts, luckily, were more liberal than the bureaucrats I mentioned. They had agreed that I could do what I wanted, and did not tie me to any "project."

I worked a great deal—at home in our own apartment, visiting my host institute only intermittently, when I had something to arrange or when there was an interesting lecture to listen to. They had invited me initially for a year, but when it turned out that I was not finished with the work and asked for another three months, they agreed without hesitation.

I was fortunate, while working at home in isolation, to have a lively and interesting intellectual climate around me.* There were erudite colleagues to talk to. I volunteered to give a series of lectures at the university on the socialist economy. The graduate students as well as the faculty members who attended were my guinea pigs, the first audience whose reactions to my ideas I could observe. I was surrounded after each lecture by a swarm of people offering friendly observations and suggestions.

Later, when *Economics of Shortage* came out and people read in the foreword that I had written it in Sweden, some readers wondered whether I had not missed the Eastern European atmosphere and daily life as I wrote about the shortage economy and the socialist system. Not I! I had amassed plenty of experiences before I reached Stockholm. What I needed for writing the book was peace and quiet— distance from the bitter conflicts, petty struggles, exasperation, and tussles of life at home.

I mentioned in the previous chapter some of the perceptions—writings, debates, and personal experiences—that preceded and prepared the way for the book. In fact, my interest in the shortage economy goes back much further in my intellectual history, for I had devoted a chapter of my candidacy dissertation to the subject. Over the intervening twenty years, I had returned to the question repeatedly from several angles, but so far, the many years' work had produced only fragments that I had accumulated in my mind. Now suddenly, amid the calm of Swedish life, the pieces of the puzzle fell into place.

---

* I mentioned in the previous chapter how my observations in America had schooled me in democracy. That political education continued in Sweden. I will never forget how Prime Minister Olof Palme appeared on television to concede electoral defeat after his Social Democrats had been in power for forty-four years. No doubt it was a devastating moment for him, but he controlled himself perfectly. He smilingly announced the defeat and said, in the most natural manner, that he would hand over his office to the victors. I realized that democracy was most easily recognized by the way that the government allowed itself to be dismissed and replaced in a civilized fashion.

When I set about writing the book, I advanced with dizzying speed, often finishing a chapter a week.* Much of it was ready in my mind and just needed to be written down. And as I have often found, several questions and the strands connecting them were clarified for me in the course of writing.

Many earlier works on economics had referred to the problems of shortages in the socialist economy. Perhaps a couple of paragraphs would be devoted to this topic in an article, or even a whole chapter in a book. *Economics of Shortage*, however, was the first monograph devoted entirely to the subject. As I explained in its introduction, I sought diligently for earlier works that I could cite. Where I found theoretical forerunners, I gave references in the book in the customary manner. Similarly, the people who gave me advice or were involved in the preparatory research are mentioned in the book, with thanks for their assistance.† I do not claim, therefore, that all the ideas appearing in the book were first conceived or first written down by me. But I can say that my basic inspiration did not come from arguments put forward earlier by others. Nor can I point to a single book and say that *Economics of Shortage* continues where it left off. Nonetheless, I was strongly influenced indirectly by certain works—for example, by Marx, Keynes, and Hirschman.‡ But those influences, discussed in earlier chapters, were not confined to the subject of chronic shortage in the socialist system.

That is not to say I was not influenced strongly by the theoretical knowledge gained from my reading since 1955, my empirical research in Hungary, my personal discussions, lectures I had heard, debates held at conferences, and my experiences during lengthy periods spent abroad. *Overcentralization* was written by a *naive* researcher observing reality with open eyes. *Economics of Shortage* was the work of a *professional* economist, an appropriately trained member of his trade, who better

---

* When each individual chapter was completed, Zsuzsa immediately read it and commented on it. This habit had already begun to develop during the years before writing the *Economics of Shortage*, but by the time of the completion of the new book, it was so fixed that I could not have imagined finishing a new work without it. My wife rewarded each chapter with a box of fine Swedish chocolate creams. (I was not obliged to watch my cholesterol in those days.) Could that have increased my speed of composition?

† The book has two appendices of mathematical economics, in which I was assisted as coauthor by Jörgen Weibull and András Simonovits.

‡ I drew particular inspiration from *Capital*. Marx regarded unemployment neither as the random error of market adaptation nor as the consequence of wrong economic policy, but as a specific feature of the capitalist system. Marx was one of the great pioneers of the approach that attempts to recognize and explain the system-specific dysfunctional features that are deeply characteristic of politico-socioeconomic structures. My respect for him is compatible with my radical break from Marxism as a comprehensive worldview and political program.

finds his way around the world of economics, society, and politics by relying on the literature and his own experience.

Let me return for a moment to something I referred to at the beginning of the chapter: I took to Stockholm several kilos of notes I had taken of what I had read. In fact, I hardly looked at those notes as I wrote the book, and the same is largely true of my other works as well. I obviously have in mind the ideas I have found in published sources and manage to remember them at the right moments. Actually looking up sources or notes on them as I write would bog me down and interrupt my line of thought. Perhaps I would then adhere to them too closely, instead of using my own head. It is enough for me to go back to the sources and check references as I revise my first draft.

The message of the book

I had twin purposes in writing *Economics of Shortage*. On the one hand, I wanted to give a comprehensive picture of how the socialist system operates. On the other hand, I sought to present methodically the phenomena, causes, and effects of a chronic shortage economy. Or perhaps it would be better to avoid setting up dichotomies and say that I aimed in discussing the shortage economy to present a broader, deeper picture that went beyond the causes and effects of the specific phenomenon. The shortage economy is that *part* of something through which I set out to present the *whole*. Since instances of shortage are met with every day by citizens of socialist countries, they would sense that this concerned them and their lives. The title *Shortage* was itself a provocation, getting straight to the heart of the matter. The book was to generalize from *everyday life* and raise those generalizations to the level of comprehensive theory.

I might have achieved the latter aim more easily if I had begun by describing the phenomenon in the sphere of consumption, since everyone without exception is always playing the role of a consumer. But that would have defied the logic of the presentation, because the roots of the problem lie in production. So I began with the operation of enterprises and their procurement of inputs. (I had also had some recent experience of procurement while constructing our condominium.)

Instances of shortage occur in all economies. Travelers are unable to travel at the desired time because the last airplane ticket is snapped up in front of them. There is a queue at the cinema to see the latest successful film. These instances are sporadic and brief events, not very serious. It is appropriate to refer to a *shortage economy* if the shortages appear in all or almost all spheres of the economy: in firms and households; in the allocation of products, services, and labor; and in current utilization and investment. The shortage is *chronic*, not temporary. Supply falls short of demand, and the difference is often very large—in other words, shortage is *intense*.

Briefly, the shortage economy shows extensive, chronic, intense shortages all through the economy. The market does not fluctuate temporarily around an equilibrium between supply and demand. It deviates permanently from what in an earlier chapter was called the Walrasian equilibrium. Chronic shortage is the *normal state* for the system, not an unusual event.

Shortage (and I will not repeat "extensive, chronic, and intense" each time) has serious consequences.

Shortage often means that buyers have to buy something other than what they had intended. Such forced substitution eats into the satisfaction of consumption. Procuring scarce goods requires lengthy searches and time-consuming queuing. A given volume of consumption yields less welfare for consumers in a shortage economy than for those in a well-supplied market economy.

Intermittent, incomplete deliveries of materials and semifinished products and components, coupled with a labor shortage, cause much friction and obstruction in production, thereby lessening the productivity of labor.*

Producers in a shortage economy have no trouble selling their output, for which there are eager buyers. There is no competition among producers to win buyers. So shortage removes one of the main incentives to technical development, making it one of the fundamental causes of the technical stagnation under the socialist system.

So far, I have listed direct economic losses from shortage. No less important is its effect on people's overall well-being.† The superiority of the producer or seller degrades human relations. Buyers are at the producer's or seller's mercy and are often placed in a humiliating situation. Distribution of many products and services can be resolved only through a rationing system or administrative allocation. This

---

* It was the joint effect of several factors that resulted in a wider range of products, higher labor productivity, and availability of more advanced technology after the change of system. Several studies based on thorough statistical analyses have demonstrated that the producers' competition for customers has proved the most important factor. Reading studies written by Carlin et al. in 2001 and Djankov and Murrell in 2002, I realized that the changes in production following the post-socialist transition supported one of the main findings of *Economics of Shortage*.

† Foreign students (and younger Hungarians) can have no idea what tortures shortage can bring. When I sought to explain the housing shortage in my lectures, I would bring up the case of a young couple who were legally divorced but were forced to remain in the same apartment. The old wife and the new were obliged by the housing shortage to live in one home, sharing a kitchen and bathroom. Whenever I told the story, the audience would laugh. They found this depressing and demeaning situation funny.

becomes an important weapon in the bureaucracy's hands, enabling it to strengthen its power over people's lives.

The last statement may suggest that the authorities created the shortage economy on purpose, but that is not true. Sellers reap advantages, since the buyers cannot pick and choose or reject goods; however, every seller is concurrently a buyer as well, trying to procure a range of goods and services, and while doing so he or she is in a weak and demeaning position. Many members of the bureaucracy (unless they are highly privileged) will suffer the personal inconveniences of a shortage economy. Nobody wants it, but it appears nonetheless. If it depended on a few people, they could be compelled to end it and alter the strength of the buyer and seller on the market. But it does not involve anyone's free will, for it is created by the *system itself*. Whether the actors like it or not, the chronic shortage economy appears and constantly reproduces itself.

No single factor can satisfactorily explain how shortage appears and reproduces. A full explanation involves grasping a more complicated mechanism of cause and effect. One important link in this causal chain is what I called in the book the "soft budget constraint." This concept and the theory explaining it elicited much response and it took off on a career of its own, independent of *Economics of Shortage*. I will therefore devote a separate chapter to it.

The final link in the causal chain is the institutional system of the socialist economy. Let me quote from the last pages of *Economics of Shortage*, the "final remarks": "Definite social relations and institutional conditions generate definite forms of behavior, economic regularities and norms. These cannot be invalidated by decisions of the state. Government decision and state plan have not prescribed the investment tension, the chronic labor shortage, the tendency toward price-drift, and so on, and no government decision or state plan can eliminate them as long as the conditions exist that maintain these phenomena."[1] The shortage economy is an intrinsic, system-specific attribute of the socialist system that reforms may alleviate but can never abolish.

That was the message of my book *Economics of Shortage*.

Self-censorship

The book spoke important truths. I put down each word convinced I was writing the truth and nothing but the truth. But I also knew the book could not tell the *whole* truth.

We were living in the Stockholm suburb of Lindingö, on an island in the bay. I vividly remember walks through the seashore woods with my wife, as we repeatedly discussed what should go into the book and what not.

The starting point was that the book should address primarily Hungarian readers, and we would be living in Hungary again when we left Sweden.* How far could I go in a manuscript intended above all for publication back home, as a legally printed and distributed book? I was also thinking from the start of the book's possible fate in other socialist countries. Would it be publishable? If not, would it be declared "hostile" and would those who perused it be liable to persecution?

Before traveling to Sweden, we had seen András Kovács's famous 1968 film *Walls*, which depicts swordsmen fighting in a darkened room, fearing they will collide with the walls but not knowing where those walls are. So they only dare move in the center of the room.† Audiences understood quite clearly what Kovács was referring to.

Not only was I aware that there were walls, but I also knew where they ran. Although the room for maneuver in Hungary was much greater than in Romania or Albania, there were still political constraints on the content of legal publications.

I also took into account the fact that I had built up a significant international reputation by the latter part of the 1970s, and that prestige gave me a measure of protection. This consequently pushed somewhat further out the walls that could constrain what I had to say. I should add that I wanted not just to go up to "my" walls but to transcend them. This was precisely the book in which I sought to increase the space defined by the walls and loosen the constraints as well for others who would follow my example.

But even given all this, I could say at most that I had some leeway. I could not write in a legally published book all that I thought on the subject.

I wanted to avoid three issues. First, I did not want to talk explicitly about the Soviet Union, the Soviet bloc countries' relations with the Soviet Union, or their trading and economic ties with each other. Second, I did not want to get embroiled in the role of the Communist Party in the socialist economy. Third, I did not want to say how things would change if state ownership gave way to private ownership.

---

* I discussed these matters with my wife in detail, and we always managed to reach agreement in the end. Yet I, as author, bore full individual responsibility for what appeared in the book. So I feel justified in using the first-person singular to present the resulting line of argument.

† I quote the film script (A. Kovács 1968, p. 37), with directions inset in italics. Benkő, a main character, comments on what is happening.
The two fencers begin to look for each other.
Benkő: See how they are afraid of the walls? Yet they are quite far from them.
They play on, avoiding each other but always moving in the center of the room.
Benkő: The room is far bigger but they are not using it, so they look clumsier than they really are.

These were obviously not secondary questions. They played a fundamental part in understanding the socialist system. I did not want to state half-truths about them, but I could not allow myself to say anything other than the truth. The best course seemed to be to *keep quiet* about them.

But I wanted to point this lacuna out to discerning readers. I stressed in the introduction what the book would *not* cover—for example, the role of the party. I said the analysis would only cover state-owned enterprises, omitting the "second economy" and "informal sector."

Rather than dropping hints, I thought it was more important for the reader to be caught up by the wave of the exposition and adopt the logic of the book. If that happened, the readers would be able to *think further* driven by their own intellectual power. The book ends with chapter 22. The decision to end the book where it does was taken after long and careful deliberation. Among the considerations was a hope that readers would be able to infer an unwritten twenty-third chapter for themselves. The book did not note that the cause of the general, intense, and chronic shortage economy was the Communist system and that a change of system was required before the shortage could be ended for good. The book did not state that the essential features of the system were not susceptible to reform. Nonetheless, many readers clearly read that claim into it.*

I have given only a factual description of how self-censorship operated as I composed *Economics of Shortage*. I will return at the end of the chapter to the political and ethical dilemmas involved.

Publishers' referees

Westerners unfamiliar with the workings of the Communist system would assume that it included formal institutions of censorship. Some countries had them in the early period of socialism, but the consolidated system did not need them any more. The tasks of censorship were delegated to the people responsible ex officio for the written (or broadcast) word: the editor of a newspaper, the director of a publishing house, the chair of the television or radio organization. The task could be delegated to subordinates, in the usual way, but doing so did not absolve the editor of responsibility. He or she had to give an account of what was published to superiors (directors of state publishing firms reported to the Publishing Division of the Ministry of

---

* One reader of the book at the time, a physicist with an interest in politics and economics, described to me not long ago what an experience it had been to read *Economics of Shortage* and how shaken he had been by the book's assertion that a change of system was needed. He firmly remembered after twenty-five years that this proposition had appeared in the book, until I actually showed him that it appeared nowhere in so many words.

Education and Culture, for example). Ultimately, however, leaders of all state institutions were responsible to the Communist Party. If someone in the party (in practice, some party leader or assigned functionaries at the party headquarters) did not like what was to be published, that person had ways of preventing its publication or applying sanctions after the event.

The reins were kept very tight in tougher times. Any piece of writing the slightest bit problematic—criticizing too strongly or signaling any other kind of deviation—would be rejected by the editor in his or her capacity as censor. Or if the editor were uncertain, the piece would be sent up to party headquarters for an opinion. For if the editor published such a piece on his or her own initiative and it created a political storm, there would be serious reprisals.

When my book was completed, the Kádár regime was in a relative "soft" phase. Let us take one by one the processes my book went through.

First, the director of the publishing firm did not resist its publication. The editor in chief, László Fébó, was enthusiastic and did all he could to further it. Authors of academic books in the West are used to having the publisher choose referees for the book without consultation with the author and get unbiased opinions from them. The anonymity prevents the author from growing angry at negative comments that they may make. In contrast, in the socialist countries the referee was named on the book's title page and had to openly take professional and, more problematically, political responsibility for the work. In some cases, the author might have a quiet word with the editor in chief about who the referee should be. This is what happened in my case. Since not all the necessary qualities might be combined in one person, there should be one referee of professional reputation and another with political weight and influence.

After some discussion, it was decided that András Bródy, a colleague of mine at the Institute of Economics, would fit the first role.[2] No one could question his professional standing, as he had become a well-known name at home and abroad. I had been close friends with Bródy at one time, but our relations had become somewhat more distant. I knew he had not been altogether pleased with one or two of my earlier works. Nonetheless, Bródy took the political risk of coming out wholly in favor of the book. He expressed his report with a generosity worthy of a true scholar, saying I had presented socialism in *Economics of Shortage* in the same way that Adam Smith had presented capitalism. I remain truly grateful for Bródy's encouragement and support.

The other reader was Lajos Faluvégi, who was finance minister at the time.[3] (He later rose to the higher position of president of the National Planning Office.) He was an economic expert and not a party cadre, but his opinion was respected and trusted in higher party circles. He was among the committed reformers.

I am a little embarrassed when I now tell the story of Faluvégi's reader's report for the first time. A dear friend of mine, Andrea Deák, was a member of the minister's confidential staff. It often happens with high-ranking statesmen that materials put out in their name, such as speeches they deliver, are written not by them but by one of their staff. Andrea Deák was charged by the minister with drafting the reader's report on *Economics of Shortage*. Except that the text was composed not by Andrea, but by me! I cannot say who made the first move in this—whether Andrea asked me to do it, or I offered. I certainly knew the book better, which made the job easier for me. I wrote it in a moderate tone, recognizing the book's merits (without praising them to the skies) and saying nothing about the book's far-reaching implications.

All this took place in great secrecy. Neither the publisher nor anyone else knew who the real author of the report was. Nor did it matter, in fact. When Andrea handed the draft to her boss, she took responsibility for it. If there were anything the matter, Faluvégi would have raised it with her. More importantly, Faluvégi, who obviously perused the book before signing the report, would have to take responsibility should there be later complaints from party circles.

The publisher now had two favorable, supportive reader's reports and the book had passed the Hungarian "censorship" procedures. Its editors and readers did not ask for a line to be altered.* I had gauged well where the walls ran. Whatever amputations of my ideas had to be done, they were carried out by me in advance.

First impressions

I remember the joyful moment in Egyetem tér, opposite the University Church, in 1980, when my wife and I first saw the book in a bookshop window. The first printing soon sold out and a literary weekly published a note under the title "Shortage of 'Shortage.'"[4] There were altogether three printings in Hungarian.

The book appeared almost simultaneously in English. I had agreed with the helpful and understanding editor at North-Holland that *Economics of Shortage* would

---

* The publisher's designers, whom we consulted about the cover, smilingly presented alternatives. One, eventually chosen, simply had lettering on it. The other bore a color picture of a nude figure before a mirror: the emperor's new clothes! The drawing still hangs on my office wall. It is reproduced in the set of photos published in this book.

My wife held a veritable seminar on *Economics of Shortage* for the great graphic artist János Kass, who produced a brilliant series of drawings inspired by it. These I received as a birthday present from Zsuzsa and they hang in our home to this day. The artist later continued the series and they appeared as illustrations for volumes of my studies published in Hungary and Japan. One of these drawings is also included among the photos.

be published by them even if for some reason the Hungarian edition should not be authorized.

Later came editions in French and Polish, and then in Chinese, the last in a printing of 100,000 copies; in China it won the title of "best seller of the year" in the nonfiction category in the following year. It was published in Czechoslovakia as well but not distributed commercially, merely passed from hand to hand in scholarly institutes. The Russian edition was circulated as a samizdat. Not until the end of the Gorbachev era was it published legally. Then it was a big success, selling 70,000 copies.

The spread of the ideas in the book was helped by a lecture I delivered as chairman to the 1978 conference of the international Econometric Society, summarizing its main points. The lecture was published in the journal *Econometrica*.[5]

Reviews appeared in several of the leading economics journals in the West, almost all of them favorable. Whether reviews appeared in socialist countries depended on how hard or soft a line the regime took. It was particularly important that a detailed, favorable appraisal appeared in Russia, thanks to the courage of the economist R. G. Karagedov.[6] His review of the English edition made it much easier for the samizdat Russian text to circulate there.

The number of citations in the works of Western and Eastern economists reached the hundreds in the next few years. The book began to be used in teaching. I was delighted when I heard that Rajk College, at the Karl Marx University of Economics in Budapest, was holding "*Shortage* seminars" year after year, to discuss the book chapter by chapter.

That interest instigated my first invitation to the university to deliver public lectures on *Economics of Shortage* to large audiences. (Previously I had conducted only seminars attended by small numbers.) Every week the grand lecture hall was packed with students and others from outside the university.*

A dispute with the "disequilibrium" school

I do not want to suggest that the book marched triumphantly forward from start to finish. Some people made a wry face at it. Some did not even feel the subject was relevant. A good few, in Hungary and abroad, voiced reservations or were expressly critical. This chapter gives two samples of the dissenting opinions. (I will deal in a later chapter with a debate over the interpretation of *Economics of Shortage*

---

* One juncture in the first lecture that won appreciation was when I explained forced adaptation and people's humiliation and conformism by quoting a popular song by the talented singer Zorán Sztevanovity: "The beer's lukewarm, but it'll still do for us."

between advocates and opponents of Hungary's reform of its system of economic management.)

In the early 1970s two American economists, Robert J. Barro and Herschel I. Grossman, had devised an original model for studying markets that display a state of excess supply or excess demand instead of Walrasian equilibrium.[7] These they termed *disequilibrium models*. Such an approach has an obvious affinity with the problems I raised first in *Anti-Equilibrium* and later, in a more developed state, in *Economics of Shortage*.

The theoretical structure of the Barro–Grossman model was later adopted and used for econometric calculations by the British economist Richard Portes, whose studies were focusing on socialist economies at the time. Portes founded a school: he and his colleagues and followers designed a succession of disequilibrium models for various socialist economies.[8]

I had met Richard when he was in Budapest at the end of the 1950s as a graduate student of planning. We had seen each other intermittently since that time and generally interpreted economic problems in similar ways. At this point, however, a sharp disagreement arose between us.

I objected to the way that Barro and Grossman, and Portes and his followers after them, described the consumer market as a *macro* aggregate. The state of the market, according to the distorted image presented by this type of model, shows now general excess supply and now general excess demand, and may switch back and forth between the two states of disequilibrium. How could it be said of an economy like Poland's, where people suffered from acute shortage, that it might switch for even short periods of time to a state of general excess supply? Econometric calculations could confirm such a conclusion only if false assumptions and definitions had been incorporated into the model when it was built.

My book underlined that shortage cannot be characterized satisfactorily using aggregate measures. In a socialist economy, usually shortage and surplus exist side by side. Because of poor adaptation, the two did not preclude each other: grave shortages of certain products and services could appear while unsold stocks and unutilized service capacities were building up in a prodigal fashion.

Furthermore, shortages cannot be measured with the usual statistical indices on which Portes and his associates based their calculations. If actual purchases coincide with demand, then the observed data for purchases and sales reflect demand adequately. But if buyers cannot carry out their buying intentions, who knows how large the real, original, unsatisfied demand was? The information known about it becomes less and less reliable as the frequency rises with which buyers react to shortage by buying something other than they had intended. Forced substitution partly or completely soaks up excess demand.

Another objection I had was that the Portes models described only a consumer market, isolating it from the investment market. Yet the focus of the problems was precisely the continual tension in the investment sphere: those running the economy and the managers of state-owned enterprises had an insatiable "investment hunger" and urge to expand, ensuring that the demand in this market always exceeded the supply of available resources.

Portes and associates had one huge advantage over me in these debates. They gleaned data from the statistics available to them. They were then able to make mathematical-statistical calculations, which undoubtedly impressed everyone. I could do little else than appeal to intuition or common sense; I could not oppose the quantified Portes models with likewise quantified Kornai models.*

New methods were required if shortages were really to be measured. We set about fashioning such a new kind of measurement. A good example is the indicator devised by Attila Chikán, director of Rajk College, who, with the help of his colleagues, produced quantifications based on Hungarian data. Enterprise inventories on the output side tend to fall in a shortage economy, as buyers try to buy up anything they can. In contrast, hoarding tendencies appear on the consumption side. Firms are afraid of future shortages and, like hamsters, stock up on materials and semifinished products. The ratio of output stocks to input stocks is an expressive indicator. If it decreases, it signals that the shortage is intensifying; if it increases, the shortage is easing.

Other shortage indicators started to be observed and systematically collected (e.g., the length of the queues for various products and services, and the distribution and frequency of forced substitution). It would take five or ten years for the work to pay off, as long time series would have to be observed before conclusions could be drawn from the figures. I had just set about the task when the shortage economy slipped away! Thank goodness it did, but the change meant that the debate remained forever unresolved. I stick by my logical arguments, but I have never been able to refute the conclusions of Portes and associates with other, more convincing, calculations.

Such polemics in Hungary often sour the personal relations between the debating partners. Luckily, that did not happen between Portes (later Sir Richard) and me. They remained as cordial and friendly as they had been before our argument began.

---

* Some of the early results looked rather promising. In Hungary, it was mainly my colleagues and students who started empirical research in the spirit of the theory developed in *Economics of Shortage*. Some researchers in other countries also undertook investigations based on the theory. Of particular interest in this regard are articles published by Gérard Roland in 1987 and 1990.

A dispute with an orthodox Russian economist

The other debate occurred in Athens in 1981, at a roundtable conference of the International Economics Society, chaired by the great British economist Sir John Hicks.* I devoted my lecture to the main ideas in my still new book, emphasizing that shortage was a system-specific trouble of the socialist planned economy. One speaker in the debate was Professor V. R. Khachaturov, then president of the Soviet Economic Association, who strongly opposed my position. He did not deny that instances of shortage could occur. (Could occur? Hungary was then a land of plenty compared with the Soviet Union, where the acute housing shortage was coupled with regular absences of staple foods and everyday items of clothing from the stores.) These instances, he said, arose from planning errors. Raise the standard of planning and the problem would be overcome.

Also present was Leonid Kantorovich, the great mathematical economist and pioneer of the theory of linear programming, who was a co-winner of a Nobel Prize in 1975. He was there, but he kept quiet.

Hicks in his summary spoke in tones of agreement about my lecture, but he did not comment on my disagreement with Khachaturov. Like other Western economists of that era at East–West meetings, he did not want to become openly involved in a debate between two economists from socialist countries.†

Khachaturov's remarks and his vehement tone confirmed my initial belief that the message of *Economics of Shortage* had strong political overtones.

Helping to erode the system

I have given examples of the written and oral reception of my book, in terms of editions, publications, reviews, and citations. More important still than that tangible influence was how it affected the thinking of intellectuals living under the socialist system.

Many years later, I visited our new local doctor for the first time. He greeted me like a long-lost friend. He had read *Economics of Shortage* and he said—I am quoting his words—that it had changed his view of the world. Thereafter he had looked

---

* I mentioned him earlier; he had championed the publication of my first book in English.

† I first met at that conference with Professor Wu Jinglian, later one of the architects of the Chinese reform. He said he found my argument convincing. He hoped that people in China would become familiar with my ideas and that they would influence his country's development. We have met several times since. He has been a driving force behind Chinese editions of my books.

at the socialist economy with different eyes. Not long after, I was in Krakow, Poland, and heard just the same remark from a Polish sociologist.

The same statements appeared in writing, not just in private conversation. Let me confine myself to opinions of Russian economists.* Daniel Yergin and Joseph Stanislaw, in a 1998 book about the change of system, recall a conversation they had with Yegor Gaidar, the country's prime minister at the time of the great economic turn. They sum up Gaidar's opinion as follows: "The one living economist who could claim to have influenced the minds of a whole generation living under communism was Kornai. He meticulously dissected the centrally planned system and demonstrated its irrationality and self-destructiveness. He also demonstrated the inadequacies of its would-be variant, market socialism." They continue by quoting Gaidar himself: "He was the most influential on all of us in the 1980s.... His analysis of the economy of shortage, in the early 1980s, had a great impact on all of us. He was addressing our problems. We knew all his books."[9]

David E. Hoffman, a former Moscow correspondent of the *Washington Post*, wrote a book a few years ago called *The Oligarchs: Wealth and Power in the New Russia*, in which he reminisces about the group of young Soviet economists surrounding Gaidar and Anatoly Chubais. Let me quote him: "Then came a sudden bolt of inspiration. They were profoundly inspired by a two-volume, 630-page book published in 1980 by a Hungarian economics professor, János Kornai. *Economics of Shortage*, more than any other text, offered an insight into the failings of Soviet socialism." Hoffman quotes a member of the group: "The book first arrived in Leningrad as smuggled photocopies and instantly 'became a Bible.' We had some ideas initially, but the book was kind of a catharsis. It pushed our thinking forward. You met a person and you said, 'Have you read Kornai?' And then it was a starting point for discussion."[10]

This is what I would point to if I were asked what accomplishment in my life I am proudest of. I am gratified that my book won acclaim from many intellectuals and shocked economists and also members of other professions into seeing the socialist system differently.

---

* The reaction in Hungary was reviewed in a study published by Attila Chikán in 2004. I would also like to mention another set of statistics that concern the impact in Hungary. In 1989, two Hungarian researchers, György Such and István János Tóth, published a "scientometric" study analyzing in detail who is cited and how often in Hungarian economics literature. This included a table that ranked authors' citations over five-year periods (p. 1207). In the two periods between 1963 and 1972, Marx stood in first place. Between 1973 and 1978, Marx was still first, followed by Lenin and Kornai. The order reversed between 1978 and 1982, when my citations came out on top, and so it remained between 1983 and 1987, when there were twice as many citations of my works as of Marx's in papers written by Hungarian economists.

After the Berlin Wall came down, many theories gained currency about the antecedents to the event. Credit was claimed by a variety of political forces east and west of the Iron Curtain. Some pointed to Reagan's toughness and American military pressure, others to the clever planning of Gorbachev. Some thought the actions of the dissidents—Andrei Sakharov, Václav Havel, Adam Michnik, and so on—were decisive, and others put the "reform communists" at the top of the list. As I myself see it, the wrong question was being raised. Although the change in 1989–1990 took place incredibly fast, it was preceded by a long process of weakening and deterioration in the socialist system. As is true of all complex, wide-ranging historical processes, the erosion can be explained by several concurrent factors. I find all "single-factor" explanations intellectually suspect, because they simplify the complexity of historical processes to the extreme, and usually mask some political intent or desire for self-aggrandizement.

One major factor that played an important preparatory role, though it was not the biggest or only cause, was the fundamental alteration that steadily took place in the thinking of the leading political, economic, and cultural strata under the socialist system. No regime, not even a dictatorship, can survive without a group of supporters who believe in its legitimacy and viability. One foundation for the structure of the socialist system was the existence of Communists who believed in their cause, thought the problems would be temporary at most, and were impelled to make sacrifices by a messianic sense of mission. Hitler and his accomplices did not rely only on repression and military commands to fight World War II to the end. There remained to the last people who believed in the cause. The grave of the socialist system was dug in part by the dissipation of belief and trust in the system. The ring of socialist sympathizers broke. The inner circle, the cadres, lost their conviction and began to seek other answers.

That intellectual erosion came about mainly because of personal experience: the woes of the economy, Russian losses in the Afghan War, the bitterness of the public. The writings that reached the politically minded intelligentsia at that time helped people in interpreting their experiences and hastened the decay. I could list several. In first place, I put Solzhenitsyn's *Gulag Archipelago*, which created quite a sensation at the time; but works by George Orwell and Arthur Koestler were also being read, after a hiatus of several decades. *Economics of Shortage* added an element of its own to the image of communism that was developing. The three authors just mentioned were concerned with the brutality, the cunning, and the untruthful and inhuman nature of the repression. My book addressed calmly and objectively other layers of its readers' thoughts and feelings. It undermined the naive idea that socialism could be given a "human face" and thereby rendered capable of fulfilling its mission. Lenin, quite rightly, stated that socialism would triumph if it achieved higher productivity than capitalism. Readers of *Economics of Shortage* understood that no such triumphant superiority would ensue.

I do not know how many of the politically active intelligentsia knew my work directly or at second hand, and how many remained uninfluenced by it. No such survey has ever been conducted. But I found myself that many people who might be expected to take up the book, if only because it was "in fashion" for a couple of months and was being spoken of among the intelligentsia, never did so.* That too warns me against exaggerating its effects. But even by a realistically modest estimate, its influence was certainly wide.

The political and ethical dilemmas of publication again

After returning from Stockholm, I met at the Academy guesthouse in Mátraháza with Ferenc Donáth, one of the leading members of the intelligentsia opposing the Kádár regime, who has been referred to in earlier chapters. I was working on the final chapters of *Economics of Shortage*. We ate at the same table and often took walks in the woods, talking earnestly about science, scholarship, politics, and the economy.

On one walk, Donáth said he was editing a *Festschrift* in honor of István Bibó.† It could be anticipated that legal publication of the book would not be possible, and for this reason it would have to be put out in the form of samizdat. Several famous people had offered to contribute. Would I do so? I answered no, clearly and decisively. Since Donáth was well aware of my general views about legal and illegal publication and of what I was engaged in at the time, he did not press me. He simply took note of my refusal.

I did not sense from what he said then or later that he bore me any grudge at all. We met later on several occasions for interesting, confidential discussions. He came

---

* I read the diary of the well-known Hungarian author Ferenc Karinthy, which includes accounts of his reading. We were personally acquainted, which might also have attracted his attention to the book, but it is clear that Karinthy never read *Economics of Shortage* and it was not referred to in the circles in which he moved. Gábor Klaniczay, the noted historian, explains in his fascinating memoirs what books influenced his generation, members of the Hungarian intelligentsia born in the 1950s. Mine is not among them.

† It was originally János Kenedi's idea to produce a *Festschrift* for Bibó's seventieth birthday. Work started on the book after Bibó's death. Ferenc Donáth took the job of chairman of the editorial committee, and was joined by György Bence, Sándor Csoóri, Árpád Göncz, Aliz Halda, János Kenedi, János Kis, Pál Réz, Jenő Szűcs, and Zádor Tordai as members. The book was offered for legal publication to the Gondolat Publishing House, which—obviously after consultation with higher party circles—rejected it. So it was published in samizdat form in 1981. It eventually appeared in print after the change of system, in 1991, under the editorship of and with a foreword by Pál Réz.

to me while I was in Munich in the summer of 1983, when he was receiving medical treatment there. Later I visited him in a hospital in Budapest; I was astounded to see how bravely he bore the suffering of his mortal illness, with his accustomed ironic smile on his face. We followed two very different strategies in life, but that did not impede our friendship or mutual respect.

Ferenc Donáth was by no means the only close acquaintance of mine involved in illegal or semilegal organization work under the Kádár regime, who nonetheless took note of my decisions with tact and human understanding. I always felt they respected the path I had chosen for myself and appreciated what I had accomplished.

I recounted in chapters 5 and 7 how I decided in 1955–1956 not to try to influence events with illegal publications and how I confirmed my decision in 1957. I had already set my course toward becoming a professional economist and member of the Western profession, exerting influence through legally printed publications. From the outset, that meant making some concessions. I was prepared to make them as long as they did not conflict with the prohibitions dictated by my conscience.

I tried to follow that strategy in life consistently, and it was consistent with it to write *Economics of Shortage* but not to contribute an article to the Bibó *Festschrift*.

Self-censorship called for some bitter sacrifices. There may be social scientists, or more probably writers or poets, who find intellectual enjoyment in concealing their meaning between the lines and cunningly outwitting watchful political censors. I found no such joy in it. I tried almost obsessively, and still do, to say everything I have to say clearly and unambiguously. I felt as self-mutilation my having to leave it to readers to discover what I had been unable to say. Self-censorship is a demeaning process, and one reason why I experienced the change of system as a new liberation was that it freed me of such repeated feelings of bitterness.

Those who wrote for purposes of illegal publication may have felt, justifiably, that they were unconstrained. They could write all they believed at the time to be the full truth. I envied them that opportunity.*

It is an unpleasant, painful experience to say no to a friend who shares the same political purposes as yourself. It is as if you were letting down a comrade-in-arms. I found myself several times in the situation of being expected to provide an article for a samizdat publication or sign a letter of protest. I consistently declined all such invitations.

I did not want to switch back and forth between two strategies. I was not simply trying to avoid the periods of being silenced and denied chances to publish that awaited protesters. I also wanted to keep my privilege of being allowed to travel to

---

* Years after I had broken with Marxism, when my views about Marx's ideas had matured, I could have produced a polemical article on the subject. But I could never have done so legally, and my conclusions therefore remained unwritten.

the West. I can safely say it was not for the sake of tourist experiences. Each new visit abroad confirmed that I could only be a full, expert member of my profession if I met regularly with Western colleagues and spent long periods in the foremost seats of Western learning, gaining up-to-date knowledge from primary sources. Living in the inbred intellectual world of Eastern Europe increases the danger that one's thinking will remain provincial. Those of my generation who stepped into the world of international scholarship only after the change of system soon found they were at a disadvantage.

Some seek to justify their lives to themselves in hindsight, arguing that they made the one acceptable, moral decision and allowing only small leeway on each side in their lenient moments. Those who are more radical they view as hotheads, doing more harm than good by their thoughtlessness. Those making more concessions have bargained with the authorities and sold their virtue to the powerful.

I am more tolerant in my moral judgments of others' activities, but I do not accept unprincipled moral relativism. Some concessions go too far and amount in my eyes to betrayal. Some people bluster needlessly and do no good to their cause by picking fights. I despise the political chameleons, choosing their opinions like underwear and always ready to sacrifice principles for the hope of political power or lucrative business.

But I have to admit with conviction that there are several morally acceptable strategies in life, indeed several that are worthy of respect. I deeply admire and respect those who risked their livelihoods and freedom, and if need be their lives, in illegal struggles for democracy and human rights.

Let us stay with my problem of choice, however. It would be self-serving to argue that a samizdat publication could reach only a couple of hundred readers, usually within a single country, while a legal, self-censored publication such as *Economics of Shortage* reached tens of thousands, inside and outside Hungary, in many countries in the world. That is true, but there is an immediate counterargument: samizdat publications let their authors express themselves more radically, while I could only hint in some cases. I see the two as complementary, not rival, forms of publication under a dictatorship. I am delighted there were people brave and self-sacrificing enough to edit and distribute illegal papers. As a believer in Hungarian democracy, I am proud they were my contemporaries. I live in the secure knowledge that their writings and mine gave reciprocal support to each other.

14

A Breakthrough—1979 Onward

The Soft Budget Constraint

A few days before I began writing this chapter, the journal with the broadest readership among economists, the *Journal of Economic Literature*, published a review by Eric Maskin, Gérard Roland, and me of the literature on the soft budget constraint.[1] I first used the expression in print in 1979. The concept has become widely known over the past twenty-five years.

The meaning and significance of the concept

I took over the expression "budget constraint" from the microeconomic theory of the household. Let us assume a household is drawing up a budget. It has to plan its spending so that its expenses are covered by its earnings, which can be augmented by earlier savings that have built up. The total sum of financial resources available to the household is its budget constraint, which its expenditures cannot exceed.

Now let us look at how a state-owned enterprise does business under the socialist system. If all goes well, earnings cover expenditures and there is a profit. But what happens if expenditures exceed earnings and its financial resources run out? Here we can distinguish two possibilities. One is that the firm is left to its own resources. Then the budget constraint is *hard* and persistent losses will mean that it fails after a time. On the other hand, some superior body may rush to its aid and bail it out financially. In that case, the budget constraint is *soft*: there is no real curb on the firm's spending. It will survive even if spending exceeds income plus initial capital over a long period.

The story sounds familiar to all who know what happened in economies under the socialist system. The problem was especially acute in countries like Hungary that took tentative steps toward reform—for instance, by giving managers a profits-based incentive. Loud words were spoken about the need for profits, but in practice the real incentives behind them were destroyed. If a firm was profitable, that was fine. If it was making a loss, no matter—it would be saved from failure. This plainly shows how a sham market economy differs from a real one. The latter has losers as well as winners.

A soft budget constraint does serious damage. Even if prices are reasonable, firms will not be sensitive enough to the signals from prices, costs, and profits. A hard budget constraint automatically metes severe punishment to firms that are uncompetitive and post losses. A soft budget constraint gives immunity from punishment and tolerates inefficiency. This situation disposes producers to place orders irresponsibly (i.e., causes demand to run away); for if the bills cannot be paid, they will be picked by the body that bails the producers out. This was the main cause of the oversized investment plans in the socialist system, which often started with low spending targets and ended with alarming levels of excess spending.

The budget constraint, whether hard or soft, ultimately shows firms' managers what is worth attending to.* If the constraint is hard, they have to pay attention mainly to the efficiency and profitability of production. If it is soft, the most important thing for managers is to cultivate connections "above," where financial support and bailouts can be obtained in troubled times. It becomes more useful to pace the corridors of power and lobby superiors than to supervise what goes on in the factory.

Why did this idea of the soft budget attract such notice and spread so widely? Primarily because it identified a relevant phenomenon apparent to all—a syndrome with comprehensible, explainable causes and regularities and with consequences that are undoubtedly severe. From the outset I emphasized that although the phenomenon was more widespread under socialism, it occurred elsewhere too, in market economies based on private ownership. Although I concentrated initially on identifying the soft budget constraint in firms' behavior, I noted its presence in other organizations, such as health services, educational and nonprofit organizations, and local government. Moreover, symptoms of the syndrome can even be seen in whole economies if it becomes usual for international financial institutions or the world financial community to bail entire countries out when they enter a financial crisis.

But the idea's widespread acceptance is not explained just by practical relevance. The theory's structure was a fortunate fit with mainstream economic thinking. All who studied microeconomics were familiar with the idea of a budget constraint. It is easy to advance a new line of thought by enlarging and sharpening the meaning of a well-known concept. In an earlier chapter I wrote that our ideas about autono-

---

* Of course there are intermediate grades between extreme softness and extreme hardness. This and many other aspects of the softness of the budget constraint received detailed treatment in my works on the subject. The aim in this autobiography is to outline the central features of an idea in such a way that noneconomists can also grasp it. The theory is therefore expounded here in a very simplified form.

mous control had not spread because they did not fit into the routine thinking of mainstream economists in several important respects. Now, luckily, the opposite was the case. This idea's acceptance and diffusion were helped because a theory based on the familiar-sounding concept of "budget constraint" was immediately congenial and interesting.

The antecedents

My theoretical thinking about the soft budget constraint went back a long way. In chapter 7 I discussed how Hungarian state enterprises, as soon as profit incentives were introduced, pleaded that they should be compensated if losses were made. I wrote an article in 1958 asking "Should the profit-sharing [system] be corrected?" The problem had bothered me ever since: I felt there was something important behind it.

In 1972, Andreas Papandreou—the future prime minister of Greece, then teaching economics at a Canadian university—sent me an inscribed copy of *Paternalistic Capitalism*. His book drew my attention to an important social phenomenon: the paternalistic features in many types of society. What intrigued me most, of course, was how these appeared in a socialist society.

Even during Hungary's most brutally repressive period, the Communist dictator liked to play the part of a "father devoted to his people." This stern father figure gave way to a smiling one as the dictatorship in Hungary eased. In terms of political structure, paternalism means that the authorities retain in their own hands decisions that in other societies would be made by the individual, the family, the immediate community, or the lowest level of organization (for instance, the firm). So in earlier times the right to make family decisions was vested in the father, who had a duty to look after the family. A paternalistic society treats its members as minors, almost as infants. It does not expect them to look after themselves and thinks it natural that they should await remedies from above for all their woes.

I had in mind a line of argument to link paternalism with bailing out troubled firms in a socialist society. I first presented this idea in a lecture at the University of Oslo. To describe this relation between state and firm, I used the analogy of a family bringing up children. I distinguished five degrees of paternalism, from 4 to 0. Degree 4 involves *grants in kind and their passive acceptance*. This is the case with a newborn child receiving everything from its parents and not needing to ask for anything. Degree 3 entails *grants in kind with wishes actively expressed*. The child is older and still receives everything from its parents, but can talk and convey its wishes to adults. These grades resemble the relation between state and firm in an economy with strict central planning. The state provides a production plan and the resources to complete it. If the dictatorship is hard, the firm is not even consulted (Degree 4). If the repression has eased a little, there is an opportunity for the firm and the authorities to bargain over the plan indicators (Degree 3).

Degree 2 is styled *financial allowance*. The child (e.g., a typical American college student) has left home but is not yet independent. The parents provide pocket money and pay for living expenses and tuition. If the money runs out, the child turns to his or her parents for more, usually with success. In the analogous economic situation, the firm receives a financial allocation for an investment project and controls how it is spent—but if it runs out, the extra is usually paid by the state after all.

I called Degree 1 *self-supporting but assisted* and Degree 0 *self-supporting and left to itself*. The child has grown up. He or she is usually earning enough for self-support, but what happens in times of financial trouble? The family may rush to the rescue (Degree 1) or decide that the child is now responsible for his or her own destiny (Degree 0). Turning to the firm, Degree 1 reflects a market-oriented, semireformed socialist economy, in which the firm is autonomous but is helped out if there are chronic losses. Degree 0 describes circumstances free of paternalism and with strong market competition. If the firm fails, that is its problem. It cannot expect anyone to pay its debts.

This graphic description of the degrees of paternalism in terms of the family and society was later included in *Economics of Shortage*. Speaking in Oslo, I did not yet employ the phraseology of soft and hard budget constraints, but the book expressed the paternalism model in these new terms. Degree 2 of paternalism and especially Degree 1 made up the situation I termed the soft budget constraint, and Degree 0 the hard budget constraint.

The term did *not* come to me from thinking about the role of the budget constraint or trying to refine the concept. My starting point was a *real economic phenomenon* and observed practice. The phrase occurred to me almost by accident. I was preparing a series of lectures for Stockholm University and writing mathematical equations to model the operation of a state-owned enterprise, including its lower output constraints and the upper constraints of usable resources. For completeness's sake, I had to add financial constraints as well. Although a "budget constraint" does not customarily appear in the standard microeconomic model of a profit-maximizing firm, I wrote it into my model. But it immediately occurred to me that it is not an effective constraint! A firm would be incapable of overcoming a resource constraint—for example, a raw material quota; but if its budget constraint is soft, it knows that its superior body will bail it out in time of trouble.

So I used the expression "soft budget constraint" in the lecture. I remember how two professors in the audience, Bengt-Christian Ysander from Sweden and the

American Harvey Lapham, came up to me afterward along with a student, Lars Svenson (now a well-known economist) and said they had much appreciated the idea of a soft budget constraint. Those few encouraging words induced me to think over the expression more carefully and work on the associated theoretical problems.

Thereafter, describing and analyzing the soft budget constraint, as a characteristically dysfunctional feature of the socialist system, played prominent roles in my lectures and articles on the shortage economy and the socialist economy in general.

The history of knowledge certainly contains instances of theories emerging from someone's head in a complete and mature form. That has never happened with me. Starting with the 1958 Hungarian article, and through the review article published in the *Journal of Economic Literature* in 2003, the underlying idea remains: yet the intervening forty-five years have altered in many ways how I describe the method, explain the causes, and present the consequences. My current position appears in the 2003 article and my 1992 summarizing work *The Socialist System: The Political Economy of Communism*. Let me point to two changes that distinguish the earlier and later positions, because these go beyond narrow professional considerations.

In the early publications, my explanation of what causes softness in the budget constraint emphasized the state's paternalist role. Having created them, a socialist state, as a responsible parent, cannot abandon its "children," the state-owned enterprises. Moreover, the state has to safeguard the livelihood of the firms' employees. Many people read that as the final point of the causal analysis, but in fact this was not the end. Even back then I posed the question strongly to myself: *Why* does the state in the socialist system behave like that? How does its acceptance of a "caring" role tie in with its demand for undivided power? How does it fit into the political structure and official ideology? Chapter 22, the last chapter of *Economics of Shortage*, dealing with paternalism, should have been followed by one more chapter, a discussion of these deeper levels of relationships, but this remained unwritten. Self-censorship, as I mentioned in the previous chapter, prevented me from writing that chapter.

Luckily, plenty of readers could imagine how the sequence of ideas in *Economics of Shortage* should continue. However, not all were capable of taking my line of thought further on their own. They thought that I had nothing more to say. I wondered at the time and I am still wondering now, what did these colleagues think about me? Did they seriously believe that I, while spending a large part of my time in Budapest, was not aware of the nature of the communist political system—even if I did not write about it explicitly?* Of course, I did clearly see that the political

---

* I kept finding for decades that some Western colleagues had no idea that I, as a citizen of a communist country, might be restricted by censorship or self-censorship. Their incomprehension never ceased to amaze me.

structure leaves its mark on the relationship between the state and the firm. I had tried vainly to leave hints between the lines. The final pages of the book spoke in very general terms of the role of "the institutional system," but, it seems, that was not sufficient for some readers.

I explained in the previous chapter the bitter price I paid to ensure legal publication of *Economics of Shortage* and some of my other works. My decision to end the exposition of the causal chain of shortage at paternalism led to many misunderstandings. I can call this result an unfortunate component of the "price" of legality. The barriers of self-censorship fell as I published *The Socialist System* in 1992, where at last I could state my *whole* argument about the soft budget constraint.

Turning to the second development in my thinking, I saw then as now a chain of cause and effect between the soft budget constraint and shortages, but now I attribute a *different emphasis* to the strength of the relation.

Before a comprehensive, chronic, intense shortage economy can develop in a country, it is *necessary* for the budget constraint on firms that account for most of the production to be soft, but that is not a *sufficient* condition. Other factors must also take effect: a ban on free enterprise, administrative restrictions on competition from imports, distortions in the price system, and so on. *Economics of Shortage* placed too much emphasis on the soft budget constraint. That weakness cannot be explained by self-censorship and the need for voluntary curtailment to ensure legal publication. The main reason is that the analysis was not yet sufficiently mature.

Another side of that bias appears in the account of the consequences of the soft budget constraint. Shortage was the main subject of the book, and so its main emphasis was on exploring how that syndrome affected "runaway" demand. This influence is very important, but more important still is what became the main concern of all scholars dealing with the subject: the ill effects of the soft budget constraint on productivity, competitiveness, and incentives. *Economics of Shortage* also pointed these out, but I would now stress it even more, putting it at the top of the list of harmful effects emanating from the soft budget constraint.

Empirical confirmation

I felt it was important to confirm the theoretical diagnosis in practice. In 1983 Ágnes Matits, a young lecturer at the Karl Marx University of Economics, and I set about compiling a database of the main financial figures for all Hungarian state-owned enterprises over a number of years. We entered about 1.3 million data into computers that were, of course, much less effective than those of today. Ágnes and her colleagues translated the figures into an easily handled form. We made various instructive econometric analyses showing the complexity of the channels through which enterprise profits were repeatedly reallocated. It was impossible to recognize the figures for "final profits" that ultimately appeared on the enterprise books after a zigzag process of bureaucratic redistribution, so far had these departed from the original profits or losses produced. The calculations certainly confirmed that bureaucratic redistribution had siphoned off a high proportion of the profits made by the initially most profitable enterprises to those originally posting losses. Big profit makers were being penalized and loss makers were being unduly rewarded. That result gave us some tangible evidence of the existence of the soft budget constraint. Ágnes Matits and I jointly published the calculations in the book *The Bureaucratic Redistribution of Company Profits* in 1987.

Other authors also produced empirical work to test theories having to do with the soft budget constraint even before the collapse of the Soviet empire, but they did so rather sporadically. If we jump forward in time, it can be seen that research got real momentum only in the 1990s. That was the time for a breakthrough in thinking. Western experts arriving in post-socialist countries suddenly began to realize that the soft budget constraint was one of the economic evils inherited from the previous system. At the same time, many began to understand that hardening the budget constraint was one of the key tasks of achieving a transition to a market economy. A series of studies based on carefully gathered statistical data and econometric examinations were elaborated. In addition, hardly a report by the World Bank or the European Bank for Reconstruction and Development on socialist or post-socialist economies failed to deal with the question of how the soft budget constraint affected firms.

Mathematical modeling of the phenomenon

As with the empirical examinations, in the case of the mathematical modeling of the soft budget constraint syndrome I also felt that I should begin to develop a formal theoretical examination on my own. I found an excellent associate in Jörgen Weibull.* Jörgen did not like the expression "soft budget constraint," but he warmed to the notion of paternalism. We managed to devise a mathematical model to confirm that when loss-making firms are helped in a paternalistic way, the corporate

---

* I had met Jörgen as a student during my time in Sweden, but as fate would have it, he became not only a coauthor but also the husband of our daughter and father of our two Swedish grandchildren.

Our study of paternalism was written in the early 1980s. We started work on it during one of Jörgen's visits to Budapest, and completed it through correspondence between Stockholm and Budapest. In today's Internet-dominated world, this would be nothing remarkable, and coauthors now quite frequently produce their papers while physically distant from each other.

sector becomes less cautious in placing its orders, and demand increases more than when all firms have to stand their ground in a competitive environment.[2]

An interesting model along similar lines was being devised at Princeton too. Richard Quandt, always so eager to help when I was teaching there, now began research on the theory of the soft budget constraint. He and his colleagues prepared a series of studies on the subject, demonstrating, for instance, the "Kornai effect"— that is, proving the theoretical connection between softness of the budget constraint and increase in input demand from firms.[3]

The theoretical turning point came with a model created by Eric Maskin, a Harvard professor of economics, and Mathias Dewatripont,[4] then still a Ph.D. student. By that time, in the early 1990s, I was teaching at Harvard and talked a great deal with Eric about the socialist economy, including the problems of the soft budget constraint. He and Mathias had already been working for a while on the well-known game theory problem of "commitment." This holds that the connection between "players" (the participants cooperating or in conflict in a given situation) develops differently according to whether all parties abide by their previous commitments or subsequently change their stance and depart from them. Is their behavior consistent over time or inconsistent? The two theoretical economists realized that my soft budget constraint is a *special inconsistency phenomenon*.

Take a simple example. A big bank joins in funding an investment project of a firm by providing a loan. It pledges to enforce observance of the original loan contract. Whatever may happen, it will expect the firm implementing the investment project to stand on its own feet. The investor firm finds itself in financial trouble and cannot fulfill the original conditions of the loan contract, whereupon the bank, despite its pledge, offers financial assistance, showing a willingness to alter the loan conditions or provide further credit.

The model analysis showed a bailout to be in the bank's narrow financial interest. Once it had put money in the project, it was rational to throw good money after bad.

The Dewatripont–Maskin model was especially interesting and important in two ways. First, it enriched the causal analysis. It was no longer confined to cases in which an organization bailing out a loss-making firm had political, macroeconomic, or social motivations.* Even simple self-interest would prompt a profit-oriented bank to rescue and aid a loss-making firm to which it has lent money. The truth of this observation can be seen in business practice. Big banks, for a time, are prepared

---

* When does some rescue operation or other become justified? Are the expected macroeconomic or social effects of a bailout more important than the more remote and persistent effects on the behavior of those hoping for a similar rescue? Discussion of such important and intellectually stimulating normative questions exceeds the scope of this autobiography.

to rescue ill-performing, unreliable clients. Doing so may be less awkward and generate smaller losses than just writing off the debt.

The other attraction of the Dewatripont–Maskin model was that it addressed the problem with the apparatus of mathematical game theory. Economists' interest had turned to game theory in the 1990s—hundreds of researchers gladly used its methodology. It was the hot field of research. Those eager to apply and understanding well this fascinating, elegant, and flexible technique could now describe the soft budget constraint through its easily understandable model.

The first Dewatripont–Maskin model was followed by several variants. Each clarified aspects, origins, and effects of the syndrome from different angles.

The story behind the first summarizing article

Let us now go back in time. By 1984, the soft budget constraint (among other things) had been mentioned in several of my articles and in *Economics of Shortage*, and I felt that the time had come to write an article expressly on the subject to summarize my thinking about it. I wanted the article to receive a great deal of publicity, but not just among Sovietologists and specialists in Eastern Europe. I trusted that if other economists also learned about this still little-known idea, it might inspire them to apply the concept to the market economy as well.

The resulting article did not contain mathematical models. It was expressed in words from start to finish. There were some illustrative tables, but the figures in them were allowed to speak for themselves. No mathematical-statistical analyses of the data were included, and no econometric analysis was applied to support the statements.

I submitted it to one of the field's most prestigious journals, the *American Economic Review*. A few months later, I received a reply from the editor. The article had been sent to three referees for review. One of them recommended publication after small changes, but the other two criticized it strongly. The editor commented that the tone of the two critical reviews was harsh and perhaps excessively so. Nonetheless, he thought it better if I put my thoughts in survey form, not for his journal but for the *Journal of Economic Literature*. It was his understanding that I had already agreed to write such an article for that journal.[5]

This polite dismissal was based on an error of fact. I was indeed working on a study for the other journal, but the subject was different: a comprehensive survey and evaluation of economic reform in Hungary. There was hardly any overlap between the two pieces.

To put it plainly, the *American Economic Review* had rejected my article. I offered it to the journal *Kyklos*, where it was accepted without alteration.[6] Since then, it has become one of the most frequently cited of all my publications.

I could console myself with the thought that other, greater men and women have likewise had their work rejected. Many years later, two American researchers, Joshua S. Gans and George B. Sheperd, asked several noted economists about such experiences.* Many of them, from Sir Roy Harrod, one of the creators of modern growth theory, to Milton Friedman and Paul A. Samuelson, the best-known U.S. economists of the twentieth century, had similar experiences. Some leading journals had rejected the papers they submitted, which included works that later became classics of economic theory. Serene in the knowledge that my case was far from exceptional, I might as well drop the matter.

But there is an interesting sequel to the story. A few years later, Yingyi Qian (then still a Harvard graduate student, now a professor at the University of California at Berkeley) likewise submitted an article to the *American Economic Review*; its subject was how shortage under the socialist system relates to the softness of the budget constraint. He examined that relation with an ingeniously devised mathematical model, a variant of the Dewatripont–Maskin model mentioned above. In the manner customary for the journal, he presented theoretical propositions in precise, mathematical language, along with their strict proofs. The article made due reference to its intellectual sources: *Economics of Shortage*, the *Kyklos* article, and the Dewatripont–Maskin study. It formed an important part of Yingyi's doctoral thesis. Eric Maskin and I were his teachers and officially appointed thesis advisers. We both read the manuscript, and, as thesis advisers are expected to do, gave advice. The author expressed his thanks for that in the article.

Yingyi Qian's article raised relevant questions and added to the extensive literature on the subject original thoughts expressed with exemplary exactitude and clarity. The editors, in my view, were right to accept and publish it. I can say, with a clear conscience, I felt not a scrap of envy toward my junior. I had friendly relations with Yingyi in his student days and they have deepened since. I always tried to clear the way for him, and he has given me professional assistance, and, whenever we met, friendly and affectionate attention.† It fills me with joy that one of my kindest and best students published his study in one of economics' most prestigious forums.

* I was asked too, but refrained from telling the story at the time. Now that an account has appeared in the *Journal of Economic Literature* of how the idea of the soft budget constraint spread, I think the time has come to tell the story, and these memoirs, by placing the incident in context, provide the best framework for doing so.

† When my wife and I made our second visit to China, Yingyi spared the time to fly over specially from the United States to help me communicate with Chinese colleagues. We had trouble with interpreters, and on several occasions he was prepared to translate instead. He was proficient, he joked, in three languages: English, Chinese, and Kornai-ese!

But why did the journal reject the first article and accept the second? Although I raise the question from the standpoint of the one rejected, my personal story points to *general* problems. What criteria are used by reviewers charged with deciding what writings to publish? How does the act of publishing affect academic careers? On a deeper level, what behavior is encouraged in academics by today's practices of publication, appointment, and promotion?

Some lessons from the incident

Before starting to offer an answer, I would like to point out that I have put forward big, far-reaching questions, and it is beyond the scope of this autobiography to address them fully. The causal analysis will be partial, covering only what relates to my story.* I do not deal with many other, no less significant aspects of the selection criteria applied, or with all their beneficial or harmful effects. For example, I do not discuss the useful influence of the high professional standards demanded by editors and referees in their selection of papers for publication in these journals, although I regard these as extremely important.

The process for selecting papers for leading journals includes elements of chance. Both possible kinds of error are obviously made: articles worthy of publication are rejected, and ones unworthy of it are published. The decisions are made by people, and nobody is infallible. The question is whether there are *systematic* errors. Is there some kind of regular and recurrent distortion in the practice of acceptance and rejection? Many think there are several kinds of distorting tendencies, and I would like to discuss just one of these in detail.

Truly important, forward-looking new ideas in the social sciences rarely are first expressed in a perfectly accurate, faultless way.† They often appear in the form of a hazy or only half-lucid conjecture, beginning a long process of reflection and understanding. Sometimes an erroneous but thought-provoking statement initiates a fruitful line of inquiry, as experiments to disprove the error lead researchers closer to the truth.

Mathematics has played an important part in research since it joined the arsenal of economics. But as far as I can trace matters, exciting and relevant insights have usually been put forth initially by a pioneer researcher in words, not in mathematical

---

* I consider only the problems of the social sciences, as I lack close knowledge of how natural scientists work or of the processes leading to their discoveries.

† Certainly, there are exceptions. Arrow's Impossibility Theorem is probably one—a truly brilliant, original discovery expressed in a precise mathematical form from the moment of its appearance.

models. First came the prose of Adam Smith, about the coordinating action of the invisible hand, and only much later Léon Walras's mathematical theory of equilibrium, which is somewhat inaccurate, according to present knowledge. Still later came the perfect accuracy of Kenneth Arrow and Gérard Debreu. First there was John Maynard Keynes and his more or less inaccurate ideas about interest and liquidity preferences, then the IS-LM (investment–savings, liquidity–money supply) model of John Hicks, which demonstrated and sharpened these ideas in mathematical form.[7] First John Rawls expressed his theory of justice, and then Arrow set about formalizing one of Rawls's theses.[8] First Joseph Schumpeter published a book on the role of the entrepreneur that was devoid of mathematical analysis.[9] Decades later, Philippe Aghion and some other economists managed to frame Schumpeter's ideas in terms of concise, strict mathematical models.[10]

Although I am simplifying to an extreme, let me distinguish three consecutive (though sometimes temporally overlapping) phases in economic research—or, more precisely, in the birth and career of the really essential new discoveries. In the first, someone recognizes and states the problem, and presents the first conjectural solution to the "puzzle." In the second, someone "cleans up" the line of argument, renders the conceptual apparatus accurate, clarifies the assumptions and abstractions needed to arrive at provable conclusions, and provides logical proof of the propositions. The third and final phase consists of drawing conclusions, which may raise further theoretical questions while also offering practical lessons for economic policy.

In the first phase, a major role is played by intuition, the ability to recognize problems, imagination, and the ability to link isolated observations and statements in a new way. Analysis with mathematical models appears mainly in the second phase as a technique of exceptional (and, in the study of certain topics, even indispensable) importance. The third phase—drawing theoretical conclusions—involves cognitive processes similar to those at work in the first phase. Practical conclusions rely chiefly on sound knowledge of reality and a critical sense that enables one to compare theoretical theses with practical applications.

I am not saying that these three successive phases constitute a universally valid model for every essential discovery in economics. I know researchers who begin already in the first phase to write mathematical formulas, outline models, or perhaps represent the relationship in geometrical diagrams, and I know others who avoid such techniques. The process that occurs is often iterative: initial experience in the second phase prompts the researcher to rethink the first phase—in other words, to clarify the question being raised and to devise new conjectures. Where scientific research is going on collectively, the tasks of the various phases will often be done by different researchers. The emphasis in my comments is not on temporal order but on distinguishing the looser and stricter components in the cognitive process.*

In my experience, the giants of mathematical economics are quite aware of the complexities of the cognitive process and the division in roles. I have never heard an Arrow or a Koopmans comment dismissively on ideas (or their creators) that are inaccurately or semi-accurately presented but contain an essential insight, or denigrate those who create them.† As the British economist Wildon Carr remarked discerningly, "It is better to be vaguely right than precisely wrong."[11]

Let us go back to the selection criteria of learned journals. Where should valuable, novel, but half-finished ideas appear? Should only fully formed, precisely expressed works appear in print in the most prestigious journals? Should they accept a piece only if they are dead certain that the author is not mistaken?‡

It would not matter if the *American Economic Review*, for instance, specialized in papers generated in what I have called the "second phase" of research, so long as other, no less prestigious journals gave space to "first phase" materials as well. There, along with mature writings, pieces could also appear in which authors presented first conjectures and half-finished ideas.§

---

* My critical observations actually have two distinguishable emphases: the impatience with which selection is made among half-formulated new ideas and the prejudices that exist against a nonformalized, verbal style of presentation. In practice, the two problems are often entwined, and thus it is reasonable to treat them together.

† I remember clearly when a mediocre mathematical economist made derogatory remarks about Hirschman's *Exit, Voice, and Loyalty* (1970), which I discussed in an earlier chapter. This little book expounds brilliant new ideas, in a new way. Our economist dismissed it all as long-winded and woolly. He could not see the point in writing at such length on such a simple subject.

‡ It does not take much insight on the part of an editor or a referee, once an important theory has emerged or even been worked out in full, to say whether some new little twist on the well-tried model makes sense. But it takes a sharp eye to select half-finished theories and suppositions, distinguishing what is promising and may grow into a mature theory from what is valueless, uninteresting, or confused, and then publish the former and reject the latter.

§ I can also give an example from the story of my own publications. In 1978, at the Chicago and Geneva conferences of the Econometric Society, I presented some of the main ideas of *Economics of Shortage*, which I was then writing. It was written in "prose" from start to finish, without any mathematical models. The theoretical ideas were not quite mature. Nevertheless, Hugo Sonnenschein, the editor in chief of *Econometrica* at the time, decided to publish it. I believe that the publication of a paper so far from the usual profile, completely devoid of mathematics, was a somewhat exceptional event in the history of *Econometrica*, and it can be credited to Professor Sonnenschein's courage in taking the initiative and to his openness to unorthodox ideas.

I said "no less prestigious" just now, because luckily there are journals prepared to publish promising half-finished products. But usually these are second-tier publications, which count for far less when it comes to job appointments and promotions. We are at the conjunction of two major problems here: how leading journals choose what to publish and how leading research universities choose faculty. I was astonished when I first heard a Swedish researcher say half-ironically that having two articles in *Econometrica* was enough of a reference for an appointment to a professorship in Sweden. If that statement is not exactly right, there is certainly some truth in it. Beginners with a fresh Ph.D., seeking to rapidly advance their academic career in the West, should not try to come up with revolutionary new (but raw) ideas. The sure way is to take a theory that is well-known and accepted in the profession, along with a tried and accepted mathematical model of it. These need to be modified slightly, so that every definition is precise and every proposition faultlessly proved. There is a good chance the article will be accepted by one of the top-rate journals.* And the surest way to a dazzling career is an array of publications in top journals edited according to those criteria.

I find the process of selection described above harmful. It deters people from trial and error. Journal editors feel that the risk of a mistake is too great. Yet only from among many misses could a real bull's-eye arise from time to time! The system accustoms researchers to caution when they should be trained to be brave. The very title of an article published by the Swiss economist Bruno Frey in 2003 is sufficient to point out the seriousness of the problem: "Publishing as Prostitution? Choosing between One's Own Ideas and Academic Failure."

The leading economics journals today do not give young researchers any real opportunity and incentive to try their wings. This is a self-reinforcing, expanding process. Ever more journals are setting out to be an *American Economic Review* in miniature and aping its editorial principles. Ever more second- and third-rank universities are trying to follow the top five or ten and requiring assistant professors to apply every brain cell to produce papers that can be shoved through the publication meat grinder, leaving them no energy for ideas that are dangerous (i.e., unlikely to be published). Out of young people selected for an academic career in this manner will the future referees for the leading journals be chosen, and they will prefer writings like their own. The given approach is then conserved. Journals will become increasingly uniform in their articles' style, content, format, structure of discussion, and methodologies.

Let me go further and say that such biased American publishing standards for hiring, retention, and promotion are increasingly being followed by the departments of

---

* It is not worth launching a *great* new subject, because it will inevitably call for extensive treatment, whereas the leading journals favor short, concise contributions.

economics and by economics journals in other countries as well. More perilous still, perhaps, is that the bad example of economics research in America is starting to be followed by other social sciences, such as sociology and political science. Sometimes people in these disciplines are threatened: write models for the phenomena you study or we will not count your work as scientific. Primarily in economics but increasingly in other social sciences, mathematical methods are seen as giving "respectability" to a contribution. Though the idea could be conveyed more simply in everyday language, it is wiser to present it in a more complicated way, using mathematical formulas. Though this form of expression is harder to comprehend, it will appear more scientific. Often the mathematical formula or equation seems to dangle from the argument like a pendant; it has no explanatory function and is introduced simply to look more impressive.

My critical remarks are not aimed at the formalization of theories or employment of mathematical techniques as such. I have always been a believer in and modest practitioner of these methods myself. All I oppose is the exaggeration and bias—aggressively granting a monopoly to one method or approach. Most of all, I would like trials, intellectual experiments, innovation, and originality to receive more support and appreciation.

I often think wistfully how I was not able to spend my life in the peaceful academic world of the United States. I am confident enough to think I could have advanced there from lecturer to full professor. How many diversions and blind alleys could I have escaped and how directly could I have progressed! But at other times, I feel it was lucky that things took a different course. Never since I set out as a researcher have I yoked myself to a dogmatic discipline imposed from outside. I have preferred to be an outsider than to become a mechanical "pattern copier." I may have gone off track many times for that reason, but I managed to retain my intellectual independence.

There has recently been an extensive international debate on this problem—the selection practices of leading journals and their effect on the development of economics.* I hope that my comments may contribute to this discussion. I have analyzed the problem at length because I am convinced that the story of my paper is not an isolated case. I have taken this opportunity not to offer yet another venting of complaints by a rejected author but to address an important and widespread phenomenon.

A few chapters earlier, I reported on the proposal for reform that I made at the Institute of Economics in Budapest. In 1971 I was arguing that much greater weight

---

* One of the debate's main initiators is Glenn Ellison, who was until recently editor in chief of the leading theoretical mathematical economics journal, *Econometrica*, and took a sharply critical view of current publication practices.

should be given to publications when making appointments and promotions. Let Eastern Europeans also compete in the prestigious international journals, I urged. I admit that distortions in the selection processes of the Western economics profession were somewhat less familiar to me thirty-five years ago than they are now. Nonetheless, even knowing of those harmful distortions, I would not withdraw my advice of that time: Eastern European authors should do all they can to get published in journals of international standing. I extend the metaphor I introduced in chapter 11, of exports to the Western market. For Hungarian (or, more generally, Eastern European) products to improve, it is essential that they be forced to measure up in demanding Western markets. This remains true even if we know that these are not perfect markets. Several factors distort the ideal selection expected from a perfect market: monopolies, superior strength of big companies, customer prejudice against unknown producers, and so on. We cannot cocoon ourselves within our national borders; we must not be provincial and allow ourselves to be satisfied with success on the familiar domestic terrain. Doing so will lead only to complacency and deteriorating standards of quality.

Therefore I maintain my advice regarding publication, despite my critical view of the international economics profession, especially in the context of decisions on promotion and professorial appointments in Hungary.

15

Amicable, Dispassionate Criticism—1968–1989
The Hungarian Reform Process: Visions, Hopes, and Reality

Yugoslavia, after breaking with the Soviet bloc and Soviet political hegemony in 1948, went on in 1949 to reject Stalin's system of economic control in favor of a home-grown "self-management" system. Hungary, however, was the first country inside the Soviet bloc to try combining a communist political system with market economics. The command economy was eliminated in 1968. No longer were there central instructions on what state-owned enterprises should produce, or central distribution of materials, energy, labor, or wages. The "classic" Stalinist model was replaced by a formation known initially as the New Economic Mechanism.

It can be said without nationalistic bias that Hungary's reform process had significance beyond its borders. The development raised hopes in all places where initiative was being stifled by the rigidity of the command economy. Many at the time saw Hungary as an example to follow. Its experiences influenced the Chinese reform and the thinking of economists in the Soviet Union and Eastern Europe. It was scrutinized by Western economists specializing in the communist economies.

Half-fulfilled, half-blighted hopes

The turning point of 1968 was followed by two hectic decades. As relations of political power changed, the reform process stopped and started several times; it sometimes went into reverse, if anti-reform forces were uppermost. The forward-looking tendencies ultimately prevailed, and by the end of the 1980s, the features of a market economy were demonstrably stronger in Hungary than they had been in 1968. But it all remained a hybrid, an inconsistent combination of bureaucracy and market, right up to the change of system in 1989–1990.

What developed in the state sector of the Hungarian economy was a sham, something false and artificial. The detailed planning commands ended and decision-making rights passed to management. But what kind of independence was it if the manager was picked by the party committee and the ministry, who retained the right to hire and fire? Prices on a real market are set by agreement between buyer and seller. Here many of the prices continued to be set not directly by buyer or seller, but by a central pricing office. In the better case, it tried to "simulate" a market and find the right prices for the existing supply/demand ratio. In the worse case, there was not even an attempt to simulate the market price. Prices were determined from the outset in such a way that some products or even enterprises were permanent loss makers, while high prices guaranteed a profit for others. Because the role of profits increased, the management of a firm had to pay far more attention to profitability than it had done in the old days. But the profit incentives were not the real thing either, owing partly to the distortion of prices, as mentioned above, and partly to the bureaucratic redistribution of profits. If one enterprise made "too much" profit, its gains were skimmed off and redistributed among the loss makers. This was a competition that guaranteed winners, but no losers. The budget constraint, in other words, had stayed soft.

Those who had hoped that the market mechanism would gain ground could be only half content. The same blend of satisfaction and frustration was felt by those who would have liked the most important decisions to remain with the central authorities, despite the partial decentralization. The idea was for the previous *direct* regulation—planning instructions—to be replaced by *indirect* regulation, with measures of monetary and fiscal policy, interest rates, exchange rates, tax rates, and state subsidies conveying the intentions of the economy's central directors to the producers and consumers.

But it proved to be a daydream.* "I saw a vision," I wrote in 1982, "as if I first entered a modern dispatcher room of a factory, with various 'regulators': hundreds of buttons and switches, instruments and signal lamps. Dispatchers were bustling about pressing now this button, turning now that lever. And then I got into the workshop, and I saw that materials were pushed about in wheelbarrows and that the foreman shouted himself hoarse. True, production is carried on, but quite independently of when and which button is pressed in the impressing dispatcher room. No wonder, the dispatcher room and the workshop were not connected."[1]

The connecting cable was missing. What did interest or exchange rates matter if enterprises were still not sufficiently sensitive to prices and costs? Such sensitivity was dulled because the central, bureaucratic redistribution of profits meant that profitability was still not a matter of a firm's life and death. Managers' careers depended far more on their connections to higher authorities than on their market successes.

The bureaucrats continued to hold the reins on the managers, but they tried to do so more loosely. This relaxation had an advantage as well, for it left room for initiative at the enterprise level and for some influence from market impulses. Shortages

---

* László Antal (1982) aptly called this the "regulatory illusion."

of many products and services ceased, although the shortage economy remained in some areas of prime importance, such as trade in many imported goods, the rental housing sector, telephone services, and health services.

Introducing decentralization more widely on a micro level ran parallel with slackening macroeconomic discipline. By the time the region was on the threshold of the change of system, the countries experimenting with decentralizing reforms—Hungary and later Poland—saw the sharpest increases in inflation, while mechanisms holding back wages loosened and foreign indebtedness spiraled upward. The old Stalinist administrative discipline was no longer curbing unfavorable macroeconomic tendencies, but real profit incentives, real competition, and real market forces were not yet having an adequate disciplinary effect. The countries introducing partial reforms performed worse than did the heavy-handed Communist dictatorships, such as Husák's Czechoslovakia and even Ceauşescu's Romania, where better current account figures and more stable wage and price levels were obtained at the cost of a declining standard of living.

The 1968 reform concentrated on implanting a new economic mechanism in the state sector. It was almost as a by-product of this reform process that production and service provision by the nonstate sector began to broaden. These forms of ownership were a heterogeneous set. There were the so-called small cooperatives, already more or less independent, in contrast to the entities, called simply cooperatives, that were actually run by executives appointed by the party-state. Then there were small firms of artisans, traders, and service providers whose ownership was truly private. One curious form was known as the VGMK (*vállalati gazdasági munkaközösség*, or intra-enterprise economic labor partnership), forming a little privately owned island within a state-owned enterprise. Finally, there was a burgeoning "second economy," in which tens or possibly hundreds of thousands of people worked for themselves, while holding down jobs in the "first economy" on which they labored halfheartedly. One of the prime features of the Hungarian reform process was that even if encroachment on the monopoly or predominance of state ownership typical of classical socialism was not encouraged, a blind eye was turned to it.

From a naive reformer to a critical analyst

The account of the Hungarian reform just given is too brief to go into detail about an extremely complex process. It just pinpoints what I saw and still see as the characteristic features of the New Economic Mechanism. Such a short description cannot follow the dynamics of the process; it instead provides only a still picture of the Hungarian economic mechanism in the 1980s. What I need to convey in this book is above all how I stood in relation to the process of renewing the socialist system. What did I think of it and what did I do about it?

The chapter title gives 1968 as the starting year, because that was when the command economy was abolished and the New Economic Mechanism officially began. But the story begins much earlier, of course. Although the subject has been mentioned in earlier chapters, let me tell the story so far and my part in it, at the risk of repeating myself somewhat.

I began in 1954 with strong interest and belief in the idea of renewing the socialist economy, and with enthusiasm for it. My book on overcentralization, although it was a positive analysis of the old mechanism, was imbued with that belief. As a continuation of that work, I began with several colleagues in the summer of 1956 to draw up a proposal for reform. I was still influenced by the ideas of reform socialism when, in the early days of the 1956 Revolution, I formulated an economic program for Imre Nagy, the prime minister.

That belief was dispelled after the defeat of the revolution, in the wake of the brutal reprisals. The stage of my career when I was a "naive reformer" ended,* and the belief that I had held in earlier periods was never resurrected in me again. Thereafter, I never expected an economy controlled by the Communist Party to be compatible with respect for individual freedom and human rights. *Political and ethical* considerations led me to disillusionment with the Eastern European brand of "market socialism." It on the one hand implied the assumption that the Communist Party should retain power (or at least implied resignation about that prospect), but on the other hand sought, for efficiency's sake, to blend that retention of power with the market coordination so successful in the capitalist countries.

I did not dawdle over my reply in 1957 when the party center asked me to join a new reform committee. I did not want to hobnob on committees with people who had crept back in the wake of Soviet tanks, shut friends up in prison, and breathed revenge.

That deep aversion continued to be a barrier to my joining the committees set up in the 1960s by the party center. I was appalled at the thought of having to listen to the latest whispers so that I might discover whether Comrade X, that week's party boss in charge of the economy, could be won over to the idea of exchange rates based on the marginal-cost criterion or remained a firm adherent of the average-

---

* I first used the expression in 1986 in an article for the U.S. *Journal of Economic Literature* (1986c), whose title is quoted in the subtitle of this chapter. In the study, I termed "naive reformers" György Péter, father of the idea of reform in Hungary; Włodzimierz Brus, the leading intellectual in the Polish reform movement; and Ota Sik, the main economist of the Prague Spring. I would put Gorbachev in the same category. Many economists have undergone a "naive reformer" phase, each over a different period. (Some have never abandoned such beliefs.)

cost criterion. I wanted no part in cobbling together a compromise committee recommendation that would eventually be discussed and at best endorsed in a party forum.

Many of the influential Hungarian intelligentsia in the Kádár period came into some kind of personal contact with György Aczél, the paramount controller of cultural affairs. It is not the task of this chapter to asses Aczél's work or weigh precisely when his actions did harm or good. I do not pass judgment on those who dined with him regularly or very occasionally, danced attendance on him for favors, or, with true self-sacrifice, made applications to him on behalf of imprisoned colleagues. I see it as mainly symbolic that I was one of the few "leading intellectuals" never to have sought out Aczél.*

I recognize that my conduct was not consistent in this respect. I avoided Aczél like the plague, but I was not embarrassed, as I have mentioned earlier, to ask Rezső Nyers (who had been exiled to our institute as its director after falling from the inner leadership of the party, but remained a member of the Central Committee) to look into obtaining a home phone for me. I did not take part in the committees or working groups at the party center, but I remained close friends with a colleague who held an office in the party organization at my workplace and was even its secretary for a time. I did not class people by whether they were party members or not. Yet somewhat inconsistently, I kept out of the active work of preparing the reform because doing so would have connected me organizationally with the leadership of the Communist Party and I felt that it would have put me among the fellow travelers surrounding the party center.†

I mention only as a second factor, albeit one tying in strongly with the primary, political factor, the nature of the behavior and tasks I had set myself after 1956. I drew a strict distinction—I admit all too strict—between two functions: that of an expert adviser influencing political decisions and that of a scientific researcher.‡ At this point, I am not discussing the question of what relationship exists between the

---

* In the fall of 1980 he sent me a message via Lajos Faluvégi, then head of the Planning Office, expressing displeasure at an article of mine on the conflict between socialist ethics and efficiency. (As will be seen later, he was not alone in faulting the article.) I listened and said simply, "We appear to disagree." I later received the critical comments in writing from Faluvégi.

† János Szentágothai, president of the Hungarian Academy of Sciences, must have been encouraged by one of the economist academicians to inquire of me ironically, "Why are you so fussy? Why are you so afraid of getting mud splashed on your immaculate toga?"

‡ The person called adviser in this line of thought is not a professional politician such as, for instance, the leader of a party organization or movement, a member of the legislature, or someone in a high government position. The adviser holds a civilian job to make a living, although much of his or her energy is spent on influencing political events.

two in a democracy. I am solely focusing on that situation in which the dilemma had arisen for my colleagues and me—that is, when a totalitarian government had recourse to the advice of expert advisers. The two roles call for different training and impose different patterns of behavior on those who wholeheartedly perform one or the other. Successful advisers need to be shrewd tacticians with a talent for maneuvering. They need to be flexible and able to compromise. These are virtues in the political arena but cause serious risk in scientific research. Those who believe inexorably in what they say may radiate certainty in political life, but a scientific researcher has to remain objective, weighing arguments and counterarguments with rationality, not faith, and retaining a good measure of doubt even about the beliefs he or she has accepted. Those who seek to shape society to match their own vision will find it hard to retain the characteristics expected of a scholar.

I do not like to do anything halfheartedly. I could not devote one half of my brain and heart to the tasks of an adviser to a government—a government that I would like to see disappear from the political scene—while remaining a researcher with the other. Perhaps others could, but not me. I feared that if I tried, I would fail in both roles.

I apologize to the reader for bringing up this dilemma again and again. I cannot even promise that it will be absent from the later chapters, because it has followed me throughout my life. In completely different historic situations and in relation to different specific choices, I have always found the choice between political involvement and complete concentration on my academic work a hard one. It is thus one of the main themes of my autobiography, and some repetition is inevitable.

Ultimately, having gone beyond the naive reformer period in my life, I became a critical analyst of the reform of the socialist economy. There was no question of my turning my back on the problem. It deeply concerned me even in the years when I did not write a word about it. Whatever book or article I read, I repeatedly thought about how its arguments would apply to the socialist economy. Nor was this special interest confined to study. I watched carefully what changes were taking place in the practice of economic management.

Some years later, problems of the reform became central to my research as well. *Anti-Equilibrium* already impinged on these questions in several ways. As I wrote *Economics of Shortage*, I sought to show how dysfunctional features typical of the socialist economy were explained by fundamental attributes of socialism that partial reforms *within* the system could at most alleviate, not resolve. Attention to the soft budget constraint was expressly drawn by study of the semireformed, seemingly profit-oriented Hungarian economy.

I later wrote several studies whose main thrust was to describe and analyze the reform. These, in their subject matter, resembled the works my colleagues were producing. We published in the same Hungarian journals. On occasions, we both spoke in the same Hungarian or international forum.

My writings plainly expressed my sympathy for the idea of reform. I was not rooting for the other side; I would have rejoiced to see the reform succeed. Nor was there anything special in the fact that I criticized the state of the reform, for "reform economists" did likewise and no less strongly. Yet there was an essential difference between their approach and mine. A confident reformer's watchword was "not yet." The price system was not good yet. The state bureaucracy was still intervening too much in corporate affairs. The financial market did not operate yet, and so on. But "not yet" has to be temporary. Eventually, things have to improve.

In contrast, I did not believe in that optimistic scenario. My sentiments then were those of a reform skeptic. My friend Mihály Laki ironically termed us both "fastidious reformers." We and some like-minded colleagues were averse to the aspects of reform I described a page or two earlier as false, fabricated, and simulated. This was not a real market economy—and the way it was going, it was not going to become one.

Come the 1970s and 1980s, a long time had passed since my confidence in a renewal of socialism had been broken by political and ethical trauma. Since then, I had been studying the Western literature in my field, I had gained firsthand knowledge of the developed Western economy, and I had thought through, critically and rationally, the relations between private ownership, public ownership, bureaucracy, and the market. This rational process, conducted as an economist and social scientist, convinced me that in an economy in which public ownership predominated, the market could not play the main role in coordinating economic processes. The two features were incompatible. The problem was not that some characteristic of the market economy did not "yet" prevail. The truth was that only a capitalist economy could operate a *genuine*—not a sham or simulated—market economy.*

That conviction left me ambivalent even about the propositions of the most ardent reformers. In what ways were their proposals going to bring a real market economy closer? Were they not fostering illusions? Were they not raising vain hopes in many naive, benign people with semi-socialist convictions that the market, dominance of state ownership, and a political structure that professed "anti-capitalist," Marxist-Leninist principles could all be reconciled? They could think, a few more firm measures of reform and off we go down a "third road," which is and yet is not socialism, which is a market economy without being real capitalism or bearing

---

* Marx's economic theory implies a suspicion of the market. Orthodox Marxist-Leninists who accused the proponents of market reforms of holding "anti-Marxist" views were absolutely right. I refrained from actually saying this in my work, because I did not want to offend the conscience of reformers who readily declared themselves Marxist.

all its ugly features. There was a fundamental theoretical divide setting me apart from the reform economists, with their continuing belief in the feasibility of market socialism.

I became involved in many kinds of debate, sometimes conducted face to face; but at other times my opponents contended with me and targeted my views and stance indirectly. The arrows showered on me from many directions. Let me relate a few typical episodes that show best where I stood at the time.

"Instead of saying what should be done..."

One legendary figure in the reform period was Tibor Liska. We clashed strongly on several occasions, but I still recall fondly his fervent, charismatic speeches and respect his wit, outspokenness, loyalty to his principles, and refusal to engage in cheap tactics. Liska was the prophet of a curious kind of socialist capitalism or capitalist socialism. His vision was for every citizen to receive a due proportion of society's collective wealth as starting capital, to be managed as an entrepreneur in an economy otherwise operating along market lines.* Liska sketched some points on the blueprint with minute thoroughness, but other aspects, no less important, remained blurred. Into the notions were mixed Tibor's pure faith in the fine moral postulate of equal opportunity, his respect for the spirit of enterprise typical of capitalism, and his conviction that any utopia could be realized if the will was strong enough.†

Liska was a guru, surrounded by disciples. He held gatherings to which he invited famous economists; they would try to argue dispassionately, but Liska always floored them with a few punchy arguments and won by a knock-out. He once invited me to such an intellectual boxing match. I said my piece in my usual style, objectively weighing up the state of the half-reformed Hungarian economy, the strengths and weaknesses of Liska's ideas, and the realistic possibilities and limitations of social transformation.[2] Tibor got angry. It would be interesting to quote his actual words, but they were unfortunately not recorded. So I will try to reconstruct what he said on the basis of how he remembered it: "[Kornai's lecture] was the kind of theorizing that considers what shit is worth, how deep it is, and what kind of shit it is, rather than how we can get out of it. Which is a fundamental

---

* Understandably, some followers of Liska, after the change of system, fought strongly for "voucher" privatization with free distribution of state property to citizens.

† Liska wrote his oft-mentioned work *Econostat* in 1966, but for twenty-two years it was circulated only in samizdat form. It was first published in 1988, in the final days of the Kádár era. But Liska never systematized his reform visions or summarized them in a concise form. Today's readers can get the best overview from an essay by his son, Tibor F. Liska (1998).

difference, because if somebody wants to analyze shit, and ponder the question of whether it comes up to my neck or runs into my mouth or stings my eyes, he is a long way from the person who says never mind what it is worth, what matters is that we get out of it quick."[3]

It would have been good if I had been able to think of some sharp and witty retort, but duels of that kind were never my forte. All I could come up with were some cool, dry counterarguments—for example, that the task of science was to observe and understand reality—which bounced off the emotionally roused audience. I said that we did not need confused nightmares from Hungarian economists. They had to know Hungarian reality and the reality of a true market economy thoroughly in order to choose a realistic path to an improved situation.

One of the outstanding figures among the Hungarian reform economists was László Antal, a senior fellow at the Financial Research Institute. He was not a prophet like Liska. He was an eagle-eyed observer, one of the best experts on prevailing conditions in the Hungarian economy, and an analyst with a rational mind and good judgment. Unlike me, he was an active reformer through and through, and taking part in decision making was (and I think remained) a passion and a necessary element of his life. It was more important to him to be offering good advice behind the scenes to those with the real power to decide than for people to notice his publications at home. And he attached no significance whatsoever to making his ideas known to colleagues abroad. In 1983, the literary weekly *Élet és Irodalom* (*Life and Literature*) did an interview with him. "You like to call yourself a reform economist," remarked the reporter, Sándor Szénási. "Does that imply some special position compared with the 'average' expert?" And Antal replied, "If I have to make a distinction, I would say there are economists who simply play the part of an observer and describer, who give diagnoses from an ethical and, incidentally, risk-free position, but do not make recommendations. Although I recognize that they have a right to do so, that basic position annoys me. I confess very openly to striving to influence decisions."[4]

If the shoe fits, wear it. Even at the time, I took Antal's remark to be referring to me. I felt that as well as Antal, quite a few other reform economists looked with similar disapproval on my attitude toward the reform.

At this point, let me repeat an idea I expressed in relation to samizdat writers in an earlier chapter. I do not find just a *single* type of behavior morally justified—my own—or feel "annoyed" by the other types of behavior. Some behaviors I reject and morally condemn, but I consider several attitudes to be morally justified, not just one. It was good to have people politicizing actively from exile. It was beneficial to have people at home struggling illegally, risking police persecution. It was advantageous to have "reformers" trying to convert the official leaders of the socialist economy to better ways. But it was also useful to have objective analysts exploring the real nature of the system through scientific investigation. And ultimately, it was good that a sensible division of labor developed among these forms of behavior and ways of life.

To be sure, sometimes I felt revulsion against the reform economists and their compromises with the possessors of power, but I eventually managed to suppress such feelings and never expressed them in public. What prevailed was an insight that their activity did more good than their concessions did harm. This feeling may not have been reciprocated by some reform economists. I can only go by the words they spoke and wrote. I have no way of telling what such colleagues of mine thought deep down.

There is one further remark I would like to make about behavior. I have argued for the *utility* of analyzing the socialist system scientifically, which was my behavior. Let me stress, as I have in earlier chapters, that theoretical criticism proved a useful *instrument* in the process of weakening the foundations of the Communist order and eventually bringing it down and superseding it. Important though this function may be, I would not want to narrow the role of social science down to being a political instrument in a good cause. Thought has *intrinsic* value. Thought and comprehension are a joy in themselves to some people. That has always been so, and it will stay so as long as there are people who consider science their mission in life.

Efficiency and socialist ethics

In 1979 I was invited to Ireland to deliver the Geary Lecture, named after the renowned economist and statistician R. C. Geary. There I presented in a more developed form the line of argument that I had first come out with in India.*

I contrasted systems of values of two types. One asked what demands had to be met for the market mechanism to promote the greatest efficiency in economic activity, and the other what demands were made by socialist morality. The exposition led to the conclusion that it was impossible to meet both sets of requirements at once. I could not prove that "impossibility theorem" with a strict mathematical model—I am sorry to this day that no one has worked on the problem. I simply argued for the supposition and illustrated it by pointing to the inconsistencies in the Hungarian reform. The obligation of solidarity as displayed in assisting weaker

---

* I never simply read out a prepared text in a lecture hall. My method was first to expound arguments orally—several times, if possible—honing them from one lecture to the next and learning from the audience reactions. Only when I felt the lecture had sufficiently matured would I set about writing it down.

members of society, for instance, could conflict with economic competition, if those falling behind suffered real disadvantage and hardship.

My words were addressed mainly to those who too easily reconcile socialist beliefs with support for market reform, as if this unusual blend were free of all conflicts.

When I had finished, R. C. Geary himself asked a question. He was very pleased to see there was no unemployment in the communist countries; indeed, there was a shortage of labor. In the West, on the other hand, it was good that everything was available and goods shortages were unknown. Could the advantages of the two systems not be combined, without the drawbacks of each?

I answered as I did in the final section of a later article, published in *Valóság (Reality)* and the *Cambridge Journal of Economics* in 1980:

It is understandable…that the idea arose that an "optimum economic system" must be designed.…Those setting this aim envisage something like a visit to a supermarket. On the shelves are to be found the various components of the mechanism, incorporating the advantageous qualities of all systems. On one shelf, there is full employment as it has been realized in Eastern Europe. On another, there is the high degree of workshop organization and discipline [found] in a West German or Swiss factory. On a third shelf is economic growth free of recession, on a fourth, price stability, on a fifth, rapid adjustment of production to demands on the foreign market. The system designer has nothing to do but push along his trolley and collect these "optimum components," and then compose from them at home the "optimum system." But this is a naive, wishful day-dream. History does not provide such supermarkets, in which we can make our choice as we like.…The choice of system lies only among various "package deals."[5]

The study, which came out later in several languages, attracted strong notice, for it went against the vision of a "socialist market economy" that would operate harmoniously.

I cannot resist a short digression at this point, to recall an episode connected with the study I have just mentioned. Around that time, the figure of László Lengyel appeared in Hungarian public life. He first sharpened his wits against the well-known economic historians Iván T. Berend and György Ránki, who refuted his remarks. He and Miklós Polgár then contributed to the discussion on my efficiency versus ethics article, putting forward two ideas. First, the interests of specific groups lay behind all ethical concepts. Secondly, it was untrue that the contradictions discussed in my article caused the problems associated with reform.

The soapbox Marxism of the first statement was not worth responding to, but I did not want to leave the second unanswered. I responded sharply, calling on the authors to debate honestly. I had stated in the introduction of my paper that I was not undertaking a *causal* analysis. Nothing in my study ascribed the woes of the Hungarian economy or the difficulties of reform to the conflict between the two systems of values described. Their comment twisted the article's message in other respects as well.

I have had critical remarks written about me on countless occasions, but I am not in the habit of reacting. If I did not agree with something, I simply carried on without debating it in most cases. If I considered the criticism valid, then its influence would be most apparent in my subsequent writings. What I felt was unacceptable in the Lengyel–Polgár piece was its infringement of the unwritten ethical rules of debate.*

László Lengyel returned to the incident in an autobiographical interview given to Elemér Hankiss: "Our style of debate came from the implacable, derisive, disparaging manner of Marx, or rather from scientific bad manners. . . . I attacked Kornai, Berend, and Ránki derisively in the 1970s. However right I may have been in everything, I recognize that I wanted to expose them personally."[6] The sincerity of the self-criticism is praiseworthy, but I return to the episode precisely because I see that Lengyel condemns only his earlier bumptious manner. The problem was not merely with the *style* of the criticism, but with its ethically unacceptable method. Lengyel remembers wrongly when he remarks on "however right" he may have been. Having reread the dispute now, I realize again that their criticism was wrong even in its substance. They distorted my arguments to construct arbitrary statements that they attributed to me and then quarreled with. I return to this old controversy because today this kind of debating still persists; in fact, it is now getting even more widespread. It is unacceptable that it has become commonplace in Hungarian public life, the press, and intellectual writings to twist and distort an opponent's message and then start to refute or reject the falsified statement.

The importance of property rights

One of those who contributed in 1983 to the debates on reform in *Valóság* was the sociologist and economist Andrea Szegő.[7] She stressed that she did not want any restoration of Stalinism, but she argued for stronger central control, imposed by more up-to-date methods. Her assault on the reform process from the "left" includes several approving references to *Economics of Shortage*. What she understood from the book was that public ownership gives rise to a shortage economy— that is, that production is constrained not by demand but by the centrally located resources. So long as public ownership remains predominant, the reform cannot

---

* Serious injury had been involved earlier when I was branded by the ideologists of Kádárite repression. Then the criticism was politically and intellectually unacceptable, but I did not feel *morally* outraged. Those critics stood on the other side of the intellectual barricade, but they did not falsify my ideas. They criticized what I had really stated and really thought.

change the underlying nature of the socialist system. Public ownership is more compatible with centralized control than with the market mechanism.*

Soon thereafter, the reform economists took issue with Andrea Szegő. From this point of view, the article Tamás Bácskai and Elemér György Terták published in 1983 was typical. They refuted the "leftist" interpretation of my ideas and emphasized that my works give support to the reform.†

I felt embarrassment as I read these arguments. Of course, I sincerely wished the reform every success. I thought any kind of restoration of "leftism" would be harmful. In *that* sense, I was on the reformers' side. On the other hand, Andrea Szegő was the one who had understood my basic theoretical idea, not those who were trying to defend me from her. If you want a market system, you will have to want private ownership as well. If you insist on public ownership being predominant, do not be surprised when bureaucratic control keeps returning. All the cunning of reformers intent on blending public ownership with market coordination cannot make the operation of the economy permanently smooth, effortless, and untroubled. I expressed this point in more detail in a later piece of writing: there is natural affinity between private ownership and market coordination on the one hand and public ownership and bureaucratic coordination on the other.[8] Attempts to match public ownership with the market involve artificially constructing regulations to make up for the absence of such affinity.

I made it clear, in the studies I published in 1981 and 1986–1987 assessing the Hungarian reform process, how important I thought it was for a lively and varied nonstate sector to appear and develop. There and only there is the market a real one.

Radical advocates of reform placed "ownership reform" on the agenda in the 1980s.[9] Márton Tardos, one of the leading intellects among the reform economists, proposed establishing "holding companies" similar to such associations familiar in modern capitalism. The holding companies instead of the ministries would own the state-owned enterprises, and their management would exercise the "rights of ownership."

The proposal took sham "simulation" of real capitalism in an economy dominated by the Communist party-state to grotesque extremes. Think for a moment:

---

* Andrea Szegő later, in 1991, criticized *Economics of Shortage* from a Kaleckian point of view, and distanced herself from my theories.

† Neither the coauthor nor the readers, including myself, could have had any idea at the time that the enthusiastic reformer Tamás Bácskai had been for many years—as mentioned in chapter 9—a secret police informer. It was the same Tamás Bácskai now "defending" me who in 1960 had thought it important to inform the political police that I had broken with Marxism.

heads of the bureaucracy would appoint other bureaucrats and tell them: "Act as if you were owners...." My question, in an article confronting the visions of reform socialism with reality, was this: "Can ownership interest be simulated by an artificially created body which is commissioned (by whom? by the bureaucracy?) to represent society as the 'owner'?"[10]

Later, after the change of system, I continued my polemic against "market socialism." The subject is still on the agenda, if for no other reason than that ways to reform society, politics, and the economy are still being sought in China, Vietnam, and Cuba, and the vision of market socialism still has its attractions.

The Lange model and the reality of Hungarian reform

The Hungarian reform was discussed in the West as well as in Hungary. At home, the situation was more or less apparent to everyone who took part to an appreciable degree in the exchange of views. They differed largely over what could be *expected* of the reform and what its prospects were. Abroad, on the other hand, I often found superficial accounts with a textbook flavor. At the time, the most frequently consulted textbook on the theory of comparative economic systems was the 1980 work by Paul R. Gregory and Robert C. Stuart, which had this to say about the reform of Hungarian economic management: "In a general way, NEM [the New Economic Mechanism] bears a close resemblence to the Lange model."[11] A serious mistake! Let me remind readers of chapter 7, where Oskar Lange's theory of socialism has already been discussed. He conceived of an economy in which all firms would be publicly owned. The center would exercise control over firms exclusively in reaction to surplus supply or surplus demand by, respectively, lowering or raising prices.

Hungarian practice was quite different. Only a relatively narrow field of economic coordination had anything resembling Lange-type control: prices were set centrally and not rigidly, but with frequent changes. Most prices were otherwise determined. In addition, the state bureaucracy employed a myriad of other tools of intervention in the processes of the economy. The competition between state-owned enterprises was not genuine, as it was distorted by the softness of the budget constraint. The final, perhaps vital difference from the Lange model was that public ownership was no longer absolute. Luckily a private sector had appeared, and with it a real, not a simulated, market.

Unfortunately, the confusion over concepts has remained and the task of clarifying them is hopeless. If the expression "market socialism" is reserved for Oskar Lange's original idea, an economy that combines public ownership with market coordination, then the 1968–1989 period in the Hungarian economy was *not* market socialism at all. But the expression is not a registered trademark whose use is limited to what Lange meant by it. Let us turn the labeling procedure around. There is a system in which the Communist Party is in power and which officially describes itself as socialist. There appear in this system some elements of market coordination, confined to a restricted sphere and distorted by various bureaucratic influences. Who can stop this hybrid system's own ideologists from calling it "market socialism"—or, if that does not appeal, reversing the words to come up with "socialist market economy"? No regime can be denied the right to name itself. At the same time, as I have tried to point out in my works, when the history of economic thought is being taught in the classroom, it is important not to confuse the theoretical model with its historical realization.

A detour: Another piece of Hungarian reality

The word "reality" appears in the title of the previous section. If we are talking about that now, we should not stay up there, on the bright, exalted plane of theoretical argument. Somewhere deep down in the darkness, other events are occurring. Someone took notes busily when I put my thoughts on market socialism and the Hungarian reform forward at an American–Hungarian seminar, or in a lecture in New York.

As I was gathering material for these memoirs and looking through archival materials from the former secret services, I found documents making it clear that the political police received reports from its agents operating abroad on some lectures of mine.

One report was included in the "Daily Operative Information Report" of December 10, 1981.[12] This was a daily summary of the most important new information from the tens of thousands of staff in the vast network of agents and the political police machine. Its primary recipient was the top member of the political police hierarchy, the minister of the interior. Copies also went to the chiefs of the interior ministry's secret police apparatus, and an extract was sent to Communist Party and government leaders. Point 6 of the December 10 daily report described how, at a Hungarian–American seminar held recently in Budapest, "János Kornai, the well-known Hungarian expert, disclosed to the Americans confidential and detailed information on the internal situation of COMECON, the difficulties of the Soviet economy, and the problems in the relationships between Hungary and some other socialist countries. Kornai gave a detailed analysis of Hungary's economic difficulties and problems. Prior to their arrival in Budapest, the American economists visited Poland. They wanted, with Kornai's assistance, to check the authenticity of the economic policy information they had gained there—with success, according to our source."[13]

An investigation began immediately, of which I knew nothing at that time. It was finally agreed that I had not committed any breach of state secrets and no proceedings would be taken against me. (Let me note here that I kept strictly to the principle of not using secret data in lectures or discussions of any kind, even if it seemed ridiculous that they should be classified.) Another Daily Operative Information Report, dated April 26, 1985, has also emerged from the secret files.[14] Point 7 mentions that I gave a lecture in a New York institution on March 7. It claims that the institution operated "under the patronage of the CIA." On the instructions of police Major General Y. Y., deputy head of the department, a new investigation was started. Of course, as in the other case, I had no knowledge of this. "Let Department III/II-1 investigate Kornai," was the major general's order. "Investigation" meant getting out my records again,* the first document leading to a second and a third and so on— all those holding incriminating data on me. I cannot follow the order in which they reviewed these files. It seems certain that they had another look at the summary compiled after the 1981 report mentioned above. The handwritten index card summarizing my case gives my details: "János Kornai, Hungarian economist, member of the Economic Institute of the Hungarian Academy of Sciences, honorary professor (failed recruitment)." Then follows the reference numbers of the files containing data on me. The last handwritten entry on this card[15] is "III/II-20:85 guest prof. in the USA. Invited by CIA to ea."†

It is worth recalling these events while trying to reconstruct the nature of the political and social structure behind the reform process. In the foreground, the Hungarian and Western intelligentsia befriended each other and debated seriously about Oskar Lange and prices. Behind the scenes, the informing, snooping, and betrayal still went on.

Looking back with today's eyes

Let us return to the world of economic reform. I was relieved to find, as I reread my studies on Hungarian reform, that I could still endorse what I wrote at that time.

---

* "They can tap all my telephone calls / (when, why, to whom.) / They have a file on my dreams and plans / and on those who read them. / And who knows when they'll find / sufficient reason to dig up the files / that violate my rights" (from Attila József's poem "A Breath of Air," written in 1934; József 1997, pp. 96–97).

† I assume that "ea" meant "lecture" (*előadás*). Undoubtedly they quote the 1985 report and take it for granted that it was a "CIA lecture."

The most I would do if these works were being republished would be to add a few explanatory notes in places where self-censorship originally inhibited me from saying all I wanted at the time. There was good reason to note that my studies pointed to the ambiguity of the reform process and tried to dispel the false hopes they aroused.

I can give myself this retrospective endorsement for the *positive* description and analysis, but the *assessment* is another matter. These days, I would give the reform better marks for performance. It is easy to be wise after the event, as they say. My only defense is that knowledge of later events was needed before any even-handed judgment of these phenomena could be made.

Assume for a moment that the Soviet empire had not collapsed and Eastern Europe had stayed under party-state rule. Halfway reform, a curiously illusory, misleading ideology, and partial achievements might have helped to conserve the Kádár system. The compromises won by the reformers could have put off real, radical change.*

Luckily that is not what happened. Once the change of system had occurred, a hybrid, quasi-market reform proved a good preparatory school, when looked at with today's eyes. Members of the leading economic team of reform socialists (or the more talented and expert of them) were somewhat used to how the market works; why one must pay attention to costs, prices, and profits; what a private contract signifies; and so on. Many learned what it meant to be an entrepreneur in the private sector of the reform period, and that schooling gave Hungary something of an edge over the other post-socialist countries.

That edge, unfortunately, largely disappeared after fifteen years, just as the edge of a good education does in an individual's career. Initially it makes progress easier, but those with a poorer education, given energy and good fortune, may later catch up or even overtake the early leaders. That is what happened with the economic transformation of the central Eastern European countries. Czechoslovakia's attempts at reform had been smothered in 1968 by one of the strongest dictatorships and most centralized economies among them. On top of that, the country broke into two not long after the change of system. Yet it has not lagged behind Hungary, the leading reformer under socialism, in establishing and running the institutions of a market economy.

That brings us to a knotty question. What are we really judging? Are events in the 1970s and 1980s to be scored on what they would mean for the nation's *future* twenty years later? Perhaps such an assessment is proper from the long-term

---

* This resembles somewhat the ambiguous effects today of the Chinese reform, which to some extent stabilize and lend legitimacy to the power of the Communist Party.

historical perspective of a large collective entity. But people have only one life. Looking with today's eyes and feelings at how Hungarians and Czechs spent the period 1968–1989, I would say Hungarians enjoyed more lenient practices. The air was freer. It was easier to travel. There were more goods and modern culture flowing in from the West. Life was more livable.* Commonplace though it may sound, Hungary was—as they used to say in Hungary at the time—the most cheerful barrack in the camp, certainly a better place than Czechoslovakia or East Germany or Romania. The reforms in the economy were closely tied to the easing of the rigor and rigidity of the Stalin period. With hindsight, I see that as a greater, more precious achievement than I did at the time.

---

* Parents whose thinking opposed the regime and who happened to have young or adolescent children in the hardest era of oppression were faced with a severe dilemma. If they spoke openly at home, children who were not fully mature or sufficiently cautious might talk about their parents' views where they should not. However, if caution and self-protection kept parents from speaking honestly with their families, they deprived them of necessary political enlightenment and did not offset the misleading influences of the press, the propaganda machine, and even school.

Fortunately, we had no such problems. We could speak frankly with the children on sensitive political issues. We were on the same wavelength as them. The generational conflict that often divides parents and children in fundamental political and ethical questions was unknown to us. A factor that assisted our mutual understanding was the less oppressive atmosphere prevailing when our children started to take an interest in social and political issues, allowing people to talk more openly at home and elsewhere. This relative openness contributed to what I characterized earlier as a more livable life.

16

Harvard—1984–2002

I was strolling in the park of the Institute for Advanced Study at Princeton in the autumn of 1983 when I saw Albert Einstein coming toward me in a short-sleeved shirt and sandals on bare feet. I could not believe my eyes. It all fitted—face, flowing white hair, expression, dress—so what on earth was happening? Was I seeing things?

It turned out a film was being made, on the authentic location where Einstein had worked from the time he arrived in America. There he would walk happily in the park, immersed in thought.

We had been living there for some weeks by then, at 45 Einstein Drive, in a little house on an estate designed by a fellow countryman of mine, Marcel Breuer.

A Princeton institution

The Einstein cult lives on at Princeton and his intellect still inspires those who arrive here. Before turning to my personal experiences, let me say a little about the Institute for Advanced Study there, for it is rare in America to find a research institute not affiliated with any university. Almost all scholars and scientists in the United States spend much of their time teaching. Many American colleagues of mine envied the way research fellows at the academy institutes of the Soviet Union and Eastern Europe were relieved from teaching (or even barred from it). When Einstein arrived in America, his scientist hosts thought he at least should not be forced to spend all day teaching students. There should be an institute founded at which Einstein could devote all his energies to research. And impossible though it might be to find a second or third Einstein, there should at least be a few other outstanding scientists recruited as permanent fellows. Thereafter, their intellectual appeal would draw talented guest fellows from all over the world, each to spend a year there, far from their own universities or institutes, relieved of all teaching and administrative tasks, and able to put everything into researching a subject of their choice.

A foundation was formed by donations from rich and generous American sponsors and the institute began work soon thereafter. Initially it was used as the ideal research station mainly by theoretical physicists and mathematicians. John von Neumann, the Hungarian mathematical genius, spent all his years in America there. (He gave his name to the other road on the estate where we lived, Neumann Drive.) Kurt Gödel, the giant of mathematical logic, worked there too. The great physicist J. Robert Oppenheimer was director from 1947 to 1966. In 1973 the School of Social Sciences was founded, and each subject was headed by a professor. In the academic year 1983–1984, when I was there, Albert Hirschman was the professor looking after economics, Michael Waltzer was responsible for political science, and Clifford Geertz oversaw anthropology. All three were among the foremost scholars in their disciplines.

The institute had expanded over the years, but its initial structure had remained: a small permanent faculty surrounded by six or seven times as many visiting fellows, chosen by the permanent fellows and changing each year. Right from the beginning, researchers from various disciplines gathered there; one of the attractions of the place is the interdisciplinary character of the work.

I felt that the invitation was a great honor, and the year I spent there was among the most interesting and inspiring of my life. Anyone who wants to equip a special heaven for men and women of scholarship and science should take the Princeton institute as a model. The buildings are set in a huge park with a little lake in the middle; a little further away is a private wood with a stream running through it and paths set among the dense trees—an ideal hideout for those like me, who like to cogitate while walking through natural surroundings. Society can be found among colleagues over an excellent lunch.

Selecting those to be invited is done partly on the basis of material submitted by the applicants and partly through evaluations by the institute's permanent fellows. Albert Hirschman had gathered economists who stuck out in some way, departing from neoclassical dogma in some respect. It was an interesting company indeed. I found Axel Leijonhufvud there, a Swedish American professor well-known for his reinterpretation of Keynes. Conversation partners included George Akerlof, whose witty article on "lemons" (defective cars) put him among the founders of the theory of asymmetric information, work for which he had received a Nobel Prize. Don McCloskey, with his stammer and invariably interesting and novel opinions, was there. His work on the "rhetoric" of economics had attracted great attention. (To simplify his argument to the utmost, truth in social science consists and consists only of the things of which one can convince one's colleagues using the methods currently fashionable and widely accepted.)*

To be frank, I had something of a creative block at the time. I had finished what I wanted to write in the aftermath of *Economics of Shortage* and I still did not know what the next big task should be. I struggled bitterly to find a way forward.

My reading in "normal" years would tie in mainly with my current research. I now used my heavenly freedom at Princeton for more general study and information gathering. I read Robert Dahl and Charles Lindblom on democracy and "polyarchy," John Rawls's theory of justice, Thomas Schelling's spirited ideas on strategy, the work of other fellows at the time (such as Leijonhufvud, Akerlof, and McCloskey, of course), and books by Amartya Sen and Oliver Williamson, who visited the institute to deliver seminar lectures. These are a few examples of the works that were a great intellectual experience for me during that year.†

Meanwhile, the idea taking shape inside me was for a single work summarizing all I had recognized and learned about the socialist system over decades of research. While I was at the institute, I drew up the first outline of the work that would not appear for a decade: *The Socialist System.*

That is precisely what is so splendid about the contribution to science made by the generous institutional and financial framework that research organizations similar to the Princeton Institute for Advanced Study provide. My intentions were not yet clear to me when I arrived, but my long-term plans crystallized during the year to the point that I could write the first outlines. In the end, it was another eight or ten years before my initial ideas at Princeton had matured and I could submit the manuscript of a book to a publisher. Researchers pleading for public or private funds have to append to each plea a detailed account of what they plan to do. There is a great need, though, for another form of funding—one that does not impose strict conditions.‡ Those who are invited to the Institute for Advanced Study, of course, have said in their applications what they would like to concern themselves

---

* No one could have imagined then that the athletic Don would have sex reassignment surgery a few years later and continue his illustrious career as Deirdre McCloskey. McCloskey deserves respect for the remarkable courage he showed in acting on self-knowledge and making that extremely difficult decision.

† My readings also reflect a desire to go beyond the subject matter of *Economics of Shortage* and to include issues of political structure, ideology, and social relations in my analyses.

‡ I may consider myself lucky to have had the chance at numerous institutions in the West to do research of my choice, at my own pace. For instance, as I mentioned in the chapter on writing *Economics of Shortage*, I had no obligations of any kind at the International Economic Research Institute of Stockholm University.

with, but there is no legally binding, bureaucratic contract stipulating when they have to complete the study. As my case demonstrates, those who arrive at Princeton are given almost boundless freedom. The institute accepts a risk that nothing concrete will result from generous support. The only guarantee—if they choose well whom they invite—is that a scientist who has a passion for research anyway will make the best of the freedom and time provided.*

The phone rang one day while I was at Princeton. It was Michael Spence, chairman of the economics department at Harvard University, inviting me to deliver a public lecture.† When I mentioned this to Albert Hirschman, long a Harvard professor before coming to Princeton, he gave a fleeting smile that I did not quite know what to make of at the time. Anyway, I gladly accepted the invitation and gave the lecture a few weeks later.

How Harvard appoints its professors

Before telling the story of my own appointment, let me jump forward in time and go through the appointment procedure at Harvard University as I saw and experienced it when I was involved in selection as a faculty member.

A full professor at an American university enjoys tenure, a job for life, under a curiously asymmetrical working contract.‡ Tenured professors may resign at any

---

* I write in some detail about the way the Princeton institute operates (the conditions of invitation, the requirements researchers are expected to meet, etc.) because it served as a model for other institutes of advanced study, including Collegium Budapest, the first such in Central Europe, where I have been a permanent fellow from its founding.

† The organization of Harvard University, like that of other American universities, follows a different pattern from Continental European universities, including Hungary's. Units are called by different names. At Harvard, a "school" or "faculty," headed by a dean, is a much broader unit than its Hungarian counterpart. Economics belongs to the Faculty of Arts and Sciences, which embraces all social and natural sciences. A school is made up of departments, but these are also much broader entities than a "chair" or an "institute" in most Continental universities. American departments are headed by a chair, who is responsible for coordinating the department's teaching work and administration. He or she is only first among equals in relation to the faculty members. Not even associate or assistant professors are the chair's subordinates. They do their teaching and research independently. That is radically different from the situation in a German or Hungarian *Lehrstuhl*, with its vertical relations of superiority and subordination between department head and members of the department.

The supreme head of a university is called a president in the United States and a rector in Hungary and many other countries.

‡ Tenure at Harvard and some other universities is confined to the full professors, the highest-ranking members of the faculty. However, a number of universities extend this to the middle-ranking associate professors as well.

time if they do not like the job or if they receive a better offer elsewhere, whereas the university cannot dismiss them if dissatisfied with their performance.*

Although the expediency of that legal arrangement is disputable, it has wide support because the full safety it provides is considered the most important guarantee of academic freedom. No one can have his or her livelihood threatened for political or scientific views expressed. The system's defenders cite the McCarthy period, when many American university professors were protected by tenure from political persecution.

As it is difficult to get rid of tenured university professors, great thought has to go into selecting them. There are no rules here applicable to all American universities. I can recount only the procedure at Harvard, based on my experience and on *The University: An Owner's Manual* by Henry Rosovsky, who as long-serving dean of the biggest faculty at Harvard, the Faculty of Arts and Sciences, was in a prime position to gain insight into the matter.

Let us take a hypothetical example. The Department of Economics needs a professor to teach corporate finance. The selection process at the first level is controlled exclusively by the committee of full professors, with neither the lower-ranking professors nor the students playing any part. The regular monthly meeting of professors first deals with the idea itself. Is this really the field that needs to be strengthened? If the matter is agreed on, a "search committee" is appointed. This little group then spends several months on the problem. Its members read the recent literature on the subject, make inquiries, and, after a number of discussions, come up with a candidate. They set the bar as high as possible. Let me quote Rosovsky on the selection criteria: "who is the brightest, most interesting, and promising? . . . who is the best person 'in the world' fitting the job description? . . . who is the world's leading authority?"[1] One old Harvard colleague of mine put the expectations of the candidate like this: "As a result of his contributions the discipline in his field changed, that is, it became different from what is was before his work."

The search committee does more than put a name forward with a few lines of recommendation. The chair of the committee delivers a veritable lecture on the candidate's work, to convince the department's other professors that the candidate meets the high criteria. Each member of the search committee contributes a personal opinion. Then comes the debate. Opinions are expressed by those who know the candidate personally or have read his or her work. Are his or her research findings as excellent and pathfinding as the search committee members rate them? What is his or her research potential for the future? Comments are made and reservations are expressed by those with objections to the candidate. The candidate's personality is

---

* There are commonsense exceptions, of course—e.g., if a professor commits a crime.

discussed. If anyone knows, teaching ability and students' opinions are considered. But these factors, I found to my surprise, are never decisive. What really matter are scholarly achievement and perceived future research potential.

A long debate ensues, but even then there is no decision. First, the department chair sends a letter to several well-known experts in the subdiscipline (in this example, corporate finance). The letter will inquire about several names, including the one recommended by the search committee, without saying which is being considered for the appointment. The addressees are asked to rank the names and justify the order. Since those asked do not know which name Harvard has in mind, their responses are called "blind letters." This amounts to a kind of closed-circle opinion polling among those most knowledgeable about the subject.

The candidate's biography and list of publications and two or three papers are handed to the professors for study, and his or her other works are made available. The assignment is to become acquainted at first hand with the candidate's work. A few months later, the proposal is resubmitted to the professors' meeting and the exchange of views recommences. Perhaps they will reach a consensus at the second meeting. If not, the matter is put on the agenda a third time and everyone's vote is recorded. If the candidate has a majority, that brings the first act, but not the selection drama, to an end.

Only now does the department head approach the candidate officially to learn whether he or she wishes to join. There is no applying for the job.* *Invitations* to a full Harvard professorship are issued to those thought worthy by their future colleagues. The answer is for the most part affirmative, but of course, in some cases, the candidate expresses thanks for the honor and declines—for instance, because his or her present position is preferred, or a move is undesirable for family reasons. In that case, the procedure starts again with the search committee putting forward a new name.

Suppose the candidate is ready to have his or her name put forward. At this stage, the acceptance still only expresses willingness in principle, in the knowledge that the second and third parts of the appointment process are still to come. The next step is to discuss with the dean the financial terms, in which the department has no say. Pay is a strictly private matter. No one in the department knows how much their colleagues receive, and neither does the department chair. Economists are relatively cheap to hire, because they need only to be given a salary and perhaps financial

---

* Most new appointments as full professor are filled by outsiders. The procedure differs somewhat if an insider is being promoted. Then the associate professor concerned decides whether to submit to the procedure of "tenure review." This is a risky decision, because it often ends with a refusal of tenure, which comes as a dreadful blow. Many people prefer to take the preventive measure of departing for another university, where they are offered a more senior, tenured post.

assistance in finding accommodation if there is a move involved.* The expensive acquisitions are physicists or chemists, who may ask for laboratories costing several million dollars and staff to assist them. Full professors have no fixed scale of pay into which a new appointee might be slotted. Pay and all other material conditions are subject to an agreement between the dean and the appointee.

Once the dean and the candidate have agreed, the dean proposes the appointment to the president of the university. Each department member writes a letter to the dean explaining his or her vote for or against the candidate. The president receives these statements and the blind letters.

A majority of department votes and the dean's approval are necessary but not sufficient for an appointment. The university needs to know the department is not dominated by a clique of friends or people sharing a scientific, political, or world view, intent on bringing in a kindred spirit at all costs. So there has to be a further impartial check, and for this, the president appoints an ad hoc committee. One member will be a Harvard professor conversant with the subject but working in another department of the university (e.g., an economist working in the Business School). The president also invites two outside experts from other U.S. universities or even from abroad. The members of the ad hoc committee receive the candidate's papers and, if they accept the task, read the candidate's work thoroughly.

Then the president, dean, and members of the ad hoc committee meet in complete secrecy in the president's office. (Because I was an ad hoc committee member myself for an appointment in another department, I could observe the procedure.) The occasion begins with the hearing of "witnesses." The chair of department attends only as the first witness, summing up the majority view of the department. He or she is questioned by the committee members and then leaves. Then come other witnesses, mainly experts in the candidate's subdiscipline. Also heard as witnesses are those who oppose the appointment. The committee members are keen to hear the opponents' arguments in detail. After the witnesses have been examined, the chair of the ad hoc committee calls on each member to state and explain his or her support or opposition. No vote is taken, as this committee is not authorized to decide. The president closes the meeting by inviting everyone to lunch.

Finally comes the last phase, the president's decision.† In most cases, the recommendation of the department and the dean is accepted, but in some, it is rejected. A presidential rejection always causes a big stir.

* To be sure, economists' salaries are relatively high, as there is high demand for their services on the labor market outside the academy. The best are called on by the government and by business, and the competition pushes salaries upward.

† Strictly speaking, the decision is taken by the highest body of Harvard University on the president's recommendation. But this is a formality; the true ultimate decision is the president's.

The process, beginning with an initial determination of the vacancy and ending with the official appointment, can easily last for a year or two.

I was astounded when I arrived at a deeper understanding of this procedure. I had been used to the biased, often cynical handling of "personnel matters" back home. Of course, professional considerations played a part in Hungary too, but what really counted were the candidate's connections. What forces would try to promote or reject the appointee? Would the decision be reached on political grounds, or in return for personal loyalty, or in expectation of reciprocal favors, or just out of cronyism? I was impressed that the Harvard criterion was achievement in the field. Professors willingly identified with the university's criteria of prestige: they wanted to make selections that would bolster Harvard's number one position.* Many busy people spent long hours in numerous meetings to ensure the appointment was a good one. The faculty feel that this is the *most important* matter on which they have to decide. If the professors are worthy, then everything will be fine; but if they are not good enough, then the university will surely sink into mediocrity.

No one would say the long-employed traditional procedure works perfectly. Perhaps some participants in the selection process are biased and beside purely academic criteria are actually influenced by personal feelings or pressures coming from outside. Such phenomena are hidden, and I could not observe them. Also, mistakes occur even if everyone is exclusively considering academic criteria. Some appointees fail to meet the department's expectations; conversely, outstanding scholars may be overlooked. Legends are told about the case of Paul Samuelson, who had studied at Harvard under Schumpeter. His Ph.D. thesis, *Foundation of Economic Analysis*, became a classic.[2] He was a brilliant mathematician in a period when that was still not a general requirement in the economics profession. Yet Harvard did not offer him a post,† and he went to the Massachusetts Institute of Technology, also in Cambridge. There he reorganized the Department of Economics, which under his intellectual influence became one of the centers for studying international economics. Samuelson was the first American economist to be awarded a Nobel Prize.

---

* A large section of the public regards Harvard as the most prestigious American university. Recently, many institutions have published rankings of universities, as measured in various ways. Here I quote only one source, the *Times Higher Education Supplement*, which regularly ranks the world's universities according to a combination of criteria (opinion research among academics, number of citations of teachers' publications, teacher/student ratio, etc.). The 2004 survey put Harvard University in first place, with a score of 100, compared with 88 for the second university and 79 for the third.

† Why not? Some people explain the snub simply as anti-Semitism. Others say that the old-school professors with no insight into mathematics feared Samuelson's sharp mind and critical comments.

The remarkably high standard set for selection may contribute to what outsiders call "Harvard arrogance." Like those at other institutions proud of their traditions and achievements, the professors of Harvard do not feel they are looking down their noses, but outsiders often perceive an attitude of condescension and resent it.

Though the appointment procedure has its drawbacks, I observed and served it with awe and respect as long as I took part in it.

Moving to Cambridge

It is time to get back to my appointment. I wondered, as I worked on these memoirs, if I might, after all these years, gain access to the papers, minutes, and blind letters of the procedure. I asked advice of my experienced colleagues, who were decidedly against my making any such request. They reminded me of something I really knew in any case. One of the fundamentals of the procedure is confidentiality. Those who speak on the appointment of a candidate do so in the firm belief that their comments will never, under any circumstances, get back to the candidate concerned. That encourages them to make negative observations as well, without threatening future relations between colleagues, if they should happen to work together later or attend the same conferences. However, the advice ran that it would not be a breach of confidentiality if I simply asked one or two members of faculty what they remembered of the events.

Based on what I learned later about the various stages of the general procedure, the main lines of the story became clear. It was felt in the economics department at Harvard some time in 1983–1984 that they needed a specialist in the communist economies. The search might have gained urgency because Abram Bergson was preparing to retire. He was the most prestigious American scholar in Sovietology and, apart from that, made an important contribution to the theory of welfare economics with the introduction of the social welfare function named after him. At some point in the search process, my name came up. I was personally known well by colleagues at several American universities. Some I could count as friends, but I happened not to have close relations with anyone at Harvard, apart from meeting in passing with a professor or two. So they wanted to get to know me.

I was invited first to give a lecture, followed by dinner and a professional discussion over the tablecloth. Next came an invitation to fill the prestigious Taussig guest professorship for 1984–1985. I was to move there and the department would find me accommodation. I would teach just one course and spend the rest of the time on research. I gladly accepted the invitation and moved from Princeton to Cambridge.

There I delivered for the first time the series of lectures that I would hone and expand in subsequent years, until it became my book *The Socialist System*. I became acquainted with Harvard, and at the same time—as it is by now evident—the Harvard economists were making my acquaintance. They had already called for my biography and several publications when I was asked to be a guest professor. I would imagine that the material was at the time being passed around in the search process.

Finally came the day I described earlier as the end of the first act. Professor Jerry Green, chairman of the Harvard University Department of Economics, told me the department had decided to invite me to be a full professor. The dean was ready to discuss terms.

(Now, twenty years later, I asked Jerry Green by letter what he could say about those events. Let me quote from his reply: "we commissioned a subcommittee to read some of your work and report to the group. The outcome was never in doubt.... Your appointment in our Department was by unanimous vote.... I cannot imagine that anyone would mind me telling you that at this time, so many years later."[3])

By the time events reached that stage, I already had three other offers: one from the London School of Economics, my first port of call in the West, and another from the University of California at Los Angeles. But the real rival to the Harvard invitation was Stanford, which had passed the stage of faculty voting and was making a firm offer. I met the dean at Harvard and then traveled to Stanford with my wife, to see the potential there. I had narrowed down the choice to those two: Stanford or Harvard.

There were many attractions at Stanford. I hardly knew anyone at Harvard, while at Stanford I had many friends: I had known Kenneth Arrow, Tibor Scitovsky, Alan Manne, and Masahiko Aoki since my first visit in 1968. It was a splendid team, in constant rivalry with Harvard and MIT. Apart from that, there was nature, the beauty of California, the sea, the forests, and the excitements of San Francisco. With two such splendid choices, it was very hard to reach a decision.

My wife and I literally became ill from the tension this caused. The chairman of the department at Stanford lent us his seaside home for a weekend. There we were, full of good news and enticing prospects in exquisite natural surroundings, and I contracted an excruciating lumbago that left me hardly able to walk. The cramp was certainly caused by stress. Meanwhile my wife had a high fever. The Scitovskys arrived for us in a car to take us to Stanford.

Finally, we decided with great difficulty that I should accept Harvard, for some weighty professional reasons. The concentration of intellectual power looked even greater there than in any other university, especially if MIT and the other universities in the Boston area are taken into account. This was certainly true for my discipline. Harvard and the other research centers in its neighborhood contained many more people working on the economies of the Soviet Union, Eastern Europe, and China and on comparative economic systems than Stanford did.

We were thrilled by California, but we also came to know and love Boston, which seemed the most English and European of any American city. There was another important factor. I had stipulated in both cases that I would spend only half my time in America and the other half working in Hungary on unpaid leave. This both universities had accepted, if none too willingly, as they would have preferred to have all my energies. Once I had decided to commute back and forth in that way, Boston gained the attraction of being a continent's width nearer to Budapest than San Francisco.

I reached agreement with the dean. I was promised assistance in finding and furnishing a permanent home, and the university would pay our annual airfares between Budapest and Boston. At the same time, I was warned that this was only a proposal and I would have to wait for the final decision, which could still be negative.

We spent the following weeks in tense expectation engendered by that knowledge. (It later became clear to me that the meeting of the ad hoc committee was taking place.) The decision finally came, and I became a full professor at Harvard University.

We began looking for an apartment and finally found one in a condominium that was approaching completion. In line with custom in the Anglo-Saxon world, buildings are given names. Where we lived was called University Green, and was on the part of Mount Auburn Street close to the university campus and to Harvard Square. This famous center of life in Cambridge has the heart of the university on one side, including Harvard Yard, the grassy expanse containing the oldest block of lecture halls, main office buildings, and residences. Other parts of the square contain office buildings, restaurants, banks and stores, and, most importantly, large bookshops open late into the night. On Saturday and Sunday, Harvard Square fills with street musicians, other performers, and merchants, sometimes making up a huge street fair. To be near Harvard Square is to be at the throbbing heart of the city, which made the apartment all the more attractive.

My wife and I traveled home for the 1985–1986 academic year. When in fall 1986 we arrived back in Cambridge, we stayed for the first few nights in the Faculty Club, but we could hardly wait to take possession of the new apartment. When it was ready, it stood completely empty. We borrowed a couple of mattresses from friends and slept on them until we had bought furniture.

The joys and cares of teaching

It was my fate to begin regular teaching at an age when others have decades of teaching experience behind them and can do it almost without preparation.

Let us compare my position with that of a typical Harvard teacher of, say, microeconomics. He would have learned the material thoroughly as a student, and as he had studied at a good university he could also have observed the methods his teachers used in their courses. He would have been appointed an assistant professor before thirty, and by fifty or sixty, he would have been lecturing on the same things for twenty to thirty years. All he had to do was alter his presentation to accommodate any worthwhile new ideas in the literature and update his statistics. He could easily build his own research into some of his lectures. He might, as was permissible and widespread, base a course on the structure of a well-tried textbook or blend material from several books and add original findings and insights.

At the age of fifty-six I had to start from scratch. The main subject on which I lectured was titled "The Political Economy of the Socialist System." My teaching was addressed exclusively to graduate students in programs leading to a master's degree or a doctorate. Some Western textbooks touched on the subject and I assigned occasional chapters as recommended reading, but I wanted to present the subject in my own way. I had never attended any other professor's lectures on the same subject, so I could not know how others were doing what I had to do. I made use of the huge published literature, of course, but ultimately I shaped all I wanted to say and all the material I wanted to present, from the first sentence to the last.

Furthermore, mine was not a settled, developed subdiscipline such as standard microeconomics or macroeconomics. There the reality defined by the theory is relatively fixed, and changes from year to year are almost imperceptible. In contrast, talking about the socialist economy was like shooting at a moving target. I started teaching at Harvard in the mid-1980s, by which time the Communist camp was in ferment and one event of world-historical importance was followed by another. In the Soviet Union it was the time of glasnost and perestroika. In Beijing's Tiananmen Square millions demonstrated—and the protest was followed by bloody reprisals.[*] And finally, in 1989 the Berlin Wall was falling. I had to recast the course as "The Political Economy of Socialism and the Post-Socialist Transition." Although what I had said before the change of system about the communist economy and the reforms within the system remained valid and of interest to students, I had to

---

[*] During the dramatic occurrences in Beijing, my wife and I were practically glued to the television, watching live the eruption—and suppression—of the Chinese student movement. Anybody who had lived through 1956 in Hungary could see many similarities. We had deep sympathy for my Chinese students and shared their apprehension as the events unfolded.

shorten the first part of my syllabus and make space to explain the problems of the transition. Fresh news kept arriving in abundance, but of course I could not use the university rostrum to present a press briefing. I had to try to provide a deeper, systematic analysis.

I do not think my colleagues quite realized what a tough challenge I faced. I had to catch up to acquire what the others already had by virtue of a Western university education and experience, while tackling the intellectual difficulties of the subject. I had to overcome doubts and hesitation and even feelings of professional inferiority before standing in front of a class at Harvard—young people, selected very carefully from the best applicants, and used to listening to lectures with a critical ear.

I must have blundered at times. My irremediable Hungarian accent was no joy for the students. But I can say with satisfaction that I managed to win their attention and respect. I attracted unusually large audiences for someone teaching an optional course for graduates, and the initial numbers tended to increase rather than dwindle,* not least because world events pushed the problems of the communist system into the public eye. But another factor was that word went around about my classes.

The professors are not the only ones at Harvard who assign grades. A questionnaire is handed out to the economics students at the end of the year, on which they write their anonymous assessments of their teachers' work and hand them in to the department. I still proudly keep those course evaluations. There were some criticisms—several students faulted the selection of compulsory and recommended readings, for instance. I was afraid many of them would object because I rarely wrote equations on the blackboard or provided mathematical models. Some found my lectures less "technical," but that feature drew relatively few negative comments. The number of remarks with an opposite sign was considerably higher. This, it turned out, was actually a reason why some students gladly came to my lectures: they found my "prosaic" style refreshing. I would often bring up personal experiences and firsthand observations. Sometimes I referred to films or novels that could offer a graphic picture of the characteristics of the communist system. Students appreciated that approach, which gave authenticity to an account of a faraway world. Also making lectures more engaging were my candid answers even to personal, even nosy questions. The philosophy and methodology of my oral lectures and my writings that I used as teaching material departed in many ways from the approach in other courses. Far from scaring people off, this difference proved to be one of the attractions of my lectures. Several respondents praised the fact that I was

---

* I made a bet with my wife, at the start of each academic year, about how many students would enroll in my course. We each wrote a number and put it in an envelope and the winning guess was the nearest. My guesses were always the more pessimistic, but she won each time. That meant she could choose the restaurant for a celebratory supper.

not just teaching economics in a narrow sense but including analysis of the political structure, ideology, and social relations. Once Schumpeter, one of the greatest figures in integrated social science, had taught in the department, but fifty years later, students encountered an interdisciplinary approach only rarely.

I do not want to exaggerate the worth of the questionnaires in providing feedback. It was not a survey of *all* Harvard Ph.D. students. The respondents made up what is known to opinion pollsters as a self-selected sample. My course was not a compulsory subject. Students chose to attend, but once they had enrolled, they were obliged to go to class and take the examination. Those who did so were interested in the subject in the first place and had heard from students from previous years what they might expect. I do not say the approach I took was especially attractive to Harvard students. I draw a much more modest and limited conclusion. Amid all the excitement and struggles, it was reassuring to find year after year quite a few students who took intellectual delight in my courses and received thought-provoking responses to their questions from my lectures and writings.

Diversity and tolerance

Although my lectures differed from others' in spirit, that was by no means unusual. Harvard University (and many other institutions of American higher education) strove expressly for diversity. Students could choose from a range of intellectual strands, philosophies, and scientific schools of thought.

Amartya Sen divided his time between the economics and philosophy departments and for many years ran a philosophy seminar with Robert Nozick. When Nozick's *Anarchy, State and Utopia* appeared, he was viewed as a brilliant new star in the firmament of libertarianism.* Sen was at the opposite end of the political spectrum. He researched problems of poverty and famine and called unconditionally for the state to play a redistributive role. The difference in their views never disturbed their sincere friendship and it gave their joint seminar its spark of excitement.

There were various schools of economic thought within our department and representatives of political views that not merely differed but were bitter rivals. Among the faculty were Steve Marglin, a radical left-wing economist, and a few old-style Keynesians. Another member was Robert Barro, who engaged in theoretical research while contributing regularly to the conservative *Wall Street Journal* on daily policy issues. Certain professors served in presidents' administrations for longer or

---

* Nozick came to alter his earlier, radically libertarian views on several issues. A bold thinker, excellent writer, and man of warm humor and kindness, he died in 2002, at the peak of his powers.

shorter periods, before returning to the university. By the time I arrived, John Kenneth Galbraith was over 80 and retired, but he still came into the department periodically. (We also saw his erect, lanky figure regularly at the swimming pool.) Apart from the enormous reputation he had gained with his books, he had belonged to the circles of Presidents Kennedy and Johnson and served as U.S. ambassador to India. Martin Feldstein coordinated the massive organizational and educational task of providing undergraduate teaching in economics on a mass scale. He belonged to the other political hemisphere, having served President Reagan as senior adviser for several years. Another colleague was Larry Summers, until he left teaching for public service as vice president of the World Bank. He was later deputy secretary, then secretary of the treasury in the Clinton administration. Thereafter he returned to Harvard. Although he nominally remained a member of the faculty of the economics department, he became president of the university in 2001. Following his resignation, effective the end of the 2006 academic year, he is expected to return to the department as a distinguished professor. The economics department, like the philosophy department, had its pair of professors—in its case, Robert Barro and Gregory Mankiw—who would display their clashing views before the audience at their joint seminars.

All these people might argue strongly with each other in teaching or lecturing, or in their public appearances, and were known to sympathize with different sides of the political spectrum, but there were never arguments engendered by politics or worldview at departmental meetings. The debates and differences of view did not preclude fruitful cooperation. Perhaps I was the only one to marvel at that while everyone else thought it was natural.

Among our good friends were a couple in which the man was a Republican and the woman a Democrat. We were amused when the sharp-tongued wife would make teasing comments on her husband's conservative views before friends, but none of that troubled the "peaceful coexistence" in which they had lived for decades. We were reminded of a Hungarian friend, who told us sadly after the change of system how difficult it was to sit down to a family meal with their grownup children, as the young couples were so intolerant of each other's political views.

Ethical rigor

I was much impressed by the weight attached by Harvard professors to observing the ethical requirements of their position. It would be interesting and enlightening to report on how American universities changed after vigorous moves were made against sexual harassment of students and a ban on faculty-student relationships was imposed.* I had no personal experience of such incidents and the gossip that must have flown around did not reach me. "Politically correct" behavior in those fervid years meant that a male professor should be distant even with his female colleagues and behave as if he did not notice they were female. I unhesitatingly behaved at Harvard just as I had in Budapest, complimenting female colleagues on their dress or hairstyle if I thought they were attractive and perhaps bantering a little if I did not, paying little heed to whether that was politically correct. I felt my female colleagues were better pleased with a human approach than a sanctimoniously formal one.

However, that is not the aspect I would like to treat here in detail. Let me instead say a word about the ethical problems having to do with teaching and research.

Basic theoretical research, research for practical applications, and commercial applications of research findings are closely linked these days. Where does academic activity performed altruistically for the cause of science end and financially motivated work begin? There is no desire at Harvard University to hypocritically dodge this issue.† Grants from business are a major source for financing research. So the university tries to go beyond the issue of what is *legally* allowed or disallowed and apply clear standards expressing what is *ethically* permissible or unacceptable.

At the university a distinction is drawn between two kinds of conflict: conflict of interest and conflict of commitment. A professor at the university or other member of the university staff is ethically obliged to respect the university's material interests. For instance, university laboratory equipment should not be used for research without paying the university a fee, if remuneration for the research is being received from a business firm. And if two types of assignment are performed at once—for example, university work and contract work for the firm—the second must not be done to the detriment of the first.

University faculty are sometimes charged with assignments by U.S. intelligence agencies and secret services. This is not the kind of spying seen in films, where the secret agent breaks into an office and steals military data. Let us stay with economists: it was well known that the CIA would regularly call on U.S. experts for estimates of the GDP of the Soviet Union, because official Soviet statistical reports were thought, justifiably, to be unreliable. That was a serious scientific task and no American economist politically committed to his or her country would see anything

---

* In a student newspaper, Galbraith confessed to committing this sin as a young assistant professor. Soon after, he married the student and they have been together ever since.

† A committee of professors chaired by one of Harvard University's leading office holders was formed to produce a detailed report on the problem, put forward specific recommendations for regulating contacts and collaboration between the university and the business world, and draft principles to resolve potential conflicts.

objectionable in it. True, but what of the university's independence and political integrity if faculty are acting for intelligence agencies? Can university staff be allowed to receive secret financial remuneration for military or intelligence-directed research? What political criticism might this arrangement expose the university to domestically and internationally?

The university analyzed the problem and drew up a rule: No research qualified as "secret" could be done within the campus. As for work done as consulting, everyone was to act according to his or her own conscience about accepting financial support from intelligence agencies or the military for research appearing under his or her own name. But let the researchers report such work. If the results were published, let them declare that the work was funded by the Pentagon or the CIA.

However stable, considered, and detailed the rules and regulations may be, there will still be borderline cases between the permissible and the impermissible. Various ethics committees were formed at Harvard with this in mind. A Harvard professor or other faculty member can turn for advice to them, or in simpler cases to a single committee member.* If a committee learns of an act that may be ethically problematic, an inquiry may begin.

I would not want to give the impression that ideal conditions prevail at Harvard or other leading American universities, from an ethical point of view. The problem is not simply that dubious incidents occur—that happens, inevitably, wherever people work. But unfortunately, it can also happen that the heads of the university and the university community fail to address such cases appropriately, to take a stand on them, or to make their position on them public.

Whenever I have talked to university friends about a specific case of that kind, I have found that they want to impose a high ethical standard and seek to strengthen the world reputation of Harvard and American academic life in general. It would be good if they would express their opinion openly as well.

---

* I once asked advice after receiving a present from a student, on whether to accept it. As the gift was a symbolic expression of gratitude of no appreciable value and exams were over, I was advised I could accept it rather than offending the student by refusing it.

17

At Home in Hungary and in the World— 1985 Onward

Harvard University wanted me full-time when I was offered a professorship. It was made plain that the university would put all its clout behind an application for American citizenship. If I did not want that, I could at least apply with university support for a "green card" (permanent residence). I turned down all the proposals. As I said earlier, I insisted in my negotiations with the university on being free to spend half my time in Hungary. Why?

What tied me to Hungary

I would like to fulfill an earlier promise and return to the problem of emigration. I did not leave Hungary after the 1956 Revolution, when a surge of refugees left for the West. I turned down offers of university jobs at Cambridge in England and Princeton in America, which would have meant leaving Hungary. Now, in 1985, as I dealt with Harvard (and other U.S. universities making concurrent offers), I rejected the idea of emigration again. (I date the chapter from 1985, when the question once more became urgent.) On this matter I cannot plead family reasons. Of our three children, one lives in Hungary, one in Sweden, and one in the United States.[*] Our

---

[*] Our son Gábor studied economics, but where he really learned what it means to found and successfully manage a company was not at the university but in practicing his vocation. He takes great pleasure in teaching management at the University of Pécs, giving up some of the free time left to him from directing his successful IT company. Our daughter Judit also graduated from the Budapest University of Economics; she now works as program director at the Business School of the Stockholm University of Economics, organizing extension courses for leading players in the world of business. Our son András is the only one who has turned his back on economics: he has a Ph.D. in mathematics and another in linguistics. Today, as his main activity, he does applied research in America in the most exciting of areas—development of the Internet. He enjoys traveling to Budapest, where he assists Ph.D. students as a visiting professor at the University of Technical Sciences. I cannot help feeling a bit of parental pride. We are most proud that all of our three children are working hard, and that they have always stood on their own feet.

seven grandchildren also live in these three countries. If we live nearer to one of our children's families, it means we are a greater distance from the others. So other reasons were what influenced our choice. I repeatedly discussed these decisions with my wife. We agreed not just on the final decision but on the reasons for it. But in keeping with the style of these memoirs, let me tell my tale in the first-person singular, as I am relating my own thoughts and feelings.

I had a myriad of emotional ties to Hungary. I had always been moved and delighted on returning from abroad to cross the Chain Bridge or Elizabeth Bridge and see the view of Budapest unfold. I owned two copies of works by Arany, Ady, Attila József, and other Hungarian poets, and of Karinthy's writings—one in our Budapest home and one in our American. I had a portrait of Bartók on the wall of my room at Harvard.

I think in Hungarian. I never read my lectures; I always deliver them, even in English, freely. I can express myself with ease in English, but I much prefer to write in Hungarian and I do that much better. When publishing a book, I call on a professional translator to put the Hungarian manuscript into English. I count in Hungarian and dream in Hungarian on the rare occasions when I recall what was said.

There is no sense in saying I love the Hungarian people. My conscious philosophy and feelings revolt against such general statements about groups. There are some Hungarian citizens I like and some to whom I am indifferent, whom I reject, with whom I am angry, whose sins I count as unpardonable. But I am the same with Americans, Germans, or Israelis. I have real, true friends in Hungary and abroad, but my friends with whom half a word tells all and to whom I am bound by our entire past, which likewise binds them to me, are confined only to Hungary.

Hungary is the country whose destiny concerns me most. I know more about its history than about that of any other country. Ever since I can remember, I have been concerned about what goes on in Hungary. Even while spending a full year in America, I kept an eye on events from the outside (although with great empathy). We still had Hungarian papers delivered, and when the Internet came, we kept up to the minute with Hungarian news. What really interested us deep down were events in Hungary.

Any sense of national superiority is alien to me, but I was filled with delight when István Szabó's *Mephisto* won an Oscar, when Hungarians gained Olympic medals, when I could talk to American friends about László Németh's play *Galileo*, or when the conversation turned to the Budapest school that taught John (János) von Neumann, Eugene (Jenő) Wigner, and William (Vilmos) Fellner, or there was praise in the *New York Times* for Ildikó Enyedi's film *Twentieth Century* or a piano recital by András Schiff. And it always felt good, in America, China, or the Soviet Union, to hear praise for the pioneering role played by Hungarian economists in the international discourse on socialism. I call that feeling of pleasure national pride, for want of a better expression.

I am not given to pathos; I do not refer to the words of our second national anthem, "here must you live and die."* I prefer the drier idiom of an economist and talk of requiring consistency of myself. This I stated earlier in another context. I stuck by my Hungarian passport, though denied the chance to travel for years and required to apply an exit permit each time I wanted to leave the country. Should I change passports now that travel had become easier at last? I resigned myself to staying in Hungary in periods of repression and strong restrictions on freedom, and to all the drawbacks of Hungarian citizenship. Should I renege just as the old system was loosening and breaking up?

My reasons are dominated by sentimental ties, but I must add that there were also other, professional considerations behind my decision not to emigrate. I had specialized in the socialist system and the post-socialist transition, subjects with which many people in the West dealt as well. What gave my work special authenticity was that everything from my first book to my last article was written by someone who had himself seen and experienced what went on. I have done much research on *general* subjects, but I have based it on Hungary as an *example*. Many articles of mine state that approach from the outset: the main title defines the general subject and the subtitle adds "in the light of Hungarian experience." I have never worried that readers may suspect provincialism in that. I have felt that the real intellectual challenge was exactly when—after comparative fact-finding and gathering of information—I could move from particular observations to the general conclusions.

Individuals have a sovereign right to choose where they want to live. According to my values, it is quite acceptable for someone born in Hungary to decide to move elsewhere. A variety of reasons may underlie such a move: escape from persecution, disillusionment with the social milieu, or simply a feeling that he or she will be happier elsewhere.

Anyone active in politics can express political protest by emigrating, as was done by Lajos Kossuth, Mihály Károlyi, Oszkár Jászi, and Béla Bartók, and by many democratic politicians after 1945. It is a heroic gesture involving great sacrifice. Of course, I do not view this course as morally inferior to staying at home—or as superior, for that matter. Can those who oppose an oppressive regime express their stand only by leaving the country? Is the mere act of staying therefore evidence of knuckling under? That type of rigid classification is unacceptable to me. People can

* These words, cited frequently in Hungary, come from the poem "Appeal" by the great Hungarian poet Mihály Vörösmarty (1800–1855). The last four lines of the first stanza, addressed to "Hungarian," run (literally), "Nowhere in the wide world but this / has any place for you; / though fate's hand bless or scourge you, / here must you live and die."

keep their heads down in exile or walk tall in their native land. A moral judgment on someone's life must rest on deeds, not simply on the choice of country to live in.

Comparisons: Life in Cambridge and in Budapest

Moving back and forth, six months here and six months there, certainly encourages comparisons. What is better or worse in one or the other and what is simply different? We did not compare "America" with "Hungary" or "Eastern Europe," just the thin slices of a huge cluster of phenomena in each hemisphere that we met with. I am not contrasting two systems or two cultures here. Such a comparison has appeared in countless books and studies; I have written this and that about it myself. All I want to convey are some personal memories and impressions. I was once asked in a questionnaire what three things I liked and what three things I disliked about America. That seems a good framework.

I was charmed by the smiles on American faces. I do not mean that there is some imperative to "keep smiling," but rather that good humor is commoner among professors and students, sales staff and waiters, reporters and interviewees on breakfast shows, than it is in Hungary. People in the United States must have their cares and woes too, but they do not display them for all to see. My first American secretary, Madeline LeVasseur, was nursing first her mortally ill mother and then her slowly dying husband, with infinite self-sacrifice. She had a hard life. But when I walked in the office, she always had a smile; she was far from being a complainer. Another secretary in the department was young, attractive Susan, who underwent a cancer operation followed by therapy that made her hair fall out. She joked and smilingly showed her new wig and hat, asking in a charmingly natural way whether they suited her complexion.

Whenever we returned from a stay in the States, we were greeted by a chorus of complaints—all quite justified, but the question here is not just the gravity of the troubles but the approach to them. When we were still beginners at going backward and forward, we would say on returning to Budapest, when asked how we were, "Oh, fine." People would then ask again: "Are you really fine? Of course, well, it is easy for you, living in America." Later I grew more cautious. I prepared a few complaints in advance, and when I had done so, we were on the right wavelength straightaway.

We were glad to find that the Americans we had business with were honest and honorable in their dealings. Here I am not trying to say which social system or which country breeds more abuse of official power, corruption, or political mendacity. I am thinking of life's little encounters. When I pay for something in a store, do I get the right change? If a tradesman says he is coming at 9 on Wednesday, does he turn up on time? If you receive information over the telephone, is it accurate? If I leave a message on someone's voice mail, does that party return the call? We were disappointed in people's reliability and honesty far less often in Cambridge than in Budapest.

There is a "gray" economy in America as well, although with somewhat narrower scope than in Eastern Europe. But when we met it, it seemed to work on morally more acceptable principles than at home. We had need of a handyman when we moved in, a jack-of-all-trades to drill holes, move electric outlets, and assemble bookcases. Steve appeared after work and did everything, except for putting up the curtains. He worked for a firm supplying curtains by day, and he did not feel it would be right for him to compete with his employer in his moonlighting.

People's professionalism and working discipline are impressive. Whatever the field or level on which you were in contact with people, you could feel they knew their job and did it conscientiously. That was not confined to the highly qualified, such as our primary care physician, who kept up with the latest medical developments and reacted immediately if opinion on some therapy or medication changed. It applied equally to the video technician or car mechanic or house painter. Our impression was that they were better trained and were devoted more completely to their work than their Hungarian counterparts were. There was less loafing and chatting on the job. We began to compile a mental picture of a type: the hardworking American. Not everyone belonged to the type there and, of course, expert, hardworking people are not unknown in Hungary—and their number seems to be growing nowadays; but I think I am right in saying that the type is more prevalent in America. It is among the major sources of the country's high growth and productivity.

Now let us turn to our three negative experiences. Let me begin with the language, which gave me a lot of trouble. Of course, that was not the fault of the wonderfully expressive English language itself. But for someone who grew up in another country, its unfathomable pronunciation and astonishingly rich vocabulary are practically impossible to master. The problem clearly lay with my language abilities. Let me recall two of many early blunders. The state police, during my driving test in Boston, showed me traffic signs and I had to say what they meant. One of them I said unhesitatingly meant "No hijacking." What I meant was "No hitchhiking." This caused great mirth, but I was given my license just the same. Another time I was lecturing on the problems of inventories and managed to say "whorehouse" instead of "warehouse" on three occasions, to my students' delight. My linguistic skills later improved, but I still had difficulties up to my last day if I had to decipher the strange English of my Chinese or Japanese students or to interpret rapid-fire information supplied over the phone.

As for the second example, there is a graver problem. I was troubled by the curious provincialism of public thinking, even if the "province" was a sizable one. The United States is strongly introspective, despite the central position it holds in the political, economic, and scientific world. A good way of showing this quality is to analyze the highly influential news programs on the three main TV networks. There is seldom an item that is not about America. If they do report on an event abroad, you can be fairly sure there will be an American angle to it. Europe, especially its smaller countries, is much more open toward the world.

Finally, something I feel ambivalent toward: the eternal optimism and belief in action found in Americans. If there is a natural disaster in a region and people are interviewed, they do not appear to be crushed by it or demand federal intervention or aid. Instead they say something like "We will manage" or "Yes, we will start over." And they immediately start talking about their plans. The self-help attitude toward adversity is splendid and exemplary indeed.

But this readiness for action is often combined with naiveté and a tendency to underestimate just how complex the situation is. Americans confronted with a problem are certain it can be solved. They cannot conceive that a problem without a solution could exist. They often come up straightaway with a proposal that will set things to rights. Unfortunately, the approach often rests on an oversimplified description of the situation and thus the suggested solutions are primitive.

Rapid action can often work wonders. While European Hamlets and Oblomovs hesitate or resign themselves to inaction, Americans may mobilize their forces. In other cases, sudden action can lead the wrong way. Remember (and here we jump forward in time) the American advisers who knew straightaway, after the collapse of communism, what should be done and started proposing uniform measures everywhere. Sometimes this worked, and sometimes it had disastrous consequences.

A center of world culture

I sense gross exaggeration when some snobbish Hungarian intellectuals talk in superior tones of how primitive and uncultured the Americans are. There are coarse, uncultured Americans, of course, just as there are plenty of such people in Hungary or elsewhere in Europe. But I was in the lucky position of living in one of the world's centers of science and culture. Boston and its suburbs contain seven universities, with two of the leading ones—Harvard and MIT, only ten minutes away—on a single street, Massachusetts Avenue. I met scholars with impressive knowledge in many places in the world, but perhaps I can safely risk the statement that the concentration of sharp minds, talents, and education found there is unique.

The Budapest Museum of Fine Art would be glad to own the Van Gogh, Gauguin, Max Beckmann, Klimt, or even László Moholy-Nagy paintings to be found in Harvard's museum, let alone the treasures in the great Boston gallery, the Museum of Fine Arts.

We only had to take the subway for a few minutes to reach Symphony Hall, the home of the Boston Symphony Orchestra, one of the finest orchestras in the world. What concerts we heard there! Any famous musician visiting the United States counts it an honor to be invited to Boston. We had two other fine concerts halls available: the warm-sounding, wood-paneled Jordan Hall and the great lecture theater of Harvard, Sanders Hall. After attending concerts for a number of years, we would see more familiar faces in the audience than we would back home in the Academy of Music.

We went to plenty of movies. However big the stock in the video rentals, they cannot afford the pleasure of a film theater. (At the time, we were delighted all the more to see a film as soon as it came out. These days, the same can be done in Budapest.) Some that we saw never reached Budapest—for instance, *Vanya on 42nd Street*, a magical adaptation of Chekhov's play *Uncle Vanya*, and *Thirty-two Short Films about Glenn Gould*, presenting the eccentric genius at the piano.

As for books, we had three large bookstores with infinite stocks in Harvard Square, a couple of minutes away from our apartment. Always full of students and other book lovers, they even stayed open at night. When our Swedish grandchildren arrived, the first thing they would do was to rush down to the bookstores in the Square. Looking through the books, we came across all the latest titles. (We frequently browsed through the Sunday supplement of the *New York Times* or the *New York Review of Books* in the hopes of guidance in the face of the seemingly endless supply of books.)

If the culture in Boston was not enough, we had New York and Washington close enough to be accessible. Hardly a year went by without a few days' visit to one or the other. Adding the concert halls, opera houses, theaters, and galleries of those two great cities to those of Boston, we had almost infinite choice. We had the constant feeling of missing something we should have seen or heard because we lacked time or had other engagements.

Friends

Friendship is essential to me. Of course, friendships can vary in intensity, sincerity, and frequency of contact, but the borderline between acquaintances and friends is always clearly discernible. It gives me pleasure to be close to those around me, whatever the nature of the relationship may be.

As I have mentioned before, I feel good at my workplace if I can be on friendly terms with my immediate colleagues. I have been very lucky in this respect. My secretaries at Harvard were charming, kind people. I have already talked about Madeline. Kate Pilson and I usually began each morning with a discussion, not just about the tasks for the day but about political events, films, and reading experiences. Lauren LaRosa put a booklet of her own poems in my hand, as a kind token of trust. I have not seen any of them for many years, but I correspond with all three and we sometimes talk on the telephone.

I was never in a managerial position, but I have had one or more research assistants to help me. I felt it was a special privilege that from 1985 to 1997, Mária Kovács—Marcsi, as she is called by friends—worked with me. After finishing her studies at the prestigious Rajk College of the Karl Marx University of Economics, she agreed to work for me full-time. She helped with everything: collecting data, editing my manuscripts, maintaining correspondence, keeping in touch with people, and administering my documents. She was familiar with my work in such detail that I did not even have to say what I wanted before she knew. When I started at Harvard, she agreed to accompany us to America each time.

Marcsi was followed by Ágnes Benedict and then János Varga. They too, like Marcsi Kovács, "commuted" with us between Budapest and Cambridge. Each came for an initial two years and then volunteered to continue for a further year.

These three young people were not only my assistants, but my dear friends, whom my wife and I viewed as if they were our children or grandchildren. (They were between the two generations in age.) We were glad to help them if they had any problem. We often met off-campus, and they were fond of my wife Zsuzsa's cooking.

Warm friendships developed in my teacher–student relations with those to whom I was a Ph.D. adviser, and they assisted me in my research and writings. Anna Seleny, Yingyi Qian, Chenggang Xu, Carla Krüger, Jane Prokop, Alexandra Vacroux, Karen Eggleston, and John McHale belong not only in lists of acknowledgments or as coauthors, but as kind memories. We met not just at the university but as families too. I have remained in touch with them all since they and I left Harvard, talking to some of them frequently and others more rarely.

We needed some domestic help and found a job-wanted notice stuck on a tree. We called the number and a charming girl soon appeared, Susan Ryan-Vollmar. She had recently finished college and wrote short articles and verses from time to time. While retaining her literary ambitions, she wanted to earn a livelihood in domestic work. We came to terms and thereafter she came to our apartment to clean. After we had become friends, we began to persuade her to resume her studies and enroll at the university again. That is what she did. She took a higher-level journalism course, found a job at a small paper, and then moved to a leading Boston paper, where she is now deputy to the chief editor.

When Susan had been coming for a while, she asked whether we would mind if she brought a friend to help her. Thereafter, the cleaning was done in tandem by Susan, the journalist, and her partner, Linda Croteau, a teacher at a junior high.

They remained faithful to us. However high Susan's career soared and however Linda was burdened by her teaching, feelings of friendship prompted them to keep helping us in our home. These were interesting encounters. They worked hard, for they were both unbeatably meticulous and thorough cleaners.* When they stopped for a pause, we would talk about current political events and books we had read. When I had a difficulty expressing myself in English, I could turn to Linda or Susan for guidance. We felt the excitement of family members when we were told that Susan was expecting a child. We heard by phone, after we had left America, that she gave birth to a second.

Once, at the swimming pool, Zsuzsa got into a conversation with a good-looking, white-haired, athletic woman. The chats led to friendship. Mimi Berlin, who taught Russian history at Harvard's Extension School, and Gerry Berlin, an excellent lawyer, amateur clarinetist, and former human rights campaigner, became two of our closest friends. It became a tradition that when we arrived in Cambridge from Europe, we spent the first evening in their home, enjoying a lovely meal; and when we left, we said good-bye to Cambridge by having a delicious dinner prepared by Mimi. We have had the good fortune to meet them in Budapest as well since we left the States.

We spent many interesting evenings with Robert and Bobby Solow, often going to concerts with them. Every economist knows what Solow means for the science of economics. It is an enthralling experience to hear him lecture.† I know nobody else who is able to explain such difficult and complex ideas in such a crystal-clear manner, without any condescension, spiced with sparkling wit and humor. Around the dining table we were able to enjoy the same great intellect, and in addition the very humane attention, interest, and helpfulness he showed toward his friends.

The majority of our friends were university colleagues. Zwi Griliches and his wife Diana, Dale and Linda Jorgenson, our fellow countryman Francis Bator (Feri Bátor)

---

* Susan and Linda were among the guests at the dinner in my honor when I retired from Harvard University. We sat at big round tables and neighbors began asking each other who was who. They were surrounded by university professors, and when the question of their jobs came up, their first answer was that they were the cleaning women in János Kornai's household. The others were a little surprised. Even at liberal Harvard, it was unusual for cleaning women to appear at a gala dinner of professors. It later emerged that they were a journalist and a teacher as well.

† Our daughter Judit was still deliberating which university she should apply to when in 1972, on her first trip to America, she accompanied me to a conference where one of the speakers was Robert Solow. She decided that if economics was such an interesting subject, it would be worth enrolling in the university of economics. Later she became slightly disappointed—not all lecturers are like Solow.

and Jae Roosevelt, Amartya Sen and Emma Rothschild, Robert and Nancy Dorfman, Frank and Mathilda Holzman, Robert Schulman and his wife, Judit Fejes: where shall I stop? Some of these dear friends—Zwi Giliches, Robert Dorfman, the Holzmans—are now deceased, and we sorely miss them.

Domestic parties are a common way to socialize in America. A large number would come together and spend a long time standing with drinks in their hands, circulating and talking to this person or that. That superficial conversation was usually followed by a sit-down dinner, in which it was customary to talk to each neighbor in turn, even for an hour or two and even if they were previously unknown. If you were not lucky with your neighbors, the pleasantries could pall after a while.

I have to say that in all the time we spent in America, we never gave a single party of that kind; and if we were invited to such affairs, we tried, within the bounds of politeness, to excuse ourselves. The kind of gathering we like is one where the hosts invite two, three, or four guests and everyone contributes to a single conversation. If a subject comes up, we discuss it intensely rather than jumping to the next topic every five minutes.

I find small talk irritating. Someone explained to us that it is not done in American academic circles to talk about problems in one's own profession, because that would be impolite to those outside the field. We once had three couples to our house, including two great economists and an equally famous political scientist, with their wives, who were also researchers and artists, respectively. We were returning hospitality to them all. Initially, we were delighted to think what stimulation lay ahead, but instead, the conversation was on conventional, neutral subjects, as our guests carefully avoided discussion of professional issues. We learned our lesson. We later tried to steer the conversations with an occasional question or contribution, to create discourse that was interesting and illuminating. And when our friends saw that we liked that kind of socialization, they respected our wishes. The party invitations dwindled. Instead we were asked to the smaller, conversational gatherings we love. If I had to rank what we enjoyed most in Cambridge, I would certainly put in one of the first few places our sparkling, varied social life, so full of intellectual excitement.

One reason why our guests were eager to call was that they always found something special to eat. One of Zsuzsa's cakes became famous in Cambridge. A more distant acquaintance, we were told, was inquiring how she could get herself invited to the Kornais' because she would like to try the famous almond cake as well.

I felt at home in the Harvard Faculty Club. Hardly a week went by without a lunch or two there with colleagues or guests. Those passing a lifetime in Western universities probably found its attractions self-evident. In Cambridge, I became attached to that kind of get-together: intimate conversation over the tablecloth, mainly about problems in our subject, but politics, the arts, and personal matters might come up as well.

Yet however close our friendships with our newfound American friends were, we lacked something: a shared past. Our friends in Hungary were being decimated as the decades went by. Some dropped away, or we dropped away from them because we had grown apart or because our thoughts and public activity had taken different directions. Friendships were being tested. History is a stern examiner of fidelity, loyalty, and character. But the friendships that withstood these ordeals were the stronger for it, incomparably more intense than the less deeply rooted friendships initiated in later years.

If the subject of repression in a Communist country came up with Americans, our friends would immediately think of the McCarthy period. We wondered how they could compare the harassment of a few hundred people who lost jobs or were otherwise persecuted with the ruthless repression in the Rákosi era and the brutal reprisals of 1957–1958, for instance, when as punishment for ten days of revolution 229 people in one small country were murdered by judicial sentence and thousands spent years behind bars.[1] What could Americans grasp of the meaning of a totalitarian system? They, on the other hand, felt we could not comprehend what endangering and curtailing rights signified in a society accustomed to freedom. But it was in vain that they and we sought to understand, through rational argument and historical knowledge, what the other might be feeling. Nothing was the same as going through it and sensing personally what repression meant.

There was the same trouble with speaking about the Holocaust. All our friends, Jews and non-Jews, felt strongly about and condemned that ghastly crime, but they had not worn a yellow star themselves. The fate of the Jews preoccupied many of our American friends more than it did us, yet empathy, solidarity, and sense of moral responsibility remain different from a trauma experienced personally.

The shared experiences of a difficult life strengthen the ties that bind us with our friends in Hungary. When we returned after a long absence, we could hardly wait to hear what our friends would report. We shared in the excitement when the pace of change accelerated and signs that the Kádár system was weakening and the Soviet empire breaking up proliferated. In Budapest as in Cambridge, we kept away from the newly fashionable parties, large gatherings, and intellectual salons, confining ourselves, here as well, to small gatherings and sensible discourse. We had long conversations, for instance, with the historian Péter Hanák and his wife Kati, with Pál Lőcsei and Éva Kende, and with András Nagy and Ágnes Losonczy.* We met the

---

* My meetings with Péter Kende and his wife, Hanna B. Kende, were exceptional. Péter had not been able to return to Budapest until the change of system, and so we seized every opportunity to see each other when I was abroad.

Litváns not only for dinners in their flat but for walks in the Buda hills. We were very fond of the company of my colleagues and former students, such as Mihály Laki, Kati Farkas, Tamás Bauer, János Gács, Mari Lackó, András Simonovits, and Zsuzsa Kapitány. Continuing in Budapest the pleasant customs of the Faculty Club, I happily met in a restaurant with Éva Csató, with whom I had worked on *Szabad Nép*; Ilus Lukács, a translator of *Economics of Shortage*; or Ágnes Matits, with whom I had done a large empirical survey on the soft budget constraint. In all these cases, we had come to know each other through work, and they all became long-lasting friends.

We found among our Hungarian friends something for which none of our American ties could have compensated us.

Among the economists of Europe and the world

From 1983 on, since my stay in Princeton, I have spent half my time in the United States. That did not turn me into a half American. For one thing, I have many ties to other countries than Hungary and the United States and to their citizens.

I had started much earlier to take responsibilities that extended across national boundaries, when in 1972 I was elected, on Tinbergen's suggestion, vice president of the Development Planning Committee of the United Nations. I held the post until 1977. There I joined Indian, Mexican, French, Soviet, Dutch, and Polish economists in devising economic policy proposals for developing countries, to put before other UN agencies.

Later, I was active in the international association of mathematical economists, the Econometric Society. I was elected first to the Executive Committee, and in 1978 was made president.* While performing the duties of the presidency, I made a special point of promoting the cause of involvement in the society's congresses of economists from socialist countries, so helping to bring them into the circles of economics in the Western world.

I did my best to promote that cause in various other ways as well. Whenever I had the opportunity, I was eager for colleagues from the Soviet Union and Eastern Europe to be invited to international events, either as visiting researchers or visiting professors.

My activity with the European Economic Association (EEA) coincided with my time at Harvard. It was founded through the efforts of the Belgian professor Jacques

---

* Under the two-stage election system of the Econometric Society, one of several candidates is first chosen as president elect and is active for a year getting to know the tasks involved in the presidency. In the next year, his or her name appears on the ballot as the single candidate for president.

Drèze, whom I respected not only for his exceptional scientific achievements but also for his commitment to public service. I supported him, too, as one of the founders. My discovery of what Europe stands for did not start with Hungary's accession to the European Union in 2004. The establishment of the EEA with Drèze as its president came in 1986, when the Iron Curtain was still in place. In the following year, there were two candidates for president, Frank Hahn and myself. I had known Hahn since my very first visit to England, for a conference at Cambridge in 1963. As I mentioned in chapter 10, he had written an article deeply critical of my book *Anti-Equilibrium*, "The Winter of Our Discontent." We had friendly relations. He had been helpful when I had asked him to assist Tamás Lipták in finding a job after he emigrated. To return to the election, it is customary in that case to ask both candidates if they accept nomination. We both did, and I won the majority of votes.

I again worked to bring colleagues from socialist countries into the society, as I had earlier with the Econometric Society. I managed to ensure that invitations to the first congress in Vienna went out to several promising economists then unknown in the West. They included Leszek Balcerowicz, later a leading figure in the Polish change of system; the sociologist Tatiana Zaslavskaya, whose critical studies of the Soviet system would earn her world fame; and the young Vladimir Dlouhý, destined to be a party leader and minister in the Czech government after the change of system.

I had the following to say in my president's report to the 1987 annual congress: "I am a citizen of a socialist country. It is understandable that the participation of Eastern European economists in our Association is an issue of special concern for me." I listed some of the special difficulties that Eastern Europeans faced and asked for assistance from Western colleagues, "who are lucky enough not to know the kind of difficulties their Eastern European colleagues are faced with. Many of us citizens of Eastern Europe frequently have the bitter feeling that intellectuals in the West identify Europe with Western Europe. Let us be reminded: the border of the continent is not the river Elbe. We, too, wish to be regarded as Europeans."[2]

It is the president's privilege and duty to choose the scholarly theme for the annual congress, which governs the subject matter of the presidential address and the two keynote lectures. I thought the most important subject for our part of the world was freedom, and I called my lecture "Individual Freedom and Reform of the Socialist Economy."[3] I asked Amartya Sen to be one of the keynote speakers and he chose "Freedom of Choice: Concept and Content" as a title.[4] The other keynote speaker was Assar Lindbeck, whose study was titled "Individual Freedom and Welfare-State Policy."[5]

I tried in my lecture to clarify through Hungary's example how decentralization, expansion of private ownership, mitigation of shortage, and loosening of bureaucratic constraints on the labor market not only boosted economic efficiency but raised individual liberty and freedom of choice as well. I emphasized the importance of the shift in the socialist world away from the "maximum state" toward a reduction in the state's role and an increase in individual freedom.

A visit to China

My wife and I spent four weeks in China in the summer of 1985, at the invitation of the Chinese Academy of Social Sciences and the World Bank. First, we attended a conference in Beijing on the problems of state-owned enterprises. It was instructive, but much more lay ahead. I had taken part in many conferences, but what happened next was unlike any previous experience of mine before.

The Chinese had asked seven foreign economists to comment on the country's situation and prospects. The others, in addition to me, were the Yale professor James Tobin, the great U.S. macroeconomist (recipient of the Nobel Prize a few years later); Otmar Emminger, former president of the West German Bundesbank; Michel Albert, former president of the French Planning Commission; Sir Alexander Cairncross, an Oxford professor who was one of the chief economic advisers to the British government and the Labour Party in the 1960s; Aleksander Bajt, a Yugoslav economist and noted expert on "self-management"; and Leroy Jones, an American professor who had written a book on South Korean planning.*

These seven economists and the Chinese colleagues accompanying them were received by Prime Minister Zhao Ziyang for a two-hour discussion.† He told us what problems most concerned them and on which they would like to hear responses from Western scholars.

On the next day, we and a group of Chinese economists were flown to Chongqing, where we boarded a boat that started off down the Yangzi River. We were given

---

* One of the main figures preparing the meeting of Western and Chinese economists was Ed Lim, who at the time directed the Office of the World Bank in China. His work was a good example of how a Western consultant can best serve transition in a socialist country. He did not produce his own recipe for adoption by the locals, come what may. Instead, he tried to present a wealth of alternative paths. From the list of economists above, it can be seen that the Chinese wanted to become familiar with the American, Western European, and East Asian experiences, and with Eastern European ideas of reform—and Ed Lim was really helpful in meeting their desire.

† Zhao Ziyang was one of the pioneers of Chinese reform. The paramount leader of the changes was Deng Xiaoping, but Zhao is considered the architect and main organizer of the first fundamental reforms. He was the one Chinese leader to enter Tiananmen Square and speak to student leaders during the days of protest in 1989. After the protest was crushed, he was sacked as premier; he remained under house arrest until his death in January 2005.

luxury tourist treatment. Splendid Chinese cooking was served and there was even a swimming pool on deck. However, we did not get much time for recreation and relaxation.

Our hosts worked us hard. Each foreign guest was assigned a half day's discussion, beginning with a lecture, after which the senior Chinese colleagues would ask questions. The leading Chinese economists did not want to take a public stand in the debate on the most sensitive issues of the reform. And it seemed that for the younger ones it was not proper to ask questions. They had obviously decided to talk it all over among themselves and draw conclusions after the foreign guests had returned home.

China was through the first stage of reform by then. Although this process was described to us in terms that fit in with the party line, what had happened in fact was that socialist agriculture, including the great Chinese innovation of "communes," had been jettisoned. In its place, as a consequence of a peasant movement that swept away any kind of resistance, farming based on private ownership had been resurrected again. The dire shortages of food gave way to plenty. China went far further in agricultural reform than Hungary had, a point more noteworthy than the difference between the vigorous Chinese villages and the tired, inefficient farms of the Soviet kolkhoz system, which were not suitable for further development. The big question after the success with agriculture was what to do with the rest of the economy.

While I was in America preparing my lecture, I tried to gain as thorough a knowledge of the Chinese situation as possible. I thought it was especially important to clarify the ways in which China resembled and differed from Hungary. I was not thinking so much of obvious distinctions: populations of a billion and ten million respectively, Asian versus European culture, or differences between Chinese and Hungarian (or Eastern European) history. What they would most want to know from me was what they could learn from the experiences of the Hungarian reform —what was worth adopting and what problems to avoid. Preparing for my lecture meant analyzing the similarities and differences of situation and scope between the two reforms.

I felt at the first conference in Beijing and later while talking to Chinese economists and business leaders that in a certain sense I was at home in China, despite the distance and the historical and cultural differences. All the phenomena that came up and the cares and woes were familiar. The difficulties they combated were the same as the ones preoccupying us in Hungary. They would certainly have learned a lot of interesting things from the American macroeconomist or the West German central banker, but we Eastern Europeans understood best the realm of ideas in which they were living as well.

Hungary, back in 1968, had abolished the command economy based on central plan directives. It had been shown that the economy, which was still dominated by state ownership and directed by the Communist Party, could nonetheless work. The bureaucratic and the market mechanisms could coexist, although the friction between them was great. When I was in Budapest, I was highly critical of the incomplete, inconsistent nature of the reform; nevertheless, I thought that the abolition of the command economy in China would take the reform process another big step forward. That was a positive lesson, which I certainly wanted to underline to the Chinese leadership. I also wanted to draw attention to the troubles and dangers attending that step: the inconsistency of the Hungarian reform, the "soft budget constraint," and the distortions in the price system. China in the mid-1980s had extremely ambitious growth plans. I pointed to the risks entailed in a rush to growth: the extent of the danger of inflation and of neglect of some sectors. I reminded colleagues of the importance of harmony in Chinese thinking and culture. I advised harmonious development instead of rush and forced growth.

At that time, what was equally depressing both in Hungary and China was the persistence of political repression, the absence of liberty and rights. We could detect some indirect signs of that. At the usual European or American economics conferences, it is easy to tell from the mood in the hall, the faces of the audience, and the content of the responses whether a lecture has been well received. That was impossible to fathom on the boat. I could not read a thing from the faces of the audience or the chairman. I had to fall back on other indicators of success or failure. During breaks, I would be surrounded by many young Chinese economists, excitedly putting questions in none-too-good English but making themselves understood. They began to discuss with me how they would initiate the publication of my books. I will return to that; but for the moment, let us stay on the boat.

From time to time, we would stop for a half day's break and the boat would cast anchor. One day we went to a market in a riverbank village and saw for ourselves the results of the agricultural reform: the varied supply of fine fruits, vegetables, fish, shellfish, and turtles and the wide variety of meats. Another day we went to the Three Gorges, one of the most famous tourist sights in China. We went in rowboats to enjoy this natural wonder. There was already talk of flooding the district and building a giant dam that would leave the Three Gorges under water. This was indeed built a few years later, and the natural wonder can no longer be seen. We ended our voyage at Wuhan, where I lectured at the university.

It emerged later that the "boat conference," in Chinese *Bashan Lun* (as it would become known in the economic press there), had a marked influence on Chinese economic thinking. The proceedings were published in a book and the lectures reported on in periodicals.[6] Chinese economists have often cited the advice received from the participants and to this day still recall the boat conference as an outstanding event.

A year later, in 1986, my book *Economics of Shortage* appeared in Chinese. It sold 100,000 copies and was reprinted in 1998. The book served as theoretical background when the command economy was eliminated in China, and it has been used as a textbook wherever economics was taught. Including that one, altogether eight of my books appeared in Chinese. When I visited China again years later, it was moving to have university teachers, a city mayor, and business managers tell me time and time again, "I am a disciple of yours."

Feeling at home

Our main home remained in Hungary all through the period. But we tried not to live a temporary life in Cambridge. Our apartment there was as carefully furnished as the one in Budapest. We displayed pictures and personal memorabilia. We made the acquaintance not only of friends in the strict sense but of people from the concierge to the hairdresser, and the doctor to staff at the swimming pool, whom we met in everyday life. We felt at home at Harvard, in Cambridge, in the Boston area, in the United States.

I relate this in the plural because Zsuzsa and I did not just react spontaneously to the shorter or longer journeys, including several stays of several months. After a while, we had a conscious agenda. Wherever we went, we wanted to feel at home. If technically or financially possible, we would try to make our physical and social surroundings more personal. The task was made easier, of course, because we moved in the academic world. Although national, cultural, and historical differences are great, we would soon meet in India, Japan, or Mexico with professors or students; before too long, we would find common ground and share with them many aspects of our lifestyle and interests. We felt at home instantly in that globalized academic world.

It gives me great pleasure to assert that I have friends not only in Hungary and in the United States, but also in many other countries; we mutually follow each other's work, from time to time exchange letters, and if it is possible meet in person. At this point, I would like to call attention to the names of those whose interest went beyond the reading of my work, or perhaps beyond writing of reviews and commentaries, who were willing to contact publishers in their countries for the sake of my writings, and sometimes even undertook the tasks of translating and editing my books. In France Marie Lavigne, Bernard Chavance, and Mehrdad Vahabi; in China Xiaomeng Peng; in Vietnam Nguyen Quang A; in Japan Tsuneo Morita; in the Czech Republic Karel Kouba; and in Poland Tadeusz Kowalik and Grzegorz

Kołodko helped selflessly, making huge sacrifices of time and energy to get my works to the readers in their countries.

I observed above that everywhere in the "globalized" world of academics, we feel right at home. I do not want to present that feeling in a one-sided way. Commuting between Hungary and America, with frequent journeys to all parts of the world, meant that while feeling at home everywhere, I stayed somewhat alien everywhere. There was nowhere I could warm to entirely, because time was already up: we had to go to the next place. Returning to Budapest, we were sorry to leave our dear American friends, not to meet my students, and not to hear that concert in the following month, which we would have been glad to attend. Time and time again we felt regret about missing things happening at one place while we were at the other place. We always had to say good-byes.

There was a joke often told in Budapest in the 1970s and 1980s. Old Kohn emigrates to America. He lives there for a while, but does not enjoy himself and returns home. When he applies for an emigration passport a second time, they ask him, "Say, Mr. Kohn. Where do you actually like to be?" "On the road," he replies.*

We would recall this joke if we happened to feel ill at ease somewhere. Others would mention with a little malice, if the subject of our constant "commuting" arose, that we seemed to like being on the road. Yet that did not characterize our basic mental state when we were traveling all the time. Travel was tiring and we would rather be at home.

What tired us was not just the baggage, notes, books, and so on that had to be packed at one end and unpacked at the other. The visa applications and other administrative tasks also started anew with the preparations for a journey. And adjusting to the time difference always exhausted us.†

I am not thinking of the physical tiredness that travel brings as people get older. Much more of a burden than the effort to get from one place to another was the doubling of our lives. Every activity pursued in Hungary, every thread tying us to Hungary, had its equivalent in America. We had a home here and a home there, a

---

* The joke paints a somewhat overly rosy picture of the ease of emigration. But by then, those not banned from traveling could do so quite easily, and as long as you did not say explicitly that you did not want to return, in practice it was possible to go. For that matter émigrés did not receive settlement permits in the States automatically, either.

† Whenever we could, we had a stopover in Stockholm on our way back to Europe from Cambridge, to spend a few days with Judit, Zsófi, and Anna. Judit prepared our favorite dishes for us, cared for us with tender love, and helped us to adjust to life in Europe. She tactfully pretended not to notice that I kept falling asleep at the dinner table, owing to jet lag. Refreshed by intimate chats lasting for hours on end, we were ready to leave, fully rested, for Budapest.

car here and a car there.* Both here and there, we paid motor vehicle tax and insurance, filed income tax returns, had bank accounts, maintained catalogued, numbered files of my documents, and so on, and so forth. I was receiving a salary from one employer at any one time,† while on unpaid leave from the other, but that did not mean I had to handle problems at only one workplace. I always took with me problems and responsibilities from the other place of work and dealt with them by e-mail, letter, fax, or telephone. So the combined burden was not 50 + 50 percent of each job but surely more than 100 percent.

In spite of our constant change of location, Zsuzsa worked doggedly on her own research, the examination of Hungarian housing distribution and housing policy. While she used her time in Cambridge to learn about Western experiences and make international comparisons, she was determined to continue her work on her original topic, despite all the difficulties caused by the distance.

This curious double life called for great effort, constant commuting, and much travel to other parts of the world as well.‡ But it was worth it. I received the many advances of Western life at first hand and embedded myself in an academic community in the forefront of the economics profession, while keeping my roots in Hungary.

Much is said in Hungary and elsewhere about the brain drain. The world's richest countries, especially the United States, attract talent and thereby weaken the intellectual strength of the countries from which the talented are drawn. The lifestyle that I chose when accepting my Harvard appointment exemplifies one useful defense against the brain drain. It was possible to have a foot in America and another in the old country where I was born and bred.§

* Our beloved secondhand 1980 Volkswagen Golf served us faithfully, battered in body but with a sound engine, until we finally left the States in 2002.

† Many people around us must have thought I was receiving full salaries from both places.

‡ It was a great relief to have staff in both places to help me in my presence and absence. I have mentioned my kind and attentive American secretaries and my research assistants. All my work in Budapest was eased by Ica Fazekas and later Kati Szabó. Julianna Parti was the regular editor and conscientious administrator of my publications, while her husband, Brian McLean, was the regular translator of my texts written in Hungarian. They were so familiar with my concerns and intent on lightening my tasks, even in my absence, that their handling of my requests was almost automatic. In terms of assistance and friendship, I was in an enviable position—better even than that of Western colleagues.

§ There is no point in skipping over the fact that the choice has material consequences. Let us consider Hungarian scholars and researchers who were actually offered a university position in America. Those who chose a full-time job in America and emigration (and quite a few Hungarian researchers decided to do that) enjoyed significant material extras in their working life and later in retirement, compared with colleagues who stayed in Hungary. The solution

We often heard American friends conclude that our curious lifestyle meant we were "enjoying the best of both worlds." I know that Harvard, Cambridge, and Boston are not "America," but they are the best that America can give to an intellectual thirsty for scholarship and culture. (To avoid a charge of Harvard arrogance, perhaps I should say *among* the best.) At the same time, Hungary was the "happiest barrack" in the other camp. Certainly, being an academic researcher in Hungary offered me a more interesting and worthwhile life than most other citizens of Communist countries enjoyed. I am grateful to fate for making that possible.

---

that I chose, and to which I draw others' attention as a possibility, reduces these extras to more or less half. A researcher who chooses a 50–50 solution sacrifices some of the surplus offered for the sake of half staying at home. But it also enables him or her to build up a much stronger financial position than would be possible if depending exclusively on income as a researcher in Hungary.

18

Synthesis—1988–1993

The Socialist System

I made the decision to write a comprehensive work on the socialist system in 1983, while I was at the Institute of Advanced Study in Princeton. My reading there served as intellectual preparation and I wrote an outline at that time.

The work gained new impetus when I began teaching at Harvard University. I first gave an overall course on the political economy of socialism in 1984. The earliest forerunner to the book was a duplicated set of notes handed to students in 1986.

My university lectures drew an international audience. Among the listeners were a Chinese student who had been sent down to a village in Mao's time, and a young Polish economist with firsthand knowledge of a planned economy, while many others knew nothing about the workings of the socialist system. Some were strongly anti-communist, but others were members of the German and American New Left, naively clinging to their beliefs and oblivious to the real nature of totalitarianism. I gave the course several times and it altered and developed from year to year. I was urged on by the questions and arguments to make myself clear to several types of students (and later, readers). There is no better preparation for a work perhaps destined to be a textbook than to present the material several times to an interested audience of students.

How the book was written

I drew up a first draft and divided the material into chapters in the spring of 1986. Shortly thereafter, I had a splendid new opportunity to continue the work in peace in Helsinki, at WIDER—the World Institute for Development Economics Research, part of the UN University—thanks to the director, Dr. Lal Jayawardena. My wife and I moved there in May 1988 for more than half a year and received every possible support, including a comfortable, congenial apartment and perfect working conditions.

The peace and quiet were ideal. Helsinki is usually cool in the summer, but when we were there, it was pleasantly warm and we swam in the Baltic as well as the Olympic pool. For citizens of a country cut off from the sea, it was a singular experience to spend a few months directly on the coast and admire the wonderful colors of the sunset. After a long day's work, it would still be light enough at ten o'clock to take a walk along the lovely seashore, on the nearby historically preserved island, or by one of the bays. There my wife and I would talk over what I had written that day or planned to write in the morning. In the midst of working very hard indeed, we found much that refreshed us: buying fresh fish from the boats moored beside the market, going to concerts in the Finlandia House or the rock church, and making excursions to Finland's magical lakes.

WIDER was a draw for economists from all over the world, and many of our friends among them visited us there. Jacques Drèze interrupted a long sea voyage in a sailboat to do so. Our Harvard friends Steve Marglin and Amartya Sen came over; and on another occasion, we had as a dinner guest Edmond Malinvaud, the mentor of my early works. We met there with Sukhamoy Chakravarty, the splendid Indian economist, and a charming Swedish friend, Bengt-Christian Ysander.* We had many interesting and thought-provoking discussions with local people, the director and the fellows of WIDER, and economists from Finland.

The calm and the inspiring natural and intellectual surroundings certainly helped the work proceed at a pace that matched what I had managed with *Economics of Shortage* in Sweden. Each week, I was ready with a new chapter.† Also facilitating my speed, besides the ideal surroundings, was the fact that *The Socialist System* summarized my research career so far, so that it had, in a sense, been preceded by thirty-two years' work (or by five years of direct preparation). Once I sat down to the computer on my desk in Helsinki, I could type almost continuously, because what I wanted to write had largely taken shape in my mind.

The book contains not only ideas that had been maturing for years but a sizable supporting apparatus of tables, diagrams, statistics, references, quotations, and bibliography. I am lucky I had a team to help me, drawn from my students in Hungary and the United States; it included my former university students in the strict sense and others who saw themselves as followers of my ideas, with whom I had professional and personal ties. That intellectual closeness meant my requests were met quickly and flexibly, wherever I happened to be—Helsinki, Budapest, or Cambridge.

---

* It was a last meeting with both friends, as each died young, at the peak of his powers.

† This was the first, rough draft, of course. Like *Economics of Shortage*, the book underwent several rounds of correction—for instance after it had been read by invited colleagues, who made comments of great value to subsequent revisions.

Meanwhile, the news from home was of a disintegrating system and mounting intellectual and political opposition; but for as long as I was in Helsinki, events in Hungary remained for me just a rumble of distant artillery. I would be in a state of astonishment for a while after a telephone conversation with Budapest that woke me up to the critical condition of the socialist system, the last agonies of the Eastern European regimes, the embittered feelings of the public, and the day-to-day political struggles. But I deliberately tried to divorce my ideas from these influences. I spent those months concentrating so hard on writing the book that it absorbed me almost entirely. I was fueled by the feeling that the work was important and going well, whatever might happen. I felt then and recall now, fifteen years later, that my months in Helsinki were among the happiest of my life, perhaps even the happiest of all. Everyone who loves his or her trade, whether a carpenter, a sculptor, or a road builder, takes delight in creating something new. I am fortunate that I have experienced this joy on many occasions, but perhaps never so strongly as in Helsinki in the summer of 1988.

We returned to Budapest in the fall of 1988. By that time, the rumbles of artillery were closer. I was more than half done with the book, but a good deal of work remained to be done on it. From that time on, my writing continued in a much more distracted manner, first in Budapest and then in the first half of 1989 in Cambridge. In the second half of that year, I laid *The Socialist System* aside, feeling that I had to have my say on the change of system and put forward some timely economic policy proposals; I did so in the *Passionate Pamphlet*, the subject of the next chapter. I mention it here because I was working almost in parallel on *The Road to a Free Economy* (the *Pamphlet*'s English version) and its variants in other languages, as well as other studies and lectures on tasks of the change of system, on the one hand, and on the later chapters of *The Socialist System*, on the other. Or perhaps it would be more accurate to say I jumped excitedly and impatiently back and forth between the two themes. They and my teaching at Harvard vied for my time and capacity. While I tackled a subject of the moment, I was sorry to have left the great summary work. When I returned to it, I felt guilty for paying too little heed to everyday economic policy. With the two competing commitments, I still managed—whether in Budapest or Cambridge—to devote days or weeks to the book and, in the summer of 1991, two whole months. I was reassured, whenever I turned aside from immediate calls on me and returned to the text, that what I had written seemed quite "robust." The socialist system in Eastern Europe and the Soviet Union had collapsed in 1989 to 1991. Many people, including experts, felt they had to revise their pronouncements on the subject. It was soothing to find I did not have to change an iota of what I had written in the first half of the book. The description and analysis had withstood the first historical storm surge. The second half, on reforms, would have to be changed and augmented in several places. Although the draft had predicted ultimate failure for partial reforms, that was not the same as analyzing how the failure actually happened.

Finally, in 1991, after three years, I finished writing *The Socialist System*.

Although the text was written in Hungarian, the English translation was soon ready. It is one of the few works of mine to appear a little earlier in English than in Hungarian.

An intention to synthesize

My prime purpose was to sum up the main findings of my research so far. I had dealt with many topics over the decades and tried to answer successive new questions, as if speeding through the annals of economics. Although distinct, these works complemented one another and covered various parts of the whole. I kept returning to the same subjects (such as the disequilibrium phenomena)—indeed, in my own judgment, treating them successively with increasing sophistication. I might even venture to say that the chain of works forms a kind of arc. I now wanted to devise an analytical framework to give logical order to the conclusions in the separate parts of my work so far.*

At the same time, I did not want to limit the work solely to the review of my own findings. I intended to incorporate into the conceptual structure all the conclusions and ideas of others that I also thought were important. I had learned a lot from works of my Hungarian colleagues and of foreign researchers. I am specifically high-lighting those influences that the lively Hungarian economic milieu had shed on me. In addition, I was influenced not only by works published in print but also by the conversations taking place around me, the spirited Hungarian discourse on the troubles of socialism and on the possibilities of improvement. The book's citations and long bibliography can guide the reader through the points were I had integrated the thoughts of others. However, I must add: I was not setting out to write a history of economic thought on the theory of socialism that would calmly report all the debated and perhaps mutually inconsistent alternative positions held.

I emphasized in the foreword to the Hungarian edition of *Economics of Shortage* that it would not cover the complete political economy of socialism, just part of it. I

---

* As well as my past academic work, I also wanted to summarize my direct experiences. Having read my autobiography this far, the reader will understand that the inspiration for what I wrote on the centralization and totalitarian nature of power, the shortages, the erosion of my belief in the socialist ideal, and many other phenomena came from personal experiences as well as from books.

stressed the point with a numerical warning: while a book presenting the socialist economy in full covers 100 percent of that subject, *Economics of Shortage* covers only 30 percent. The time had come to aim at *completeness* and write a book that set out to cover 100 percent. Not in the sense of encompassing every detail, of course, which is impossible and not the goal for a scholarly work intent on condensing and generalizing.* The analysis should be complete in the sense of identifying all the *essential* features of the socialist system and discussing all the attributes necessary and sufficient for the politico-socioeconomic organism that we call the *socialist system* to emerge and operate.

Economics of Shortage did not discuss the political structure and ideology of the system, which (after the introductory chapters) is the point where *The Socialist System* starts. It differs from numerous other summarizing works of "comparative economics" in taking as its starting point, as the most typical political feature, the autocracy of the Communist Party rather than central planning or state ownership. I explained in the chapter on *Economics of Shortage* how earlier discussion of that point was ruled out by the political climate and consequent self-censorship. I decided when I started drafting the new book in 1983 that I would go beyond those bounds. In my Harvard lectures of 1984, I began to express freely my views on the roles of the Communist Party, political structure, and official ideology. I began my argument by explaining the role of the Communist Party in the notes I handed to students in 1986, as in the later book. In that sense, I was finally able to write *genuine* political economy.

I did not want to confine my subject matter to the shared, overlapping themes of economics and political science. I sought to include other approaches, such as those of sociology, social psychology, and political philosophy, so that *The Socialist System* would count not just as a study of economics but as a work of social science, integrating all those disciplines.

Most works on the socialist economy undertake a *partial* analysis, examining some well-circumscribed sphere or certain characteristics of the system. I was interested in shedding light on how the parts made a *whole*. There is a strong interaction between politics, the economy, social relations, and ideology, which together shape the behavioral regularities of the various groups and social roles. I like to call this

---

* In the same foreword, I calculated that if the 600 pages of *Economics of Shortage* presented 30 percent of a full analysis, the full task would need 2,000 pages. But when I eventually completed the book that aimed at total comprehensiveness, I sought even greater compression. I tried so hard that the comprehensive work of 2,000 pages became a book of "only" 600 pages. The overlap with *Economics of Shortage* is less than 30 percent, as I condensed it into two or three of the twenty-four chapters of *The Socialist System*.

approach the *system paradigm*.* That paradigm has a long history, and one of its great figures is Karl Marx. He also wrote partial studies, but in his chief work, *Capital*, he sought to present capitalism as a system. He was interested in knowing how the characteristic relations in the society of his time were related to each other and how they reciprocally determined their existence. The great influence of Marx on my thinking is emphasized in the preface to *The Socialist System*, which was written in 1991—the very year when citing Marx went definitively out of fashion, even among those who had hitherto liked to quote him frequently. Marx's influence on me appears primarily in the application of the system paradigm.

The preface mentions Joseph Schumpeter and Friedrich Hayek alongside Marx. Schumpeter's *Capitalism, Socialism and Democracy* and Hayek's *Road to Serfdom* are exemplary products of the system paradigm, and in that sense they, too, exercised great influence on my thinking.†

When I was working on my comprehensive book, I could not just simply "join" one or another school of social theory. Anybody trying to fit *The Socialist System* into some kind of familiar box would run into trouble. It cannot be described as a Marxist, neoclassical, Keynesian, or Hayekian work.

I wanted the book to do more than sum up what I had to say on the subject itself, the socialist system. I wanted the analysis of this particular system to illustrate the approach and the scientific methodology whose use I was attempting to promote.

Positive analysis and values

I wanted to avoid a *normative* approach in the book. I did not even ask what a "good society" was or whether the socialist vision of Marx, Lenin, or their successors was suited to producing it. I gave such questions a wide berth and aimed at a *positive* approach. There is a group of countries where the Communist Party has long exercised absolute rule. The group included twenty-six countries and a third of the world's population in the mid-1980s. All I wanted to present was what *actually* marked their political, social, and economic life, not what that life ought to be like if socialism operated as its adherents desired.

---

* Because of its frequent use in various and ambiguous ways, "paradigm" has an ill-defined meaning in common parlance. I use it in the sense introduced by Thomas Kuhn in a brilliant book in 1962: a typical approach, outlook, methodology, apparatus, and style of argument shared or applied similarly by a group of researchers.

† John Maynard Keynes is also listed as a prime intellectual influence. That is the case, but his invaluable help was primarily with problems of macroeconomics and disequilibrium. His work was not imbued with what I call the "system paradigm," and so I do not mention him here.

The book was not intended to judge. It would have been cheap and easy to do that after the fall of the Berlin Wall. As I wrote in the preface, "One almost needs a modicum of bravery today to write about the socialist system in a tone of scientific dispassion that avoids harshly critical epithets."[1]

But a determination to produce an objective positive analysis does not preclude imbuing the account of the socialist system's main features with the *values* that form the basis of my worldview. I attach especially high value to the values of freedom, human rights, human dignity, and individual sovereignty. Hard though I tried to express myself objectively, I thought it right to strongly condemn violations of these values.

Economic performance stands a grade lower in the hierarchy of my value system, but still has high value. I assessed it using customary economic criteria: how the welfare of the population developed, what the growth rate was, how rapid technical development was, and how capable the economy was of making and applying innovations. Ultimately, I applied the criterion set by Lenin at the start of the socialist transformation: the contest between capitalism and socialism would be won by the system achieving higher productivity. The book showed why defeat of the socialist system was inevitable according to Lenin's own criterion.

I hesitated over which name to use for the subject of the book: socialist or communist system. Political writings and common parlance in the West favored the epithet "communist." But the ruling Communist Parties followed Marxist parlance in reserving the word "communism" for an unattainable utopian state in which everyone would draw on goods according to their needs. They preferred the word "socialism," which promised less. When choosing between these two expressions I took the position that if firms, associations, parties, and states could choose their own names, why deny that right to the socialist system, an even bigger entity? If that system (or the leading group that ruled it) called itself socialist, let it do so. There was no reason for me to reserve the name for some idealized normative notion of "true" socialism and deny it to twenty-six countries in the real world. Those twenty-six countries made up "existing socialism," and I would call them socialist.

General models

Comparative economics usually focuses its attention on the Soviet Union, describing the antecedents to the 1917 revolution and then the emergence, stabilization, development, and fragmentation of the Soviet system, augmenting this treatment with the historical development of the satellite countries. "Soviet-type economy" is a commonly used expression. China is usually treated as an important special case.

There is good reason for an approach that identifies each country's individuality and differences from other countries in historical development. That approach does contribute to understanding the socialist system. However, in my comprehensive work I wanted to use another method. I was aiming for generalization—setting aside the variety among those twenty-six countries and distilling from them what they had in common. If essential common features are found to characterize a particular group of countries, it is right to talk of their ensemble as a distinctively separate system. The task next becomes pinpointing these essential (and *only* these essential) traits.

The goal when creating a general model is not to provide as detailed a description as possible. To keep to the subject of the book, I did not try to describe the myriad historical and other attributes distinguishing the Soviet Union, later Eastern Europe, and finally China and Vietnam. On the contrary, I wanted to show what was *common* to the operation of the Soviet, Albanian, and Chinese political regimes and economies. The art in creating general models is to see how sparing and parsimonious one can be in selecting main features.* There should be as few main features as possible—enough, but not more than is needed, for an adequate characterization.

For the general discussion, I divided the history of the socialist system into three stages. The first was transition from capitalism to mature socialism. That period in the Soviet Union ended with collectivization of agriculture and the first great trials (of 1936–1938), which dealt a final blow to the intraparty opposition. So in the Soviet case, it lasted about twenty years—longer than the road back from socialism to capitalism. In Eastern Europe, as a result of the Soviet military occupation, the first stage was far shorter than it had been in the Soviet Union, the first country to step on the socialist road.

The book calls the system in the second stage *classical socialism*. All the main features of the system now prevail in consolidated form. Some readers disliked the term "classical." Some felt it suggested praise, although it offered no value judgment and simply conveyed that the system in the early period was now mature and possessed all its main features. Others, who had a sentimental attachment to socialism, thought it unfortunate to identify the beginning of the classical period with the great show trials, executions, and mass deportations and imprisonment.

The socialist countries moved away from the classical state in the third stage, displaying various directions and lines of reform within the socialist system. There were attempts to "perfect" central planning with reorganizations and modern

---

* "Parsimonious" is a word from the principle of constructing theories known as Occam's razor, after the fourteenth-century English philosopher William of Occam or Ockham. He proposed that a theory should always be based on as few premises as possible: that is, one should be parsimonious with one's assumptions.

computer technology. Yugoslavia experimented with self-management. There in Yugoslavia, then in Hungary, and later in other socialist countries, the idea was to introduce a market mechanism while retaining the Communist monopoly of power and predominance of state ownership. Each introduction was coupled with some easing of political repression. Reform went hand in hand with deterioration of the system.

The threefold division into periods allows for a historical dimension, but again in model form. What is described is the course of the *system*, not the history of each country.

The development of the socialist system was much influenced by the ideas of Marx, Lenin, Stalin, Mao, and others. For example, the book takes issue with those who want to exonerate Marx from intellectual responsibility for the socialist system's lack of efficiency. Marx did not intend things this way, they claim—it was just that his ideas were not properly put into practice. The truth is that the key element of the program of social transformation put forward by Marx was the elimination of private property and the market and their replacement with public property and bureaucratic coordination. What ultimately caused socialism to fail was that it did implement Marx's program; those who proclaimed the program with such messianic fervor must therefore bear the intellectual responsibility for its historical outcome.

But I am not among those who claim that what had developed was inspired exclusively by ideas, and that it realized *exactly* what socialism's prophets and leaders had planned. A large contribution was also made by spontaneous, evolutionary development. I expressed in *The Socialist System* the idea that the Communist Party, on coming to power, set about implementing a program that included eliminating private ownership and the market. This acted like a genetic code, initiating and guiding the process. Then the institutions became subject to a process of natural selection. Experiments were made with various ways of constructing a state and managing the economy. What did not prove viable under the prevailing conditions vanished after a while, and what did good service to the operation of the system became incorporated into it. Marx and Engels did not provide a detailed blueprint, propose compulsory plan targets, or prescribe that the personnel departments of each organization should be linked to the political police. Those aspects developed along the way, out of the logic of actual conditions.

One of the underlying ideas in the book concerns the affinity among the various elements of the classical socialist system, due not least to the natural selection process among institutions and consequent evolutionary development. They fit together like cogs in a machine of tyranny. Classical socialism is totalitarian and brutally oppressive, but it forms a *coherent* whole.

That coherence is broken by the reform processes. The repression eases and centralization slackens, making life more bearable but concurrently undermining the system. The fine Prague Spring slogan of "socialism with a human face" is a flight of fancy. The more human the face, the less capable of operating the system becomes.

Once those calling themselves sincere Communists lose their blind faith, the system is left without support. As "political reform" advances and real choices can be made between ideologies, faiths, and political representatives, most people do *not* choose the ruling system.

The second half of *The Socialist System* lays out this line of argument in detail, taking the various trends of reform and showing how each one led into a blind alley.

Too late or too early?

After the Hungarian edition of *The Socialist System* appeared, I was interviewed by Gábor Karsai, who wrote an adept and appreciative review of the book in the business weekly *Figyelő* (Observer). During our conversation, he asked me whether I was not late with the book. I must say that his question, asked in all goodwill, struck deep. It was phrased like this in the paper: "If Kornai had managed to finish [the book] four or five years earlier and get it published in Hungarian, of course... it would have become an economics best seller, like *Shortage*. A book to be devoured by intellectuals who consider themselves well-educated and a basis of scientific reference for the then awakening camp of those seeking to change the system." A few lines later came, "Who has time today to read what is after all a specialized book about the past, of almost 700 pages?"[2]

I quoted in the preface to *The Socialist System* a passage from Simon Schama's recent exciting historical work on the French Revolution: "Chou Enlai, the Chinese prime minister, when asked what he thought of the significance of the French revolution, is said to have replied, 'It's still too early to say.' After two hundred years it may still be too early (or too late) to say."[3] I added, "That ironically ambiguous comment of Schama's is what I would like to latch onto: it is too early, or possibly too late, after the passage of two hundred years, for a social researcher to comment on a great event. Be that as it may, the author of this book does not intend to wait. I accept all the risks and drawbacks of proximity to the events."[4]

I *could* not complete the book earlier and I did not *want* to do so any later.

I needed a long period of preparation for an extremely ambitious undertaking. I had to set about rethinking the synthesis time and time again. Early in the 1990s, so many slipshod writings were appearing whose authors had hastily cobbled together a few true or half-true propositions about communism. I wanted to contribute a finer work, in which every argument was thought through and strictly logical and every reference accurate, and the whole was amply illustrated with convincing data.

I felt I had to hurry. I remember entertaining at lunch at the Harvard Faculty Club a visiting Budapest sociologist and well-known figure in the democratic opposition. He asked what I was working on and I said I was writing my comprehensive account of the socialist system. I cannot forget his astonished expression. "Are you crazy?" his look seemed to be asking. "Spending your time on that? Now?" His derisive reaction was understandable. As I have just said, after 1989–1990 I was constantly being distracted from the book by tasks of the moment. If I were not capable of forcing myself then to write *The Socialist System*, regardless of the looks in others' faces, it would have stayed trapped inside me unwritten. I needed self-discipline and a sense of vocation to finish the book down to the last table and reference and send it off to the press.

It would have been a shame to let this go to waste. Others, of course, will write about the period later. Perhaps some will look back after several centuries, as Chou Enlai recommended, and be able to take a much more objective view. But they will be relying on our writings as a source. We were the eyewitnesses. That status gave special significance to the testimony of my generation, at least in Eastern Europe, for we were there as observers and participants from start to finish.

Recognition from East and West

The book brought a strong response from the economists' profession. More than forty reviews came out, or at least came to my attention. It was translated into German and French, and then into the languages of several then (or still) socialist countries: Bulgaria, Russia, and Vietnam. The mere presence of Vietnam is interesting. Think of a country where the Communist Party still holds a monopoly of power; there appears a book discussing dysfunctional consequences of that political structure for the economy and other spheres of society. Think of a country where "reform socialism" is the official party line; there appears a book underlining the hybrid and incomplete nature of such a process.*

Most of the reviews were very favorable. Let me quote two. The late Alec Nove, then the leading Soviet expert in Britain, called it "a truly remarkable achievement. Kornai's book can be read with much profit by citizens of both east and west, by economists and by whoever is interested in politics, by specialists in the affairs of communist-run countries and by student beginners. It is well organised, shows a

---

* There have also been moves to publish the book in China. The translation is ready, but it is still not certain whether the publisher will receive official approval.

mastery of the material and is a model of clarity of exposition. Its author combines a detailed knowledge of how 'eastern' institutions worked with an enviable grasp of relevant economic theory."[5] His article concludes by declaring that the book describes "with consummate skill the essential features of the system as it was, and why attempts to reform it have been so conspicuously unsuccessful. For this he deserves our gratitude and a large readership."[6]

Professor Richard Ericson of New York's Columbia University put it this way: "This is a truly monumental work, summarizing a lifetime of thought.... A masterful work, full of wisdom and insight."[7]

Rejection from right and left

The appreciative notices also contained some criticisms on matters of economics, of course. Some reactions went much further and rejected my whole message. Again, let me give two examples, as I did with the praise.

A long review appeared from Václav Klaus and Dušán Tříska, at a time when Klaus was serving as finance minister and leader of his party. His career later took off and he became prime minister. At present, he is president of the Czech Republic. Tříska was minister of privatization at the time of the review.

They had not a good word to say about my book. Their main objection—not only to this book, but to my whole oeuvre, they said—was that I had diverged unnecessarily from the tried methodology and conceptual framework of mainstream economics. This divergence, they opined, was unnecessary. The communist system did not show a single feature that could not be examined in the customary way, with optimization models and the arsenal of conventional micro- and macroeconomics.

The tone of the criticism became extremely irritated over my book's analysis of the Communist Party. The role of the public sphere, in their view, could be clarified fully in terms of public choice theory, which stated with general validity that a politician displayed behavior tending to maximize his or her power and material interests. To cover the case of the Communist Party, you simply had to augment that model with the well-known economic theory of monopoly. The Communist Party, like any monopolist, obstructed free entry to the political market.

University departments of political science, if they took this review to heart, would immediately dissolve and let their members retrain as neoclassical economists.

I am not in the habit of disputing with reviewers, and memoirs are the last place for professional polemics. Instead, let me ask one question—a psychological one, not one having to do with economics. What could possibly have prompted two senior politicians, up to their necks in major party matters and affairs of state, to write a detailed personal attack on a scholarly work and its author?

The other sharp rejection came from the opposite end of the political spectrum, from Tamás Krausz, a Hungarian historian.* Of his many complaints, perhaps the most important is that my work lacks a historical approach. He objected to the use of "sterile models robbed of specific historical bases." Elsewhere, he concludes, "From the historical point of view... the most basic methodological shortcoming in Kornai's work is not technical in nature, but the fact that he does not view the world economy as a structured unified whole, ruled by historically developed structural particularities (such as the system of linkages between the countries of the center, the semi-periphery, and the periphery; the structure of the division of labor; the relations of exclusion and exploitation; the unequal exchange and political and power relations, etc.)." I cannot resist adding another quotation:[8] "The realm of 'good' and 'bad' appears in the work as a struggle of two basic principles in the world: economic rationality and pure market logic on the one hand, and irrational state exploitation on the other."[†]

To Klaus and Tříska the fault of my book is that it does not stick loyally to the thoughts and apparatus of the neoclassical mainstream. Yet in Krausz's eyes, and here I quote him, I am "Hungary's coryphaeus of liberal economics."[9]

You cannot please everyone at once. If you have your own intellectual profile and your own sharply defined position, you cannot expect unanimous agreement or recognition for your work. It is not surprising, in fact it is understandable—and to me more reassuring than saddening—that *The Socialist System* did not appeal to Václav Klaus or Tamás Krausz.

A bizarre episode

I was informed toward the end of 1988 that I would shortly receive the order of merit "For a Socialist Hungary." It was bizarre indeed to be receiving that order while busily writing a book that rejected the socialist system.

I phoned a senior official at the Hungarian Academy of Sciences and told him I would not accept the award. It would be better if he could intervene and stop the procedure in its tracks. We argued. He asked me why I had accepted my earlier State Prize. I said it was because I saw it as recognition from the realm of scholarship, whereas the government was giving me this decoration with a clear political

---

* It is not within the scope of this book to identify the place of Tamás Krausz's work among the intellectual groupings of radical socialism. All I say here is that his views on my book seem to place him in what is known in the West as the New Left.

† I looked through my book several times to find a word about the irrationality or exploitative nature of the state, but without success.

purpose. I then hastened to put my position in a letter to several other Academy officials.

My intervention was unsuccessful. The Academy could not or would not halt the award process. I then received notice from my fellow academician, Brunó F. Straub, head of state of the People's Republic of Hungary, to come and receive the award. The news appeared in the official gazette. I therefore addressed a letter to the president: "I respectfully report that I do not accept the award. . . . The award has a political character and a political appearance. I disagree with the government's program and its general and economic policy. I have refrained for several decades from expressing my dissent in the form of oppositional actions. I would like to refrain no less from the opposite: accepting a government award that would express even tacit assent."[10]

Fending off the award "For a Socialist Hungary" and writing a book summing up my work, I took leave of the decisive experience of my life: the socialist system.

19

Turning Point—1989–1992
The Road to a Free Economy

They started to pull down the Berlin Wall on November 10, 1989.

I have often been asked whether I thought that would happen. Or to put it another way, had I reckoned on the collapse of the Soviet and East European socialist system?

My book *The Road to a Free Economy* (originally titled in Hungarian *Passionate Pamphlet in the Cause of Economic Transition*) appeared in the bookstores in November 1989. An effective retort might be that a tome is not written in a day; here is the evidence that I was expecting the collapse sometime before it happened.

The actual story is more complicated, though. I will try to give a faithful account.

The bounds of prediction

Had I forecast the collapse of the regime? Yes and no.

Yes: several hundred pages in *The Socialist System* support the hypothesis that internal reforms cannot save the system. Instead, they undermine its foundations. The more the oppression is lifted and the more bureaucratic discipline loosens, the less possible it becomes to maintain the old power relations.

No: Neither my book nor any other scientific analysis of the socialist system stated (or could have stated) exactly *when* the end was nigh.

We have arrived at a major problem of the philosophy of science, to which I can devote only a sentence or two. One way Einstein's theory of relativity could be tested was to derive from it a prediction about how the sun bent the rays from the stars. The theoretical assumption was tested and confirmed by astronomers during the solar eclipse of May 29, 1919.[1] The prediction was dead accurate, and Einstein was lauded worldwide. But laws governing the paths of heavenly bodies are far simpler than those of societies consisting of millions of people. It would show unwonted intellectual arrogance for a social scientist to claim prescience based on *scientific theory* about when and where a revolution or war would erupt.

Yes: Those with inside knowledge of the socialist system sensed increasing signs of disintegration in 1986 and 1987. The imminence of the crisis was apparent less in its economic woes (the Soviet economy had been worse off before—for instance, when Hitler's forces occupied the western parts of the country) than in mounting disenchantment among the political, economic, and military elite.*

As we drew near to the great event of the fall of the Berlin Wall, which in retrospect is generally agreed to mark the first day of a new historical era, processes signaling the end of the old regime were already at work: talks between the authorities and the opposition on Polish parliamentary elections, and Hungarian roundtable negotiations.

In any case, from the point of view of the great collapse the most important factor was not what happened in Hungary or Poland, although that certainly contributed to the erosion. The decisive events occurred in the Soviet Union. Although the reforms introduced in the second half of the 1980s did not achieve what Mikhail Gorbachev, their initiator and leader, had hoped—they did not lead to a renewal of socialism or strengthening of the Soviet Union—their effect proved to be of great significance in world history. The atmosphere became freer, the system "softened," and with this, a basic change occurred in Soviet foreign policy and military doctrine. Earlier, Soviet tanks had been dispatched to Hungary, Czechoslovakia, and even Afghanistan. It seemed, a few years before the collapse of the empire, that the Soviet Union would not be capable of such an intervention again, inside or outside its borders. That was a premonition, not any exact scientific prediction. Not that such foresight did not call for expert knowledge and the thorough grasp of the system necessary to evaluate the various observations, but a measure of intuition was needed as well. I count myself among those who guessed we were moving, indeed careering toward a crisis.

No, again: Though people felt the speed of events, no one was able to predict their amazing acceleration. It is easy to be wise in hindsight and even devise a mathematical model. The so-called chaos theory describes complex systems that—given a certain constellation of parameters—move on a more or less regular path, but can suddenly collapse if there are even small changes in a few parameters. That is what happened.

Everyone was guessing. Perhaps some experts in communism can confirm from their writings or utterances that they foretold the crash accurately five months

---

* Some recalled words of Lenin: "For a revolution to take place it is not enough for the exploited and oppressed masses to realise the impossibility of living in the old way, and demand changes; for a revolution to take place it is essential that the exploiters should not be able to live and rule in the old way" (1964 [1920], p. 97).

ahead. Even that proves nothing about when or how accurately such a unique occurrence in world history can be predicted. After all, there are usually winning tickets in lotteries, against odds of several million to one.

I must say the acceleration of events exceeded my wildest dreams.

Resolutions in the park of Harvard's Business School and on Budapest's Gellért Hill

I tried to prepare intellectually for imminent radical changes. I looked at books about Latin American military dictatorships and the initial experiences of democracies that replaced them. I returned to my macroeconomic textbooks to refresh my knowledge. I spoke to historians and quizzed them about how the crumbling and then collapse of great empires took place.*

I had several discussions at Harvard with my fellow professor Jeffrey Sachs about the prospects for radical change. He and his Czech-born wife Sonia were friends who had helped us settle down in Cambridge and taken us around Boston. Sachs had gained a great name for himself when his advice provided the basis for curbing hyperinflation in Bolivia. That had probably swayed Lech Wałesa and his economist advisers when they approached him to be economic adviser to Solidarność, before the collapse of communism. Sachs began to be strongly interested in Eastern Europe at that time, as I did in macroeconomic stabilization. So we had plenty to talk about.

More important than preparing myself technically was to decide how to behave if a political turn ensued. I wrote at the end of chapter 7 what strategy in life I had charted for myself after the 1956 Revolution. I could rightly say in the run-up to 1989 that I had behaved accordingly, with a few none-too-important inconsistencies. But now a new period in my life was starting.

I had lived hitherto under a political regime to which I was rationally, morally, and emotionally opposed. Now there was hope that democracy would arrive, a political and economic system that I considered acceptable. So the time was right to think of my future strategy in life. Should I make some essential career change at last?

I do not like to improvise. I do not always make good decisions on first impulse when forced to it. But I can think ahead about what situations may arise, and I like to prepare in advance rules of thumb, general criteria governing choice for making specific decisions.

---

* I remember a talk I had among friends around 1987, in which I asked this question in the presence of two eminent Hungarian historians. They stared at me in wonder. Although they were politically active, my analogy had never occurred to them before.

Among our favorite strolling places in Cambridge was the park of Harvard Business School, just across the river. There my wife and I chewed over these dilemmas as we walked in the early spring of 1989. News was coming from Budapest of events that stirred our feelings as well. The Opposition Roundtable had been launched on March 22, followed by "triangular" talks on June 10, with the party in power, the political opposition, and, as the "third party," representatives of non-governmental organizations. Then most exciting of all was something only glimpsed on U.S. television: the reburial on June 16 of Imre Nagy and his martyred associates, including Miklós Gimes, whose memory was still alive in my mind.

Arriving home at the end of the academic year, we heard important news almost every day. Just one example: the Hungarian government opened its western borders on August 1. East Germans who previously could not cross the West German border in their own country started flooding in great numbers across the Hungarian–Austrian border, trying to get to the West across Hungary. Mounting numbers of them waited for weeks in this country, mainly in Budapest, while the Hungarian government made its great decision to breach the Iron Curtain and let them across the border.

One of our favorite places for a Budapest stroll was Gellért Hill. We had hard emotional and ethical problems to address, which I will return to more than once. We managed on one walk to formulate the most important decisions. My wife and I discussed these things together, but I was the active one in public life and mine was the strategy we were mainly trying to clarify.

Our most important decision was that I would make no essential change in the direction of my career. Faced with the choice of being a politician or a scholar, I had stuck to the latter for thirty-two years and I would continue to do so.

I had broken with the Communist Party in 1956 and joined no other movement since. I would stick by that. I would not become a member of any of the newly forming parties, nor would I join any of the political movements.

My economic policy concept, political ideas, value system, and world outlook were firm. I had no reason to change them. I wanted to be consistent and true to my standpoint so far.

This continuation of my established path was primarily dictated by *principles*, not obstinacy or inability to change. In talking about the decisions I took in that historic period, I repeat what I have mentioned already as one of the guiding ideas in my life: I attach special value to consistency in my opinions of myself and others. A situation may arise in which people who have passed the highest moral test feel they must alter their opinion or value system concerning the basic issues of life. But I loathe those people who change their worldviews easily under the spell of power or money.

One essential change was required of me as the one-party system gave way to free elections and a multiparty system. I needed to be available with suggestions for helping my country back on its economic feet and for accomplishing the transition to a market economy. I had been focusing on positive scientific work. From then on, I had to give adequate emphasis to a normative approach and consider economic policy, too.

How *The Road to a Free Economy* was written

I received an invitation early in August 1989 to express my ideas on the economic tasks facing the country. The meeting took place in the large conference hall of KOPINT (Konjunktúra és Piackutató Intézet, the Institute for Economic and Market Research), and it was packed tight. The audience included several leaders and economic advisers from the emerging or already operating parties and movements that made up the opposition to the regime and many scientific researchers, including some who were later to hold leading political positions.

I had been thinking about the subject of the lecture for some months. I had tried to follow the thoughts forming in the minds of experts and members of the emerging parties and the proposals being incorporated into their programs.

I was well prepared for the lecture. Nevertheless, I went to deliver it in a state of great tension and excitement, though this was not apparent in my demeanor or tone of voice. Many members of the audience were spending those weeks dashing from one meeting to the next. I suppose for them my lecture was one of many, but for me the occasion was a special event and a turning point. Thirty-three years earlier, in the summer of 1956, I had been a young, naive reformer putting forward comprehensive proposals before the Institute of Economics. A few weeks later, I had been charged by Imre Nagy's closest associates with preparing an economic program that was never compiled and never presented to Parliament by the revolutionary government as originally intended. I had not come up with a comprehensive set of proposals since. The lecture opened a new phase in my personal career and I experienced the moment with great inner emotion.

My hour's lecture was followed by lively comments in support of and opposition to what I had said, questions and answers.

Two days later, I felt an extremely painful spasm in my lower back: lumbago, or *Hexenschuß* (witch's shot), as the Germans aptly call it. You feel unable to move an inch. I dragged myself gingerly to bed and spent the next ten weeks flat on my back. The doctors determined that the excruciating pain came from a nerve trapped between two vertebrae. I was prescribed injections, strong drugs, and later exercises and swimming to loosen the spasm.

Jumping ahead in time, let me mention that I paid a visit in 1990 to Professor Sarno of New York, a specialist outside the mainstream of rheumatology—another profession with a mainstream!—whose theory was that spasms in the organs of locomotion and other irregularities could be traced back to tension and stress. He gave me some useful advice on how to prevent such problems. Diagnosing as my own amateur doctor, I think that this is what surely happened to me in the summer of 1989. I fell literally ill from the feeling of great responsibility that now I *could*—and, because of an inner imperative, I *should*—contribute to the program for national recovery. Even if there were no others, this would be a cogent argument against my assuming any role as a politician. What would happen if a politician fell ill whenever there was an important public appearance to be made?

As the pain became more bearable, I wished to continue with the work. I wanted first to turn my lecture into an article, but as I began to express myself, it soon became apparent that this was going to be a book, not an article. I had always written out all my studies and books myself, for a long time on a typewriter and more recently on a computer. This time I had no choice but to make an exception and dictate the text. The hard task of turning the dictation from my sickbed into a text ready for the press fell to my immediate colleagues. This work dragged on for weeks.

It is heart-warming to look back on the many affectionate and helpful gestures surrounding me. My kind friend, the rheumatologist Dr. Géza Bálint, often visited my sickbed, and he personally took care of me. When I began to recover, another friend, the physiotherapist Eszter Draskóczy, began to direct my exercises. If my wife had to go anywhere and I could not be left without supervision, as was the case early in my illness, my sister-in-law Mariann Dicker or a friend of ours would be beside me. I had a string of visitors, and as the manuscript progressed, I gave it to several people for comment. Economists from several political organizations came to consult with me. Journalists turned up too. I remember my first meeting with the unforgettable Katalin Bossányi; sitting down with uninhibited ease on the side of my bed, she held a microphone in front of me and began a lengthy interview.

The Road to a Free Economy was ready on the sixth weekend of my stay in bed. I had never had so energetic or kind an editor as Ágnes Erényi to see a book through. By a miracle (by the standards of the time), she had it in the bookshops by mid-November.

Initial reactions

First comments on the book began to appear in the Hungarian press (dailies, weeklies, and monthlies) within days of its launch. A short appreciation by Gáspár Miklós Tamás was called "The Kornai Bomb." Even though there had been an ongoing and wide-ranging discussion, both orally and in writing, about the handling of the crisis and the transformation ahead, *The Road to a Free Economy* had certainly burst into the course of the debate.

One of my doctors, between tapping on my back and administering an injection, remarked, "Even the faucets are flowing with Kornai now." Within a few weeks, at least fifty pieces appeared in connection with the book. All kinds of voices were heard. Many welcomed the book enthusiastically. Others took an intermediate approach, at points agreeing and at other points disagreeing with my position, and a number of commentators expressed strong opposition to my proposals. The objections were mainly raised in a well-reasoned, cultured way, but some crude personal attacks also appeared in the press. Here I was confronted again with the kind of argumentation I mentioned in an earlier chapter: Take your opponent's remarks, give an essential point a twist, take it out of its context, and then quarrel with *that* proposition.

The book became a best seller and was reprinted several times. It took about three months for the debate to reach a climax, and then it died down. The press and public opinion went on to something else.

I should have gone back to America in September 1989 for the start of the academic year, but my illness meant we went to Cambridge only toward the end of the calendar year. From there, we watched the debate subside. Meanwhile the English text was being prepared.

The American edition was given the title *The Road to a Free Economy: Shifting from a Socialist System: The Example of Hungary*, the main title echoing Hayek's classic *Road to Serfdom*. Both the title and foreword made clear that the specific proposals were for Hungary, but the author had tried to frame them in a way that lent them relevance to economic transformation in other countries as well. Editions in other languages appeared. Taking them in order of appearance, they came out in Russian (three editions from three different publishers), Czech, Slovak, French, Italian, Spanish, Polish, Ukrainian, Estonian, Japanese, Serbian, Tamil and Sinhalese (both spoken in Sri Lanka), Chinese (first in the People's Republic, and later from another publisher in Taiwan), and, finally, Vietnamese.*

The reactions were strong and swift in each case. Articles appeared in prestigious papers from the *New York Times* to *Le Monde* and from *Neue Zürcher Zeitung* to the *Financial Times*.[2] Reactions were mixed, as they had been in Hungary, ranging from enthusiastic appreciation, through a blend of praise and reservations, to angry rejection. It was disliked especially by those eager to replace state socialism with a non-communist but still non-capitalist system of some kind.

---

* Altogether, the book appeared in seventeen languages. As far as I know, this is the record for any work of social science by a Hungarian author.

I revised the original Hungarian for the English-language edition, making some corrections and additions and responding to observations made about the Hungarian edition. I also published the changes in the Hungarian economics journal *Közgazdasági Szemle*.[3] Editions in all other languages were based on that revised English text.

I gave some lectures and published articles in journals closely connected with *The Road to a Free Economy*, broadening the application of some points and exploring others in more detail.

I was asked in 1990 to deliver the annual lecture in the Netherlands in honor of Jan Tinbergen. I was lucky to see him again—tired physically, but mentally fresh as ever—for he had been a mentor of mine early in my career. I used the lecture to expound my views on the principles of privatization.[4]

In 1992, the American Economic Association did me the great honor of inviting me to deliver the Ely Lecture at its annual congress. There I spoke on the role of the state in the post-socialist period.[5] The lecture included a sentence for which I have been much criticized since, although I still stand by it: the socialist system gave rise to a "premature welfare state."

I also delivered in 1992 the Myrdal Lecture in Stockholm, in honor of the great Swedish economist Gunnar Myrdal. I spoke of tightening up financial discipline and hardening the budget constraint.[6]

When I refer to *The Road to a Free Economy* in what follows, I include the texts of these lectures, which is why I have ended the period in the chapter title with 1992. Let me now summarize the main proposals in the book and the connected lectures and add some of the immediate reactions. I add an assessment made with today's eyes.

An end to simulation

The Road to a Free Economy sharply criticized the inconsistent ideas for changing ownership relations in the final stage of reform socialism. There was to be a capital market without real private capital, cross-ownership of stakes in state-owned enterprises, "holding companies" managed by state bureaucrats behaving like owners, enterprise self-management like Yugoslavia's, and so on. I wrote that I was

fed up with this practice of simulation. We have already tried our hand at simulating quite a number of things. The state-owned firm simulates the behavior of the profit-maximizing firm. Bureaucratic industrial policy, regulating the expansion or contraction of various branches of production, simulates the role of competition. The Price Control Office simulates the market in price determination. The most recent additions to this list are the simulated joint stock companies, the simulated capital market, and the simulated stock exchange. Together, these developments all add up to Hungary's Wall Street—all made of plastic! . . . These same banks, joint stock companies, and stock exchange are but fakes. What is going on here is a kind of peculiar "Monopoly" game, in which the gamblers are not kids but adult officials, who do not play with paper money but risk real state funds.[7]

Hungarian economists who had been seeking to advance reform of the socialist economy by cooperating with enlightened members of the economic and party elites receptive to change winced at the criticism. They had been actors and initiators, even chief ideologists, in that process. I have given in detail in an earlier chapter my assessment of their activity and the relationship of this group to my work. I can now say, rereading the reactions to *The Road to a Free Economy* fifteen years later, that the leading "reform economists" were the ones who rejected my proposals most sharply, sometimes in a crude, insulting tone unworthy of debate among intellectuals.

The economist Iván Szegvári wrote, "Kornai's book has so far caused stupefaction, strong antipathy and intellectual digestive disorders among this country's economists... The confusion has been caused primarily because Kornai questions a number of axioms of the economics of Hungarian reform. This is extremely uncomfortable retrospectively and in terms of the future. Retrospectively because it obliges people to confront their intellectually too comfortable claims as reformers that the truth, i.e., the content of true reform, is known and has simply been sabotaged by politics, state administration, or the internal and external forces of reform generally."[8] András Semjén saw a social psychological effect behind the angry retorts. The book, he writes, "states that the emperor is naked, that it is fruitless to clothe state property in fancy dress for that will not mean it behaves like private property. It was not enough for us to forget our 'Soc. pol. econ.'* Now it turns out that several ostensible achievements of the reform economic ideas we formed as an antidote are simply ballast from which we have to be freed!"[9]

The most important point in the book, if its messages had to be ranked in that way, would certainly be that, in my opinion: The patching and darning of socialism had to end. There was no third road. That position was stated unequivocally in the Hungarian text, but in the English, I wanted to emphasize it further through the title. The use of a definite article—*The Road*, not *A Road*—deliberately stresses that in my view, there is no third road. The post-socialist countries, as they break with the socialist system, have to follow the road that leads to the capitalist system.[†]

---

* The officially instilled "socialist political economy" of the pre-reform period.

† I was honored in 1991 to be invited to deliver the Tanner Lecture at Stanford. (Earlier lecturers had included Raymond Aron, Kenneth J. Arrow, Saul Bellow, Joseph Brodsky, Michel Foucault, Jürgen Habermas, Václav Havel, Robert Nozick, Karl Popper, John Rawls, Richard Rorty, and Helmut Schmidt.) My title was "Market Socialism Revisited" (1993b); in the lecture, I defined in more detail than in earlier studies or *The Road to a Free Economy* what social and political factors stood in the way of applying Oskar Lange's theoretical vision.

The subject seemed to have been dropped from the agenda for a while, but the vision of a third road (or third way, as many authors call it) is imperishable and is just beginning to revive. Capitalism is inevitably replete with injustices and infringements of human dignity. People are all the angrier with the prevailing conditions when economic troubles appear. Few people have any desire to see the old regime back, but many people turn a sympathetic ear to calls for rejecting the new regime. The flood of ideas includes the "third road" versions of the old: romantic, "people's" anti-capitalism; Nazi-style hatred of bankers; campaigning against plutocracy and robber capitalism; and New Left demonization of multi-national corporations and globalization. Many of these standpoints should be criticized not so much for their economic content but rather for their hazy analysis and conceptual confusion. That is the case with the moderate social democratic proposals that actually go no further than quiet reform of the relation between the state and the economy; still, they sound better if they too are called the "third way."

Looking back, I think that *The Road to a Free Economy* had the virtue of trying to speak the plain, simple truth at a time when economic thinking in Eastern Europe was full of fudged concepts and ideas. It called a spade a spade. That is still a pertinent requirement today.

For the healthy development of the private sector

The book saw the transformation of ownership relations as the prime economic task of the change of system. I followed the line of argument I had presented in *The Socialist System*, showing that ownership relations lie deeper and are more decisive than forms of coordination (such as the relative weight of market forces or bureaucratic regulation). The aim should not be a *socialist* market economy or even just a market economy (the phrase was popular at the time), but a real, *capitalist* market economy in which private ownership played a dominant role.

I would like here to raise the position I expressed in the book to an international plane. Economists at that time recommended one of two courses of action. One strategy that was first recommended by *The Road to a Free Economy* supported the *organic development of the private sector*. The prime tasks were to dismantle the great barriers to private enterprise and liberalize entry into production. Start-ups of new private firms had to be allowed and even encouraged. The property rights of the state-owned enterprises should not be squandered but should be sold at fair prices. Free distribution of state property should be avoided. If a state-owned enterprise was not viable it had to be liquidated. All these developments had to be accompanied by a hardening of the budget constraint.

Such a change in ownership relations could be accomplished only gradually, not at a gallop, and it has therefore been known in Western debates as the *gradualist strategy*.

The rival proposal focused on disposing of state property as quickly as possible. This was the strategy of *accelerated privatization*. Proponents argued that as the old state-owned enterprises could not be sold overnight, the state should not wait for a proper buyer but should distribute to every citizen vouchers representing state assets. Each citizen has a right to his or her share of the state property; and by lodging the voucher with an investment fund, every individual would gain a stake in the enterprises formerly owned by the state. Those who recommended this approach were not against new private firms being started, but they wished to focus the attention of politicians, economists, and the state administration on voucher privatization instead. *The Road to a Free Economy* argued strongly that plans for free distribution were misguided: "It leaves me with the impression that Daddy state has unexpectedly passed away and left us, his orphaned children, to distribute the patrimony equitably....The point now is not to hand out the property, but rather to place it into the hands of a really better owner."[10]

I was able to become acquainted with the opinions of Milton Friedman and Paul Samuelson, two great and perhaps the two best-known scholars of American economics, on the pace of privatization.* Milton Friedman made his remarks in a letter. He recognized the value of my work, and agreed with several of the book's proposals. However, he did not concur with my gradualist views on privatization.†

In my answer, I argued for my own view, not just in the matter of privatization but in connection with other issues too, and then added: "I feel that there is a common cause to our disagreement and that is the difference in distance from the area we are discussing. I look at this area from the inside, from Budapest, Warsaw or Prague, and I feel that the given point of departure must be taken into account realistically. I admit at the same time that somebody looking at these countries from a much longer distance may see important issues that are lost to those who are

---

* Kenneth Arrow, Martin Feldstein, Richard Musgrave, and Jeffrey Sachs also made comments on the book when it was still in rough translation. Limitations of space prevent me from discussing their comments.

† Friedman distanced himself from me on another issue as well. He fiercely opposed the recommendation that during the time of transition, exchange rates should be fixed by the state. He saw this as incompatible with the requirements of market freedom. I was not able to share his view. Like others, I was convinced that in the first few stormy years of transition, there was a need for fixed exchange rates. This "anchor" would help the new relative prices form and stabilize.

perhaps too deeply involved in local situations. Therefore I welcome your critical remarks and I will certainly think them over again."[11]

Samuelson first made his comments during a conversation over lunch in the MIT Faculty Club, and a few weeks later he published an article in an American daily.* The first half of the piece deals with reform in China, and then he turns to my new book. "I have just seen its [i.e., the *Passionate Pamphlet*'s] English translation and recommend it highly." He expounds several of the book's proposals, including those aimed at the development of the private sector: "The citizenry, Kornai insists, should develop 'social respect' toward the private sector. Envy and equating of profit-earners with crooks and sharks is counterproductive. Hungary is in need of a *new middle class* [emphasis his]. Napoleon spoke slightingly of England as a nation of shopkeepers. Kornai is no Napoleon."[12]

Let us return to the two types of strategy for developing the private sector. Behind the alternatives lay a choice of values. Advocates of integral development attached special importance to society's undergoing restratification and embourgeoisement, in order to produce a new middle class of owners and entrepreneurs, while believers in free distribution worshipped speed. "Speed was regarded as absolutely essential," wrote Václav Klaus and Dušan Tříska in an article about my book *The Socialist System*, "and therefore no strategy was regarded as feasible unless it was capable of producing results fast."[13]

The view of the "accelerators" gained the upper hand in the debates among Western economists in Washington's international financial institutions, politicians, and academic economists at leading universities. A few thought as I did and favored gradualism, but ours was a minority view in the West. Most of the Western advisers who influenced the governments undergoing post-socialist transition favored the strategy of accelerated privatization.

The course of events differed from country to country. In some, high proportions of state assets were handed out free; in others, small proportions or hardly any. Russia was the prime case of forced-pace privatization, which there contributed greatly to encouraging an almost irreversible, unfortunate process of world-historical weight as it produced an extreme concentration of assets in the hands of a few "oligarchs."

Hungary also had loud and influential advocates of a handout scheme and a bill to that effect was introduced in Parliament. But ultimately, the strategy of accelerated privatization was rejected in favor of the kind of sequence of events recommended in *The Road to a Free Economy*. No one could say whether the book played a direct role in that decision.

---

* Even the title of the article is highly flattering: "For Plan to Reform Socialism, Listen to János Kornai" (Samuelson 1990).

Most experts ten to fifteen years later agree, in hindsight, that the gradualists were right.*

It is also worth mentioning a mistake in the arguments about ownership in *The Road to a Free Economy*. My proposals did not rule out an influx of foreign capital and pointed to the advantages of foreign direct investment. But I did not stress that enough. I did not foresee that such investment would be the strongest motor of the Hungarian economy and the new private sector, playing a pivotal part in developing exports and technology.

Responsibility for public funds

If the private sector is to increase gradually, not in leaps and bounds, then the state-owned sector cannot disappear suddenly. State property and private property will continue to exist side by side for a considerable time. *The Road to a Free Economy* expressed my distrust of state ownership. I objected to the head of a state-owned enterprise being viewed as an entrepreneur and receiving the independence and commercial freedom allowed a manager responsible to real owners for a company's performance. Those doing business with state money are not entrepreneurs. I was especially afraid of schemes that sought to hand companies over to their employees but actually allowed them to fall into the hands of the managers.

You have to beware of the claws of the executives of state-owned enterprises, I urged, and experience would prove me right. It is a shame I made a clumsy attempt to translate a good idea into legislative language. (For instance, I proposed that Parliament approve the main state-sector allocations.) Those who battled consistently during the market socialist reforms to enhance the power of heads of state-owned enterprise scolded me sarcastically for trying to reinstate the Stalinist planning system.[†]

Sadly, the real warning in *The Road to a Free Economy* was ignored. The operation and privatization of the state-owned enterprises, less dominant but still numerous, came to be surrounded by abuses and corruption. The administrative and political controls were insufficient, the privatization procedures lacked transparency, and the press and the public lost track of what was happening. Of course, these difficulties were not confined just to Hungary; they accompanied the privatization process in every country in the region.

---

* Jeffrey Sachs agreed with me initially, but then became an advocate of acceleration. I remember the conversations in which we tried in vain to persuade each other. Much later, when he saw the developments in Russia, he conceded that I had been right.

† It is interesting to reflect on the fact that the proposals on state-owned enterprises aroused protests only in Hungary, where they would have robbed executives of privileges hard-won through the reforms. They were not targeted by any of the many criticisms from abroad.

My book actually set out to explore a much more general issue: how public spending can be publicly controlled through democratic processes. Supervision of state-owned enterprises is just one aspect of such control, albeit an important one. I illustrated the point in the book with a topical problem of the time:

There is debate now about whether Hungary should undertake to host the 1995 World Expo. The issue is scheduled to go before Parliament...I propose the following.

Those government officials, committee members, and ministerial commissioners who assume responsibility for the motion should offer as mortgage their own personal assets: their condominium flats, private houses, second homes, cars, and art objects....Of course, the value of these assets will cover only a fraction of the expected investment costs. But these mortgages should still represent a considerable part of these persons' total material wealth accumulated during their life work.

The bill on the World Expo should hold out the prospect of a lavish bonus for the drafters of the motion, with the proviso that the event will come off as promised. The same bill should prescribe the full foreclosure of the mortgages in case the exhibition is a failure.

In my opinion these conditions would make it perfectly clear to the drafters what it is like to run a risk that might affect their own pocket.[14]

That ironical parable was quoted several times in Parliament. In the end, the government decided against holding the World Expo, though I would not say we drew any closer to the condition to which the proposal was drawing attention: the assumption of consistent personal responsibility by those spending public money.

Surgery for stabilization

Looking back today, I see both pertinent and erroneous ideas in the chapter of *The Road to a Free Economy* dealing with macroeconomics.

I feel it was right to stress the need to curb inflation. The region faced a real danger that inflation would speed up. Several post-socialist countries suffered a mounting problem with this in subsequent years. Inflation in Hungary had been rising year by year in the years leading up to the change of system,[15] reaching 17 percent in the year *The Road to a Free Economy* came out.* The emphasis on restoring budgetary equilibrium was also justified. But there was no consensus on these matters when *The Road to a Free Economy* appeared. Many saw high inflation and a high budget deficit as natural accompaniments of the transformation, and therefore as not worth combating nor even possible to tackle. The need for fiscal and monetary discipline was far from self-evident.

One key assumption in the book's macroeconomic proposals proved wrong: that production would not fall. Some experts saw that the radical changes in domestic

---

* The book's strongly worded advice was rejected by the government. Inflation rose further; the cost of living went up by 35 percent in 1991.

structure, the shrinkage of Eastern European markets, and the competition caused by goods coming from abroad as imports were gradually liberalized would reduce demand for domestically produced goods, causing a chain-reaction downward spiral in supply and demand and leading to a deep recession.

The Road to a Free Economy caused a stir by calling for *rapid* macro stabilization and related price liberalization, as opposed to a *gradual* alteration in ownership relations. I prescribed surgery for the sick Hungarian economy. Let me start this account with a note on terminology. The phrase "shock therapy" became widespread in international debates at the time, but I avoided it as far as I could, for two reasons. Those advocating shock therapy were pressing for very rapid action on both privatization and restoration of the macro equilibrium, whereas I was a gradualist on ownership relations while advocating swift and radical action in macro stabilization. So I was concerned to have the word "stabilization" in my formula. My other quarrel with the phrase concerned its dreadful associations. By that time, people in Hungary were already familiar with Ken Kesey's novel *One Flew over the Cuckoo's Nest*, which had also been made into an excellent movie. The rough, rebellious hero (played by Jack Nicholson in the film) is forced to take electroconvulsive treatment (ECT) that destroys his mind. The usefulness of ECT in psychiatry is debatable, but the very analogy would have been counterproductive and misleading. In stabilizing the economy, the "shock" is probably not an instrument of treatment. It can rather be viewed as a side effect, perhaps worth tolerating for the sake of favorable results expected in the end.

To return to the debates of 1989–1990, I became isolated in Hungary with my proposal for stabilization surgery, which was not accepted by other economists or any influential political forces. This rapid, radical solution was put into effect in some other countries, notably Poland, the Czech Republic, and Russia. In the first two, it was remarkably successful, refuting the prediction of some *Passionate Pamphlet* critics that stabilization surgery was doomed from the outset.* In the case of Russia, experts at home and abroad still debate whether the stabilization carried out with dramatic speed and many victims was necessary or should have been avoided, and whether it was ultimately beneficial or instead detrimental to the country's future development.

As readers can see, I have returned to my 1989 book with self-critical eyes. I have not shrunk from criticizing my earlier views, but I have to say that I cannot reach a

---

* The expression "stabilization surgery" brought out the black humor in my critics. "The operation succeeded but the patient died," they quipped, or "Doctor, are we operating or doing a postmortem?" Joking aside, it has been shown in many countries that speeding up stabilization has both advantages and drawbacks, so that the outcome may ultimately be favorable or unfavorable; but viewing the process as a deadly threat seems to have been a strong exaggeration.

firm conclusion concerning this issue. The populist economic policy of "goulash communism" survived in Hungary for many years after 1989. Governments came and went, but each tried to postpone restoring the macroeconomic equilibrium with what would necessarily be painful and unpopular measures. These populist features brought the country to the brink of crisis in 1995 (as I will discuss in the next chapter). At that juncture, there were politicians and economists ready to acknowledge that it would have been better to have accepted in 1990 the proposals in *The Road to a Free Economy* and introduced a package to restore macro equilibrium. It would have been painful to do so in 1990 or 1991, but the burden on the public would have been lighter than it was five years later. Moreover, it would have been easier to gain acceptance for the necessary sacrifices amid the initial euphoria over the change of system than it became after many had become disillusioned.

"What if…" questions are of interest in historical analysis, but ultimately they cannot be answered. It can certainly be said that the *political will* for stabilization surgery was lacking and the country's economic situation was not yet critical enough to force it into being.

On balance

Looking back on the books of those crucial years, I wonder whether I timed my tasks and divided my energies well. Should I not have rushed to publish *The Socialist System* sooner instead? Should I not have held on to *The Road to a Free Economy* longer and honed its ideas?*

I have answered the first question in the previous chapter, where I declared that no, I was not trying to contribute to issues of the moment with *The Socialist System*. If it is not boastful, I would say I meant the book for posterity, for people who would want as reliable a comprehensive eyewitness account as possible. So let the evidence be accurate. I attached importance to every sentence and every description and did not want to rush anything.

The *Road to a Free Economy*, on the other hand, was designed to contribute to the topical issues of *tomorrow*—the near future and the transition from socialism to capitalism. I felt that if I was a bit ahead of the field in having my thoughts pre-

---

* I was invited by the World Bank in 1999 to give a lecture in Washington. My lecture's title was "Ten Years after *The Road to a Free Economy*: The Author's Self Evaluation" (2001). I took several aspects of my proposals and assessed what had happened and how I saw them now. Some I could still support, but some I criticized ten years after. I was naive again. I thought the tenth anniversary of the change of system would prompt many responsible decision makers and influential advisers to reexamine their earlier ideas self-critically. It was not to be. I am afraid that I remained alone in my quixotic act of self-auditing.

pared, I had a duty to advance them as soon as possible. As I pointed out in the personal postcript, "I tried to write the study very quickly, although that is no excuse, of course, for any errors it may contain. In any case I refrained on this occasion from the repeated textual revisions permitted in more leisurely research."[16] I knew that this approach was risky. Haste might easily leave faults uncorrected. Those publishing later could learn from the debate on the first work to appear. Many authors duly came up, a year or two later, with more considered, thorough proposals, although these were not invariably nearer the mark.

One means of minimizing inaccuracies and exaggerations is teamwork. Economic policy issues had come up earlier, at the roundtable negotiations, although there the political and constitutional questions of the change of system had been the center of attention.[17] As I was writing the book at high speed, alone in bed, the economic policy program of several of the parties and other political organizations were either in the making or already completed.[18] There were two distinguished committees at work in Budapest working in the usual committee way,[19] preparing materials, calling periodic meetings, holding debates, reaching agreements, and, finally, producing proposals. Their conclusions resembled mine in many ways, but were far less strongly expressed, provocative, and effective in inciting a wide debate.

I am aware that circumspect preparation of legislation, government rulings, or great plans of action calls for collective thinking, teamwork, and consensus. I admire colleagues who give much of their time and energy to committee work, but frankly, I have always tried to avoid tasks of that kind. I like to express *my position* clearly and shrink from involvement in making concessions to reach general consent. That too is necessary, I know, but I like to leave it to those who are more flexible, more diplomatic, and less irritable when they are obliged to concede. The democratic process of decision making calls for a preparatory stage when alternative views are expressed in the rougher form found before the edges are smoothed. Then comes the stage of setting these against each other and devising an *acceptable* proposal. Here as elsewhere, I believe in the division of labor and, if possible, I position myself at the first stage. I do not usually need anyone's leave to do so, just my own initiative and a willingness to risk expressing myself strongly.

Reactions were mixed again. One reviewer called my drawing up a national economic program by myself a "unique intellectual achievement." Others disliked my acting as a "lone warrior." Rereading the book and the debate, my feelings were mixed. I looked at the reaction abroad with professional interest without any particular emotions, but the Hungarian debate moved me emotionally. Even though I was not as deeply excited as I had been eighteen to twenty years earlier, I was touched again by the mood of a historic moment. Real turning points are rare for whole nations and just as exceptional for individuals.

It was good to think that writing *The Road to a Free Economy* had given me a part in those events as well. Whether any of my proposals were right or wrong, accepted or rejected, I can certainly say I had an appreciable influence on public thinking. All the questions I addressed were in the air in Hungary at the time, being argued over by various political groups and referred to briefly in program materials that the parties were just producing, but their form was still fluid and, from the point of view of intellectual discipline, disjointed. I see *The Road to a Free Economy*'s significance in the way it *structured* an amorphous debate, stating priorities and setting the agenda.* Once it had burst into the Hungarian discourse, the debate about what we should be debating became less controversial. It even influenced those who angrily rejected what I had written, without noticing that they too were discussing what the book had put into the public mind.

The good feelings as I read the book and the debate on it in Hungary were joined by some bad memories, too. I was struck by an unfriendly, even antagonistic tone in some comments. I have a thin skin and find it hard to put up with abuse, especially if it comes from people I have been close to in the past. That (among other things) just shows I am not fit to be a politician. But what were a few crude lapses in the tone of this debate compared with what became a daily occurrence in Hungarian public life? How could I swallow the insults flung at me and continue a public speech unperturbed while I was put out by unfair articles that turned my words around—positively mild compared with the style now commonly employed?

After a while, I got over my bitterness and did not give much thought to the attacks for many years. It was a typical case of Freudian repression. The events were in my unconscious; when recalled, they triggered not only a rational reappraisal but the old emotional reaction.

The book was not in the shops before Pál Réti, an editor of the business weekly *HVG*, interviewed me. One of his questions was, "Do you not think your program would gain acceptance more easily if it were some party's, not 'above party'?"

I wrote and published the book before the country's first free general elections. I addressed it primarily to the future Parliament and government that would form out of the democratic process, at a time when I still could not know their political makeup. This was my answer to the journalist: "I do not imagine we should put our trust in some advisory body above parties that would listen to my proposals and then implement them. That can only be done if some party or parties with the support of a majority in Parliament adopts them and there is no opposition force

---

* To use a term popular with Hungarian political analysts and journalists in 2004, it thematized the economic debate. The expression "thematization" is among the most fashionable at the moment. Fashions like this fade as quickly as they come. It may easily happen that later readers of this book no longer understand the expression.

outside Parliament that could obstruct them." Then the interviewer asked me a follow-up: "Would you be prepared to be an adviser in the future, or even take a political role?" I replied, "I would like to remain fundamentally a man of science; I do not want to be a minister, a member of Parliament, or an appointed adviser."[20] I added that if a member of the new government was interested in my opinion, I would be glad to state it.

But that is the subject of the next chapter.

20

On the Boundaries between Science and Politics—1990 Onward

Highway and Byways
Struggle and Hope
Welfare, Choice, and Solidarity in Transition

Let us return to March 1990, when Jeffrey Sachs and I organized a conference to which we invited several economists from countries undergoing a change of system; all were working in universities and academic institutes and known to have an interest in practical politics as well. It was held at the UN University's WIDER institute in Helsinki, where I had earlier started writing *The Socialist System*. We had exciting debates about stabilization, privatization, and the political alternatives for the transition. Toward the end of the second session, a Czech economist announced that he could not stay any longer and had to hurry home. Half ironically and half seriously, he added, "Anyone not in Wenceslaus Square now will not be a minister."

His haste paid off; he was soon made a minister. It is interesting today to look down the list of participants. Most served for longer or shorter periods in the 1990s as minister, central bank governor, or legislator, or in other high political posts.*

As for me, I did not rush to any Hungarian Wenceslaus Square. I was sounded out by various political factions right at the beginning and later on as well as to whether I wanted to enter the political arena. I was offered various posts—minister, chief party adviser, member of Parliament. Once it was leaked to the papers that I was being considered for the presidency of the central bank. In fact, I respectfully declined all offers at the sounding-out stage. I can honestly say I was not tempted by any prospect of political power.

I was not appointed to any high post and so could not be dismissed from any. Because I did not climb hurriedly up the ladder, I did not fall off its top with similar alacrity, as many did. I abided by the resolutions referred to earlier, staying basically in the field of research and teaching. Yet I had ceased to feel that forces opposed to my principles exercised undivided power in the country. In a democracy, everyone bears responsibility for what is happening. I had to acknowledge that I faced a new

---

* The same applied in Hungary, where many leading political personalities on all sides were drawn from the academic and university world.

situation as a researcher and teacher as well. From then on, I would be working on the boundaries between science and politics.

Positions on Hungary's macroeconomic policies

Declining politically powerful offices by no means meant I had become indifferent to the events of Hungarian politics. On the contrary, I tried to observe and understand what was going on during the post-socialist transition, whether I was in Budapest or Cambridge, and I published a succession of pieces on topical issues, almost all going beyond straight analysis and making economic policy recommendations. Let me mention just a few of the subjects: the principles of privatization, how to strengthen financial discipline, the need to alter the role of the state, and the values to be applied in reforming the pension system or health care.

The research behind those writings was combined with a new spate of intense study. All I had learned before, I tried to refresh and augment with recent findings in micro- and macroeconomics. I had not had anyone around me in my youth whom I could ask for guidance. Now I was fortunate in living in one of the world's intellectual centers of economics. If I wanted advice, I could consult with the best experts on any question.

The studies appeared in professional journals. Classifying my work by my own system of values, I would say that the studies I wrote in this period for a learned audience, like the books discussed in previous chapters, were my essential achievement, not just for the research results they embodied but for their contribution to economic policy making. But I would also assess with a critical eye the occasions that prompted me to put my ideas before a wider public.

Many intellectuals gladly use the columns of the daily papers to spread their conclusions and recommendations more promptly, frequently, and widely. They also seize opportunities to speak to hundreds of thousands on television. I am aware that doing so can serve the public interest well if a convincing case is made for a good cause. I do not want to advance any "elitist" or "aristocratic" arguments for using this form of publication only in exceptional cases. I take a liberal view on this as on other matters of conduct. I respect those who undertake to appear often in the mass media, provided they do it well, but I also respect the conduct of those who avoid such appearances. As for me, I nervously and reluctantly bring myself to carry out such tasks, and therefore I take on such things quite rarely. I have opinions on many matters, but I usually decline to offer an immediate reaction to most questions.* Clever politicians are capable of delivering a pertinent, concise sound bite

---

* I was often sought by television presenters and journalists in the United States as well, eager for short, sharp reactions on the latest events. I declined on all but a few occasions.

that sums up their position. I find that style of utterance very inconvenient. If I cannot have time to express my arguments, I would rather say nothing at all.

My face is not known on television and I am not stopped and asked questions in the street. Sometimes I briefly envy the experts and scholars who have gained a nationwide reputation on television and in the press, but then I dismiss such vain thoughts and feel glad that I have kept to my own genre.

I mentioned there were some exceptions to the general rule. I have sometimes been prompted—mainly by problems seen in the Hungarian economy—to write a lengthy article on macroeconomic concerns of the day.* I wrote a long piece in 1992 in the daily *Magyar Hírlap* (*Hungarian Newspaper*), on the macroeconomic problems at the time.[1] I was depressed by the stagnation in the economy and urged cautious adjustment, a "half-turn" leading to greater stress on growth in the real economy. That article led to the notion of a half-turn becoming something of a by-word in Hungary. Its subsequent usage confirmed my views on the danger of loosing an idea or a clear, apt expression into the political arena. The reasoning in the article was accurate and it contained caveats about the need to apply the concept circumspectly, but in vain. Who could stop an idea from being used in battle, as the interests of various political forces dictated?

I was spurred by an increasingly worrying macroeconomic situation to speak out again in 1994. There was a battle inside me between concern for equilibrium, aroused especially by the deterioration of the current account, and a conviction that too restrictive an intervention would stifle economic growth. Other economists had already sounded the alarm, but I pondered over the matter for a while. Finally, I made up my mind, too. I wrote, at a gallop, a journal-length article titled (in the later English translation) "Lasting Growth as the Top Priority: Macroeconomic Tensions and Government Economic Policy in Hungary." Pressed by my always helpful friend Katalin Bossányi, I let the daily *Népszabadság* (*People's Freedom*) publish it.[2] It was no small gesture for a newspaper to publish serially five full-page articles. That length allowed me to present the subtleties of my thoughts and argue my points in detail.

The series of articles, which began to appear at the end of August 1994, can be seen as a forerunner and intellectual preparation for the later adjustment and stabilization program. I was concerned at the distortion of the consumption/investment ratio in favor of the former. Wages and public expenditures were running away and thereby worsening at an increasing pace the equilibrium position of the economy, especially the current account. In that respect, my articles not only raised the

---

* There were cases in which I had personal reasons to speak out—I would be interviewed when a book of mine came out, or on a birthday with a round number. On those occasions, I would normally agree to the flattering request and answer the press's questions.

prospect of unpopular, painful rules of economic policy but said they could not be avoided. At the same time, I pointed out that the adjustment had to be made in a way that would save Hungary from the drastic recession that usually accompanies stabilization and adjustment reforms.

The reactions were varied and mutually contradictory, as they have been to other, similar appeals. Some people approved, others thought my proposals were not radical enough, and yet others distorted or misinterpreted what I was trying to say. Some intellectual amends came later, when the study was rated highly by expert observers far from the political wrangles of Hungary. The *Festschrift* compiled for my seventieth birthday contains detailed comments on the piece from Robert Solow, one of the greatest living authorities on macroeconomics. He noted approvingly that "first, growth is just too important . . . to be put on the back burner; second, a contracting GDP will make it far more difficult to achieve the other stabilization goals; and third, more years of stagnation or decline will only make it harder to get growth going again if the time ever comes to do so."[3] The study's philosophy, according to Solow, pointed beyond a momentary situation in Hungary and would have relevance later and beyond Hungary's borders as well.

When Finance Minister Lajos Bokros came forward in March 1995 with the government's adjustment and stabilization program (the "Bokros package"), I felt a duty to support him wholeheartedly. I initiated a television interview, in which I sought to explain to viewers in plain language why the painful adjustment and sacrifices had become necessary. This presentation appeared later in printed form as "A Steep Road."[4]

I also initiated a meeting with Iván Szabó, a highly respected member of the opposition and the last finance minister in the 1990–1994 government headed by the Hungarian Democratic Forum, and attempted to convince him of the need for the drastic package. I suggested he should try to persuade his fellow members of Parliament on the opposition benches not to take a stand against the adjustment program. I had the impression that he agreed with my arguments. At any rate, he did not counter them, but my initiative had no effect. The opposition of the time attacked the adjustment program with maximum force.

Some items in the package were then challenged in the Constitutional Court. At that point I went to see László Sólyom, president of the court—not in secret lobbying but in line with legal practice, acting as an amicus curiae and giving the judge my views as a citizen with no axe to grind, before judgment was reached.* I put to him detailed economic arguments as to why the rapid, radical measures were needed. The kind of crisis that loomed had to be averted at all cost. The Mexican crisis not long before had caused that country enormous losses. In such an emer-

---

* László Sólyom was elected president of the Republic in 2005.

gency, it was in keeping with the spirit of the constitution to resort to drastic measures that would take place immediately, without advance warning. The ruling that was issued reversed important items in the package, showing that my arguments had not won approval in the court either.

Later, in 1996, when time had passed and statistics could shed light on the outcome, I published in Hungary and presented in Paris at a conference of the Organization for Economic Cooperation and Development a paper titled "Adjustment without Recession: A Case Study of Hungarian Stabilization." It used international data to measure the achievement of carrying out such painful surgery without the drop in production and leap in unemployment seen in such places as Latin America, where these side effects always resulted from the adjustment programs that followed each financial crisis.

Most economists agreed with my evaluation, but there were some dissenters. György Matolcsy rejected my arguments. Even his title quarreled with mine: "Adjustment with Recession." I recommended great circumspection in all my macroeconomic writings: measures must be calibrated to bring *lasting* growth that moves and maintains the economy on a course of balanced and sustainable growth. Matolcsy already gave signs of preferring the path that he later followed as a minister of the economy: *forcing* growth, using excessive fiscal stimuli to nudge the economy off the path of sustainable growth toward eventual equilibrium troubles.

In 1996 the interviews I gave before and after the stabilization program and the articles I wrote for newspapers and journals were gathered into a volume: *Struggle and Hope: Essays on Stabilization and Reform in a Post-socialist Economy.* The title reflects some of my feelings about events and something of the country's psychological state as well.

I felt my strength and my weakness simultaneously during the battles around the Bokros package. My macroeconomic analyses, whose conclusions I had stated orally and in writing, certainly helped to clarify the tasks ahead and make the sacrifices more acceptable to many people. But a personality like Keynes (to take another research economist as an example) would certainly have achieved more in my place. He would have been better able to persuade waverers and opponents, and he would have been more tenacious about speaking to as many people as possible in their own language. I generally trust, excessively and often naively, I admit, in the power of the written word, in the effect of a book or an article, and I do not usually set out to lobby for my proposals. I was alarmed by the near-crisis that preceded the introduction of the program, and that alarm induced me to take on an unaccustomed role.

The program, at great cost, produced a radical adjustment that brought impressive results after a few years: the equilibrium indicators improved and growth accelerated. But unfortunately, there was no way to resolve once and for all the difficult problems that arose in the mid-1990s. Just a few years later almost everything started all over again. The popularity-pursuing, improvident wage-raising, state-money-dispensing spirit of "goulash communism" did not vanish with the Kádár regime. It lives on and haunts us still. Governments, whether left-wing or right-wing, headed by conservative nationalist or socialist political forces, have pursued populist economic policies from time to time. The detrimental economic tendencies of old have repeatedly risen again.

Disturbances appeared again on the Hungarian financial scene in 2003. One after the other, acclaimed economists were penning articles in the press, urging action and criticizing monetary and fiscal policy. The situation prompted me to give a longish interview to the daily *Népszabadság*, underlining that my macroeconomic philosophy had not changed since I wrote the series of articles for the paper in 1994. At my request, the headline was again "Lasting Growth Is the Main Priority."[5]

Unfortunately, more than a year passed before the warning in the interview was heeded, though it was in tune with statements by several other economists. We called for "restraint" in state expenditure, restrictions on the galloping program of housing credit, and curbs on wages, which were rising much faster than productivity. It is a shame that redirection of the economy onto a path of sustainable growth was so long delayed and so hesitant.

Reform of the health system

I had touched on the problems of reforming the welfare state at the time of the postsocialist transition when I lectured in 1992 at the invitation of the American Economic Society. There I described the structure that had grown up under the Kádár regime as a "premature welfare state," as it had undertaken obligations it could not fulfill, obligations that were out of proportion to the country's resources. I managed, if nothing else, to ensure that thereafter, some fellow researchers would look on me with anger and scorn, in the belief that the social achievements of the socialist system had to be defended from me, not from the grip of real and inescapable disproportion. One old friend of mine has not even spoken to me since I wrote those words. I also managed to ensure that the circle of experts in the issues related to the welfare state would reject all my ideas out of hand without considering my arguments and distort them by quoting them out of context.

But the problems I pointed to in 1992 worsened rather than ceasing of their own accord. I later understood that they were not specific to Eastern Europe. The welfare state is in crisis not only there, where it was born prematurely, but in its original birthplace, northern and Western Europe, too. We face one of the gravest incongruities of our time. Here is one of the great achievements of the twentieth century, which has made life more secure for millions. Interfere with it and there is understandable hissing from all who fear that the reform will undermine their security. On the other hand, the prevailing demographic trends and pace of development of increasingly expensive new medical technologies have made it impossible to fund the welfare state in its present form and at its present extent by the present means. The severity of the conflict is apparent not only in the resistance to the Hungarian or Polish reforms but in the political storms, demonstrations, and protests elicited by somewhat meek and inconsistent attempts at reform in France (under the right-wing government of Alain Juppé) and Germany (under the left-wing cabinet of Gerhard Schröder) as well. Yet all governing forces that truly feel responsible for their country, whether left-wing or right-wing, must take action to contain the expenditures of the welfare state.

The question has been preoccupying me ever since I encountered it. I attempted to tackle the problem from various directions. One approach was to conduct an international comparison by econometric means, in conjunction with a former student of mine, John McHale, an Irishman now teaching in Canada.[6] Then László Csontos, who died young, and István György Tóth, of the research institute TÁRKI (Társadalomkutatási Intézet, or Social Research Institute), joined me in sounding out the Hungarian public on how various alternatives for reform would be received.[7] I worked with another team on measuring the size of gratuities paid to medical doctors, using data gathered from frank discussions and interviews with patients and recipients.[8]

In 1998, I published a short book in Hungarian on health care reform.[9] It had a mixed reception. Some people agreed that my proposals were timely and feasible. Others were enraged, accusing me of speaking for a political party or preparing the ground for greedy, profit-hungry capitalists, who would be merciless to patients. The affronted critics could not hear that I was proposing not radical, traumatic, precipitous changes but rather balanced, cautious reform aimed at a compromise between mutually incompatible demands.*

The book was not advocating uninhibited, unlimited market competition at all, although it also described the opposite of that as damaging. We cannot rest content with leaving a monopoly of state care and public financing in this sector or allow every decision on pensions, health, and other welfare services to remain exclusively with paternalistic politicians and bureaucrats.

---

* Pál Kovács, a politician who focused on health issues and was a former health minister, decided to be funny instead of arguing seriously against the proposals. Asked by a television reporter what use he would make of the book, he said the thickness was just right for putting under the leg of a wobbly desk he had.

Most health economists and politicians focused on health care who examine the need and possibilities for reform start from the sector's special situation and tasks and its funding problems. They look only secondarily at ethical aspects or fail to mention them at all. Those concerned about ethical implications can try to work out for themselves what principles lie behind a given idea for reform, if any. My book did the reverse. It started from a declared set of values and ethical principles and tried to deduce the practical course from them.

My book put up front two basic postulates. One was the principle of individual sovereignty. A desirable transformation should broaden the decision-making province of the individual in welfare services and narrow that of the state. That principle applies not only to decision making but also to the individual's responsibility for his or her own life. We had to give up letting a nanny state make choices for us.

The other postulate was the principle of solidarity. We must help the suffering, troubled, and disadvantaged. This position, unlike the libertarian stance of those seeking to minimize the role of the state, sees the redistributive role of the state as permissible and necessary, so long as it sets out pragmatically to relieve those in need.

On the subject of my research into health care reform, it is worth mentioning that this new field of interest also penetrated my teaching at Harvard University. I organized a seminar with John McHale to examine reform of the welfare state from an international perspective. Guest lectures were given, in some cases by recognized experts in the field and in others by students. The topics discussed included reform of the American pension system (the lecturers were Martin Feldstein and Peter Diamond), World Bank recommendations for pension reform in Eastern Europe, reform of the health care sector in China, methods of reducing unemployment (on which Professor Edmund Phelps of Columbia University lectured), changes in the distribution of wealth in various regions of the world, and so on. The audience listened to these lectures very attentively, and both the students and teachers, including myself, who followed the course were able to draw many thought-provoking conclusions from a rich body of knowledge offering a broad international perspective.

To return to my 1998 book on health care reform, the debates it provoked—less the printed reviews than calm, personal conversations—made it clear to me where I had not argued convincingly enough. I set out to revise it in conjunction with a former student of mine at Harvard, Karen Eggleston, who had specialized in health economics. The revised and expanded edition appeared in English in 2001 as *Welfare, Choice and Solidarity in Transition: Reforming the Health Sector in Eastern Europe*.[10] The new version argues for the same principles and the same main line of reform, but rests on a broader base of international material; it analyzes critically other countries' positive and negative experiences with their health systems and the changes occurring in them. It presents a more detailed and precise plan for reform than the earlier Hungarian edition did and weighs more carefully the features specific to the health sector. It explains the risks and dangers of organizing the sector on purely commercial lines. But rather than scaring people away from involvement by the private sector, it describes methods of intervention and regulation and the equalizing and redistributive mechanisms for containing the dangers. It seeks to look objectively at the advantages and drawbacks of various incentive schemes.

Initial reactions to the English edition were very favorable, and to the delight of its authors, it has also appeared in Polish, Chinese, and Vietnamese. A revised and expanded version in Hungarian came out while I was writing these memoirs. It reached the public at a time when a sharp debate is taking place on reforming the health system. The exchange of expert views has been supplanted by a hostile political battle. Public figures ostensibly championing the common weal but representing the interests of narrow groups within the sector have been clashing vehemently on television. Who knows whether the calmer, more objective tones of our book will be heard?

Considering the reactions to my macroeconomic contributions and to the first health book, I wonder in general whether any attention will be given to what I say when the final decisions in economic policy are made.

Do they ask you? Do they heed you?

Friends at home and abroad have sometimes inquired whether I get asked about economic policy matters and, if so, whether any heed is paid to my replies. I would like to give a clear, concise answer, but I cannot.

There are several possible answers. Let us begin with a literal one. Do Hungary's economic policy makers ask me to express my opinions in face-to-face conversation?

The first finance minister after the change of system was Ferenc Rabár; I had known him well in the 1960s, during the period of "two-level planning," when I asked him to join the large team. We met several times later when he worked at IIASA (the International Institute for Applied Systems Analysis) at Laxenburg, near Vienna, and then at the National Planning Office. I arrived in Hungary in 1990 during the summer vacation and Rabár phoned to ask me for a meeting. I went to his ministry and wanted to sit down at the conference table, but he smiled and offered me his chair, saying I should sit there. He told me eagerly how much he agreed with the *Passionate Pamphlet*. We met on further occasions and he always listened to my recommendations attentively.

Mihály Kupa, whom the same government asked to be Rabár's successor, set up a broad and varied informal advisory group. It included István Hetényi, a knowledgeable, highly qualified, and experienced economist, who had served as a deputy president of the Planning Office and then as finance minister up to 1986. Another member was György O'sváth, Prime Minister József Antall's personal economic adviser. There were members politically inclined toward the Alliance of Free Democrats (Szabad Demokraták Szövetsége, or SZDSZ) or the Association of Young Democrats (Fiatal Demokraták Szövetsége, or FIDESZ)—neither being a member of the coalition. When Kupa invited me to join, I hesitated but accepted. He would always listen to his advisers' opinions and I had several personal meetings with him as well. I was pleased that he was open to my ideas, although troubled by the thought that our relations might be construed as approval for government policies about which in many respects I had strong objections and reservations. The ambiguous situation ended when Kupa was dismissed. Political analysts say this was because he went too far for the government's liking in transforming the economy and applying macroeconomic discipline.

I concluded from my experience during Kupa's period as minister that I had to stick more strictly to my original principles. If a member of a democratically elected government asked me, in individual cases, for my opinion, I would gladly give it. But whatever political forces were in power, I would not take on any formal appointment as a "government adviser" or accept membership in officially appointed advisory bodies. I wanted to avoid even implying that my advice marked political approval for the government in power. Anyone formally appointed as a government adviser would be expected to show loyalty, even if his or her sharp criticism or separate opinions were not made public. I, in contrast, wanted to retain every opportunity to voice my opinion and criticism publicly.

During the fifteen years of parliamentary democracy, up until the end of 2004, we had in all ten finance ministers. At times, I was the one initiating the meeting; in other instances, it was the minister eager for the talks. Some of them were not interested to know what I thought of the economic situation or the tasks ahead.*

I have also met from time to time with other leading figures in political and public life and exchanged views with them, or expressed my opinion in writing.

In 1991, I was approached by János Kis, then president of the SZDSZ, a liberal party, to join his party's advisory body as a regular guest. Let me quote from my reply of April 14, 1991:

---

* After their dismissal I went to those with whom I had a friendly relationship before their ministerial appointment, because I wished to make clear that whether they sat on the ministerial plush seat or had been dislodged from that perch, nothing had changed in our relations as colleagues.

I would gladly discuss the country's problems with you.... However, I cannot comply with the flattering request that I regularly attend meetings of the Political Advisory Body. Allow me to explain that refusal. An important factor determining my political and professional conduct and specific acts is a desire to retain my independence, my political and intellectual autonomy. That, among other things, led me to decide since 1956, when I broke with the Communist Party, not to join any party or political movement, and I never have. It is clear to me that regular participation in the meetings of the body would not imply party membership. But this will be a grouping tied to the party, and therefore to undertake regular cooperation would be incompatible with the principles I have just expressed.... It is compatible with the principle just outlined to express my individual opinion to party leaders and economic advisers who attach importance to hearing my views. I will decide from case to case, on the basis of the policy of the parties concerned, the person requesting the advice, and a subjective assessment of the subject matter, whether to agree to such a conversation.... I am convinced that the principles I have outlined are acceptable in terms of political ethics. Far be it from me, however, to think that this is the only acceptable behavior. Parties have great need of active politicians. I have nothing in common with those who reject parliamentary democracy resting on the rivalry of parties.... Personally, too, I have much respect for those who devote themselves to party work and are ready to sacrifice to this calling the successes they would certainly have gained in other occupations.[11]

I would also like to quote extracts from a letter I sent from America on October 24, 1992, to Viktor Orbán, the president of FIDESZ, who had asked me to comment on the party's draft economic program:

I do not feel that the expression of basic principles is focused enough.
· The word "liberalism" is to be endorsed, but its content has been left unclear. It should be underlined that it refers mainly to freedom: let individuals enjoy their rights, let entrepreneurs do business, let the state refrain from elbowing its way into everything, and so on.
· The expression "pragmatism" is unclear to most people. You have to spell out better that you want to combine firm principles with flexibility, that you oppose the rigidly doctrinaire, that you are prepared for practical compromises....
· Missing from the list are three ideas that I take to have basic importance. I will just mention them as key words; they need to be worked on:
(a) *Modernization.* Up-to-date technology, modern lifestyles, up-to-date morality and social contacts—not retrieving the "old."
(b) *Honesty and legality* in business and politics. Measures against deception, cheating, corruption, shiftiness, cronyism, ethical conflict of interest, and illegality.
(c) *Security and predictability.* The government has to keep its promises; what it says has to have credibility.

Among my comments on the economic proposals were these:

The key question is for [the program] to point out clearly how it aims to put the country on its feet, lead it onto a new growth path and create jobs, without fueling inflation.... The matter must not be solved by monetary stimulus.... Greater emphasis is needed on openness to foreign capital, adding how harmful xenophobia and nationalism are.... The draft's mention of "great systems" [of state redistribution] is beside the point. What do you want to do about decentralizing and privatizing the health and welfare programs? . . . Talking in general about the welfare program, I would go not for populist promises but above all for making the future course predictable.[12]

I continue to espouse the same principles that I voiced in that letter twelve years ago.

A meeting or an exchange of letters does not in itself demonstrate real interest. That depends on the other side. Some partners I felt were clearly paying attention to what I said, thinking over my arguments, comparing them with other points of view, and drawing conclusions. But in some cases, partners in conversation seemed to show only a semblance of interest and only wanted to hear the sound of their own voice. They may have started a discussion only after their political views had solidified or sought to fortify their choices by going through the motions of exchanging views in writing or asking advice. If I really agreed with them, they could cite my agreement in other conversations. If I did not happen to agree, advice could be sought from others until someone who agreed with them was found. I have to admit, I shrink from such exchanges of views, but they certainly happen in a portion of cases. The risk of acceding to a sham request is one that everyone giving informal opinions to politicians has to take.

One repeated occurrence when I met a leading figure in politics or government at a meeting or celebration was the remark, "Oh, so you are back home, are you? I thought you were in America. I would really like to talk to you. I will be in touch." We would leave it at that and weeks would go by, but no invitation ensued. I have had five or ten similar conversations with one old acquaintance or another. Perhaps the person concerned sincerely felt it would be useful to hear my views, but then the course of day-to-day events intervened and it turned out that the need for advice and a calm conversation with an academic was not so urgent.

I think it is unacceptable for a politician to use conversations with advisers such as myself exclusively for PR purposes. It is as if they were bragging to the public about what profound practitioners of science and experts in economics were giving them advice. While I was still inexperienced, I fell for one or two such clumsy acts of propaganda. I later developed defensive reflexes and became more cautious, seeking to clarify in advance what subject the politician wanted to hear my opinions on. I tried to be especially careful in those instances when the press and television cameras had been invited. It was not that I wished to keep my meetings with politicians secret. I was flattered by the invitations and had no reason to keep quiet about them: I am ready to give my opinion to those who are really interested. I am glad to do this, and in such cases I am not bothered by doing it in public—but I do not wish to play a part in an empty promotional game.

It will be clear by now that I have mulled over these matters a great deal. There is a dividing line somewhere between the role of a politician and that of an academic with feelings of responsibility and commitment to society. I cannot accept the first, but I want to accept the second. I sometimes felt I had overstepped my self-imposed line and sometimes that I had not gone near enough to it. But just where does the boundary run?

These incidents provide a glimpse into my psychological and behavioral inhibitions, which hold me back from making frequent public contributions on questions that would inevitably involve me in political storms. I am happier to draw back into research work, where I feel at home and can better exploit my comparative advantages, to use an economist's term.

The actual effect

So far, I have tackled only the first question in the previous subtitle. Was I asked? Let me now take up the question of whether people listened.

In seeking to say whether I have been heeded, I do not want to narrow the matter down to confidential, face-to-face conversations or statements, criticisms, or proposals made in private letters. I prefer to state openly in my books, articles, and other publications what I think is really important—unless doing so conflicts with some major national security or economic interest. Have all these statements affected events?

Let me begin with some remarkable statistics. My name or some writing of mine was mentioned in the Hungarian Parliament forty-six times between 1990 and 2003.[13] These days, measuring citations is a science in itself, with researchers vying to see which of their works is cited and how often, normally in academic journals. Those interest me as well, of course, but this is a different racetrack! It is satisfying to find MPs quoting my works in debate, especially as I have consciously avoided their daily political battles.

Almost all referred to my work approvingly, in support of their opinion. Two-thirds of the mentions came from members of parties now in government (the Hungarian Socialist Party and the Alliance of Free Democrats) and a third from those of parties in opposition (the Association of Young Democrats, the Hungarian Democratic Forum, the Christian Democrats, and the Independent Smallholders' Party). Most cited *The Road to a Free Economy*, but some mentioned *Economics of Shortage, Struggle and Hope*, or the health reform book. Frequency peaked in 1995, during the stabilization and adjustment period. As an academic, I found it flattering to read in the parliamentary minutes how two MPs argued about which understood my writings better.

But mentions in Parliament, however valuable, say nothing about whether my work affected the actual course of the transformation. I am afraid I cannot give a reliable answer to that. I have always advocated multicausal analysis in methodology. If a causal explanation for a complex phenomenon is sought, attribution to a single cause is exceptional indeed. And if there are several influences, establishing their relative weights is very difficult.

That some processes in Hungary and other post-socialist countries moved in the direction I advised in my writings does not mean that my writings prompted them to do so. It could be coincidence and the real impetus could have come from else-where.* It is also possible that my writings had some influence, but other factors were much stronger. In the end, of course, the possibility that some of my ideas had an important effect, often by indirect influence, on the thinking of the decision makers cannot be excluded either.

Strong, wide-ranging measures to harden the budget constraint came earliest in Hungary. The assessment of J. Barkley Rosser Jr. and Marina V. Rosser, in one of the best-known textbooks of comparative economics, points to the strong intellectual influence of my work on that outcome, and their assessment seems convincing.† It is undeniable that I was the most prominent advocate of hardening the budget constraint in the whole post-socialist region and my writings on the subject were widely discussed.

With other, more comprehensive, questions, all that can be said is that the proposal was advanced by a chorus of which I only was a member or at most one of several leaders. I was among those who advocated gradual privatization, for instance, and rejected the third way—still the most important issue in the debates. I was also one among the like-minded intellectuals who contributed to a body of opinion strongly advocating that macroeconomic equilibrium be reconciled with the requirements of growth. I think the hypothesis that I had influence in those matters can be maintained, but it cannot be proved.

Apart from possible effects on politicians and economic decision making, there is another side to consider: whether my ideas influenced *public thinking,* the thinking

* One story by Frigyes Karinthy tells of a benign lunatic who stands at a busy crossroads and directs the traffic like the conductor of an orchestra. Every event that occurs completely independently of him, he experiences as if it had happened at his command: "The two cars are now turning the corner...Good...Opposite there should be a tram. Hang on, what's this? Here soldiers should be coming...Aha, here they are. They're coming from over there..." (1975 [1914], p. 329). I do not at any cost wish to resemble Karinthy's character, waving his baton around.

† "Hungary has by far the hardest budget constraint of any of the formerly socialist economies....Arguably this reflects the immense policy influence of János Kornai in his native country" (Rosser and Rosser 2004, pp. 377–378).

of the people outside the spheres of power, especially the intelligentsia and those in business. I cannot give an answer based on any survey. As I have mentioned when talking about *Economics of Shortage*, I received sporadic feedback. Sometimes a doctor treating me, sometimes a neighbor, sometimes a historian I ran into would say that he or she had read something of mine and found it convincing. One recurring piece of praise was that the person concerned had understood the problem and tasks better from reading my article than from official pronouncements. That his or her writings have helped readers to find their bearings is an achievement in itself for any scholar. However pleasant it may be to hear such appreciation, it is impossible to say how widespread it is.

Monetary policy making

In 1995, I was asked by György Surányi, president of the National Bank of Hungary, if I would agree to join the Central Bank Council, the main policy-making body for monetary policy. I asked for time to think about it, as I wanted to know the constitutional and political position of the council.* The decisive factor inducing me to comply with his request was the guaranteed *independence* of the central bank. By law, the Central Bank Council was independent of the government and political parties. Its members were proposed by the prime minister in consultation with the president of the National Bank of Hungary and had to be endorsed by Parliament, while the ultimate appointment fell under the authority of the president of the republic.

I was recommended for my first three-year term by Gyula Horn, prime minister when the socialist-liberal coalition governed, and for my second by Viktor Orbán, prime minister who led the conservative coalition. On both occasions, all government and opposition members of the parliamentary committees concerned (economic and budgetary) supported my nomination. At the committee hearings, I was asked technical questions that lacked a political edge, and I did my best to give objective answers. I found it comforting and reassuring that I could rely on a broad consensus. I wanted the political world to see in me a man of independent ideas, guided not by commitments to any political party but by his professional and moral conscience. That successive governments, on opposite sides in a sharp political struggle, were prepared to entrust me with such responsibility is evidence that I succeeded in my efforts.

I worked on the council for almost six years, preparing hard for each meeting and often going beyond the call of duty by submitting a written opinion in advance. I

* New legislation on the direction of monetary policy was introduced in 2001. What I am describing here of my time as a council member reflects the earlier legal framework.

tried to familiarize myself with the latest figures and other information and thoroughly study the theoretical literature pertinent to items on the agenda as well as analyses of similar situations in the past. This I did quietly, in the background, behind closed doors. The Central Bank Council had to make short- and medium-term decisions about monetary policy—and interest rate policy in particular. In cooperation with the government, it had to develop the institutional constraints that determined the exchange rate's room to maneuver.* Hungarian monetary policy won worldwide recognition at that time, with leaders of international financial activity citing Hungary as an example for other transition countries. I can say without boasting that my work, too, contributed to those achievements.

Meanwhile I learned much. I could look deeply into how economic policy was devised at the highest level. Preparing for each major decision was a professional challenge. It was reassuring to find the debates were calm, especially before political storms came to surround the National Bank. Arguments were answered with arguments, not feelings. The atmosphere was that of a group of colleagues who respected each other.

In August 2001, a few weeks before my appointment expired, I resigned from the Central Bank Council in an open letter addressed to the president of the republic. I felt that the newly passed legislation had altered the legal framework of council membership. Under the new law all members of the newly formed Monetary Council become employees of the National Bank of Hungary (and consequently of its president), a position that undermines their independence.† The new situation was incompatible with the principles I had laid down for myself.

At that time it was impossible to foresee the blunders the monetary policy makers later committed, but there were signs that problems would arise. In the past it had not bothered me that the meetings of the council were closed and the public did not know what views members took. But I now feared I would be in a perpetual minority and, willingly or not, have to assist a monetary policy that I disagreed with—

---

* In economic parlance, this is called an exchange rate regime. For example, a choice has to be made between fixing the exchange rate or letting it float freely. Or should there be leeway for market forces to play a part, but with the limits of movement of the exchange rate fixed in advance? In the latter case, how wide should the band be within which the exchange rate fluctuates?

† According to the earlier law on central banking, some of the members of the Central Bank Council were chosen from those holding high positions within the bank ("internal members"), while others (including me) came from the world of scholarship ("external members"). The latter kept their university or research institute positions as full-time jobs, and took part in the formation of monetary policy only as an additional activity. This outsider status ensured them full personal independence.

without having the opportunity to voice my private opinion to the economic profession and the citizens of the country.

Perhaps a better political tactician or diplomat than I could have worked usefully in that situation, for instance by intervening, successfully or less successfully, to forestall erroneous ideas of other members. I felt I had neither the will nor the ability for the task.

I look back with a clear conscience on six years spent taking part in successful monetary policy making, and on how, freed from the constraints of council membership in 2002, I was at liberty to criticize monetary-policy mistakes in the press and in professional discussions.

Comments on transformation in other countries

The political events of 1989–1990 brought a sudden demand for foreign advisers in all post-socialist countries. I would not join in making any general judgment here. I knew advisers who sought to get to know thoroughly the area they were going to, prepared carefully and cautiously for their task, and put their proposals forward in all modesty. Unfortunately, another type of adviser appeared as well: economists with no local knowledge but all the more intent on imposing their ideas.

I was approached from several directions to take part in planning the post-socialist transition of one country or another. Invitations to visit and exchange views in their countries came from many foreign colleagues and friends whom I had known in the period of intellectual resistance to the socialist regime.

It follows from what I have been saying that I had to decline most of these invitations. Most, but not all. I certainly did not want to tour several countries with my ideas and persuade people to accept them instead of other people's. But I felt it was not right to shrug off the requests altogether. My knowledge might ease the efforts of the transforming countries to find their paths, and in turn, I could learn a lot during my travels. I visited Russia and several other Eastern European countries, giving lectures and having long discussions with economists and economic policy makers there. I was also in Washington several times at the invitation of the International Monetary Fund and the World Bank, likewise to present my ideas at lectures and contribute to informal discussions. I was a member for several years of the scientific council at the European Bank for Reconstruction and Development (EBRD) that aided the transition of the European post-socialist countries by granting them investment loans and offering them policy advice.

So far as accurate self-judgment is possible, I would say that I escaped the sin of intellectual arrogance. I did not claim, as I heard with my own ears more pushy colleagues do, that there was only one road, which happened to be the one they were advising. I always stressed that it was not for us foreigners to say. The decisions had to come from local people who really knew the situation; they bore the responsibility for choosing. All we could do was convey to them experience we had gained in other countries and conclusions we drew from theoretical writings. The more cautious and modest foreign advisers were, the greater the chance they would be heeded.

It was an especially moving experience to visit China in 1999 and again in 2005 and to see Vietnam for the first time in 2001. It would have been a big mistake in either country to prescribe with doctrinaire rigidity the same recipe served up in post-socialist Eastern Europe. If these two countries reminded me of anything, it was not the Eastern Europe of the 1990s but the Hungary of the late Kádár period in the 1980s. They were far along the road of economic reform and the spread of a market economy and private ownership—in many ways further than 1980s Hungary had been. But there were still only traces of political reform. The Communist Party's monopoly of power and political repression remained. It was forbidden to question publicly the ideology or rhetoric of Marxism-Leninism. People with opposing ideas faced reprisals if they tried to organize an independent movement. Visiting foreigners had to remember where they were, putting their message in ways that would not only please the radical opponents of present conditions but would also not scare off the hesitant or those who had only half-accepted the idea of political reform.

My visits to China and Vietnam were also a special intellectual experience because I felt at home in that world. I speak no Chinese or Vietnamese, but in another sense, I could talk to them in their language, because my experience gave me insight into the mentality of those disillusioned with socialism, seeking a path, or still hesitant about reform. And as I heard from a few people in frank, friendly talks, they could accept me as a conversation partner much more easily than American, French, or German economists, because they sensed that I myself had been through phases of development similar to their present ones. What I had to say had credibility.

I am glad that successive books and articles of mine are appearing in those two countries. Perhaps they too will contribute to the intellectual enlightenment in preparation for the future course of reform. It would be good to see the day when democracy emerges also in these two distant countries, to which I feel close. That future pleasure depends on two conditions: that I live long and they speed up their changes.*

* In 2004 I wrote a study at the request of a university institution in Florida about the lessons of the Eastern European transformation for Cuba, if it should some time turn toward democracy and a market economy. That was an intellectual challenge similar to the one I felt in relation to the problems of China and Vietnam.

21

Continuation—1990 Onward

What the Change of System Does and Does Not Mean
Honesty and Trust

Let me turn to the other side of my activity, the work I feel is most important and my true vocation: research and teaching.

Interpreting the change of system

The change of system opened a new stage in my life because in 1990 I began to feel again a duty to take a *normative* approach, to think about practical proposals regarding economic policy for Hungary and other countries in the throes of transition. At the same time, I attached no less importance to a *positive* approach of grasping the current situation objectively, describing and analyzing its causes, and doing related theoretical work.

Understanding the concept of a system has been a central topic throughout my scholarly career. I had been engaged for decades in comparing contemporaneous systems. There was now a unique chance to observe and interpret what it meant for different systems to appear consecutively. Though everyone keeps using the expression "change of system," there is still no consensus about what it means. Indeed, some current interpretations are strongly opposed, and the disagreement causes confusion in political discourse.

I clarified this problem for myself as I worked on my book *The Socialist System*, whose title underscores that "system" is a central concept in it. Although I have mentioned them already, let me sum up here the three characteristics that I see as distinguishing the "great" systems: (1) political structure and associated dominant political ideology, (2) property relations, and (3) coordination mechanisms (the relative weight of market coordination, bureaucratic coordination, or other mechanisms). The numbering is not random but refers to the rank order of the three principal components. These three characteristics go on to determine other important features of the system: behavioral regularities, enduring market forces, and so on.

The characteristic features of the classical socialist system are a monopoly of power held by a Communist Party opposed to private ownership and to the market and the predominance of public ownership and bureaucratic coordination. The characteristic features of the capitalist system are a regime friendly toward private ownership and toward the market and the predominance of private ownership and market coordination. The change of system occurred when the socialist system yielded to a new system exhibiting the characteristics of capitalism.

I have striven here to characterize the two systems and the change of system as concisely as possible, using the fewest possible criteria. Let me therefore warn readers what does *not* belong to the change of system as I interpret it.

I do not attach a value judgment to it. It is not that I refrain from judgment, as I will explain in a minute, but the concept itself is positive, descriptive, and value-free. I may rejoice over the change of system while you deplore it, but we could still agree on what the term means. It is utterly misleading to confuse expectations of a "good" society with a positive definition of the new system. The socialist system is no evil empire and the capitalist system no social embodiment of justice and freedom. We are discussing here a general model of two real, historical structures.

"Change of system" denotes a radical transformation of structures, institutions, social relations, and typical interactions, and not the changing of the guard of any individual or group. Of course, there is a correlation between the process of structural and institutional change and the process of change in the roles and positions of individuals. The former entails the latter to some extent and after some delay; the former is unquestionably the determining force while the latter is more of a side effect.

A final proviso regarding political structure: a change of system may still occur even if the new way of governing is not a democracy, but some kind of tyranny or authoritarian regime such as a military dictatorship. My definition requires only that it should be "friendly" to the features of a capitalist economy—private ownership and the market—and not impede but rather assist their expansion. The political structure of a socialist system may give way to the terror of a Pinochet-style military junta, seizure of power by a family clique from the old *nomenklatura* (as happened in several Central Asian countries), or long-term hegemony for a group still styled a Marxist-Leninist party (a possible scenario in China or Vietnam). Eastern Europe had the inestimable luck to undergo a change of system in which the political structure changed from dictatorship to democracy.

A capitalist economy can exist without democracy, as many historical examples show. But the opposite is not the case. No democracy can exist without a capitalist system,[*] as logical argument and historical experience confirm.

---

[*] One qualification should be added to this statement: I am speaking of democracy operating in a modern industrial society. Clearly, the democracy of the ancient Greeks, a historical forerunner, was related to a different economic order.

"What a Change from Socialism to Capitalism Does and Does Not Mean" is the title of a study of mine expressing these ideas; it appeared in the *Journal of Economic Perspectives*, one of the most widely read journals of economics in the United States.* Although the piece explores the subject on the plane of theories of socioeconomic change, it carries a political message as well. Demagogic, populist remarks are often made about how the change of system has not occurred yet. I am afraid those who preach from such texts have no idea what "system" or "change of system" really means.

Of course, the mere fact that the transition between the great systems has occurred, that capitalism has succeeded socialism, leaves many questions open. There are many types of capitalism. Some assign a significant role to the state and some a less significant. Some have obtrusive and some unobtrusive inequalities in the distribution of power, rights, or wealth and income. Some provide stronger and some weaker incentives to technical advance, and so on. The real issue for further debate is not whether the change of system has occurred, but what specific direction the changes are taking. The connecting normative question is, What direction would we like to go? And that brings us to the issue of value judgments.

Expectations and frustrations, optimism and pessimism

Many people in Hungary and the Eastern European region are disappointed. They expected the change of system to bring something different, something greater and better. I am not thinking just of those who actually did badly—losing their jobs, descending the income scale, or being deprived of privileges. Disillusionment is also found among many members of the intelligentsia, who have not lost financially or have even benefited, who have not suffered any personal harm and may have gained extra recognition. They are embittered by the widespread dishonesty and mendacity they see, and by the dissipation of state wealth. They shudder at the sterile verbal battles in politics, the undiscovered corruption, the revelations that are never followed up or that fail to even take place, and the interpenetration of business and politics. It offends their sense of justice to see flaunted wealth and dire poverty juxtaposed.

I share those feelings of bitterness and indignation. But I would not add that I am disillusioned. Disillusionment comes from having expected more, and my expectations must have been more modest than those of many friends and acquaintances who feel that the change of system has let them down.

---

* A longer version was published earlier in Britain (1998a). The journal's chief editor called me to ask for a shorter version for a millennium issue published in 2000. It also appeared in Hungarian and several other languages.

I mentioned in an earlier chapter a piece I published in 1980. There I referred ironically to those who see history as a convenient supermarket, where the attractive features of various systems are put in the shopping basket and taken home in a combination that best meets one's taste. History offers "packages," including "existing" capitalism with its own immanent, system-specific problems.

In 1983, I wrote a study titled "The Health of Nations," briefly reviewing the pathologies of seven grave diseases: inflation, unemployment, shortages, excessive growth of foreign debt, disturbances of growth, malignant inequalities, and bureaucratization.[1] (Plenty of others could be added to the list, of course.) I then took the risk of saying that there is no such thing as a disease-free socioeconomic system, but we can choose our diseases. Let us be glad to have developed a social system that suffers from only two or three of those diseases. In the worst cases, countries suffer from four or five.

I was not surprised to find that the transition from socialism to capitalism brought mass unemployment. The most we could do was to struggle to keep it down, but it could not be overcome altogether. I was not surprised that income differences suddenly grew. Radical equalization would be impossible, but it was worth making an effort to help the needy and guarantee to all the conditions required for human dignity.

A number of factors tended to make my expectations more realistic than those of my peers. I am a professional researcher specializing in comparative social science—it is my trade. My studies had been focused for decades on exploring the nature of socialism and capitalism and comparing them. And my image of the developed capitalist countries had come not from books or short visits as a tourist, but from daily experience over periods amounting to several years. I took the opportunity to compare the written accounts with what I saw with my own eyes and can safely say I have no illusions about capitalism.* Despite its detrimental and morally nasty features, I concluded I would sooner live under the capitalist system than in the happiest barrack in the socialist camp.

I have to add another explanation of why the change of system did not disillusion me. Deeply ingrained in me is a rule of analysis: positive and normative approaches to a phenomenon need to be kept strictly separate. We all have a right to our dreams—how sad if poets gave them up. But I am irritated at people who style

---

* I see similarities between two clusters of illusions. The New Left built fantasies on a socialist utopia and turned in disgust from the socialism that actually appeared. At the same time, many members of the intelligentsia before the change of system built up a distorted picture of "the West" and its democracy and market economy. Faced with real capitalism, they were aghast, as they compared it not with realistic expectations but with their own imagined utopia.

themselves social scientists and mix utopia with reality, especially if they make a virtue of their mental confusion and shrug it off when their dreams are compared with realistic possibilities.

I am sometimes more or less alone in the company of intellectuals with my view that the change of system we have been living through is really a huge achievement. My feeling of taking part in a fortunate turning point in history did not end with the first euphoria of 1989–1990. It persists today, a decade and a half later.

Once upon a time, I would try to bring home from the West in a suitcase the many things in short supply. Now the choice is bigger in Budapest than in Boston. I once had to use personal connections to get a telephone line installed. Now the telephone companies are competing for my patronage. Perhaps I, as author of *Economics of Shortage*, am the only one to attach huge significance to the elimination of chronic shortage? No one else remembers how we grumbled before, not even the older people?

At one time, I had to seek approval from the party secretary and personnel officer at work before I could even apply for an exit "window" in my passport. Now I can board a train or a plane whenever I want. At one time, we used to knowingly wink at each other if someone managed to smuggle a critical comment on the regime into a printed piece. Now the only ones who do not assail political leaders in the newspapers or on television are people who do not want to. It is not *self-evident* to me, something to be taken for granted, that we have come remarkably far. If I mention this to friends, they agree: "Oh yes, you are right, but...," they will say, and then return to their complaints and lists of irritating or repellent occurrences.

I do not say I am not disillusioned with anything. Some problems have occurred for which I was not prepared, and even those I had anticipated were sometimes more serious than I had thought they would be. I say that self-critically. I am not talking of damaging or even disgusting events that were impossible to predict, but of things I could have predicted if I had thought over more deeply and fully what changes were likely to occur.

For instance, I made some naive assumptions about how Parliament would work. They can be found in *The Road to a Free Economy*, among other places. I expected too much of the separation of the branches of power—from the ability of the legislature to oversee the executive. Perhaps I was thinking of the relationship between the U.S. president and Congress during one of the great moments in the history of the American democracy. The Watergate story was a major experience for me, when senators and representatives, including members of President Nixon's own Republican Party, conducted with total consistency an inquiry that ended with the president's resignation. Then there were the many Senate and House committee meetings that I would watch on television, where the legislators would try to oversee the work of the administration, often exceeding the bounds of party interest. But "often" is an important word here, for they did not always rise above party interest.* It is naive to hope, even in a well-established democracy, that the mere fact of having been elected to the legislature will raise someone to moral heights on which he or she will think solely of the interests of constituents and country, irrespective of party or government allegiance. I should have been more circumspect in gauging how the government and the parliamentary majority work together under customary, normal conditions. I have had to learn that lesson from the performance of the new democracies in Hungary and other Eastern European countries.

I was not prepared for the nationalistic or related upsurge that burst upon the former socialist world. I had expected some of these developments, but not that they would have such a marked effect on political and intellectual life and human relations.

The Soviet Union and Yugoslavia, as ethnically heterogeneous federations, fell apart. In the former Yugoslavia, one war after another broke out. In the territory of the Soviet Union, a war took place between Azerbaijan and Armenia, while the conflict with the Chechens continues to this day. Even where armed conflict did not occur, repressed feelings of national independence flared up. Czechoslovakia split into two states. Whether the intensity is greater or lesser, tension exists between neighboring countries in Eastern Europe because of the situation of minorities. Ethnic minorities are demanding rights; the Russians, for instance, hitherto the dominant ethnic group, have suddenly found themselves a minority, even an oppressed one, in several new countries.

Alongside these international conflicts with a strong national dimension, single countries have undergone related developments that are similarly damaging and repulsive. I would list here xenophobia, disdain for neighboring peoples, and instances of an anti-Gypsy or anti-Semitic mentality, appearing first sporadically and later with greater force, until they have almost gained social acceptance.

I described in the first two chapters of the book what it meant for me as a child and an adult to have been born a Jew. Of course, I did not forget about this during the intervening half century, but it had no significance for me. It was immaterial to me that Marx was a Jew and Stalin was not; first I believed in both, later turned against both. It was immaterial to me that Rákosi was a Jew and Kádár was not; first I trusted both, later broke with and opposed both. And it was immaterial to me who the Jews were among those who influenced me, attacked me, published

---

* Believers in American democracy within the country and outside worry that regulations designed to forestall terrorist attacks also limit human rights. I hope that the forces of American democracy will be able to protect their achievements, as they have done many times before.

me, excluded me from university teaching, or invited me to take up a professorship. I am no racist. It is immaterial *to me* who counted as a Jew under the Nuremberg Laws or the Hungarian law requiring a yellow star to be worn. My Jewishness sprang to mind again when I read an article by the Hungarian poet Sándor Csoóri declaring it was hopeless, after Auschwitz, to expect Jews living in Hungary to be true Hungarians.* Was I not Hungarian enough in his eyes?

I am not prepared to accept from anti-Semites or other racists any classification according to race or religion. I can describe my awareness of myself in this respect by saying I am a Jew in self-defense, to defend my human dignity. If you are an anti-Semite, then I declare with my head held high that I am a Jew. I am not otherwise concerned with such immoral and repellent discriminations among people.

I must say I had not expected to see the day when some people put the "Jewish question" back on the agenda. The period since the change of system has disillusioned me in that respect as well—here too, I admit, because my foresight was weak.

I have spoken forcefully enough about the distressing happenings and how some caught me unaware to ensure that readers do not see me as an uncritical observer of the changes. The society we live in is in ferment, mixing bad with good, beautiful with tawdry. There are no objective rules for calculating the proportions. Each person must experience this curious blend in a subjective fashion.

I find many pessimists in the society around me. "Now what do you say to this?" friends begin and tell me a new ghastly tale. What can I say? It would sound like official optimism or the kind of claptrap that Communist people's instructors and rural agitators used to spout if I began sketching the positive features of the change of system and the likely achievements in the future. It is enough in an autobiographical book to confine myself to my own story of pessimism and optimism.

Before the systemic change, I tended toward a variant of pessimism. Pessimism cannot preclude action, I argued in 1983 in the "Health of Nations" study mentioned earlier. I quoted Camus's novel *The Plague*. Rieux, the physician, is talking to his friend Tarrou, who has been helping him combat the plague. "'Yes. But your victories will never be lasting; that's all.' Rieux's face darkened. 'Yes, I know that. But it's no reason for giving up the struggle.'"[2]

I write as follows in my preface to the American edition of *Contradictions and Dilemmas* in 1986: "I must warn the reader: this is not an optimistic book. But

---

* "With the Council Republic, the Horthy era, and particularly with the Holocaust, the chances of intellectual and spiritual integration came to an end. Now it is liberal Hungarian Jewry that wants to assimilate Hungarians both in style and mentality. To this end it has erected a parliamentary platform for itself that it could never do before" (Csoóri 1990, p. 5).

neither is it pessimistic. There has been a Hungarian tradition for centuries: you are resigned or desperate or angry and a happy outlook is uncertain or improbable—and yet, you work hard and honestly for improvement. Those who have read classics of Hungarian drama or poetry (some are translated into English), or have listened to Bartók's music, will know exactly this contradictory mood. Perhaps a member of a gray and non-philosophical profession, like that of an economist, can follow the same tradition."[3]

In me, the mix of optimism and pessimism has tipped toward optimism since the change of system. It would be irresponsible to sketch in a few lines a balance of the favorable and unfavorable aspects of the changes in progress in the country and the world—even another long book would be insufficient for that. I will mention only a few phenomena to illustrate the kinds of changes that have affected my attitude toward life. I do not deny the problems and I face up to them, but I see a different future since the chance of freedom has opened up before hundreds of millions of people in the post-socialist region. Following that opening, a new, great wave of democracy has augmented other, earlier waves of democracy. In historical terms, the area of the world under tyranny has narrowed and the area covered by democratic institutions, stronger or weaker, has widened considerably. Though the process may be coming to a halt in some places or even going into reverse, I am convinced that such setbacks can last only briefly. I too shiver to learn of the dreadful deeds of extremists and I sense what the unforeseeable consequences may be if weapons of mass destruction come into the hands of terrorists. Nevertheless, I believe that the historical process of the spread of democracy, in line with the trend of former decades and centuries, will continue.

Production is growing everywhere, though unevenly, technology is developing, and the quantity of resources available for human consumption has grown. I am fully aware that there always are new difficulties to overcome. Still, I am not going to bewail the woes of a consumer society or an aging society or the spread of computers. To me, it is an advance if lights burn in villages and sewage is piped away, if epidemics are stemmed and life expectancy is extended, and if people are better linked by modern information technology and telecommunications. I have turned into an optimist who recognizes the problems and wishes to alleviate them.

Collegium Budapest

Following the change of system, my working conditions in Budapest altered substantially. I had been on the staff of the Institute of Economics of the Hungarian Academy of Sciences since 1955, discounting nine years of forced removal to other institutions.

I was invited in 1992 to join Collegium Budapest, an institute that was just being founded. I accepted, became a founding fellow, and shifted the focus of my activity in Budapest to my new place of work. My feelings on leaving the Institute of Economics were mixed, as such feelings tend to be. I was linked to it by many emotional ties, friendships, and memories, and I remained close friends with many of the members there.*

The foundation of Collegium Budapest was initiated by Professor Wolf Lepenies, rector of the Wissenschaftskolleg zu Berlin (WIKO). The Berlin institute had been set up along the lines of the Institute for Advanced Study at Princeton, where, as I explained earlier, there were splendid opportunities for invited fellows to spend periods of up to a year on their thinking, writing, research, and study, free of teaching or administrative obligations. Professor Lepenies and his close colleague Joachim Nettelbeck, secretary of WIKO, thought the time had come to found an institute for advanced study in Eastern Europe as well. After some hesitation and examination of the possibilities in Poland and the Czech Republic, they chose Hungary for the sister organization and began recruiting a team of sponsors, including several Western European governments and foundations.

Professor Lepenies asked me for my cooperation at the start of the negotiations. I could not accept the rectorship, not least because I spent half my time at Harvard, but I agreed to join the small team leading Collegium Budapest as a permanent fellow.

I gladly directed some of my energies to promoting the activity of the new institute—for instance, by taking part each year in choosing the fellows who would be invited. Collegium Budapest operates in Hungary as an international institute that strives to host a balanced proportion of Hungarians (from Hungary and other countries) and foreigners from East and West. It is also an interdisciplinary institute, which is one of its main attractions. Inspiring lunchtime conversations may involve a musicologist and a geneticist, a philosopher and a historian. All fellows are required to report on their work to the others at a seminar, in a way that practitioners of other disciplines can follow. Great attention is paid when fellows are chosen so that the disciplines represented are appropriately balanced.

Some of the fellows work alone in their research field. Others organize themselves into groups. From time to time, a focus group to research a specific theme is formed. I initiated and organized such a group on three occasions. The most recent one I directed in conjunction with Professor Susan Rose-Ackerman of Yale, on the subject

---

* I mentioned in chapter 11, when describing life at the Institute of Economics, that it became a tradition for my group to have lunch together at 11:30 A.M. My long years of service left their trace. The former members of the Kornai Group still working there continue to have lunch first, at 11:30, not just when I visit them but on other days as well.

of "Honesty and Trust in the Light of Post-socialist Transition," included researchers in economics, sociology, political science, anthropology, philosophy, and jurisprudence from fourteen countries. More than forty studies resulted, from which the material for two volumes was chosen. The books were published in 2004.[4]

As I was engaged in the project, I discovered what high walls divided the various social sciences from each other. It became apparent repeatedly, as members of the focus group introduced their work to each other, that members of each discipline really understood only their own idiom, conceptual frameworks, and accustomed methods of research. All know well the classical literature and latest, most fashionable theories in their own subject. But they are poorly informed about the language, literature, and methodology of other fields. Whenever exponents of one profession in our little group had to address and make themselves understood by those of another, unwonted intellectual clarity was required. It was repeatedly confirmed, for instance, that what is self-evident to economists is by no means so to sociologists or lawyers, working with different axioms and approaches, and vice versa. Members of the focus group not only acquired specific knowledge and research findings, they also found the interdisciplinary cooperation an intellectual experience with lasting consequences.

Working for Collegium Budapest often involved difficult or delicate decisions. Many battles had to be fought to protect the integrity and the intellectual and political independence of this unique institution in Hungary. It was not easy to be tactful and decisive in warding off attempted interference and political pressure. My work on this was done away from the public eye, with no kind of public appreciation, but I place it among the great successes of my life.

I am now the sole academic member who has worked at Collegium Budapest from the outset. Since receiving the title of permanent fellow emeritus, I have been absolved from administrative duties, while continuing to take part in the life of the institute as a researcher. The surroundings there still delight me intellectually and aesthetically, just as they did on the first day I walked in. When I walk out of the doors in the evening hours, I look up at the floodlit tower of the Matthias Church. I am enchanted by the streets and squares of Buda Castle District and feel, time and again, what a privilege it is to be working in this captivating environment, in such calm conditions.

A splendid intermezzo: My seventieth birthday

The previous section was about work and so is the next, but I will slip in between the two an occasion of a more personal nature, which took place at Collegium Budapest.

My wife Zsuzsa prepared the celebrations for my seventieth birthday in great secrecy. As I discovered afterward, the rector at the time, Gábor Klaniczay, gave her every assistance and offered the premises for the affair.

On the evening of the event, I was asked to dress up, as Zsuzsa said she wanted to take me out to dinner. I even put on a tie. We got in the car and went up to Collegium Budapest, and there the secret was out: a birthday banquet! Zsuzsa had invited fifty-two people, including all the members of the family at home and abroad as well as our closest friends. Everyone came and everyone kept the secret until the last minute. I really had no idea until we arrived on the premises.

When everyone had arrived, we went into the lecture hall, where Zsuzsa spoke first. She began by thanking those who had helped her organize the occasion, mentioning first our dear friend Péter Hanák, the historian, who had taken part in the early preparations but had departed from us before the occasion was held. She would have said more, but her voice broke after the first few sentences and tears filled her eyes, so that she could not continue. She left the rostrum in a storm of applause.

That touching scene was followed by a performance of a string quartet by Mozart, my favorite composer. My friend Lajos Vékás, founding rector of Collegium Budapest and a great music lover, had secured the Auer Quartet to play that evening.

Then came some cheerful speeches in which friends recalled some entertaining episodes of days gone by. Péter Kende remembered our times together in the first year of elementary school. When he had had a birthday party at his house and his parents had suggested he invite me, he had said, "Oh no, not Hansi, he is a fighter!" I could hardly believe my ears! Me, a fighter?

Then came György Litván, followed by András Nagy, who talked of our days at the Institute of Economics. Those who know me well are aware that hardly a meal goes by without my dropping something on my shirt or suit. This happened in the early days of the Institute of Economics with a brand-new suit. Friends offered to whisk the trousers off to the cleaners to have the stain removed. I was locked up in my office in my underpants when the telephone rang. Sadly, the cleaners could not do it until tomorrow and they asked for my kind patience until then. Luckily, it was a joke and my trousers were returned amid laughter not much later.

Mihály Laki also told of some amusing experiences of his. He was holidaying at Mátraháza and I was there too, working intensely. However, I went off for a walk with them when they invited me, but as we set off, I looked at my watch and said, "I have an hour to spare for this walk." The story is credible. Even today, when I set out for a walk, I look at my watch and say what the "Laki time" is.

We went in to dinner. At the dinner table, my son András spoke humorously in the name of my children, and then Zsófi, my Swedish granddaughter, spoke kind words on behalf of the grandchildren in perfect Hungarian. Finally, Judit Rimler was the spokesperson for our friends, handing over to me ceremoniously a special plaque, "The Order of the Top Dog." This was a great honor indeed, as dogs were what Judit valued most.

I was happy and moved as I looked around the table. It was a unique occasion to have our three children, our grandchildren, and all our close family in Budapest at once. And alongside them were many friends. This was not a circle of friends who met regularly. Some knew each other, but others were meeting for the first time. What bound them together that evening was the kind intention of congratulating me.

I have been feted before. It is a family tradition with us to have a series of events to mark a birthday, not just short congratulations and a couple of presents. I am proud and flattered to have been part of several other, more formal celebrations. Such events took place when I received honorary doctorates from several universities, when the French ambassador in Budapest invited friends of mine to the presentation of my Legion of Honor, and when colleagues and friends greeted me at Collegium Budapest on my seventieth and seventy-fifth birthdays. For my seventieth birthday, I was honored also to be presented with two *Festschrift* volumes, by their editors—János Gács and János Köllő, and Eric Maskin and András Simonovits, respectively.[5] Each such gathering was a pleasure to me, but the one Zsuzsa conjured for my seventieth birthday stands out as an occasion when I especially felt how much affection and great warmth surrounded me. It was one of the happiest moments in my life.

Harvard: Teaching and farewell

The twice-yearly commute between Budapest and the United States continued after the change of system. At Harvard University as well, I had to meet the new expectations that the 1989–1990 turn of events had presented.

Harvard has traditionally been one of the intellectual centers of research into the Soviet Union and the communist system, owing to several factors. This was where Alexander Gerschenkron, a writer of classic economic history, worked after he left the Soviet Union. So did Wassily Leontief and Simon Kuznets, both Nobel Prize–winning economists. All three retained their interest in what was happening in the eastern half of the world. All who had an interest in the Soviet Union, the communist system, and Eastern Europe would turn up eventually at the Russian Research Center. There was also a famous center for Far Eastern studies at the university, with some outstanding China experts on its staff. During my years at Harvard, I maintained a lively connection with these research centers and with many researchers working there, and gave lectures on numerous occasions.

The fall of the Berlin Wall caused great commotion. For a while, there was hardly a professor whose interest did not turn to the new post-Soviet states and Eastern Europe. The time and energy of some faculty extended to one or two lightning visits or a couple of conferences. Others, including some exceptional talents, devoted themselves fully to the post-socialist transition for several years.

The telephone would ring and it would emerge that some fellow professor of mine was off to Budapest or some other ex-socialist country and wanted to be briefed on how things stood. I was invited to speak at a succession of Harvard seminars. Once I had to explain in a single lecture, to a thousand undergraduates in a vast introductory course on economics, how the socialist system worked and what the transformation entailed. It was a memorable moment to address them in the lovely wood-paneled Sanders Theater, where my wife and I also attended concerts regularly.

During the years that followed the change of system, I would organize "dinner seminars" in the Faculty Club and invite all the professors connected in some way with research, teaching, and advice on the post-socialist transition. We met regularly, and every participant would report over the dinner table about his or her experiences; interesting discussion and often strong clashes of views would follow.

The new situation intrigued the students as much as it did the professors. My course on the socialist system always attracted large numbers, usually more than did the other optional, voluntary seminars offered to students in the doctoral program. Now the numbers multiplied again. As the 1990s progressed, ever more of the students were from the former socialist countries—with a good many Russians, Ukrainians, Romanians, Bulgarians, Uzbeks, and, as before, Chinese among them. It was a special delight to have several Hungarian students there.

Teaching for me always involves a great deal of preparation, but it now became a difficult task indeed. The political turn and change of system posed a big challenge to comparative economics, "Sovietology," and all specialists in Eastern European research. Some simply gave up the area, feeling it would be impossible to make future use of the knowledge they had acquired. Others, like me, rolled up their sleeves and got on with it.

What I had to say about the socialist system had *matured*, and decades of research and library reading lay behind it. The institutions, political and economic structure, and legal system of the post-socialist region, on the other hand, were (and still are) changing continuously and quickly. I had only *not yet mature*, provisional material to pass on, as I frankly told my students. But I thought even that to be more useful than saying nothing at all.

Being a "transitologist" is obviously just a transitory experience, as the name itself indicates: when the transition period ends, this peculiar task and occupation will also cease to exist. But if this nonrecurring opportunity could be used well, the result would be an inestimable experience useful for many different purposes. History was offering a laboratory in which we could see how a great transformation took place over what was, in historical terms, an incredibly short time. Looking back, I am not sorry I got together with a few others to engage in transition studies, but I am sorry that economics (or, to go further, social science) did not exhaust the fantastically exciting and informative research opportunities then available.

When I first started teaching about the transition, I felt that I would not be able to give an adequate account on my own. I set up a series of lectures and invited some of the "big guns" on the subject. Large numbers of students came to hear the lectures and pose interesting questions. Nonetheless, I heard increasingly from the students in private conversation that the material was difficult to grasp systematically. Each lecturer brought a different outlook, research method, and set of preconceptions to the lecture hall, which is as it should be; but the students could not organize what they heard. When the outlines of the transition began to sharpen, I tried to give a series of lectures based on a unified structure and line of thought. This format they willingly accepted. But I did not try to do what I had done with my course on the socialist system a decade earlier and put the message of my lectures in book form. Although there is a need for summarizing monographs on the transition, they have been left to a younger generation to supply.

As the years went by, it seemed time for me to start thinking about the future. As a preamble, let me say a little about the conditions for retirement in the United States. Discrimination on grounds of age is forbidden by American law. Employers may dismiss employees for whom they have no further need at age 30 or age 70, for that matter, but the law does not allow employers to force their employees to retire on the dot of, say, 60 or 65. As a rule, "age" cannot be grounds for dismissal. This type of protection is combined with a further privilege in the case of tenured university professors. As I mentioned initially when describing the institution, they cannot be dismissed by the university except under extraordinary circumstances. Ultimately, all that means is that unlike in Europe, there is no compulsory retirement age for the privileged category to which I belonged. University professors in the States themselves decide when to retire. If they like, they can remain active for as long as they are physically capable of it.

There is a relatively small state pension at around subsistence level, to which every citizen who has contributed to Social Security is entitled. In addition, the university pays premiums into a nonprofit, private pension fund for all its active faculty. The accumulated premiums and yield are received on retirement, but no sum is guaranteed. It primarily depends on years of service and on earnings. Other determining factors are the investment portfolios chosen by the employee and the yields earned on those investments.

What does retirement mean for a university professor in the States? Regarding income, he or she faces several options: a lump-sum payment, an annuity, and so on. He can ask that after his death an annuity be paid to his widow, etc. If a teacher has taught about four to four and a half decades and has progressed through the usual rungs of the university career ladder, then retirement does not bring about a drastic reduction in income. At the same time, retirement brings relief from teaching and administrative tasks. But if retired faculty wish to do research, their applications for funding are usually supported by the university, and they are entitled to use of a university room and other support. They can remain in the stimulating atmosphere of the university, go to the library, frequent the university swimming pools, drop into the Faculty Club, and remain a full member of the subsidized university health plan. In sum, a university professor in the States loses little, financially or intellectually, while shedding many commitments. It is no wonder that most choose to retire eventually.

My case was different. I was not required by law or contract to go into retirement, but my wife and I had to think carefully about whether we could stand the double burden of two jobs as time went by. How long could we manage packing up, traveling, and unpacking twice a year? How long could we perform the many administrative tasks associated with our parallel lives in Budapest and Cambridge, let alone the extra effort of having two places of work? We did not want to wait until an unexpected illness made the decision for us. Instead, we decided to wind up the American part of our working lives while we still had the strength to accomplish the task efficiently.

Retiring for us, unlike my American colleagues, has meant not only a relief and a reduced load from giving up teaching but great losses as well. Moving back to Hungary has taken us away from the incomparable intellectual and cultural stir that is Harvard, Cambridge, and Boston. An office at the university, use of the world's largest academic library, and the chance to lunch in the Faculty Club with old colleagues are empty privileges for me—I cannot avail myself of them.

We decided after much reflection to make 2001–2002 the last academic year when I would teach at Harvard. After that, we would return home for good.

I told my students they would be the last I would teach. I remember fondly the kind celebration they treated me to after my last lecture, and the warm words all wrote anonymously on their official assessment forms for the department.

Many elderly people in Budapest have told me that their colleagues and superiors bid them farewell on their retirement at quite meaningless, formal celebrations. I can report with good feelings that my retirement party was sincere, friendly, and rich in content. Dale Jorgenson praised my professional and public work in a short lecture that emanated not only respect but also the thoroughness so typical of him. The next speaker was Eric Maskin, who by then was an economist not at Harvard University but at the Institute for Advanced Study in Princeton; he had come to Cambridge specially for this event. Dotting his address with many humorous anecdotes, he spoke of how we had worked together on the theory of the soft budget constraint and how we had dealt with students we had shared, a group of extremely talented Chinese. Jeffrey Sachs related that if he had written something and showed it to me, he felt almost anxious, because he knew that I would assess what came into my hands rigorously and impartially. The most important thing he picked out in my work was that I had told the truth in a world where tyranny and falsehood reigned. In that, in respect for truth, he compared me with Adam Michnik and Václav Havel. That conclusion I felt to be an enormous compliment.

After my three fellow economists, my son András took the floor to relate with his customary kind humor what scholarship and Harvard meant to me, according to his family experience.

I also spoke, in a partly ironic, partly serious tone. I could not and did not want to show how touched I was. It is hard to say in prose what Schubert's music can tell so well: one can be happy and sad at the same time. I was imbued with a great feeling of having spent eighteen years in that intellectual environment where I learned, taught, and made friends. It was a painful thought that I had to leave all that behind.

The ceremonies were followed by farewell after farewell: saying good-bye to friends, taking a little walk through familiar streets and squares in Boston, having a last nighttime look at our beloved Harvard Square and even a short browse through the bookstores that stay open so late.

We said goodbye to András, his wife Ági, and the children, whom we would now see only occasionally, when they visited home. Distance makes it particularly difficult for us to follow the growing up of Mishka, now a young boy, and of Dani and Nóri, who are just going through a most charming period of starting school.

We began to dismantle the apartment on Mount Auburn Street, where every feature and object had been acquired and placed with such care. Some items we gave away and some we dispatched to Budapest. Boxes and crates filled up. The movers came and put them in a shipping container and sent them on their way to Budapest.

It was as if we were watching a movie of our first days in the Mount Auburn Street apartment. There we are again, sleeping on inflatable rubber mattresses on the floor for a few days. I fix myself a provisional desk and bookshelf in my study, with the computer and the files I am working on. There is always something to do or write, up to the very last moment. "A steadfast tin soldier" is what Zsuzsa calls me on such occasions, alluding to Hans Christian Andersen's tale. We also take some video footage of these amusing yet heartbreaking final days.

The day came at last and we set off for Europe. At first, as always before, we broke the journey home in Stockholm, to spend a few days with our daughter, Judit, and grandchildren Zsófi and Anna. Then we flew home to Budapest, where my son Gábor and his family, Tünde, Julcsi, and Tomi, met us at the airport. We hope we can return to Cambridge from time to time in the future, but it will not be the kind of return to our American home that we had year after year when we came back after spending several months in Budapest. A stage in our lives had irrevocably ended.

Back at home

When we arrived in Budapest, the move itself occupied us for a good while. Climbing up three flights of stairs to the apartment in Dobsinai utca where we had lived for twenty-eight years had become too tiring. We sought a house with an elevator and finally found our dream apartment in Óbuda. We furnished it with reminders of beloved places in the past. It has furniture, pictures, and books bought in Cambridge next to furniture, ornaments, and books upon books brought from our former Budapest apartment.

Anyone who has moved knows how tiring it is. In our case, it was especially complicated, as we had to combine two homes, an American and a Hungarian, into one. Harder even than the physical fatigue was the emotional burden of selection. What should we keep, what give to others, and what throw away? We had seen elderly American friends face the same problem when moving from spacious suburban homes to something more compact in town. Now we were bemused by mounds of familiar furniture, books, and old papers. Nonetheless, the move came at a good time. Making dates with tradespeople and arguing with them, obtaining installations and cladding materials, fitting in books, records, and video tapes, and a thousand other tasks of moving absorbed our attention and left us no time for nostalgia or for repeated reliving of the sorrow of leaving Cambridge.*

"Have you gone crazy? You wanted to come back *here*, when you had it all—job, home, splendid environment—over there?" We have been asked that more than once.

---

* Our experience in building the house in Dobsinai utca was an inspiration behind the writing of *Economics of Shortage*. I could have written a good comparative case study about housing construction in 1974 and 2002, describing how the seller's market had turned into a buyer's market and supply constraint into a demand constraint on the economy. On the first occasion, we needed personal contacts to obtain a bathtub with a manufacturing fault and second-grade clinker bricks. On the second, we were able to choose surfacing materials and installations from a huge range of supplies in stores stuffed with goods.

And we have been surrounded since by much that repels and outrages us. If I turn on the television or radio news, I often switch it off again quite quickly. I do not want to hear all the abuse, exposés and sham exposés, the strident tone that assaults my ears, or the superfluity of empty promises and superficial information.

I encounter too much impoliteness and absence of human tact in other spheres of life as well as politics. I may be irritated by the impatient honking of a driver forced to wait at the lights for a second, or the lack of concern shown by staff in a store or restaurant.

Yet I feel at home in this world. Even the ugly is familiar. I know my way. I know or guess why a driver is angry or a girl in a store thinks of things other than her work.

There was an old joke about a Hungarian delegation to China. Mao Zedong asks the delegates what Hungary's population is. On hearing, he replies, "How nice for you! If there are so few of you, then everybody must know everybody."

Being a Harvard professor in America opens many doors, but I was a tiny, unknown point in that vast country. Not so here. I have spent seventy-seven years here. I know a great many people, if not everyone. And if I am not generally known, quite a lot of people know who I am. If I want the ear of a minister, he will receive me. If I phone the chief editor of a paper I do not need to take long to introduce myself.

Though the physical distance from my son András and his family has grown, we are now closer to Gábor and his family, who live in Budapest. Judit and her daughters in Sweden are easier to reach from Budapest than from Cambridge as well, not to mention the fact that we are now fellow members of the European Union. It is particularly pleasing that we can speak about serious subjects with our grown-up grandchildren—Julcsi, a high school teacher, and university students Zsófi, Anna, and Tomi—and that I can count on Tomi's expert assistance when I have a problem with my computer. (Of course, there is no sense in thinking in terms of such trade-offs. The absence of one child or grandchild cannot be compensated for by having another nearer at hand.)

We have become accustomed again to living permanently in Hungary, except for occasional short visits elsewhere. We miss, of course, the feeling we had during earlier years, when we were tired of the confusion at home, that we would soon be on the plane again, leaving Hungary's tensions and problems behind in favor of the peace, calm, and beauty that Cambridge offered.* When we are filled with such

---

* But such peace and calm was provided by that world to Hungarians who traveled there for only a few months at a time. We ultimately remained outsiders. We did not experience the political storms or public tensions with the intensity that our American friends did.

regrets, we console ourselves with another thought. We have finally arrived at a position where we do not have to start worrying toward the end of the summer about starting to pack up and move on or starting to revise my lecture notes. For eighteen years, we followed a rhythm of six-month or yearlong periods, and the commuting back and forth cut up the passing years into chunks. Now the time passes evenly.

We are at home.

"What are you working on?"

That is what I am always being asked when I meet friends or acquaintances. I can hardly imagine being able to answer "Nothing." I am an emeritus twice over, as both Harvard and Collegium Budapest honored me with the title. I would have a right to stop working. We could live comfortably without the income that my continued work may bring.

The time is bound to come when I do stop, but for now I still have an answer.

My term as president of the International Economic Association (IEA) entails various duties. The events of my presidency will culminate with the 2005 IEA World Congress, scheduled to take place in Morocco, with hundreds of participants and a huge number of papers. I have many people helping me, of course, but ultimately, the president bears responsibility. I have begun to prepare my presidential address, and, as will be expected of the first Eastern European president, I intend to address problems of post-socialist transition—or, more generally, the characteristics of great historic transformations. I plan to continue exploring these issues as my main area of research even after completing my presidential duties.

Meanwhile, I have laid aside other tasks to write my memoirs. It has been an unusual genre for a researcher who has spent decades writing monographs and academic articles. It is time to stop. The rest of my work is waiting for me.

Endnotes

The following abbreviations are used for the Hungarian archives cited in the notes:

ÁBTL   Állambiztonsági Szolgálatok Történeti Levéltára (Historical Archives of Hungarian State Security)

IH   Információs Hivatal Levéltára (Archives at the Information Office of the Republic of Hungary)

MOL   Magyar Országos Levéltár (National Archives of Hungary)

MTALt   Magyar Tudományos Akadémia Levéltára (Archives of the Hungarian Academy of Sciences)

OHA   Oral History Archívum (Oral History Archives)

PIL   Politikatörténeti és Szakszervezeti Levéltár (Archives of Political History and Trade Unionism)

1 My Family and Youth—1928–1944

1. On the Jewish hostages held in the Rabbinical School on Rökk Szilárd utca, see Braham 1981, 1:482–483; Brámer 1997 [1972].

2. Fóthy 1945. Though Fóthy's book does not mention my father by name, it discusses the lawyers who were transferred from Rökk Szilárd utca to Horthy-liget, then shortly afterward to the death camps.

3. Braham 1981, 2:325; Thassy 1996, pp. 372–376, 394–396, 418–419.

2 How I Became a Communist—1945–1947

1. Stalin 1953 [1940], 6:47.

2. Ady 2004, p. 724.

3. Lukács 1973 [1945], 1978 [1950].

4. For what Mann said at the beginning of the 1920s, see Réz 1961.

3   On a Communist Newspaper—1947–1955

1. ÁBTL V-145-288-a, pp. 514–515. Date: June 14, 1950.
2. Kornai 1951d, p. 5.
3. Kornai 1951c.
4. Kornai 1951b, p. 1.
5. Kornai 1951a, p. 1.

4   Waking Up—1953–1955

1. I was unable to reconstruct what exactly I had read of Kardelj's after 1953. I refer to Kardelj's memoirs as my source: the editors enclosed some relatively important works of his in an appendix, including his work on self-management, found in speeches and articles delivered on the subject between 1945 and 1955 (Kardelj 1982). I presume that some of these came into my hands at the time.
2. Lange 1968 [1936–1937].
3. Kornai 1954b.
4. Kornai 1954c.
5. I. Nagy 1954, p. 169.
6. I. Nagy 1954, p. 132.
7. Kornai 1954a.
8. In recalling the events of the "rebel" meeting, I drew on the following sources: Aczél and Méray 1960; Kende 1966; Lőcsei 1995; C. Nagy 1994; Szalay 1994. The minutes of the meeting are in MOL M-KS 276. f. 89/206 ő.e., which contains the documents of the Agitation and Propaganda Department of the MDP KV concerning *Szabad Nép*, including the minutes of the meetings held on October 22, 23, and 24, 1954; the resolution passed at the meeting; and the report on the meeting by the Agitprop Department.
9. Aczél and Méray 1960.
10. MOL M-KS 276. f. 89/206. ő.e. pp. 161–219.
11. MOL M-KS 276. f. 53/205. ő.e. pp. 1–3, 7–76.
12. MOL M-KS 276. f. 53/206. ő.e. pp. 31–51, 73–79.
13. MOL M-KS 276. f. 53/206. ő.e. p. 34.
14. MOL M-KS 276. f. 53/206. ő.e. pp. 73, 74, 76.
15. MOL M-KS 276. f. 53/208. ő.e., and 276. f. 53/206. ő.e.
16. Magyar Dolgozók Pártja Központi Vezetősége 1955.
17. MOL M-KS 276. f. 53/228. ő.e.

5 The Beginning of a Research Career—1955–October 23, 1956

1. Liska and Máriás 1954.

2. Hegedűs 1990.

3. Heller 1988.

4. Péter 1954, 1956.

5. Kende 1955. The manuscript is in the possession of the author.

6. ÁBTL V-145-288/document 2, pp. 325–326. Sándor Fekete's confession in his own hand, points 2 and 5. Date: December 18, 1958.

7. Péteri 2001, p. 51; for a broad survey, see Péteri 1997.

8. Kornai 1994b [1959], pp. viii–ix.

9. Kornai 1994b [1959], p. 27.

10. Kornai 1994b [1959], p. 112.

11. Kornai 1994b [1959], p. 114.

12. Kornai 1994b [1959], p. 146.

13. Kornai 1994b [1959], p. 215.

14. Kornai 1994a [1959], p. 236.

15. MTALt TMB 891/368. The minutes of the debate of János Kornai's dissertation. Date: September 24, 1956. See also Esze 1956.

16. MTALt TMB 891/368, p. 41. I have quoted György Péter directly from the records, with only a few minor linguistic corrections.

17. At the time, Mária Augusztinovics's married name was Gerő Tamásné (Mrs. Tamás Gerő). Her contribution to the debate is recorded in the minutes under her married name.

18. MTALt TMB 891/368, pp. 2–11.

19. A copy of the proposal is held in my private collection of documents.

20. Kornai 1956.

6 Revolution and After—October 23, 1956–1959

1. ÁBTL V-150-352/doc. 1, p. 442. Date: April 16, 1957. MOL XX-5-h. 1. d. 3. k. pp. 92–97. Date: 13 July, 1957. My involvement in developing the government program went onto my criminal record. (My criminal record file number is ÁBTL C-R-N 0082-479-2. The copy I have seen is dated December 21, 1966. There must have been a similar file before that.)

2. Vida 1992, p. 34.

3. Gimes 1956.

4. Halda 2002, p. 167.

5. Kornai 1990a [1957], p. 6.

6. Esze 1956.

7. Péter 1957.

8. G. Ripp 1957, p. 3.

9. Molnár 1957, p. 45.

10. Gulyás 1957–1958, p. 31.

11. Kornai 1994b [1959].

12. "Bureaucrats at Large" 1960; R.N.W.O. 1959; Devons 1959.

13. Spulber 1960, p. 763.

14. Nove 1960, p. 389.

15. MOL M-KS XX-5-h. 50. d. 1. k. pp. 48–54. Date: March 20, 1957; MOL M-KS XX-5-h 52. d. 1. k. pp. 10–13. Date: May 8, 1958.

16. MOL M-KS XX-5-h, 1. d. 4. k. pp. 57–59. Date: April 16, 1957.

17. MOL M-KS XX-5-h. 86. d. vol. 5, pp. 49–67. Interrogation report of P. P. The report to which the interrogating officer refers can be found on p. 51. Gimes's plans to establish a newspaper and the actual production of the paper are discussed on pp. 51–54. Date: April 10, 1957.

18. MOL M-KS XX-5-h. 1. d. 4. k. pp. 57–59.

19. MOL M-KS XX-5-h. 86. d. 4. and 5. k.

20. The study by Hungaricus went out immediately after it was written; only a limited number of mimeographed copies were available to a narrow circle of people. A printed edition of the Hungarian text did not appear until 1989.

21. Fejtő wrote an article in 1957 about the "Hungaricus" study. The study itself was published unabridged in French by the Imre Nagy Institute in Brussels in 1959.

22. ÁBTL V-145-288/document 3, pp. 482–492. J. Vassiliou's interrogation report. Date: June 11, 1959. See also Vasziliu 1999.

23. ÁBTL V-145-288/document 2, p. 327. Sándor Fekete's confession in his own hand, point 11. ÁBTL V-145-288/document 3, pp. 482–492. J. Vassiliou's interrogation report. Date: June 11, 1959. See also Vasziliu 1999. ÁBTL V-145-288/document 9, pp. 156–160, 233.

24. Novobáczky 1956, p. 1.

25. ÁBTL V-145-288/document 3, pp. 482–492. J. Vassiliou's interrogation report. Date: June 11, 1959. ÁBTL V-145-288/document 2, p. 326. Sándor Fekete's confession in his own hand, point 7.

26. ÁBTL V-145-288/document 2, p. 327. Sándor Fekete's confession in his own hand, point 8.

7   My Universities—1957–1959

1. Samuelson 1980.

2. Arrow 1951.

3. Hayek 1975 [1935].

4. Hicks 2001 [1939].

5. Samuelson 1983.

6. Tinbergen 2004 [1954].

7. Hayek 1975 [1935].

8. Lange 1968 [1936–1937], p. 70.

9. Kende 1959.

10. Kornai 1959.

11. Kende 1964.

12. Kornai 1958.

8   The Economic Application of Mathematical Methods—1957–1968

1. Kornai and Lipták 1959.

2. Kornai and Lipták 1962b.

3. Bródy 1970.

4. Samuelson 1983.

5. Kornai and Lipták 1962a.

6. Kornai and Lipták 1971 [1965].

7. Arrow 1971.

8. Malinvaud 1967.

9. Arrow 1973b [1963].

9   Traveling to the West—1963 Onward

1. Kornai 1967b.

2. Malinvaud and Bacharach 1967.

3. Juhász 1934.

4. ÁBTL M 13417/1. The report about me and an assessment of it can be found on p. 35 in the file. The agent, according to the report, talked to me on June 10, 1960. The thick dossier that contains, among other things, the report about me was opened on June 25, 1957.

5. The order to draw up a report on me has the reference number IH IV/1-A and is dated April 15, 1964. The reference numbers of R. R.'s reports on me are 35-634/65 and 2/B-530, and are dated May 4, 1965.

I should note here that I quote in these endnotes the reference numbers that can be found in the document copies the Information Office (IH) made available to me. I assume that the originals of these documents were picked from files in the records of the legal predecessor of the IH, which had their own reference numbers, for internal use. I do not know these numbers.

The same holds true for every document that the IH made available to me and that future notes cite.

6. IH 134-216/64. X. X.'s report on me. Date: March 2, 1964.

7. IH VI/4-A. Date: March 26, 1964.

8. Kenedi 1996, p. 438. Kenedi states in a footnote that his glossary was based on the classified *Állambiztonsági Értelmező Szótár* (Dictionary of State Security Terms), published by the Interior Ministry in 1980, which he augmented from other sources.

9. The first professional evaluation was written on the occasion of a passport application in 1966. This evaluation is later referred to in another document, from which I took the excerpt quoted above. The later document is IH 40-27-245/64, 213-3019, dated July 12, 1964.

10. The barely legible reference number on the photocopy is IH III/I-1-A. 8153.

11. Koopmans and Montias 1971.

12. The IH reference number is missing. It appears on pp. 18–22 among the copied documents received from the IH connected to the Montias case.

13. IH 34-4-797/1965. Date: April 23, 1965.

14. Captain Z. Z.'s report. IH 34-A-1027/1965. Date: May 26, 1965.

15. IH 34-4-797/1965. Date: April 23, 1965. Handwritten order on p. 1.

16. IH 59/2581-4/1965. Date: November 22, 1965.

17. IH 189-193/66. Date: May 18, 1966. IH 189-191/66. Date: May 19, 1966. IH 189-220/66. Date: June 6, 1966.

18. Bolygó 1966.

19. Montias 1976; Kornai 1978.

20. ÁBTL 0004-470-5-MRG, p. 24. Date: April 1, 1971.

21. ÁBTL 0004-470-5-MRG, p. 47. Date: January 29, 1989.

22. Montias 1982, 1989, 2002.

10   Against the Current—1967–1970

1. Kornai 1967a.

2. Kornai 1968.

3. Neumann 1963 [1955], pp. 100–101.

4. Kornai 1991, p. 367. For the idea of the "mathematical crystal," see Heisenberg 1967 [1958], pp. 231–232.

5. Arrow 1974, p. 254; Simon 1979, p. 508.

6. I read the quotation from Haydn in a weekly paper, but I have been unable to trace its source. I have nevertheless used it, because it seems credible that it should really come from Haydn and because it illustrates my point.

7. Hahn 1973, p. 330.

11 Institute, University, and Academy—1967 Onward

1. From Attila József's poem "Vigasz" (Consolation), 1933; József 2003, p. 390.

2. Kornai, Kovács, and Schmidt 1969.

3. A copy of the letter is held in my collection of documents.

4. It was Tibor Huszár who called my attention to the source of the story of my election as an academician: MOL M-KS 288. f. 36/1. ő.e. p. 9.

5. MOL M-KS 288. f. 5/675. ő.e. p. 10.

6. MOL M-KS 288. f. 5/675. ő.e. p. 10.

7. MOL M-KS 288. f. 5/682. ő.e. p. 3.

8. MOL M-KS 288. f. 5/682. ő.e. p. 7.

12 Pathfinding and Preparation—1971–1976

1. Kornai 1972.

2. Kornai 1972, p. 5.

3. Hirschman 1988 [1958]; Streeten 1959.

4. The letter of invitation is held in my collection of documents.

5. Kornai and Martos 1973.

6. Kornai and Martos 1981.

7. Kornai and Martos 1981.

8. Kornai 1974.

13 Pieces Falling into Place—1971–1980

1. Kornai 1980, p. 569.

2. A copy of András Bródy's reader's report is held in my collection of documents.

3. A copy of Lajos Faluvégi's reader's report is held in my collection of documents.

4. The short article, signed (bes), came out in the October 4, 1980, issue of the weekly paper *Élet és Irodalom.*

5. Kornai 1979.

6. Karagedov 1982.

7. Barro and Grossman 1971.

8. A typical example of the line of thinking represented by Barro, Grossman, and Portes is Portes and Winter 1980.

9. Yergin and Stanislaw 1998, p. 277.

10. Hoffman 2002, pp. 89–90.

14   A Breakthrough—1979 Onward

1. Kornai, Maskin, and Roland 2003.

2. Kornai and Weibull 1983.

3. Goldfeld and Quandt 1988, 1990, 1993.

4. Dewatripont and Maskin 1995.

5. My correspondence with the journal's editor and the readers' reports are held in my collection of documents.

6. Kornai 1986b [1980].

7. Hicks 1937.

8. Arrow 1973a.

9. Schumpeter 1983 [1934].

10. Aghion and Howitt 1998.

11. I came across this saying in a paper whose author mistakenly ascribed it to Keynes, but the credit actually belongs to Wildon Carr. See Shove 1942, p. 323.

15   Amicable, Dispassionate Criticism—1968–1989

1. Kornai 1983a, p. 229.

2. Kornai 1982.

3. I took this quotation from an interview Tibor Liska gave to OHA (interview 39, p. 346). I have only made small linguistic changes to the written transcript of the interview.

4. Szénási 1983, p. 7.

5. Kornai 1986b [1980], p. 137.

6. Lengyel 2002, pp. 157–158.

7. Szegő 1983.

8. Kornai 1984.

9. Tardos 1982, 1988a, 1988b.

10. Kornai 1986c, pp. 1733–1734.

11. The quotation is taken from the first edition of the textbook (Gregory and Stuart 1980, p. 299). In the later editions, the authors gave a more accurate treatment of the new Hungarian economic mechanism (for the most recent, see Gregory and Stuart 2004).

12. Müller 1999 gives a detailed description of the purpose of the "Daily Operative Information Report" and the methods and organization of gathering and systematizing information.

13. ÁBTL NOIJ III/1-218-265/6, p. 3. Date: December 10, 1981.

14. ÁBTL NOIJ III/II-80, p. 5. Date: April 26, 1985.

15. ÁBTL, handwritten note, annexed to document ÁBTL NOIJ III/II-80A.

16   Harvard—1984–2002

1. Rosovsky 1990, pp. 194–195.

2. Samuelson 1983.

3. The letter is held in my collection of documents.

17   At Home in Hungary and in the World—1985 Onward

1. Szakolczai 2001, p. 92.

2. Kornai 1988b, pp. 737, 739.

3. Kornai 1988a.

4. Sen 1988.

5. Lindbeck 1988.

6. In 1985, the publishing house of the Chinese newspaper *Economic Daily* brought out a selection of the material of the conference. Translated into English, the title is *The Management and Reform of the Macroeconomy: A Selection of Presentations Held at the International Conference on the Management of the Economy.* As I was not able to identify the editor(s), the publication is not included in this volume's references.

Some of the papers that were submitted to the conference are held in my collection of documents.

18   Synthesis—1988–1993

1. Kornai 1992c, p. xxi.

2. Karsai 1993, p. 19.

3. Schama 1989, p. xiii.

4. Kornai 1992c, p. xix.

5. Nove 1992, p. 23.

6. Nove 1992, p. 23.

7. Ericson 1994, pp. 495, 497.

8. Krausz 1994, p. 158.

9. Krausz 1994, p. 157.

10. A copy of my letter is held in my collection of documents.

19   Turning Point—1989–1992

1. Coles 1999.

2. Passel 1990; Bosworth 1990; Salgó 1990; Gy 1991; Denton 1990.

3. Kornai 1990b.

4. Kornai 1992b.

5. Kornai 1992a.

6. Kornai 1993a.

7. Kornai 1990c, pp. 72–73.

8. Szegvári 1990, p. 5.

9. Semjén 1990, p. 7.

10. Kornai 1990c, p. 82.

11. Copies of the exchange of letters are held in my collection of documents.

12. Samuelson 1990, p. 7.

13. Klaus and Tříska 1997 [1994], p. 167.

14. Kornai 1990c, pp. 78–79.

15. Központi Statisztikai Hivatal 1996, p. 314.

16. Kornai 1990c, p. 211.

17. The documents of the roundtable conferences were published in eight volumes. Volume 5 contains important documents on economic policy: Z. Ripp 2000, pp. 15–79, 571–633.

18. For a survey of the economic policy program of the various parties and political organizations, see Laki 1989, 1990.

19. For the work of the Blue Ribbon Committee, the participants were Hungarian and foreign experts; the Bridge Group contained only Hungarian economists. Both committees made their proposals public in the spring of 1990. See Kék Szalag Bizottság 1990; Híd-csoport 1990.

20. Réti 1989, p. 5.

20   On the Boundaries between Science and Politics—1990 Onward

1. Kornai 1992d.

2. Kornai 1995b.

3. Solow 2000, p. 408.

4. Kornai 1997b, pp. 100–120. The interview, conducted by László Zsolt Szabó, was broadcast by Duna TV on April 9, 1995.

5. Blahó 2003.

6. Kornai and McHale 2000.

7. Csontos, Kornai, and Tóth 1996, 1998.

8. Kornai 2000a.

9. Kornai 1998a.

10. Kornai and Eggleston 2001 (in Hungarian, Kornai and Eggleston 2004a).

11. Copies of the exchange of letters are held in my collection of documents.

12. A copy of the letter is held in my collection of documents.

13. The speeches made in Parliament can be found on the CD *Országgyűlési Napló 1990–2002* (Parliamentary Journal, 1990–2002) published by Arcanum Publishers, and on the Internet. We counted, grouped according to various criteria, the references found there. The tables summarizing the results are in my collection of documents.

21 Continuation—1990 Onward

1. Kornai 1983b.
2. Camus 1991 [1948], p. 128.
3. Kornai 1986b [1980], p. ix.
4. Kornai and Rose-Ackerman 2004; Kornai, Rothstein, and Rose-Ackerman 2004.
5. Gács and Köllő 1998; Maskin and Simonovits 2000.

Chronology

The criterion for including events in the chronology is not actual historical weight—some very important ones are omitted—but a much narrower one: to inform readers of historical events lying in the background of episodes described in the autobiography. It is quite apparent from some entries that the events they cover did *not* take place in Hungary. The other events did, even if this is not spelled out in the text.

1921: April 14	Count István Bethlen forms a government, the white terror that followed the short-lived Hungarian Soviet Republic of 1919 having died down. A consolidated semi-authoritarian, semi-parliamentary political regime is established.
1933: January 30	Adolf Hitler becomes German chancellor.
1938: March 12–13	Austria is annexed to Germany.
1938: May 29	The first so-called Jewish Act places ceilings on the proportion of Jews in some professions and ranks of public service.
1939: March 15	German forces occupy Bohemia and Moravia.
1939: May 5	Parliament passes the second so-called Jewish Act, further cutting employment quotas for Jews and adding more restrictions.
1939: September 1	Germany attacks Poland, precipitating World War II.
1941: April 6	German forces attack Yugoslavia.
1941: April 11	Hungary joins Germany in the war against Yugoslavia.
1941: April 16	A government order forces Jewish males in Hungary to do labor service.
1941: June 22	Germany attacks the Soviet Union.
1941: June 26	Hungary enters the war against the Soviet Union on Germany's side.
1941: August 8	The third Jewish Law forbids marriage between Jews and non-Jews.
1941: December 12	Hungary declares war on the United States.
1943: January 12–February 3	The Hungarian army suffers a catastrophic defeat on the Russian front by the Don Bend.
1944: March 19	German forces occupy Hungary.
1944: May 15	Provincial Jews in Hungary begin to be rounded up for deportation.

1944: June 6	The Normandy landings begin.
1944: August 27	The first Soviet troops cross the Hungarian frontier.
1944: October 15	The head of state, Governor Miklós Horthy, calls for an armistice in a radio broadcast. The Arrow-Cross Party, Hungary's Nazis, seizes power. On the next day, Horthy appoints the Arrow-Cross leader, Ferenc Szálasi, prime minister and resigns.
1944: December 21	A provisional parliament meets in Debrecen, eastern Hungary, which has been liberated from German/Arrow-Cross rule. A provisional national government forms the next day.
1944: December 26	The ring of Soviet forces around Budapest is closed and a siege of the city begins.
1945: January 18	The siege of Budapest ends in Pest, on the left bank of the Danube.
1945: February 4–11	Churchill, Roosevelt, and Stalin hold the Yalta Conference.
1945: February 13	The Soviet army frees Budapest from the Germans and their Hungarian Nazi allies after a siege lasting a month and a half.
1945: April 12	Fighting on Hungary's territory ends.
1945: August 6	The atomic bomb is dropped on Hiroshima.
1945: September 2	Japan's unconditional surrender brings World War II to an end.
1945: November 4	In parliamentary elections, the right-wing Smallholders' Party receives 57 percent of the vote.
1946: March 5	Visiting the United States, Churchill talks in a speech at Fulton, Missouri, of an "iron curtain" descending across Europe.
1946: August 1	The biggest hyperinflation in financial history is halted by the introduction of the forint, the new Hungarian unit of currency.
1946: November 28	The first stage of wholesale nationalization of the Hungarian economy covers the biggest industrial installations.
1948: June 12	A merger between the Hungarian Communist Party and the Social Democratic Party results in a de facto one-party system.
1948: June 28	COMINFORM, the Soviet-led international Communist body, condemns Tito and the Yugoslav Communist Party.
1949: January 25	COMECON, the body governing economic cooperation among the socialist countries, is formed in Moscow.
1949: September 16–24	A public treason trial modeled on the great Soviet show trials takes place, with László Rajk, a leading Communist, as the main accused.
1949: October 15	László Rajk and his fellow accused are executed.
1949: December 10	Parliament enacts the First Five-Year Plan.
1949: December 28	Firms with more than ten employees are nationalized.
1951: June 17	*Szabad Nép*, the principal daily, publishes a government order calling for deportation of "former exploiters" from Budapest.

1953: March 5	Stalin dies.
1953: June 17	There is an uprising in Berlin against the Communist system and Soviet occupation of East Germany.
1953: June 27–28	The Communist Party (MDP) Central Leadership passes a "June resolution" on errors made in Hungary and ways to remedy them.
1953: July 4	Imre Nagy becomes Hungary's prime minister.
1953: July 26	Internment (in concentration camps without trial) and deportation end. The day before, a partial amnesty is declared.
1955: March 9	*Szabad Nép* publishes a Communist Party Central Leadership resolution renouncing the previous post-Stalinist party line.
1955: April 14–18	Imre Nagy is dismissed as prime minister and deprived of all offices in the Communist Party.
1956: February 14–25	At the 20th Congress of the Communist Party of the Soviet Union, Khrushchev delivers a speech revealing Stalin's crimes.
1956: June 28	There is a workers' uprising in Poznan, Poland.
1956: October 19–21	In a turn in Polish politics, Gomulka is elected party first secretary and an amnesty and reforms are announced.
1956: October 23	Revolution breaks out in Budapest.
1956: October 24	Imre Nagy is appointed prime minister. Fighting between rebels and Soviet and Hungarian armed forces breaks out in various parts of Budapest. Unrest begins to spread to other cities.
1956: October 29	Soviet troops begin to withdraw from Budapest. On the next day, Imre Nagy announces an end to the one-party system and forms a coalition government embracing revived political parties that had operated before the Communist takeover.
1956: October 29	The second Arab-Israeli War begins.
1956: November 1	Hungary withdraws from the Warsaw Pact.
1956: November 4	Soviet troops attack Budapest. A new regime under János Kádár, loyal to the Soviet Union, is imposed.
1956: November 11	Armed resistance in Budapest ends.
1956: November 22	Imre Nagy and his associates are kidnapped and held prisoner in Romania.
1957: September 10	The UN General Assembly begins debating the "Hungarian question."
1957: October 4	The Soviet Union successfully puts its Sputnik, the world's first artificial satellite, into orbit round the globe.
1958: June 16	Imre Nagy, prime minister of the revolutionary government; Pál Maléter, his defense minister; and the journalist Miklós Gimes are executed.
1959: March 19	An order on agricultural production cooperatives heralds a new wave of collectivization in Hungary.
1961: August 13	Construction of the Berlin Wall begins.
1961: August 26	Death sentences carried out on a group of '56 rebels mark the end of a series of political executions.

1963: March 22	A wide amnesty is declared for people prosecuted for acts during the '56 Revolution.
1964: August 7	U.S. Congress passes the Gulf of Tonkin Resolution, authorizing direct military intervention in Vietnam.
1966: May 16	The Cultural Revolution begins in China.
1968: January 1	Hungary's New Economic Mechanism comes into force.
1968: January 3–5	The reform communist Alexander Dubček becomes first secretary of the Communist Party in Czechoslovakia.
1968: May 2	The University of Nanterre, near Paris, is closed by its dean. Student demonstrations begin in Paris in the next few days.
1968: August 20–21	Soviet, Bulgarian, Polish, Hungarian, and East German forces invade Czechoslovakia, oust the Dubček government, and bring the "Prague Spring" to an end.
1969: July 21	A U.S. spaceship lands on the moon.
1970: December 14–18	The Polish authorities fire in several places on workers striking because of price increases.
1972: May 22–30	U.S. President Nixon visits Moscow. The SALT-1 arms control treaty is signed.
1972: November 14–15	The Communist Party (MSZMP) Central Committee passes a resolution on curbing economic reform.
1975: August 1	The Helsinki Agreement is signed, an important event in political détente.
1976: September 9	Mao Zedong dies.
1978: January 6	A U.S. delegation headed by Secretary of State Cyrus Vance visits Budapest to return the Holy Crown, a symbol of Hungarian statehood.
1979: December 26–27	Soviet troops march into Afghanistan.
1981: early December	The first issue of the illegal journal *Beszélő* appears.
1981: December 13	General Jaruzelski declares a state of emergency in Poland. The Solidarity trade union organization is banned and its leaders arrested.
1982: May 6	Hungary is admitted into the International Monetary Fund.
1982: July 7	Hungary is admitted into the World Bank.
1985: March 11	Mikhail Gorbachev becomes the new general secretary of the Communist Party of the Soviet Union.
1985: June 14–16	Opposition intellectuals hold a meeting at Monor, near Budapest.
1985: November 19–20	The first of several Gorbachev–Reagan summit meetings takes place.
1986: February 25–March 6	The Congress of the Communist Party of the Soviet Union accepts a program of *glasnost* (openness) and *perestroika* (transformation).
1986: October	A document summarizing the position taken by Hungarian reform economists, *Change and Reform*, is prepared.
1987: August 23	Anti-Soviet demonstrations occur in Lithuania, Latvia, and Estonia.

1987: September 27	The Hungarian Democratic Forum is founded at a meeting in the east Hungarian village of Lakitelek. It will receive the most votes in the first round of the first free general elections in 1990 and go on to form a coalition government.
1988: May 20–22	The Hungarian Communist Party removes as its general secretary János Kádár, who has led the country for thirty-two years.
1989: February 10–11	The leading body of the Hungarian Communist Party comes out in favor of introducing a multiparty system.
1989: June 13	"National Roundtable" negotiations on a peaceful transition begin between the political forces in power and those in opposition.
1989: June 16	Imre Nagy and his fellow martyrs are reburied in Budapest.
1989: November 9	Demolition of the Berlin Wall begins.
1990: April 8	Free elections are held in Hungary.
1990: May 29	Boris Yeltsin is elected president of the Russian Federation.
1990: June 25	Slovenia declares independence; the breakup of Yugoslavia begins.
1990: October 3	The two German states are reunified.
1991: June 19	Withdrawal of Soviet forces from Hungary is completed.
1991: July 1	The Warsaw Pact, the military alliance of the Communist countries, is dissolved.
1991: December 26	The Soviet legislature declares the dissolution of the Soviet Union.
1997: July 8–9	It is announced that NATO has begun negotiations with Czechoslovakia, Hungary, and Poland on membership.
2001: September 11	Terror attacks are made on the World Trade Center in New York and the Pentagon building near Washington, D.C.
2004: May 1	Hungary is among the ten new members of the European Union, eight of them former socialist countries.

Glossary

Sources for the glossary are on file with the author and may be obtained from him on request.

Aczél, György (1917–1991)   Hungarian Communist politician, who joined the party in 1935. In 1945, he became a functionary of the Communist Party. He was imprisoned on falsified charges in 1949, but freed in 1954. He was deputy minister of culture from 1957 to 1967; then the secretary of the party committee in charge of cultural affairs; and, from 1974 to 1982, a deputy prime minister. From the mid-1960s until the mid-1980s, he was the main political controller of cultural life. His policy was more permissive than that in many other Soviet-bloc countries. Aczél treated cultural life as a network of his personal connections, and he tried to manage it by combining, on the one hand, threats and penalties with, on the other hand, benefits and privileges personally determined by him.

ÁVH (Államvédelmi Hatóság, State Security Authority)   The political police, modeled on the Soviet Cheka and its successors, founded in Hungary in February 1945. During the 1956 Revolution, it became the prime target of popular rage and was dissolved. From the outset, its officers were recruited from Communists; though nominally they reported to the prime minister, its top leadership was under the direct control of Mátyás Rákosi (see entry below), the Communist Party leader. The ÁVH carried out the repressive actions of the party-state in the Stalinist period. Its members referred to it as the "fist of the party."

Babits, Mihály (1883–1941)   Influential figure in Hungarian literature during the first half of the twentieth century. Babits was a lyricist who left a lasting impression on many other genres in addition to poetry. He translated the works of Sophocles, Dante, Shakespeare, and Verlaine into Hungarian. He held a permanent position at the periodical called *Nyugat*, where he served as editor from 1929 until his death. Babits was an exceptionally erudite man, whose excellent sense of form was coupled with great moral sensitivity as well as a philosophical predisposition. *A History of European Literature* (1935) is not literary history in a strict sense: it is a set of interlaced essays, in which the practicing poet "reads through" the literature of Europe from the classical Greco-Roman tradition to the beginning of the twentieth century.

Berlin Wall   The system of fortified walls around West Berlin, isolating it from East Germany and dividing the city. Political oppression and a low standard of living caused more than a million East German citizens to leave the country for good via the open zone frontier in West Berlin between 1949 and 1961. On August 12–13, 1961, the East German authorities built the Berlin Wall around the Western zones of the city to prevent any more people from leaving. It became a symbol of cold war division. After months of mass defections and demonstrations, the crisis-ridden Communist leadership opened the borders of the German Democratic Republic on November 9, 1989, and holes were made in the wall. Final demolition of the wall system began in February 1990.

Betlen, Oszkár (1909–1969)   Hungarian Communist journalist. He was imprisoned for nine months for communist activity in 1931 and then deported to his native Pozsony (by then renamed Bratislava, in Czechoslovakia), where he became a Slovak Communist Party functionary. After spending World War II in German concentration camps, he joined the Hungarian Communist daily *Szabad Nép* in 1946 and was its editor in chief from 1951 to 1954. He typified the Stalinist mentality and ideology in the Hungarian press.

Bibó, István (1911–1979)   Hungarian legal scholar, essayist, and politician. A professor at the University of Szeged from 1946 to 1950, he was one of the foremost left-wing, non-communist political thinkers in Hungary in the postwar years before the Communists took power. The turn toward Stalinism in 1948–1949 motivated him to withdraw from public life. He served as state minister in the government of Imre Nagy on November 2–4, 1956. Arrested in 1957, Bibó was sentenced to life imprisonment in 1958 but released in the 1963 amnesty. He then worked as a researcher at the Central Statistical Office until his retirement. His funeral turned into a demonstration against the Kádár regime; in fact, it was one of the earliest public actions by the opposition of the time.

Bierut, Bolesław (1892–1956)   Polish Communist politician. A communist activist between the two world wars, he completed party school in the Soviet Union before joining the staff of Comintern. He was imprisoned in Poland for communist activity from 1933 to 1938, then left for the Soviet Union in 1939 and worked for the notorious political police of the time, the NKVD (Narodnyĭ Komissariat Vnutrennikh Del, the People's Commissariat of Internal Affairs). He returned home in 1943. He became head of state in 1945, general secretary of the Polish United Workers' Party in 1948, and prime minister in 1952, a post from which he resigned in 1954. He was the personification in Poland of a Stalinist type of dictatorship.

Change of system   The term widely used in Hungary for the near-simultaneous collapse of the communist system in 1988–1989 in the Soviet Union and in the countries of Central and Eastern Europe, as dictatorship was replaced with democracy, a single-party with a multi-party system, a socialist economy dominated by state ownership with a market economy based on private ownership. The serious inner crisis of the Communist state party led to the resignation of János Kádár (see entry below) in May 1988, after he had spent thirty-two years in power. From the Hungarian National Roundtable talks (see entry below) there emerged an agreement on the road map of how to return to democracy. The former Communist state party, the MSZMP (Magyar Szocialista Munkáspárt, or Hungarian Socialist Workers' Party), dissolved itself early in October 1989, and a new Republic of Hungary was declared on October 23. Free general elections were held in March 1990 and a non-communist government was formed: this juncture is considered the starting point of the change of system.

COMECON   The Council for Mutual Economic Assistance, an international economic organization (1949–1991). Founded in Moscow in January 1949 by the Soviet Union and six East European socialist countries, COMECON had the official purpose of assisting and coordinating the economic development of the socialist countries. But under Soviet direction, it actually forced compulsory specialization on its member countries, causing grave distortions in their economic structures. A further undeclared task was to isolate the countries of the socialist camp from the Western countries. COMECON broke up after the political change of system in Eastern Europe.

Commune, Hungarian Soviet Republic, 1919 A regime of Soviet Russian-style proletarian dictatorship, also known as the Commune or the Republic of Councils, which ruled Hungary for 133 days from March 21 to August 1, 1919. It replaced the democratic government brought to power in the so-called Aster Revolution of October 31, 1918. After the Communist and Social Democratic parties merged in March 1919, Communists under the leadership of Béla Kun took over the country. But under the pressure of an invasion by Romanian forces, popular dissatisfaction, inflation, and supply shortages caused by a blockade, the Commune leaders resigned and fled abroad on August 1.

Constitutional Court A body of special judges with independent legal status formed at the time of the change of system, patterned on similar courts in the European democracies, to protect democratic constitutionalism. The Constitutional Court is independent of the political parties, the executive and legislative branches of government, and the other parts of the juridical system, including the Supreme Court. It started work on January 1, 1990. Among its tasks are to examine whether legislation or international treaties conflict with the constitution, to interpret the constitution, to declare laws and actions unconstitutional, and to examine complaints made on grounds of constitutional law. Its rulings on constitutionality cannot be challenged. The Constitutional Court has eleven members, whose appointments must be confirmed by a two-thirds majority vote in Parliament. Their terms last nine years and each constitutional judge may be reappointed once.

Eötvös Collegium Hungary's oldest and most famous college, in Budapest. Modeled on Paris's École Normale Supérieure, it was established in 1895 to provide the finest possible teacher training. Education in the Collegium displayed not just high professional standards but a tolerant, democratic-liberal spirit, which in those times was a rarity. The college was closed in 1949 as the Stalinist system was consolidating and the premises were turned into a student hostel.

Esterházy, Péter (1950–) Hungarian author of several novels, short stories, and articles for the press. He is a member of one of the best-known aristocratic families in Hungary. In *Celestial Harmonies: A Novel*, published in 2000, he simultaneously recalls his childhood years during the Communist era and recounts his family's history spanning many centuries. Two years later, in his novel *Revised Edition*, he felt compelled to supplement the earlier picture with the newly learned information that his father, Mátyás Esterházy, had been recruited as an informer by the secret police of the Communist era. Esterházy's prose is usually characterized as "postmodern." He is considered a great master of language, as in his writings he in effect regenerates Hungarian itself. He is one of the best-known writers in the country.

Farkas, Mihály (1904–1965) Hungarian Communist politician. A functionary of the international Communist youth organization before World War II, Farkas did party work in several West European countries before returning to the Soviet Union at the end of 1944. He became deputy general secretary of the Hungarian Communist Party in 1945 and served as defense minister from 1948 to 1953. He developed his own personality cult in the military; he was notorious for his brutality and his vengeful nature. Along with Mátyás Rákosi (see entry below), he was most to blame for the cruel, repressive actions of the Stalinist era. Rákosi tried to shift all responsibility onto him, with such success that Farkas was arrested even before the 1956 Revolution. He was sentenced to fourteen years' imprisonment in 1957 but released under the 1960 amnesty. He subsequently worked as a publisher's reader until his death.

German occupation of Hungary   Hungary entered World War II in 1941, on Germany's side. By early 1944, Hungary seemed a decreasingly reliable ally, as the changing course of the war had made Governor Miklós Horthy (see entry below) hesitant, and his prime minister, Miklós Kállay, was known to have pro-British sympathies. On Hitler's orders, the German army occupied Hungary on March 19, 1944, with hardly a shot being fired. Deportation of the Jewish population to the death camps began soon afterward.

Gerő, Ernő (1898–1980)   Hungarian Communist politician. Between the wars he was a Comintern agent, and he served in the Spanish Civil War as a commissar. In 1945, he became minister of transportation and was active in raising the prestige of the Communist Party in Hungary. He was minister of the interior from 1953 to 1954, and became first secretary of the Communist Party when Mátyás Rákosi was ousted in July 1956. As one of the inner circle of four leaders (with Rákosi, József Révai, and Mihály Farkas; see their individual entries) during the Stalinist years of the early 1950s, he dealt mainly with economic affairs. He was the best bureaucrat and the best organizer in the party. He fled to the Soviet Union during the 1956 Revolution, but was able to return to Hungary in 1960. After being expelled from the Communist Party in 1962 for the illegal acts he had committed in the Rákosi period, he worked as a translator.

Glasnost (literally, "openness"; Russian)   A political initiative announced in 1986 by Mikhail Gorbachev, general secretary of the Communist Party of the Soviet Union, at the same time as perestroika (see entry below). Under certain restrictions, it significantly increased freedom of criticism of the system of state and society in the Soviet Union. Masses of critical articles written in a spirit of glasnost began to appear in the Soviet papers, enlivening the country's intellectual scene and stimulating debate on numerous shortcomings in the Soviet system. The years of more open criticism strengthened the public demand for democratic transformation and contributed substantially to the processes that eventually brought an end to the Soviet Union and the socialist camp.

Goulash communism   A label applied by the Western press to the consolidated Kádár system beginning in the late 1960s and still more in the early 1970s, in a reference to the Hungarian beef dish. Living standards for much of Hungarian society had improved by that time; consumption rose, repression eased, and rights and freedoms broadened to some extent.

Great distribution systems   A generally accepted expression in Hungary for the financing of education, health care, pension, and family support systems inherited from the Kádár period. A broad system of social welfare was built up in Hungary under socialism that had some major achievements but was extremely wasteful. Financing these redistributive systems has subsequently become increasingly difficult, or even impossible. Essential reforms were carried out after 1990 in several areas (such as the pension system), but only minimal changes were made in others.

Horthy, Miklós, Nagybányai [a particle denoting nobility] (1868–1957)   National leader between the world wars. A Hungarian naval officer, Horthy was promoted to rear admiral and put in command of the Austro-Hungarian fleet in 1918. During the 1919 Hungarian Soviet Republic, he raised a "national army" in Szeged (then occupied by Entente forces) and marched on Budapest in November 1919, meeting no resistance. In March 1920, he became governor (head of state) of a kingdom of Hungary that had no king, and his name is associated with the conservative, nationalist period between the wars. He was forced by the Germans to resign in October 1944 and put under house arrest in Bavaria. He spent the last twelve years of his life in exile in Portugal.

Hungarian National Roundtable Talks   Discussions in 1989 about the transfer of power from the Communist party-state and a transition to democracy. The leaders of the Hungarian Socialist Workers' Party (Magyar Szocialista Munkáspárt, or MSZMP) became the first Communists in the Soviet bloc to declare in favor of a multiparty system. Dozens of opposition groups and parties then began to form. On March 22, 1989, these set up the Opposition Roundtable, which aimed at reaching a common position. The MSZMP and its satellite social organizations sat down with representatives of the Opposition Roundtable in June 1989 to determine legal and political conditions for the transition. This series of talks, which became known as the National Roundtable, led in September to agreement on a scenario for the change of system (see entry above). Some of the opposition groups attending the talks eventually did not sign the agreement, issuing dissenting opinions on particular issues.

Hungarian Revolution, 1956 (October 23–November 4)   It began with a demonstration of Budapest students on October 23 and developed that night into an armed uprising. On October 24, a government was formed by the popular reform communist Imre Nagy. The revolutionaries fought successfully against the Hungarian state security forces and the Soviet army, which had to withdraw from Budapest. On October 30 a multiparty coalition government formed. In response to the first signs of a Soviet armed intervention in the making, the Nagy government declared Hungary's neutrality and left the Warsaw Pact. Soviet forces attacked Budapest again on November 4 and installed a countergovernment under János Kádár (see entry below); fighting lasted another week. This was the biggest uprising against the Soviet Union in any Soviet bloc country. Its defeat was followed by several years of reprisals, and the lawful prime minister, Imre Nagy, was among those executed.

Jászi, Oszkár (1875–1957)   Hungarian social scientist, politician, and political commentator. In 1900 he founded the journal *Huszadik Század* (Twentieth Century), which he also edited, and he founded the National Bourgeois Radical Party in 1914. As a friend and adviser of Mihály Károlyi (see entry below), he was an influential political figure in the Hungarian democratic revolution of 1918, holding for a while the minority affairs portfolio in the Károlyi government. During the Hungarian Commune of 1919 (see entry above), he left for Vienna, where he became one of the main émigré figures. Jászi was the leading theorist of Hungarian bourgeois radicalism, a sharp critic of the Soviet system, and the greatest authority on national and minority questions in Central Europe. As an adversary of communism, he could not return home to Hungary after 1945.

Kádár, János (1912–1989)   Hungarian Communist politician. A member of the illegal Communist Party before the war, he was imprisoned several times. As interior minister from 1948 to 1950, he was one of those carrying out the repressive acts of the Stalinist system. He himself was arrested on fabricated charges in 1951, and released in 1954. He was appointed a minister in the Imre Nagy government during the 1956 Revolution, but on November 4 he formed a countergovernment in the service of the Soviet Union. He became head of the new Hungarian Socialist Workers' Party and effective leader of the country in November 1956, holding that position until May 1988. He is associated with the bloody reprisals after the

1956 Revolution and with the creation and leadership of a less repressive, "soft" dictatorship after 1963.

Karinthy, Ferenc (1921–1992)   Hungarian author, translator, and journalist, son of Frigyes Karinthy (see entry below); known to everyone by the nickname Cini. After first studying linguistics, he turned to writing and was a freelance contributor to the dailies *Szabad Nép* and *Magyar Nemzet* in 1951 to 1953. Besides his novels and plays, his lifework includes newspaper articles and a diary kept for decades and published after his death. His humor, love of life, and enthusiasm for sports made Cini a special phenomenon in the Hungarian intellectual elite.

Karinthy, Frigyes (1887–1938)   Hungarian author, poet, and translator. A well-known literary personality, he is one of the most complex figures of Hungarian literature, a genius clown best known for his huge output of humorous and grotesque writings. His collection of parodies (*That's How You Write*) puts the styles of Hungarian and non-Hungarian authors in various genres in front of a distorting mirror. He left a lasting impact on Hungarian urban idiom, as he created outstanding work in every literary form from journalism to drama, from the novel and short story to poetry. Recovering in Sweden after surgery for a brain tumor in 1936, he wrote *Journey around My Skull*, describing with brilliant objectivity his illness and its treatment.

Károlyi, Mihály (1875–1955)   Hungarian politician. A member of an old and extremely wealthy aristocratic family, he entered parliament in 1910. He established an opposition party in 1916, during World War I, putting forward a program of universal franchise, a secret ballot, and peace with the Allies. During the democratic revolution of October 1918, he was called on to be prime minister and then provisional president of the republic from January 1919 until the proclamation of the Hungarian Soviet Republic in March; he left the country in July 1919. Károlyi spent the following decades in Paris and London, increasingly becoming a fellow traveler of the Communist Party. In 1923, when Hungary was under a conservative nationalist government, he was convicted in absentia of treason and had his property confiscated. He returned to Hungary in 1946 and accepted the position of ambassador in Paris in 1947, but he resigned in 1949 in protest against the Rajk trial (see entry below) and went into exile again.

Kossuth, Lajos (1802–1894)   Hungarian politician. Kossuth was finance minister of the first Hungarian independent parliamentary government (1848), the main political leader of the Hungarian War of Independence (1848–1849), and head of state of the briefly independent Hungary (1849). Prior to 1848, he was the main advocate of the internal liberal and radical reforms; but after the defeat of the War of Independence (1849), Kossuth viewed the regaining of Hungarian independence as his most important objective. From 1849 on, he lived in exile, first in England and then later in Italy, maintaining this status even after 1867 in protest against the *Ausgleich* (compromise) signed with Vienna. He popularized the cause of Hungarian independence in England and the United States with long lecture tours in 1851–1852. He lived in Turin, Italy, from 1861 until his death. Kossuth was one of the most important and most popular figures of Hungarian history, a foundational political author and speaker, and his writings and speeches are often quoted in his country.

Kulaks   The name given to the wealthy strata of peasants in Stalin's Soviet Union, declared to be "class enemies" of the proletariat. Hungary followed the same pattern in 1948–1949.

Those placed on the kulak list were subject to high taxation and delivery obligations that were impossible to meet. Many were relocated or imprisoned. Their situation eased under the first Imre Nagy government; the kulak list was abolished in 1954.

"Left wing" in the Hungarian reform debate   A sizable opposition to the New Economic Mechanism introduced in January 1968, which attacked the attempt at reform in Hungary. Some politicians and members of the Communist intellectual elite were concerned that the equality, collectivism, and social justice hitherto proclaimed as socialist values would be abandoned. They saw the rejection of central planning and the limited independence given to enterprises as gains by a "petty bourgeois acquisitiveness" and "individualism" that were alien to the communist worldview. In the conservative wing of the Hungarian party apparatus, a so-called worker opposition developed that gained support from the strengthening neo-Stalinist political line of Leonid Brezhnev's Soviet Union. Because of pressure from this group between 1972 and 1974, numerous reform measures in the New Economic Mechanism program were held up for years. Voices opposed to reform and preferring a Soviet-type model of economic management based on the communist worldview continued to be raised by Hungarian intellectuals until the change of system (see entry above).

Mass organizations   Blanket Communist term for various large-scale social organizations and associations subsumed into the party-state. In Hungary and the other countries under the socialist system, each held a monopoly in its own field—one trade union movement, one women's association, one youth league, one writers' union, and so on. Their governing bodies governed in name only, as decisions were actually made by the party-state and implemented by officers hired and fired by the party-state. They functioned to channel the party's ideas and wishes to the stratum of society that each covered (workers, youth, women, etc.).

Népszabadság (People's Freedom)   The largest-circulation political daily in Hungary. It first appeared during the 1956 Revolution, on November 2, published by the newly established Hungarian Socialist Workers' Party (Magyar Szocialista Munkáspárt, or MSZMP). Its predecessor as the organ of the ruling party had been *Szabad Nép*—a paper on which the author of this book had worked—which ceased publication during the revolution. *Népszabadság* even took over the issue numbering of *Szabad Nép* and became the central daily of the state party during the Kádár period. On October 8, 1989, during the change of system, it became an independent socialist daily; it dropped the word "socialist" from its masthead in 1994.

Örkény, István (1912–1979)   Hungarian author. He studied chemical engineering and then pharmacy. His first book appeared in 1941, but he was called up for labor service in 1942, taken prisoner in 1943, and remained a Soviet prisoner of war until 1946. On his return, he worked as a publisher's reader and wrote for newspapers. After being banned from publishing for several years because of his conduct in the 1956 Revolution, Örkény worked as an engineer in a drug factory; he began to live by his writing again in 1963. He found his own voice during the 1960s in his *One-Minute Stories*, where he depicted the grotesque and absurd aspects of everyday life. Of his plays, *The Tót Family* and *Catsplay* have been the most popular in Hungary and abroad, and they have been adapted for the movie screen as well.

Party college   An institution found in most socialist countries. These schools, which were often residential, offered a variety of courses on Marxist-Leninist philosophy, political economy, and party history. Access was granted only to those recommended by the Communist Party. Hungary's Communist Party established party college ideological training for its new functionaries in the spring of 1945. The most elite school was the one on Karolina út, Budapest. A recommendation for training in a party college was a sign of the party's confidence in a person.

People's colleges   Boarding colleges operated in Hungary from 1945 to 1949 that enabled talented young people from poor worker and peasant families to gain a higher education. The predecessor institution of the people's colleges, which was named first Bólyai College and later Győrffy College, had been established at the end of the 1930s. New colleges were initiated by alumni of Győrffy College. The number of colleges grew and a national federation, NÉKOSZ (Népi Kollégiumok Országos Szövetsége), was founded in 1946. As the movement came under Communist control, students from people's colleges played a prominent role in establishing the communist system in the country. However, beginning in the spring of 1948, this overly autonomous organization found itself in the crossfire of attacks initiated by the Communist Party. It was dissolved in July 1949 and the colleges closed.

"People's writers"   A movement that emerged in the late 1920s. The Hungarian term *népi írók* is problematic in English, as neither "people's" nor "popular" reflects the meaning of *népi*. It refers to the way in which the interests of the writers in the movement were oriented toward the common people. The most active members had a peasant background or a commitment to the peasantry, and they described in their literary and sociological works the backwardness of Hungarian society and the plight of the peasantry within it. They saw the existing middle classes of noble origin and the "alien" urban bourgeoisie as having lost credibility, and their solution to what they saw as the crisis for the Hungarian nation was to educate the peasantry, who would then replace those strata with a new middle class. The movement's ideas were marked by agrarian-democratic radicalism and respect for an idealized peasant way of life. Behind these political ideas and thinking were heterogeneous worldviews, as adherents ranged from fellow travelers of the Communist Party through left-wing socialist believers in Western European–style democracy and right-wingers to some followers of the extreme right wing in Hungary. The program of protection for the nation and Hungarian culture as envisaged by some "people's writers" was tinged with racism, anti-Semitism, and xenophobia. The movement's golden age lasted until the end of the 1940s, but it still exerts a strong influence on Hungarian intellectual life. Major writers in the movement include László Németh, Gyula Illyés, József Erdélyi, Péter Veres, Géza Féja, János Kodolányi, and Ferenc Erdei.

Perestroika (literally, "transformation"; Russian)   An experiment in reform associated with Mikhail Gorbachev, general secretary of the Communist Party of the Soviet Union. Perestroika, instituted in 1986, was meant to reform the structure of the state and society, with the aim of bolstering the power of the Soviet Union. But perestroika collapsed after some years, as its economic reforms failed and social discontent increased. The reforms proclaimed as a strengthening transformation in fact launched a process that led to the Soviet regime's political disintegration.

Petőfi, Sándor (1823–1849)   Hungarian poet. He was not even 20 when he burst onto the scene of Hungarian poetry, and in only a few years he became the most popular poet and the leading figure of his generation, owing in particular to his intense and prophetic temperament. In his political poetry, he championed people's rights and advocated national independence. The revolution of March 15, 1848, began when the crowd took his incisive poem "Rise, Hungarians" to the press and had it printed without its being cleared by the Austrian censor. The incident came to symbolize the struggle for freedom of the press. He played a key part in the revolution as one of the leaders of the influential March Youth. He ran for a seat in the legislature, but his radical republican views left him politically isolated and he was not elected. At the end of 1848, he took part as an officer in the War of Independence from the Habsburgs, and he disappeared in the battle of Segesvár (Sighişoara) against the Russian Tsarist army. For a long time, the people were unable to accept that he had died. Legends spread that he had hidden or was in prison in Siberia. He is Hungary's best-known poet.

Polish roundtable talks A series of talks between February and April 1989 that initiated the process of democratic transformation in Poland. Public dissatisfaction over the economic crisis and the consequent wave of strikes led to representatives of the party-state sitting down to negotiate with the leaders of Solidarity (see entry below), a previously outlawed organization that was legalized again in February 1989. At the talks, held in public, the party-state leaders agreed to hold partially free elections. According to the agreement, all the seats in the Senate, the newly established upper house of the legislature, were to be filled in unrestricted elections, while in the decision-making Sejm 65 percent of the seats were reserved for the state party. To the surprise of the Communist leaders, all the Senate seats and all 35 percent of the lower house seats open to free election were won by Solidarity candidates. The Communists were obliged to accept the Solidarity candidate, Tadeusz Mazowiecki, as prime minister, after which Solidarity formed a coalition government with the state party. Truly free elections were then held in 1991.

Prague Spring The 1968 reform communist experiment in Czechoslovakia, designed to produce "socialism with a human face." It began when the party leadership under Alexander Dubček adopted a program of political and economic reform. The Soviet leadership feared that the process would lead to the development of political forms approaching the pattern of the Western democracies. After diplomatic pressure had failed to persuade the Czechoslovak leaders to reverse their course, forces of the Warsaw Pact invaded the country on August 20, 1968, and ended the reform. Dubček was replaced soon after. His successor, Gustáv Husák, brought into being one of the most repressive anti-reform socialist systems in Eastern Europe.

Rajk, László (1909–1949) Hungarian Communist politician. He spent most of World War II in prison in Hungary, but for a short while after his release, he took part in the armed resistance to the Germans. In 1945, he was one of the most popular men in the Communist Party, especially among young intellectuals. As minister of the interior from 1946 to 1948, he engineered several show trials. He himself was arrested in 1949, underwent a public show trial after the Soviet pattern, and was condemned to death and executed with several others. He was rehabilitated in 1955 and his reburial on October 6, 1956, attended by a hundred thousand people, turned into a demonstration against Stalinism.

Rákosi, Mátyás (1892–1971) Hungarian Communist politician. Rákosi had been a high functionary in the Hungarian Soviet Republic of 1919 before emigrating and working for the international communist organization Comintern. Returning to Hungary secretly in 1925, he was arrested and sentenced to fifteen years' imprisonment. In an exchange arranged with the Soviet government, the Hungarian government let him emigrate to the Soviet Union in 1940. He returned to Hungary in 1945 as paramount leader of the Communist Party. By 1948, he had liquidated all other political forces and overseen the creation of a Soviet-type one-party system, and he became prime minister in 1952. Rákosi, who had a good sense of politics and was relatively erudite, is associated with the introduction of Stalinist repression into Hungary. He did not simply copy the Soviet system but also made an effort to guess Stalin's wishes in advance and surpass them. In June 1953, the post-Stalin Soviet leadership forced Rákosi to resign as prime minister, but he remained leader of the Communist Party and again assumed the paramount position in 1955. In July 1956, he was relieved of all posts and he left for the Soviet Union, where he died in exile.

Révai, József (1898–1959) Hungarian Communist politician and Marxist ideologue. A founding member of the Hungarian Party of Communists in 1918, he went into exile in 1919, in Vienna, Prague, and then Moscow, returning to Hungary only in October 1944. He was one of the inner circle of four leaders (with Mátyás Rákosi, Ernő Gerő, and Mihály Farkas; see their individual entries) during the Stalinist years of the early 1950s, editing the main Communist daily, *Szabad Nép*, from 1945 to 1950 and serving as minister of culture from 1949 to 1953. He was Hungary's chief ideologist and paramount leader of cultural life in that period, but the political changes initiated by Imre Nagy in 1953 deprived him of real power.

"Right wing" in Hungary, 1953–1956 This faction within the Hungarian Communist Party was composed mainly of politicians and intellectuals supporting the reform program of Imre Nagy. The group was accused of "right-wing deviation endangering the party and socialism" in April 1955, as the Stalinist forces of Mátyás Rákosi (see entry above) steadily regained supremacy. The committed believers in reform were almost all set aside and dismissed during 1955. In the spring of 1956, the intellectuals began to organize an anti-Stalinist movement whose public events, such as Petőfi Circle debates and the reburial of László Rajk (see entry above), played an important role in preparing for the revolution of October. Out of former "right-wing deviant" survivors of the post-1956 purges came several prominent figures in the democratic opposition in the Kádár period.

Samizdat (self-publishing; from the Russian *sam* + *izdatelstvo*) A piece of political writing or literature duplicated and distributed in a socialist country illegally, without official approval. Samizdats began to appear in Hungary in the mid-1970s.

Siege of the Radio, 1956 A peaceful protest outside the Hungarian Radio building in central Budapest on October 23, 1956, which turned into an armed clash. A large crowd intent on having the demonstrators' "sixteen points" read on the air had gathered by afternoon at the building, which was guarded by state security forces. This the Communist leaders would not allow the radio to do. Still unarmed, the crowd was further angered when the Communist Party leader, Ernő Gerő (see entry above), threatened reprisals in a speech broadcast at 8 P.M. The security police fired several times to disperse the crowd, but by then people had obtained weapons and laid siege to the building about 10 P.M. Hostilities lasted until dawn, when the insurgents gained control. It was one of the first events signaling the start of the armed uprising and the Hungarian Revolution (see entry above).

Solidarity (translation of the Polish Solidarność) Polish trade union organization and political movement founded in September 1980 as a result of widespread strikes in the shipyards of the port of Gdansk in August. It was the first independent trade union in the Soviet bloc. Faced with Solidarity's growing influence, General Wojciech Jaruzelski, first secretary of the Communist Party and prime minister of Poland, declared martial law in December 1981, outlawing the trade union and interning its leaders. But Solidarity continued to operate underground, and in 1989, the Communist leadership recognized it as a participant in the Polish roundtable talks (see entry above).

Smallholders' Party (Független Kisgazdapárt, or FKgP) The Independent Smallholders', Land Workers', and Citizens' Party, founded as an opposition peasant party in 1930, under the Christian-nationalist Horthy system. It became the biggest political party immediately after World War II, drawing its members mainly from people opposed to the ideas of the Left and from those who were religious. Though it won the first free elections in November 1945 by a wide margin, under Soviet pressure it nonetheless formed a coalition with the left-wing parties. Zoltán Tildy of the FKgP was the first president of the republic. But under the guise of the coalition, and relying on a combination of political guile, illegal techniques, and the active participation of the Soviet authorities, the Communists had destroyed the FKgP completely by 1947, when its most important leaders were in prison or in exile. Some of its politicians were prepared to bargain, however, lending legitimacy to the Communist takeover and even assisting in running the Stalinist system. By the following year, the party had become insignificant, and it disappeared altogether as the one-party system developed. The FKgP was revived for a few days during the 1956 Revolution, when Tildy became a minister in the Imre Nagy government. The FKgP reemerged again with the change of system in 1989 and proved to be the third strongest party in the first free elections. It then shifted toward populism and was torn apart by internal dissensions after the turn of the millennium.

Széchenyi, István (1791–1860) A member of one of Hungary's wealthiest and most respected aristocratic families, who became widely known in 1825 when he donated a year's income from his estates toward the founding of what became the Hungarian Academy of Sciences. The 1830 appearance of his book *Credit*, outlining his economic and political ideas, is counted as the beginning of Hungary's Age of Reform. His books had great influence on public thinking. Széchenyi helped to organize the regulation of the Danube and the building of the Chain Bridge, the first permanent link between Buda and Pest. He was the minister of transportation and public works in the first Hungarian independent parliamentary government (1848). His contemporaries as well as posterity regard him as "the greatest Hungarian," an epithet bestowed on him by none other than Lajos Kossuth (see entry above), with whom he had been engaged in an ongoing public debate during the 1840s about the country's transformation. In September 1848 he became deranged and entered a mental hospital, where he remained until his death. There he wrote pamphlets protesting against the tyranny of the Habsburg monarchy; their illegal distribution led to his being harassed by the police. He took his own life.

Szerb, Antal (1901–1945) Literary historian, novelist, essayist. His two major works, the 1934 *History of Hungarian Literature* and the 1941 *History of World Literature*, describe the great historical changes in literature. In writing these books, he was influenced by Oswald Spengler's philosophy of history. They display exceptional analytical power, relaxed style, and subtle humor. A high school teacher, he was awarded the honorary title of a university professor in 1937 but was never appointed to a university post. His novels, such as *Journey by Moonlight* and his mystical crime story *Pendragon Legend*—which are quite popular in Hungary and have been only recently introduced to Western readers—synthesize several genres: crime story and travelogue meet fiction and essay. He was of Jewish origin and raised from birth as a Catholic. In 1942, he lost his job, his books were banned, and he could no longer publish. He was called up for labor service in 1943 and 1944, and he died in February 1945 as a result of brutal treatment in a west Hungarian labor camp.

Tiananmen Square (literally, "Heavenly Peace Square"; Chinese) A vast square in central Peking, and in April 1989 the main scene of protests by Chinese students calling for political reforms. On June 3 and 4, 1989, the Chinese Communist Party leaders sent in the army to clear the square of demonstrators and suppressed the student movement. According to the official reports of the Chinese government, this event had no casualties. Some unofficial sources put the number of those killed at several hundred, others at several thousand.

Ulbricht, Walter (1893–1973)   East German Communist politician. He joined the leadership of the German Communist Party in 1923 and gained a seat in the Reichstag in 1928. He fled abroad in 1933, after Hitler came to power, and worked for the international communist organization Comintern. He returned to Germany from the Soviet Union in 1945 and became paramount leader of the German Democratic Republic, where he was associated with the installation of a Stalinist system. Ulbricht was forced to resign all Communist Party posts in 1971, but he remained head of state until his death.

Wenceslaus Square (Václavské náměstí)   A square in the historic city center of Prague. It was an important venue during the Czechoslovak change of system, also known as the "velvet revolution." A series of demonstrations began there in November 1989, after the fall of the Berlin Wall. On November 17, demonstrators heading for Wenceslaus Square were attacked by internal security forces and more than 500 were injured in the incident. Thereafter, demonstrations of hundreds of thousands became common in Prague. Under this pressure, the whole leadership of the Communist Party was dismissed and Gustáv Husák resigned as head of state. A coalition government was formed with members of the Civic Forum, the party with which the democratic opposition was associated. At the end of December Václav Havel, the well-known opposition playwright, was elected president, and in June 1990 the opposition Civic Forum went on to a resounding victory in the parliamentary elections.

Work contests   Movements in Stalinist countries aimed at raising production. The most famous was launched in the mid-1930s in the Soviet Union and named for the coal miner A. G. Stakhanov, who met his quota several times over. Enterprises had to exceed their plan targets and individuals their piecework quotas. The first such campaign in Hungary occurred in spring of 1949. Exceptional performers were given the title "Stakhanovite," as well as financial rewards or apartments or holiday accommodation, amid loud publicity. The often unrealistic results attained in work contests led to increases in work quotas, to the detriment of workers. They weakened solidarity among workers. The fate of the Stakhanovites is well portrayed in Andrzej Wajda's 1977 film *Człowiek z marmuru* (Marble man).

References

Works of János Kornai

Sole Author

Kornai, János. 1948. Marx Tőké-je magyarul (Marx's *Capital* in Hungarian). *Társadalmi Szemle* 3 (8–9), pp. 615–619.

———. 1951a. A megnövekedett feladatok terve (Plan for increased tasks). *Szabad Nép*, January 9, p. 1.

———. 1951b. A munkaidő jobb kihasználásáért (For the better utilization of working hours). *Szabad Nép*, July 4, p. 1.

———. 1951c. A takarékosság—a munkaverseny egyik központi feladata (Economic efficiency—the key task in a work contest). *Szabad Nép*, March 18, p. 1.

———. 1951d. Kövessük a csepeli példát (Let us follow the example of Csepel). *Szabad Nép*, April 7, p. 5.

———. 1954a. A Központi Vezetőség iránymutatásával tovább a júniusi úton (Further along the June road with the Central Leadership pointing the way). *Szabad Nép*, October 11, p. 3.

———. 1954b. A villamosenergia kérdése (The question of the electric power). *Szabad Nép*, February 11, p. 1.

———. 1954c. "Egy évtized" Nagy Imre elvtárs válogatott beszédei és írásai ("One decade": Selected speeches and writings of Comrade Imre Nagy). *Szabad Nép*, October 6, pp. 2–3.

———. 1955. A "Tőkéről" és a szocializmus közgazdasági kérdéseiről (On "Das Kapital" and the economic questions of socialism). Manuscript.

———. 1956. Gyökerestül irtsuk ki a bürokráciát (Uproot bureaucracy once and for all). *Szabad Nép*, October 14, pp. 3–4.

———. 1958. Kell-e korrigálni a nyereségrészesedést? (Should the profit-sharing [system] be corrected?). *Közgazdasági Szemle* 5 (7), pp. 720–734.

———. 1959. "Mennyiségi szemlélet" és "gazdaságossági szemlélet" (The "quantitative outlook" and the "economic outlook"). *Közgazdasági Szemle* 6 (10), pp. 1083–1091.

———. 1967a. Anti-Equilibrium. Esszé a gazdasági mechanizmus elméleteiről és a kutatás feladatairól (Anti-Equilibrium: Essay on the theory of economic mechanism and on the tasks of research). Mimeographed. MTA Közgazdaságtudományi Intézet, Budapest.

———. 1967b. Mathematical Programming of Long-Term Plans in Hungary. In *Activity Analysis in the Theory of Growth and Planning*, edited by Edmond Malinvaud and M. O. L. Bacharach, pp. 211–231. London: Macmillan; New York: St. Martin's Press.

———. 1968. Anti-Equilibrium. Mimeographed. Institute of Economics, Hungarian Academy of Sciences, Budapest.

———. 1972. *Rush versus Harmonic Growth: Meditation on the Theory and on the Policies of Economic Growth*. Amsterdam: North-Holland.

———. 1974. Az adaptáció csikorgó gépezete (The creaking mechanism of adaptation). Mimeographed. MTA Közgazdaságtudományi Intézet, Budapest.

———. 1975. *Mathematical Planning of Structural Decisions*. With contributions by Tamás Lipták and Péter Wellisch. 2nd enl. ed. Amsterdam: North-Holland; Budapest: Akadémiai Kiadó. (First ed. published in 1965.)

———. 1978. John Michael Montias: The Structure of Economic Systems. *Journal of Comparative Economics* 2 (2), pp. 277–292.

———. 1979. Resource-Constrained versus Demand-Constrained Systems. *Econometrica* 47 (4), pp. 801–819.

———. 1980. *Economics of Shortage*. Amsterdam: North-Holland.

———. 1982. Comments on Tibor Liska's Concept of Entrepreneurship. *Acta Oeconomica* 28 (3–4), pp. 455–460.

———. 1983a. Comments on the Present State and Prospects of the Hungarian Economic Reform. *Journal of Comparative Economics* 7 (3), pp. 225–252.

———. 1983b. The Health of Nations: Reflections on the Analogy between the Medical Sciences and Economics. *Kyklos* 36 (2), pp. 191–212.

———. 1984. Bureaucratic and Market Coordination. *Osteuropa Wirtschaft* 29 (4), pp. 306–319.

———. 1986a. *Contradictions and Dilemmas*. Cambridge, Mass.: MIT Press.

———. 1986b [1980]. Efficiency and the Principles of Socialist Ethics. In *Contradictions and Dilemmas: Studies on the Socialist Economy and Society*, pp. 124–138. Cambridge, Mass.: MIT Press.

———. 1986c. The Hungarian Reform Process: Visions, Hopes, and Reality. *Journal of Economic Literature* 24 (4), pp. 1687–1737.

———. 1986d. The Soft Budget Constraint. *Kyklos* 39 (1), pp. 3–30.

———. 1988a. Individual Freedom and the Reform of the Socialist Economy. *European Economic Review* 32 (2–3), pp. 233–267.

———. 1988b. Report from the President to the Members of the European Economic Association. *European Economic Review* 32 (2–3), pp. 737–739.

———. 1989. *Indulatos röpirat a gazdasági átmenet ügyében* (Passionate pamphlet in the cause of economic transformation). Budapest: HVG Kiadó.

————. 1990a [1957]. *A gazdasági vezetés túlzott központosítása* (Overcentralization in economic administration). Budapest: Közgazdasági és Jogi Könyvkiadó.

————. 1990b. Kiegészítések a "Röpirathoz" (Complements to the "Pamphlet"). *Közgazdasági Szemle* 37 (7–8), pp. 769–793.

————. 1990c. *The Road to a Free Economy: Shifting from a Socialist System: The Example of Hungary*. New York: W. W. Norton. (Originally published in Hungarian in 1989.)

————. 1991. *Anti-Equilibrium: On Economic Systems Theory and the Tasks of Research.* 3rd ed. Amsterdam: North-Holland. (First ed. published in 1971.)

————. 1992a. The Postsocialist Transition and the State: Reflections in the Light of Hungarian Fiscal Problems. *American Economic Review* 82 (2), pp. 1–20.

————. 1992b. The Principles of Privatization in Eastern Europe. *De Economist* 140 (2), pp. 153–176.

————. 1992c. *The Socialist System: The Political Economy of Communism*. Princeton, N.J.: Princeton University Press; Oxford: Oxford University Press.

————. 1992d. Visszaesés, veszteglés vagy fellendülés (Recession, idling, or prosperity). *Magyar Hírlap*, December 24, pp. 12–13.

————. 1993a. The Evolution of Financial Discipline under the Postsocialist System. *Kyklos* 46 (3), pp. 315–336.

————. 1993b. Market Socialism Revisited. In *The Tanner Lectures on Human Values*, edited by Grethe B. Peterson, pp. 3–41. Salt Lake City: University of Utah Press.

————. 1994a. A legfontosabb: A tartós növekedés (Lasting growth as the top priority). Parts 1–5. *Népszabadság*, August 29, p. 11; August 30, p. 11; August 31, p. 11; September 1, p. 11; September 2, p. 11.

————. 1994b [1959]. *Overcentralization in Economic Administration: A Critical Analysis Based on Experience in Hungarian Light Industry*. Translated by John Knapp. Oxford: Oxford University Press. (Originally published in Hungarian in 1957.)

————. 1994c. Péter György, a reformközgazdász (György Péter, the reform economist). In *Egy reformközgazdász emlékére: Péter György, 1903–1969*, edited by János Árvay and András B. Hegedűs, pp. 75–89. Budapest: Cserépfalvi Könyvkiadó–T-Twins Kiadó.

————. 1995a. *Highway and Byways: Studies on Socialist Reform and Postsocialist Transition*. Cambridge, Mass.: MIT Press.

————. 1995b. Lasting Growth as the Top Priority: Macroeconomic Tensions and Government Economic Policy in Hungary. *Acta Oeconomica* 47 (1–2), pp. 1–38.

————. 1997a. Adjustment without Recession: A Case Study of Hungarian Stabilization. In *Lessons from the Economic Transition: Central and Eastern Europe in the 1990s*, edited by Salvatore Zecchini, pp. 123–152. Dordrecht: Kluwer Academic Publishers, OECD.

————. 1997b. *Struggle and Hope: Essays on Stabilization and Reform in a Post-Socialist Economy*. Cheltenham, U.K.: Edward Elgar.

————. 1998a. *Az egészségügy reformjáról* (On the reform of the health system). Budapest: Közgazdasági és Jogi Könyvkiadó.

———. 1998b. *From Socialism to Capitalism. What Is Meant by the "Change of System"?* London: Centre for Post-Collectivist Studies.

———. 2000a. Hidden in an Envelope: Gratuity Payments to Medical Doctors in Hungary. In *The Paradoxes of Unintended Consequences*, edited by Lord Dahrendorf and Yehuda Elkana, pp. 195–214. Budapest: CEU Press.

———. 2000b. What the Change of the System from Socialism to Capitalism Does and Does Not Mean. *Journal of Economic Perspectives* 14 (1), pp. 27–42.

———. 2001. Ten Years after *The Road to a Free Economy*: The Author's Self Evaluation. In *Annual Bank Conference on Development Economics 2000*, edited by Boris Pleskovich and Nicholas Stern, pp. 49–66. Washington D.C.: World Bank.

———. 2004. *What Can Countries Embarking on Post-Socialist Transformation Learn from the Experiences So Far?* Cuba Transition Project. Miami: Institute for Cuban and Cuban-American Studies, University of Miami.

Coauthor

Bognár, Géza, Róbert Gál, and János Kornai. 2000. Hálapénz a magyar egészségügyben (Gratuity payment in the Hungarian health care system). *Közgazdasági Szemle* 47 (4), pp. 293–320.

Csontos, László, János Kornai, and István György Tóth. 1998. Tax Awareness and Reform of the Welfare State: Hungarian Survey Results. *Economics of Transition* 6 (2), pp. 287–312.

Kornai, János, Zsuzsa Dániel, Anna Jónás, and Béla Martos. 1971. Plan Sounding. *Economics of Planning* 11 (1–2), pp. 31–58.

Kornai, János, and Karen Eggleston. 2001. *Welfare, Choice and Solidarity in Transition: Reforming the Health Sector in Eastern Europe*. Cambridge: Cambridge University Press.

———. 2004. *Egyéni választás és szolidaritás. Az egészségügy intézményi mechanizmusának reformja Kelet-Európában* (Welfare, choice, and solidarity in transition: Reforming the health sector in Eastern Europe). Budapest: Nemzeti Tankönyvkiadó.

Kornai, János, János Kovács, and Ádám Schmidt. 1969. Észrevételek Intézetünk munkájához: Munkastílus, irányítás, nevelés, szervezet (Comments on the work of our institute: Working style, administration, education, and organization). Mimeographed. MTA Közgazdaságtudományi Intézet, Budapest.

Kornai, János, and Tamás Lipták. 1959. A nyereségérdekeltség matematikai vizsgálata (The mathematical analysis of profit incentives). Mimeographed. Közgazdasági és Jogi Könyvkiadó, Budapest.

———. 1962a. Kétszintű tervezés: Játékelméleti modell és iteratív számítási eljárás népgazdasági távlati tervezési feladatok megoldására (Two-level planning: A game-theoretical model and iterative computing procedure for solving long-term planning problems of the national economy). *MTA Matematikai Kutató Intézetének Közleményei* 7/B (4), pp. 577–621.

———. 1962b. A Mathematical Investigation of Some Economic Effects of Profit Sharing in Socialist Firms. *Econometrica* 30 (1), pp. 140–161.

———. 1971 [1965]. Two-Level Planning. In *Selected Readings in Economic Theory from Econometrica*, edited by Kenneth J. Arrow, pp. 412–440. Cambridge, Mass.: MIT Press.

Kornai, János, and Béla Martos. 1973. Autonomous Control of the Economic System. *Econometrica* 41 (3), pp. 509–528.

——— (eds.). 1981. *Non-Price Control*. Amsterdam: North-Holland.

Kornai, János, Eric S. Maskin, and Gérard Roland. 2003. Understanding the Soft Budget Constraint. *Journal of Economic Literature* 41 (4), pp. 1095–1136.

Kornai, János, and Ágnes Matits. 1987. *A vállalatok nyereségének bürokratikus újraelosztása* (The bureaucratic redistribution of a firm's profit). Budapest: Közgazdasági és Jogi Könyvkiadó.

Kornai, János, and John McHale. 2000. Is Post-Communist Health Spending Unusual? A Comparison with Established Market Economies. *Economics of Transition* 8 (2), pp. 369–399.

Kornai, János, and Susan Rose-Ackerman (eds.). 2004. *Building a Trustworthy State in Post-Socialist Transition*. New York: Palgrave Macmillan.

Kornai, János, Bo Rothstein, and Susan Rose-Ackerman (eds.). 2004. *Creating Social Trust in Post-Socialist Transition*. New York: Palgrave Macmillan.

Kornai, János, and Jörgen W. Weibull. 1983. Paternalism, Buyers' and Sellers' Market. *Mathematical Social Sciences* 6 (2), pp. 153–169.

Works of Other Authors

Aczél, Tamás, and Tibor Méray. 1960. *The Revolt of the Mind: A Case History of Intellectual Resistance behind the Iron Curtain*. New York: Praeger.

Ady, Endre. 2004. *Ady Endre összes versei* (The complete poems of Endre Ady). Budapest: Osiris.

Aghion, Philippe, and Peter Howitt (eds.). 1998. *Endogenous Growth Theory*. Cambridge, Mass.: MIT Press.

Akerlof, George A. 1970. The Market for "Lemons": Quality Uncertainty and the Market Mechanism. *Quarterly Journal of Economics* 84 (3), pp. 488–500.

Antal, László. 1982. Fejlődés kitérővel—A magyar gazdasági mechanizmus a 70-es években (Development with a detour: The Hungarian economic mechanism in the 1970s). *Gazdaság* 14 (2), pp. 28–56.

Arrow, Kenneth J. 1951. Alternative Approaches to the Theory of Choice in Risk-Taking Situations. *Econometrica* 19 (4), pp. 404–437.

——— (ed.). 1971. *Selected Readings in Economic Theory from Econometrica*. Cambridge, Mass.: MIT Press.

———. 1973a. Rawls's Principle of Just Saving. *Scandinavian Journal of Economics* 75 (4), pp. 323–335.

———. 1973b [1963]. *Social Choice and Individual Values*. 2nd ed. New Haven: Yale University Press. (First ed. published in 1951.)

———. 1974. General Economic Equilibrium: Purpose, Analytic Techniques, Collective Choice. *American Economic Review* 64 (3), pp. 253–272.

Arrow, Kenneth J., Samuel Karlin, and Herbert E. Scarf. 1958. *Studies in the Mathematical Theory of Inventory and Production*. Stanford: Stanford University Press.

Babits, Mihály. 1998 [1936]. *Az európai irodalom története* (The history of European literature). Budapest: Merényi.

Bácskai, Tamás, and Elemér György Terták. 1983. Mesterséges érdek—növekedési kényszer (Artificial interest—Compulsion to growth). *Valóság* 26 (10), pp. 91–94.

Baráth, Magdolna. 1999. Az MDP vezetése és a rehabilitáció (The leadership of the MDP and the rehabilitation). *Múltunk* 44 (4), pp. 40–97.

Barro, Robert J., and Herschel I. Grossman. 1971. A General Disequilibrium Model of Income and Employment. *American Economic Review* 61 (1), pp. 82–93.

Bauer, Tamás. 1981. *Tervgazdaság, beruházás, ciklusok* (Planned economy, investment, cycles). Budapest: Közgazdasági és Jogi Könyvkiadó.

Bergson, Abram. 1948. Socialist Economics. In *A Survey of Contemporary Economics*, edited by Howard S. Ellis, pp. 412–448. Philadelphia: Blakiston.

Blahó, Miklós. 2003. A fő cél a tartós növekedés. Interjú Kornai Jánossal (The main aim is lasting growth: Interview with János Kornai). *Népszabadság*, January 25, pp. 23, 27.

Blanchard, Olivier. 1999. An Interview with János Kornai. *Macroeconomic Dynamics* 3 (3), pp. 427–450.

Böhm-Bawerk, Eugen von. 1975 [1949]. *Karl Marx and the Close of His System*. Clifton, N.J.: A. M. Kelley. (Originally published in German in 1896.)

Bolygó, János. 1966. Mit kutatott professzor Montias Magyarországon? (What did Professor Montias research in Hungary?). *Magyar Nemzet*, July 3, p. 7.

Bosworth, Barry P. 1990. Which Way to the Market? *New York Times Book Review*, May 27, p. 17.

Boulding, Kenneth E. 1966. *Economic Analysis*. 4th ed. New York: Harper and Row. (First ed. published in 1941.)

Braham, Randolph L. 1981. *The Politics of Genocide: The Holocaust in Hungary*. 2.vols. New York: Columbia University Press.

Brámer, Frigyes. 1997 [1972]. Koncentrációs tábor a Rabbiképző épületében (Concentration camp in the Rabbinical Seminary building). In *Évkönyv*, edited by Sándor Scheiber, pp. 219–228. Budapest: Magyar Izraeliták Országos Képviselete.

Bródy, András. 1956. A hóvégi hajrá és gazdasági mechanizmusunk (End-of-month rush and our economic mechanism). *Közgazdasági Szemle* 3 (7–8), pp. 870–883.

———. 1970. *Proportions, Prices, and Planning: A Mathematical Restatement of the Labor Theory of Value*. Budapest: Akadémiai Kiadó. (Originally published in Hungarian in 1969.)

"Bureaucrats at Large." 1960. *Times Literary Supplement*, April 15, p. 244.

Camus, Albert. 1991 [1948]. *The Plague*. Translated by Stuart Gilbert. New York: Vintage International. (Originally published in French in 1942.)

Carlin, Wendy, Steven Fries, Mark E. Schaffer, and Paul Seabright. 2001. *Competition and Enterprise Performance in Transition Economies: Evidence from a Cross-Country Survey*. EBRD Working Paper 62. London: EBRD.

Chikán, Attila (ed.). 1989. *Készletek, ciklusok, gazdaságirányítás. A magyar gazdaság készletalakulása és befolyásoló tényezői, 1960–1986* (Stocks, cycles, economic management: The position of the Hungarian economy's stocks and the factors influencing it, 1960–1986). Budapest: Közgazdasági és Jogi Könyvkiadó.

———. 2004. A hiány szerepe az átmenet szellemi előkészítésében (The role of "The Economics of Shortage" in the intellectual preparation for the change of system). *Magyar Tudomány* 49 (7), pp. 698–707.

Coles, Peter. 1999. *Einstein and the Total Eclipse*. Cambridge: Icon Books.

Csoóri, Sándor. 1990. Nappali hold. II. rész (Daytime moon: Part 2). *Hitel* 3 (18), September 5, p. 5.

Dahl, Robert A. 1979 [1971]. *Polyarchy: Participation and Opposition*. New Haven: Yale University Press.

Debreu, Gérard. 1965 [1959]. *Theory of Value: An Axiomatic Analysis of Economic Equilibrium*. New York: Wiley.

Denton, Nicholas. 1990. On the Brink of Transformation. *Financial Times*, September 17, p. 2.

Deutscher, Isaac. 1968 [1949]. *Stalin: A Political Biography*. Oxford: Oxford University Press.

Devons, Ely. 1959. A Study in Central Planning: Evidence from Inside. *The Guardian*, October 22, pp. 10–11.

Dewatripont, Mathias, and Eric S. Maskin. 1995. Credit and Efficiency in Centralized and Decentralized Economies. *Review of Economic Sudies* 62 (4), pp. 541–555.

Djankov, Simeon D., and Peter Murrell. 2002. Enterprise Restructuring in Transition Economies: A Quantitative Survey. *Journal of Economic Literature* 40 (3), pp. 739–792.

Donáth, Ferenc (head of the editorial board). 1981. Bibó-emlékkönyv (In memory of Bibó). 2 vols. Samizdat.

Dorfman, Robert, Paul A. Samuelson, and Robert M. Solow. 1987 [1958]. *Linear Programming and Economic Analysis*. New York: Dover Publications.

Draaisma, Douwe. 2004. *Why Life Speeds Up When You Get Older: How Memory Shapes Our Past*. Cambridge: Cambridge University Press.

Durant, Will. 1991 [1926]. *Story of Philosophy: The Lives and Opinions of the Greater Philosophers*. New York: Simon and Schuster.

Ericson, Richard E. 1994. Book Review. *Journal of Comparative Economics* 18 (3), pp. 495–497.

Esterházy, Péter. 2003. Mik vogymuk. 1. könyv. (What are we: Book 1). *Élet és Irodalom*, May 9, p. 3.

Esze, Zsuzsa. 1956. Egy kandidátusi értekezés vitája (Discussion of a candidate's dissertation). *Közgazdasági Szemle* 3 (11–12), pp. 1483–1495.

Eucken, Walter. 1951 [1940]. *The Foundations of Economics*. Chicago: University of Chicago Press.

Fejtő, Ferenc. 1957. La première autocritique des "Communistes Nationaux" hongrois. *France Observateur* 8 (January 31), p. 6.

Fóthy, János. 1945. *Horthyliget—A magyar ördögsziget* (Horthy-liget—The Hungarian Devil's Island). Budapest: Müller Károly Könyvkiadóvállalat.

Frey, Bruno S. 2003. Publishing as Prostitution? Choosing between One's Own Ideas and Academic Failure. *Public Choice* 116 (1–2), pp. 205–223.

Frisch, Ragnar. 1961. A Survey of Types of Economic Forecasting and Programming, and a Brief Description of the Channel Model. Mimeographed. Oslo: University of Oslo.

Friss, István. 1957. Népgazdaságunk vezetésének néhány gyakorlati és elméleti kérdéséről (Some empirical and theoretical questions of managing the economy). *Népszabadság*, October 2, pp. 3–4.

Gábor, R. István, and Péter Galasi. 1981. A *"második gazdaság": Tények és hipotézisek* (The "second economy": Facts and hypotheses). Budapest: Közgazdasági és Jogi Könyvkiadó.

Gács, János, and János Köllő (eds.). 1998. A *"túlzott központosítástól" az átmenet stratégiájáig: Tanulmányok Kornai Jánosnak* (From "overcentralization" to the strategy of transition: Studies for János Kornai). Budapest: Közgazdasági és Jogi Könyvkiadó.

Gáll, Ernő. 2003. *Napló* (Diary). Vol. 1. Budapest: Polis Könyvkiadó.

Gans, Joshua S., and George B. Shepherd. 1994. How Are the Mighty Fallen: Rejected Articles by Leading Economists. *Journal of Economic Perspectives* 8 (1), pp. 165–179.

Gimes, Miklós. 1956. Magyar Szabadság (Hungarian freedom). *Magyar Szabadság*, October 29, p. 1.

Goldfeld, Stephen M., and Richard E. Quandt. 1988. Budget Constraints, Bailouts and the Firm under Central Planning. *Journal of Comparative Economics* 12 (4), pp. 502–520.

———. 1990. Output Targets, the Soft Budget Constraint and the Firm under Central Planning. *Journal of Economic Behavior and Organization* 14 (2), pp. 205–222.

———. 1993. Uncertainty, Bailouts, and the Kornai Effect. *Economics Letters* 41 (2), pp. 113–119.

Gregory, Paul R., and Robert C. Stuart. 1980. *Comparative Economic Systems*. Boston: Houghton Mifflin.

———. 2004. *Comparative Economic Systems*. 7th ed. Boston: Houghton Mifflin.

Grossfeld, Irena. 1989. Disequilibrium Models of Investment. In *Models of Disequilibrium and Shortage in Centrally Planned Economies*, edited by Christopher Davis and Wojciech W. Charemza, pp. 361–374. New York: Chapman and Hall.

Gulyás, Emil. 1957–1958. Az árutermelés, értéktörvény és pénz a szocializmusban (Production, the law of value, and money in socialism). Manuscript.

Gy [pseud.]. 1991. Skizze eines Reformprogramms am Beispiel Ungarns. *Neue Zürcher Zeitung* Fernausgabe, June 30–July 1, p. 7.

Haberler, Gottfried von. 1964. *Prosperity and Depression: A Theoretical Analysis of Cyclical Movements*. 5th ed. London: Allen and Unwin. (First ed. published in 1937.)

Hahn, Frank. 1973. The Winter of Our Discontent. *Economica* 40 (159), pp. 322–330.

Halda, Alíz. 2002. *Magánügy. Dokumentum/regény* (Private affair: Documentary/novel). Budapest: Noran.

Hašek, Jaroslav. 2000 [1973]. *The Good Soldier Švejk and His Fortunes in the World War*. Translated by Cecil Parrott. London: Penguin. (Originally published in Czech in 1920–1923.)

Hayek, Friedrich A. von (ed.). 1975 [1935]. *Collectivist Economic Planning: Critical Studies on the Possibilities of Socialism*. Clifton, N.J.: A. M. Kelly.

———. 2001 [1944]. *The Road to Serfdom*. London: Routledge.

Hegedűs, András. 1990. A bolsevik grand-seigneur tragédiája (The tragedy of the Bolshevik *grand seigneur*). *Pesti Hírlap*, November 3, p. 8.

Heisenberg, Werner. 1967 [1958]. Az elemi részek (Elementary particles) (Lecture presented in Budapest). *Válogatott tanulmányok* (Selected papers), pp. 219–237. Budapest: Gondolat.

Heller, Farkas. 1988. *Közgazdaságtan* (Economics). 2 vols. 5th ed. Budapest: Közgazdasági és Jogi Könyvkiadó. (First ed. published in 1912–1920.)

Hicks, John R. 1937. Mr. Keynes and the Classics: A Suggested Interpretation. *Econometrica* 5 (2), pp. 147–159.

———. 2001 [1939]. *Value and Capital: An Inquiry into Some Fundamental Principles of Economic Theory*. New York: Oxford University Press.

Híd-csoport. 1990. Híd a közeli jövőbe (Bridge to the near future). *Közgazdasági Szemle* 37 (4), pp. 442–458.

Hirschman, Albert O. 1988 [1958]. *The Strategy of Economic Development*. Boulder, Colo.: Westview Press.

———. 1970. *Exit, Voice, and Loyalty: Responses to Decline in Firms, Organizations, and States*. Cambridge, Mass.: Harvard University Press.

Hoffman, David E. 2002. *The Oligarchs: Wealth and Power in the New Russia*. New York: Public Affairs.

Huizinga, Johan. 1996. *The Autumn of the Middle Ages*. Translated by Rodney J. Payton and Ulrich Mammitzsch. Chicago: University of Chicago Press. (Originally published in Dutch in 1919.)

Hungaricus [Sándor Fekete]. 1959 [1956–1957]. *Quelques enseignements de la révolution nationale et démocratique hongroise*. Brussels: Imre Nagy Institute.

———. 1989 [1956–1957]. *Az 1956-os felkelés okairól és tanulságairól* (On the causes and lessons of the 1956 uprising). Budapest: Kossuth Könyvkiadó.

József, Attila. 1997. *Winter Night: Selected Poems*. Translated by John Bátki. Oberlin, Ohio: Oberlin College Press.

———. 2003. *József Attila összes versei* (Complete poems of Attila József). Budapest: Osiris.

Juhász, Andor. 1934. *Halló, itt London!* (Hallo, it's London!). Budapest: Révai.

Kalecki, Michał. 1965. *Theory of Economic Dynamics: An Essay on Cyclical and Long-Run Changes in Capitalist Economy*. 2nd ed. London: Allen and Unwin. (First ed. published in 1954.)

Karagedov, Rajmond G. 1982. Mechanizm funkcionirovaniya socialisticheskoy ekonomiki (Mechanism of the function of a socialist economy). *Isvestija Sibirskava Otdeleniya Akademij Nauk SSSR* 3 (11), pp. 115–128.

Kardelj, Edvard. 1982. *Reminiscences: The Struggle for Recognition and Independence: The New Yugoslavia, 1944–1957.* London: Blond and Briggs–Summerfield Press. (Originally published in Serbo-Croatian in 1980.)

Karinthy, Ferenc. 1994. *Napló* (Diary). Budapest: Littoria.

Karinthy, Frigyes. 2001 [1914]. A felelős ember (The man in charge). In *Humoreszkek*, 2:155–157. Budapest: Akkord.

Karsai, Gábor. 1993. A szocializmus genetikai programja (The genetic program of socialism). *Figyelő* 37, November 11, pp. 17–19.

Kék Szalag Bizottság 1990. *[A Bizottság] Gazdasági Programjavaslata* (Recommendations for an economic program). Budapest: Kék Szalag Bizottság.

Kende, Péter. 1955. Kritikai jegyzetek a marxizmus gazdasági tanaihoz (Critical remarks on the economic theories of Marxism). Manuscript.

———. 1959. L'intérêt personnel dans le système d'économie socialiste. *Revue Economique* 10 (3), pp. 340–364.

———. 1964. *Logique de l'économie centralisée. Un exemple: la Hongrie.* Paris: Société d'Éducation d'Enseignement Supérieure.

———. 1966. *A Szabad Nép szerkesztőségében. Tanulmányok a magyar forradalomról* (In the editorial offices of Szabad Nép: Studies on the Hungarian revolution). Munich: Aurora.

Kenedi, János. 1981. *"Tiéd az ország, magadnak épített"* (The country is yours, you build it for yourself). Paris: Magyar Füzetek Könyvei.

———. 1996. *Kis állambiztonsági olvasókönyv. Október 23.—március 15.—június 16* (Small state security reader: October 23—March 15—June 16). 2 vols. Budapest: Magvető.

Keynes, John M. 1997 [1936]. *The General Theory of Employment, Interest, and Money.* Amherst, N.Y.: Prometheus Books.

Klaniczay, Gábor. 2003. *Ellenkultúra a hetvenes-nyolcvanas években* (Counterculture in the '70s and '80s). Budapest: Noran.

Klaus, Václav, and Dušan Tříska. 1997 [1994]. Review of János Kornai's *The Socialist System: The Political Economy of Communism.* In *Renaissance: The Rebirth of Liberty in the Heart of Europe*, by Václav Klaus, pp. 163–169. Washington, D.C.: Cato Institute.

Koestler, Arthur. 1993 [1941]. *Darkness at Noon.* Translated by Daphne Hardy. New York: Bantam Books.

Koopmans, Tjalling C. 1957. *Three Essays on the State of Economic Science.* New York: McGraw-Hill.

Koopmans, Tjalling C., and John M. Montias. 1971. On the Description and Comparison of Economic Systems. In *Comparison of Economic Systems*, edited by Alexander Eckstein, pp. 27–78. Berkeley: University of California Press.

Kovács, András. 1968. Falak (Walls). *Új Írás* 8 (3), pp. 28–48.

Kovács, Imre. 1989 [1937]. *A néma forradalom* (The silent revolution). Budapest: Cserépfalvi–Gondolat–Tevan.

Központi Statisztikai Hivatal. 1996. *Magyar Statisztikai Évkönyv, 1995* (Hungary's statistical yearbook, 1995). Budapest: Központi Statisztikai Hivatal.

Krausz, Tamás. 1994. A történetietlen politikai gazdaságtan (A nonhistorical political economy). *Eszmélet* 6 (24), pp. 157–178.

Kuhn, Thomas S. 1996. *The Structure of Scientific Revolutions.* 3rd ed. Chicago: University of Chicago Press. (First ed. published in 1962.)

Laczik, Erika. 2005. Egy besúgó tisztikereszttel (An informer with an Officer's Cross). *Magyar Nemzet,* January 29, pp. 1, 5.

Laibson, David, and Richard Zeckhauser. 1998. Amos Tversky and the Ascent of Behavioral Economics. *Journal of Risk and Uncertainty* 16 (1), pp. 7–47.

Laki, Mihály. 1989. Az új politikai szervezetek a gazdaságpolitikáról és a gazdaságirányításról (The new political organizations about the economic policy and economic management). *Tervgazdasági Fórum* 5 (4), pp. 1–16.

———. 1990. Rendszerváltás küszöbén. Az ellenzéki pártok gazdaságpolitikai programjai (On the threshold of the change of system: The economic policy programs of the opposition parties). Mimeographed. Közgazdasági Információs Szolgálat, Budapest.

Lange, Oskar. 1968 [1936–1937]. On the Economic Theory of Socialism. In *On the Economic Theory of Socialism,* edited by Benjamin E. Lippincott, pp. 57–143. New York: McGraw Hill.

Leijonhufvud, Axel. 1968. *On Keynesian Economics and the Economics of Keynes: A Study in Monetary Theory.* New York: Oxford University Press.

Lengyel, László. 2002. *A távol közelében. Kérdez: Hankiss Elemér* (Near to far away. The interviewer: Elemér Hankiss). Budapest: Helikon Kiadó.

Lengyel, László, and Miklós Polgár. 1980. Gazdasági elvek, etikai elvek—és a valóság (Economic principles, ethical principles, and reality). *Valóság* 23 (9), pp. 101–107.

Lenin, Vladimir I. 1964 [1920]. Left-wing Communism: An Infantile Disorder. In *Collected Works,* 31:17–118. Moscow: Progress Publishers.

Lerner, Abba P. 1975 [1944]. *Economics of Control: Principles of Welfare Economics.* New York: A. M. Kelley.

Lindbeck, Assar. 1977. *The Political Economy of the New Left: An Outsider's View.* 2nd ed. New York: Harper and Row. (First ed. published in 1971.)

———. 1988. Individual Freedom and Welfare State Policy. *European Economic Review* 32 (2–3), pp. 295–318.

Lindblom, Charles E. 1977. *Politics and Markets.* New York: Basic Books.

Liska, Tibor. 1988 [1966]. *Ökonosztát: Felkészülés a mechanizmusreformra* (Econostat: Preparation for reforming the mechanism). Budapest: Közgazdasági és Jogi Könyvkiadó.

Liska, Tibor, and Antal Máriás. 1954. A gazdaságosság és a nemzetközi munkamegosztás (Economic efficiency and the international division of labor). *Közgazdasági Szemle* 1 (1), pp. 75–94.

Liska, Tibor F. 1998. A Liska-modell (The Liska Model). *Közgazdasági Szemle* 45 (10), pp. 940–953.

Lőcsei, Pál. 1995. "Politikai és lelkiismereti lázadás volt..." (It was a political and moral rebellion). *Respublika* 2 (13), pp. 36–40.

Lukács, György. 1973 [1945]. On the Responsibility of Intellectuals. In Lukács, *Marxism and Human Liberation: Essays on History, Culture and Revolution*, edited by E. San Juan Jr., pp. 267–276. New York: Delta.

———. 1978 [1950]. *Studies in European Realism: A Sociological Survey of the Writings of Balzac, Stendhal, Zola, Tolstoy, Gorki, and Others.* Translated by Edith Bone. London: Merlin Press.

Magyar Dolgozók Pártja Központi Vezetősége (Central Leadership of the Hungarian Workers' Party). 1955. A Magyar Dolgozók Pártja Központi Vezetőségének határozata a politikai helyzetről és a párt feladatairól (The decision of the Central Leadership of the Hungarian Workers' Party on the political situation and the party's tasks). *Szabad Nép*, March 9, pp. 1–2.

Malinvaud, Edmond. 1967. Decentralized Procedures for Planning. In *Activity Analysis in the Theory of Growth and Planning*, edited by Edmond Malinvaud and M. O. L. Bacharach, pp. 170–208. London: Macmillan; New York: St. Martin's Press.

Malinvaud, Edmond, and M. O. L. Bacharach (eds.). 1967. *Activity Analysis in the Theory of Growth and Planning.* London: Macmillan; New York: St. Martin's Press.

Marx, Karl. 1992. *Capital: A Critique of Political Economy.* Translated by Ben Fowkes (vol. 1) and David Fernbach (vols. 2 and 3). London: Penguin Books. (Originally published in German in 1867, 1885, and 1896.)

Marx, Karl, and Friedrich Engels. 2002 [1888]. *The Communist Manifesto.* Translated by Samuel Moore. London: Penguin Books. (Originally published in German in 1848.)

Maskin, Eric S., and András Simonovits (eds.). 2000. *Planning, Shortage, and Transformation: Essays in Honor of János Kornai.* Cambridge, Mass.: MIT Press.

Matolcsy, György. 1997. Kiigazítás recesszióval. Kemény költségvetési és puha piaci korlát (Adjustment with recession: Hard budget constraint and soft market constraint). *Közgazdasági Szemle* 44 (9), pp. 782–798.

McCloskey, Deirdre N. 1998. *The Rhetoric of Economics.* 2nd ed. Madison: University of Wisconsin Press. (First ed. published in 1985.)

McKenzie, Lionel W. 1959. On the Existence of General Equilibrium for a Competitive Market. *Econometrica* 27 (1), pp. 54–71.

Molnár, Endre. 1957. Revizionista nézetek a szocialista állam gazdasági szerepéről (Revisionist views on the economic role of the socialist state). *Társadalmi Szemle* 12 (2), pp. 44–59.

Montias, John M. 1976. *The Structure of Economic Systems.* New Haven: Yale University Press.

———. 1982. *Arts and Artisans in Delft: A Socio-Economic Study of the Seventeenth Century.* Princeton, N.J.: Princeton University Press.

―――. 1989. *Vermeer and His Milieu: A Web of Social History*. Princeton, N.J.: Princeton University Press.

―――. 2002. *Art at Auction in 17th Century Amsterdam*. Amsterdam: Amsterdam University Press.

Müller, Rolf. 1999. Napi operatív információs jelentések, 1979–1989 (The daily operative information reports, 1979–1989). In *A Történeti Hivatal Évkönyve 1999*, edited by György Gyarmati, pp. 251–284. Budapest: Történeti Hivatal.

Nagy, Csaba. 1994. Lázadás a Szabad Népnél 40 évvel ezelőtt. Beszélgetés Lőcsei Pállal és Méray Tiborral (Rebellion at *Szabad Nép* 40 years ago: A conversation with Pál Lőcsei and Tibor Méray). *Kritika* 23 (10), pp. 10–11.

Nagy, Imre. 1954. *Egy évtized. Válogatott beszédek és írások (1948–1954)* (One decade: Selected speeches and writings, 1948–1954). Budapest: Szikra.

Neumann, John von. 1963 [1955]. The Impact of Recent Developments in Science on the Economy and on Economics. In *Collected Works*, 6:100–101. New York: Macmillan.

Nove, Alec. 1960. Overcentralization in Economic Administration. *Economica* 27 (108), pp. 389–391.

―――. 1992. No Third Way? *New Statesman and Society*, June 19, p. 23.

Novobáczky, Sándor. 1956. Különös emberek (Strange people). *Irodalmi Újság*, October 6, p. 1.

Nozick, Robert. 1998 [1974]. *Anarchy, State and Utopia*. Oxford: Blackwell.

Nyíri, Sándor. 1994. A Péter György elleni büntetőeljárás (The criminal case against György Péter). In *Egy reformközgazdász emlékére: Péter György, 1903–1969* (In memory of a reform economist: György Péter, 1903–1969), edited by János Árvay and András B. Hegedűs, pp. 45–47. Budapest: Cserépfalvi Könyvkiadó–T-Twins Kiadó.

Ortega y Gasset, José. 1993 [1932]. *The Revolt of the Masses*. New York: W. W. Norton. (Originally published in Spanish in 1929.)

Orwell, George. 1966 [1949]. *Nineteen Eighty-four*. Harmondsworth: Penguin.

Papandreou, Andreas G. 1972. *Paternalistic Capitalism*. Minneapolis: Univesity of Minnesota Press.

Passel, Peter. 1990. Socialist Eggs, Market Omelet. *New York Times*, April 11, p. 2.

Péter, György. 1954. A gazdaságosság jelentőségéről és szerepéről a népgazdaság tervszerű irányításában (On the importance and significance of economic efficiency in the plan-based management of the economy). *Közgazdasági Szemle* 1 (3), pp. 300–324.

―――. 1956. A gazdaságosság és a jövedelmezőség jelentősége a tervgazdaságban (The importance of economic efficiency and profitability in the planned economy). *Közgazdasági Szemle* 3 (6), pp. 695–711; (7–8), pp. 851–869.

―――. 1957. A gazdasági vezetés túlzott központosítása. Kornai János tanulmányáról ("Overcentralization in Economic Administration": On János Kornai's study). *Magyarország* 1 (1), p. 2.

Péteri, György. 1997. New Course Economics: The Field of Economic Research in Hungary after Stalin, 1953–56. *Contemporary European History* 6 (3), pp. 295–327.

————. 1998. *Academia and State Socialism: Essays on the Political History of Academic Life in Post-1945 Hungary and Eastern Europe.* Highland Lakes, N.J.: Atlantic Research and Publications.

———— (ed.). 2001. *Intellectual Life and the First Crisis of State Socialism in East Central Europe, 1953–1956.* Trondheim Studies on East European Cultures and Societies, no. 6. Trondheim: Program on East European Cultures and Societies.

Phillips, Albin W. 1958. The Relation between Unemployment and the Rate of Change of Money Wage Rates in the United Kingdom, 1861–1957. *Economica* 25 (2), pp. 283–299.

Pigou, Arthur C. 2002 [1952]. *The Economics of Welfare.* 4th ed. New Brunswick, N.J.: Transaction Publishers. (First ed. published in 1920.)

Pogonyi, Lajos. 2003. A munkásosztály megsemmisítése. Interjú Vajda Mihállyal (The annihilation of the workers' class: Interview with Mihály Vajda). *Népszabadság*, October 15, p. 14.

Portes, Richard, and David Winter. 1980. Disequilibrium Estimates for Consumption Goods Markets in Centrally Planned Economies. *Review of Economic Studies* 47 (1), pp. 137–159.

Qian, Yingyi. 1994. A Theory of Shortage in Socialist Economies Based on the "Soft Budget Constraint." *American Economic Review* 84 (1), pp. 145–156.

Rainer, M. János. 1999. *Nagy Imre—Politikai életrajz* (Imre Nagy: A political biography, vol. 2, 1953–1958). Budapest: 1956-os Intézet.

Rawls, John. 1999. *A Theory of Justice.* Rev. ed. Cambridge, Mass.: Harvard University Press, Belknap Press. (First ed. published in 1971.)

Réti, Pál. 1989. Miénk az ország (The country is ours). *Heti Világgazdaság*, November 11, pp. 3–5.

Révész, Sándor. 1999. *Egyetlen élet. Gimes Miklós története* (One single life: The story of Miklós Gimes). Budapest: 1956-os Magyar Forradalom Történetének Dokumentációs és Kutatóintézete–Sík Kiadó.

Réz, Pál. 1961. Thomas Mann and Hungary—His Correspondence with Hungarian Friends. *New Hungarian Quarterly* 2 (3), pp. 84–99.

———— (ed.). 1991. *Bibó-emlékkönyv* (In memory of Bibó), by Ferenc Donáth. Budapest: Századvég; Bern: European Protestant Hungarian Free University. (First available in a samizdat edition, 1981.)

Ripp, Géza. 1957. Revizionizmus "az új gazdasági mechanizmus" leple alatt (Revisionism under the veil of the "New Economic Mechanism"). *Népszabadság*, July 23, p. 3.

Ripp, Zoltán (ed.). 2000. *A rendszerváltás forgatókönyve. Kerekasztal-tárgyalások 1989-ben* (The script of the change of system. The roundtable negotiations in 1989). Vol. 5. Budapest: Új Mandátum.

R.N.W.O. 1959. Iron Curtain Economy. *Financial Times*, December 28, p. 12.

Roland, Gérard. 1987. Investment Growth Fluctuations in the Soviet Union: An Econometric Analysis. *Journal of Comparative Economics* 11 (2), pp. 192–206.

————. 1990. On the Meaning of Aggregate Excess Supply and Demand for Consumer Goods in Soviet-Type Economies. *Cambridge Journal of Economics* 14 (1), pp. 49–62.

Rosovsky, Henry. 1990. *The University: An Owner's Manual*. New York: W. W. Norton.

Rosser, J. Barkley, Jr., and Marina V. Rosser. 2004. *Comparative Economics in a Transforming World Economy*. 2nd ed. Cambridge, Mass.: MIT Press. (First ed. published in 1996.)

Salgó, István. 1990. Les propositions de l'économiste János Kornai provoquent un vif débat. *Le Monde*, April 20, p. 3.

Samuelson, Paul A. 1980. *Economics*. 11th ed. New York: McGraw-Hill. (First ed. published in 1948.)

———. 1983. *Foundations of Economic Analysis*. Enl. ed. Cambridge, Mass.: Harvard University Press. (First ed. published in 1947.)

———. 1990. For Plan to Reform Socialism, Listen to János Kornai. *Christian Science Monitor*, April 4, p. 7.

Sartre, Jean-Paul. 1990 [1957]. *Existentialism and Human Emotions*. New York: Carol Publications. (Originally published in French in 1946.)

Schama, Simon. 1989. *Citizens: A Chronicle of the French Revolution*. New York: Alfred A. Knopf.

Schelling, Thomas C. 1980 [1960]. *The Strategy of Conflict*. Cambridge, Mass.: Harvard University Press.

Schneider, Erich. 1962. *Money, Income, and Employment*. Translated by Kurt Klappholz. New York: Macmillan. (Originally published in German in 1949.)

Schumpeter, Joseph. 1983 [1934]. *The Theory of Economic Development: An Inquiry into Profits, Capital, Credit, Interest and the Business Cycle*. Translated by Redvers Opie. New Brunswick, N.J.: Transaction Books. (Originally published in German in 1911.)

———. 1987. *Capitalism, Socialism and Democracy*. 6th ed. London: Unwin. (First ed. published in 1942.)

Scitovsky, Tibor. 1992. *The Joyless Economy: The Psychology of Human Satisfaction and Consumer Dissatisfaction*. Rev. ed. New York: Oxford University Press. (First ed. published in 1976.)

Semjén, András. 1990. A műtétet az orvosnak is túl kell élnie (The operation must be survived by the surgeon, too). *Figyelő*, February 22, p. 7.

Sen, Amartya K. 1977. Rational Fools: A Critique of the Behavioural Foundations of Economic Theory. *Philosophy and Public Affairs* 6 (2), pp. 317–344.

———. 1988. Freedom of Choice. *European Economic Review* 32 (2–3), pp. 269–294.

———. 1997 [1982]. *Choice, Welfare and Measurement*. Cambridge, Mass.: Harvard University Press.

Shove, Gerald F. 1942. The Place of Marshall's *Principles* in the Development of Economic Theory. *Economic Journal* 52 (208), pp. 294–329.

Simon, Herbert A. 1979. Rational Decision-Making in Business Organizations. *American Economic Review* 69 (4), pp. 493–513.

Simonovits, András. 2003. A magyar szabályozáselméleti iskola (The Hungarian school of control theory). *Közgazdasági Szemle* 50 (5), pp. 465–470.

Solow, Robert. 2000. Stability and Growth: Commentary on a Commentary. In *Planning, Shortage, and Transformation: Essays in Honor of János Kornai*, edited by Eric S. Maskin and András Simonovits, pp. 407–412. Cambridge, Mass.: MIT Press.

Spengler, Oswald. 1991 [1965]. *The Decline of the West.* Abridged by Helmut Werner; English abridged ed. prepared by Charles Francis Atkinson. New York: Oxford University Press. (Originally published in German in 1918–1922.)

Spulber, Nicolas. 1960. Overcentralization in Economic Administration—A Critical Analysis Based on Experience in Hungarian Light Industry. *American Economic Review* 50 (4), pp. 763–764.

Stackelberg, Heinrich von. 1952 [1943]. *The Theory of the Market Economy.* London: William Hodge.

Stalin, Joseph V. 1949 [1940]. *Dialectical and Historical Materialism.* Moscow: Foreign Languages Publishing House. (Originally published in Russian in 1938.)

————. 1953 [1940]. On the Death of Lenin—A Speech Delivered at the Second All-Union Congress of Soviets, January 26, 1924. In *J. V. Stalin, Works,* 6:47–53. Moscow: Foreign Languages Publishing House.

Streeten, Paul. 1959. Unbalanced Growth. *Oxford Economic Papers,* n.s. (11), pp. 167–190.

Such, György, and István János Tóth. 1989. A magyar közgazdaságtudomány a Közgazdasági Szemle tudománymetriai vizsgálatának tükrében (Hungarian economic science in the mirror of the scientometric analysis of *Közgazdasági Szemle). Közgazdasági Szemle* 36 (10), pp. 1163–1241.

Szabó, Zoltán. 1986 [1936]. *A tardi helyzet* (The Tard story). Budapest: Akadémiai Kiadó–Kossuth Könyvkiadó–Magvető.

Szakolczai, Attila. 2001. *Az 1956-os forradalom és szabadságharc* (The 1956 Revolution and War of Independence). Budapest: 1956-os Intézet.

Szalay, László. 1994. Előhang 1954-ből: a Szabad Nép taggyűlése (Overture from 1954: The Communist Party membership meeting at *Szabad Nép). Világosság* 35 (10), pp. 48–56.

Szegő, Andrea. 1983. Érdek és gazdasági intézményrendszer (Interest and the economic institutional system). *Valóság* 26 (6), pp. 22–36.

————. 1991. The Logic of a Shortage Economy: A Critique of Kornai from a Kaleckian Macroeconomic Perspective. *Journal of Post Keynesian Economics* 13 (3), pp. 328–336.

Szegvári, Iván. 1990. Az egységesség mítosza. Vita az "Indulatos röpirat"-ról (The myth of unity: Debate on the "Passionate pamphlet"). *Figyelő,* February 11, p. 5.

Szénási, Sándor. 1983. Pató Pál elvtárs. Interjú Antal Lászlóval (Comrade Pál Pató: An interview with László Antal). *Élet és Irodalom,* November 11, p. 7.

Szerb, Antal. 2003a [1941]. *A világirodalom története* (History of world literature). Budapest: Magvető.

————. 2003b [1934]. *Magyar irodalomtörténet* (History of Hungarian literature). Budapest: Magvető.

Tamás, Gáspár Miklós. 1989. A Kornai-bomba (The Kornai bomb). *Heti Világgazdaság,* November 11, p. 66.

Tardos, Márton. 1982. Program a gazdaságirányítási és szervezeti rendszer fejlesztésére (A program to develop the system of economic management and the system of organization). *Közgazdasági Szemle* 19 (6), pp. 715–729.

———. 1988a. A gazdasági szervezetek és a tulajdon (Economic organizations and ownership). *Gazdaság* 22 (3), pp. 7–21.

———. 1988b. A tulajdon (Property). *Közgazdasági Szemle* 35 (12), pp. 1405–1423.

Thassy, Jenő. 1996. *Veszélyes vidék* (Dangerous territory). Budapest: Pesti Szalon.

Tinbergen, Jan. 2004 [1951]. *Econometrics*. London: Routledge. (Originally published in Dutch in 1941.)

———. 1981 [1969]. The Use of Models: Experience and Prospects. *American Economic Review* 71 (6), pp. 17–22.

Vasziliu, Georgiosz. 1999. *"Nagyon jó egyetemre jártam, a magyar forradalom egyetemére" Georgiosz Vasziliu elmondja életét Hegedűs B. Andrásnak* (I studied at a very good university: The university of the Hungarian revolution; Vassiliou Georgios speaks about his life to András B. Hegedűs). Budapest: 1956-os Intézet.

Veres, Péter. 1997 [1939]. *Gyepsor. Elbeszélések, versek* (Gyepsor: Stories and poems). Budapest: Szabad Föld.

Vida, István. 1992. Sajtófogadás 1956. november 3-án. A Nagy Imre-per irataiból (Press conference on November 3, 1956: From the documents of the Imre Nagy case). *Rubicon* 3 (7), pp. 31–34.

Yergin, Daniel, and Joseph Stanislaw. 1998. *The Commanding Heights: The Battle between the Government and the Marketplace That Is Remaking the Modern World*. New York: Simon and Schuster.

Index